Edited by Hans-Jörg Schmid
Entrenchment and the Psychology of Language Learning

Language and the Human Lifespan Series

Bilingualism Across the Lifespan
Factors Moderating Language Proficiency
Edited by Elena Nicoladis and Simona Montanari

Entrenchment and the Psychology of Language Learning
How We Reorganize and Adapt Linguistic Knowledge
Edited by Hans-Jörg Schmid

Innovative Investigations of Language in Autism Spectrum Disorder
Edited by Letitia R. Naigles

María Blume and Barbara C. Lust
Research Methods in Language Acquisition
Principles, Procedures, and Practices

Entrenchment and the Psychology of Language Learning

How We Reorganize and Adapt
Linguistic Knowledge

Edited by
Hans-Jörg Schmid

DE GRUYTER
MOUTON

American Psychological Association • Washington, DC

Copyright © 2018 by the American Psychological Association and Walter de Gruyter GmbH. All rights reserved. Except as permitted under the United States Copyright Act of 1976, no part of this publication may be reproduced or distributed in any form or by any means, including, but not limited to, the process of scanning and digitization, or stored in a database or retrieval system, without the prior written permission of the publishers.

This volume is text- and page-identical with the hardback published in 2016.

Published by
American Psychological Association
750 First Street, NE
Washington, DC 20002-4242
www.apa.org

Walter de Gruyter GmbH
Genthiner Strasse 13
10785 Berlin / Germany
www.degruyter.com

To order in the United States and Canada:
APA Order Department
P.O. Box 92984
Washington, DC 20090-2984
Tel: (800) 374-2721; Direct: (202) 336-5510
Fax: (202) 336-5502; TDD/TTY: (202) 336-6123
Online: www.apa.org/pubs/books/
E-mail: order@apa.org

To order in Europe:
HGV Hanseatische Gesellschaft für Verlagsservice mbH
Holzwiesenstr. 2
72127 Kusterdingen / Germany
Tel.: +49 (0)7071 9353 – 55
Fax.: +49 (0)7071 9353 – 93
Online: www.degruyter.com
E-mail: orders@degruyter.com

Other customers, including those in the United Kingdom, may order from either publisher.

Typeset in DG Meta Serif Science by Circle Graphics, Inc., Columbia, MD

Printer (U.S. & Canada): United Book Press, Baltimore, MD
Printer (Europe): CPI books GmbH, Leck, Germany
Cover Designer: Mercury Publishing Services, Inc., Rockville, MD

The opinions and statements published are the responsibility of the authors, and such opinions and statements do not necessarily represent the policies of the American Psychological Association or Walter de Gruyter GmbH.

Library of Congress Cataloging-in-Publication Data
Names: Schmid, Hans-Jörg, editor.
Title: Entrenchment and the psychology of language learning : how we reorganize and adapt linguistic knowledge / edited by Hans-Jörg Schmid.
Description: First Edition. | Washington, DC : American Psychological Association, [2016] | Series: Language and the human lifespan. | Includes bibliographical references and index.
Identifiers: LCCN 2016038801| ISBN 9783110634891 | ISBN 3110634899
Subjects: LCSH: Language and languages—Study and teaching—Psychological aspects. | Cognitive learning. | Cognitive grammar. | Psycholinguistics.
Classification: LCC P53.7 .E68 2016 | DDC 401/.93—dc23
LC record available at https://lccn.loc.gov/2016038801

British Library Cataloguing-in-Publication Data
A CIP record is available from the British Library.

Bibliographic information published by the Deutsche Nationalbibliothek
The Deutsche Nationalbibliothek lists this publication in the Deutsche Nationalbibliografie; detailed bibliographic data are available in the internet at http://dnb.dnb.de.

Printed in the United States of America and Germany
First Edition

Contents

Contributors —— vii

Hans-Jörg Schmid
Introduction —— 3

I Setting the Scene

Hans-Jörg Schmid
1 **A Framework for Understanding Linguistic Entrenchment and Its Psychological Foundations** —— 9

II Linguistic Perspectives on Entrenchment

Ronald W. Langacker
2 **Entrenchment in Cognitive Grammar** —— 39

Martin Hilpert and Holger Diessel
3 **Entrenchment in Construction Grammar** —— 57

Hendrik De Smet
4 **Entrenchment Effects in Language Change** —— 75

Anatol Stefanowitsch and Susanne Flach
5 **The Corpus-Based Perspective on Entrenchment** —— 101

Alice Blumenthal-Dramé
6 **Entrenchment From a Psycholinguistic and Neurolinguistic Perspective** —— 129

Dirk Geeraerts
7 **Entrenchment as Onomasiological Salience** —— 153

III Cognitive Foundations of Linguistic Entrenchment Processes

Atsuko Takashima and Iske Bakker
8 **Memory Consolidation** —— 177

Robert J. Hartsuiker and Agnes Moors
9 **On the Automaticity of Language Processing** —— 201

Ethan Jost and Morten H. Christiansen
10 Statistical Learning as a Domain-General Mechanism of Entrenchment —— 227

Fernand Gobet
11 Entrenchment, Gestalt Formation, and Chunking —— 245

Anne-Kristin Cordes
12 The Roles of Analogy, Categorization, and Generalization in Entrenchment —— 269

Franziska Günther, Hermann J. Müller, and Thomas Geyer
13 Salience, Attention, and Perception —— 289

IV Entrenchment in Language Learning and Language Attrition

Anna L. Theakston
14 Entrenchment in First Language Learning —— 315

Brian MacWhinney
15 Entrenchment in Second-Language Learning —— 343

Rasmus Steinkrauss and Monika S. Schmid
16 Entrenchment and Language Attrition —— 367

V Deconstructing Entrenchment

Philip Herdina
17 Entrenchment, Embeddedness, and Entanglement: A Dynamic Complexity View —— 387

Stephen J. Cowley
18 Entrenchment: A View From Radical Embodied Cognitive Science —— 409

VI Synopsis

Hans-Jörg Schmid
19 Linguistic Entrenchment and Its Psychological Foundations —— 435

Index —— 453

About the Editor —— 475

Contributors

Iske Bakker, PhD
Donders Institute for Brain, Cognition and Behaviour
Radboud University
Nijmegen, The Netherlands

Alice Blumenthal-Dramé, DrPhil
Department of English
University of Freiburg
Breisgau, Germany

Morten H. Christiansen, PhD
Cognitive Science Program
Cornell University
Ithaca, NY
Haskins Labs and Department of Child Language
Aarhus University
Aarhus, Denmark
Department of Language and Communication
University of Southern Denmark
Odense, Denmark

Anne-Kristin Cordes, DrPhil
Institute for German Studies
Faculty III—School of Linguistics and Cultural Studies
Carl von Ossietzky University of Oldenburg
Oldenburg, Germany

Stephen J. Cowley, PhD
Center for Human Interactivity and the COMAC Cluster
University of Southern Denmark, Slagelse
Slagelse, Denmark

Hendrik De Smet, PhD
Department of Linguistics
University of Leuven
Leuven, Belgium

Holger Diessel, PhD
Department of English
University of Jena
Jena, Germany

Susanne Flach, MA
Department of English Philology
Freie Universität Berlin
Berlin, Germany

Dirk Geeraerts, PhD
Department of Linguistics
University of Leuven
Leuven, Belgium

Thomas Geyer, PhD
Department of Psychology
Ludwig-Maximilians-Universität München
Munich, Germany

Fernand Gobet, PhD
Department of Psychological Sciences
University of Liverpool
Liverpool, England

Franziska Günther, DrPhil
Department of English and American Studies
Ludwig-Maximilians-Universität München
Munich, Germany

Robert J. Hartsuiker, PhD
Department of Experimental Psychology
Ghent University
Ghent, Belgium

Philip Herdina, DrPhil
Department of English
Leopold-Franzens-Universität Innsbruck
Innsbruck, Austria

Martin Hilpert, PhD
Department of English
University of Neuchâtel
Neuchâtel, Switzerland

Ethan Jost, MA
Department of Psychology
Cornell University
Ithaca, NY
fMRI Lab
Memorial Sloan Kettering Cancer Center
New York, NY

Ronald W. Langacker, PhD
Department of Linguistics
University of California, San Diego
La Jolla, CA

Brian MacWhinney, PhD
Department of Psychology
Carnegie Mellon University
Pittsburgh, PA

Agnes Moors, PhD
Department of Psychology
University of Leuven
Leuven, Belgium
Department of Psychology
Ghent University
Ghent, Belgium

Hermann J. Müller, PhD
Department of Psychology
Ludwig-Maximilians-Universität München
Munich, Germany

Hans-Jörg Schmid, DrPhil
Department of English and American Studies
Ludwig-Maximilians-Universität München
Munich, Germany

Monika S. Schmid, PhD
Department of Language and Linguistics
University of Essex
Colchester, England

Anatol Stefanowitsch, PhD
Department of English Philology
Freie Universität Berlin
Berlin, Germany

Rasmus Steinkrauss, PhD
Departments of European Languages
 and Applied Linguistics
University of Groningen
Groningen, The Netherlands

Atsuko Takashima, PhD
Donders Institute for Brain, Cognition
 and Behaviour
Radboud University
Nijmegen, The Netherlands

Anna L. Theakston, PhD
ESRC International Centre for Language and
 Communicative Development (LuCID)
School of Psychological Sciences
University of Manchester
Manchester, England

Edited by Hans-Jörg Schmid
Entrenchment and the Psychology of Language Learning

Hans-Jörg Schmid
Introduction

Linguistic communication is among the most highly automatized forms of human behavior. Effortlessly and with stunning speed, speakers and hearers access and retrieve linguistic knowledge from memory and apply lower level and higher level cognitive abilities such as perception, attention, categorization, and inferencing while producing and comprehending utterances. For this to be possible, linguistic knowledge must be organized in maximally and immediately accessible and retrievable formats.

In the wake of Chomsky's claim in the 1960s that language is a highly specialized and largely autonomous cognitive module, linguists and psychologists lost sight of the psychological foundations shared by language and nonlinguistic cognition. Although most linguists focused their attention on the description of linguistic structures and structural principles of language, most psychologists studied behavior and its cognitive and neuronal basis without worrying too much about the potential influence of language and its representations in the mind.

Over the past 20 years, this division of labor has begun to crumble. With the development of cognitive–linguistic, usage-based, and complex–adaptive models of language, linguistics has begun to emancipate itself from its self-imposed isolation and has found a foothold in the cognitive sciences alongside cognitive psychology, neuropsychology, social psychology, and other related fields. Many linguists have developed a keen interest in the role played by domain-general neurocognitive abilities and processes in the emergence and storage of linguistic knowledge. In contrast, many psychologists have not yet ventured far into linguistics, partly because what is still perceived as "mainstream" linguistics (i.e., Chomskyan autonomous linguistics) did not seem to offer much that would have made that effort worthwhile. Potential effects of the omnipresence of language and linguistic thought on human behavior, input processing, and learning are frequently not considered as falling within the remit of psychological inquiry.

The notion of *entrenchment* epitomizes like no other the opportunity to establish a new meeting ground for psychology and linguistics. It captures the idea that linguistic knowledge is not autonomous, abstract, and stative but is instead continuously refreshed and reorganized under the influence of communicative events in social situations. Linguistic entrenchment can essentially be regarded as a lifelong cognitive reorganization process, the course and quality of which are conditioned by exposure to and use of language on one hand and by the application of domain-general cognitive abilities and processes to language on the other. Memory, categorization, analogy, and abstraction, as well as perception and attention, are crucially involved in entrenchment, as are routinization and automatization, and imitation and emulation.

The aim of the present volume is to bring together expertise from linguistics, psycholinguistics, neurology, and cognitive psychology to develop a joint vision of entrenchment, memory, and automaticity in linguistic and nonlinguistic cognition and to provide a realistic picture of the psychological and linguistic foundations of linguistic knowledge and language learning. The chapters collected could be of equal interest to linguists wishing to understand the psychology behind language and for psychologists who are willing to integrate linguistic aspects into their work. The notion of entrenchment mainly explains how linguistic knowledge emerges from language use and may therefore have a particularly strong appeal to supporters of usage-based theories of language. However, given its wide purview of linguistic perspectives and psychological processes, the present volume might serve as an incentive for linguists and psychologists of all persuasions to learn more about the ways in which linguistic knowledge is constantly reorganized and adapted.

The present book is divided into six parts. Part I (Setting the Scene) provides an expanded conceptualization of entrenchment, including its main facets and empirical evidence. Part II (Linguistic Perspectives on Entrenchment) begins with two chapters detailing the role of entrenchment in cognitive grammar (Chapter 2 by Ronald W. Langacker) and construction grammar (Chapter 3 by Martin Hilpert and Holger Diessel). The next three chapters look at entrenchment from the diachronic perspective (Hendrik De Smet, Chapter 4), the corpus-based perspective (Anatol Stefanowitsch and Susanne Flach, Chapter 5), and the experimental perspective (Alice Blumenthal-Dramé, Chapter 6). The final chapter in Part II proposes an understanding of entrenchment in terms of onomasiological salience (Dirk Geeraerts, Chapter 7).

In Part III (Cognitive Foundations of Linguistic Entrenchment Processes), the psychological perspective dominates. The six chapters assembled here deal with the psychological foundations of entrenchment. The first four deal with the key cognitive affordances behind entrenchment: memory (Atsuko Takashima and Iske Bakker, Chapter 8), automatization (Robert J. Hartsuiker and Agnes Moors, Chapter 9), statistical learning (Ethan Jost and Morten H. Christiansen, Chapter 10), and gestalt formation and chunking (Fernand Gobet, Chapter 11). The two remaining chapters discuss two major sets of psychological determinants of entrenchment processes: categorization, generalization, and analogy (Anne-Kristin Cordes, Chapter 12); and attention, perception, and salience (Franziska Günther, Hermann J. Müller, and Thomas Geyer, Chapter 13).

The three chapters in Part IV (Entrenchment in Language Learning and Language Attrition) investigate the role of entrenchment in first-language acquisition (Anna L. Theakston, Chapter 14), second-language learning (Brian MacWhinney, Chapter 15), and language attrition (Rasmus Steinkrauss and Monika S. Schmid, Chapter 16).

Part V (Deconstructing Entrenchment) consists of two chapters offering critical views of the notion of entrenchment and some of its premises and implications. One approaches entrenchment from the perspective of dynamic complexity theory (Philip Herdina, Chapter 17), the other from the perspective of radical embodiment cognitive science (Stephen J. Cowley, Chapter 18).

Finally, Part VI (Synopsis) synthesizes all the chapters by highlighting central insights and directions for future research.

I Setting the Scene

Hans-Jörg Schmid
1 A Framework for Understanding Linguistic Entrenchment and Its Psychological Foundations

1.1 Introduction

This chapter introduces the main facets of the notion of entrenchment and highlights its role as a potential mediator between linguistic and psychological approaches to the study of linguistic knowledge, language learning, and their psychological foundations. The larger part of the chapter surveys empirical evidence for entrenchment processes and their linguistic effects from a variety of sources. It also discusses consequences of these findings and proposes an integrative framework for the study of entrenchment.

1.2 Entrenchment—A Multifaceted Concept

The main elements of the concept of entrenchment have a long history dating as far back as the 19th century (see, e.g., Blumenthal-Dramé, 2012, p. 11; Bybee, 1985, p. 117; Paul, 1920, e.g., pp. 12–14, 49–50, 94–95; de Saussure, 1916, e.g., pp. 122–127, 177; Wray, 2002, p. 8). The credit for introducing the term *entrenchment* into linguistics, however, goes to Ron Langacker (1987), one of the founding fathers of cognitive linguistics. According to him, there is a

> continuous scale of entrenchment in cognitive organization. Every use of a [linguistic] structure has a positive impact on its degree of entrenchment, whereas extended periods of disuse have a negative impact. With repeated use, a novel structure becomes progressively entrenched, to the point of becoming a unit; moreover, units are variably entrenched depending on the frequency of their occurrence. (p. 59)

Langacker's description rests on two key assumptions that are still associated with entrenchment today: First, repetition and rehearsal increase the *strength of representations*, whereas disuse may cause decay (see also Langacker, 1987, p. 100, 1991, p. 45); second, repeated usage of a given linguistic structure causes it to be processed as a *holistic unit*. Although Langacker's account portrays both facets in terms of degrees, their characters seem to differ: The understanding in terms of strength of representation evokes a purely quantitative, gradual, potentially asymptotic trajector, whereas the understanding in terms of a holistic chunk promotes the picture that a qualitative change from analytic and declarative to holistic and procedural processing takes place at some point (see Blumenthal-Dramé, 2012, pp. 67–69, 186–187). From a psychological point of view, the first facet can be explained in terms of memory consolidation, while the second one involves a chunking process that can find an end point in a gestaltlike chunk that is emancipated from its component parts and defies analytical processing.

In a more recent publication, Langacker (2008) relates both facets of entrenchment to the process of automatization, understood in terms of a reduction of conscious monitoring:

> Automatization is the process observed in learning to tie a shoe or recite the alphabet: through repetition or rehearsal, a complex structure is thoroughly mastered to the point that using it is virtually automatic and requires little conscious monitoring. In CG [cognitive grammar] parlance, a structure undergoes progressive **entrenchment** and eventually becomes established as a **unit**. (p. 16; emphasis in original)

As a first rough approximation, then, entrenchment can be understood as referring to a set of cognitive processes—mainly memory consolidation, chunking, and automatization—taking place in the minds of individual speakers. In addition, the term *entrenchment* has been used to denote not only these cognitive processes but also the effects they have on the representations of linguistic structures, that is, their products or resultant states. It is in this sense that we can talk about *degrees* or *strengths of entrenchment* and about *entrenched linguistic structures*. The main determinant of entrenchment identified in early work (see Bybee, 1985, p. 117; Langacker, 1987, p. 59) and much researched subsequently is frequency of exposure to and use of linguistic structures (see also Divjak & Caldwell-Harris, 2015).

1.3 Empirical Evidence for Entrenchment

Empirical evidence for entrenchment processes and their determinants and effects comes from four main sources: psycholinguistic and neurolinguistic experiments, quantitative corpus-linguistic investigations, studies of language change, and patterns of language use in context. In what follows, the major insights and claims from these sources are summarized, divided into work on frequency effects on entrenchment in terms of strength of representation (Section 1.3.1); frequency effects on entrenchment in terms of chunking and holistic units (1.3.2); effects of repetition in linguistic, situational, and social contexts on entrenchment (1.3.3); and other determinants of entrenchment (1.3.4). The superscript letters in Sections 1.3.1 through 1.3.4 serve as cross-references to the framework for the study of entrenchment proposed in Section 1.5 (see specifically Table 1.1).

The cognitive and linguistic effects of discourse frequency undoubtedly constitute the most intensively researched field relating to entrenchment. Recent surveys of

Tab. 1.1: Survey of Cognitive Entrenchment Processes and Their Cognitive and Linguistic Effects

Repetition-related determinant	Type of association affected	Psychological affordances	Cognitive effects	Linguistic effects
– Token repetition of word-forms and fixed strings	– Symbolic association	– Memory consolidation – routinization	– Increase in representational strength of symbolic association of specific form–meaning pairing[a]	– Faster and more effortless processing of words[a] and expressions[d] with less interference from paradigmatic neighbors[b] – Faster resolution of lexical[c] and syntactic ambiguities[e] – Early acquisition of words[f] – "Entrenchment" in a narrow sense (Braine & Brooks, 1995) in acquisition[l] – Stability of morphological form[m] – Resistance to analogical pressure and change[n, r] – Reduction of phonological form and bleaching of meaning[o] – Increase in frequency of usage[a, l]
– Type repetition of variable construction (lexical or grammatical)	– Symbolic association	– Memory consolidation – Routinization – Categorization – Schematization	– Emergence of, and increase in, representational strength of variable schema[a, h] (in cooperation with paradigmatic and syntagmatic associations)[j]	– Constructionalization[p] – Productivity[q] – Innovation[r] – New meanings, polysemy, partly under the influence of pragmatic associations[s]
– Token repetition of identical sequence of elements	– Syntagmatic association	– Memory consolidation – Routinization – Chunking – Automatization	– Increasing holistic processing of specific sequence of elements[w] – Automatic processing of chunk once started[a, d] – Priming effects between parts of sequence[a, e] or sequences of larger constructions[a, g]	– Fusion, coalescence, formulaic language (idioms, routine formulae, irreversible binominals), collocation[y] – Form: phonetic and morphological reduction[x] – Meaning: reduction of semantic specificity (grammaticalization),[a, b] loss of compositionality (lexicalization)[a, c] – Tightening of internal syntagmatic bonds[a, a] – Loosening of paradigmatic associations of composite parts[z]

(continues)

Tab. 1.1: Survey of Cognitive Entrenchment Processes and Their Cognitive and Linguistic Effects (Continued)

Repetition-related determinant	Type of association affected	Psychological affordances	Cognitive effects	Linguistic effects
– Type repetition of functionally identical sequences with variable slots	– Syntagmatic association	– Memory consolidation – Routinization – Chunking – Categorization – Schematization	– Emergence of complex schematic constructions with variable slots (in cooperation with symbolic and paradigmatic associations)[j]	– Constructionalization[p] – Productivity[q] – Innovation[r]
– Token repetition	– Paradigmatic association	– Comparison	– Preferential selection[u]	– Increase in strength compared to paradigmatic competitors[t] – Attractor for analogical change[v]
– Type repetition	– Paradigmatic association	– Comparison – Analogy	– Emergence of complex schematic constructions with variable slots (in cooperation with symbolic and syntagmatic associations)[j]	– Basis for analogical change and pressure[s] – Grammatical categories (word classes)[j] – Word fields, paradigmatic relation[k]
– Token or type repetition in specific context	– Pragmatic association	– Memory consolidation	– Rich memory of exemplars[a,f] – From episodic to semantic memory[a,i]	– Semantic change caused by invited inference, context absorption[a,h] – Emergence of connotations[a,i] – Emergence of register-specificity[a,k] – Support for chunking[a,l]

Note. For more details about the effects of entrenchment that are listed in this table, see Sections 1.3.1–1.3.3 and corresponding superscript notations. For more details about the types of associations, see Section 1.5.

frequency effects from a range of different perspectives are provided by Blumenthal-Dramé (2012, pp. 27–65, et passim), Bybee (2003), Diessel (2007), Divjak and Caldwell-Harris (2015), Divjak and Gries (2012), Gries and Divjak (2012), Jurafsky (2003), Krug (2003), and Lieven (2010).

1.3.1 Frequency Effects on Entrenchment in Terms of "Strength of Representation"

Psycholinguistic experiments on lexical frequency effects in production and comprehension arguably have the longest tradition. In general, lexical decision tasks as well as reading-time and eye-tracking experiments have shown that frequent words are recognized, accessed, and retrieved faster, with less effort and with less interference from paradigmatic neighbors than rare ones and that the same goes for frequent meanings of lemmas as opposed to rare meanings[c] (Dell, 1990; de Vaan, Schreuder, & Baayen, 2007; Forster, 2007; Giora, 2003; Gregory, Raymond, Fosler-Lussier, & Jurafsky, 2000; Hauk & Pulvermüller, 2004; Jescheniak & Levelt, 1994; Jurafsky, Bell, Gregory, & Raymond, 2001; Just & Carpenter, 1980; Knobel, Finkbeiner, & Caramazza, 2008; Rugg, 1990; Sandra, 1994). For morphologically complex words such as compounds (e.g., *lifecycle*) and derivations (e.g., *undress*, *happiness*), additional effects of the frequencies of the constituents on processing and storage have been demonstrated (e.g., Blumenthal-Dramé, 2012; Bybee & McClelland, 2005; Hay, 2001). Frequent compounds and word pairs (e.g., *car accident*) and multiword expressions (e.g., *call it a day*) are activated faster than rare expressions of these types[d] (Jurafsky, 2003, p. 62). Although the effects of frequency on larger syntactic constructions are less well supported by experimental evidence (Jurafsky, 2003, p. 63), it has been shown that frequency affects sentence parsing and the resolution of ambiguous syntactic structures[e] (e.g., Diessel, 2007; Hare, McRae, & Elman, 2004; Jurafsky, 1996; Roland & Jurafsky, 2002). For example, the verb *remember* is more frequently complemented by a noun phrase (*he remembered the problem*), whereas the verb *suspect* favors clausal complements (*he suspected the problem was serious*). Sentences that meet the expectations arising from this probabilistic tendency are processed with less effort than those that do not—for example, *he remembered the problem was serious* and *he suspected the problem* (Diessel, 2007, p. 113; Jurafsky, 1996).

Evidence for frequency effects has also been found in research on first-language and second-language learning from a usage-based perspective (e.g., Childers & Tomasello, 2001; Cordes, 2014; Ellis, 2009; Gries & Divjak, 2012; Kidd, Lieven, & Tomasello, 2010; Lieven, 2010; Lieven & Tomasello, 2008; MacWhinney, 1999, 2004; Redington, Chater, & Finch, 1998). Although it is uncontroversial that frequent words are acquired earlier than rare ones,[f] it has been shown that both children and second-language learners seem to be able to use more nuanced probabilistic information about co-occurrence tendencies while building up their lexicon and constructing a grammar (Diessel, 2007;

Ellis, 2006; Saffran, 2001; Saffran, Aslin, & Newport, 1996; see also Jost & Christiansen, Chapter 10, this volume).

A fundamental insight, which is paralleled by evidence from the study of language change (discussed later in the chapter), is that the repetition of identical tokens in the input (known as *token frequency*) results in increased entrenchment in terms of the strength of the corresponding specific representation,[g] whereas repetition of varied items sharing commonalities of form or meaning (*type frequency*) facilitates categorization, abstraction, generalization, and the emergence of variable schemas[h] (Abbot-Smith & Tomasello, 2006; Goldberg, 2006, 2009; Lieven & Tomasello, 2008, p. 174; Matthews, Lieven, Theakston, & Tomasello, 2005; Tomasello, 2003, pp. 173–175). For instance, the repetition of a fixed sequence such as *what's that* strengthens the representation of this form–meaning-function complex, whereas the repetition of expressions such as *give me* (or *gimme*) *the doll, give me the book, give me the cup*, and so on, encourages the formation of a variable schema "give me *X*" (see also in this volume Cordes, Chapter 12; Theakston, Chapter 14). The process of schematization requires an intricate interplay of an emerging symbolic association between forms and meanings/functions, of syntagmatic associations between the component parts of a schema (e.g., *gimme* + X), and of the paradigmatic associations between the elements that can fill the variable slot in a schema (*the doll, the book, the cup*).[i] These paradigmatic associations, which are based on the psychological processes of comparison and analogy, also make up the starting point for the emergence of grammatical categories such as word classes and clause constituents[j] (Lieven, 2014; Tomasello, 2003, pp. 169–173) and for the paradigmatic dimension of lexical networks, such as word fields and sense relations.[k] With regard to the productive use of such schemas and their slot fillers by children, it has been demonstrated that their frequency distribution encourages entrenchment of certain combinations and thus constrains overgeneralizations[l] (Ambridge, Pine, Rowland, & Young, 2008; Braine & Brooks, 1995; Brooks & Tomasello, 1999; Theakston, 2004). For example, children are less likely to overgeneralize complementation patterns for frequent verbs (e.g., *read me a book*) than for rare ones (e.g., *examine me a book*) in production and are also more willing to accept frequent ones than rare ones as grammatical. Ambridge, Pine, Rowland, and Chang (2012) showed that this effect persists in adult language.

Corpus-based studies of frequency effects have tested the assumption that the frequencies of occurrence of lexical elements and syntactic constructions in large corpora mirror degrees of entrenchment and strengths of representation[a] (Arppe, Gilquin, Glynn, Hilpert, & Zeschel, 2010; Blumenthal-Dramé, 2012; Schmid, 2000; see also Stefanowitsch & Flach, Chapter 5, this volume). The rationale on which these studies are based is that frequencies of occurrence in large, balanced corpora not only can serve as an approximation of the kind of repetitiveness that the average speaker produces and is typically exposed to but can actually provide clues as to the potential effects of this exposure on the cognitive systems of individual speakers. In view of the methodological gap between corpus data and degrees of entrenchment (see Mukherjee,

2005, p. 225; Schmid, 2010, 2013), it is particularly important that some studies have attempted to produce converging evidence from different sources by relating corpus-based measures to behavioral data collected in experiments (Divjak, 2008; Gries, Hampe, & Schönefeld, 2005, 2010; Schmid, 2013; Wiechmann, 2008). Questions to be considered include the following: Is relative or absolute frequency relevant for entrenchment, or do the two have different effects on entrenchment (Croft, 2008; Haspelmath, 2008; Schmid, 2014)? Are different types of relative frequencies relevant for different facets of entrenchment—for example, relative frequency to paradigmatic competitors, relative frequency to functional or onomasiological competitors, or relative frequency to relative frequencies of syntagmatic partners (see Divjak & Caldwell-Harris, 2015; Geeraerts, Grondelaers, & Bakema, 1994; Glynn & Fischer, 2010; Schmid, 2010; Schmid & Küchenhoff, 2013; Stefanowitsch & Gries, 2003)? Is the use of transitional or conditional probabilities superior in explanatory power to relative string frequencies (Blumenthal-Dramé, 2012; Bybee & Scheibman, 1999; Divjak, 2008; Jurafsky, 1996; Krug, 2003, pp. 33–39)?

The study of language change is another field in which entrenchment has been tied to discourse frequency (see De Smet, Chapter 4, this volume). Again, this is despite the fact that there is a considerable methodological gap between collective language change (i.e., conventionalization), which provides the data and explananda, on the one hand, and individual entrenchment, on the other hand. Cognitive processes such as routinization and automatization (e.g., Bybee, 2003; Croft, 2000, pp. 72–76; Haiman, 1994; Krug, 2003; Paul, 1920, pp. 49–50) and cognitive principles such as economy (Bybee, 1985; Croft, 2008; Haspelmath, 2008) have been held responsible for frequency-based types of language change. The shortcut between conventionalization and entrenchment is explicitly discussed, for example, by Blumenthal-Dramé (2012, p. 24); Croft (2000, p. 162); Paul (1920, pp. 12–14, 94–95); Rohde, Stefanowitsch, and Kemmer (2000); Schmid (2013); and Zenner, Speelman, and Geeraerts (2012, p. 769).

Diachronic frequency effects have to be interpreted in a highly differentiated way with regard to whether they affect the phonological or the morphological forms or the meanings and usage conditions of constructions, whether the constructions are morphologically simple or complex, and whether they are formally fixed or include variable slots. In addition, as mentioned earlier, the distinction between token frequency and type frequency has to be taken into consideration. The main claims concerning the entrenchment aspect of *strength of representations* (see Section 1.3.2 for chunking effects) are as follows: High token frequency of specific items, especially irregular ones such as *went*, *told*, or *spoke*, has a conserving effect on their morphological form (Bybee, 2007, p. 10; Diessel, 2007), which makes them resistant to paradigmatic analogical pressure and change; and high token frequency of specific items also has a reducing effect on their phonetic form (e.g., present-day English *free* and *friend* both derive by fusion from the Old English diphthongal stem *freo-* or *frio-*) and a bleaching effect on their meanings (Bybee, 2003, 2006; Bybee & Thompson, 1997; Krug, 2000). Type frequency of variable schemas also shows seemingly contradictory effects: On the one hand, high type frequency combined with some degree of dispersion among the fillers of variable slots has the effect of facilitating the emergence of constructions (*constructionalization*; Traugott & Trousdale, 2013); this allows for productivity (*Mary baked me cake*), increases the potential for innovation (*Mary smiled me a kiss*), and provides the basis for change caused by analogical pressure (Himmelmann, 2004; Traugott & Trousdale, 2013, p. 18). On the other hand, highly frequent fillers of the variable slot are strongly represented compared with paradigmatic competitors and thus selected preferentially, almost by default (e.g., *give* in the ditransitive construction *Mary gave me the book*); they function as analogical attractors for less frequent items and contribute to the resistance to change (Bybee, 2006, 2010a; Traugott, 2008).

1.3.2 Frequency Effects on Entrenchment in Terms of Chunking and Holistic Units

Language change has also provided a massive body of insights into entrenchment in terms of "chunking" and the development of composite structures into holistic units (again, see De Smet, Chapter 4, this volume). The main type of evidence—which, as before, relies on a shortcut from conventionalization to entrenchment—comes from processes affecting the phonetic and morphological forms of repeated strings of words. High string token frequency, that is, the repetition of identical sequences of elements, has been found to be conducive to the phonetic and morphological reduction of complex words and word strings. Fusion and coalescence have been interpreted as symptoms of an increasing holistic processing and storage of repeated multiword sequences and other types of formulaic language (Bybee, 2003, 2007, p. 324; Bybee & Scheibman, 1999; Haspelmath, 2008, 2011). Whether these changes are the product of high relative frequency (Haspelmath, 2008) or absolute frequency (Croft, 2008); whether other measures, such as transitional probabilities, are more predictive (Bybee & McClelland, 2005; Hoffmann, 2005; Krug, 2003); and whether it is really frequency that is ultimately and solely responsible for formal reductions (Haspelmath, 2014) has yet to be determined.

The overall picture is again quite complex: On the one hand, formal reduction, fusion, and coalescence, as in *bye* from Early Modern English (*God*) *be wy you*, *because* from Middle English *by cause*, *lord* from Old English *hláfweard* 'loafkeeper,' or, more recently, *gonna* and *wanna* from *going to* and *want to* are interpreted as indicating the emancipation of emerging holistic units from their component parts and their paradigmatic relations[2] (Blumenthal-Dramé, 2012, p. 20; Bybee, 2007, p. 301; Peters, 2009); these effects are regarded as contributing to an increasing autonomy of representation (Blumenthal-Dramé, 2012, p. 4, et passim; Bybee, 2003, pp. 617–618). On the other hand, while strengthening their internal syntagmatic bonds,[a,a] chunks with grammatical function tend to reduce their external syntagmatic autonomy, thus becoming more dependent on their grammatical cotext (Lehmann, 2004, p. 155). As far as semantic aspects are concerned, long-term diachronic fusion is typically accompanied by a reduction in the semantic specificity of sequences with grammatical function[a, b] (e.g., *going to* from 'locomotion' to 'future intention'; see, e.g., Bybee & Pagliuca, 1985) and by semantic changes leading to a loss of compositionality for sequences with lexical meanings such as compounds (e.g., *lord*, noted earlier; see, e.g., Brinton & Traugott, 2005).

Although fixed multiword chunks such as *what's that*, *more milk*, or *gimme hug* also play a key role in the early phases of first-language acquisition (Tomasello, 2003, 2009), these holophrastic units are not the result of a gradual chunking process, at least not in the minds of the child learners, but are learned and processed as chunks to begin with. It is only later that they are decomposed and can form the basis for early pivot schemas (*more milk, more tea, more toast* > "more *X*") and more complex and variable schemas, for example, "give *X Y*" (Tomasello, 2003).

Experimental studies on adult language have pursued the idea that frequent chunks (*good morning*) and more or less fixed formulaic sequences (*many happy returns, all the same, if you know what I mean*) are processed in a holistic manner, that is, by means of an access-and-retrieval rather than an online, computational procedure[w] (Pawley & Syder, 1983; Wray, 2002, 2008; for a recent survey of experimental work, see Conklin & Schmitt, 2012). Such single-step memory retrieval can be interpreted as a symptom of the routinization and automaticity of processing (Logan, 1988). A second feature of chunk processing that is commonly associated with automaticity (Bargh, 1992; Moors & De Houwer, 2006) is autonomy in the sense that once started, the processing is completed without further monitoring[a, d] (see Hartsuiker & Moors, Chapter 9, this volume). The frequent co-occurrence of linguistic elements sequentially ordered in running text is assumed to have both a lexical and a syntactic priming effect[a, e] (Hoey, 2005; Pickering & Branigan, 1999; Pulvermüller, 2010), which presumably uses neuronal sequence detectors. As a consequence, the later portions of fixed and semi-fixed expressions are to some extent predictable. Lexical items have been shown to act as primes for both lexical items (Jones & Estes, 2012) and for syntactic structures (Newman, Ratliff, Muratore, & Burns, 2009; Segaert, Kempen, Petersson, & Hagoort, 2013). The outcomes of these experiments crucially depend on the types of sequences tested, however. Variables to be taken into consideration include frequency (of parts and chunks), length, fixedness, idiomaticity, discourse function, and other pragmatic constraints. The elements tested range from more or less fixed and noncompositional idioms (e.g., *shoot the breeze, pull someone's leg*; see Conklin & Schmitt, 2012; Gibbs, 1980; Siyanova-Chanturia, Conklin, & Schmitt, 2011; Swinney & Cutler, 1979; Underwood, Schmitt, & Galpin, 2004), phrasal verbs (*heat up, slow down*; see Cappelle, Shtyrov, & Pulvermüller, 2010), semiprefabricated phrases (e.g., *don't have to worry, why don't you*; Arnon & Snider, 2010; Tremblay & Baayen, 2010; Tremblay, Derwing, & Libben, 2009; Tremblay, Derwing, Libben, & Westbury, 2011), and irreversible binomials (e.g., *bread and butter, law and order*; Siyanova-Chanturia, Conklin, & van Heuven, 2011) to less strongly connected but still to some extent predictable collocations (e.g., *run a shop, crack a joke*; Jurafsky, 1996; McDonald & Shillcock, 2003; Sosa & MacFarlane,

2002). The evidence collected so far seems to be quite conclusive as regards the holistic storage and processing of prototypical, that is, noncompositional idioms. In contrast, the extent to which other, less fixed and more transparent combinations are indeed processed as chunks and the role played by discourse frequency for chunking has turned out to be much less easy to determine[y] (see Blumenthal-Dramé, Chapter 6, this volume). One of the many remaining riddles is that the best candidates for holistic processing, idioms, belong in general to the least frequently occurring formulaic sequences.

Collocations and collostructions, that is, associations between grammatical constructions and lexical elements filling variable slots (e.g., *give* in the ditransitive noun phrase [NP]–verb [V]–NP–NP construction), have been in the focus of corpus-based research on entrenchment for some time (see Evert, 2004, for a survey, as well as Ellis & O'Donnell, 2014; Schmid & Küchenhoff, 2013; Stefanowitsch & Gries, 2003; Wiechmann, 2008; Zeschel, 2012). Although collocations can be explained from a psychological perspective as a loose form of chunking (see Gobet, Chapter 11, this volume) based on syntagmatic co-occurrence tendencies, collostructions involve schematization and are conducive to the emergence of paradigmatic relations between the lexical items that are more or less likely to occur in the variable slot. Typically, grammatical constructions show the tendency to attract one or two lexical items particularly frequently. This skewed distribution facilitates the acquisition of schematic constructions in first-language (e.g., Casenhiser & Goldberg, 2005; Childers & Tomasello, 2001; Goldberg & Casenhiser, 2006) and second-language acquisition (Ellis, 2009) and contributes to the role of these anchor words as prototype-like analogical attractors[q] (discussed earlier). Recently, the problems in measuring frequency and exploring the relation between various types of frequency counts and hypothetical degrees and types of entrenchment have been highlighted (e.g., Arppe et al., 2010; Blumenthal-Dramé, 2012; Lieven, 2010; Schmid, 2010; Schmid & Küchenhoff, 2013).

1.3.3 Effects of Repetition in Linguistic, Situational, and Social Contexts on Entrenchment

The evidence reviewed so far indicates that frequency of occurrence, no matter how it is measured and operationalized, at least partly conditions both types of entrenchment processes. However, frequency as such is no more than an idealized and mechanical approximation of repeated use and exposure by individual speakers taking place in concrete situations. What pure frequency counts can certainly not inform us about are the manifold ways in which repeated exposure can affect the cognitive and linguistic system depending on the linguistic, situational, and social contexts of specific usage events (see in this volume Herdina, Chapter 17; Cowley, Chapter 18). Frequency counts also overlook the fact that entrenchment as a repetition-conditioned cognitive process can only become effective if the traces of processing events "survive," as Pickering and Garrod (2004, p. 218) put it, a particular communicative event and are carried over to the next. In addition, it is only in communicative situations that replication and subsequent propagation, that is, spread of communicative knowledge among speakers, can take place (Croft, 2000, p. 38). In fact, experimental work on diverse types of linguistic structures suggests that frequency as such may be a less good a predictor of behavioral measures than context-related variables such as contextual diversity (Adelman, Brown, & Quesada, 2006; McDonald & Shillcock, 2001) and dispersion across text types (Baayen, 2010). This is in line with basic tenets of usage-based models (Kemmer & Barlow, 2000, p. xxi) and exemplar-based models (e.g., Bybee, 2006, pp. 716–718; Bybee & McClelland, 2005; Pierrehumbert, 2001), which also assume rich storage of contextual information relating to previous linguistic experience.[a,f]

Effects of the wider linguistic context on syntactic choices have also been investigated under the label of syntactic or structural priming[a,g] mentioned earlier. The focus in the present context, however, lies not on the immediate linguistic environment but instead on the tendency to repeat syntactic structures used or heard in preceding sentences and to comprehend them faster and with less effort (Bock, 1986; Chang, Dell, & Bock, 2006; Reitter, Keller, & Moore, 2011; Segaert et al., 2013; Snider, 2007). Whether the observed persistence effects (Szmrecsanyi, 2005) are to be explained in terms of transient residual activation in short-term memory or as an early form of implicit procedural learning (Bock & Griffin, 2000) remains controversial.

Lexical and structural priming across sentence boundaries and particularly across speaker turns is conducive to repetition and imitation and is therefore likely to influence the automatization and memory consolidation underlying entrenchment. The tendency of speakers in conversation toward processes known as *replication* (Croft, 2000), *accommodation* (see Auer & Hinskens, 2005; Giles, Coupland, & Coupland, 1991; Giles & Ogay, 2006; Trudgill, 1986, p. 1–38), *alignment* (e.g., Jaeger & Snider, 2013; Pickering & Garrod, 2004), and *co-adaptation* (Ellis & Larsen-Freeman, 2009, p. 91) can also be related to these effects. This takes us to a higher, interactional level of situational aspects of entrenchment, where imitation, emulation, and joint activity come into play as determinants of repetition and memory consolidation (Auer & Hinskens, 2005; Garrod & Pickering, 2009). Interestingly, according to Garrod and Pickering (2007), the sociocognitive process of alignment is largely automatic (see also Hartsuiker & Moors, Chapter 9, this volume). The claim that joint activity and joint attention in concrete situations contribute to repetition and entrenchment in first-language acquisition is well supported by research in the usage-based framework (Tomasello, 2003, 2009).

Context effects become visible in terms of increasing strengths of representation and chunking, each on both the individual cognitive microlevel and the collective macrolevel. New and increasingly more strongly entrenched meanings associated with existing forms can arise by means of absorbing existing or new pragmatic associations from context[a,h] (Boye & Harder, 2012, p. 17; Bybee, 2003, p. 618; Croft, 2000, pp. 130–140; Heine, Claudi, & Hünnemeyer, 1991, Chapter 3; Kuteva, 2001, p. 150; Nicolle, 2011; Traugott & Dasher, 2004, pp. 34–41). Well-known examples include the addition of causal meanings to originally temporal conjunctions such as *after*, *since*, or *as* on the basis of the common inference *post hoc ergo propter hoc* (König & Traugott, 1988). If it is assumed that context-dependent, pragmatic information is retained in episodic memory, while knowledge of concepts and words is stored in semantic memory, these changes can be interpreted as involving a shift or transfer from episodic to semantic memory[a, i] (see Takashima & Bakker, Chapter 8, this volume). The same process can be held responsible for gradual connotative enrichment of meanings[a, j] and knowledge about the register specificity of words and expressions,[a, k] which are also derived from rich experience of exemplars in specific situations (Schmid, 2014). Finally, the study of language acquisition (Behrens, 2009; Tomasello & Rakoczy, 2003), conversational patterns (Auer & Pfänder, 2011; Günthner, 2011; Hopper, 1987; Nattinger & DeCarrico, 1992), and language change (e.g., Bybee, 2010a, 2010b; Traugott, 2008) strongly indicate that formulaic sequences are supported by pragmatic associations and patterns in discourse (see also Schmid, 2014).

1.3.4 Other Determinants of Entrenchment

Frequency and repetition in context are not the only factors affecting entrenchment processes and their outcomes. Instead, a wide range of other variables play a role, in part by acting directly on entrenchment processes and in part by indirectly influencing repetition and thus frequency. Theoretical models of entrenchment should be informed about these factors, and empirical work investigating entrenchment must keep an eye on them as potential confounding variables (see Herdina, Chapter 17, this volume). The following brief overview is divided into linguistic factors, processing-related factors other than frequency and repetition, speaker-centered factors, and other context-related factors.

The main linguistic factor influencing the outcome of entrenchment processes is the grammatical structure of the language in question. Although entrenchment processes as such are arguably universal (Bybee, 2003, p. 622), the specific ways in which they affect first the representations of individual speakers and eventually the conventional system of the language will differ depending on the basic typological (isolating, agglutinative, fusional) and other structural characteristics. The nature of the linguistic units subjected to entrenchment processes differs considerably across language types, and so, presumably, will the outcomes of entrenchment. For example, because string chunking is largely a process involving elements in linear sequence (Bybee, 2002), it is likely that the outcome of chunking differs depending on whether the language has fixed or flexible word order. The length of potential chunks, which is partly influenced by typological factors as well, is also likely to affect degrees of entrenchment (Blumenthal-Dramé, 2012, p. 40).

Other processing-related factors, in addition to repetition and rehearsal, include the perceptual salience of linguistic forms and of extralinguistic referents as well as the cognitive salience of concepts (Geeraerts, Grondelaers, & Bakema, 1994).

The relation between attention, salience, and entrenchment is far from trivial (Schmid, 2007; see also Günther, Müller, & Geyer, Chapter 13, this volume). On the one hand, because salient forms and referents are more likely to attract attention and therefore invite repeated processing, they are also more likely to become entrenched. Once entrenched, these routines are activated more quickly and with less effort and are therefore more likely to be repeated. Obviously, this gives rise to a feedback loop in which frequency comes to serve as both a cause and an effect of entrenchment[a,1] (Barlow & Kemmer, 2000, p. x; Schmid & Günther, 2016; see also Geeraerts, Chapter 7, this volume). Although this seems to involve the danger of a circular argumentation (Blumenthal-Dramé, 2012, p. 43), feedback loops of this type are common not only in cognitive processing, but also in diffusion processes in social systems. On the other hand, while entrenched form–meaning pairings are unlikely to attract attention, less entrenched constructions, such as rare words, are highly salient. This is shown in the inverse frequency effects reported from experiments on structural priming in which low-frequency combinations of verbs and constructions emerge as more likely to be repeated than high-frequency ones (e.g., Snider, 2007, p. 96).

Processing mode may have an effect as well. Because chunking processes are usually traced back to articulatory economy (e.g., Bybee, 1985), it is often assumed that individual entrenchment and long-term collective conventionalization of this type are fostered more by frequency in speech than by frequency in written text (Krug, 2003, p. 32). Whether the processing of spoken language is also more conducive to entrenchment in terms of strength of representation and schematization than the processing of written language has yet to be shown. The fact that many speakers are highly aware of the appropriateness of words and constructions in specific situational contexts supports the assumption that contextual information is stored alongside formal and semantic aspects. Blumenthal-Dramé (2012, p. 40) reviewed studies suggesting that the potential for mental imagery and emotional arousal may have an effect on entrenchment.

If entrenchment relates to the minds of individual speakers, it is, more or less by definition, subject to individual, speaker-related differences (Barlow, 2013; Dąbrowska, 2012, 2015; Schmid & Mantlik, 2015; Street & Dąbrowska, 2010). Most of these are hard to grasp and control methodologically because their sources are hidden in the exposure and usage histories of individual speakers, which, in turn, are influenced not only by familiar social variables such as region, gender, education, training, and social roles (Geeraerts, 2005) but also by personal routines and experiences. In addition, individual preferences for analytical and holistic perceptual processing may well have an effect (de-Wit & Wagemans, 2015). Age undoubtedly plays a key role because neuroplasticity, and with it the potential for cognitive reorganization, decreases over time (Blumenthal-Dramé, 2012, pp. 44–47; Seidenberg & Zevin, 2006). Even if entrenchment is conceived of as a lifelong learning process, there can be no doubt that linguistic reorganization is particularly dynamic during the so-called *critical* or *sensitive period* (Lenneberg, 1967), that is, before the age of approximately 14 years. Furthermore, entrenchment processes and their outcomes crucially depend on whether speakers are acquiring and developing their first, second, or a later language, because entrenched first-language routines have a strong transfer and interference effect on the learning of later languages (MacWhinney, 2008; see also MacWhinney, Chapter 15, this volume). Feedback effects of languages learned later on the first language and especially on other nonnative languages learned earlier are also well attested (see Cenoz, Hufeisen, & Jessner, 2001).

Finally, because entrenchment is subject to the use of language in social situations, key social parameters of the other interlocutors are likely to play a role, both directly and mediated by other variables, such as salience. The extent to which accommodation, imitation, and alignment take place and can have an effect on short- and long-term entrenchment depends on the social roles and the (overt and covert) prestige of the interlocutors vis-à-vis the speaker. Research in communication accommodation theory (Giles, Coupland, & Coupland, 1991) has shown that speakers are more willing to converge in their use of language if they feel solidarity. Finally, the prestige of sources and media that provide input (e.g., newspapers, magazines, TV, Internet) and the speakers and writers, respectively, also influence entrenchment.

1.4 Consequences for Understanding the Psychological Foundations of Entrenchment

The discussion so far has demonstrated that entrenchment processes can be made responsible for a wide range of cognitive and linguistic effects. Before a proposal integrating these effects is made (see Section 1.5), it is important to summarize the psychological foundations of entrenchment and point to missing links between insights on linguistic entrenchment and the underlying psychological processes.

First, entrenchment in terms of variable strengths of representations suggests memory-based interpretations (see Takashima & Bakker, Chapter 8, this volume): Rehearsal affected by repeated exposure and use results in memory consolidation; disuse causes decay and attrition (Langacker, 1987, p. 57). Although a single exposure may leave memory traces strong enough to persist (de Vaan, Schreuder, & Baayen, 2007), it has to be assumed that memory consolidation requires repetition, ideally in different communicative situations, and the retaining of memory traces from one communicative event to the next. Sleep has been shown to be conducive to memorizing new words (Dumay & Gaskell, 2007). Automaticity could come into play here as an effect of increasingly routinized reactions to communicative demands in social situations by means of implicit statistical learning. For example, for most people, it is a highly automatic routine requiring little monitoring and conscious effort to greet family members or colleagues when they see them for the first time in the morning. Because a large proportion of everyday conversation is formulaic (see the references provided in Conklin

& Schmitt, 2012, p. 46), automaticity may well complement memory consolidation as an important cognitive process (see Hartsuiker & Moors, Chapter 9, this volume). The boundary between stored knowledge of linguistic routines and the automatic skill of applying them in the right context does not seem to be clear-cut.

This leads to the second main facet of entrenchment: holistic processing and storage of complex chunks (see Gobet, Chapter 11, this volume). As pointed out earlier, the autonomous processing of fixed chunks, in the sense of unmonitored completion once begun (Bargh, 1992), points toward an account in terms of high degrees of automaticity, as does the tendency to align linguistically with interlocutors (Garrod & Pickering, 2009). However, language production as such (see Garrod & Pickering, 2009) is of course clearly not an entirely automatic cognitive process, and so memory and other higher cognitive abilities definitely have a role to play. If we want to understand how knowledge of language and linguistic competence can emerge by means of entrenchment, the details of how memory, learning, and automatization work together have to be spelled out in greater detail.

This, thirdly, is not enough, however. As the discussions in Sections 1.3.1 and 1.3.2 have shown, entrenchment in terms of strength of representation and entrenchment in terms of chunking are inextricably intertwined with schematization. As soon as entrenched routines involve variable forms or contain variable slots, schematization comes into play. If one accepts the reasonable working definition of Blumenthal-Dramé (2012, p. 4), which states that entrenchment denotes "the strength of autonomy or representation of a form–meaning pairing *at a given level of abstraction in the cognitive system*" (emphasis added), it becomes clear that schematization is an inevitable part of entrenchment, not least because constructional schemas undoubtedly lie at the heart of language learning, linguistic knowledge, and the generative capacity of speakers to form sentences. From a psychological point of view, the decision to include schematization as a key entrenchment process widens the agenda even further to include categorization, generalization, and abstraction as relevant cognitive processes underlying schematization (see Cordes, Chapter 12, this volume).

Fourth, a model of entrenchment has to factor in the psychosocial processes mentioned in Section 1.3.3: imitation, emulation, accommodation, alignment, and co-adaptation, as well as the range of social variables affecting their effects (see Section 1.3.4). A solid understanding of these processes is essential because they act as mediators between the cognitive processes taking place in the minds of language users and the communicative factors that lie behind frequency-based repetition and the way it affects speakers' cognitive systems and the collective linguistic system (Schmid, 2015). Models of language as a complex adaptive system (Ellis & Larsen-Freeman, 2009; Frank & Gontier, 2010; Five Graces Group, 2009; see also Herdina, Chapter 17, this volume) or as distributed cognition (Cowley, 2011; Cowley & Vallée-Tourangeau, 2013; see also Cowley, Chapter 18, this volume), as well as sociocognitive models of linguistic knowledge (Geeraerts, 2005; Geeraerts, Kristiansen, & Peirsman, 2010; Kristiansen, 2008; Zenner, Speelman, & Geeraerts, 2012) target these aspects.

1.5 Toward an Integrated Framework for the Study of Entrenchment and Its Psychological Foundations

In light of the preceding discussion, the following working definition of entrenchment is suggested: *Entrenchment* refers to the ongoing reorganization and adaptation of individual communicative knowledge, which is subject to exposure to language and language use and to the exigencies of domain-general cognitive processes and the social environment. Specifically, entrenchment subsumes processes related to

1. different strengths of the representations of simple and complex linguistic elements and structures,
2. degrees of chunking resulting in the availability of more or less holistically processed units, and
3. the emergence and reorganization of variable schemas providing the means required for generative linguistic competence.

The linguistic effects that can result from these basic entrenchment processes are numerous, diverse, and, in part, seemingly contradictory. Conceptual and terminological confusion is increased because the term *entrenchment* has been used to refer to a variety of things: cognitive processes and their cognitive and linguistic effects, as well as collective processes and their long-term linguistic effects on the language system. Terms denoting more specific entrenchment processes such as *chunking*, *fusion*, and *analogy* have also been used to refer to both individual cognitive and long-term collective conventionalization processes.

To demonstrate that entrenchment is nevertheless a valuable and coherent concept with considerable explanatory power, the remainder of this introduction sketches out an integrative framework for the study of entrenchment and its psychological foundation. In this proposal,

- cognitive processes taking place in the minds of individuals (entrenchment) are distinguished from social processes effecting long-term language change (conventionalization);
- cognitive processes are distinguished from cognitive effects;
- cognitive effects are distinguished from linguistic effects;
- determinants and predictors of entrenchment are distinguished from entrenchment processes, and these in turn from cognitive and linguistic effects;
- effects of repetition of specific tokens and exemplars (token frequency) are distinguished from effects of repetition of abstract types and schemas (type frequency); and
- effects of entrenchment in linguistic forms are distinguished from effects on linguistic meanings.

As a first step, the nature of the entities that serve as input to entrenchment processes is redefined. Usage-based models usually assume that entrenchment operates over constructions and constructional schemas that are characterized as form–meaning pairings. Furthermore, they claim that these constructions and schemas are related to each other in a massive associative memory network organized mainly in terms of hierarchical relations (see Hilpert & Diessel, Chapter 3, this volume). The present proposal diverges from this idea in two important ways: First, it rejects the distinction between constructions serving as nodes in the network and relations between nodes and instead assumes that linguistic knowledge is available in one format only, namely, associations. These associations come in four types: symbolic, syntagmatic, paradigmatic, and pragmatic. Second, entrenchment processes are seen as operating over these four types of associations in the network rather than over constructions, which, in turn, are regarded as more or less strongly entrenched symbolic associations between forms and meanings (for more details, see Schmid, 2014, 2015). This decision is partly motivated by concerns (Schmid, 2013; see also Blumenthal-Dramé, 2012) that as soon as one claims that a "construction" is "represented" in a speaker's mind, both the gradual and the dynamic aspects inherent in the concept of entrenchment are left behind. The four types of associations are defined as follows:

- *Symbolic* associations link linguistic forms and meanings in language processing and thus afford the semiotic potential of linguistic signs and constructions.
- *Syntagmatic* associations link forms and meanings processed sequentially in language production and comprehension.
- *Paradigmatic* associations link associations during ongoing language processing to competing associations, that is, to associations that could potentially enter the focus of attention in the given linguistic and situational environment.
- *Pragmatic* associations link symbolic, paradigmatic, and syntagmatic associations with perceptual input garnered from external situations.

While all four types of associations are portrayed as being activated in the course of ongoing language processing, entrenchment is brought about by the routinization effected by the repeated processing of identical or similar stimuli. This is exactly what is predicted by emergentist and usage-based models of language.

The precise ways in which these four types of associations are affected by entrenchment processes is summarized in Table 1.1 (see Section 1.3). The table focuses on frequency and repetition as the main determinant of entrenchment and distinguishes between types of repetition, cognitive effects, and linguistic effects. Details about these effects can be found in Sections 1.3.1 through 1.3.3. In addition, suggestions concerning possible psychological affordances underlying entrenchment are listed.

The table should be read from left to right. The first line, for example, states that the token repetition of identical word forms and fixed strings increases the representational strength of the symbolic association between these forms and the corresponding meanings by means of memory consolidation and routinization, which has the numerous linguistic effects listed in the right-hand cell. The additional determinants of entrenchment discussed in Section 1.3 are not included in the table but form part of the general framework of entrenchment. The goal of this proposal, in addition to highlighting the dynamic quality of entrenchment processes, is to show that the large diversity of entrenchment processes can be reconciled in a unified framework if types of inputs to entrenchment processes, determinants, and effects of entrenchment are systematically distinguished. It would be exaggerated to claim that everything falls into place once this is done, but a small step forward may be accomplished.

1.6 Conclusion

The proposed framework in this chapter is bound to raise a lot of questions, but it may still serve as a starting point for the investigation of entrenchment processes and the interpretation of empirical data and findings. The contributions to this volume will equip readers with everything they need to form their own ideas of entrenchment and its psychological foundations in memory and automatization.

References

Abbot-Smith, K., & Tomasello, M. (2006). Exemplar-learning and schematization in a usage-based account of syntactic acquisition. *The Linguistic Review*, *23*, 275–290. http://dx.doi.org/10.1515/TLR.2006.011

Adelman, J. S., Brown, G. D. A., & Quesada, J. F. (2006). Contextual diversity, not word frequency, determines word-naming and lexical decision times. *Psychological Science*, *17*, 814–823. http://dx.doi.org/10.1111/j.1467-9280.2006.01787.x

Ambridge, B., Pine, J. M., Rowland, C. F., & Chang, F. (2012). The roles of verb semantics, entrenchment, and morphophonology in the retreat from dative argument-structure overgeneralization errors. *Language*, *88*, 45–81. http://dx.doi.org/10.1353/lan.2012.0000

Ambridge, B., Pine, J. M., Rowland, C. F., & Young, C. R. (2008). The effect of verb semantic class and verb frequency (entrenchment) on children's and adults' graded judgements of argument-structure overgeneralization errors. *Cognition*, *106*, 87–129. http://dx.doi.org/10.1016/j.cognition.2006.12.015

Arnon, I., & Snider, N. (2010). More than words: Frequency effects for multi-word phrases. *Journal of Memory and Language*, *62*, 67–82. http://dx.doi.org/10.1016/j.jml.2009.09.005

Arppe, A., Gilquin, G., Glynn, D., Hilpert, M., & Zeschel, A. (2010). Cognitive corpus linguistics: Five points of debate on current theory and methodology. *Corpora*, *5*, 1–27. http://dx.doi.org/10.3366/cor.2010.0001

Auer, P., & Hinskens, F. (2005). The role of interpersonal accommodation in a theory of language change. In P. Auer, F. Hinskens, & P. Kerswill (Eds.), *Dialect change* (pp. 335–357). Cambridge, England: Cambridge University Press. http://dx.doi.org/10.1017/CBO9780511486623.015

Auer, P., & Pfänder, S. (Eds.). (2011). *Constructions: Emerging and emergent.* http://dx.doi.org/10.1515/9783110229080

Baayen, R. H. (2010). Demythologizing the word frequency effect: A discriminative learning perspective. *The Mental Lexicon, 5,* 436–461. http://dx.doi.org/10.1075/ml.5.3.10baa

Bargh, J. A. (1992). The ecology of automaticity: Toward establishing the conditions needed to produce automatic processing effects. *The American Journal of Psychology, 105,* 181–199. http://dx.doi.org/10.2307/1423027

Barlow, M. (2013). Individual differences and usage-based grammar. *International Journal of Corpus Linguistics, 18,* 443–478. http://dx.doi.org/10.1075/ijcl.18.4.01bar

Barlow, M., & Kemmer, S. (Eds.). (2000). *Usage-based models of language.* Stanford, CA: CSLI.

Behrens, H. (2009). Usage-based and emergentist approaches to language acquisition. *Linguistics, 47,* 381–411. http://dx.doi.org/10.1515/LING.2009.014

Blumenthal-Dramé, A. (2012). *Entrenchment in usage-based theories: What corpus data do and do not reveal about the mind.* http://dx.doi.org/10.1515/9783110294002

Bock, K. (1986). Syntactic persistence in language production. *Cognitive Psychology, 18,* 355–387. http://dx.doi.org/10.1016/0010-0285(86)90004-6

Bock, K., & Griffin, Z. M. (2000). The persistence of structural priming: Transient activation or implicit learning? *Journal of Experimental Psychology: General, 129,* 177–192. http://dx.doi.org/10.1037/0096-3445.129.2.177

Boye, K., & Harder, P. (2012). A usage-based theory of grammatical status and grammaticalization. *Language, 88,* 1–44. http://dx.doi.org/10.1353/lan.2012.0020

Braine, M., & Brooks, P. (1995). Verb argument structure and the problem of avoiding an overgeneral grammar. In M. Tomasello & W. Merriman (Eds.), *Beyond names for things: Young children's acquisition of verbs* (pp. 353–376). Hillsdale, NJ: Erlbaum.

Brinton, L. J., & Traugott, E. C. (2005). *Lexicalization and language change.* Cambridge, England: Cambridge University Press. http://dx.doi.org/10.1017/CBO9780511615962

Brooks, P., & Tomasello, M. (1999). How children constrain their argument structure constructions. *Language, 75,* 720–738. http://dx.doi.org/10.2307/417731

Bybee, J. L. (1985). *Morphology: A study of the relation between meaning and form.* http://dx.doi.org/10.1075/tsl.9

Bybee, J. L. (2002). Sequentiality as the basis of constituent structure. In T. Givón & B. F. Malle (Eds.), *The evolution of language out of pre-language* (pp. 109–134). http://dx.doi.org/10.1075/tsl.53.07byb

Bybee, J. L. (2003). Mechanisms of change in grammaticization: The role of frequency. In B. Joseph & R. Janda (Eds.), *Handbook of historical linguistics* (pp. 602–623). http://dx.doi.org/10.1002/9780470756393.ch19

Bybee, J. L. (2006). From usage to grammar: The mind's response to repetition. *Language, 82,* 711–733. http://dx.doi.org/10.1353/lan.2006.0186

Bybee, J. L. (2007). *Frequency of use and the organization of language.* http://dx.doi.org/10.1093/acprof:oso/9780195301571.001.0001

Bybee, J. L. (2010a). *Language, usage and cognition.* http://dx.doi.org/10.1017/CBO9780511750526

Bybee, J. L. (2010b). Usage-based theory. In B. Heine & H. Narrog (Eds.), *The Oxford handbook of linguistic analysis* (pp. 69–78). Oxford, England: Oxford University Press.

Bybee, J. L., & McClelland, J. L. (2005). Alternatives to the combinatorial paradigm of linguistic theory based on domain general principles of human cognition. *The Linguistic Review, 22,* 381–410. http://dx.doi.org/10.1515/tlir.2005.22.2-4.381

Bybee, J. L., & Pagliuca, W. (1985). Cross-linguistic comparison and the development of grammatical meaning. In J. Fisiak (Ed.), *Historical semantics—Historical word-formation* (pp. 59–83). http://dx.doi.org/10.1515/9783110850178.59

Bybee, J. L., & Scheibman, J. (1999). The effect of usage on degrees of constituency: The reduction of *don't* in English. *Linguistics, 37*, 575–596. http://dx.doi.org/10.1515/ling.37.4.575

Bybee, J. L., & Thompson, S. A. (1997). Three frequency effects in syntax. In L. J. Matthew & J. Moxley (Eds.), *Proceedings of the 23rd annual meeting of the Berkeley Linguistics Society* (pp. 378–388). Berkeley, CA: Berkeley Linguistics Society.

Cappelle, B., Shtyrov, Y., & Pulvermüller, F. (2010). *Heating up* or *cooling up* the brain? MEG evidence that phrasal verbs are lexical units. *Brain and Language, 115*, 189–201. http://dx.doi.org/10.1016/j.bandl.2010.09.004

Casenhiser, D., & Goldberg, A. E. (2005). Fast mapping between a phrasal form and meaning. *Developmental Science, 8*, 500–508. http://dx.doi.org/10.1111/j.1467-7687.2005.00441.x

Cenoz, J., Hufeisen, B., & Jessner, U. (Eds.). (2001). *Cross-linguistic influence in third language acquisition: Psycholinguistic perspectives*. Bristol, England: Multilingual Matters.

Chang, F., Dell, G. S., & Bock, K. (2006). Becoming syntactic. *Psychological Review, 113*, 234–272. http://dx.doi.org/10.1037/0033-295X.113.2.234

Childers, J. B., & Tomasello, M. (2001). The role of pronouns in young children's acquisition of the English transitive construction. *Developmental Psychology, 37*, 739–748. http://dx.doi.org/10.1037/0012-1649.37.6.739

Conklin, K., & Schmitt, N. (2012). The processing of formulaic language. *Annual Review of Applied Linguistics, 32*, 45–61. http://dx.doi.org/10.1017/S0267190512000074

Cordes, A. K. (2014). *The role of frequency in children's learning of morphological constructions*. Tübingen, Germany: Narr.

Cowley, S. J. (Ed.). (2011). *Distributed language*. http://dx.doi.org/10.1075/bct.34

Cowley, S. J., & Vallée-Tourangeau, F. (Eds.). (2013). *Cognition beyond the brain: Computation, interactivity and human artifice*. http://dx.doi.org/10.1007/978-1-4471-5125-8

Croft, W. (2000). *Explaining language change: An evolutionary approach*. Harlow, England: Longman.

Croft, W. (2008). On iconicity of distance. *Cognitive Linguistics, 19*, 49–57. http://dx.doi.org/10.1515/COG.2008.003

Dąbrowska, E. (2012). Different speakers, different grammars: Individual differences in native language attainment. *Linguistic Approaches to Bilingualism, 2*, 219–253. http://dx.doi.org/10.1075/lab.2.3.01dab

Dąbrowska, E. (2015). Individual differences in grammatical knowledge. In E. Dąbrowska & D. Divjak (Eds.), *Handbook of cognitive linguistics* (pp. 650–668). http://dx.doi.org/10.1515/9783110292022-033

Dell, G. S. (1990). Effects of frequency and vocabulary type on phonological speech errors. *Language and Cognitive Processes, 5*, 313–349. http://dx.doi.org/10.1080/01690969008407066

de Saussure, F. (1916). *Cours de linguistique générale* [Course in general linguistics]. Paris, France: Payot.

de Vaan, L., Schreuder, R., & Baayen, R. H. (2007). Regular morphologically complex neologisms leave detectable traces in the mental lexicon. *The Mental Lexicon, 2*, 1–23. http://dx.doi.org/10.1075/ml.2.1.02vaa

de-Wit, L., & Wagemans, J. (2015). Individual differences in local and global perceptual organization. In J. Wagemans (Ed.), *Oxford handbook of perceptual organization* (pp. 713–735). Oxford, England: Oxford University Press.

Diessel, H. (2007). Frequency effects in language acquisition, language use, and diachronic change. *New Ideas in Psychology, 25*, 108–127. http://dx.doi.org/10.1016/j.newideapsych.2007.02.002

Divjak, D. (2008). On (in)frequency and (un)acceptability. In B. Lewandowska-Tomaszczyk (Ed.), *Corpus linguistics, computer tools and applications—State of the art* (pp. 1–21). Frankfurt, Germany: Peter Lang.

Divjak, D., & Caldwell-Harris, C. L. (2015). Frequency and entrenchment. In E. Dąbrowska & D. Divjak (Eds.), *Handbook of cognitive linguistics* (pp. 53–75). http://dx.doi.org/10.1515/9783110292022-004

Divjak, D., & Gries, S. T. (Eds.). (2012). *Frequency effects in language representation.* http://dx.doi.org/10.1515/9783110274073

Dumay, N., & Gaskell, M. G. (2007). Sleep-associated changes in the mental representation of spoken words. *Psychological Science, 18*, 35–39.

Ellis, N. C. (2006). Language acquisition as rational contingency learning. *Applied Linguistics, 27*, 1–24. http://dx.doi.org/10.1093/applin/ami038

Ellis, N. C. (2009). Constructing a second language. In N. C. Ellis, C. Nick, & D. Larsen-Freeman (Eds.), *Language as a complex adaptive system* (pp. 90–123). Chichester, England: Wiley-Blackwell.

Ellis, N. C., & Larsen-Freeman, D. (Eds.). (2009). *Language as a complex adaptive system.* Chichester, England: Wiley-Blackwell.

Ellis, N. C., & O'Donnell, M. (2014). Construction learning as category learning: A cognitive analysis. In T. Herbst, H.-J. Schmid, & S. Faulhaber (Eds.), *Constructions collocations patterns* (pp. 71–97). http://dx.doi.org/10.1515/9783110356854.71

Evert, S. (2004). *The statistics of word cooccurrences: Word pairs and collocations* (Unpublished doctoral dissertation). Institut für Maschinelle Sprachverarbeitung, University of Stuttgart, Germany.

Five Graces Group [Becker, C., Blythe, R., Bybee, J., Christiansen, M. H., Croft, W., Ellis, N. C., Holland, J., Ke, J., Larsen-Freeman, D., & Schoenemann, T.]. (2009). Language is a complex adaptive system: Position paper. In N. C. Ellis & D. Larsen-Freeman (Eds.), *Language as a complex adaptive system* (pp. 1–26). Chichester, England: Wiley-Blackwell.

Forster, K. I. (2007). Visual word recognition: Problems and issues. In G. Jarema & G. Libben (Eds.), *The mental lexicon. Core perspectives* (pp. 31–53). Amsterdam, the Netherlands: Elsevier.

Frank, R. M., & Gontier, N. (2010). On constructing a research model for historical cognitive linguistics (HCL): Some theoretical considerations. In M. E. Winters, H. Tissari, & K. Allan (Eds.), *Historical cognitive linguistics* (pp. 31–69). Berlin, Germany: De Gruyter Mouton.

Garrod, S., & Pickering, M. (2007). Automaticity in language production in monologue and dialogue. In A. Meyer, L. Wheeldon, & A. Krott (Eds.), *Automaticity and control in language processing* (pp. 1–20). New York, NY: Psychology Press.

Garrod, S., & Pickering, M. J. (2009). Joint action, interactive alignment, and dialog. *Topics in Cognitive Science, 1*, 292–304. http://dx.doi.org/10.1111/j.1756-8765.2009.01020.x

Geeraerts, D. (2005). Lectal variation and empirical data in Cognitive Linguistics. In F. J. Ruiz De Mendoza Ibanez & M. S. Pena Cerval (Eds.), *Cognitive linguistics: Internal dynamics and interdisciplinary interaction* (pp. 163–189). Berlin, Germany: Mouton de Gruyter.

Geeraerts, D., Grondelaers, S., & Bakema, P. (1994). *The structure of lexical variation. A descriptive framework for cognitive lexicology.* http://dx.doi.org/10.1515/9783110873061

Geeraerts, D., Kristiansen, G., & Peirsman, Y. (Eds.). (2010). *Advances in cognitive sociolinguistics.* http://dx.doi.org/10.1515/9783110226461

Gibbs, R. W., Jr. (1980). Spilling the beans on understanding and memory for idioms in conversation. *Memory & Cognition, 8*, 149–156. http://dx.doi.org/10.3758/BF03213418

Giles, H., Coupland, N., & Coupland, J. (1991). Accommodation theory: Communication, context and consequence. In H. Giles, N. Coupland, & J. Coupland (Eds.), *Contexts of accommodation: Developments in applied sociolinguistics* (pp. 1–68). http://dx.doi.org/10.1017/CBO9780511663673.001

Giles, H., & Ogay, T. (2006). Communication accommodation theory. In B. B. Whaley & W. Samter (Eds.), *Explaining communication: Contemporary theories and exemplars* (pp. 293–310). Mahwah, NJ: Erlbaum.

Giora, R. (2003). *On our mind: Salience, context, and figurative language.* http://dx.doi.org/10.1093/acprof:oso/9780195136166.001.0001

Glynn, D., & Fischer, K. (Eds.). (2010). *Quantitative methods in cognitive semantics: Corpus-driven approaches.* http://dx.doi.org/10.1515/9783110226423

Goldberg, A. (2006). *Constructions at work: The nature of generalization in language.* Oxford, England: Oxford University Press.

Goldberg, A. (2009). The nature of generalization in language. *Cognitive Linguistics, 20*, 93–127.

Goldberg, A., & Casenhiser, D. (2006). Learning argument structure constructions. In E. V. Clark & B. F. Kelly (Eds.), *Constructions in acquisition* (pp. 185–204). Stanford, CA: CSLI.

Gregory, M., Raymond, W., Fosler-Lussier, E., & Jurafsky, D. (2000). The effects of collocational strength and contextual predictability in lexical production. *Chicago Linguistic Society, 35*, 151–166.

Gries, S. T., & Divjak, D. (Eds.). (2012). Frequency effects in language learning and processing. http://dx.doi.org/10.1515/9783110274059

Gries, S. T., Hampe, B., & Schönefeld, D. (2005). Converging evidence: Bringing together experimental and corpus data on the associations of verbs and constructions. *Cognitive Linguistics, 16*, 635–676. http://dx.doi.org/10.1515/cogl.2005.16.4.635

Gries, S. T., Hampe, B., & Schönefeld, D. (2010). Converging evidence II: More on the association of verbs and constructions. In J. Newman & S. Rice (Eds.), *Experimental and empirical methods in the study of conceptual structure, discourse, and language* (pp. 59–72). Stanford, CA: CSLI.

Günthner, S. (2011). Between emergence and sedimentation: Projecting constructions in German interactions. In P. Auer & S. Pfänder (Eds.), *Constructions: Emerging and emergent* (pp. 165–185). http://dx.doi.org/10.1515/9783110229080.156

Haiman, J. (1994). Ritualization and the development of language. In W. Pagliuca (Ed.), *Perspectives on grammaticalization* (pp. 3–28). http://dx.doi.org/10.1075/cilt.109.07hai

Hare, M., McRae, K., & Elman, J. L. (2004). Admitting that admitting verb sense into corpus analyses makes sense. *Language and Cognitive Processes, 19*, 181–224. http://dx.doi.org/10.1080/01690960344000152

Haspelmath, M. (2008). Frequency vs. iconicity in explaining grammatical asymmetries. *Cognitive Linguistics, 19*, 1–33. http://dx.doi.org/10.1515/COG.2008.001

Haspelmath, M. (2011). The gradual coalescence into "words" in grammaticalization. In H. Narrog & B. Heine (Eds.), *The Oxford handbook of grammaticalization* (pp. 342–355). Oxford, England: Oxford University Press.

Haspelmath, M. (2014). On system pressure competing with economic motivation. In B. MacWhinney, A. Malchukov, & E. Moravcsik (Eds.), *Competing motivations in grammar and usage* (pp. 197–208). http://dx.doi.org/10.1093/acprof:oso/9780198709848.003.0012

Hauk, O., & Pulvermüller, F. (2004). Effects of word length and frequency on the human event-related potential. *Clinical Neurophysiology, 115*, 1090–1103. http://dx.doi.org/10.1016/j.clinph.2003.12.020

Hay, J. (2001). Lexical frequency in morphology: Is everything relative? *Linguistics, 39*, 1041–1070. http://dx.doi.org/10.1515/ling.2001.041

Heine, B., Claudi, U., & Hünnemeyer, F. (1991). *Grammaticalization: A conceptual framework.* Chicago, IL: University of Chicago Press.

Himmelmann, N. P. (2004). Lexicalization and grammaticization: opposite or orthogonal? In W. Bisang, N. P. Himmelmann, & B. Wiemer (Eds.), *What makes grammaticalization: A look from its fringes and its components* (pp. 21–42). Berlin, Germany: Mouton de Gruyter.

Hoey, M. (2005). *Lexical priming: A new theory of words and language.* http://dx.doi.org/10.4324/9780203327630

Hoffmann, S. (2005). *Grammaticalization and English complex prepositions: A corpus-based study.* New York, NY: Routledge.

Hopper, P. (1987). Emergent grammar. *Berkeley Linguistics Society, 13*, 139–157.

Jaeger, T. F., & Snider, N. E. (2013). Alignment as a consequence of expectation adaptation: Syntactic priming is affected by the prime's prediction error given both prior and recent experience. *Cognition, 127*, 57–83. http://dx.doi.org/10.1016/j.cognition.2012.10.013

Jescheniak, J. D., & Levelt, W. J. M. (1994). Word frequency effects in speech production: Retrieval of syntactic information and of phonological form. *Journal of Experimental Psychology: Learning, Memory, and Cognition, 20*, 824–843. http://dx.doi.org/10.1037/0278-7393.20.4.824

Jones, L. L., & Estes, Z. (2012). Lexical priming: Associative, semantic, and thematic influences on word recognition. In J. S. Adelman (Ed.), *Visional word recognition: Vol. 2. Meaning and context, individuals and development* (pp. 44–72). Hove, England: Psychology Press.

Jurafsky, D. (1996). A probabilistic model of lexical and syntactic access and disambiguation. *Cognitive Science, 20*, 137–194. http://dx.doi.org/10.1207/s15516709cog2002_1

Jurafsky, D. (2003). Probabilistic modelling in psycholinguistics: Linguistic comprehension and production. In R. Bod, J. Hay, & S. Jannedy (Eds.), *Probabilistic linguistics* (pp. 39–76). Cambridge, MA: MIT Press.

Jurafsky, D., Bell, A., Gregory, M., & Raymond, W. D. (2001). Probabilistic relations between words: Evidence from reduction in lexical production. In J. Bybee & P. Hopper (Eds.), *Frequency and the emergence of linguistic structure* (pp. 229–254). http://dx.doi.org/10.1075/tsl.45.13jur

Just, M. A., & Carpenter, P. A. (1980). A theory of reading: From eye fixations to comprehension. *Psychological Review, 87*, 329–354. http://dx.doi.org/10.1037/0033-295X.87.4.329

Kemmer, S., & Barlow, M. (2000). Introduction. In M. Barlow & S. Kemmer (Eds.), *Usage-based models of language* (pp. vii–xxvii). Stanford, CA: CSLI.

Kidd, A., Lieven, E. V. M., & Tomasello, M. (2010). Lexical frequency and exemplar-based learning effects in language acquisition: Evidence from sentential complements. *Language Sciences, 32*, 132–142. http://dx.doi.org/10.1016/j.langsci.2009.05.002

Knobel, M., Finkbeiner, M., & Caramazza, A. (2008). The many places of frequency: Evidence for a novel locus of the lexical frequency effect in word production. *Cognitive Neuropsychology, 25*, 256–286. http://dx.doi.org/10.1080/02643290701502425

König, E., & Traugott, E. C. (1988). Pragmatic strengthening and semantic change: The conventionalizing of conversational implicature. In W. Hüllen & R. Schulze (Eds.), *Understanding the lexicon* (pp. 110–124). http://dx.doi.org/10.1515/9783111355191.110

Kristiansen, G. (2008). Style-shifting and shifting styles: A socio-cognitive approach to lectal variation. In G. Kristiansen & R. Dirven (Eds.), *Cognitive sociolinguistics: Language variation, cultural models, social systems* (pp. 45–88). http://dx.doi.org/10.1515/9783110199154.1.45

Krug, M. (2000). *Emerging English modals: A corpus-based study of grammaticalization.* http://dx.doi.org/10.1515/9783110820980

Krug, M. (2003). Frequency as a determinant in grammatical variation and change. In G. Rohdenburg & B. Mondorf (Eds.), *Determinants of grammatical variation in English* (pp. 7–67). http://dx.doi.org/10.1515/9783110900019.7

Kuteva, T. (2001). *Auxiliation: An enquiry into the nature of grammaticalization.* Oxford, England: Oxford University Press.

Langacker, R. W. (1987). *Foundations of cognitive grammar: Vol. 1. Theoretical prerequisites.* Stanford, CA: Stanford University Press.

Langacker, R. W. (1991). *Foundations of cognitive grammar: Vol. 2. Descriptive application.* Stanford, CA: Stanford University Press.

Langacker, R. W. (2008). *Cognitive grammar: A basic introduction.* http://dx.doi.org/10.1093/acprof:oso/9780195331967.001.0001

Lehmann, C. (2004). Theory and method in grammaticalization. *Zeitschrift für Germanistische Linguistik, 32*(2), 152–187. http://dx.doi.org/10.1515/zfgl.2004.32.2.152

Lenneberg, E. H. (1967). *Biological foundations of language.* Chichester, England: Wiley-Blackwell.

Lieven, E. V. (2010). Input and first language acquisition: Evaluating the role of frequency. *Lingua, 120,* 2546–2556. http://dx.doi.org/10.1016/j.lingua.2010.06.005

Lieven, E. V. (2014). Language-learning from a usage-based approach. In T. Herbst, H.-J. Schmid, & S. Faulhaber (Eds.), *Constructions collocations patterns* (pp. 9–32). Berlin, Germany: De Gruyter Mouton.

Lieven, E. V., & Tomasello, M. (2008). Children's first language acquisition from a usage-based perspective. In P. Robinson & N. C. Ellis (Eds.), *Handbook of cognitive linguistics and second language acquisition* (pp. 168–196). New York, NY: Routledge.

Logan, G. D. (1988). Towards an instance theory of automatization. *Psychological Review, 95,* 492–527. http://dx.doi.org/10.1037/0033-295X.95.4.492

MacWhinney, B. (Ed.). (1999). *The emergence of language.* Mahwah, NJ: Erlbaum.

MacWhinney, B. (2004). A multiple process solution to the logical problem of language acquisition. *Journal of Child Language, 31,* 883–914. http://dx.doi.org/10.1017/S0305000904006336

MacWhinney, B. (2008). A unified model. In P. Robinson & N. Ellis (Eds.), *Handbook of cognitive linguistics and second language acquisition* (pp. 341–371). New York, NY: Routledge.

Matthews, D., Lieven, E., Theakston, A., & Tomasello, M. (2005). The role of frequency in the acquisition of English word order. *Cognitive Development, 20,* 121–136. http://dx.doi.org/10.1016/j.cogdev.2004.08.001

McDonald, S. A., & Shillcock, R. C. (2001). Rethinking the word frequency effect: The neglected role of distributional information in lexical processing. *Language and Speech, 44,* 295–323. http://dx.doi.org/10.1177/00238309010440030101

McDonald, S. A., & Shillcock, R. C. (2003). Low-level predictive inference in reading: The influence of transitional probabilities on eye movements. *Vision Research, 43,* 1735–1751. http://dx.doi.org/10.1016/S0042-6989(03)00237-2

Moors, A., & De Houwer, J. (2006). Automaticity: A theoretical and conceptual analysis. *Psychological Bulletin, 132,* 297–326. http://dx.doi.org/10.1037/0033-2909.132.2.297

Mukherjee, J. (2005). *English ditransitive verbs: Aspects of theory, description and a usage-based model.* Amsterdam, the Netherlands: Rodopi.

Nattinger, J. R., & DeCarrico, J. S. (1992). *Lexical phrases and language teaching*. Oxford, England: Oxford University Press.

Newman, S. D., Ratliff, K., Muratore, T., & Burns, T., Jr. (2009). The effect of lexical priming on sentence comprehension: An fMRI study. *Brain Research*, *1285*, 99–108. http://dx.doi.org/10.1016/j.brainres.2009.06.027

Nicolle, S. (2011). Pragmatic aspects of grammaticalization. In H. Narrog & B. Heine (Eds.), *The Oxford handbook of grammaticalization* (pp. 401–412). Oxford, England: Oxford University Press.

Paul, H. (1920). *Prinzipien der Sprachgeschichte* [Principles of the history of language]. Halle, Germany: Niemeyer.

Pawley, A., & Syder, F. H. (1983). Two puzzles for linguistics theory: Nativelike selection and nativelike fluency. In J. C. Richards & R. W. Schmidt (Eds.), *Language and communication* (pp. 191–226). New York, NY: Longman.

Peters, A. (2009). Connecting the dots to unpack the language. In R. Corrigan, E. A. Moravcsik, H. Ouali, & K. M. Wheatley (Eds.), *Formulaic language: Vol. 2. Acquisition, loss, psychological reality, and functional explanations* (pp. 387–404). http://dx.doi.org/10.1075/tsl.83.08pet

Pickering, M. J., & Branigan, H. P. (1999). Syntactic priming in language production. *Trends in Cognitive Sciences*, *3*, 136–141. http://dx.doi.org/10.1016/S1364-6613(99)01293-0

Pickering, M. J., & Garrod, S. (2004). Toward a mechanistic psychology of dialogue. *Behavioral and Brain Sciences*, *27*, 169–190. http://dx.doi.org/10.1017/S0140525X04000056

Pierrehumbert, J. B. (2001). Exemplar dynamics: Word frequency, lenition and contrast. In J. Bybee & P. Hopper (Eds.), *Frequency and the emergence of linguistic structure* (pp. 516–530). http://dx.doi.org/10.1075/tsl.45.08pie

Pulvermüller, F. (2010). Brain embodiment of syntax and grammar: Discrete combinatorial mechanisms spelt out in neuronal circuits. *Brain and Language*, *112*, 167–179. http://dx.doi.org/10.1016/j.bandl.2009.08.002

Redington, M., Chater, N., & Finch, S. (1998). Distributional information: A powerful cue for acquiring syntactic categories. *Cognitive Science*, *22*, 425–469. http://dx.doi.org/10.1207/s15516709cog2204_2

Reitter, D., Keller, F., & Moore, J. D. (2011). A computational cognitive model of syntactic priming. *Cognitive Science*, *35*, 587–637. http://dx.doi.org/10.1111/j.1551-6709.2010.01165.x

Rohde, A., Stefanowitsch, A., & Kemmer, S. (2000). Loanwords in a usage-based model. *Chicago Linguistic Society: Papers from the General Session*, *35*, 265–275.

Roland, D., & Jurafsky, D. (2002). Verb sense and verb subcategorization probabilities. In P. Merlo & S. Stevenson (Eds.), *Sentence processing and the lexicon: Formal, computational, and experimental perspectives* (pp. 325–346). http://dx.doi.org/10.1075/nlp.4.17rol

Rugg, M. D. (1990). Event-related brain potentials dissociate repetition effects of high- and low-frequency words. *Memory & Cognition*, *18*, 367–379. http://dx.doi.org/10.3758/BF03197126

Saffran, J. R. (2001). Words in a sea of sounds: The output of infant statistical learning. *Cognition*, *81*, 149–169. http://dx.doi.org/10.1016/S0010-0277(01)00132-9

Saffran, J. R., Aslin, R. N., & Newport, E. L. (1996). Statistical learning by 8-month-old infants. *Science*, *274*, 1926–1928. http://dx.doi.org/10.1126/science.274.5294.1926

Sandra, D. (1994). *Morphology in the reader's mental lexicon*. Frankfurt/Main, Germany: Peter Lang.

Schmid, H.-J. (2000). *English abstract nouns as conceptual shells. From corpus to cognition*. http://dx.doi.org/10.1515/9783110808704

Schmid, H.-J. (2007). Entrenchment, salience and basic levels. In D. Geeraerts & H. Cuyckens (Eds.), *The Oxford handbook of cognitive linguistics* (pp. 117–138). Oxford, England: Oxford University Press.

Schmid, H.-J. (2010). Does frequency in text really instantiate entrenchment in the cognitive system? In D. Glynn & K. Fischer (Eds.), *Quantitative methods in cognitive semantics: Corpus-driven approaches* (pp. 101–133). http://dx.doi.org/10.1515/9783110226423.101

Schmid, H.-J. (2013). Is usage more than usage after all? The case of English *not that*. *Linguistics*, *51*, 75–116.

Schmid, H.-J. (2014). Lexico-grammatical patterns, pragmatic associations and discourse frequency. In T. Herbst, H.-J. Schmid, & S. Faulhaber (Eds.), *Constructions collocations patterns* (pp. 239–293). http://dx.doi.org/10.1515/9783110356854.239

Schmid, H.-J. (2015). A blueprint of the entrenchment-and-conventionalization model. *Yearbook of the German Cognitive Linguistics Association*, *3*, 1–27. http://dx.doi.org/10.1515/gcla-2015-0002

Schmid, H.-J., & Günther, F. (2016). Toward a unified socio-cognitive framework for salience in language. *Frontiers in Psychology*, *7*. http://dx.doi.org/10.3389/fpsyg.2016.01110

Schmid, H.-J., & Küchenhoff, H. (2013). Collostructional analysis and other ways of measuring lexico-grammatical attraction: Theoretical premises, practical problems and cognitive underpinnings. *Cognitive Linguistics*, *24*, 531–577. http://dx.doi.org/10.1515/cog-2013-0018

Schmid, H.-J., & Mantlik, A. (2015). Entrenchment in historical corpora? Reconstructing dead authors' minds from their usage profiles. *Anglia*, *133*, 583–623. http://dx.doi.org/10.1515/ang-2015-0056

Segaert, K., Kempen, G., Petersson, K. M., & Hagoort, P. (2013). Syntactic priming and the lexical boost effect during sentence production and sentence comprehension: An fMRI study. *Brain and Language*, *124*, 174–183. http://dx.doi.org/10.1016/j.bandl.2012.12.003

Seidenberg, M. S., & Zevin, J. D. (2006). Connectionist models in developmental cognitive neuroscience: Critical periods and the paradox of success. In Y. Munakata & M. Johnson (Eds.), *Processes of change in brain and cognitive development. Attention and performance XXI* (pp. 585–612). Oxford, England: Oxford University Press.

Siyanova-Chanturia, A., Conklin, K., & Schmitt, N. (2011). Adding more fuel to the fire: An eye-tracking study of idiom processing by native and nonnative speakers. *Second Language Research*, *27*, 251–272. http://dx.doi.org/10.1177/0267658310382068

Siyanova-Chanturia, A., Conklin, K., & van Heuven, W. J. (2011). Seeing a phrase "time and again" matters: The role of phrasal frequency in the processing of multiword sequences. *Journal of Experimental Psychology: Learning, Memory, and Cognition*, *37*, 776–784. http://dx.doi.org/10.1037/a0022531

Snider, N. (2007). *An exemplar model of syntactic priming*. Stanford, CA: Proquest.

Sosa, A. V., & MacFarlane, J. (2002). Evidence for frequency-based constituents in the mental lexicon: Collocations involving the word of. *Brain and Language*, *83*, 227–236. http://dx.doi.org/10.1016/S0093-934X(02)00032-9

Stefanowitsch, A., & Gries, S. T. (2003). Collostructions: Investigating the interaction of words and constructions. *International Journal of Corpus Linguistics*, *8*, 209–243. http://dx.doi.org/10.1075/ijcl.8.2.03ste

Street, J., & Dąbrowska, E. (2010). More individual differences in language attainment: How much do adult native speakers of English know about passives and quantifiers? *Lingua*, *120*, 2080–2094. http://dx.doi.org/10.1016/j.lingua.2010.01.004

Swinney, D. A., & Cutler, R. A. (1979). The access and processing of idiomatic expressions. *Journal of Verbal Learning & Verbal Behavior, 18,* 523–534. http://dx.doi.org/10.1016/S0022-5371(79)90284-6

Szmrecsanyi, B. (2005). Language users as creatures of habit: A corpus-based analysis of persistence in spoken English. *Corpus Linguistics and Linguistic Theory, 1,* 113–150. http://dx.doi.org/10.1515/cllt.2005.1.1.113

Theakston, A. (2004). The role of entrenchment in children's and adults' performance on grammaticality judgment tasks. *Cognitive Development, 19,* 15–34. http://dx.doi.org/10.1016/j.cogdev.2003.08.001

Tomasello, M. (2003). *Constructing a language. A usage-based theory of language acquisition.* Cambridge, MA: Harvard University Press.

Tomasello, M. (2009). The usage-based theory of language acquisition. In E. L. Bavin (Ed.), *Cambridge handbook of child language* (pp. 69–88). Cambridge, England: Cambridge University Press.

Tomasello, M., & Rakoczy, H. (2003). What makes human cognition unique? From individual to shared to collective intentionality. *Mind & Language, 18,* 121–147. http://dx.doi.org/10.1111/1468-0017.00217

Traugott, E. C. (2008). The grammaticalization of *NP of NP* constructions. In A. Bergs & G. Diewald (Eds.), *Constructions and language change* (pp. 21–43). Berlin, Germany: Mouton de Gruyter.

Traugott, E. C., & Dasher, R. B. (2004). *Regularity in semantic change.* Cambridge, England: Cambridge University Press.

Traugott, E. C., & Trousdale, G. (2013). *Constructionalization and constructional changes.* http://dx.doi.org/10.1093/acprof:oso/9780199679898.001.0001

Tremblay, A., & Baayen, H. (2010). Holistic processing of regular four-word sequences: A behavioral and ERP study of the effects of structure, frequency, and probability on immediate free recall. In D. Wood (Ed.), *Perspectives on formulaic language: Acquisition and communication* (pp. 151–173). London, England: The Continuum International.

Tremblay, A., Derwing, B., & Libben, G. (2009). Are lexical bundles stored and processed as single units? *Working Papers of the Linguistics Circle of the University of Victoria, 19,* 258–279.

Tremblay, A., Derwing, B., Libben, G., & Westbury, C. (2011). Processing advantages of lexical bundles: Evidence from self-paced reading and sentence recall tasks. *Language Learning, 61,* 569–613. http://dx.doi.org/10.1111/j.1467-9922.2010.00622.x

Trudgill, P. (1986). *Dialects in contact.* Oxford, England: Blackwell.

Underwood, G., Schmitt, N., & Galpin, A. (2004). The eyes have it: An eye-movement study into the processing of formulaic sequences. In N. Schmitt (Ed.), *Formulaic sequences: Acquisition, processing, and use* (pp. 153–172). http://dx.doi.org/10.1075/lllt.9.09und

Wiechmann, D. (2008). On the computation of collostruction strength: Testing measures of association as expressions of lexical bias. *Corpus Linguistics and Linguistic Theory, 4,* 253–290. http://dx.doi.org/10.1515/CLLT.2008.011

Wray, A. (2002). *Formulaic language and the lexicon.* http://dx.doi.org/10.1017/CBO9780511519772

Wray, A. (2008). *Formulaic language: Pushing the boundaries.* Oxford, England: Oxford University Press.

Zenner, E., Speelman, D., & Geeraerts, D. (2012). Cognitive sociolinguistics meets loanword research: Measuring variation in the success of anglicisms in Dutch. *Cognitive Linguistics, 23,* 749–792. http://dx.doi.org/10.1515/cog-2012-0023

Zeschel, A. (2012). *Incipient productivity. A construction-based approach to linguistic creativity.* Berlin, Germany: De Gruyter Mouton.

II Linguistic Perspectives on Entrenchment

Ronald W. Langacker
2 Entrenchment in Cognitive Grammar

2.1 Introduction

While linguistic descriptions have to be justified in their own terms, they should at least be plausible from the psychological standpoint. As a guiding strategy, therefore, cognitive grammar (CG) aims at maximal coverage of language structure on the basis of some minimal assumptions about cognition. It adopts the working hypothesis that a viable descriptive framework can be formulated relying only on cognitive phenomena—entrenchment being one—that are either well established or easily demonstrated. Although CG, as a linguistic framework, says nothing specific about their neural basis or psychological implementation, ascertaining their role in language contributes to their empirical investigation. The following discussion of entrenchment considers its nature, its linguistic manifestations, and some theoretical issues it bears on.

2.2 Linguistic Units

A language comprises a structured inventory of conventional linguistic units (Langacker, 1987a). In this context, *structured inventory* means that units are connected by relations of symbolization, composition, and categorization—they constitute an *assembly*. Being *conventional* and being *linguistic* are matters of degree. So is entrenchment, the basis for a structure having the status of a *unit*. Entrenchment is not specific to language but a general phenomenon observable in any kind of learned human activity. A matter of cognition, it is the *individual* counterpart of conventionalization, the *social* process of structures becoming standard in a speech community.

The term *structure* is problematic with regard to language. A physical structure (e.g., a building) consists of parts (chunks of material substance) connected in a particular configuration; it is not only stable through time but fully manifested at any given moment. By contrast, linguistic structures are nonmaterial, consisting in *processing activity*. As such, their manifestation is transient rather than continuous, and, because activity occurs through time, they are not fully manifested at any one moment. Furthermore, although linguistic structures are implemented by neural networks, they do not consist in the physical configuration of these networks, but in how they function through and over time.

Entrenchment is a key to bridging the gap between microlevel neural activity and the stable, macrolevel elements invoked by linguists to describe language structure (see Smolensky, Goldrick, & Mathis, 2014). The neural substrate comprises an immense population of neurons and their synaptic connections. Driven by its summed inputs, a neuron has a fluctuating activation level (firing rate) and tends to activate or inhibit others as determined by connection strengths. Macrolevel structures reside in the interaction of large assemblies of neurons. We can usefully speak of a *pattern of activity*: a complex neural event consisting in the total activity of a particular assembly over a certain span of time. Defined in this general fashion, however, every pattern is unique. If examined in sufficiently fine-grained detail, no two events are precisely identical in terms of the neurons involved, their activation levels, and the timing of subevents. How, then, can structure emerge?

Three related factors are involved. First, certain patterns must count as being "the same." It may be that they are similar enough for the differences to be negligible. If dissimilar, they may still be alike in terms of how they function as part of a more elaborate pattern (e.g., serving to activate another subpattern). Nonidentical patterns can thus be effectively equivalent—inherently or functionally—for processing purposes. This leads to a second factor: *recurrence*, in which "the same" pattern occurs on multiple occasions. Recurrence is a kind of stability through time (a kind possible for neural events), and as such it represents an aspect of "structure." To qualify as a structure, however, it is not sufficient for a pattern to recur. A third factor is that the recurrence is not just accidental but ascribable to features of the neural substrate, which enable and facilitate the pattern's occurrence under certain conditions. This *potential* to occur at any moment represents a kind of continuity through time.

We can speak of structure to the extent that neural processing is organized by recurrent patterns of this sort. Of the substrate features responsible for this organization, some are innate (hardwired), but many reflect adjustments resulting from previous activity. The term *entrenchment* refers to these adjustments. A basic mechanism is Hebbian reinforcement, wherein the coactivation of neurons strengthens the connection between them (Feldman, 2006; Hebb, 1961). It has the higher level consequence, essential for cognition, that the occurrence of a pattern enhances its potential for occurring again.

A *unit* is characterized in CG as an *established pattern* of activity: a complex neural event with a significant potential for recurrence owing to entrenchment (adjustments in the substrate). The word *entrenchment* suggests that a unit is established gradually, through many occurrences, each effecting a minimal adjustment in connection strengths; it reflects the notion that the emergence of linguistic structures is a gradual process based on repetition. If this is true for the most part, it must also be acknowledged that in some circumstances, a unit is established by just a single occurrence: One exposure may be enough to learn a new word or even a memorable sentence. But because this involves an adjustment in the substrate, we can still speak of entrenchment in a slightly broader sense.

Status as a unit is a matter of degree because each occurrence contributes to its further entrenchment and subsequent ease of activation. Even at early stages, a unit learned incrementally has some influence on language processing, and established units can be entrenched even further. At some point, a unit is well enough established (deeply enough entrenched) that it constitutes "an event waiting to happen": Once initiated, it will run to completion if not deflected from this course. Metaphorically, we might describe this in terms of momentum and the unleashing of potential energy stored in synaptic connections. In psychological terms, it correlates with automatization (see Hartsuiker and Moors, Chapter 9, this volume), whereby a thoroughly mastered routine is executed without close monitoring. From the dynamic systems perspective (see Herdina, Chapter 17, this volume), a well-entrenched unit is an *attractor*—a region in state space toward which the system gravitates when in its vicinity.

The reality of units and the linguistic structures they constitute might be challenged along the following lines: cognition resides in dynamic processing activity, marked by continuity and inherent variability, so positing discrete units and static structures is both misguided and misleading. This argument is valid if directed against the classic view of language based on the "building-block metaphor." In the present account, however, units are not at all like building blocks, and structures are anything but static. Instead they consist in organized activity. Rather than being *static*, they are characterized by *stability* in the guise of potential for recurrence. Variability is inherent, because recurrence is not a matter of exact identity but of overlap or functional equivalence, and although the emergence of units implies a certain coherence and consistency, there is no expectation of their being discretely bounded.

Units are as real as the neural substrate and its electrochemical activity. They emerge from such activity in much the same way that waves emerge in the ocean. Although emergent, a wave is an actual phenomenon with real-world consequences (you can surf on one; it can capsize a boat). For an accurate assessment of their properties, it is important to recognize the nonfundamental nature of such entities. Denying their existence would be pointless, however: Being fundamental is not the same as being real (Langacker, 2006).

The existence of units does not entail the possibility, even in principle, of arriving at a definitive list. One reason is that entrenchment is a matter of degree, so what to count as a unit is somewhat arbitrary. Like a wave, moreover, a pattern of activity cannot be precisely delimited; although bounded (it does not extend indefinitely), there is no specific point where it begins or ends. Nor are units separate or independent: Patterns adapt to one another; they often overlap; some are included in others. Additional units are constantly emerging as new associations are forged through the coactivation of established patterns.

In brief, linguistic ability comprises a vast assembly of interconnected units. Consisting in patterns of neural activity, these are variable and constantly being adjusted. We can nonetheless speak of structure because this activity is highly organized. Units emerge through entrenchment, which thus provides the very basis for cognition and language structure.

2.3 Development of Units

Units being established patterns of activity, one dimension of variation is the degree of entrenchment: How well established they are. Each occurrence of a unit reinforces it, enhancing the ease (hence the likelihood) of its recurring. For a well-entrenched unit, the effect may simply be to maintain it by countering the tendency for unused patterns to weaken. We see this tendency, for example, when it is difficult to remember the name of a person we have not encountered for a long time.

Frequent occurrence does more than just maintain a unit. With sufficient rehearsal, its execution becomes faster, less effortful, and essentially automatic. This is partially due to the pattern being *streamlined*, making it simpler and more efficient. Aspects of streamlining are sketched in Figure 2.1, where ellipses are patterns of activity and solid lines indicate entrenchment. The larger ellipses represent more inclusive patterns that incorporate the others.

First, as shown in diagram (a), efficiency is achieved by subpatterns overlapping and adapting to one another and by the elimination of less essential elements. Providing phonological illustration are coarticulation effects and the reduction of unstressed vowels, for example, *unprofessional* being rendered as [m̩prəfɛ́šn̩l].

More radically, as shown in diagram (b), streamlining involves the reconfiguration of a unit, so that the same overall effect is achieved more directly. This happens when certain portions (C) of the original pattern (AB) constitute an implicit solution to the same processing task. C being immanent in AB, it is progressively reinforced as the latter recurs; and being inessential to the task, other facets of AB may gradu-

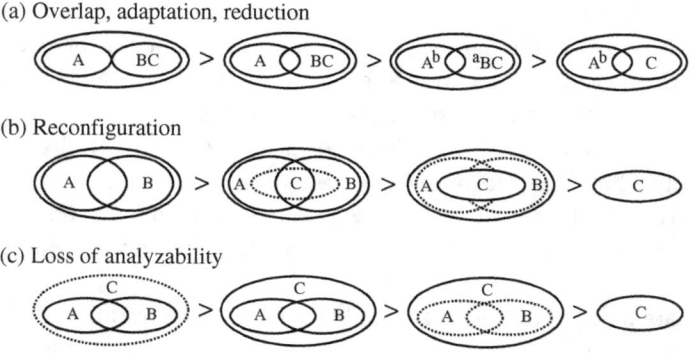

Fig. 2.1: Developments affecting units.

ally fade away. An example is French *quatre-vingts* ("eighty"), which expresses a numerical value as a multiple of 20; because the French number scale is basically decimal otherwise, the expression tends to be reconstrued as directly indicating a multiple of 10.

The example also illustrates the loss of *analyzability*, represented in diagram (c). When units (A and B) first combine to form a complex structure, their activation is instrumental in evoking the composite whole (C). Owing to adaptation and to other inputs, C is a structure in its own right, more than just the sum of its parts. Once established as a unit, C can be accessed directly, in which case A and B as such are activated only weakly, and eventually not at all. Thus *compute* has greatly diminished salience in *computer*, and *profess* no longer figures in *professor*.

Like individual units, the assembly of units constituting language structure is constantly changing through use. Variability is inherent because patterns of activation can never be precisely identical. Units are activated, to varying degrees, on the basis of multiple inputs in a larger processing context (including their prior activation level), all of which has a shaping influence. Although the variation is often negligible, it can be quite substantial. Should it recur, the adaptation of a unit may itself undergo entrenchment, resulting in a more inclusive unit comprising the original pattern, its variant manifestation, and relevant features of the context. One such case is a conditioned allophone, for example, [t] being rendered as [d] when intervocalic. Another is the adapted sense of a lexeme, for example, *red* as applied to hair.

This is shown in Figure 2.2a, where A^0 is the original unit, and A^1 its variant manifestation in a certain context (C). The dashed arrow indicates that A^1 consists in a distorted realization of A^0: It is A^0 that is elicited and being executed, but owing to the context, A^1 is the pattern that actually occurs. This entire configuration, where A^0 is manifested as A^1 in C, is subject to entrenchment as a unit. Ipso facto, A^1 is then a unit also. Eventually (by a process akin to loss of analyzability), it may be activated directly, independently of A^0 and even C. The result is that A^0 and A^1 are coexisting (and potentially coequal) variants.

There can be multiple variants, some retaining their status as *extensions* (adapted realizations) vis-à-vis A^0 or a prior extension. As sketched in Figure 2.2b, A^0 thus

(a) Context-induced variant

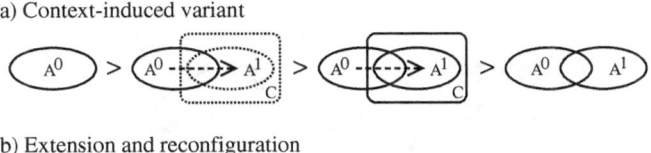

(b) Extension and reconfiguration

Fig. 2.2: Variation of units.

develops into an assembly of overlapping units that differ in regard to salience (degree of entrenchment, represented by thickness of lines) and the possibility of independent activation. As determined by use, the assembly not only grows but can also be reconfigured; for example, Figure 2.2b shows A^1 becoming independent of A^0 and more salient. An array of this sort is described by cognitive linguists as a *complex category* (with A^0 as prototype) and modeled as a kind of network (Lakoff, 1987; Langacker, 1987a, Chapter 10; Taylor, 2004). However, the discreteness of the network metaphor should not obscure the fact that units and assemblies are variable and adaptable: consisting in overlapping patterns of activity with indeterminate boundaries, they define a continuous field of possibilities (Allwood, 2003; Langacker, 2006).

An important feature of assemblies is that units are connected by overlap, consisting in partially shared processing activity. As a limiting case, one unit may be wholly included in another. A special case of inclusion is *elaboration*, indicated by the solid arrow in Figure 2.3a. It is a difference in granularity: A^0 is a coarse-grained structure, whereas A^1 is more specific. The activity comprising A^0 inheres in that of A^1, the additional activity of which is responsible for its finer-grained detail.

An elaborative relation can come about in various ways. First, as shown in Figure 2.3b, an established unit (A^0) supports the emergence of a more elaborate structure (A^1) through the recurrence of activity representing more specific detail. When multiple structures arise in this fashion, we can say that A^0 is *differentiated* into A^1 and A^2. An alternative is *schematization*, which often results from extension. Figure 2.3c shows A^0 as being extended to A^1 and then A^2. It depicts the special case in which, in contrast to Figure 2.2b, all three structures share some essential processing activity. Because the activation of this subpattern is inherent in that of the more inclusive structures, it can be entrenched and established as a unit. Should it represent their coarse-grained commonality, this unit constitutes a *schema* (A) having the more elaborate structures (A^0, A^1, A^2) as *instantiations*.

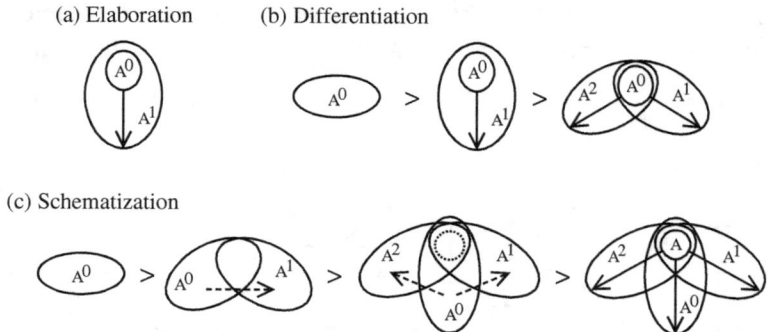

Fig. 2.3: Overlap of units.

2.4 Units in Action

A person's ability in a language consists in a vast assembly of conventional units connected by overlap, inclusion, and association. These are embedded in the total array of units—established patterns of neural activity—responsible for cognition in the broadest sense (including perception and motor control). Although they inhere in the minds of individuals, units are not isolated from external factors. Rather, they are shaped by interaction with the physical and social world and provide the basis for further interaction.

Supporting a given unit are numerous other units connected to it either directly or indirectly. Because they emerge from language use, which draws on a wide range of capacities and any aspect of general or contextual knowledge, linguistic units incorporate many others that are not all specific to language. Once established, linguistic units play a role in subsequent language processing, their activation serving to realize the latent potential they embody. This is a special case of *categorization*, broadly understood as the evocation of established structures for the structuring of current activity. In this broad sense, categorization includes the role of units in both comprehension and production, for example, contributing to either the formation or the apprehension of complex conceptions. Likewise, it figures not only in perception but in physical actions, because these involve the execution of established motor routines (Fuster, 2003).

Using *apprehension* as a cover term, we can speak of categorization when the activation of a unit is instrumental in the apprehension of a *target*. As an "event waiting to happen," a well-entrenched unit is readily elicited with appropriate input and will run its course unless disrupted. The target, on the other hand, consists in current activity awaiting interpretation: In terms of being a coherent structure, it may still be inchoate or only fragmentary. Categorization occurs when this activity (along with other input) serves to activate the unit, the execution of which contributes to completing and organizing the target structure. Metaphorically, we can say that the unit *captures* the target.

This is sketched in Figure 2.4, where U is a unit, T is an inchoate target, and shading indicates current activation. In Figure 2.4a, T is more inclusive than U but not in any way inconsistent with it. Categorization begins with local patterns of activity representing features of T, some of which overlap with U. If the overlap is enough to activate U, its execution provides the context for further processing of T, filling in certain gaps and imposing its organization. There being no inconsistency, U is realized in undistorted fashion as part of T, which is generally more elaborate. We can say that U is *recognized* (or *immanent*) in T, or conversely, that T is *apprehended as* an instance of U (Langacker, 2009b, 2009c).

Categorization does not require full consistency, however. Figure 2.4b represents the case of U and T overlapping despite some conflicting specifications. Although the

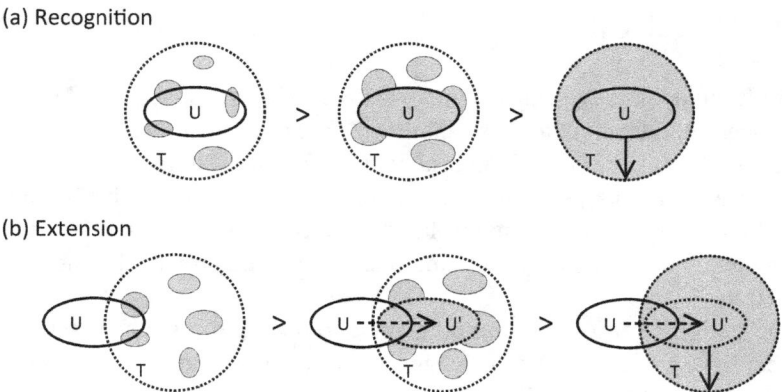

Fig. 2.4: Categorization.

overlap may still be sufficient for U to capture T and effect its categorization, their inconsistency results in U having a distorted (or adapted) realization, U'. Hence it is U' that structures T, which is apprehended as an *extension* from U.

Sounds and conceptions count as language only when categorized by linguistic units. A target expression activates a wide array of units, each serving to apprehend some facet of it. The units evoked differ in size, specificity, and domain (sound, meaning, lexicon, grammar). Collectively these categorizations constitute the expression's linguistic structure (Langacker, 2008, Chapter 8). Each categorization represents an implicit assessment of the target's status vis-à-vis established linguistic precedent: When T conforms to the precedent U embodies, apprehension is a matter of simple recognition; extension is required when it deviates from this precedent. These assessments provide the basis for what linguists refer to as *grammaticality* or *well-formedness*, but for units reflecting a socially established norm, a better term would be *conventionality*. In any case, the demands of language use are such that some deviation from precedent is normal and usually not even noticed. Still, every usage event has an impact, contributing to the maintenance, further entrenchment, or adaptation of activated units.

An expression's structure consists in numerous categorizations each pertaining to some aspect of it—a local target within the whole. On the basis of overlap, each such target activates a unit that serves to capture it. But a given target overlaps to some extent with many units, any of which has the potential to categorize it. Assuming that only one is activated for this purpose, what determines the choice?

A number of factors come into play. One is degree of entrenchment, which translates into inherent ease of activation. Another basic factor is extent of overlap with the target. This favors the selection of specific units over schematic ones because their more elaborate content affords a greater potential for overlap. A third factor is prior level of activation. In particular, a unit's selection is facilitated by residual activation from its recent occurrence. There is also the effect of other inputs, such as priming by the activation of related structures. The effect is negative in the case of competing alternatives, where each inhibits the others. Because these factors interact and are matters of degree, the outcome is not predetermined but varies depending on the overall circumstances. It is not the case, for example, that the unit selected for categorization is always the most deeply entrenched, or the one that most closely matches the target.

Despite their simplistic nature, the foregoing notions deal straightforwardly with basic linguistic phenomena. Most fundamental is the apprehension of a target as a well- or ill-formed instance of language use (Figure 2.4), whether through the activation of a single unit (e.g., in the articulation of a speech sound) or many units (in the processing of a complex sentence). To be sure, because apprehension consists in capture and completion by categorizing units, deviations from the norm can easily go unnoticed: This happens when the execution of U overrides the deficiencies of T. Proofreading errors are a case in point.

Also handled straightforwardly is the formation of complex structures through the combination of simpler elements. An important point is that the "computation" involved (even for instances of general rules) is just a matter of coactivation and Hebbian reinforcement. Suppose that A and B are independently established units that happen to be coactivated, as shown at the left in Figure 2.5a. In the form of strengthened synaptic connections, their co-occurrence leaves a trace (dashed-line ellipse) facilitating the recurrence of this overall pattern. Each recurrence leaves another trace that further strengthens it, until a unit emerges subsuming A and B as subpatterns. With enough repetition—*token frequency*—this higher level unit becomes well entrenched and is easily elicited. Through input overlapping with A and B, it can then be activated as a whole for categorization of a target.

Consider next the emergence of a general combinatory "rule." This is sketched in Figure 2.5b, where B is a schema having B^1, B^2, B^3, ... as elaborations. As before, the coactivation of A and B^1 leaves a trace facilitating the recurrence of this overall pattern. However, because B is immanent in B^1, connections involved in the co-occurrence of A and B are also strengthened (dashed-line ellipse). This facilitates the coactivation

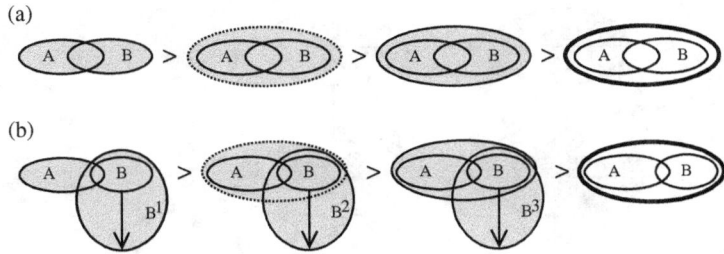

Fig. 2.5: Effects of token and type frequency.

of A and other instantiations of B (B^2, B^3, etc.), and each such occurrence helps establish a partially schematic unit with A and B as subpatterns. It is not required that any particular combination occur with any frequency—at the extreme, each might occur just once, so that none is established as a unit. However, the greater the number of instantiations occurring in the pattern, the more the schematic unit is entrenched. If most occur in it, this schema will be stronger than competing alternatives, and hence accessible for the categorization of new combinations. Thus, *type frequency* results in productivity.

Like entrenchment, however, productivity is a matter of degree. On the one hand, a productive pattern may fail to apply in certain cases. On the other hand, a discernible pattern may be largely or wholly nonproductive, that is, inaccessible for the apprehension of new instances. Whether a particular unit is activated to categorize a target is not determined by the unit and target alone. It also depends on the overall configuration of units, as well as levels of activation due to priming and other inputs.

In a neutral context, the main factors in the choice of categorizing unit are entrenchment and extent of overlap with the target. Candidate units compete for activation, and because they are mutually inhibitory, one emerges victorious and effects the categorization. Examples of how this works are provided in Figure 2.6. For the sake of clarity, overlapping structures are represented separately; their overlap is conveyed indirectly by dashed and solid arrows, respectively indicating relations of extension and elaboration. The structures involved are past-tense verbs (specific or schematic). No attempt is

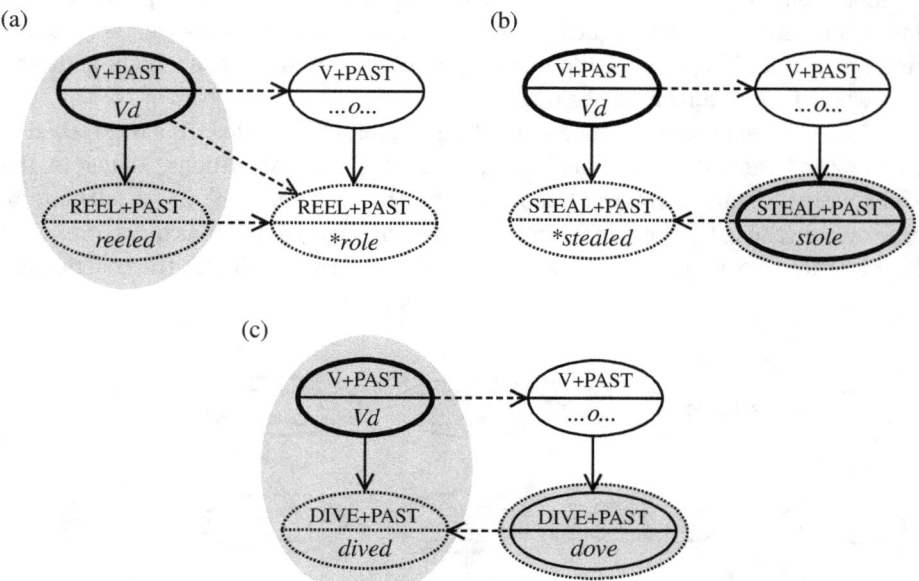

Fig. 2.6: Competition for activation.

made to show their full complexity: They comprise both component structures and the composite whole, each residing in the symbolic relation between a form and a meaning.

In Figure 2.6a, the schema labeled (V+PAST/Vd) embodies the regular rule of past-tense formation in English. The schema labeled (V+PAST/...o...) is the reinforced commonality of "irregular" verbs such as *stole, drove, rode, broke, spoke,* and *froze*. Both are presumed to be units, but owing to a vast difference in type frequency, the former is deeply entrenched and the latter only minimally. Suppose, then, that the target is the preterite of a verb, for example, *reel*, whose past-tense form is too infrequent to be established as a unit. In speaking, overlap with potential categorizing units is provided by the intended meaning (REEL+PAST). In listening, it is provided by perception of the form (*reeled*); but, in either case the difference in entrenchment ensures that (V+PAST/Vd) will be activated for the target's categorization. The disparity is great enough that (V+PAST/...o...) will rarely, if ever, win the competition—for all intents and purposes, it is inaccessible for the assessment of new combinations. My intuition, in fact, is that even if presented with *role*, clearly understood as the past tense of *reel*, I would apprehend it as a distorted realization of the general pattern (and of *reeled*), not as a well-formed realization of the schema it instantiates.

Suppose, next, that the target is the past-tense form of *steal*. In this case, the requisite form is a well-entrenched unit, *stole*, as shown in Figure 2.6b. Because the target is just its contextual manifestation, this fully specific unit competes with the general pattern for activation as the categorizing structure. Further, because (STEAL+PAST/*stole*) overlaps the target in virtually all respects, and the schematic (V+PAST/Vd) to a much lesser extent, the former will usually win the competition. Indeed, the form **stealed* is apprehended as an ill-formed realization of *stole* even though it instantiates the regular pattern. This is known as *blocking* (or *preemption*): Owing to its greater specificity (hence its capacity for overlap), a well-entrenched irregular form occurs in lieu of one that would otherwise be expected.

A pattern's accessibility for apprehension of a certain target is not absolute but dependent on the specific array of relevant units and their degree of entrenchment. Given the strength of the general pattern, for example, **stealed* might well occur with sufficient priming or as an error due to a heavy processing load. Although it is hard to imagine **role* as the past tense of *reel*, new instances of some minor patterns do indeed occur, for example, *brung* as the past tense of *bring* (Bybee & Slobin, 1982). Furthermore, the competition for activation does not invariably result in a clear-cut victory. Like *stole*, for instance, *dove* is an established unit but is less frequent and not so well entrenched. Hence, competition for the past tense of *dive* may well end in a draw: Entrenchment favors (V+PAST/Vd), whereas overlap favors (DIVE+PAST/*dove*). So if both categorizations are effected, as in Figure 2.6c, the choice of *dived* versus *dove* results in fluctuation or uncertainty. Of course, a form that is only minimally entrenched (e.g., *strove*) is likely to lose the competition to its regular counterpart (*strived*). From the diachronic perspective, therefore, these factors have the well-known consequence that frequent irregular forms are the most resistant to regularization.

2.5 Theoretical Issues

Entrenchment bears on a broad range of fundamental linguistic issues. It comes into play to the extent that language is learned (as opposed to being innately specified), referring to both the fact of learning and its thoroughness. For the most part, entrenchment correlates with frequency: Prior occurrences determine its degree, which in turn determines the likelihood of subsequent occurrences.

Entrenchment thus figures in the general issue of whether frequency is relevant for describing language structure. From the standpoint of cognitive-functional linguistics, the effects of frequency cannot be relegated to a separate domain of "performance" or "use," because structure is basically just the execution of established usage patterns (units). We have seen, for example, that the entrenchment of specific and schematic structures is a main factor in assessing the well-formedness of particular expressions (Figure 2.6). Moreover, frequently occurring instances of general patterns are themselves entrenched as units, often with their own special properties (like the effects of streamlining, or fine-grained phonetic details). So although frequency per se need not be represented, its effects are essential to a full and accurate description (Bybee, 1994, 2006; Bybee & Hopper, 2001). They are readily accommodated in *usage-based* models of language (Barlow & Kemmer, 2000), which posit the entrenchment of specific instances as well as the schematized structures representing their reinforced commonality.

The effects of entrenchment are pertinent to a central notion of construction grammar: the original definition of a *construction* as not being strictly predictable from other patterns (Fillmore, Kay, & O'Connor, 1988; Goldberg, 1995). This characterization was criticized (Langacker, 2005) as confounding the question of whether a construction exists—that is, whether it constitutes a unit—with the problem of demonstrating its existence to other linguists. Goldberg (2006, 2009) subsequently acknowledged that entrenched structures count as constructions even if fully regular. Yet although this amendment is well justified, the original definition can be maintained if interpreted as referring to effects of entrenchment. An entrenched unit is bound to differ from the corresponding novel structure, if only in terms of rapid execution or streamlining (Langacker, 2009a). To be sure, these effects will often be too subtle for use as a diagnostic.

Entrenchment being both fundamental and ubiquitous, it is only to be expected that fixed (formulaic) expressions have a massive role in both acquisition and ongoing language use (Dąbrowska, 2000; Diessel & Tomasello, 2001; Langacker, 1987a, pp. 35–36; Pawley, 1985; Tomasello, 1992). Yet since recurrence is observed at different levels of specificity, and for selected aspects of complex expressions, entrenchment also gives rise to (partially) schematic patterns, as in Figure 2.5b. Language use is thus a mixture of formulaicity and creativity, which cannot be neatly separated. The absence of a nonarbitrary boundary informs a basic tenet of CG and other versions of construction grammar: that lexicon and grammar reside in a continuum of symbolic structures (form–meaning pairings).

Lexical meanings are the subject of several contentious issues, all involving the question of how many senses to posit for a lexeme. Because established senses constitute semantic units, entrenchment is a pivotal factor.

One view is that lexical senses should not be posited at all—that a lexeme exhibits a continuous field of semantic potential (Allwood, 2003; Zlatev, 2003). Furthermore, if senses are thought of as being discrete, separate, and exhaustive of the options (the most simplistic interpretation of the network model of polysemy), they should in fact be rejected. Here, however, units are viewed dynamically as overlapping patterns of activity that are variable (being influenced by the larger context) and adapted as needed for the apprehension of new experience. So a lexeme does indeed support a continuous, open-ended field of potential meanings. Crucially, however, this field is contoured by prior usage, so that certain locations are favored by easy access (i.e., they function as attractors). The more accessible locations can be recognized as established lexical senses, and although their delimitation (hence their number) may to some extent be arbitrary, to ignore their existence would be even more misleading. Analogously, a certain arbitrariness in counting the peaks in a mountain range does not imply that there are none.

As shown by Tuggy (1993), entrenchment offers a straightforward approach to a classic problem of lexical description: the issue of *vagueness* versus *polysemy*. The distinction hinges on the relative entrenchment of schematic and more specific meanings, and because this is a matter of degree, the results of standard diagnostic tests are often not clear-cut. The lexeme *uncle* is vague because the specific values *maternal uncle* and *paternal uncle* are nonsalient in Western Anglophone culture. Thus, it is unproblematic for instances of each to be included in the referent of *uncles* because this invokes the schematic meaning "parent's brother." Judgments are less clear-cut in the case of *painters*: Can the referent consist of an artist and a house painter? There is uncertainty because these incongruous senses coexist with the schematic meaning "one who paints." By contrast, *nails* can hardly be interpreted as including both carpentry nails and fingernails because their evident similarity is not entrenched as an accessible schematic meaning. *Nail* is *polysemous* to the extent that these specific meanings are connected by semantic overlap. The term *homonymy* applies to the end point of the scale, where the apprehension of semantic relationships requires a leap of imagination (e.g., *spring* as a season, a mechanical device, or a source of water).

The validity of positing multiple senses for a lexeme (polysemy) is sometimes questioned. A proposed alternative is *monosemy*, in which a single schematic meaning gives rise to a lexeme's myriad uses through a variety of interpretive strategies (Reid, 2004; Ruhl, 1989; Wierzbicka, 1988, 1996). Arriving at a specific interpretation is a creative process involving general and contextual knowledge as well as capacities such as metaphor, metonymy, and inference. Adhering to monosemy encourages the search for an abstract common meaning, and by strictly delimiting what counts as "linguistic," it avoids the unconstrained proliferation of senses. By itself, however, a single schematic meaning does not allow the prediction of which conceivable interpretations are actually entrenched and conventionally exploited. From the standpoint of CG, the units representing these interpretations—being essential for normative language use—can hardly be considered nonlinguistic (Langacker, 2004). Counting those with a low degree of entrenchment (a minimal trace of prior occurrences), a lexeme may in fact have a large number of established or incipient senses. This does not, however, imply that they proliferate without limit: although any specific boundary would be arbitrary, some degree of entrenchment and conventionality is required.

Another issue where entrenchment comes into play is whether certain lexical categories—noun and verb in particular—are language universals. Arguing against their universality is the fact that, in certain languages, any lexeme is freely used in either capacity. However, the status of noun and verb as *lexical* categories is seen as a secondary issue in CG. The claim is rather that they are universal *grammatical* categories, semantically definable in terms of their *profile* (conceptual referent): A noun refers to a "thing," and a verb to a "process" (Langacker, 1987b, 2009b, 2013). In all languages, grammatical constructions (notably, nominals and clauses) serve the function of singling out and describing these two sorts of referents.

Consider, then, a language in which lexemes have no intrinsic category: In CG terms, they impose no profile on the conceptual content they invoke. A lexeme seldom occurs in isolation but is normally used in constructions implying a particular kind of referent (e.g., with a demonstrative, or marked for tense). Because it then subserves the construction's referential function, the lexeme is contextually interpreted as referring to the profiled entity—in effect, it is *apprehended as* a noun or verb for immediate purposes. For many lexemes, this is likely to happen on numerous occasions, in which case their categorization as noun or verb is subject to entrenchment; to the extent that this occurs, we can speak of *lexical* nouns and verbs. As a general matter, appearance in constructions is a main factor in determining a lexeme's category (Goldberg, 1995). It may be that languages simply differ in their preference for establishing a *primary* categorization.

Although often asked, the question of whether a certain feature is attributable to a lexeme or to an encompassing construction is basically misguided because it rests on the "building block" view of semantic composition. Instead, composite meanings arise through the coactivation and adaptation of overlapping patterns of neural activity, so that often a specification cannot be localized. In *red hair*, for example, the atypical import of *red* is certainly due to the larger context (its combination with *hair*, as well as general knowledge). It is thus a *contextual variant* of *red*. But at least originally, it is a variant of red, being *apprehended as* an extension from its basic value (Figure 2.2a). Once established as a unit, a variant sometimes becomes more autonomous, being accessible outside the original context or without evoking the basic sense.

However, because units are learned and used in context, they never achieve absolute autonomy but only degrees of *decontextualization*. They are abstracted from *usage events* (instances of language use, in all their specific detail) by the reinforcement of recurring commonalities. An emerging unit thus retains recurring features of the context, abstracting away from those that fail to be reinforced. If it occurs in varied contexts, none of which predominates, it will be autonomous vis-à-vis any particular one. As recurring patterns, however, its appearance in some of these contexts will also be established as units.

Thus, a linguistic unit is never fully discrete or independent. Because it retains at least a schematic vestige of the contexts supporting its emergence, it is best conceived as a *point of access* to an assembly of indefinite extent. In particular, units representing its appearance in larger constructions are not extraneous but inherent to its characterization. A full description of *red*, for instance, includes its adapted realization in *red hair*. Likewise, *ready* serves as point of access to the larger structures [*ready* [*to* v]] and [*ready* [*for* N]]. A unit of this sort, where a lexeme appears in a certain structural frame, is accessible via each: [*ready* [*to* v]] not only figures in the overall characterization of *ready*, but also instantiates the constructional schema [ADJ [*to* v]]. These are alternate ways of viewing the same assembly.

In this we find a solution to the classic problem of *distribution*: how to ensure that lexemes occur in the right environments. Distribution is problematic only given the common view of lexemes as context-independent elements ("building blocks") that have to be "inserted" in structural frames (Chomsky, 1965). It is handled straightforwardly in a *dynamic usage-based model* like CG, where structure consists in overlapping patterns of activity (Langacker, 2000). On this view, lexemes are never independent to begin with but are abstracted (via selective entrenchment) based on their occurrence in specific expressions. What we recognize as a lexeme belongs to more encompassing structures (entrenched to different degrees) representing the contexts from which it emerges. These larger units, which can be specific (*red hair*) or schematic ([*ready* [*to* v]]; [*ready* [*for* N]]), directly specify a lexeme's potential for occurrence in particular environments. Of course, it can also be used in a new construction because well-entrenched schemas are easily activated for this purpose. For instance, a novel past-tense form emerges through coactivation of a verb and the general pattern [V+PAST/vd].

A final issue is the nature of linguistic "rules." In the view presented here, *structure* resides in recurring patterns of activity, and "rules" take the form of *units*, that is, established patterns of any sort (processing routines). Units run the gamut in terms of size, nature, internal complexity, entrenchment (hence, ease of activation), and generality (ranging from highly specific to maximally schematic). A language comprises a vast *assembly* of connected units, some of which are activated in the apprehension of particular expressions. Computation ("rule application") consists in *coactivation* of overlapping patterns.

On this account, a single processing model accommodates the full spectrum ranging from general, productive patterns (like [V+PAST/vd]), to minor, essentially nonproductive ones (e.g., [V+PAST/...o...]), to cases of lexical idiosyncrasy (e.g., *was* as the past tense of *be*). There is no need to posit distinct processing systems—one for retrieving learned expressions and another for constructing new expressions through application of general rules (Pinker & Prince, 1988)—because the same assembly of units can act in either fashion depending on the configuration of units, their degree of entrenchment, their level of schematicity, and the input. Indeed, varied empirical findings argue against the clear-cut division expected with separate systems (Plunkett & Juola, 1999; Seidenberg & Plaut, 2014; Simonsen, 2001).

The unified model sketched here relies on schematic units abstracted from usage events. Some have challenged the validity of positing schemas or abstractions of any sort, appealing instead to *analogy* with *stored exemplars* (e.g., Eddington, 2007; Skousen, 1989). The common rejection of schemas stems in part from their being conceived as separate structures, distinct from their instantiations. However, they are actually related by inclusion: Schemas consist in processing activity representing certain features of instantiating structures. Because their abstraction is simply a matter of entrenchment through recurrence (Figure 2.3c), their emergence can hardly be doubted.

In the exemplar model, each occurrence of a structure (e.g., a sound) is stored, and new occurrences are shaped by analogy with "clouds" of stored exemplars (denser clouds exerting a stronger influence). Literally, however, an exemplar cannot be "stored"—it is a transient neural event, which occurs and then is gone. What is stored is a *trace* of its occurrence in the guise of adjusted synaptic connections that facilitate occurrence of a comparable event (i.e., *recurrence*). Cumulatively, the adjustments effected by a sufficient number of similar events have a strong shaping influence on subsequent processing, in which case we can speak of a "well-entrenched pattern" or "attractor." Hence, there is no fundamental distinction between a cloud of exemplars and a schema: The difference is metaphorical rather than substantive (Langacker, 2010, 2016). On either account, linguistic ability resides in established patterns of activity (units) with varying degrees of entrenchment.

References

Allwood, J. (2003). Meaning potentials and context: Some consequences for the analysis of variation in meaning. In H. Cuyckens, R. Dirven, & J. R. Taylor (Eds.), *Cognitive approaches to lexical semantics* (pp. 29–65). http://dx.doi.org/10.1515/9783110219074.29

Barlow, M., & Kemmer, S. (Eds.). (2000). *Usage-based models of language*. Stanford, CA: CSLI.

Bybee, J. (1994). A view of phonology from a cognitive and functional perspective. *Cognitive Linguistics*, 5, 285–305. http://dx.doi.org/10.1515/cogl.1994.5.4.285

Bybee, J. (2006). From usage to grammar: The mind's response to repetition. *Language*, 82, 711–733. http://dx.doi.org/10.1353/lan.2006.0186

Bybee, J., & Hopper, P. (Eds.). (2001). *Frequency and the emergence of linguistic structure*. http://dx.doi.org/10.1075/tsl.45

Bybee, J., & Slobin, D. I. (1982). Rules and schemas in the development and use of the English past tense. *Language*, 58, 265–289. http://dx.doi.org/10.1353/lan.1982.0021

Chomsky, N. (1965). *Aspects of the theory of syntax*. Cambridge, MA: MIT Press.

Dąbrowska, E. (2000). From formula to schema: The acquisition of English questions. *Cognitive Linguistics*, *11*, 83–102.
Diessel, H., & Tomasello, M. (2001). The acquisition of finite complement clauses in English: A corpus-based analysis. *Cognitive Linguistics*, *12*, 97–141. http://dx.doi.org/10.1515/cogl.12.2.97
Eddington, D. (2007). Flaps and other variants of /t/ in American English: Allophonic distribution without constraints, rules, or abstractions. *Cognitive Linguistics*, *18*, 23–46. http://dx.doi.org/10.1515/COG.2007.002
Feldman, J. A. (2006). *From molecule to metaphor: A neural theory of language*. Cambridge, MA: MIT Press.
Fillmore, C. J., Kay, P., & O'Connor, M. C. (1988). Regularity and idiomaticity in grammatical constructions: The case of *let alone*. *Language*, *64*, 501–538. http://dx.doi.org/10.2307/414531
Fuster, J. M. (2003). *Cortex and mind: Unifying cognition*. New York, NY: Oxford University Press.
Goldberg, A. E. (1995). *Constructions: A construction grammar approach to argument structure*. Chicago, IL: University of Chicago Press.
Goldberg, A. E. (2006). *Constructions at work: The nature of generalizations in language*. Oxford, England: Oxford University Press.
Goldberg, A. E. (2009). The nature of generalization in language. *Cognitive Linguistics*, *20*, 93–127. http://dx.doi.org/10.1515/COGL.2009.005
Hebb, D. O. (1961). *The organization of behavior: A neuropsychological theory*. New York, NY: Wiley.
Lakoff, G. (1987). *Women, fire, and dangerous things: What categories reveal about the mind*. http://dx.doi.org/10.7208/chicago/9780226471013.001.0001
Langacker, R. W. (1987a). *Foundations of cognitive grammar: Vol. 1. Theoretical prerequisites*. Stanford, CA: Stanford University Press.
Langacker, R. W. (1987b). Nouns and verbs. *Language*, *63*, 53–94. http://dx.doi.org/10.2307/415384
Langacker, R. W. (2000). A dynamic usage-based model. In M. Barlow & S. Kemmer (Eds.), *Usage-based models of language* (pp. 1–63). Stanford, CA: CSLI.
Langacker, R. W. (2004). Form, meaning, and behavior: The cognitive grammar analysis of double subject constructions. In E. Contini-Morava, R. S. Kirsner, & B. Rodríguez-Bachiller (Eds.), *Cognitive and communicative approaches to linguistic analysis* (pp. 21–60). http://dx.doi.org/10.1075/sfsl.51.03lan
Langacker, R. W. (2005). Construction grammars: Cognitive, radical, and less so. In F. J. Ruiz de Mendoza Ibáñez & M. S. Peña Cervel (Eds.), *Cognitive linguistics: Internal dynamics and interdisciplinary interaction* (pp. 101–159). Berlin, Germany: de Gruyter Mouton.
Langacker, R. W. (2006). On the continuous debate about discreteness. *Cognitive Linguistics*, *17*, 107–151. http://dx.doi.org/10.1515/COG.2006.003
Langacker, R. W. (2008). *Cognitive grammar: A basic introduction*. http://dx.doi.org/10.1093/acprof:oso/9780195331967.001.0001
Langacker, R. W. (2009a). Cognitive (construction) grammar. *Cognitive Linguistics*, *20*, 167–176. http://dx.doi.org/10.1515/COGL.2009.010
Langacker, R. W. (2009b). Constructions and constructional meaning. In V. Evans & S. Pourcel (Eds.), *New directions in cognitive linguistics* (pp. 225–267). http://dx.doi.org/10.1075/hcp.24.17lan
Langacker, R. W. (2009c). A dynamic view of usage and language acquisition. *Cognitive Linguistics*, *20*, 627–640. http://dx.doi.org/10.1515/COGL.2009.027

Langacker, R. W. (2010). How not to disagree: The emergence of structure from usage. In K. Boye & E. Engberg-Pedersen (Eds.), *Language usage and language structure* (pp. 107–143). Berlin, Germany: de Gruyter Mouton.

Langacker, R. W. (2013). On grammatical categories. *Foreign Studies*, *1*, 1–23.

Langacker, R. W. (2016). Metaphor in linguistic thought and theory. *Cognitive Semantics*, *2*, 3–29. http://dx.doi.org/10.1163/23526416-00201002

Pawley, A. (1985). On speech formulas and linguistic competence. *Lenguas Modernas*, *12*, 84–104.

Pinker, S., & Prince, A. (1988). On language and connectionism: Analysis of a parallel distributed processing model of language acquisition. *Cognition*, *28*, 73–193. http://dx.doi.org/10.1016/0010-0277(88)90032-7

Plunkett, K., & Juola, P. (1999). A connectionist model of English past tense and plural morphology. *Cognitive Science*, *23*, 463–490. http://dx.doi.org/10.1207/s15516709cog2304_4

Reid, W. (2004). Monosemy, homonymy and polysemy. In E. Contini-Morava, R. S. Kirsner, & B. Rodríguez-Bachiller (Eds.), *Cognitive and communicative approaches to linguistic analysis* (pp. 93–129). http://dx.doi.org/10.1075/sfsl.51.06rei

Ruhl, C. (1989). *On monosemy: A study in linguistic semantics*. Albany: State University of New York Press.

Seidenberg, M. S., & Plaut, D. C. (2014). Quasiregularity and its discontents: The legacy of the past tense debate. *Cognitive Science*, *38*, 1190–1228. http://dx.doi.org/10.1111/cogs.12147

Simonsen, H. G. (2001). Past tense acquisition in Norwegian: Experimental evidence. In H. G. Simonsen & R. T. Endresen (Eds.), *A cognitive approach to the verb: Morphological and constructional perspectives* (pp. 129–151). Berlin, Germany: Mouton de Gruyter.

Skousen, R. (1989). *Analogical modeling of language*. Dordrecht, the Netherlands: Kluwer Academic.

Smolensky, P., Goldrick, M., & Mathis, D. (2014). Optimization and quantization in gradient symbol systems: A framework for integrating the continuous and the discrete in cognition. *Cognitive Science*, *38*, 1102–1138. http://dx.doi.org/10.1111/cogs.12047

Taylor, J. R. (2004). *Linguistic categorization: Prototypes in linguistic theory* (3rd ed.). Oxford, England: Oxford University Press/Clarendon.

Tomasello, M. (1992). *First verbs: A case study of early grammatical development*. http://dx.doi.org/10.1017/CBO9780511527678

Tuggy, D. (1993). Ambiguity, polysemy, and vagueness. *Cognitive Linguistics*, *4*, 273–290. http://dx.doi.org/10.1515/cogl.1993.4.3.273

Wierzbicka, A. (1988). *The semantics of grammar*. http://dx.doi.org/10.1075/slcs.18

Wierzbicka, A. (1996). *Semantics: Primes and universals*. Oxford, England: Oxford University Press.

Zlatev, J. (2003). Polysemy or generality? Mu. In H. Cuyckens, R. Dirven, & J. R. Taylor (Eds.), *Cognitive approaches to lexical semantics* (pp. 447–494). http://dx.doi.org/10.1515/9783110219074.447

Martin Hilpert and Holger Diessel
3 Entrenchment in Construction Grammar

3.1 Introduction

Construction grammar is a linguistic theory that aims to model speakers' knowledge of language as a large, interconnected network of symbolic units (Croft, 2001; Goldberg, 1995, 2006; Langacker, 1987). These symbolic units vary in schematicity, from concrete lexical items, such as *table* or *chair*, to highly abstract syntactic patterns, such as *wh*-questions or cleft sentences. The notion of entrenchment fits well into this view of linguistic knowledge. In line with statements in the Introduction to this volume, we understand *entrenchment* as a process that strengthens knowledge—any type of knowledge. Naturally, our focus lies on the entrenchment of linguistic knowledge. We furthermore submit that the dynamic quality of entrenchment offers a natural explanation of how the constructional network is shaped over time through language use. Any time a construction is used, the network changes in subtle ways. Constructions that are used frequently become, over time, more entrenched than constructions that are used only rarely. Any time a connection between a linguistic form and a meaning is activated, this activation influences how the form–meaning pairing will be processed on future occasions. With every usage event, speakers thus update their mental representations of the constructions in the network. Depending on its frequency of activation, each construction in the network, and each connection in the network, displays a different degree of entrenchment. This chapter elaborates on this general idea, discussing in detail how entrenchment relates to the constructional view of language. We focus on the following five issues.

Section 3.2 provides a theoretical basis and explains how the network of constructions is internally organized. The constructions that form part of the network are mutually connected through associative links. These links can represent relations between abstract constructions and their instantiations, constructions with partial structural overlap, or relations of polysemy, among several others (Diessel, 2015; Goldberg, 1995; Hilpert, 2014b). The discussion in the first section illustrates how the different parts of the constructional network are subject to entrenchment through repeated language use.

The third section examines the relations between syntactic constructions and the lexical elements that typically appear in them. Following a methodological proposal made by Stefanowitsch and Gries (2003), numerous corpus studies have found that constructions tend to exhibit uneven distributions with regard to the lexical elements they accommodate: Some elements appear much more often than would be expected by chance, whereas others are almost completely absent. For patterns such as the English ditransitive construction (Goldberg, 1995), the *way*-construction (Israel, 1996), or the

V the hell out of NP construction (Perek, in press), it is possible to determine which lexical elements co-occur with the respective pattern much more often (or less often) than would be expected. The observed asymmetries motivate the view that entrenched lexico-grammatical interrelations form an important part of linguistic knowledge.

Section 3.4 discusses the role of entrenchment in the *no negative evidence problem* (Bowerman, 1988). The point at issue is that native speakers of any language can discriminate between an utterance that is rare, but grammatically acceptable, and an utterance that is equally rare, but ungrammatical, that is, in violation of an established linguistic convention. For example, how is it that for speakers of English, *The dinosaur swam his friends to the mainland* is acceptable (see Boyd & Goldberg, 2011, p. 57), whereas *The waiter recommended me the sushi* is perceived as unacceptable? Among the solutions to this puzzle that have been proposed, the notion of *negative entrenchment* is particularly relevant in the context of this chapter.

The fifth section relates entrenchment to issues in morphology. After a brief outline of how morphology is conceived of in construction grammar, we discuss a morphological phenomenon in the grammar of English, namely, affix ordering. To illustrate, the English derivational affixes *-ize* and *-ive* allow the formation of words such as *specialize* or *collective*. Interestingly, when the two affixes are combined in a single word, only one sequence is possible: *Collectivize* is a word, **specializive* is not. This section lays out how the notion of entrenchment, as understood from the perspective of construction grammar, offers an explanation for this observation. Hay and Plag (2004) proposed a solution in terms of affix parsability, which relates to the relative entrenchment of subpart links in the constructional network.

The sixth section takes a step back and addresses whether entrenchment in the constructional network affects links between constructions, the constructions themselves, or both. How this issue relates to static versus dynamic conceptions of constructions, and the consequences of these two views, is discussed.

3.2 Knowledge of Language as a Network of Interlinked Constructions

A distinguishing feature of construction grammar is the claim that knowledge of language exclusively consists of a large network of constructions (Goldberg, 2003, p. 219). This means that linguistic knowledge, which is often strictly compartmentalized in other linguistic theories, for instance, into knowledge of syntactic rules on the one hand and knowledge of words and idioms on the other, is to be modeled as a unified repository of form–meaning pairings. Crucially, this repository is not an unordered list or "bag of constructions." It is viewed as a hierarchical network in which constructions are systematically interconnected through different kinds of associative links, some of which are reviewed in this section. It is important to emphasize two limitations of our discussion at the outset. First, our presentation of how constructions are organized in speakers' minds is a first sketch, rather than an established consensus. Researchers in construction grammar share a number of assumptions about this, but it remains to be worked out in detail how a full-scale network of a speaker's linguistic knowledge is to be modeled. Second, we do not attempt to present a complete model of the constructional network. The types of links we consider have been proposed in a number of studies, notably in Goldberg (1995), but more and different types of links could be added and are probably necessary for a realistic model of linguistic knowledge (for a discussion, see Diessel, 2015). With these caveats in mind, we now delve into the subject matter of this section.

A first type of connection between constructions is labeled with the term *inheritance*. In general terms, inheritance describes "vertical" relations in the constructional network between relatively schematic constructions and more specific constructions. Lexically specific constructions, as, for instance, the idiom *throw a fit* in *He was throwing a fit*, are related to the more schematic constructions that they instantiate, in this case the transitive construction, which combines a verb with a direct object. The transitive construction, in turn, would relate to even more schematic constructions, as, for instance, the past-tense construction or the progressive aspect construction. In the way that "an oak" is "a tree," "a plant," and "a living being" at the same time, an idiomatic sentence such as *He was throwing a fit* simultaneously instantiates a range of more abstract constructions. The relation between an abstract construction and a more concrete instantiation is called an *instance link* (Goldberg, 1995, p. 79).

Another type of relation between constructions is accomplished through *polysemy links* (Goldberg, 1995, p. 75). Polysemy describes the phenomenon that a single linguistic form is associated with a range of different but conceptually related meanings. For instance, the English preposition *over* conveys the meaning of "traversal" in the sentence *He kicked the ball over the fence*. In the sentence *We talked over three hours*, it encodes "excess." Assuming that the form *over* is represented by a single node in the constructional network, polysemy links connect that form with all of its different meanings. Other examples of polysemy links are found with the different meanings of the English ditransitive construction (*John gave Mary a book* vs. *They denied John the permission*) and the English s-genitive (*John's keys* vs. *John's promotion*), which are discussed in Hilpert (2014b, pp. 60–61). Because polysemy is often the result of meaning extension via metaphor, Goldberg (1995, p. 81) identifies *metaphorical links* as a special case of links that connect a basic sense of a construction with an extended sense. An example of a metaphorical link is the connection between the caused motion construction (*He kicked the ball over the fence*) and the resultative construction (*He mixed flour and water into a thick batter*). The two constructions share their morphosyntactic form but differ in meaning. Through the metaphor STATES ARE LOCATIONS (Lakoff & Johnson, 1980), caused motion toward a final location is linked to action that leads to a resultant state.

Another type of inheritance link connects constructions with partial similarities in their respective forms or meanings. These links are called *subpart links* (Goldberg, 1995, p. 78). Crucially, constructions that are linked through subpart links do not instantiate each other but are recognizably similar, with respect to form or meaning. For instance, the sentences *John wrote a letter* and *John wrote Mary a letter* share much of their respective structure, but through the links that we have discussed so far, they would only be connected insofar as they both instantiate a more abstract construction, say the subject–predicate construction, which then links back to both of them. Assuming that speakers recognize that the transitive construction and the ditransitive construction share a number of morphosyntactic and semantic features, these two constructions are interlinked in the constructional network, with matching parts being mapped onto one another. Unlike instance links, which were characterized earlier in the chapter as "vertical links," subpart links can thus be seen as "horizontal links" that connect different constructions at the same level of abstraction. Because a single construction may share features with several other constructions at once, subpart links relate to what is called *multiple inheritance*. Hilpert (2014b, p. 63) discussed the following example of a combined construction, a so-called syntactic amalgam, as an illustration.

Example 3.1 *The Smiths felt it was an important enough song to put on their last single.*

In this sentence, two constructions are interlaced, namely, an attributive construction with an adjective (e.g., *an important song*), and a construction in which the adverb *enough* projects a following *to*-infinitive (e.g., *It's important enough to put on a single*). The writer of the preceding example draws on both of these constructions and integrates them into a single syntactic structure. The source constructions for this integrated structure, and their interlacing, are as follows:

Example 3.2 *It was   an   important   song.*
It was   important   enough   to put on their last single.

Because Example 3.1 differs from both of these source constructions, it would be misleading to think of the relation as one of instantiation. Rather, the newly created construction displays multiple inheritance through two subpart links.

To summarize the main point of the preceding paragraphs, construction grammar models speakers' knowledge of language as a large repository of form–meaning pairings. The constructions in that repository are interlinked in different ways. We have presented a selection of links that are commonly assumed, namely, instance links, polysemy links, and subpart links. In the rest of this section, we aim to clarify how these links are subject to entrenchment.

There is general consensus among usage-based linguists that the co-occurrence of linguistic elements in language use leads to the entrenchment of the associative connections between them in memory, which in turn affects the processing and development of constructions in language acquisition and diachronic change (for an overview of frequency effects in usage, acquisition, and change, see Diessel, 2007). With regard to instance links, entrenchment facilitates the categorization of concrete utterance tokens, also called *constructs* (Fried, 2015), into constructions, that is, more general schemas. How easily is an utterance such as *John gave me a box of chocolates* processed as an instance of the ditransitive construction? There is evidence from corpus linguistics that this sentence is a highly prototypical instance of the ditransitive construction. As Bresnan, Cueni, Nikitina, and Baayen (2007) showed, a prototypical ditransitive sentence includes an animate, intentional agent (*John*) that acts on an inanimate, indefinite theme (*a box of chocolates*), which is transferred (*gave*) to a willing, discourse-given recipient (*me*). Of course, there are ditransitive sentences that deviate in one or more aspects from this prototype; but what is predicted in the constructional model of linguistic knowledge is that less prototypical instances of a construction will have weaker instance links to the overarching construction and thereby incur a greater processing cost for the listener.

Like instance links, polysemy links differ with regard to their respective degrees of entrenchment. A decontextualized instance of the English s-genitive, such as *John's apple*, is in principle ambiguous between a number of interpretations. It could be that what is referred to is an apple that John possesses, but it could also be that the expression denotes an apple that John pointed to, or a picture of an apple that John painted. The strength of a polysemy link will depend on the network of meanings that a linguistic form is associated with. In the case of the *s*-genitive, Taylor (1989) argued that "possession" is the central, most prototypical sense of the construction, which is extended to a number of other, more peripheral senses. This means that the form of the *s*-genitive construction is connected to the concept possession through a stronger link than for instance to the concept of "origin," which would be activated when we refer to a still life that John painted as *John's apple*. High frequency of use is an important correlate of prototypicality, but not the only one. Another crucial criterion for prototypicality is high connectivity to other senses, so that the prototypical sense is at the center of a network of similar senses (see Croft & Cruse, 2004, p. 78).

Finally, the entrenchment of subpart links determines how easily speakers can analyze a complex construction into its component parts. In other words, a construction with strongly entrenched subpart links will be highly transparent, whereas a construction with only weakly entrenched subpart links will appear opaque, so that speakers are more likely to process it holistically. To give an example of a strong subpart link, a salient subpart of the English ditransitive construction is the noun phrase construction that is instantiated by the string *a box of chocolates* in the sentence *John gave me a box of chocolates*. This noun phrase is easily "parsed out" from the ditransitive construction and further into its component parts. An example from the opposite end of the continuum would be the string *let alone* in sentences such as *He won't talk to me, let alone apologize*. Fillmore, Kay, and O'Connor (1988, p. 515) pointed out that the string *let alone*, despite its verbal heritage, shows the general distributional behavior of a coordinating conjunction. At the same time, it differs from *and* and *or* in several respects. Hence, speakers are unlikely to process *let alone* as an instance of a more general construction and will rather treat it as a sui generis item.

To conclude, this section has discussed how the constructions speakers know are interconnected through different types of links. The links we presented do not form an exhaustive set, and as yet, there is no complete theory as to how constructions are connected in speakers' minds. There is, however, evidence that all of the links considered in this section are subject to entrenchment. Links that are frequently activated are deeply entrenched in memory, and this affects the cognitive processes that are involved in language use: Deeply entrenched instance links facilitate the categorization of constructs; deeply entrenched polysemy links induce the listener to select a particular semantic interpretation (unless this interpretation is in conflict with the context), and deeply entrenched subpart links enhance the parsability (or compositionality) of linguistic sequences.

3.3 Collostructions: Links Between Constructions and Lexical Items

A central and recurrent finding of corpus-based research is that lexical elements show clear patterns of co-occurrence in naturally produced language. The term *collocation* captures the fact that, for example, a word such as *copyright* entertains associative ties with *infringement*, or the word *silver* is frequently followed by *lining*. Associative links of this kind are a fundamental characteristic of linguistic knowledge, as conceived of in construction grammar. Importantly, collocational links do not only connect different lexical elements, such as *silver* and *lining*, but they also link lexical elements to more abstract morphosyntactic patterns. For example, most naturally occurring instances of the English noun *damn* are produced in a single morphosyntactic frame, namely, with a negated form of the verb *give* and the indefinite determiner *a* (e.g., *I don't give a damn, Who gives a damn?*). Conversely, many abstract constructions tend to occur more often than expected with specific lexical elements. The English ditransitive construction, for instance, is strongly associated with verbs such as *give* or *send* (Stefanowitsch & Gries, 2003), and *wh*-questions with long-distance dependencies (*What do you think they will try next?*) tend to be produced with *think* or *say* as matrix verbs (Dąbrowska, 2008). In a constructional model of language, these associations are also assumed to be part of speakers' linguistic knowledge.

A stream of research into the interdependencies of constructions and lexical elements has been prompted by a series of papers by Gries and Stefanowitsch (2004a, 2004b; Stefanowitsch & Gries, 2003, 2005), who introduced the term *collostructional analysis* and proposed a suite of quantitative methods for corpus analysis. Introductions to the collostructional methods can be found in Stefanowitsch (2013) and Hilpert (2014a).[1] The main aim of a collostructional analysis is to determine which lexical items are "typical" of a given construction. This is done through relative frequency counts of lexical items in constructions and elsewhere, and the use of statistical association measures to evaluate those frequency counts. For example, given a construction such as the English resultative construction (NP$_1$ VERB NP$_2$ ADJ, e.g., *John coughed himself hoarse*), are there verbs that occur in this morphosyntactic frame more often than would be expected, given their overall text frequency? Collostructional analysis is a cover term for three related methods that share this basic question and thus allow the researcher to investigate associations between grammatical constructions and lexical items. The three methods can be described as follows.

Collexeme analysis (Stefanowitsch & Gries, 2003) investigates which lexical items typically occupy a lexical slot in a grammatical construction, as, for instance, the verbal slot in the English resultative construction. *Distinctive collexeme analysis* (Gries & Stefanowitsch, 2004a) contrasts the associative ties of two or more constructions. This facilitates the comparison of near-synonymous constructions such as the ditransitive versus the prepositional dative construction, modal auxiliary constructions such as *will* versus *shall*, or the progressive vs. the simple present. As a third option, *covarying-collexeme analysis* (Gries & Stefanowitsch, 2004b; Stefanowitsch & Gries, 2005) investigates dependencies between lexical items that occupy two different slots within the same construction. To illustrate, English gerundive complement clauses (*Failing to prepare is a recipe for disappointment*) hold a slot for an *ing*-form (*failing*) and another one for a verb in the infinitive (*to prepare*). Hilpert (2010) presented a covarying-collexeme analysis that determines typical gerund–verb combinations and allows conclusions about the semantic frames that are most strongly entrenched with the construction.

The output of a collostructional analysis is a ranked list of lexical elements that shows the relative frequency of these elements in particular constructions. A recurring result across many collostructional analyses is the observation that lexemes and

---

[1] Critical points concerning collostructional analysis are raised in Bybee (2010) and Schmid and Küchenhoff (2013). Among other things, these points concern the ranking of lexical elements, the calculation of mutual attraction, and the use of null-hypothesis significance testing. Gries (2012, 2015) has responded to these criticisms by discussing methodological points, such as the use of the Fisher–Yates exact test as an association measure, the cross-tabulation of several constructional contexts, and the inclusion of entropy and dispersion as additional model parameters. A particularly relevant question from this exchange is how the results of a collostructional analysis relate to cognitive entrenchment (see also Küchenhoff & Schmid, 2015, pp. 541–542). In most applications of the collostructional methods, a bidirectional measure of association (the Fisher–Yates exact test) has been used. Alternatively, it is possible to use directed association measures between constructions and lexical items, analogous to conditional probabilities in word-to-word associations. All of these are assumed to capture aspects of entrenchment, albeit different ones. Wiechmann (2008) presented an overview of association measures and their relative performance with regard to the prediction of reading times in eye-tracking data. In that overview, the Fisher–Yates exact test performs rather well, which motivates its use in collostructional analyses to approximate the entrenchment of links between words and constructions.

constructions co-occur if they are semantically compatible with each other. Following Goldberg (1995, p. 50), Stefanowitsch and Gries argued that the co-occurrence patterns of lexemes and constructions are semantically motivated. The verb *give*, for instance, is frequently used in the ditransitive because the lexical meaning of *give* fits the constructional meaning of the ditransitive very closely—both verb and construction denote an act of transfer. Goldberg (1995) explained the co-occurrence patterns of lexemes and constructions by a particular semantic principle, that is, the Principle of Semantic Coherence. However, although this principle accounts for the general tendency to "fuse" lexemes and constructions that are semantically related, it is important to recognize that the relationship between lexemes and constructions is not fully predictable from semantic criteria (see Goldberg, 1995, pp. 52–56; Herbst, 2014, p. 273). There are semantic idiosyncrasies that are not consistent with the principle of semantic coherence and that can only be explained by language users' experience with particular co-occurrence patterns. The entrenchment of a link between a lexical item and a construction can thus come about in two ways: either through a good semantic fit and the resulting high frequency of co-occurrence or through the mere observation that a lexical item occurs much more often than expected with a construction, regardless of their respective meanings. Let us consider a concrete example.

It is well-known that the ditransitive construction is commonly used with verbs of communication such as *tell* (e.g., *He told me the truth*). Because communication can be (metaphorically) construed as an act of transfer, the co-occurrence of verbs of communication and the ditransitive construction is semantically motivated. Note, however, that one of the most frequent verbs of communication, that is, the verb *say*, is not licensed by the ditransitive construction. When *say* is construed as a transfer verb, parallel to *tell*, it is exclusively found in the related *to*-dative construction (and not in the ditransitive; see Examples 3.3 and 3.4):

Example 3.3 a. *Peter told me the truth.*
              b. *I never told this to anyone else.*
Example 3.4 a. * *Peter said me the truth.*
              b. *I never said this to anyone else.*

Similar idiosyncrasies have been observed with other co-occurrence patterns (see Boas, 2008), suggesting that the semantic associations between lexemes and constructions are not fully productive. Because idiosyncratic constraints cannot be derived from general semantic principles, it is a plausible hypothesis that the co-occurrence patterns of lexemes and constructions are entrenched in memory. That is, speakers "know" the verbs that are (commonly) combined with particular verb-argument constructions regardless of any semantic criteria that (may) motivate the co-occurrence of particular words and constructions (for a discussion, see Diessel, 2015). This hypothesis is supported by evidence from early child language (see Theakston, Chapter 14, this volume).

3.4 Negative Entrenchment and the No Negative Evidence Problem

The earliest constructions children produce are tied to frequent verbs they encounter in the ambient language, but it does not take long before children begin to combine verbs and constructions productively, producing structures that are not generally consistent with the conventions of adult grammar (for a recent review, see Diessel, 2013).

Because parents do not systematically correct their children's errors, it is important to consider how children learn to constrain the overuse of certain schemas or rules. Bowerman (1988) referred to this question as the *no negative evidence problem*. In the generative literature, it is commonly assumed that the no negative evidence problem can only be resolved through the support of an innate language faculty that constrains the occurrence of particular grammatical patterns. However, challenging this view, usage-based linguists have argued that the overuse of grammatical constructions in early child language is constrained by the child's steadily growing linguistic experience (e.g., Ambridge, Pine, Rowland, & Chang, 2012; Ambridge, Pine, Rowland, & Young, 2008; Boyd & Goldberg, 2011; Braine & Brooks, 1995; Brooks, Tomasello, Dodson, & Lewis, 1999; Brooks & Tomasello, 1999; Stefanowitsch, 2008, 2011). Specifically, these researchers suggest that children's overgeneralization errors are eliminated be the combined effect of general semantic criteria and entrenchment.

The importance of entrenchment has been demonstrated in a series of experimental studies that were designed to test the effect of frequency on children's use of verb argument constructions (for a review, see Tomasello, 2003, pp. 175–181). In one of these studies, Brooks, Tomasello, Dodson, and Lewis (1999) exposed children of different age groups to English verbs such as *disappear* or *vanish*, which are restricted to intransitive uses. In the training phase of the experiment, the children saw physical actions that were described by the experimenter with the use of these verbs: A puppet pulled a string so that an object fell through a trap door and disappeared. In the test phase of the experiment, the children were prompted to redescribe that action. This was done in a way that encouraged overgeneralization errors, namely, through a question that directed the children's attention to the responsible agent of the action. The question "What is Big Bird doing?" was thus meant to elicit overgeneralization errors such as, "He disappeared the car." Brooks et al. (p. 1330) found that responses of this kind are more easily elicited with (infrequent) verbs that are less entrenched (and usually acquired at a later age). Children are thus relatively likely to accept "He vanished the car" as a possible sentence, while they are more reluctant to produce "He disappeared the car." This behavior suggests that the accumulative memorization of positive evidence tells children not only what is possible but also what is impossible.

Building on this research, Stefanowitsch (2008) argued that the absence of an expected co-occurrence pattern in language use leads both child and adult speakers to the conclusion that the absent pattern is not licensed by a particular schema or rule. On this view, entrenchment not only increases language users' expectations that particular words and constructions can easily fuse, it also increases their expectations that particular words and constructions are unlikely to co-occur, up to the point where certain co-occurrence patterns appear to be outright unacceptable (or ungrammatical). To flesh out this idea, Stefanowitsch (2008) offered the example of the verb *say* in the English ditransitive construction. As pointed out earlier, a sentence such as **Mary said Sue something nice* is not (usually) accepted by native speakers. Could it be that speakers form this intuition simply on the basis of their daily experience with language? Stefanowitsch (2008) argued that speakers can do this, provided that they combine the following pieces of information. First, the ditransitive construction is a relatively frequent syntactic pattern in English. Second, the verb *say* is a relatively frequent verb in English. Given that *say* is never heard in the ditransitive, but much less frequent verbs such as *buy*, *send*, or *sell* are, speakers reason (subconsciously) that this asymmetry is too robust to be a coincidence: In other words, they arrive at the conclusion that *say* is not acceptable in the ditransitive construction.

Further research on negative entrenchment has focused on the role of functionally equivalent constructions. Boyd and Goldberg (2011) and Goldberg (2011) advocated the idea that speakers form generalizations over sets of constructions that are comparable with regard to their meanings, as, for instance, the ditransitive construction and the prepositional dative construction. Through their linguistic experience, speakers learn that the verb *recommend* is commonly used in the prepositional dative construction (*John recommended the book to Mary*), while it is virtually absent from the ditransitive construction, despite the functional similarity of these two constructions. On the basis of this statistical asymmetry, speakers eventually reject ditransitive *recommend*.

Although entrenchment has a major role in children's recovery from overgeneralization errors, constraining linguistic generalizations works not only on the basis of statistical learning (see Jost & Christiansen, Chapter 10, this volume) or "negative entrenchment" (Stefanowitsch, 2008) but also includes a second factor, semantics. Following a suggestion by Pinker (1989), a number of studies have argued that the use of verbs is constrained by semantic verb classes that are associated with particular verb–argument constructions. Experimental evidence for this hypothesis comes, for instance, from a study by Ambridge et al. (2008) in which children and adults were taught novel verbs such as *tam* (meaning "laugh") or *meek* (meaning "fall") in intransitive contexts. For all of these novel verbs, it is safe to assume an identical, low degree of entrenchment. Still, when the participants were later confronted with uses of those verbs in new morphosyntactic contexts, not all examples were rated as equally acceptable. Sentences such as *The man meeked Lisa* ("made Lisa fall") were more readily accepted than sentences such as *The funny clown tammed Bert* ("made Bert laugh"). Ambridge et al. explained this as an effect of constructional semantics: The transitive construction is more strongly associated with direct physical causation. Transitive sentences with the verbs *tam* and *meek* are thus judged on the basis of verb meanings, rather than on the basis of entrenchment. This does not take anything away from the importance of (negative) entrenchment, but it shows that semantics has a role to play as well.

To draw a conclusion from these observations, a usage-based constructional view of linguistic knowledge holds that naturally occurring linguistic data contain not only positive evidence, from which children can learn the forms of a language, but also negative evidence, from which children can infer what combinations of linguistic units are not acceptable. The hypothesis that (negative) entrenchment constrains the overuse of verbs rests on the assumption that lexemes and constructions are associated with each other through specific links that determine the speakers' expectations about particular co-occurrence patterns in language use on statistical grounds.

3.5 Entrenchment in Morphological Constructions

Construction grammar has been devised as a theory of linguistic knowledge in its entirety. Everything that speakers know when they know a language is to be represented as a large network of constructions. Most research in this framework is concerned with syntactic patterns, but there has also been construction-based research in morphology. In particular, the research by Bybee (1985, 1995) is immediately compatible with central tenets of the construction-based theory of language. In fact, Bybee's research on morphology had a major impact on the development of the network model of grammar and the usage-based approach (for a review of this research, see also Bybee, 2010, and Diessel, 2011). Central assumptions of usage-based construction grammar, such as the view of linguistic knowledge as a repository of grammatical patterns, the idea that constructions are generalizations over tokens of language use, and the interconnection of constructions through formal and functional overlap, are described in Bybee (1985). More recently, Booij (2010, 2013) developed an explicitly constructional approach to morphology that draws on these ideas. Example 3.5 illustrates different morphological constructions.

> Example 3.5 *This is a wug. Now there is another one. There are two . . . wugs.*
> *If you need to reach me, I'm skypable all morning.*
> *Not quite shorts, not quite pants—shpants!*

In the simplest of terms, *morphological constructions* are form–meaning pairings with structure below the word level. Constructions of this kind allow speakers to process and produce newly coined words such as the ones shown in Example 3.5. Even a reader who has not encountered the words *wugs*, *skypable*, or *shpants* before will be able to figure out what they mean and how they function in their respective syntactic contexts. Morphological constructions give rise to words (*skypable*) and word forms (*skyping*, *skyped*), all of which are subject to conventionalization and entrenchment.

A regular plural, such as the word form *cats*, is thus a construct of the English plural construction, even though it is hardly a newly coined word form. Highly entrenched instances of morphological constructions can be observed to become more and more autonomous from the schema that gave rise to them. Bybee (2010, p. 45) gave the examples of *awful* and *wonderful*, both of which instantiate the morphological *NOUN-ful* construction but which have developed meanings that are not strictly predictable from that construction. Less entrenched instances of the construction, such as, for instance, *scornful*, are semantically more transparent. Autonomy can also make itself felt in phonological reduction, so that, for instance, the suffix -*ment* in the highly entrenched word *government* is more likely to be pronounced in a reduced fashion than the same suffix in a less entrenched word, such as *endearment*. In terms of the links between constructions that have been discussed in Section 3.2, it can thus be said that words such as *awful* and *scornful* differ in the strength of their instance links to the *NOUN-ful* construction: Constructions with relatively greater autonomy have weaker instance links to overarching patterns (Hilpert, 2015, p. 26). At the same time, *awful* and *scornful* also differ in the strength of their subpart links that connect them to their respective lexical stems. For many speakers, the connection between the adjective *awful* and the noun *awe* will be weak. By contrast, *scornful* and *scorn* are likely to be related through a strong subpart link.

The last section discussed the concept of negative entrenchment as an explanation for speakers' intuitions that certain utterances are ungrammatical. The examples that were offered to illustrate that phenomenon were concerned with combinations of lexical elements and syntactic constructions. Also in the domain of morphology, there are certain formations that speakers perceive as ungrammatical. The unacceptability of a potential word such as **unnice* finds a natural explanation in the fact that the adjective *nice*, judged by its high overall frequency, is conspicuously absent from the *un-ADJECTIVE* construction. Exposure to language use of derived adjectives, such as *unhappy*, *unfair*, or *unusual*, and simplex adjectives, such as *nice*, *recent*, or *hard*, will lead speakers to the subconscious insight that the latter do not pair with the *un-ADJECTIVE* construction.

There are also unacceptable morphological formations that require a different explanation, however. For instance, it is commonly observed that there are constraints on the way in which English derivational affixes can be combined in morphologically complex derived words. To take the suffixes -*ive* (*active*, *collective*, *relative*) and -*ize* (*generalize*, *specialize*, *stabilize*) as an example, these can only be combined in one order: -*ive* before -*ize*, not the other way around.

> Example 3.6 *nativize*
> *collectivize*
> *relativize*
> **generalizive*
> **specializive*
> **stabilizive*

Why do the two suffixes behave in this asymmetric way? An explanation that has been suggested (Siegel, 1974) posits two levels of affixes in English. The suffix *-ive* belongs to the first level, the suffix *-ize* to the second level. What is predicted is that words with Level 1 affixes may serve as a morphological base for words with Level 2 affixes, but not vice versa. Although this account predicts the correct order of affixes for most words, it does not provide a functional explanation for affix ordering.

Hay and Plag (2004) proposed an alternative account that resonates with our previous discussion of entrenchment and constructional subpart links. As was pointed out earlier, the entrenchment of subpart links for a given complex construction determines how easily speakers can analyze that construction into its component parts. Applied to morphological constructions, this means that speakers can easily parse out an affix of a complex word if that affix is linked to the overarching constructional schema through a strong subpart link. For example, the affix *-ness* in the word *sweetness* is easily parsed out as a part of the *ADJECTIVE-ness* construction. If, however, the subpart link between affix and constructional schema is weak, the word in question will be less transparent, and consequently harder to parse for a speaker. An example would be the affix *-ity* in the noun *brevity*. The affix is linked to the *ADJECTIVE-ity* construction (cf. *ability, reality, activity*, etc.), but that link is, in comparison to *-ness* and the *ADJECTIVE-ness* construction, relatively weak.

Coming back to the impossibility of **generalizive* and **specializive*, what did Hay and Plag (2004) propose? The basic claim they advanced is that parsable affixes like *-ness* can be easily added to a complex word, whereas affixes that are hard to parse out, such as *-ity*, are more constrained. In the words of Hay (2002), "an affix that can be easily parsed out should not occur inside an affix that cannot" (p. 527). This claim is supported by corpus evidence. On the basis of frequencies of derived words (e.g., *goodness, really*) and their respective bases (*good, real*), Hay and Plag determined a parsability hierarchy for 15 English suffixes. Affixes with many formations that are relatively more frequent than the corresponding bases (cf. *really* vs. *real*) are low on the parsability hierarchy; affixes for which most formations are less frequent than their bases (cf. *goodness* vs. *good*) are highly parsable. Hay and Plag then compared that hierarchy against a database of complex derived words with multiple suffixes. They found that higher parsability of an affix correlates with a higher likelihood that the affix can take a morphologically complex base. In other words, the fact that *foolishness* is a word but **goodnessish* is not is because *-ness* is more easily parsed out than *-ish*. With regard to entrenchment, ease of parsing, or transparency, translates into more strongly entrenched subpart links. Complex derived words such as *foolishness* are coined because speakers have internalized a constructional schema that links to the affix *-ness* through a strongly entrenched subpart link. Corresponding schemas for *-ish*, *-ive*, or *-ity* can be assumed to exist, but there the subpart links are not as strongly entrenched.

3.6 Entrenched Constructions or Entrenched Links?

The final section in this chapter addresses the question whether entrenchment in the constructional network affects links between constructions, the constructions themselves, or both. The most common view in construction grammar appears to be that entrenchment is a characteristic of constructions themselves, that is, of nodes in the constructional network that represents speakers' linguistic knowledge.

Much of the preceding discussion has deviated from this view and has instead focused on the entrenchment of connections in the network of constructions, that is, the relative strength of instance links, subpart links, and the symbolic links between form and meaning of constructions. So far, the entrenchment of links has not been the subject of extensive discussion in the constructionist literature (but see Diessel, 2015, and Hilpert, 2014b), but given the wide consensus that linguistic knowledge is to be understood as a network, the general idea that connections can be entrenched to different degrees should not be controversial. However, in the introduction to this volume, Schmid advances an understanding of entrenchment that views it as pertaining only to connections, not to nodes:

> Usage-based models usually assume that entrenchment operates over constructions and constructional schemas that are characterized as form–meaning pairings. Furthermore, they claim that these constructions and schemas are related to each other in a massive associative memory network organized mainly in terms of hierarchical relations (see Hilpert & Diessel, Chapter 3, this volume). The present proposal diverges from this idea in two important ways: First, it rejects the distinction between constructions serving as nodes in the network and relations between nodes and instead assumes that linguistic knowledge is available in one format only, namely, associations. (Schmid, Chapter 1, this volume, Section 1.5)

Schmid thus emphasizes that constructions are to be understood as links between form and meaning and that strongly entrenched constructions are simply strong symbolic links between a form and a meaning. This proposal is not primarily motivated by theoretical parsimony but rather by the aim of describing linguistic knowledge in inherently dynamic terms. By viewing constructions as nodes, Schmid argues, gradualness and dynamicity are left behind, and a division is created between static representations of linguistic knowledge on the one hand and dynamic language processing on the other (p. 13). We generally agree with this view. Specifically, we contend that the "connection view" of entrenchment can actually capture the insights that have been formulated in the "node view," but beyond that, there are two concrete advantages. First, the "connection view" avoids a number of undesirable consequences of the node view; second, it enables a number of connections to other research traditions that might prove fruitful. With regard to the first point, it is true that in the "node view," constructions are reified in a way that might invite the idea of static structures that speakers recall from memory whenever they use language. It is this view that has been criticized by Hopper (1987), who also argued for a more dynamic and "emergent" view of grammar. Proponents of usage-based construction grammar (e.g., Bybee, 2013) have actually been quite explicit about the fact that constructions are subject to constant change through language use. The preceding sections have made the point that different aspects of entrenchment can be usefully captured as the strength of different kinds of links, which is in line with both Schmid's proposal and many empirical findings. With regard to the second point, the "connection view" would encourage researchers in construction grammar to make more explicit how they envision the connections that hold together the network of constructions. As mentioned in Section 3.2, this remains an area in construction grammar that is still theoretically underdeveloped. At the same time, there is a substantial research tradition on distributed connectionist modeling that can be made fruitful for research in usage-based construction grammar (for a concrete example, see Lewis & Elman, 2001).

3.7 Conclusion

This chapter has attempted to flesh out how the notion of entrenchment fits into the theoretical model of linguistic knowledge that goes by the name of construction grammar. Its main point has been the claim that entrenchment has a central place in this model and that the idea of entrenchment actually provides natural explanations for a wide range of empirical phenomena, including seemingly disparate ones, like phonological reduction on the one hand and intuitions of ungrammaticality on the other. This chapter has characterized several aspects of entrenchment in terms of connections in the network of constructions that is meant to represent speakers' knowledge of language. These connections are of different kinds, linking form and meaning, abstract constructions and their instantiations, as well as constructions and their component parts. Through experience with language in use, these connections are subject to incremental changes in relative strength. It goes without saying that many aspects of this general idea still await more thorough investigation. We believe that what we have presented here represents a complex of ideas that is shared to a substantial extent by the practitioners in the field, but because construction grammar is really a family of theories, rather than a unified enterprise, there are bound to be issues that will provoke disagreement. We look forward to seeing some of these disagreements made explicit, especially in a dialogue that involves not only construction grammarians but also and specifically readers of this volume who identify with other theories and disciplines.

References

Ambridge, B., Pine, J. M., Rowland, C. F., & Chang, F. (2012). The roles of verb semantics, entrenchment, and morphophonology in the retreat from dative argument-structure overgeneralization errors. *Language*, *88*, 45–81. http://dx.doi.org/10.1353/lan.2012.0000

Ambridge, B., Pine, J. M., Rowland, C. F., & Young, C. R. (2008). The effect of verb semantic class and verb frequency (entrenchment) on children's and adults' graded judgements of argument-structure overgeneralization errors. *Cognition*, *106*, 87–129. http://dx.doi.org/10.1016/j.cognition.2006.12.015

Boas, H. C. (2008). Determining the structure of lexical entries and grammatical constructions in construction grammar. *Annual Review of Cognitive Linguistics*, *6*, 113–144. http://dx.doi.org/10.1075/arcl.6.06boa

Booij, G. (2010). *Construction morphology*. Oxford, England: Oxford University Press.

Booij, G. (2013). Morphology in construction grammar. In G. Trousdale & T. Hoffmann (Eds.), *The Oxford handbook of construction grammar* (pp. 255–273). Oxford, England: Oxford University Press.

Bowerman, M. (1988). The "no negative evidence" problem: How do children avoid constructing an overly general grammar? In J. Hawkins (Ed.), *Explaining language universals* (pp. 73–101). Oxford, England: Basil Blackwell.

Boyd, J. K., & Goldberg, A. E. (2011). Learning what not to say: The role of statistical preemption and categorization in "a"-adjective production. *Language*, *81*, 1–29.

Braine, M., & Brooks, P. J. (1995). Verb-argument structure and the problem of avoiding overgeneral grammar. In M. Tomasello & W. Merriman (Eds.), *Beyond names for things: Young children's acquisition of verbs* (pp. 353–376). Hillsdale, NJ: Erlbaum.

Bresnan, J., Cueni, A., Nikitina, T., & Baayen, R. H. (2007). Predicting the dative alternation. In G. Bouma, I. Krämer, & J. Zwarts (Eds.), *Cognitive foundations of interpretation* (pp. 69–94). Amsterdam, the Netherlands: Royal Netherlands Academy of Science.

Brooks, P. J., & Tomasello, M. (1999). How children constrain their argument structure constructions. *Language*, *75*, 720–738. http://dx.doi.org/10.2307/417731

Brooks, P. J., Tomasello, M., Dodson, K., & Lewis, L. B. (1999). Young children's overgeneralizations with fixed transitivity verbs. *Child Development*, *70*, 1325–1337. http://dx.doi.org/10.1111/1467-8624.00097

Bybee, J. L. (1985). *Morphology: A study of the relation between meaning and form*. http://dx.doi.org/10.1075/tsl.9

Bybee, J. L. (1995). Regular morphology and the lexicon. *Language and Cognitive Processes*, *10*, 425–455. http://dx.doi.org/10.1080/01690969508407111

Bybee, J. L. (2010). *Language, usage, and cognition*. http://dx.doi.org/10.1017/CBO9780511750526

Bybee, J. L. (2013). Usage-based theory and exemplar representations of constructions. In G. Trousdale & T. Hoffmann (Eds.), *The Oxford handbook of construction grammar* (pp. 49–69). Oxford, England: Oxford University Press.

Croft, W. A. (2001). *Radical construction grammar. Syntactic theory in typological perspective*. http://dx.doi.org/10.1093/acprof:oso/9780198299554.001.0001

Croft, W. A., & Cruse, D. A. (2004). *Cognitive linguistics*. http://dx.doi.org/10.1017/CBO9780511803864

Dąbrowska, E. (2008). Questions with long-distance dependencies: A usage-based perspective. *Cognitive Linguistics*, *19*, 391–425. http://dx.doi.org/10.1515/COGL.2008.015

Diessel, H. (2007). Frequency effects in language acquisition, language use, and diachronic change. *New Ideas in Psychology*, *25*, 108–127. http://dx.doi.org/10.1016/j.newideapsych.2007.02.002

Diessel, H. (2011). Review of "Language, usage and cognition" by Joan Bybee. *Language*, *87*, 830–844. http://dx.doi.org/10.1353/lan.2011.0082

Diessel, H. (2013). Construction grammar and first language acquisition. In G. Trousdale & T. Hoffmann (Eds.), *The Oxford handbook of construction grammar* (pp. 347–364). Oxford, England: Oxford University Press.

Diessel, H. (2015). Usage-based construction grammar. In E. Dąbrowska & D. Divjak (Eds.), *Handbook of cognitive linguistics* (pp. 295–321). http://dx.doi.org/10.1515/9783110292022-015

Fillmore, C., Kay, P., & O'Connor, C. (1988). Regularity and idiomaticity in grammatical constructions: The case of let alone. *Language, 64*, 501–538. http://dx.doi.org/10.2307/414531

Fried, M. (2015). Construction grammar. In A. Alexiadou & T. Kiss (Eds.), *Handbook of syntax* (2nd ed., pp. 974–1003). Berlin, Germany: Walter de Gruyter.

Goldberg, A. E. (1995). *Constructions. A construction grammar approach to argument structure.* Chicago, IL: University of Chicago Press.

Goldberg, A. E. (2003). Constructions: A new theoretical approach to language. *Trends in Cognitive Sciences, 7*, 219–224. http://dx.doi.org/10.1016/S1364-6613(03)00080-9

Goldberg, A. E. (2006). *Constructions at work: The nature of generalization in language.* Oxford, England: Oxford University Press.

Goldberg, A. E. (2011). Corpus evidence of the viability of statistical preemption. *Cognitive Linguistics, 22*, 131–154. http://dx.doi.org/10.1515/cogl.2011.006

Gries, S. T. (2012). Frequencies, probabilities, association measures in usage-/exemplar-based linguistics: Some necessary clarifications. *Studies in Language, 36*, 477–510.

Gries, S. T. (2015). More (old and new) misunderstandings of collostructional analysis: On Schmid & Küchenhoff (2013). *Cognitive Linguistics, 26*, 505–536. http://dx.doi.org/10.1515/cog-2014-0092

Gries, S. T., & Stefanowitsch, A. (2004a). Co-varying collexemes in the into-causative. In M. Achard & S. Kemmer (Eds.), *Language, culture, and mind* (pp. 225–236). Stanford, CA: CSLI.

Gries, S. T., & Stefanowitsch, A. (2004b). Extending collostructional analysis: A corpus-based perspective on "alternations." *International Journal of Corpus Linguistics, 9*, 97–129. http://dx.doi.org/10.1075/ijcl.9.1.06gri

Hay, J. (2002). From speech perception to morphology: Affix-ordering revisited. *Language, 78*, 527–555. http://dx.doi.org/10.1353/lan.2002.0159

Hay, J., & Plag, I. (2004). What constrains possible suffix combinations? On the interaction of grammatical and processing restrictions in derivational morphology. *Natural Language and Linguistic Theory, 22*, 565–596. http://dx.doi.org/10.1023/B:NALA.0000027679.63308.89

Herbst, T. (2014). Idiosyncrasies and generalizations: Argument structure, semantic roles and the valency realization principle. In S. Flach & M. Hilpert (Eds.), *Yearbook of the German Cognitive Linguistics Association* (Vol. 2, pp. 253–289). http://dx.doi.org/10.1515/gcla-2014-0015

Hilpert, M. (2010). The force dynamics of English complement clauses: A usage-based account. In K. Fischer & D. Glynn (Eds.), *Quantitative methods in cognitive semantics* (pp. 155–178). http://dx.doi.org/10.1515/9783110226423.155

Hilpert, M. (2014a). Collostructional analysis: Measuring associations between constructions and lexical elements. In D. Glynn & J. Robinson (Eds.), *Corpus methods for semantics: Quantitative studies in polysemy and synonymy* (pp. 391–404). http://dx.doi.org/10.1075/hcp.43.15hil

Hilpert, M. (2014b). *Construction grammar and its application to English.* Edinburgh, Scotland: Edinburgh University Press.

Hilpert, M. (2015). From hand-carved to computer-based: Noun-participle compounding and the upward-strengthening hypothesis. *Cognitive Linguistics, 26*, 1–36. http://dx.doi.org/10.1515/cog-2014-0001

Hopper, P. (1987). Emergent grammar. *Berkeley Linguistics Society, 13*, 139–157.

Israel, M. (1996). The way constructions grow. In A. Goldberg (Ed.), *Conceptual structure, discourse and language* (pp. 217–230). Stanford, CA: CSLI.

Küchenhoff, H., & Schmid, H.-J. (2015). Reply to "More (old and new) misunderstandings of collostructional analysis: On Schmid & Küchenhoff" by Stefan Th. Gries. *Cognitive Linguistics*, *26*, 537–547. http://dx.doi.org/10.1515/cog-2015-0053

Lakoff, G., & Johnson, M. (1980). *Metaphors we live by*. Chicago, IL: University of Chicago Press.

Langacker, R. W. (1987). *Foundations of cognitive grammar: Vol. 1. Theoretical prerequisites*. Stanford, CA: Stanford University Press.

Lewis, J. D., & Elman, J. L. (2001). Learnability and the statistical structure of language: Poverty of the stimulus arguments revisited. In B. Skarabela, S. Fish, & A. Do (Eds.), *Proceedings of the 26th Annual Boston University Conference on Language Development* (pp. 359–370). Boston, MA: Cascadilla Press.

Perek, F. (in press). Using distributional semantics to study syntactic productivity in diachrony: A case study. *Linguistics*.

Pinker, S. (1989). *Learnability and cognition. The acquisition of argument structure*. Cambridge, MA: MIT Press.

Schmid, H.-J., & Küchenhoff, H. (2013). Collostructional analysis and other ways of measuring lexico-grammatical attraction: Theoretical premises, practical problems and cognitive underpinnings. *Cognitive Linguistics*, *24*, 531–577. http://dx.doi.org/10.1515/cog-2013-0018

Siegel, D. (1974). *Topics in English morphology* (Unpublished doctoral dissertation). Massachusetts Institute of Technology, Cambridge, MA.

Stefanowitsch, A. (2008). Negative entrenchment: A usage-based approach to negative evidence. *Cognitive Linguistics*, *19*, 513–531. http://dx.doi.org/10.1515/COGL.2008.020

Stefanowitsch, A. (2011). Constructional preemption by contextual mismatch: A corpus-linguistic investigation. *Cognitive Linguistics*, *22*, 107–129. http://dx.doi.org/10.1515/cogl.2011.005

Stefanowitsch, A. (2013). Collostructional analysis. In Th. Hoffman & G. Trousdale (Eds.), *The Oxford handbook of construction grammar* (pp. 290–307). Oxford, England: Oxford University Press.

Stefanowitsch, A., & Gries, S. (2003). Collostructions: Investigating the interaction of words and constructions. *International Journal of Corpus Linguistics*, *8*, 209–243. http://dx.doi.org/10.1075/ijcl.8.2.03ste

Stefanowitsch, A., & Gries, S. (2005). Covarying collexemes. *Corpus Linguistics and Linguistic Theory*, *1*, 1–43. http://dx.doi.org/10.1515/cllt.2005.1.1.1

Taylor, J. R. (1989). Possessive genitives in English. *Linguistics*, *27*, 663–686. http://dx.doi.org/10.1515/ling.1989.27.4.663

Tomasello, M. (2003). *Constructing a language. A usage-based theory of language acquisition*. Cambridge, MA: Harvard University Press.

Wiechmann, D. (2008). On the computation of collostruction strength: Testing measures of association as expression of lexical bias. *Corpus Linguistics and Linguistic Theory*, *4*, 253–290. http://dx.doi.org/10.1515/CLLT.2008.011

Hendrik De Smet
4 Entrenchment Effects in Language Change

4.1 Introduction

Although the concept of entrenchment has made something of a splash in historical linguistics, it was never a complete stranger to the field. Take simple changes such as the semantic divergence between English *busy* and its derivative *business*, which now means 'economic activity' rather than 'the state of being busy,' or between French *maintenir*, 'hold on to,' and what used to be its present participle, *maintenant*, today meaning 'now.' Or take the formal contraction of the Dutch phrase (*het*) *mach schien* '(it) can happen' to the adverb *misschien*, 'maybe,' or of English *God be with ye* to *goodbye*. Changes like these have long been known, and even without a more articulate concept of entrenchment, one could intuit that they must involve processes that operate on frequent usage patterns. It does not take much to realize that such changes must involve something like redundant storage or chunking. What is new, however, is that the processes involved in these changes are no longer deemed curiosities, observed sporadically in the lexicon but alien to grammar proper; instead, they are now thought to be constitutive of the very texture of grammar. What is also new is that these and other changes have been integrated into a growing body of evidence, supporting a more unified theory of the relation between usage and linguistic knowledge.

Entrenchment refers to the automation process through which linguistic structures achieve "unit status" (Langacker, 1987, p. 57). As a structure gets entrenched, it becomes part of a speaker's linguistic repertoire, as a ready-made pattern that can be used largely automatically, with no effort going into creative assembly. Entrenchment is dependent on usage, increasing through repeated use and decreasing through nonuse (Langacker, 1987, p. 59). It can affect any dimension or level of linguistic structure (Langacker, 1987, pp. 57–58). Prefabs such as *I see what you mean* or *the thing is that* have unit status, to the extent that they are ready-made (parts of) syntagms. Yet any single word is also a unit, being an automated pairing of a phonological form to a conceptual structure, and so are the individual sounds of a language, each of which is an automated sequence of articulatory movements. Crucially, there is no strict dichotomy between units and nonunits (Langacker, 1987, p. 59). Entrenchment is gradual. Even among established units, degrees of entrenchment vary and will be reflected in variable ease of activation (Langacker, 1991, p. 48; for more details, see Langacker, Chapter 2, this volume).

That entrenchment changes with exposure hints at a diachronic dimension. In fact, the role of entrenchment in historical linguistic theory goes much further. The

---

I am grateful to Hans-Jörg Schmid for his comments on an earlier version of this chapter.

goal of this chapter is to provide an overview of the relations between the cognitive linguistics concept of entrenchment and the field of historical linguistics. At its best, entrenchment explains some phenomena that have always embarrassed historical linguists. For example, it brings some measure of predictability to analogical levelling (Bybee & Slobin, 1982). Historical linguists in turn have been contributing important evidence of the role of entrenchment in grammar. For instance, they have extensively documented the relation between changing usage frequency and phonetic reduction (Hooper, 1976; Krug, 1998). The theoretical cross-fertilization and resulting insights certainly justify enthusiasm. At the same time, there is no denying that there are still several issues to be resolved. Explanations based on entrenchment often seem prone to circularity; how entrenchment leads to formal reduction or semantic change is still not fully understood; it remains unclear how the gradual character of entrenchment relates to the discreteness typically associated with syntax; and entrenchment of paradigmatic relations is still much underexplored. Those issues, too, are discussed in this chapter.

The following overview sticks to the conceptual framework proposed by Schmid (Chapter 1, this volume), addressing the effects of entrenchment on pragmatic, symbolic, syntagmatic, and paradigmatic relations in grammar. These are the relations of a form to, respectively, its extralinguistic context, the meaning it encodes, the other forms with which it co-occurs in a syntactic sequence, and other forms that could take its place in a syntactic sequence.[1]

Given this diversity of relation types, the effects of entrenchment on language change appear disparate and paradoxical. Sometimes entrenchment is a conservative force; sometimes it lies at the basis of grammatical innovation. To find some unity in disparity, it helps to think of entrenchment as endowing a relation with a selectional advantage in usage. Arguably, it is this advantage over alternative choices that makes entrenched relations both conservative and prone to extension into new usage contexts. On the one hand, alternative choices are less likely to encroach on a relation that is firmly entrenched. On the other hand, entrenchment works in tandem with what Langacker (1987, p. 71) termed *partial sanction*. In verbalization, language users may opt for coding solutions that deviate from convention. They then select an expression with specifications that only partly correspond to the conceptualization to be coded. This is what leads to innovation. Because partial sanction is the source of creativity in language, it may seem to stand in direct opposition to entrenchment. In fact, however, partial sanction may well depend on entrenchment (De Smet, 2016). After all, language users are more likely to choose a deviant coding solution if that

---

1 These are all form-centered relations, and it is to these that the following discussion is restricted. But this is still a simplification. Schmid's framework can in fact be taken further to include, for instance, paradigmatic relations between meanings (as in conceptual metaphors, cf. Lakoff & Johnson, 1980); it could capture syntagmatic relations between a form and the meanings typically found in its immediate context (as in semantic prosody effects, cf. Sinclair, 1991); and so on.

solution is readily available. The easy access language users have to an entrenched expression is what allows them to select that expression despite its maladaptedness to the coding problem at hand.

Before starting off on the detailed discussion, a few preliminary notes are in order. First, in what follows I take discourse frequency as a proxy to entrenchment. This is possibly naive, because the linguistic significance of an expression's frequency may be codetermined by the frequency of its parts (Hay, 2003), the frequency of its contexts (Gries & Stefanowitsch, 2004), or the frequency of its alternatives (Schmid, 2014; see also Schmid, Chapter 1, this volume). However, simple discourse frequency has had undeniable explanatory success in diachronic research. Perhaps that is because the diachronic dimension itself introduces—in the form of frequency change—the relativity to which frequency effects are sensitive. In that light, simple frequency will also do for the purpose of this chapter.

Second, there is a tension between the psychological basis of entrenchment and the social nature of change. Language change is a social phenomenon. It spreads through and across communities and may even unfold over multiple generations of speakers. Yet it is claimed that the dynamics of change can be explained by how language is processed in the minds of individuals. This assumes that change is the summed outcome of how individuals respond to the language to which they are exposed and to which they, in turn, contribute (Keller, 1994). The danger in linking the individual to the social in this way is that one ends up talking about an idealized speaker. The move is not uncommon—think of the Chomskyan "ideal speaker-listener" or the "rational agent" of economics—but it downplays individual variation. Whether this is problematic, we do not know. It is not inconceivable that some changes depend precisely on the differences that exist in a population (see, e.g., Schelling, 1978, on processes of social change, or Labov, 2001, on the role of specific age cohorts in propagating "change from below"). Regarding the cognitive basis of language, however, the range of individual variation is only beginning to be explored (Dąbrowska, 2012, 2015). This chapter does not dig further into the issue.

Third, in much of what follows, the elephant in the room is grammaticalization. *Grammaticalization* is the process by which a lexical item adopts a grammatical function and undergoes concomitant changes to its form and syntactic behavior (Hopper & Traugott, 2003; Lehmann, 1985). For example, English *go* was and still is a verb marking spatial motion, but in the pattern *be going to* it developed into a future auxiliary, with a phonetically reduced variant *gonna* and with some new syntactic properties, such as transparency to thematic role assignment (for a detailed history, see Krug, 2000). Grammaticalizing items tend to undergo dramatic increases in their frequency, and this is what makes them so interesting in connection to entrenchment. Indeed, many of the changes that come with grammaticalization have been explained as entrenchment effects. I do not discuss grammaticalization as such here, but an occasional mention of the term is inevitable, and many of the examples that come up in the body of this chapter are instances of grammaticalization.

4.2 Pragmatic Association

Pragmatic relations become entrenched when language users store information about the contexts in which linguistic expressions are used. That this possibility exists seems uncontroversial. In fact, it is presupposed by much of sociolinguistic theory. In addition, entrenchment of pragmatic relations also offers a plausible explanation for a major body of semantic changes.

4.2.1 The Social Dynamics of Change

Language users register who uses specific expressions and under what conditions. Speakers' ability to style-shift depends on this, as do the social dynamics of change (Labov, 2001, pp. 517–518). The simplest illustration is changes from above, in which language users more or less consciously adopt a prestige form (Labov, 1994, p. 78). For example, Weerman, Olson, and Cloutier (2013) showed that although Dutch had already largely lost its inflectional case marking system, the genitive was revitalized in the 17th century and made a comeback, particularly in highly formal writing. They argued that writers at the time attached social prestige to genitive forms.

As another example, D'Arcy and Tagliamonte (2010) discussed the social factors underlying the use of English *wh*-relatives in relation to *that* and zero (as in *a friend who/that/Ø you can trust*). Of the three variables, the *wh*-relatives are the relative newcomer, having over several centuries spread from formal writing into careful speech. The development took place with the persistent backing of prescriptive grammarians, and it appears that even to this day, the choice between relative markers is socially indexical. Focusing on the present-day use of the variables in the city of Toronto, D'Arcy and Tagliamonte found (among other things) that the restrictive subject-relative pronoun *who* is comparatively favored by middle-aged and more educated women and professionals. In other words, it has the typical social patterning of a prestige form. Indeed, they found that speakers adapt their usage in light of this, with speakers making "subtle alternations in variant use in response to the social makeup of the discourse situation" (D'Arcy & Tagliamonte, 2010, p. 400). Specifically, the educated women in the study favor *who* even more strongly when speaking to other educated women. This presents straightforward evidence that through their association with specific contexts of use in the minds of language users, expressions pick up social meaning.

4.2.2 Pragmatic Strengthening

A different type of change involving entrenchment of pragmatic relations is illustrated in Example 4.1. In the example, the Mandarin adverbial *mǎ shàng* (马上), meaning 'immediately,' is used. But in fact the expression is a combination of the noun *mǎ*, 'horse,' and *shàng*, 'on,' literally meaning 'by horse.'

Example 4.1 *dào   jiā   zhī hòu wǒ mǎ shàng   gěi nǐ   dǎ diàn huà*
            arrive home after   I   immediately to you   make a phone call
            "After I come home, I'll give you a call immediately."

The connection between the two senses of *mǎ shàng* is straightforward enough. There was a time when a horse would bring someone to his or her destination with the least possible delay. Even so, for the meaning of *mǎ shàng* to change from "by horse" to "immediately" takes more than language users' inference that someone coming by horse is probably coming soon. The inference must also be remembered, and the memory trace must be so strong that the expression's inferred meaning can supersede the original meaning. The former process involves entrenchment of a pragmatic association; the latter involves partial sanction. That is, at some point a language user who wants to verbalize the meaning 'immediately' must opt for an expression meaning 'by horse,' despite its inaptness if no actual horse is being talked about.

The process through which pragmatic inferences become semanticized was labeled *pragmatic strengthening* by Traugott and König (1991). Although there is still discussion about the types of pragmatic inference most typically involved (Mosegaard Hansen & Waltereit, 2006), there is no questioning the pervasiveness of the general process in all domains of grammar (Hopper & Traugott, 2003; Schwenter & Traugott, 1995; Traugott & Dasher, 2002). For instance, pragmatic strengthening is also seen at work in the English conjunction *while* (Traugott & König, 1991, pp. 199–201). In Example 4.2, *while* marks simultaneity between two situations:

Example 4.2 *Đet lastede þa .xix. wintre wile Stephne was king.* (1154, *Oxford English Dictionary* [OED])
            "That lasted then nineteen winters during the time when Stephen was king."

In Example 4.3, its meaning is the same, but its use comes with a side effect. A language user need not mark two situations as simultaneous, even if they are. So if she or he chooses to do so, it is because the simultaneity is somehow worth drawing attention to. Often, that is when the expectations raised by one situation conflict with the simultaneous occurrence of the other situation. In Example 4.3, for instance, it is remarkable for people to escape if they are being hunted at the same time.

Example 4.3 *While men hunted after hem þai han a-wai schaped.* (c. 1350, *OED*)
            "While men were hunting after them, they escaped."

Once *while* becomes associated with contrastive contexts, it is a small step for *while* to actually come to express concessive or adversative meaning. This is illustrated in Example 4.4, where adversative meaning has superseded the original temporal meaning.

> Example 4.4 *While Adorno confines this category to "serious" music, Paddison points out that there seems no reason why it could not include a good deal of avant-garde jazz.* (1993, British National Corpus [BNC])

The occurrence of pragmatic strengthening demonstrates the permeability of the pragmatics–semantics distinction. Language users store information about the contexts in which expressions are used. If an expression is repeatedly linked to the same contextually inferred meaning, the inferred meaning can become coded meaning, shortcutting the inferential process.

4.3 Symbolic Association

In pragmatic strengthening, new symbolic relations derive from originally pragmatic relations. But entrenchment has also been argued to work its effects on symbolic relations directly. Specifically, entrenchment has been linked to semantic generalization. In theory, the connection is very reasonable. Easy availability of a strongly entrenched symbolic relation facilitates its overapplication through partial sanction. The result must be semantic change. However, the actual historical data do not easily comply with the theory. One problem is methodological. The connection between entrenchment and semantic change is difficult to demonstrate in real changes. This is because the absolute frequency increases through which growing entrenchment is to be diagnosed may just as well be the result of semantic change as its cause. In addition, there are some theoretical worries, relating to the scope and nature of the phenomenon, as well as to the precise diachronic mechanism involved. It is on these theoretical issues that the following discussion primarily focuses.

4.3.1 Bleaching

Semantic generalization, often referred to as *bleaching*, is a process through which an expression gradually expands its potential extension (i.e., the range of things to which it may apply), thereby giving up its semantic specificity (Lehmann, 1985). Bybee (2003) explicitly linked bleaching to frequency, arguing that "the mechanism behind bleaching is habituation: a stimulus loses its impact if it occurs very frequently" (p. 605). She illustrated this with the semantic change in English *can* from 'mental ability' via generalized 'ability' to 'root possibility,' where each step corresponds to the loss of a specific semantic feature. There are several problems with this example, however. For a start, different senses of *can* co-occur synchronically. Although the changes Bybee described took place in the early modern period, Coates (1983, pp. 85–102), describing present-day English, still distinguished the 'ability' sense (Example 4.5a) from 'root possibility' (Example 4.5b). If *can* simply lost semantic specifications, the verb's older more specific sense would have to have been subsumed under the newer generalized sense. The verb would not be felt by speakers to be polysemous.

> Example 4.5 a. *"I can walk far, mister Brook. I can walk all the way to the mine."*
> (Coates, 1983, p. 89)
> b. *We believe that solutions can be found which will prove satisfactory.*
> (Coates, 1983, p. 96)

Moreover, loss of semantic specifications is inconsistent with the appearance of the arguably more specific "permission" sense in *can*, as illustrated in Example 4.6.

> Example 4.6 *You can start the revels now.* (Coates, 1983, p. 88)

Finally, there is a viable alternative explanation for the semantic changes in *can*. The changes could easily have arisen through pragmatic strengthening (see Section 4.2).

As it turns out, it is difficult to find truly convincing examples of bleaching through frequency. An example that is often cited comes from Haspelmath's (1989) study on infinitive markers. These tend to follow a cross-linguistically recurrent pathway of change, starting out as markers of infinitival purpose adjuncts to end up as more or less meaningless complementizers. The change can be illustrated by the Dutch infinitive marker *om*. Deriving from a preposition meaning 'for the sake of,' it was optionally used in Middle Dutch to introduce infinitival purpose clauses, as in Example 4.7a. Present-day Dutch, however, allows uses without the original purpose meaning, as shown by Example 4.7b.

> Example 4.7
> a. [Die duvel]   quam   vor   hare   in   mans   gedane,   omme   quaetheit
>   the devil   came   before   her   in   man's   guise   in order   evil
>   haer   te   lecghene ane   (1393–1402, *Middelnederlands Woordenboek*)
>   her   to   put   to
>   "The devil came before her in human guise, in order to propose to her evil doings."
> b. *In   het   begin   vinden   die   uitwijkende   gasten   het   vervelend   om*
>   in   the   beginning   find   these   redirected   guests   it   annoying   OM
>   *hier   in   het bos   te   worden   ondergebracht.*
>   here   in   the woods   to   be   accommodated.
>   (2002, *Twente Nieuwscorpus* [TNC])
>   "At first, these redirected guests find it annoying (*in order) to be accommodated here in the woods."

This example is not fully convincing either, however. Dutch *om* infinitives actually retain their purpose meaning in the context in which they were originally used, that is, as adjuncts, as shown in Example 4.8.

Example 4.8 Wat   moet   er   gebeuren   om   herhalingen   te   voorkomen?
            what   must   PT   happen   in order   repetitions   to   prevent
            (2004, TNC)
            "What has to be done (in order) to prevent any repetition?"

Again, an alternative explanation is conceivable. The purpose meaning in instances such as Example 4.5a was in fact coded redundantly. To a speaker of Middle Dutch, the syntactic status of the infinitive clause as an adjunct would have been clear without *om* because all argument positions in the main clause are filled. Furthermore, from the syntactic analysis, the purpose meaning would have followed because expressing purpose is what Middle Dutch infinitival adjuncts did. Conceivably, it was because of semantic redundancy that *om* could be reinterpreted as a semantically empty element.[2] It is not obvious, then, that the bleaching of *om* resulted from habituation through frequent use.

Haspelmath (1999) himself offered a somewhat different take on the relation between frequency and bleaching. He understood bleaching not as semantic generalization but (at least at first) as a loss of pragmatic salience (p. 1055). Haspelmath argued that novel expressions are initially coined or adopted by speakers because they are extravagant, thereby contributing to speakers' social success, but as they then gain in frequency, they start losing their extravagance through habituation. The idea that speakers' desire to be noticed generally drives grammaticalization is contested (Traugott & Trousdale, 2013, 125). De Smet (2012) even argued that many grammatical changes happen because they are unnoticeable and inconspicuous (see Section 4.4.3). Even so, Haspelmath's inflationary cycle is perhaps likely to occur with respect to linguistic strategies that speakers often rely on to score rhetorical effect.

Intensifiers, for example, are known to have a rapid rate of turnover (Lorenz, 2002). Witness the wavelike pattern in Figure 4.1, which shows the token frequencies (normalized and then standardized to *z* scores) of *awfully*, *terribly*, and *totally* in the past 200 years of American English (based on the *Corpus of Historical American English* [*COHA*], Davies, 2010). The consecutive waves are consistent with the idea that speakers recruit relatively infrequent adverbs as intensifiers to boost expressiveness, and then abandon them again when they become too frequent. The most striking curve in Figure 4.1 is that of *totally*, which has gone through the cycle of recruitment

---

[2] Some will wonder why *om* was used in the first place. I would suggest because it facilitated parsing by flagging the beginning of an infinitive clause. This is particularly useful in a language like Dutch in which the infinitival verb comes in clause-final position. On that view, *om* was not recruited to mark purpose meaning (being compatible with purpose meaning sufficed) but to signal syntactic relations early on in sentence structure.

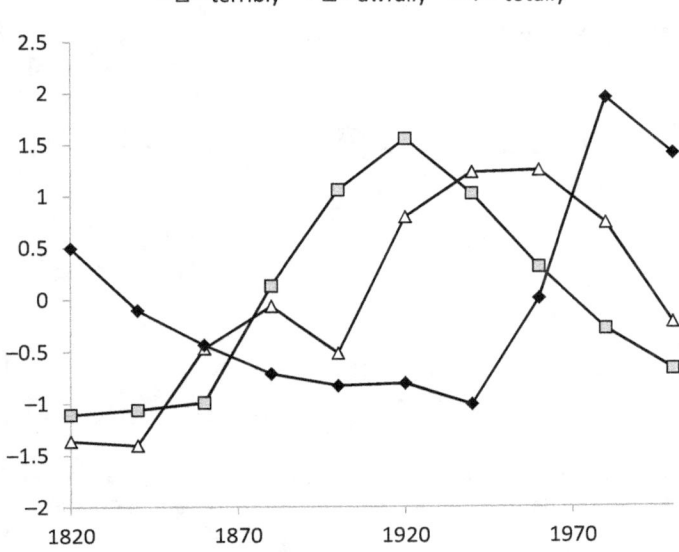

Fig. 4.1: Normalized and standardized frequencies of *awfully*, *terribly*, and *totally* in 19th- and 20th-century American English (based on the *Corpus of Historical American English*).

and abandonment twice, with not only a frequency peak in the late 20th century but also a decline in the 19th century following an earlier peak. That the cycle can be repeated in a single adverb suggests that the effect of frequency is indeed primarily on an item's pragmatics, not its semantics. If popularity in the 18th century had caused semantic bleaching, *totally* would have lost the expressiveness that motivated its recruitment as a "new" intensifier in the 20th century. From this, loss of pragmatic salience through entrenchment appears a real possibility, but its link to semantic generalization may be uncertain.

4.3.2 Proneness to Polysemy

The preceding discussion does not really satisfy the question whether symbolic relations can change under their own entrenchment. Perhaps an affirmative answer is to be sought not in semantic generalization but in the emergence of polysemy. There is robust synchronic evidence showing that frequent words tend to be more polysemous (Zipf, 1949). So from a diachronic point of view, one would want to know whether frequency causes polysemy or vice versa. In many cases, this just leads to a diachronic chicken-or-egg problem, but some lexical items are of special interest, because changes in their frequency are clearly due to external events. Consider the word *tsunami*. Figure 4.2 shows the normalized frequency of *tsunami* in the news section of *COHA* between the 1990s and 2000s. Predictably, frequency increased following the 2004 Indian Ocean

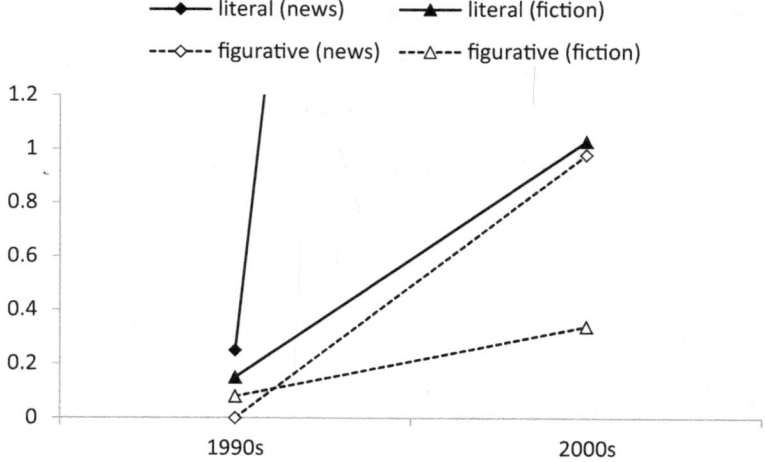

Fig. 4.2: Normalized frequencies (per million words) of literal and figurative uses of *tsunami* in news and fiction texts from the 1990s and 2000s (based on the *Corpus of Historical American English*).

tsunami—in fact, it rockets off the chart. As Figure 4.2 further shows, the frequency of *tsunami* also increased in contemporary fiction data, indicating that the word and concept became more available to speakers even in contexts unrelated to the Indian Ocean tsunami. Most interestingly, the increase affected not only literal but also figurative uses of *tsunami*, both in the newspaper data and in the fiction data. Some examples of figurative uses are given in Example 4.9. This indicates that increasing entrenchment made the word more available for metaphorical extension. It is conceivable, then, that stronger entrenchment correlates with greater proneness to semantic change.

Example 4.9 a. *talk of a romance between John Donlan . . . and the gorgeous Maria Angelica Connors . . . reported a couple of weeks ago have [sic] caused a <u>tsunami.</u>* (2008, *COHA*)
b. *The team in the Terry unit acted quickly, bringing out a stretcher and hoisting the two-hundred-and-seventy-pound former teamster onto it, then wheeling him to an area that could be screened off from other patients. But they were paddling against a medical <u>tsunami.</u>* (2009, *COHA*)

4.4 Syntagmatic Association

The process through which syntagmatic relations are entrenched is often referred to as *chunking* (see Gobet, Chapter 11, this volume). That chunking happens has been established beyond reasonable doubt, on the basis of historical evidence, among other things. Even so, there are again aspects of the process that are elusive. This section addresses the historical evidence in support of chunking and then delves into some of the areas that still deserve further exploration.

4.4.1 Constructional Split

Important historical evidence of chunking comes from semantic changes that affect whole syntagmatic sequences rather than their component parts. For instance, as Example 4.10a shows, *in spite of* originally meant 'in defiance of,' which was consistent with the meaning of *spite*, 'contempt.' Later, however, *in spite of* developed the meaning 'notwithstanding,' as in Example 4.10b, a change that was not paralleled by any change to *spite* (or to *in* or *of*, for that matter; Hoffmann, 2005). That the change exclusively affected *in spite of* and not its individual component parts must mean that speakers had already stored *in spite of* independently of the elements of which the phrase is made up.

> Example 4.10 a. *But for noy of my nobilte & my nome gret, I shuld . . . spede the to spille <u>in spite of</u> þi kynge.* (c. 1400, OED)
> "Were it not for the harm to my nobility and great name, I would encourage you to kill in defiance of your king."
> b. <u>*In spite of*</u> *his vows to stay out of trouble he always managed to find it.* (1989, BNC)

Essentially the same phenomenon is seen in words whose meaning changes in a specific syntactic constellation. For instance, Ghesquière (2014, pp. 160–176) showed that English *whole* originally meant 'intact, undivided,' as in Example 4.11a and 4.11b, but developed (among other things) into a secondary determiner establishing reference to an entity in its entirety, as in Example 4.11c. As the examples show, the original meaning of *whole* is found in attributive and predicative contexts, but the new meaning is exclusive to attributive contexts. So language users must have stored attributive *whole* independently of its more general lexical entry.

> Example 4.11 a. *Ensure that the seeds you buy are <u>whole</u> and not split or lightly crushed.* (Ghesquière, 2014, p. 161)
> b. *100g <u>whole</u> blanched almonds* (Ghesquière, 2014, p. 161)
> c. *there were at first not enough tablets available for the <u>whole</u> school.* (Ghesquière, 2014, p. 163)

Similar changes happen in morphology. One type of change is known as *derivational split* (Bybee, 1985). When derivational split occurs, the meaning of a derivational form is no longer fully predictable from the meanings of its base and the derivational pattern. For instance, *sheepish* ought to mean 'having the qualities of a sheep,' but it is now only used meaning 'embarrassed, excessively diffident.' One might question whether this still represents a sheeplike quality. It certainly underrepresents the broad range of potential sheeplike qualities (e.g., group loyalty, woolliness, having a gentle disposition). It follows that a speaker must have a separate lexical entry for *sheepish*. To use or interpret *sheepish*, a speaker cannot rely only on the meanings of *sheep* and *-ish* suffixation alone.[3]

4.4.2 Conservatism

Chunking is further evidenced by the survival of obsolete elements in specific syntagmatic combinations. Etymological dictionaries abound with examples. Old English *ræden*, 'condition,' for instance, has disappeared as a noun, but survives as *-red* in present-day English *hatred* and *kindred*. Similarly, the Middle Dutch case system has largely collapsed, but many of its forms survive into present-day Dutch in fixed expressions, such as *te mijner verdediging*, 'to my defence,' which preserves dative inflection on the possessive pronoun, or biblical *de leliën des velds*, 'the lilies of the field,' which retains genitive inflection on the possessor noun and its determiner. The only way such relic forms could have survived is through chunking.

The ability of chunks to conserve older material can be held responsible for the apparently erratic character of analogical leveling. Analogical leveling makes for a better form–meaning fit in the grammar of a language by wielding out irregularities, but its application is typically inconsistent, which seems to defeat the whole point of leveling (Harris & Campbell, 1995; Lass, 1998). For example, the irregular English past tense form *lept* has been analogically leveled to *leaped*, in line with the regular past tense formation pattern by *-ed* suffixation, yet the form *kept* (rather than **keeped*) defiantly continues to exist. Hooper (1976) accounted for this by arguing that frequent forms are more resistant to leveling. Because they are more strongly entrenched, frequent forms have a selectional advantage that allows them to persistently outcompete assembly of the regular alternative. Synchronically, this results in a concentration of irregularity in the most frequent forms of a language. In present-day English, for instance, the top 10 most frequent verbs are all irregular (*be, have, do, say, go, get, know, make, think, take*), even though irregular verbs constitute a minority overall.

What holds for morphology extends to syntax. Well-entrenched sequences can preserve old structures, against the tide of regularization. The following example comes from Harris and Campbell (1995, pp. 104–106). In Finnish, nonfinite complements of nonmotion verbs are usually formed on the basis of the so-called first infinitive, as in *yrittää tehdä*, 'try to do.' There is a class of exceptions, however, consisting

---

3 Bybee (1985) also described inflectional split, as in French *maintenant*, 'now,' which used to be the present participle of *maintenir*, 'hold on to.'

of verbs that combine with the "third infinitive," for instance, *pyrkiä tekemään*, "strive to do" (instead of **pyrkiä tehdä*).[4] Normally, third infinitives combine with verbs of motion to denote a goal, as in *mennä tekemään*, "go to do." As it turns out, the exceptional nonmotion verbs with third-infinitive complements can all be traced back historically to motion verbs; *pyrkiä*, "strive," for instance, originally meant "hurry to do." What must have happened, then, is that a number of motion verbs, including *pyrkiä*, in combination with the third infinitive underwent semantic change and lost their motion sense. The constructions that resulted were anomalous from the perspective of synchronic grammar but withstood regularization, at least in a number of dialects and with a number of verbs. Both the semantic developments and the subsequent resistance to regularization can be explained as the result of chunking.

4.4.3 Supporting Constructions

Existing chunks may also act as supporting constructions to other ongoing changes (De Smet & Fischer, in press). Innovations are more likely to succeed or proceed more quickly if they resemble an established form, even if the similarity is only superficial. For example, *as good as* first appeared as a degree modifier 'almost, virtually' with predicative adjectives and participles, as in Example 4.12a. Later its use extended to modifying verb phrases. Some of the first verb-modifying uses were with verbs in affirmative *do*-support constructions, as in Example 4.12b. Only later did *as good as* spread to other verb forms, as in Example 4.12c.

Example 4.12 a. *and hys son fell downe be fore hym as good as dede.* (1448, De Smet & Fischer, in press)
"and his son fell down before him as good as dead."
b. *And Bellarmine does as good as confesse this one . . .* (1617, De Smet & Fischer, in press)
c. *for he as good as confesseth that we are bound to . . .* (1641, De Smet & Fischer, in press)

Why did *as good as* first extend to *do*-support contexts? Presumably, in those contexts its use was supported by already well-entrenched syntagmatic associations. For instance, *do* and *good* frequently co-occurred, as in Example 4.13a, as did the concessive adverb *as good* and infinitival verbs, as in Example 4.13b.

---

4 The Finnish first infinitive is formed by the addition of the suffix *-ta /-tä* to the stem of the verb; the third infinitive by the addition of the participle suffix *-ma /-mä* in combination with the illative case ending *Vn*. In the case of *tehdä* and *tekemään*, the first- and third-infinitive forms have undergone some further changes to the stem *tek-* that are conditioned by the suffixes added.

Example 4.13 a. *one moment in hell will bee worse then all the pleasure in the world <u>did good.</u>* (1630, De Smet & Fischer, in press)
b. *we had <u>as good loose</u> somewhat, as <u>vndoe</u> our selues by law, and then loose that too.* (1615, De Smet & Fischer, in press)

In other words, entrenched syntagmatic associations gave *as good as* a selectional advantage in some syntactic contexts, explaining why it appeared there more readily than elsewhere. Because the similarities between an innovation and its supporting constructions are typically superficial, the relation is one of partial sanction.

The opposite effect also occurs. Overt deviation from a well-entrenched syntagmatic pattern may slow down change (De Smet, 2012; De Smet & Van de Velde, 2013). English determiners, for instance, raise strong expectations about the following element, which will likely be a noun, or else an adjective or (exceptionally) an adjective-modifying adverb. Elements that do not readily answer to these expectations rarely find their way into positions immediately following the determiner. *As good as* is a case in point. Although it functions as an adverb in some contexts, it certainly does not look like one. Consequently, even though it can modify predicative adjectives (see Example 4.12a), it never extended its range of use to combine with attributive adjectives (De Smet & Fischer, in press). The sequence of a determiner and what looks like a preposition (*as*) is too conspicuously deviant to sneak into the grammar. The resistance to conspicuous innovation, too, presupposes knowledge of likely syntagmatic sequences.

4.4.4 Phonetic Reduction and Loss of Compositionality

All of the foregoing simply presupposes that syntagmatic sequences are remembered and accessible as units. With high levels of entrenchment, however, the effects of chunking can go further. Chunks tend to undergo formal reduction, and lose their underlying compositionality (Bybee, 2006, 2010). Even though these effects apply to the phonetic and syntactic levels of syntagmatic structure, respectively, they often go hand-in-hand and reinforce one another. On top of that, they interact with the kind of semantic changes discussed in Section 4.4.1.

Consider the recent development of an indefinite article *yí* from *yí gè* (一个) in Beijing Mandarin, as described in detail by Tao (2006). In Mandarin, the numeral *yì* 'one' with falling tone is subject to a lexically specific tone sandhi rule: It adopts a rising tone (*yí*) when preceding another syllable with falling tone. Because the rule is applied regularly, *yì* and *yí* are in complementary distribution, and recognizable as phonologically conditioned realizations of the same numeral 'one.' In the combination *yí gè* the tone sandhi rule applies before the classifier *gè*, which is used like other classifiers to link a numeral to a noun, as in Example 4.14a. However, Tao (p. 103) showed that as *yí gè* develops into an indefinite article, the sequence undergoes phonetic reduction. Its final vowel becomes a schwa and receives neutral tone, next the intervocalic consonant is deleted, and finally the remaining vowel sequence is simplified. The result is an indefinite article *yí*, used with rising tone regardless of the tone on the following syllable, as in Example 4.14b. Being the only trace of the eroded classifier *gè*, the invariable rising tone in *yí* 'a' now formally signals the difference with the numeral *yì/yí* 'one.'

Example 4.14 a. *yí   ge   rén   yì   wǎn   shuǐ*
(adapted from Tao, 2006, p. 113)
one   CL   person   one   CL   water
"each person (gets) one bowl of water"
b. *chī   yí   táor   ba*   (adapted from Tao, 2006, p. 114)
eat   a   peach   INT
"have a peach"

The emergence of invariable *yí* "a" illustrates the interaction between reduction and loss of compositionality. On the one hand, the frequent combination *yí gè* is automated and stored as a chunk. This makes the combination vulnerable to semantic change, further obscuring its original syntax. On the other hand, it is formal reduction that consolidates the loss of compositionality by making the component parts truly unrecognizable.

Phonetic reduction can perhaps be seen as another form of partial sanction, this time between a phonological target and its phonetic realization. However, the more specific mechanisms underlying phonetic reduction are complex and not yet fully understood (Ernestus, 2014; Gahl, Yao, & Johnson, 2012). In actual speech, reduction positively correlates with speech rate. At the same time, it can be assumed that high speech rate is easier to maintain in frequent sequences because their predictability makes them easier for speakers to plan. Together, this can explain why frequent sequences are more prone to reduction (Ernestus, 2014, p. 31; Pluymaekers, Ernestus, & Baayen, 2005). Down at the level of specific articulatory gestures, Bybee (2006) linked reduction to fluency through practice. She proposed that practice improves speakers' ability to anticipate upcoming articulations in frequent sequences, which causes articulatory overlap. Finally, in diachrony, reduction may proceed in steps, with one reduced form serving as input to the next, and with extensive synchronic variation as a result. Mandarin *yí gè*, discussed earlier, is a case in point. This suggests that some reduction processes depend on language users storing variant realizations, as is maintained by exemplar-based models (Bybee, 2001, pp. 40–43). However, each of the preceding mechanisms is open to debate. First, high speech rate does not always bring reduction (Van Son & Pols, 1990). Second, practice through repetition may also lead to more accurate articulations (Baayen, Tomaschek, Gahl, & Ramscar, in press). Third, the synchronic evidence for storage of variant realizations is relatively weak (Ernestus, 2014).

Loss of compositionality raises new questions, too. Syntactic structure is generally thought of as discrete. Something is either a head or a dependent, either one constituent or two constituents, and so on. This makes one wonder whether loss of compositionality proceeds abruptly or gradually. The alleged discreteness of syntactic structure suggests the former. But the gradient nature of entrenchment suggests the latter. There is good synchronic evidence to support the idea that compositionality is gradient, particularly in morphology (Hay & Baayen, 2005), but a historical linguist would of course like to catch the process in action. To do so, one possible avenue of research is into syntactic priming effects between chunks and the syntactic structure they (used to) instantiate. Torres Cacoullos (2015) investigated the variation between the progressive and the simple forms in Spanish, illustrated in Example 4.15a and 4.15b, respectively.

> Example 4.15 a. *¿Sabes   tú   on   quién   estás   habla-ndo?*
> know.PRS.2SG you with REL   be.PRS.2SG speak-GER
> (19th century, adapted from Torres Cacoullos, 2015)
> "Do you know who you are talking to?"
> b. *Olvidas   que hablas   con un republicano?*
> forget.PRS.2SG COMP speak.PRS.2SG with a   republican
> (19th c., adapted from Torres Cacoullos, 2015)
> "Do you forget that you are speaking (lit. you speak) to a republican?"

Torres Cacoullos argued that the progressive form was in origin a combination of the locative verb *estar* (from Latin *stare* 'stand') and a gerund. As the pattern grammaticalized, it came to mark progressive aspect and, at the same time, increased in frequency. The frequency increase appears to have had striking consequences. In her early data, Torres Cacoullos found that the choice between the progressive and simple forms is sensitive to a strong priming effect, the progressive form being favored when another use of *estar* precedes in the discourse, as in Example 4.16. In her later data, the effect gradually weakens. This suggests that the progressive form ceased to be associated with the other uses of *estar*.

> Example 4.16 *no   sabemos   quién   está   dentro; habla-ndo   están.*
> NEG   know.PRS.1PL   who   be.PRS.3SG inside speak-GER   be.PRS.3PL
> (15th century, adapted from Torres Cacoullos, 2015)
> "We don't know who is inside; they are talking."

Torres Cacoullos interpreted this as evidence of a gradual change to underlying syntactic compositionality, as a result of chunking.

4.5 Paradigmatic Association

Of the four form-based relations discussed in this chapter, paradigmatic relations are the odd one out because they are the least tangible. To the analyst, it is easy enough to conceive of paradigmatic relations. The question is whether they get entrenched as units in language users' minds (for a critical answer, see Croft, 2001). If they do, it is as probabilistic second- or even third-order generalizations. Take word classes as an example. If language users can group words into a word class, they must do so on the basis of similar meanings and similar[5] distributions over syntagmatic contexts. This means that the word class only emerges by virtue of prior knowledge of the symbolic and syntagmatic relations maintained by its members. The word class is entrenched as a unit to the extent that it is emancipated from that prior knowledge. What traditional grammar calls a word class, then, is a distributional regularity that exists sui generis. The behavior of its members is predictable directly from their class membership, requiring no assessment of their similarities to other members.

That paradigmatic relations can get entrenched as units may seem plausible, but it is difficult to prove. It is therefore somewhat troubling that within the usage-based literature the issue has so far received little attention (for discussion, see Cappelle, 2006). From a diachronic point of view, the changes of interest are especially those that see an item extend its range of use to new syntagmatic contexts. To stick with word classes, consider the kind of change described by Denison (2001) and Van Goethem and De Smet (2014). In noun–noun sequences, the qualifying noun can be reinterpreted as an adjective. For instance, French *géant*, 'giant,' can still be read as a noun in a noun–noun compound in Example 4.17a, but it behaves as an attributive adjective in Example 4.17b and as a predicative adjective in Example 4.17c.

Example 4.17   a. *un calmar géant de 9 mètres et de 180 kilogrammes*
   "a giant squid 9 metres long and 180 kilograms"
   b. *une ville géante et contrastée*
   "a gigantic and diverse city"
   c. *le lit était géant et super confortable*
   "the bed was huge and super comfortable"

Invariably, there is more than one way to account for such a change. Is *géant* first reclassified as an adjective, and does its new behavior follow from its new class membership? Or is it simply attracted to new constructions because they are open to other words that denote a similar meaning and have an overlapping distribution?

---

5 Croft (2001) convincingly showed that word class membership on the basis of *identical* distributions is impossible to maintain because it either requires arbitrary selection of "relevant" distributional contexts or else leads to an uncontrollable proliferation of word classes.

Tab. 4.1: Paradigmatic Analogy in the Inflection of (Dialectal) Dutch *kloppen* ('knock')

	Stage I	Stage II	Stage III	Stage IV
Singular	*klopp-e*	*klopp-e*	*klopp-e/-en*	*klopp-en*
Plural	*klopp-en*	*klopp-e/-en*	*klopp-e/-en*	*klopp-en*

The former account involves automatic reliance on the distributional predictions of an entrenched paradigm; the latter requires active comparison over semantically and distributionally similar elements. As for *géant*, I believe the issue is impossible to resolve. However, in what follows, I turn to some cases showing that paradigms do affect language change. All examples involve formal alternations that appear to have become automated and so must have unit status.[6]

4.5.1 Paradigmatic Analogy

Sometimes language users identify an alternation between two forms in some contexts, and then extend the alternation into contexts that previously only allowed one of the forms. De Smet (2013) labeled this process *paradigmatic analogy*. A particularly elegant example is found in Aalberse (2007, pp. 140–141). Aalberse argued that in the verbal paradigms of some Dutch dialects the *-en* endings of the plural could extend to the first person singular. Initially, these dialects would distinguish between singular and plural endings, just like other varieties of Dutch (Stage I in Table 4.1). Presumably, however, the dialects had a tendency for *-n* deletion, leading to variation between *-en* and *-e* in the plural (Stage II). The variation then spread to the first person singular, where *-e* is the original form (Stage III). If, eventually, the *-en* ending won out, the singular too became exclusively *-en* marked (Stage IV). The logic underlying the crucial extensional step—Stage III in Table 4.1—is that "if the two forms *-e* and *-en* are alternates in the plural, it is possible that the language users assume that *-e* and *-en* are alternates in the full paradigm" (Aalberse, 2007, p. 141). In other words, once an alternation pattern is entrenched, the presence of one alternate (*-e*) in a context sanctions the other (*-en*) in the same context.

Paradigmatic analogy can take the appearance of a constraint on change. For example, De Smet (2013) described how subject-controlled gerund complements as in Example 4.18 over time spread to an ever-growing number of matrix verbs, including *love* (13th century); *hate* (14th century); *forbear, escape* (15th century); *fear, avoid* (16th century); *miss, omit, prefer, propose* (17th century); *remember,*

---

[6] For reasons of space, the overview is incomplete. Other types of change that depend on automated second-order generalizations might include calquing (Heine & Kuteva, 2006), the grammaticalization of zero (Bybee, 1994), or the stacking of inflectional endings to create new morphological tenses or cases (Kiparsky, 2011, p. 17).

mind, regret, enjoy, risk (18th century); *suggest, try* (19th century); *admit, consider, resent* (20th century); and so on.

> Example 4.18 a. *The cat loves being stroked, absolutely loves it!* (BNC)
> b. *Downey admitted shouting but said it was on the spur of the moment* (BNC)

What is striking in this is that despite the obvious success of gerund complements, they almost[7] never extended beyond the distribution of noun phrases. Accordingly, all of the preceding verbs are transitive verbs. There is no general restriction against intransitive verbs taking complement clauses (e.g., intransitive *long* takes *to*-infinitival complements as in *She longed to know what he was thinking*; intransitive *laugh* takes *that*-complements, as in *He laughed that now he knew why they wore rubber boots*; etc.). Therefore, the specific ban on gerund complements with intransitive verbs indicates that the distribution of gerunds is determined by a strongly entrenched paradigmatic tie to noun phrases. Knowing that gerunds historically developed from deverbal nouns (Fanego, 2004), the tie is not completely surprising. Yet it is striking that paradigmatic association between gerunds and noun phrases could constrain change to gerunds over several centuries.

4.5.2 Suppletion

In *suppletion*, inflectional forms of historically unrelated lexemes come to function as forms of a single lexeme. Although such a change is decidedly curious, it is not that uncommon, particularly in high-frequency items (Corbett, 2007). In English, the lexeme GO comprises two historically distinct roots, one supplying the past form *went*, the other supplying the remaining forms *go, goes, going*, and *gone*. In Middle English, these roots still represented roughly synonymous but distinct verbs, each with a full inflectional paradigm. Similarly, the lexemes GOOD and BAD have suppletive comparatives and superlatives *better–best* and *worse–worst*. The lexemes ONE and TWO have suppletive ordinal forms *first* and *second*. The present-day lexeme BE is even made up of three historically distinct roots supplying the forms (a) *am, is, are*; (b) *was, were*; and (c) *be, being, been*; in Old English, yet another root *sind-* was in use for present plural forms. The first person pronoun *I* has the suppletive oblique and possessive forms *me/my*; and two more suppletive roots in the plural forms: *we* for nominative and *us/our* for oblique and possessive.

Suppletion testifies to the role of paradigmatic relations twice. First, suppletive pairs often fit recurrent alternations in the language (Hippisley, Chumakina, Corbett,

---

[7] De Smet (2010, 2014) showed that there exists a handful of exceptions, but in each case, they are due to other developments interfering with the extension of gerund complements.

& Brown, 2004; Petré, 2014).[8] For example, the two suppletive series *good–better–best* and *bad–worse–worst* mirror the morphological distinction positive–comparative–superlative that is marked by means of suffixation for other monosyllabic adjectives in English: *fine–finer–finest, old–older–oldest*, and so on. In other words, in suppletion, the relation between what were historically distinct words is reorganized in terms of regular alternations available in the grammar. If an existing alternation can serve as a template for change, it must have unit status.

Second, cases of suppletion with a recorded history show that the starting point for suppletion is typically competition (Corbett, 2007; Petré, 2014). Often one or both of the lexemes involved is defective from the start (e.g., *second* is a French loan deriving from a verb 'follow' and did not have a cardinal alternate to begin with). But where their distributions overlap, the competing lexemes eventually become fully interchangeable. It is this stage of interchangeability of forms that marks the emergence of an automated paradigmatic relation. The true suppletive relation only arises as a next step, as the competition is resolved in favor of different forms in different contexts (e.g., English *beon*, 'be,' survived in the infinitive and participles but was ousted elsewhere). The prior shift from lexical (near-)synonymy to lexical identity is crucial, however, turning an incidental alternation into a fully systematic and consistent one. This marks the point at which an alternation must have achieved unit status.

4.5.3 Hypercorrection

Hypercorrection resembles paradigmatic analogy but extends across language varieties. It typically happens when a speaker adopts a variety that is not his or her own—for example, a prestige dialect—and identifies a (near-)systematic correspondence between two variants, one associated with the speaker's vernacular and one associated with the other variety. Hypercorrection takes place when the alternation is overextended, with the more prestigious variant being used in contexts where it never occurs in the target variety. The phenomenon presupposes that speakers have learned an alternation and that they apply it more or less automatically, particularly where their knowledge of actual syntagmatic sequences fails. As such, it must involve a paradigmatic association with unit status.

For example, varieties of English spoken in the north of England have the /ʊ/ vowel in words where the more prestigious standard variety has either /ʊ/ (as in *foot, good*, or *could*) or /ʌ/ (as in *hut, love*, or *sun*). Consequently, northern speakers insert /ʌ/ pronunciations when shifting to the standard variety, but in doing so they may hypercorrect and pronounce words such as *could* as /kʌd/ instead of /kʊd/ (Chambers & Trudgill,

---

[8] Note, however, that there is a danger of circularity here because suppletive relations that do not fit regular alternations may not be recognized as cases of suppletion, either because of the definition of suppletion or because they are simply harder to spot. A possible example that does not fit regular alternation patterns is the relation between English *will* and *shall* (Arnovick, 1990).

1980). The mistakes prove that such speakers lack accurate knowledge of the actual phonological sequences containing /ʌ/ in the target variety. To complement failing knowledge, they rely on the stylistically polarized alternation between /ʊ/ and /ʌ/.

As an example of hypercorrection in grammar, consider the case described by Flikeid (1992). She studies the third-person plural forms in Acadian French communities. These are small rural communities in Nova Scotia, largely isolated from one another and from the rest of the French-speaking world. The vernacular Acadian third-person plural indicative forms end in -*ont* /ɔ̃/, for example, /partɔ̃/ '(they) leave,' contrasting with normative French third-person plural forms, which end in orthographic -*ent*, phonologically zero, for example, /part/ '(they) leave.' Given this situation, the normative forms can usually be derived from the vernacular forms by truncation. However, where either the vernacular or the normative form is irregular, speakers may create a hypercorrect third form by overapplying the truncation rule. For instance, the vernacular third-person indicative plural for *croire* /krwar/, 'believe,' is irregular /krwajɔ̃/, giving rise to hypercorrect /krwaj/, as opposed to normative French /krwa/. Similarly, the vernacular third-person plural indicative for *aller* /ale/, 'go,' is /alɔ̃/, leading to hypercorrect /al/, where in fact normative French has irregular /vɔ̃/.

Interestingly, whereas hypercorrect forms such as /krwaj/ or /al/ occur only sporadically most of the time, Flikeid (1992) found one community where some hypercorrect forms have become part of the community repertoire. The forms are highly frequent, much more so than in other communities, indicating that they are likely to have been socially transmitted, in addition to being analogically generated. This at once reveals the elusiveness of hypercorrections and paradigmatic generalizations in general. Although hypercorrection relies on automated paradigmatic relations, its output may always go on to lead a life of its own, as a stored chunk (see Section 4.4). In the same vein, apparent cases of hypercorrection may in fact be or have become functionally constrained (e.g., Bullock, Toribio, & Amengual, 2014; Labov & Harris, 1986, pp. 13–17).[9] At that point, their occurrence no longer depends on automatic substitution of a vernacular form for a more prestigious form.

4.6 Conclusion

Theorizing about language use tends to assume a tension among replication and creativity, storage, and assembly. From a synchronic point of view, entrenchment would appear to sit on the replication side of usage. Perhaps the main contribution of historical linguistics is in revealing the paradoxes inherent in this contrast. Judging from its role in change, entrenchment is involved in much that is new in usage. It crucially underlies not only what is replicated but also what is newly created. In various ways,

---

9 Lass (1998) would refer to these as *exaptations*.

it is involved in the emergence of new forms, new meanings, new structures, and new structural oppositions.

At the same time, the role of entrenchment effects in language change leads to new questions and challenges. The exact mechanisms at work in many of the changes linked to entrenchment are still unclear. Bleaching and phonetic reduction, for instance, are among the effects of entrenchment most commonly cited, but neither process is fully understood at present. On top of that, the changes linked to entrenchment lead back to some of the major problem areas in linguistic theory, such as the boundaries between meaning and context and the nature of abstract syntactic relations in and across constructions. The concept of entrenchment promises a model of language that looks coherent in its outline and that may come to have real explanatory power in its application, but it is certainly a model that remains incomplete.

References

Aalberse, S. P. (2007). The typology of syncretisms and the status of feature structure: Verbal paradigms across 355 Dutch dialects. *Morphology*, *17*, 109–149. http://dx.doi.org/10.1007/s11525-007-9111-0

Arnovick, L. K. (1990). *The development of future constructions in English: The pragmatics of modal and temporal* will *and* shall *in Middle English*. Bern, Switzerland: Peter Lang.

Baayen, H. R., Tomaschek, F., Gahl, S., & Ramscar, M. (in press). The Ecclesiastes principle in language change. In M. Hundt, S. Mollin, & S. Pfenninger (Eds.), *The changing English language: Psycholinguistic perspectives*. Cambridge, England: Cambridge University Press.

Bullock, B. E., Toribio, A. J., & Amengual, M. (2014). The status of *s* in Dominican Spanish. *Lingua*, *143*, 20–35. http://dx.doi.org/10.1016/j.lingua.2014.01.009

Bybee, J. L. (1985). *Morphology: A study of the relation between meaning and form*. http://dx.doi.org/10.1075/tsl.9

Bybee, J. L. (1994). The grammaticization of zero: Asymmetries in tense and aspect systems. In W. Pagliuca (Ed.), *Perspectives on grammaticalization* (pp. 235–254). http://dx.doi.org/10.1075/cilt.109.02byb

Bybee, J. L. (2001). *Phonology and language use*. http://dx.doi.org/10.1017/CBO9780511612886

Bybee, J. L. (2003). Mechanisms of change in grammaticalization: The role of frequency. In B. D. Joseph (Ed.), *The handbook of historical linguistics* (pp. 602–623). http://dx.doi.org/10.1002/9780470756393.ch19

Bybee, J. L. (2006). From usage to grammar: The mind's response to repetition. *Language*, *82*, 711–733. http://dx.doi.org/10.1353/lan.2006.0186

Bybee, J. L. (2010). *Language, usage and cognition*. http://dx.doi.org/10.1017/CBO9780511750526

Bybee, J. L., & Slobin, D. I. (1982). Rules and schemas in the development and use of the English past tense. *Language*, *58*, 265–289. http://dx.doi.org/10.1353/lan.1982.0021

Cappelle, B. (2006). Particle placement and the case for "allostructions." *Constructions* SV1-7/2006. Retrieved from http://www.constructions.uni-osnabrueck.de/wp-content/uploads/2014/06/2006-SI-Cappelle22-80-1-PB.pdf

Chambers, J. K., & Trudgill, P. (1980). *Dialectology*. Cambridge, England: Cambridge University Press.

Coates, J. (1983). *The semantics of the modal auxiliaries*. London, England: Croom Helm.
Corbett, G. G. (2007). Canonical typology, suppletion, and possible words. *Language, 83*, 8–42. http://dx.doi.org/10.1353/lan.2007.0006
Croft, W. (2001). *Radical construction grammar: Syntactic theory in typological perspective*. http://dx.doi.org/10.1093/acprof:oso/9780198299554.001.0001
Dąbrowska, E. (2012). Different speakers, different grammars: Individual differences in native language attainment. *Linguistic Approaches to Bilingualism, 2*, 219–253. http://dx.doi.org/10.1075/lab.2.3.01dab
Dąbrowska, E. (2015). Individual differences in grammatical knowledge. In E. Dąbrowska & D. Divjak (Eds.), *Handbook of cognitive linguistics* (pp. 650–668). http://dx.doi.org/10.1515/9783110292022-033
D'Arcy, A., & Tagliamonte, S. A. (2010). Prestige, accommodation and the legacy of relative *who*. *Language in Society, 39*, 383–410. http://dx.doi.org/10.1017/S0047404510000205
Davies, M. (2010). *The corpus of historical American English: 400 million words, 1810–2009*. Retrieved from http://corpus.byu.edu/coha/
Denison, D. (2001). Gradience and linguistic change. In L. J. Brinton (Ed.), *Historical linguistics 1999: Selected papers from the 14th International Conference on Historical Linguistics, Vancouver, 9–13 August 1999* (pp. 119–144). Amsterdam, the Netherlands: Benjamins.
De Smet, H. (2010). English *-ing*-clauses and their problems: The structure of grammatical categories. *Linguistics, 48*, 1153–1193. http://dx.doi.org/10.1515/ling.2010.038
De Smet, H. (2012). The course of actualization. *Language, 88*, 601–633. http://dx.doi.org/10.1353/lan.2012.0056
De Smet, H. (2013). *Spreading patterns: Diffusional change in the English system of complementation*. Oxford, England: Oxford University Press.
De Smet, H. (2014). Constrained confusion: The gerund/participle distinction in Late Modern English. In M. Hundt (Ed.), *Late Modern English syntax* (pp. 224–238). Cambridge, England: Cambridge University Press. http://dx.doi.org/10.1017/CBO9781139507226.017
De Smet, H. (2016). How gradual change progresses: The interaction between convention and innovation. *Language Variation and Change, 28*, 83–102.
De Smet, H., & Fischer, O. (in press). Analogy: Supporting constructions in language change. In M. Hundt, S. Mollin, & S. Pfenninger (Eds.), *The changing English language: Psycholinguistic perspectives*. Cambridge, England: Cambridge University Press.
De Smet, H., & Van de Velde, F. (2013). Serving two masters: Form–function friction in syntactic amalgams. *Studies in Language, 37*, 534–565. http://dx.doi.org/10.1075/sl.37.3.04des
Ernestus, M. (2014). Acoustic reduction and the roles of abstractions and exemplars in speech processing. *Lingua, 142*, 27–41. http://dx.doi.org/10.1016/j.lingua.2012.12.006
Fanego, T. (2004). On reanalysis and actualization in syntactic change: The rise and development of English verbal gerunds. *Diachronica, 21*, 5–55. http://dx.doi.org/10.1075/dia.21.1.03fan
Flikeid, K. (1992). The integration of hypercorrect forms into the repertoire of an Acadian French community: The process and its built-in limits. *Language & Communication, 12*, 237–265. http://dx.doi.org/10.1016/0271-5309(92)90016-3
Gahl, S., Yao, Y., & Johnson, K. (2012). Why reduce? Phonological neighborhood density and phonetic reduction in spontaneous speech. *Journal of Memory and Language, 66*, 789–806. http://dx.doi.org/10.1016/j.jml.2011.11.006
Ghesquière, L. (2014). *The directionality of (inter)subjectification in the English noun phrase: Pathways of change*. http://dx.doi.org/10.1515/9783110338751

Gries, S. T., & Stefanowitsch, A. (2004). Extending collostructional analysis: A corpus-based perspective on "alternations." *International Journal of Corpus Linguistics*, *9*, 97–129. http://dx.doi.org/10.1075/ijcl.9.1.06gri

Harris, A. C., & Campbell, L. (1995). *Historical syntax in cross-linguistic perspective*. http://dx.doi.org/10.1017/CBO9780511620553

Haspelmath, M. (1989). From purposive to infinitive: A universal path of grammaticalization. *Folia Linguistica Historica*, *10*, 287–310.

Haspelmath, M. (1999). Why is grammaticalization irreversible? *Linguistics*, *37*, 1043–1068. http://dx.doi.org/10.1515/ling.37.6.1043

Hay, J. (2003). *Causes and consequences of word structure*. London, England: Routledge.

Hay, J. B., & Baayen, R. H. (2005). Shifting paradigms: Gradient structure in morphology. *Trends in Cognitive Sciences*, *9*, 342–348. http://dx.doi.org/10.1016/j.tics.2005.04.002

Heine, B., & Kuteva, T. (2006). *The changing languages of Europe*. http://dx.doi.org/10.1093/acprof:oso/9780199297337.001.0001

Hippisley, A., Chumakina, M., Corbett, G. G., & Brown, D. (2004). Suppletion: Frequency, categories, and distribution of stems. *Studies in Language*, *28*, 387–418. http://dx.doi.org/10.1075/sl.28.2.05hip

Hoffmann, S. (2005). *Grammaticalization and English complex prepositions: A corpus-based study*. London, England: Routledge.

Hooper, J. (1976). Word frequency in lexical diffusion and the source of morphophonological change. In W. Christie (Ed.), *Current progress in historical linguistics* (pp. 96–105). Amsterdam, the Netherlands: North-Holland.

Hopper, P., & Traugott, E. C. (2003). *Grammaticalization*. http://dx.doi.org/10.1017/CBO9781139165525

Keller, R. (1994). *On language change: The invisible hand in language*. London, England: Taylor & Francis.

Kiparsky, P. (2011). Grammaticalization as optimization. In D. Jonas, J. Whitman, & A. Garrett (Eds.), *Grammatical change: Origins, nature, outcomes* (pp. 15–51). http://dx.doi.org/10.1093/acprof:oso/9780199582624.003.0002

Krug, M. (1998). String frequency: A cognitive motivating factor in coalescence, language processing and linguistic change. *Journal of English Linguistics*, *26*, 286–320. http://dx.doi.org/10.1177/007542429802600402

Krug, M. (2000). *Emerging English modals: A corpus-based study of grammaticalization*. http://dx.doi.org/10.1515/9783110820980

Labov, W. (1994). *Principles of linguistic change: Vol. 1. Internal factors*. Oxford, England: Blackwell.

Labov, W. (2001). *Principles of linguistic change: Vol. 2. Social factors*. Oxford, England: Blackwell.

Labov, W., & Harris, W. A. (1986). De facto segregation of black and white vernaculars. In D. Sankoff (Ed.), *Diversity and diachrony* (pp. 1–24). http://dx.doi.org/10.1075/cilt.53.04lab

Lakoff, G., & Johnson, M. (1980). *Metaphors we live by*. Chicago, IL: University of Chicago Press.

Langacker, R. W. (1987). *Foundations of cognitive grammar: Vol. 1. Theoretical prerequisites*. Stanford, CA: Stanford University Press.

Langacker, R. W. (1991). *Foundations of cognitive grammar: Vol. 2. Descriptive application*. Stanford, CA: Stanford University Press.

Lass, R. (1998). *Historical linguistics and language change*. Cambridge, England: Cambridge University Press.

Lehmann, C. (1985). Grammaticalization: Synchronic and diachronic change. *Lingua e Stile, 20,* 303–318.

Lorenz, G. (2002). Really worthwhile or not really significant? A corpus-based approach to delexicalization and grammaticalization of intensifiers in Modern English. In I. Wischer & G. Diewald (Eds.), *New reflections on grammaticalization* (pp. 143–161). http://dx.doi.org/10.1075/tsl.49.11lor

Mosegaard Hansen, M., & Waltereit, R. (2006). On the role of generalized conversational implicature in semantic change. *Chicago Linguistic Society, 42,* 33–46.

Petré, P. (2014). *Constructions and environments: Copular, passive, and related constructions in Old and Middle English.* http://dx.doi.org/10.1093/acprof:oso/9780199373390.001.0001

Pluymaekers, M., Ernestus, M., & Baayen, R. H. (2005). Lexical frequency and acoustic reduction in spoken Dutch. *The Journal of the Acoustical Society of America, 118,* 2561–2569. http://dx.doi.org/10.1121/1.2011150

Schelling, T. C. (1978). *Micromotives and macrobehavior.* New York, NY: Norton.

Schmid, H.-J. (2014). Lexico-grammatical patterns, pragmatic associations and discourse frequency. In T. Herbst, H.-J. Schmid, & S. Faulhaber (Eds.), *Constructions collocations patterns* (pp. 239–293). http://dx.doi.org/10.1515/9783110356854.239

Schwenter, S. A., & Traugott, E. C. (1995). The semantic and pragmatic development of substitutive complex prepositions in English. In A. Jucker (Ed.), *Historical pragmatics: Pragmatic developments in the history of English* (pp. 243–273). http://dx.doi.org/10.1075/pbns.35.16sch

Sinclair, J. M. (1991). *Corpus, concordance, collocation.* Oxford, England: Oxford University Press.

Tao, L. (2006). Classifier loss and frozen tone in spoken Beijing Mandarin: The yi+ge phono-syntactic conspiracy. *Linguistics, 44,* 91–133. http://dx.doi.org/10.1515/LING.2006.004

Torres Cacoullos, R. (2015). Gradual loss of analyzability: Diachronic priming effects. In A. Adli, M. García García, & G. Kaufman (Eds.), *Variation in language: System- and usage-based approaches* (pp. 265–288). http://dx.doi.org/10.1515/9783110346855-011

Traugott, E. C., & Dasher, R. (2002). *Regularity in semantic change.* Cambridge, England: Cambridge University Press.

Traugott, E. C., & König, E. (1991). The semantics-pragmatics of grammaticalization revisited. In E. C. Traugott & B. Heine (Eds.), *Approaches to grammaticalization* (Vol. 1, pp. 189–218). http://dx.doi.org/10.1075/tsl.19.1.10clo

Traugott, E. C., & Trousdale, G. (2013). *Constructionalization and constructional changes.* http://dx.doi.org/10.1093/acprof:oso/9780199679898.001.0001

Van Goethem, K., & De Smet, H. (2014). How nouns turn into adjectives: The emergence of new adjectives in French, English, and Dutch through debonding processes. *Languages in Contrast, 14,* 251–277. http://dx.doi.org/10.1075/lic.14.2.04goe

Van Son, R. J. J. H., & Pols, L. C. W. (1990). Formant frequencies of Dutch vowels in a text, read at normal and fast rate. *The Journal of the Acoustical Society of America, 88,* 1683–1693. http://dx.doi.org/10.1121/1.400243

Weerman, F., Olson, M., & Cloutier, R. (2013). Synchronic variation and loss of case: Formal and informal language in a Dutch corpus of 17th-century Amsterdam texts. *Diachronica, 30,* 353–381. http://dx.doi.org/10.1075/dia.30.3.03wee

Zipf, G. K. (1949). *Human behavior and the principle of least effort: An introduction to human ecology.* New York, NY: Hafner.

Anatol Stefanowitsch and Susanne Flach
5 The Corpus-Based Perspective on Entrenchment

5.1 Introduction

Entrenchment is a fundamentally cognitive notion, referring to the degree to which a linguistic structure of any degree of complexity or schematicity forms an established unit of the mental grammar of a speaker. It may therefore seem that linguistic corpora, which are essentially large samples of usage data, have no particular role to play in estimating degrees of entrenchment of linguistic structures. Instead, psycholinguistic methods may be perceived as more suitable because they appear to measure the phenomenon more directly.

However, this perception is mistaken for two reasons. First, entrenchment is a theoretical construct, a hypothesized aspect of mental representations. As such, we cannot directly measure degrees of entrenchment, or even verify the existence of entrenchment, by any currently available means. Regardless of whether we attempt to measure entrenchment experimentally or on the basis of corpora, we must rely on operational definitions that approximate the theoretical construct but are not identical with it. In Section 5.2.1, we sketch ways of conceptualizing the relationship between mental representations and usage data that allow the corpus-based operationalization of the former on the basis of the latter.

Second, entrenchment as a theoretical construct has always been defined with respect to what we might loosely refer to as frequency of occurrence. Thus, it seems not only possible but obvious to turn to corpus-based operationalizations to investigate (degrees of) entrenchment. In Section 5.2.2, we discuss this issue in more detail and touch on the relationship between corpus-based measures of entrenchment on the one hand and experimental ones on the other.

Although at first glance raw frequencies of occurrence may seem to be a straightforward way of measuring entrenchment, matters are slightly more complicated. Linguistic units may differ along at least two dimensions, complexity and schematicity, and simple frequency counts are useful approximations of entrenchment only in the case of minimally complex and minimally schematic expressions. In Section 5.3.1, we discuss complexity and schematicity in more detail. In Section 5.3.2, we discuss established corpus-based measures of entrenchment for different types of units. Specifically, we deal with simple, nonschematic units in Section 5.3.2.1, with different perspectives on complex, nonschematic units in Section 5.3.2.2, and with schematic units in Section 5.3.2.3.

DOI 10.1515/9783110341423-006

Although the relationship between corpus frequency and entrenchment is overwhelmingly taken for granted in the cognitive linguistic research literature, it has recently been questioned. Section 5.4 addresses the major points of criticism.

5.2 Corpora, Cognition, and Entrenchment

5.2.1 Corpora and Cognition

It is fairly uncontroversial that linguistic corpora (collections of authentic spoken or written language use) can be a useful tool for linguistic research. There is wide agreement in applied linguistics, for example, that dictionaries, reference grammars, and to some extent language-teaching materials should be based on the analysis of corpora and use citations from corpora to illustrate the phenomena under discussion. Similarly, it is regarded as a matter of course in sociolinguistics and discourse analysis that language variation and the structure of linguistic interaction are investigated largely on the basis of samples of authentic language use. Finally, there are areas of linguistic study, such as historical linguistics, in which no other source of data exists in the first place.

There is considerably less agreement on whether corpora have a place in the investigation of the language system in the context of syntactic theorizing, let alone in contexts where it is explicitly investigated as a cognitive phenomenon. In these areas of research, psycholinguistic experiments (ranging from simple grammaticality judgments to complex stimulus-response designs) are generally seen as the most obvious, or even the only, source of empirical data. Although corpora and corpus-linguistic methods are being adopted by a growing number of researchers in syntax-theoretic and cognitive-linguistic frameworks (see, e.g., Glynn & Fischer, 2010; Gries, 2003; Gries & Stefanowitsch, 2006; Perek, 2015; Schmid, 2000; Schneider, 2014; Wulff, 2008), they are sometimes still explicitly advised against (most notably by Chomsky, 1957, pp. 15–17; see also Andor, 2004, for Chomsky's recent view on the value of corpus data) or ignored entirely.

This hesitant, sometimes downright hostile attitude toward corpora in cognitive or theoretical approaches to language is due at least in part to the assumption that their object of study is incompatible with the type of data collected in corpora. While the object of study is the language system or its representation in speakers' minds (e.g., langue, competence, i-language, linguistic cognition), corpora are widely understood to contain linguistic usage (e.g., parole, performance, e-language, linguistic interaction). However, the incompatibility is more apparent than real once the relationship between corpora and cognition is made explicit. There are two main ways in which this relationship can be conceptualized (see also Stefanowitsch, 2011).

First, and most obviously, there is what we will refer to as the *corpus-as-output* view. From this perspective, a corpus is a sample of the language use of a particular group of speakers representative for a particular speech community—a snapshot, as it were, of the linguistic performance they collectively generate on the basis of the individual linguistic representations in their minds. The corpus-as-output view is not incompatible with a cognitive approach: As in other methodological frameworks relying on the observation of naturally occurring behavior, we can draw inferences about the mental representations underlying this behavior. Specifically, we can attempt to model mental linguistic representations based on observed patterns of language use in combination with general assumptions about cognitive mechanisms employed in turning linguistic representations into linguistic action.

However, the corpus-as-output view is more straightforwardly compatible with research questions that allow the researcher to remain agnostic or even apathetic with respect to cognition, such as the research areas mentioned at the beginning of this section and much of the research that explicitly describes itself as "corpus-linguistic," regardless of whether this research is descriptive, theoretical, diachronic, or applied (e.g., Biber, Johansson, Leech, Conrad, & Finegan, 1999; Hilpert, 2013; Hunston, 2002; Hunston & Francis, 2000; Leech, Hundt, Mair, & Smith, 2009; Mair, 2004, 2006; McEnery & Hardie, 2012).

Second, there is a somewhat less obvious perspective that we will refer to as the *corpus-as-input* view. From this perspective, the corpus is a (more or less representative) sample of the language use that members of a particular speech community are exposed to during language acquisition and on the basis of which they construct their mental representations in the first place. Although this model is unlikely to appeal to generative linguists, who axiomatically minimize the relevance of the input to the process of constructing linguistic representations, it is widely accepted in usage-based models of first- and second-language acquisition (see, e.g., Ambridge, Kidd, Rowland, & Theakston, 2015; Ellis & Wulff, 2015; Lieven & Tomasello, 2008; MacWhinney, 2008; Tomasello, 2003; see also MacWhinney, Chapter 15, this volume, and Theakston, Chapter 14, this volume).

If we use corpora as a model of linguistic input, we must, of course, take care to construct them in such a way that they approximate the actual input of a given (average member of a) speech community. This is especially important in the context of first-language acquisition research because children are initially exposed to a rather restricted input of exclusively spoken language of a familiar register, to some extent adapted (consciously or subconsciously) to their limited linguistic skills (e.g., baby talk, motherese, caregiver language). To model this input, large samples of naturally occurring adult–child interactions must be collected (see, e.g., the Manchester Corpus [Theakston, Lieven, Pine, & Rowland, 2001]; and CHILDES [MacWhinney, 2000]).

Usage-based models of language are not limited to the initial period of language acquisition, however: Exposure to and experience with performance data are seen as central in the shaping and reshaping of the linguistic competence of speakers throughout their lifetimes (see, e.g., Hoey, 2005; Langacker, 1987, 1991). Although the acquisition of general grammatical schemas ("rules") is complete at some point,

Exhibit 5.1 Data Sources

BNC. British National Corpus. Available at http://www.natcorp.ox.ac.uk (Aston & Burnard, 1998).
BROWN. A Standard Corpus of Present-Day Edited American English. Available at http://www.nltk.org/nltk_data (Francis & Kucera, 1979).
COCA. Corpus of Contemporary American English. Available at http://corpus.byu.edu/coca (Davies, 2009).
ENCOW14. Corpora from the Web, English Version, Release 2014, Slice AX03. Available at https://webcorpora.org (Schäfer & Bildhauer, 2012).

---

the acquisition of vocabulary and (semi-)idiomatic expressions continues well into adulthood, and—crucial in a discussion of entrenchment—the quantitative distribution of phenomena in the input will continue to influence the representation of these phenomena. In this wider context, large, register-mixed corpora such as the *British National Corpus* (*BNC*; Aston & Burnard, 1998; see Exhibit 5.1 for the data sources used in this chapter) may not be perfect models of the linguistic experience of adult speakers, but they are reasonably close to the input of an idealized average member of the relevant speech community. In our discussion of entrenchment, we will adopt the corpus-as-input view and mention practical limits where applicable.

5.2.2 Corpora and Entrenchment

Although entrenchment is a (hypothesized) cognitive phenomenon, it does not seem to play an important role in the cognitive sciences. It is not mentioned at all, for example, in recent handbooks of psychology and psycholinguistics such as Reisberg (2013) or Traxler and Gernsbacher (2006). Instead, it originates in Langacker's (1987) *Foundations of Cognitive Grammar*, where, after a detailed discussion of the extent to which combinations of simple linguistic units may themselves be units of the linguistic system, he introduced the notion as follows:

> Linguistic units are more realistically conceived of as falling along a continuous scale of entrenchment in cognitive organization. Every use of a structure has a positive impact on its degree of entrenchment, whereas extended periods of disuse have a negative impact. With repeated use, a novel structure becomes progressively entrenched, to the point of becoming a unit; moreover, units are variably entrenched depending on the frequency of their occurrence. (p. 59)

Clearly, Langacker's (1987) idea of entrenchment is related to the psycholinguistic notion of repetition priming and its long-term effects, and in experimental studies in cognitive linguistics, the notions seem to be largely equated with each other. Entrenchment is typically operationalized in terms of reaction times and accuracy of responses to certain stimuli, that is, the same aspects of behavior that are used in psycholinguistics to operationalize long-term effects of priming (e.g., facilitation, stimulus-response binding; see, e.g., Blumenthal-Dramé, Chapter 6, this volume).

However, note that Langacker (1987) does not define entrenchment in psycholinguistic terms but in terms of language "use" (presumably both in the sense of the input that the speaker is confronted with and the language output that they themselves produce). Moreover, he explicitly refers to frequency of occurrence as the driving force of entrenchment, a point he repeats in a later work (Langacker, 2008, p. 238), where he suggests "observed frequency" as the basis for estimating degree of entrenchment empirically.

Because corpora are essentially large samples of linguistic usage data that may serve as models of the linguistic input and output of (adult) speakers, they are the most obvious place to turn to to operationalize Langacker's (1987) definition. This methodological insight is captured in Schmid's (2000) "from-corpus-to-cognition principle," which simply states that "frequency in text instantiates entrenchment in the cognitive system" (p. 39). This principle will serve as our departure point for discussing corpus-based measurements of entrenchment.

5.3 Measuring Entrenchment in Corpora

Both Langacker's definition of entrenchment and Schmid's (2000) operationalization suggest that estimating entrenchment on the basis of a linguistic corpus is straightforward: If frequency drives entrenchment, the number of times that a particular phenomenon occurs in our corpus should be a direct measure of its entrenchment in the cognitive system.

However, as we will show, this interpretation of *frequency* as "(raw) token frequency" is too narrow for all but the simplest units of language. The entrenchment of a monomorphemic word may be measured in terms of token frequency, but linguistic units may differ from such simple units along two dimensions: complexity and schematicity. The dimension of complexity concerns the internal structure of linguistic units, that is, the question of whether, and to what degree, a unit consists of identifiable subunits at the same level of articulation.[1] The dimension of schematicity concerns the question of whether, and to what degree, a linguistic unit is phonologically specified, that is, associated with a particular sound shape. Let us illustrate these dimensions in more detail before we return to the question how they relate to the notion of frequency.

---

[1] Note that morphemes typically consist of more than one phoneme (or, in the case of written language, grapheme), that is, while they are simple (unanalyzable) units at the level of linguistic signs (the *first articulation*, cf. Martinet, 1960, pp. 13–14), they are complex at the level of phonology (the *second articulation*, cf. Martinet, 1960, p. 15), the units of which could themselves be investigated in terms of their entrenchment. We do not discuss the entrenchment of phonemes or graphemes further in this chapter, but at least some of the measures discussed with respect to complex units are presumably also relevant to this issue.

5.3.1 Types of Linguistic Units: Complexity and Schematicity

Figure 5.1 shows the two dimensions as a system of axes and provides examples of (potential) units at different points.

Let us begin with the dimension of complexity. Monomorphemic words are maximally simple: They cannot be analyzed into smaller meaningful units. Multimorphemic words are slightly more complex, at least from the perspective of the analyst: They consist of at least one root and one or more affixes. Still further up the dimension of complexity, we find multiword expressions, such as adjective–noun compounds (e.g., *working class, higher education*) and fixed phrases (e.g., *a great time, a great deal, for old time's sake*). These phrases include *idioms of decoding*, the meaning of which cannot be derived from their component parts and must therefore necessarily be stored and processed as units (e.g., *great deal*). They also include *idioms of encoding*, which are semantically relatively transparent but must be stored and processed as units nevertheless because their *existence* is not predictable from its component parts. For example, someone who does not know the expression *great time* will be able to derive its meaning to some extent from the meaning of *great* and *time* when they encounter it in an appropriate context; however, they would not be able to predict a priori that this phrase can be used to describe an enjoyable situation—in French, the direct translation *grand temps* means 'high time' in the sense of urgency, and in German *große Zeit* is not a fixed phrase at all, and if used, it would most likely be interpreted as '(the)

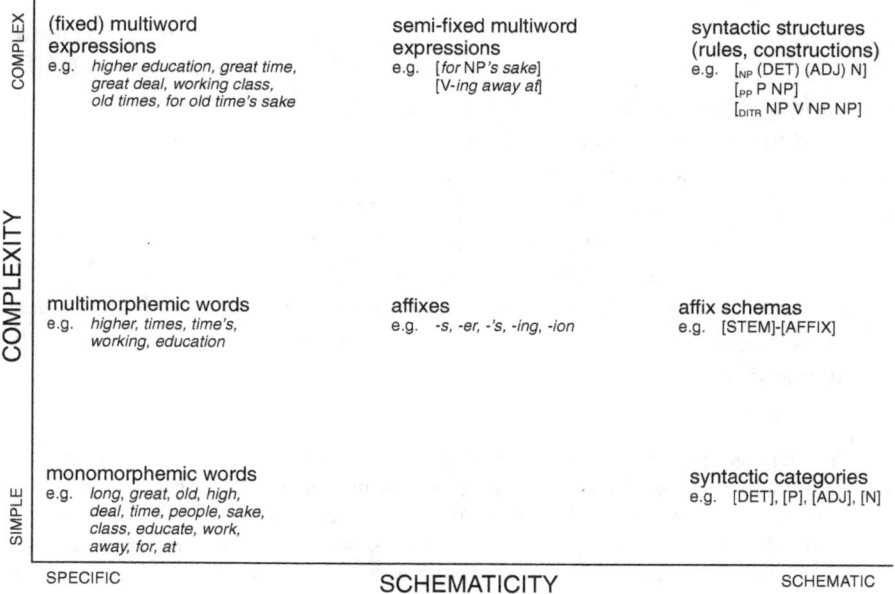

Fig. 5.1: The syntax-lexicon continuum (see Croft, 2001, p. 17; Langacker, 1987, pp. 25–27).

great age (of)' (on idioms of encoding/decoding, see Makkai, 1972, pp. 25–26; Wulff, 2013, p. 276).

Next, let us look at the dimension of schematicity. Again, we find monomorphemic words as one end point of this dimension: They are associated with a specific phonological sound shape (which is frequently invariant or at least predictable by general rules). At the other end of this dimension we find simple but maximally schematic units—syntactic categories such as determiner, adjective, and noun, for example. These are simple in that they cannot be decomposed into smaller units but schematic in that they do not have a specific sound shape associated with them. For example, although the class of adjectives shares syntactic properties (all adjectives can modify a noun, be used as a predicate with a copula, or both), there is nothing that they have in common in terms of phonology (*long* and *high* do not share any phonemes, differ in syllable structure, and the former shares its form with the verb *to long* while the latter shares its form with the noun *high*, as in *an all-time/record high*).

Diametrically opposed to the minimally schematic and minimally complex monomorphemic word are maximally schematic and complex units of grammatical structure. Depending on one's theoretical outlook, this category contains purely formal units, such as phrase structures (noun phrase, prepositional phrase, or even more abstract units such as the X-bar schema of government and binding theory or the head feature principle of Head-Driven Phrase Structure Grammar), or fully schematic meaningful constructions, such as the ditransitive construction with the meaning 'X cause Y to receive Z' (Goldberg, 1995, pp. 141–151) or the resultative construction with the meaning 'X cause Y to become Z.'

Between these extreme points, we find constructions falling along intermediate points at one or both dimensions. For example, there are the maximally complex but only partially schematic semifixed expressions variously referred to as *constructional idioms* (Jackendoff, 2002), *grammar patterns* (Hunston & Francis, 2000), and *variable idioms* (e.g., Stefanowitsch & Gries, 2003). The pattern *for NP's [noun phrase] sake*, for instance, has highly conventionalized instances such as *for God/Christ/heaven's sake*, but also productive instances such as *for her sanity's sake, for money's sake, for your job's sake* (all of which occur only once in the *BNC*). Another example is *V away at* (as in *eat/chip/hammer/work/scrub away at sth.*). Affixes (which contain a slot for the base to which they attach) may be seen as units of medium complexity and medium schematicity, and general morphological schemas such as STEM-AFFIX ("suffix") and AFFIX-STEM ("prefix") as units of medium complexity and high specificity. Depending on how a given model handles lemmas (in the sense of a construct covering all word forms derived from a particular stem), these may also be thought of as falling somewhere in the middle on both dimensions: Their form is partially specific (phonological content shared by all forms) and partially schematic (to be specified by affixes when deriving the word forms). The treatment of affixes and lemmas depends on the particular theoretical framework adopted, however, and the following discussion does not hinge crucially on this issue.

5.3.2 Usage Intensity and Entrenchment

We are now in a position to take a closer look at the relationship between frequency and entrenchment for units of different degrees of schematicity and complexity. Because we use the term *frequency* in a variety of technical ways, we adopt the ad hoc term *usage intensity* as a cover term. In our terminology, the entrenchment of a unit depends on its usage intensity in language use (as sampled in linguistic corpora); usage intensity must be conceptualized in different ways for different types of units.

Before we discuss measures of different types of units, there is an important caveat to acknowledge. In the preceding section, we used the term *linguistic unit* in the sense of form–meaning pairs—that is, Saussurean *signs* of various degrees of complexity (de Saussure, 1916, pp. 97–100) or Langackerian *symbolic units* (Langacker, 1987, pp. 58–60). Corpora, of course, do not contain such units, but only their forms. Because there is no one-to-one relationship between forms and signs/symbols, we cannot straightforwardly equate tokens in a corpus with linguistic units. For example, the string *bank* belongs to at least three linguistic units: one with the meaning 'financial institution,' one with the meaning 'land along a river,' and one with the meaning 'set of similar things' (*a bank of lights*). If we want to compare, for example, the entrenchment of the words *bank* ('land along a river') and *shore* ('land along the edge of a body of water'), we cannot simply use the frequencies of the respective strings in a corpus—24,546 for *bank(s)* and 2,281 for *shore(s)* in the *BNC*—because the former belongs to the unit 'financial institution' in approximately 95% of the hits. This must, of course, be kept in mind particularly in the case of simple units, where the strings must be manually coded for which linguistic unit they belong to before they are counted. With complex units, it is less of a problem; it is common knowledge in machine translation research that multiword units are less ambiguous than single word units (e.g., in the complex units *along the bank*, *investment bank*, and *bank of lights*, the string *bank* unambiguously belongs to the units 'land along a river,' 'financial institution,' and 'set of similar things,' respectively). This means that we can afford to be less concerned about ambiguity and manual coding the more complex the units investigated are.

5.3.2.1 Simple Units

In the case of maximally specific, maximally simple units such as monomorphemic words, usage intensity can indeed be equated with raw token frequency, that is, the number of times that the unit occurs in a given corpus. There is no reason to measure usage intensity in any other way, and indeed, there does not seem to be any alternative. Consider Table 5.1, which lists the 10 most frequent adjectives and nouns in the *BNC* (morphologically complex words are shown in parentheses).

Tab. 5.1: The 10 Most Frequent Adjectives and Nouns in the *British National Corpus*

Adjectives				Nouns			
Rank	Word	n	%	Rank	Word	n	%
1	other	129,885	0.0011586	1	time	151,754	0.0013537
2	new	113,561	0.0010130	2	people	121,584	0.0010846
3	good	76,551	0.0006829	3	way	95,351	0.0008506
4	old	52,436	0.0004678	4	(years)	88,571	0.0007901
5	(different)	47,521	0.0004239	5	year	73,009	0.0006513
6	great	43,924	0.0003918	6	(government)	61,789	0.0005512
7	(local)	43,783	0.0003906	7	day	58,802	0.0005245
8	small	41,812	0.0003730	8	man	57,589	0.0005137
9	(social)	41,629	0.0003713	9	world	57,397	0.0005120
10	(important)	38,679	0.0003450	10	life	54,903	0.0004898

Note. Unambiguously tagged words only; $N = 112{,}102{,}325$.

For the morphologically simple words, it is obvious that, with the caveat discussed earlier, their raw token frequency should be indicative of their relative entrenchment; for example, *new* should be more entrenched than *old* and *good*, and *time* should be more entrenched than *people* and *way*. As long as we base our entrenchment estimates on a single corpus (or on different corpora of exactly the same size), we can express token frequency as an absolute frequency, but we can also express it independently of corpus size as an unconditional probability p(w), that is, the likelihood that the word will occur in any given amount of text.

It is less obvious how morphologically complex words fit into the picture. In at least some cases, different forms derived from the same stem presumably contribute jointly to the entrenchment of the stem—the forms *year* and *years* taken together are more frequent than the form *people*, so we would predict the stem *year* to be more entrenched than the stem *people*. However, it is still to some extent controversial, under what circumstances morphologically complex words are actually recognized (i.e., stored and processed) as complex entities (see, e.g., Blumenthal-Dramé, 2012; Ford, Davis, & Marslen-Wilson, 2010; Hay & Baayen, 2005; Marslen-Wilson, Komisarjevsky, Waksler, & Older, 1994).

There is a wide agreement in the literature, however, that at least some morphologically complex words are stored and processed as units, especially if they are highly frequent or if they are phonologically or semantically nontransparent. For example, the adjective *important* is almost nine times more frequent than the verb *import*, the adjective *imported*, and the noun *import* combined, and the stem has a different meaning in the latter three. It is plausible to assume that *important* is treated like a simple unit by speakers, rather than being derived from the stem *import* and the suffix -*ant* when needed. This is even clearer in the case for the adjective *social*, which is theoretically derivable from the bound stem *soc(i)*- (that also occurs in *society*, *sociology*, *sociopath*, etc.) and the suffix *-al* (also found in *local*, *governmental*, etc.): again, *social* is more frequent than all other forms potentially derived from *soc-* taken together, and the stem is pronounced differently in the adjective ([səʊʃ]) than in the other words ([səs] in *society*, [səʊs] in *sociology*, *sociopath*, etc.). Again, it is plausible to assume that speakers treat the adjective *social* like a simple unit.

Whether we treat a given word as a simple unit or as a combination of a stem and one or more affixes is to some extent an empirical issue (see the literature cited earlier in the chapter) and to a large extent a theoretical decision in the context of a particular model of language. Crucially, however, whatever decision one makes, corpora will provide the token frequencies needed to determine the entrenchment of the units one has postulated. If we treat a unit as simple and specific, its entrenchment is measured by its raw frequency; if we treat a unit as complex and/or schematic, this introduces complications, which we turn to next, beginning with the issue of complexity.

5.3.2.2 Complex Units

Instead of stem–affix combinations (the status of which as complex units is at least theoretically debatable in all cases, e.g., in word-and-paradigm models of morphology, and widely debated in some cases, as in the literature cited earlier), we demonstrate the problem of measuring the entrenchment of complex units with the less debatable case of multiword units. The usage intensity of complex units can be measured in three related, but distinct, ways.

5.3.2.2.1 Frequency-Based Measurement

The first way of estimating the entrenchment of complex units is to treat them analogously to simple units and measure their usage intensity in terms of the token frequency of the expression as a whole (as, e.g., Hunston & Francis, 2000, and Sinclair, 1991, do, albeit without explicit reference to *entrenchment*). Table 5.2 shows the 10 most frequent adjective–noun pairs in the *BNC*.

At first glance, it is certainly plausible that these adjective–noun combinations are highly entrenched (at least in the British English of the 1990s). However, it is less plausible that the order of frequency reflects degrees of entrenchment—for example, it is surprising that the combination *other people* should be more entrenched than the proper name *Soviet Union*, or even the combination *young people*.

One problem with simply counting the frequency of occurrence of complex units is that this ignores the individual frequencies of their components: *other* and *people* are both much more frequent overall than *Soviet* and *Union*, so the co-occurrence is less surprising in the case of the former than in the case of the latter. In other words, raw frequency counts can be misleading in the case of complex units because they ignore the a priori likelihood of co-occurrence.

Tab. 5.2: The 10 Most Frequent Adjective–Noun Combinations in the *British National Corpus*

Rank	Bigram	n	%	n per million words
1	Prime Minister	9,461	0.00008440	84.40
2	other hand	5,566	0.00004965	49.65
3	Labour Party	4,257	0.00003797	37.97
4	long time	4,229	0.00003772	37.72
5	other people	4,126	0.00003681	36.81
6	hon. friend	4,099	0.00003656	36.56
7	local authorities	4,028	0.00003593	35.93
8	great deal	4,021	0.00003587	35.87
9	Soviet Union	3,895	0.00003475	34.75
10	young people	3,609	0.00003219	32.19

Note. Unambiguously tagged words only; $N = 112,102,325$.

5.3.2.2.2 Probability-Based Measurements

The second way of estimating the entrenchment of complex units is to take their complexity into account and to measure their usage intensity by relating the token frequency of the expression as a whole to the individual token frequencies of its component parts. The most straightforward way of doing this is to calculate the conditional probability $p(w_{n+1}|w_n)$, that is, the likelihood that we will encounter a word w_{n+1} given that we have just encountered a word w_n (calculated, obviously, by dividing the frequency of the bigram $w_n w_{n+1}$ by the frequency of w_{n+1}). This is referred to as *transitional probability* in the computational and corpus-linguistic literature (see, e.g., Bush, 2001; Bybee & Scheibman, 1999; and Krug, 2003, for work relating transitional probability directly to the notion of entrenchment; see also Saffran, Newport, & Aslin, 1996, on first-language acquisition). Note that transitional probability is equivalent to the psycholinguistic notion of *cue reliability*, that is, the reliability with which a given linguistic Phenomenon A predicts the occurrence of another Phenomenon B (see, e.g., MacWhinney, 2008; note that cue reliability and related measures are routinely derived from corpora).

Table 5.3 shows the 10 adjective–noun combinations with the highest transitional probability/cue reliability in the *BNC*, that is, the highest probability that the adjective in question will be followed by the noun in question. For reasons we discuss subsequently, we have discarded here and in all following tables all cases that occur fewer than three times and all cases in which the adjective and the noun never occur outside of the combination. We have also removed manually all cases in which the first and/or second word is erroneously tagged as an adjective or noun, respectively.[2]

---

[2] These were mostly proper names, such as *Ronny Johnsen*, or foreign language items such as *ambre solaire* (French) and *faerie queene* (Middle English), as well as a few misspelt or mistokenized items. The *BNC* is tagged using a stochastic tagger that will guess (often, but by no means always correctly) the part of speech of an unknown word based on the part of speech of the preceding word.

Tab. 5.3: Transitional Probability (or Cue Reliability) of Adjective–Noun Combinations in the *British National Corpus*

Rank	Bigram	n (Bigram)	n (Adjective)	n (Noun)	p(N|Adj)
1	ulcerative colitis	728	754	1,004	0.9655
2	corned beef	78	82	1,484	0.9512
3	arachidonic acid	72	76	4,898	0.9474
4	scrolled area	216	229	34,786	0.9432
5	stainless steel	285	307	3,647	0.9283
6	sclerosing cholangitis	68	74	200	0.9189
7	foregone conclusion	78	85	5,008	0.9176
8	varicose veins	58	64	760	0.9062
9	adoral shields	114	127	559	0.8976
10	helping hand	120	134	32,513	0.8955

At first glance, it is difficult to assess the degree to which these combinations are entrenched. On the one hand, some of them feel like strongly entrenched units (e.g., *corned beef, stainless steel, foregone conclusion*). On the other hand, combinations such as *arachidonic acid* or *sclerosing cholangitis* are likely to be unfamiliar to most members of the speech community. Thus, it is not the units themselves that are necessarily strongly entrenched, but the (directional) relationship between the second and the first element. In other words, if speakers know the adjective (which is vastly more likely in the case of *stainless* than in the case of *arachidonic*), they will be able to predict the following noun with a high degree of accuracy.

Of course, we can also measure the entrenchment of the relationship in the opposite direction, that is, the conditional probability $p(w_n|w_{n+1})$. This corresponds to the psycholinguistic notion of *cue availability* (see MacWhinney, 2008), that is, the degree to which a linguistic Phenomenon B is available as a cue to a different Phenomenon A. In the case of adjective–noun combinations, the cue availability is p(Adj|N), that is, the probability that a particular adjective will precede a given noun. Table 5.4 shows the adjective–noun pairs with the highest cue availability.

Clearly, cue reliability and cue availability measure different things: There is no overlap between the 10 adjective–noun pairs with the highest cue reliability and those with the highest cue availability, and in fact, pairs with a high cue reliability generally have a low cue availability and vice versa. Take the phrases *stainless steel* (from Table 5.3) and *global warming* (from Table 5.4). Although *stainless steel* has a high cue reliability of 285/307 = 0.9283, it has a rather low cue availability of 285/3647 = 0.0781. Conversely, *global warming* has a high cue availability of 599/683 = 0.877 but a rather low cue reliability of 599/3521 = 0.1701.

In the context of language processing, this difference is presumably relevant: If we hear *stainless*, we have a high expectation that *steel* will follow, but if we hear *global*, we do not necessarily expect *warming* (at least not in the 1990s; the cue reli-

Tab. 5.4: Cue Availability of Adjective–Noun Combinations in the *British National Corpus*

Rank	Bigram	n (Bigram)	n (Adjective)	n (Noun)	Cue reliability
1	muscular dystrophy	77	607	83	0.927711
2	false pretences	86	3,530	96	0.895833
3	cerebral palsy	102	478	115	0.886957
4	global warming	599	3,521	683	0.877013
5	still lifes	54	2,763	63	0.857143
6	intestinal pseudo-obstruction[a]	24	838	28	0.857143
7	grand theogonist	28	4,352	33	0.848485
8	multiple sclerosis	142	2,204	171	0.830409
9	major histocompatibility	36	23,581	44	0.818182
10	intestinal pseudoobstruction[a]	18	838	22	0.818182

Note. All combinations where one of the two parts occurred fewer than three times were removed beforehand; mistagged combinations were removed manually (e.g., *faerie queene, paba-udca disulphate*).
[a] All calculations are based on orthographic strings so that different spellings of the same word are counted as separate types.

ability may have changed in the meantime). In contrast, if we are unsure whether we have heard *warming* or *warning*, the absence of the adjective *global* would lead us to tend toward *warning*; but if we are unsure whether we have heard *steel* or *seal*, the absence of the adjective *stainless* would not provide much of a cue.

However, with respect to the entrenchment of the unit as a whole, the directionality of the priming relationship is irrelevant; a high probability in either direction should favor entrenchment, while a low probability should disfavor it. Thus, a combined measure may be the best indicator of entrenchment, and there are several fairly common association measures that combine the two probabilities. The most obvious of these is *cue validity* (defined as the product of the two probabilities; see Bates & MacWhinney, 1987, p. 164); others are the *Dice coefficient* (defined as the harmonic mean of the two probabilities) and *minimum sensitivity* (defined as the smaller of the two probabilities). These measures have in common that they give more weight to the smaller of the two probabilities and therefore yield similar results. Table 5.5 shows the 10 adjective–noun pairs with the highest cue validity in the BNC.

Like transitional probability/cue reliability and cue availability, the combined measures yield mixed results; although it is plausible in most (perhaps all) cases that there is a strong association between the adjective and the noun, the adjectives and nouns themselves are in many cases infrequent, and thus the combinations are unlikely to be entrenched for an average member of the speech community.

The reason many extremely rare phrases rank highly when using probability-based entrenchment measures is simply that probability-based measures are insensitive to raw frequency. A combination such as *ulcerative colitis*, which despite its terminological status is likely to be familiar to a relatively large proportion of the speech community, has almost the same probability-based entrenchment values as

Tab. 5.5: Cue Validity of Adjective–Noun Pairs in the *British National Corpus*

Rank	Bigram	n (Bigram)	n (Adjective)	n (Noun)	Cue validity
1	myalgic encephalomyelitis	7	8	7	0.8750
2	x-linked agammaglobulinaemia	5	5	6	0.8333
3	polychlorinated biphenyls	26	31	27	0.8076
4	ulcerative colitis	728	754	1,004	0.7001
5	endoplasmic reticulum	29	30	41	0.6837
6	ornithischian pisanosaurus	2	3	2	0.6667
	popular-democratic interpellations	2	2	3	0.6667
	thievin' 'aybag	2	3	2	0.6667
	triple-combed burgonet	2	2	3	0.6667
	twin-elliptic harmonograph	2	3	2	0.6667

Note. $N = 112{,}092{,}864$.

the combination *endoplasmic reticulum*, which is unlikely to be known to anyone who is not a molecular biologist, simply because the proportional frequencies of the noun, the adjective, and the combination are the same—the fact that *ulcerative colitis* is 25 times more frequent has no influence on the measures.

Although this in itself may seem to be a desirable property of probability-based measures in some contexts, it has the unfortunate consequence that the importance of rare combinations is often overestimated: Probability-based measures react more sensitively to small differences for low frequencies than for high frequencies. If, for example, the combination *ulcerative colitis* occurred one time less than it actually does (727 instead of 728 times), the cue validity would change from 0.7001 to 0.6982, a barely noticeable difference of 0.0019. If, however, the combination *twin-elliptic harmonograph* occurred one time less (once instead of twice), the cue validity would change from 0.6667 to 0.167—a drastic change of 0.5. This problem is most dramatic with rare combinations of rare words. There are a number of adjective–noun combinations in the *BNC* that only occur one to three times, but where the adjective and the noun never occur by themselves, such as *honey-throated harangueress* and *flinted knife-sharpener* (once), *ultra-religious chasidim* and *histidine-containing phosphocarrier* (twice), or the nonce-word combinations *slithy toves* (from Lewis Carroll's *Jabberwocky*) and *Vermicious Knids* (from Roald Dahl's *Charlie and the Great Glass Elevator*; three times each). All these combinations will have probability-based measures of 1, that is, they will be estimated as maximally entrenched.

One might assume that this is a problem of corpus construction, that such overestimates could be avoided if the corpus did not contain samples from scientific discourses or literary works by authors known for coining words. However, as cases such as *honey-throated harangueress* and *flinted knife-sharpener* show, even nonspecialized discourse will necessarily contain rare combinations of rare words. We can try to avoid the problems of probability-based measures to some extent by discarding rare combinations from our analysis (which is what we did earlier), but in doing so, we are combining probabilities with frequencies in an arbitrary and unsystematic way that is unlikely to yield psychologically plausible measures of entrenchment.

5.3.2.2.3 Statistical Measures

The third way of estimating the entrenchment of complex units also takes their complexity into account but measures usage intensity in terms of measures derived from contingency tests—either test statistics such as G^2 from the log-likelihood test or χ^2 from the chi-square test, or the p values of exact tests such as Fisher–Yates or the binomial test (see Dunning, 1993; Gries, 2012; Pedersen, 1996; Stefanowitsch & Gries, 2003, for discussion; see Evert, 2004, for a comprehensive overview of such measures).

Like probability-based measures, these association measures take into account the co-occurrence frequency of the elements relative to their individual frequencies, but unlike probability-based measures, they also take into account the frequency of co-occurrence relative to the overall size of the corpus. Thus, on the one hand, if two words that are independently frequent also co-occur together frequently, this co-occurrence will be treated as less important than the co-occurrence of words that mainly occur together—in this sense, statistical measures are better than frequency-based ones. On the other hand, if the combination is frequent, then a given relationship between the co-occurrence frequency and the individual frequencies will be treated as more important than the same relationship in a rare combination; in this sense, statistical measures are better than probability-based measures. Put simply, statistical association measures combine the strength of frequency-based measures and probability-based measures and are thus likely to be the best corpus-based approximation of entrenchment.

Table 5.6 shows the most strongly associated adjective–noun pairs according to the widely used G^2 statistic.[3]

It seems highly plausible that these are among the most strongly entrenched adjective–noun combinations (for British speakers in the early 1990s). All combinations are either compounds (and titles, such as *Prime Minister*, or proper names,

---

[3] Calculated as

$$G^2 = 2\sum_i O_i \cdot \ln\left(\frac{O_i}{E_i}\right),$$

where O is the observed frequency and E the expected frequency of each cell of a two-by-two contingency table containing the frequency of the bigram w_{n+1}, the frequency of w_n outside of the bigram, the frequency of w_{n+1} outside of the bigram, and the frequency of all bigrams containing neither w_n nor w_{n+1}.

Tab. 5.6: Statistical Association of Adjective–Noun Pairs in the *British National Corpus*

Rank	Bigram	n (Bigram)	n (Adjective)	n (Noun)	G^2
1	Prime Minister	9,461	11,954	23,394	152,595.99
2	hon. friend	4,099	10,548	15,867	59,728.61
3	Soviet Union	3,895	10,679	16,436	55,762.05
4	Labour Party	4,257	13,084	39,680	51,626.13
5	great deal	4,021	44,335	10,434	49,481.33
6	hon. gentleman	2,908	10,548	5,070	47,890.81
7	local authorities	4,028	44,121	12,855	47,561.11
8	other hand	5,566	135,478	32,513	45,315.17
9	local authority	3,530	44,121	18,189	37,751.86
10	wide range	2,743	11,002	19,411	35,568.47

Note. $N = 112{,}092{,}864$.

such as *Soviet Union*) or compound-like (*local authorities*), or they are (part of) fixed phrases (*great deal, [on the] other hand*). Frequent nonfixed phrases such as *long time* or *young people* are also treated as strongly entrenched, but not as strongly as they would be under the frequency-based measure; likewise, combinations with a high cue validity are treated as strongly entrenched if they are frequent (such as *ulcerative colitis*, Rank 161 according to G^2), but not if they are rare (like *twin-elliptic harmonograph*, which does not even make it into the top 10,000).

5.3.2.2.4 Discussion

Of course, it is ultimately an empirical issue which measures best approximate entrenchment (or, more precisely, which corpus-linguistic operationalizations of entrenchment correlate with which psycholinguistic operationalizations of entrenchment). The relative merits of measuring the entrenchment of multiword expressions in terms of token frequency and transitional probability have been discussed in the literature, for example, with respect to their ability to predict univerbation phenomena (e.g., cliticization of the negative particle after modals and copulas after pronouns; see Bybee, 2001; Bybee & Scheibman, 1999; Krug, 1998, 2003).

All three types of measures predict these and related phenomena with an above-chance accuracy, suggesting that all of them are somehow related to entrenchment. However, none of them consistently outperforms the others, suggesting that they measure different aspects of entrenchment that are relevant to different phenomena. Roughly speaking, token frequency measures the usage intensity of the multiword expression as such, corresponding to the entrenchment of the unit as a whole; in contrast, transitional probability measures the usage intensity of the association between the component parts of the expression, corresponding to the entrenchment of the priming relationship between them. Thus, it may be that the more the multiword expression behaves like a simple unit (i.e., the less likely it is that speakers recognize or are aware of its constituent parts), the better frequency will predict its degree of entrenchment, and the more the multiword expression behaves like a complex unit, the better probability- and/or association-based measures will do.

5.3.2.3 Schematic Units

So far, we have dealt with the dimension of complexity. Let us now turn to the dimension of schematicity, which introduces an additional complication concerning the corpus-based measurement of entrenchment. We illustrate this with two patterns of medium complexity and schematicity: the semifixed expressions [*color* NP ADJ], as in Example 5.1a and 5.1b; and [*drive* NP ADJ], as in Example 5.2a and 5.2b:

> Example 5.1 a. *Well*, color me stupid, *because I didn't want to believe he was seeing another woman.* (*Waiting to Exhale*, cit. OED, s.v. colour)
> b. *"Well,* color me surprised *. . . not."* (Herald Times, cit. OED, s.v. colour)
> Example 5.2 a. *"I don't know how these women cope. It would* drive me crazy.*"* (*BNC* JYB)
> b. *"I'm sorry! It's the storm. It's* driving me mad!*"* (*BNC* CB5).

The phrase [*color* NP ADJ], a (chiefly American English) colloquial expression meaning 'consider me ADJ,' is much less frequent than the second: It does not occur in the *BNC* at all and only 13 times in the 450-million-word *Corpus of Contemporary American English* (*COCA*; Davies, 2009); in contrast, [*drive* NP ADJ] occurs more than 150 times in the *BNC* and more than 1,000 times in *COCA*. Thus, going by frequency, [*drive* NP ADJ] should be much more entrenched than [*color* NP ADJ]. Probability-based measures will lead to the same conclusion: The cue validity of *drive* for [V NP ADJ] is approximately 0.0001, whereas that of *color* for [V NP ADJ] is approximately 0.0000002, that is, 500 times lower.[4]

At first glance, it seems intuitively correct to assign a higher entrenchment to [*drive* NP ADJ] than to [*color* NP ADJ]: Examples like those in 5.2a and 5.2b are likely to be more familiar, and thus more easily and quickly recognized and retrieved, than those in 5.1a and 5.1b. However, what is captured by these measures is not straightforwardly a fact about the patterns [*drive* NP ADJ] and [*color* NP ADJ] because the

---

4 The exact frequencies needed to perform these calculations are impossible to determine because *COCA* can only be accessed imprecisely using a web interface. We have used estimates of 116,000 occurrences for [V NP ADJ], 6,500 for the verb *color*, 92,000 for the verb *drive*, 12 for the expression [*color* NP ADJ], and 1,200 for the expression [*drive* NP ADJ]; although these are rough estimates, we are confident that they are close to the actual frequencies of occurrence.

raw frequencies confound the frequency of the patterns with the frequency of its specific instantiation(s). The specific expression *drive me crazy*, for example, is vastly more frequent than the specific expression *color me stupid*. This influences the overall raw frequency of the respective patterns, but it does not necessarily influence their entrenchment because it is primarily a fact about the specific expressions and will therefore influence the entrenchment of the specific expressions.

The entrenchment of the schema itself does not depend primarily on its token frequency (i.e., the frequency with which a speaker encounters an instantiation of the pattern) but on its type frequency (i.e., the *number of different instantiations* of the pattern encountered). It is only by virtue of encountering many instantiations of a pattern that a schematic representation emerges from the entrenched representations of individual manifestations (see, e.g., Croft, 2001, p. 28; Croft & Cruse, 2004, p. 309; Diessel, 2004, pp. 29–34; Langacker, 2008, p. 234; Taylor, 2012, p. 285, for the explicit equation of schematic entrenchment with type frequency). Conversely, the entrenchment of a schema is directly related to its productivity, that is, its ability to serve as a template for new instances (see, e.g., Bybee, 2010, p. 67; Croft, 2001, p. 28; Langacker, 2008, p. 234; Lieven, 2010, Taylor, 2012, pp. 173–174, for discussions of the relationship between entrenchment, type frequency, and productivity).

Because the type frequency depends to some extent on token frequency (the more tokens, the more opportunities for different types to occur), the two must be put into some kind of relationship. The simplest measure suggested in the literature is the type/token ratio (i.e., N_{types}/N_{tokens}), which is the percentage of tokens that are different from each other.[5]

Let us return to the example of the abstract patterns [*color* NP ADJ] and [*drive* NP ADJ]. Both expressions have a number of variable slots, including the object (which is most often the pronoun *me* in the case of [*drive* NP ADJ], and near-exclusively so in the case of [*color* NP ADJ]), and the adjectival object complement, which we focus on here to illustrate schematic entrenchment. Exhibit 5.2 shows the adjectives occurring in this slot of the two constructions in a 700-million-word slice of the *ENCOW* corpus (Schäfer & Bildhauer, 2012) together with their frequency.

Clearly, the two patterns are very different from each other as far as the distribution of their instantiations is concerned: Although [*drive* NP ADJ] is instantiated more than 20 times more frequently than [*color* NP ADJ] (1,028 vs. 46), it has fewer different instantiations (24 vs. 31). In other words, although its token frequency is higher, its type frequency is lower. The type/token ratios show the differences between the two patterns even more clearly: For [*drive* NP ADJ], it is just above 2% (24/1028 = 0.0233),

---

[5] Note that type/token ratios are not the only way to quantify the entrenchment of schematic patterns. A substantial literature discusses and tests different ways of measuring morphological productivity (for an overview, see Baayen, 2009). Because of the close relationship between schematic entrenchment and productivity, this literature is highly relevant to the discussion of corpus-based entrenchment measures even if the term *entrenchment* is rarely used there.

Exhibit 5.2 Adjectives occurring in the patterns [drive NP ADJ] and [color NP ADJ]

---

drive NP ADJ (*N* = 1,028)
crazy (495), *mad* (293), *insane* (127), *wild* (29), *bonkers* (19), *batty* (16), *nuts* (10), *mental* (8), *potty* (6), *crackers* (5), *bananas* (5), *loopy* (2), *silly* (2), *ballistic* (1), *berserk* (1), *buggy* (1), *daft* (1), *delirious* (1), *demented* (1), *frantic* (1), *loony* (1), *nutty* (1), *rowdy* (1), *scatty* (1)

colo(u)r NP ADJ (*N* = 46)
unimpressed (8), *skeptical* (6), *cynical* (2), *disappointed* (2), *jealous* (2), *amazed* (1), *blue* (1), *curious* (1), *dubious* (1), *envious* (1), *excited* (1), *fundamentalist* (1), *green* (1), *happy* (1), *hyper-paranoid* (1), *impressed* (1), *inflammable* (1), *innocent* (1), *interested* (1), *Marxist* (1), *naive* (1), *old-fashioned* (1), *pathetic* (1), *perfect* (1), *shocked* (1), *simple* (1), *slow* (1), *strange* (1), *unconvinced* (1), *unsurprised* (1), *wrong* (1)

---

whereas for [*color* NP ADJ], it is almost 70% (31/46 = 0.6739). In other words, although the specific expressions *drive sb crazy*, *drive sb mad*, and *drive sb insane* are vastly more entrenched than the specific expressions *color me unimpressed*, *color me cynical*, or any other instance of this pattern, the schematic pattern [*color* NP ADJ] is more entrenched than the schematic pattern [*drive* NP ADJ]. This may seem counterintuitive given the vast difference in token frequency between the two patterns, but note that it is also supported by the qualitative differences in productivity: The instances of [*drive* NP ADJ] are all filled by adjectives meaning "insane" and/or "angry" (i.e., synonyms of *crazy/mad*), whereas the instances of [*color* NP ADJ] are filled by a semantically heterogeneous set of adjectives.

The type/token ratio (or other measures of productivity/schematic entrenchment) can also be applied to simple schematic expressions (e.g., word classes) or fully schematic expressions (e.g., the pattern [ADJ N]), yielding measures that are generally interpretable in terms of entrenchment. For example, the tagged version of the *BROWN* corpus (Francis & Kucera, 1979) contains 7,631 distinct items tagged as (uninflected) adjectives, occurring a total of 68,588 times. Thus, the type/token ratio for the word class adjective is 0.11. Nouns have a somewhat lower but similar type/token ratio of 0.08 (13,130:164,892). In contrast, prepositions have a type/token ratio of 0.001 (132:122,620) and determiners one of 0.0004 (51:136,193), more than 100 times lower than those of nouns and adjectives. Thus, although many individual *members* of the word classes preposition and determiner are more entrenched than even the most frequent individual nouns or adjectives, the word classes noun and adjective themselves are much more entrenched than the word classes preposition and determiner. This corresponds most obviously with the fact that the word classes noun and adjective are open classes, whereas preposition and determiner are closed classes. Open classes such as noun and adjective have a high productivity: Their schematic representation is entrenched enough to allow the easy addition of new members. In contrast, closed classes have a low or even nonexistent productivity: Their schematic representations are so weakly entrenched relative to their individual members that they allow the addition of new members only occasionally (in the case of prepositions) or not at all (in the case of determiners).

With respect to fully abstract patterns, consider [ADJ N] (the default pattern for nouns modified by adjectives in English) and [N ADJ] (a rare pattern borrowed into English from French during the Middle English period and found in present-day English mainly in job titles such as *Secretary General* or *poet laureate* but also in some otherwise regular noun phrases such as *body politic* or *life eternal*). The tagged version of the *BROWN* corpus contains 23,524 different types of the pattern [ADJ N], occurring a total of 30,142 times; the type/token ratio is thus a very high 0.78, indicating a strong entrenchment of the pattern relative to its individual members (even the most frequent combination, *old man*, occurs only 66 times, accounting for just 0.2% of all tokens). In contrast, there are 22 types of the pattern [N ADJ], occurring a total of 57 times; the type/token ratio is thus a much lower 0.39, indicating a much weaker entrenchment of the pattern relative to its individual members (the most frequent member, *Attorney General*, occurs 18 times, accounting for almost a third (31.6%) of the pattern).

5.4 Corpora and Entrenchment: Further Issues

It is uncontroversial that, as a theoretical concept, entrenchment is causally related to frequency (or, more precisely, usage intensity in its different forms)—as pointed out earlier, this relation was posited by Langacker (1987) as part of the definition of entrenchment. It should also be uncontroversial that linguistic corpora are the most obvious (perhaps the only) source from which different measures of usage intensity can be reliably derived empirically. This seems so obvious that it is taken for granted in much of the corpus-linguistic literature that makes use of the notion (see, e.g., Gries & Stefanowitsch, 2004; Schönefeld, 2012; Stefanowitsch & Gries, 2003; Zeschel, 2008, 2010). It also seems to be taken for granted in experimental psycholinguistics, where stimuli are routinely controlled for frequency.

Nevertheless, the relation between entrenchment and frequency in general, or corpus frequency in particular, has been questioned from a number of perspectives, three of which we discuss in conclusion.

First, it has been argued that entrenchment does not correspond to frequency empirically (Blumenthal-Dramé, 2012). For this criticism to be viable, we would need to have a way of measuring entrenchment directly. However, as pointed out at the end of Section 5.2, entrenchment is a theoretical construct, and any empirical measure of it will be based on operationalizations that capture the phenomenon behind the theoretical construct only partially.

Corpus-based measures will capture overall usage frequency, but they will fail to capture more subtle determinants of usage intensity. The situational salience of an individual usage event may give it a weight that is disproportionate to its frequency (see in this context Schmid's notion of *contextual entrenchment*; Schmid, 2010, p. 126). For example, the ADJ-N combination *lonely hunter* is not particularly frequent; it occurs three times in the *BNC*, with a cue validity of 0.000018 and a G^2 of 33.22. Nevertheless, it is likely to be highly entrenched for readers of Carson McCuller's *The Heart Is a Lonely Hunter* (note that two of the three uses in the *BNC* occur in mentions of this novel's title). In fact, a linguistic structure may sometimes be salient precisely because it is rare but unusual. Take again the example of *honey-throated harangueress*: It is unlikely that readers of this chapter will have encountered this combination anywhere else (there is not a single hit for *harangueress* on the entire World Wide Web, and only 369 for the adjective *honey-throated*), and it is unlikely that they will encounter it ever again. Still, many are likely to remember it anyway (the authors of this chapter certainly will). Finally, verbal thought likely has an impact on entrenchment, but it will not be captured in corpora unless and until technologies for mind reading become available.

However, psycholinguistic measures are no more likely to capture entrenchment fully accurately. The response time to psycholinguistic stimuli is dependent not just on the kinds of long-term effects of priming that correspond to entrenchment; it also depends on short-term effects (e.g., the recency of the exposure to a linguistic structure, or, again, situational salience).

It should thus not be surprising if there is no perfect match between experimental and corpus-based measures of entrenchment, nor should mismatches be taken as evidence against the plausibility of corpus-based or experimental operationalizations. Each of them can, and does, contribute to our understanding of cognitive processes independently—the value of corpus methods is not *inherently* dependent on whether its results can be replicated or confirmed by experimental methods (or vice versa).

Still, the two types of operationalization are attempts to measure the same phenomenon and should be thought of as complementary. Experimental and elicitation data primarily measure potential *effects* of entrenchment, although they may, by including training phases, also manipulate the *causes* of entrenchment. In contrast, corpus data measure primarily potential *causes* (based on the corpus-as-input model), although they may also be used to investigate certain *effects* of entrenchment (based on the corpus-as-output model). Thus, it would be surprising (and problematic) if there were no correlation at all between them.

In fact, there is encouraging evidence to the effect that the two perspectives and methodological paradigms do approximate the same phenomenon because their results consistently produce converging evidence on various levels of complexity (e.g., Gries, Hampe, & Schönefeld, 2005, 2010; Wiechmann, 2008; see also Stefanowitsch, 2008, for a corpus-based discussion of "negative entrenchment," i.e., the entrenchment of the *absence* of expected combinations of units in the input; and Ambridge, Bidgood, et al., 2015, for corresponding psycholinguistic evidence). This is not to say that there is general agreement on which particular type of measure best describes or predicts which type of linguistic unit at which level of granularity (e.g., Bybee, 2010; Gries, 2012, 2015; Küchenhoff & Schmid, 2015; Schmid & Küchenhoff, 2013), but given the complexities involved in measuring frequency/usage intensity, this is hardly surprising. Crucially, these and other studies show that there is a correlation between psycholinguistic measures of entrenchment and text frequency in general.

Second, it has recently been argued that corpora are generally unsuitable for the study of entrenchment. Blumenthal-Dramé (2012, especially Chapter 8) argues that because corpora aggregate the linguistic usage of many speakers, they cannot be used for determining the entrenchment of linguistic structures in a given individual's mind. Similarly, Schmid (2010, p. 117) suggested that corpus-based measures of entrenchment are better thought of as measuring conventionalization.

It is true that a given linguistic corpus is not typically representative of the input, let alone the output of a particular individual. However, this does not constitute an argument against using corpora in the study of cognition because the same is true of experimental measures, which are also averaged across groups of subjects. As in a balanced corpus, these subjects are assumed to be, but never actually shown to be, representative of the speech community. Thus, experiments, like corpora, measure the average entrenchment of a structure in the mind of a typical member of the speech community.

Of course, the cognitive sciences are generally not actually concerned with the mental representations of particular individuals, but if they were, note that it would be much easier to construct corpora representing the input–output of a particular individual than it would be to run valid and reliable experiments on a particular individual (for a corpus-based case study of individual differences in entrenchment, see Schmid & Mantlik, 2015).

It is also plausible to assume that corpus-based measures of entrenchment may be used to measure degrees of conventionalization, but this does not preclude their use in measuring average entrenchment. Conventionalization is a theoretical construct that differs from entrenchment mainly in that it describes established linguistic structures at the level of the linguistic system itself (in syntactic theory or in grammar writing) or at the level of the speech community as an abstract entity (e.g., in sociolinguistics). Entrenchment, in contrast, describes established linguistic structures at the level of an average speaker's mental representation or at the level of the speech community as an aggregate of individuals. This is not to say that entrenchment and conventionalization are the same thing—they differ theoretically in a number of ways. It is to say that they are measured in the same way (or similar) ways—they do not differ empirically. Perhaps we could say that the corpus-as-input view is more amenable to models concerned with entrenchment, whereas the corpus-as-output view is more in line with models interested in conventionality.

Third, and finally, there is a general criticism of corpus linguistics that is also relevant to the quality of entrenchment measures derived from corpora: Although we can easily imagine a perfect corpus (or different perfect corpora for different research contexts), actually existing corpora fall well short of such perfect corpora in terms of size, sampling of text types and demographic representation. In Section 5.3, we demonstrated some of the problems caused by the inclusion of specific text types when inferring the average entrenchment of structures. However, sampling issues are not unique to corpus linguistics but are an integral part of any methodology. They must be dealt with in the short term by keeping them in mind when moving from data to model building, and in the long term by reducing them as much as possible. In the case of corpus linguistics, this means making more complete and more creative use of the resources that are already available and that encompass not just established corpora like the *BNC*, the *BROWN*-Family, and the (still expanding) *ICE*-Family, but also specialized corpora such as the Manchester Corpus of the input to and output of children during first-language acquisition (Theakston, Lieven, Pine, & Rowland, 2001) and the vast and varied text archives that are increasingly made available online (and, of course, the Internet with its huge amount of informal everyday language found on message boards, mailing lists, and the social media). Finally, it means constructing larger and more balanced corpora.

References

Ambridge, B., Bidgood, A., Twomey, K. E., Pine, J. M., Rowland, C. F., & Freudenthal, D. (2015). Preemption versus entrenchment: Towards a construction-general solution to the problem of the retreat from verb argument structure overgeneralization. *PLoS ONE, 10*, e0123723. http://dx.doi.org/10.1371/journal.pone.0123723

Ambridge, B., Kidd, E., Rowland, C. F., & Theakston, A. L. (2015). The ubiquity of frequency effects in first language acquisition. *Journal of Child Language, 42*, 239–273. http://dx.doi.org/10.1017/S030500091400049X

Andor, J. (2004). The master and his performance: An interview with Noam Chomsky. *Intercultural Pragmatics, 1*, 93–111. http://dx.doi.org/10.1515/iprg.2004.009

Aston, G., & Burnard, L. (1998). *The BNC handbook: Exploring the British National Corpus with SARA*. Edinburgh, Scotland: Edinburgh University Press.

Baayen, R. H. (2009). Corpus linguistics in morphology: Morphological productivity. In A. Lüdeling & M. Kytö (Eds.), *Corpus linguistics. An international handbook* (Vol. 2, HSK, 29.2, pp. 899–919). Berlin, Germany: Mouton de Gruyter.

Bates, E., & MacWhinney, B. (1987). Competition, variation, and language learning. In B. MacWhinney (Ed.), *Mechanisms of language acquisition* (pp. 157–194). Hillsdale, NJ: Erlbaum.

Biber, D., Johansson, S., Leech, G., Conrad, S., & Finegan, E. (1999). *Longman grammar of spoken and written English*. Harlow, England: Longman.

Blumenthal-Dramé, A. (2012). *Entrenchment in usage-based theories: What corpus data do and do not reveal about the mind*. Berlin, Germany: De Gruyter Mouton.

Bush, N. (2001). Frequency effects and word-boundary palatalization in English. In J. Bybee & P. Hopper (Eds.), *Frequency and the emergence of linguistic structure* (pp. 256–280). http://dx.doi.org/10.1075/tsl.45.14bus

Bybee, J. L. (2001). Frequency effects on French liaison. In J. Bybee & P. Hopper (Eds.), *Frequency and the emergence of linguistic structure* (pp. 337–359). http://dx.doi.org/10.1075/tsl.45.17byb

Bybee, J. L. (2010). *Language, usage and cognition.* http://dx.doi.org/10.1017/CBO9780511750526
Bybee, J. L. & Scheibman, J. (1999). The effect of usage on degrees of constituency: The reduction of *don't* in English. *Linguistics, 37,* 575–596. http://dx.doi.org/10.1515/ling.37.4.575
Chomsky, N. A. (1957). *Syntactic structures.* The Hague, the Netherlands: Mouton.
Croft, W. (2001). *Radical construction grammar. Syntactic theory in typological perspective.* http://dx.doi.org/10.1093/acprof:oso/9780198299554.001.0001
Croft, W., & Cruse, D. A. (2004). *Cognitive linguistics.* http://dx.doi.org/10.1017/CBO9780511803864
Davies, M. (2009). The 385+ million word *Corpus of Contemporary American English* (1990–2008+): Design, architecture, and linguistic insights. *International Journal of Corpus Linguistics, 14,* 159–190. http://dx.doi.org/10.1075/ijcl.14.2.02dav
de Saussure, F. (1916). *Cours de linguistique générale* [Course in general linguistics]. Lausanne, Switzerland: Payot.
Diessel, H. (2004). *The acquisition of complex sentences.* http://dx.doi.org/10.1017/CBO9780511486531
Dunning, T. (1993). Accurate methods for the statistics of surprise and coincidence. *Computational Linguistics, 19,* 61–74.
Ellis, N. C., & Wulff, S. (2015). Usage-based approaches in second language acquisition. In B. VanPatten & J. Williams (Eds.), *Theories in second language acquisition: An introduction* (pp. 75–93). New York, NY: Routledge.
Evert, S. (2004). *The statistics of word co-occurrences: Word pairs and collocations* (Unpublished doctoral dissertation). Universität Stuttgart, Stuttgart, Germany.
Ford, M. A., Davis, M. H., & Marslen-Wilson, W. D. (2010). Derivational morphology and base morpheme frequency. *Journal of Memory and Language, 63,* 117–130. http://dx.doi.org/10.1016/j.jml.2009.01.003
Francis, W. N., & Kucera, H. (1979). *Brown corpus manual: Manual of information to accompany A standard corpus of present-day edited American English, for use with digital computers* (revised and amplified). Providence, RI: Department of Linguistics, Brown University.
Glynn, D., & Fischer, K. (Eds.). (2010). *Quantitative methods in cognitive semantics: Corpus-driven approaches.* http://dx.doi.org/10.1515/9783110226423
Goldberg, A. E. (1995). *Constructions: A construction grammar approach to argument structure.* Chicago, IL: University of Chicago Press.
Gries, S. T. (2003). *Multifactorial analysis in corpus linguistics: A study of particle placement.* New York, NY: Continuum.
Gries, S. T. (2012). Frequencies, probabilities, and association measures in usage-/exemplar-based linguistics: Some necessary clarifications. *Studies in Language, 11,* 477–510. http://dx.doi.org/10.1075/sl.36.3.02gri
Gries, S. T. (2015). More (old and new) misunderstandings of collostructional analysis: On Schmid and Küchenhoff (2013). *Cognitive Linguistics, 26,* 505–536. http://dx.doi.org/10.1515/cog-2014-0092
Gries, S. T., Hampe, B., & Schönefeld, D. (2005). Converging evidence: Bringing together experimental and corpus data on the association of verbs and constructions. *Cognitive Linguistics, 16,* 635–676. http://dx.doi.org/10.1515/cogl.2005.16.4.635
Gries, S. T., Hampe, B., & Schönefeld, D. (2010). Converging evidence II: More on the association of verbs and constructions. In S. Rice & J. Newman (Eds.), *Empirical and experimental methods in cognitive/functional research* (pp. 59–72). Stanford, CA: CSLI.

Gries, S. T., & Stefanowitsch, A. (2004). Extending collostructional analysis: A corpus-based perspective on "alternations." *International Journal of Corpus Linguistics*, *9*, 97–129. http://dx.doi.org/10.1075/ijcl.9.1.06gri

Gries, S. T., & Stefanowitsch, A. (Eds.). (2006). *Corpora in cognitive linguistics: Corpus-based approaches to syntax and lexis*. http://dx.doi.org/10.1515/9783110197709

Hay, J. B., & Baayen, R. H. (2005). Shifting paradigms: Gradient structure in morphology. *Trends in Cognitive Sciences*, *9*, 342–348. http://dx.doi.org/10.1016/j.tics.2005.04.002

Hilpert, M. (2013). *Constructional change in English: Developments in allomorphy, word formation, and syntax*. http://dx.doi.org/10.1017/CBO9781139004206

Hoey, M. (2005). *Lexical priming. A new theory of words and language*. Abington, England: Routledge.

Hunston, S. (2002). *Corpora in applied linguistics*. http://dx.doi.org/10.1017/CBO9781139524773

Hunston, S., & Francis, G. (2000). *Pattern grammar: A corpus-driven approach to the lexical grammar of English*. http://dx.doi.org/10.1075/scl.4

Jackendoff, R. (2002). *Foundations of language: Brain, meaning, grammar, evolution*. http://dx.doi.org/10.1093/acprof:oso/9780198270126.001.0001

Krug, M. (1998). String frequency: A cognitive motivating factor in coalescence, language processing, and linguistic change. *Journal of English Linguistics*, *26*, 286–320. http://dx.doi.org/10.1177/007542429802600402

Krug, M. (2003). Frequency as a determinant in grammatical variation and change. In G. Rohdenburg & B. Mondorf (Eds.), *Determinants of grammatical variation in English* (pp. 7–67). http://dx.doi.org/10.1515/9783110900019.7

Küchenhoff, H., & Schmid, H.-J. (2015). Reply to "More (old and new) misunderstandings of collostructional analysis: On Schmid & Küchenhoff" by Stefan Th. Gries. *Cognitive Linguistics*, *26*, 537–547. http://dx.doi.org/10.1515/cog-2015-0053

Langacker, R. W. (1987). *Foundations of cognitive grammar: Vol. 1. Theoretical prerequisites*. Stanford, CA: Stanford University Press.

Langacker, R. W. (1991). *Foundations of cognitive grammar: Vol. 2. Descriptive applications*. Stanford, CA: Stanford University Press.

Langacker, R. W. (2008). *Cognitive grammar: A basic introduction*. http://dx.doi.org/10.1093/acprof:oso/9780195331967.001.0001

Leech, G., Hundt, M., Mair, C., & Smith, N. (2009). *Change in contemporary English: A grammatical study*. http://dx.doi.org/10.1017/CBO9780511642210

Lieven, E. (2010). Input and first language acquisition: Evaluating the role of frequency. *Lingua*, *120*, 2546–2556. http://dx.doi.org/10.1016/j.lingua.2010.06.005

Lieven, E., & Tomasello, M. (2008). Children's first language acquisition from a usage-based perspective. In P. Robinson & N. C. Ellis (Eds.), *Handbook of cognitive linguistics and second language acquisition* (pp. 168–196). New York, NY: Routledge.

MacWhinney, B. (2000). *The CHILDES project: Tools for analyzing talk*. Mahwah, NJ: Erlbaum.

MacWhinney, B. (2008). A unified model. In P. J. Robinson & N. C. Ellis (Eds.), *Handbook of cognitive linguistics and second language acquisition* (pp. 341–371). New York, NY: Routledge.

Mair, C. (2004). Corpus linguistics and grammaticalisation theory: Statistics, frequencies, and beyond. In H. Lindquist & C. Mair (Eds.), *Studies in corpus linguistics* (Vol. 13, pp. 121–150). http://dx.doi.org/10.1075/scl.13.07mai

Mair, C. (2006). *Twentieth-century English: History, variation and standardization*. http://dx.doi.org/10.1017/CBO9780511486951

Makkai, A. (1972). *Idiom structure in English.* http://dx.doi.org/10.1515/9783110812671

Marslen-Wilson, W. D., Komisarjevsky, L., Waksler, R., & Older, L. (1994). Morphology and meaning in the English mental lexicon. *Psychological Review, 101,* 3–33. http://dx.doi.org/10.1037/0033-295X.101.1.3

Martinet, A. (1960). *Éléments de linguistique générale* [Elements of general linguistics]. Paris, France: Colin.

McEnery, T., & Hardie, A. (2012). *Corpus linguistics: Method, theory and practice.* Cambridge, England: Cambridge University Press.

Pedersen, T. (1996). Fishing for exactness. *Proceedings of the South-Central SAS Users Group Conference* (SCSUG-96), 188–200. Austin, TX.

Perek, F. (2015). *Argument structure in usage-based construction grammar: Experimental and corpus-based perspectives.* Amsterdam, the Netherlands: Benjamins.

Reisberg, D. (Ed.). (2013). *The Oxford handbook of cognitive psychology.* http://dx.doi.org/10.1093/oxfordhb/9780195376746.001.0001

Saffran, J. R., Newport, E. L., & Aslin, R. N. (1996). Word segmentation: The role of distributional cues. *Journal of Memory and Language, 35,* 606–621. http://dx.doi.org/10.1006/jmla.1996.0032

Schäfer, R., & Bildhauer, F. (2012). Building large corpora from the web using a new efficient tool chain. In N. Calzolari, K. Choukri, T. Declerck, M. Uğur Doğan, B. Maegaard, J. Mariani, ... S. Piperidis (Eds.), *Proceedings of the Eighth International Conference on Language Resources and Evaluation* (LREC-12; pp. 486–493). Istanbul, Turkey: ELRA.

Schmid, H.-J. (2000). *English abstract nouns as conceptual shells: From corpus to cognition.* http://dx.doi.org/10.1515/9783110808704

Schmid, H.-J. (2010). Does frequency in text instantiate entrenchment in the cognitive system? In D. Glynn & K. Fischer (Eds.), *Quantitative methods in cognitive semantics: Corpus-driven approaches* (pp. 101–133). http://dx.doi.org/10.1515/9783110226423.101

Schmid, H.-J., & Küchenhoff, H. (2013). Collostructional analysis and other ways of measuring lexicogrammatical attraction: Theoretical premises, practical problems and cognitive underpinnings. *Cognitive Linguistics, 24,* 531–577. http://dx.doi.org/10.1515/cog-2013-0018

Schmid, H.-J., & Mantlik, A. (2015). Entrenchment in historical corpora? Reconstructing dead authors' minds from their usage profiles. *Anglia, 133,* 583–623. http://dx.doi.org/10.1515/ang-2015-0056

Schneider, U. (2014). *Frequency, chunks and hesitations. A usage-based analysis of chunking in English* (Doctoral dissertation). Albert-Ludwigs-Universität, Freiburg, Germany.

Schönefeld, D. (2012). Things going unnoticed—A usage-based analysis of *go*-constructions. In D. Divjak & S. T. Gries (Eds.), *Frequency effects in language representation* (Vol. 2, pp. 11–49). Berlin, Germany: De Gruyter Mouton.

Sinclair, J. (1991). *Corpus, concordance, collocation.* Oxford, England: Oxford University Press.

Stefanowitsch, A. (2008). Negative entrenchment: A usage-based approach to negative evidence. *Cognitive Linguistics, 19,* 513–531. http://dx.doi.org/10.1515/COGL.2008.020

Stefanowitsch, A. (2011). Cognitive linguistics meets the corpus. In M. Brdar, S. T. Gries, & M. Žic Fuchs (Eds.), *Cognitive linguistics: Convergence and expansion* (pp. 257–289). http://dx.doi.org/10.1075/hcp.32.16ste

Stefanowitsch, A., & Gries, S. T. (2003). Collostructions: Investigating the interaction of words and constructions. *International Journal of Corpus Linguistics, 8,* 209–243. http://dx.doi.org/10.1075/ijcl.8.2.03ste

Taylor, J. R. (2012). *The mental corpus: How language is represented in the mind.* http://dx.doi.org/10.1093/acprof:oso/9780199290802.001.0001

Theakston, A. L., Lieven, E. V. M., Pine, J. M., & Rowland, C. F. (2001). The role of performance limitations in the acquisition of verb-argument structure: An alternative account. *Journal of Child Language, 28,* 127–152. http://dx.doi.org/10.1017/S0305000900004608

Tomasello, M. (2003). *Constructing a language: A usage-based theory of language acquisition.* Cambridge, MA: Harvard University Press.

Traxler, M. J., & Gernsbacher, M. A. (2006). *Handbook of psycholinguistics.* Amsterdam, the Netherlands; Boston, MA: Elsevier/Academic Press.

Wiechmann, D. (2008). On the computation of collostruction strength: Testing measures of association as expressions of lexical bias. *Corpus Linguistics and Linguistic Theory, 4,* 253–290. http://dx.doi.org/10.1515/CLLT.2008.011

Wulff, S. (2008). *Rethinking idiomaticity: A usage-based approach.* London, England: Continuum.

Wulff, S. (2013). Words and idioms. In T. Hoffmann & G. Trousdale (Eds.), *The Oxford handbook of construction grammar* (pp. 274–289). Oxford, England: Oxford University Press.

Zeschel, A. (2008). Lexical chunking effects in syntactic processing. *Cognitive Linguistics, 19,* 427–446. http://dx.doi.org/10.1515/COGL.2008.016

Zeschel, A. (2010). Exemplars and analogy: Semantic extension in constructional networks. In D. Glynn & K. Fischer (Eds.), *Quantitative methods in cognitive semantics: Corpus-driven approaches* (pp. 201–219). Berlin, Germany: de Gruyter Mouton.

Alice Blumenthal-Dramé
6 Entrenchment From a Psycholinguistic and Neurolinguistic Perspective

6.1 Introduction

Across the various entrenchment definitions given in the cognitive linguistics literature, it is possible to identify the following recurring key ingredients: high frequency of use, great ease of processing, great strength of representation, high fluency of composition, and chunk status. Although the term *entrenchment* itself has little currency outside of usage-based cognitive linguistics, several strands of neurolinguistic and psycholinguistic research have investigated frequency effects on language processing and can therefore contribute to sharpening the cognitive linguistics notion of entrenchment. The present chapter aims to review this research, to discuss how it can be integrated into an empirically informed and coherent picture of linguistic entrenchment, and to outline some promising avenues for further research.

Section 6.2 provides an overview of how the notion of entrenchment has been defined in the cognitive linguistics literature, with a special focus on assumptions that are relevant to operationalizing entrenchment for experimental purposes. Section 6.3 presents experimental studies attesting to the fact that high-frequency expressions are processed with greater speed and accuracy than matched low-frequency expressions, probably as a result of enhanced fluency of composition. Section 6.4 reviews psycholinguistic and neurolinguistic research testing the relationship between chunk status and usage frequency. Section 6.5 highlights outstanding questions and sketches some possible directions in which future research might fruitfully proceed. Section 6.6 concludes the chapter.

Note that this review focuses on the entrenchment of transparent multimorphemic sequences, thus deliberately excluding relevant research on noncompositional sequences (e.g., *all of a sudden*, *kick the bucket*, *by and large*, see Croft, 2001, p. 15) and monomorphemic words (an overview of relevant research and further references can be found in Blumenthal-Dramé, 2012, and Schmid's introduction to this volume). This should clearly not be taken to imply that the notion of entrenchment is irrelevant or even inapplicable to nontransparent sequences or single words. However, by virtue of their being arbitrary form–meaning associations, such strings inherently have to be represented in a holistic fashion at some level, no matter how frequent. The maximally strong prediction that frequency on its own can induce chunk status—which, as will become clear later, must be seen as the theoretically most relevant entrenchment criterion—can only be tested on the basis of strings for which there is no logical necessity of resorting to a chunked representation, which explains the focus of the present chapter.

6.2 Defining Entrenchment

Many definitions of entrenchment in cognitive linguistics posit positive correlations among usage frequency, strength of memory representation, and ease of processing. Moreover, they share the view that entrenchment is a gradable phenomenon and that high degrees of entrenchment go along with chunk status (Croft & Cruse, 2004, p. 292; Langacker, 2008, pp. 16, 21, 38). This latter assumption was highlighted by De Smet and Cuyckens (2007), who claimed that an entrenched utterance "represents an automated, routinized chunk of language that is stored and activated by the language user as a whole, rather than 'creatively' assembled on the spot" (p. 188). As this quote illustrates, chunk status refers to the idea that a string which can be analyzed into smaller subcomponents (e.g., *I don't know*) is perceived as a unit, with unit status implying retrieval in a single step rather than access to its component parts (*I, do, not, know*) and their composition.

The presumed correlations among usage frequency, representation format, and processing ease directly follow from a number of premises that are distinctive of usage-based models of language. First, these models assume that people's language representations are continuously updated as a function of their everyday experience with language. This implies the more specific claims that every single string encountered in language use, no matter how complex, leaves a trace in memory and that memory traces determine the size and nature of mental units (Abbot-Smith & Tomasello, 2006; Bybee & McClelland, 2005; O'Grady, 2008). Second, unlike received models of language, usage-based models allow for massive representational redundancy, meaning that chunked and compositional representations (involving single morphemes along with rules for their composition) for one and the same string can coexist. Thus, the assumption that people have a chunked representation for a high-frequency expression such as *I don't know* does not exclude that they also have at their disposal (and to some extent even coactivate) separate representations for the individual component morphemes of this expression (*I, do, not,* and *know*) as well as relevant grammatical knowledge (e.g., knowledge about negation or word order in declarative sentences; Bybee, 2007, p. 301).

It is interesting to note that entrenchment definitions vary as to how they precisely model the impact of usage events on memory representation. Models broadly fall into two classes: holistic and syntagmatic. *Holistic* views (i.e., those focusing on part–whole relations) emphasize that every single usage event strengthens the memory trace for a complex, unanalyzed string as a whole (Hay & Baayen, 2005). This is thought to enhance the string's relative prominence in the cognitive system, making it more easily accessible than its individual component parts (for which autonomous

	Holistic	Syntagmatic
High-frequency whole	**[I don't know]** [I] [don't] [know]	Idontknow
Low-frequency whole	[You won't swim] **[You] [won't] [swim]**	You won't swim

Fig. 6.1: Different ways of modeling the impact of string frequency on mental representation.

representations are thought to exist owing to partial overlap between different strings stored in memory). Conversely, a string that is only rarely encountered is assumed to be weakly represented as a whole and therefore less readily activated than its component parts. Holistic models can thus be said to interpret frequency effects in terms of competition between representations for wholes and their parts (see Figure 6.1, Holistic column).

By contrast, *syntagmatic* accounts highlight sequential relations within strings. More specifically, they posit that every use of a given string increases the degree of syntagmatic fusion between its component morphemes. This development is thought to go along with a weakening of the connections between the coalescing morphemes and mentally related entries, notably paradigmatic alternatives, semantically related entries, and other forms of the same morphemes (Bybee & Torres Cacoullos, 2009). Conversely, morphemic identity is supposed to be preserved in low-frequency strings (see Figure 6.1, Syntagmatic column).

In the Holistic column, brackets indicate mental units. The units' relative representation strength is reflected by bold versus light font, and their relative time course of activation is indicated by line indentation. The top cell shows the cognitive precedence of a high-frequency string over its component parts. The bottom cell illustrates the opposite scenario. In the Syntagmatic column, the degree of syntagmatic fusion as a function of string frequency is expressed by word spacing. Note that this figure is a gross oversimplification in that it assumes that all subcomponents are equally strongly represented and that it does not take into consideration the status of substrings such as *you won't* or *don't know*.

Note that these perspectives are not as far apart conceptually as they might initially appear—they might even be seen as capturing exactly the same information in formally different ways. Thus, both accounts challenge the received view that the morphemes of all transparent language sequences are indiscriminately accessed in online processing. Rather, the extent to which a (descriptive) morpheme is separately accessed depends on the usage frequency of the sequence in which it is embedded. As a result, on both accounts, the constituent morphemes of higher frequency sequences are cognitively less prominent than those of lower frequency sequences. Both perspectives are therefore perfectly in line with the usage-based tenet that frequency is more than a superficial performance phenomenon affecting the efficiency of computational operations on context-independent primitive building blocks of language.

The main conceptual difference resides in the fact that under the holistic view, memory traces of different grain size and representation strength compete for priority in online processing. By contrast, under the syntagmatic view, the relevant knowledge is available in a precompiled format that condenses information about the relationship between memory traces into a single representation. However, it is not clear at present how these two perspectives can be empirically distinguished (Docherty & Foulkes, 2014), and they are often treated as not being mutually exclusive—witness the following quote, in which Bybee (2007) explicitly claims that both the level of holistic accessibility and the level of syntagmatic fusion coevolve under the effect of frequency:

> Each token of use of a word or sequence of words strengthens its representation and makes it more easily accessed. In addition, each instance of use further automates and increases the fluency of the sequence, leading to fusion of the units. (p. 324)

However, most entrenchment definitions are neutral as to the representational dimension along which units arise:

> With repeated use, a novel structure becomes progressively entrenched, to the point of becoming a unit; moreover, units are variably entrenched depending on the frequency of their occurrence. (Langacker, 1987, p. 59)

Langacker's (1987) definition also nicely illustrates a further feature shared by most entrenchment definitions: It traces the evolution from less to more entrenched sequences. However, it is important to note that although from a usage-based perspective, this direction of evolution is certainly not precluded, it cannot be taken to hold across the board. Unlike received theories of language, usage-based models do not posit morphemes and rules to represent ontogenetic priors from which all complex expressions are necessarily derived. Rather, in line with the holistic view, unanalyzed exemplars encountered in natural language use are considered to be the atoms of language, with morphemes and combinatory rules representing emergent abstractions (Arnon & Snider, 2010; Lieven & Tomasello, 2008).

This implies that a cognitive development from more to less entrenched representations is not only conceivable but possibly even the default case, at least during certain developmental periods. Thus, a child might grasp the overall communicative function of the expression *I don't know* (and even use it appropriately) well before being able to separately handle its constituent parts and the relevant grammatical rules (see Theakston, Chapter 14, this volume). By contrast, the scenario taken for granted by most entrenchment definitions applies to situations where the cognitive prominence of a complex string increases relative to that of connected representations. For example, someone starting a new job as a shop assistant might come to represent an expression that is highly frequent in the relevant field (e.g., "Please enter your PIN") in an increasingly entrenched fashion (for a similar example, see Schmid, 2014, p. 249).

6.3 Entrenchment and Ease of Processing: Experimental Perspectives

6.3.1 Interpreting Ease of Processing

The last years have seen a huge increase in neurolinguistic and psycholinguistic studies examining the effects of usage frequency on the processing of transparent multimorphemic strings. These studies have exploited different tasks (e.g., self-paced reading, decision tasks, or memory tests), technologies (from pen-and-paper tasks via eye-tracking to brain mapping methods such as electroencephalography and functional magnetic resonance imaging [fMRI]), and dependent variables (response times, response accuracies, different eye movement measures, as well as more and less direct measures of neural activity) and have typically identified a positive correlation between processing ease and frequency.

Although this finding has often been interpreted in terms of holistic storage, it is important to emphasize from the outset that most of these studies actually give no reason to reject the null hypothesis that higher frequency strings are simply assembled with greater ease and efficiency than matched lower frequency counterparts. As a result, they cannot be taken to unequivocally support usage-based models over competing models that consider frequency as a mere performance phenomenon affecting the efficiency of computations, without challenging the cognitive status of the underlying building blocks.

One way to think about these competing models is that they consider frequency to modulate the accessibility of the component morphemes of a string (e.g., *I don't know* is processed more quickly than *you won't swim* because *I*, *don't*, and *know* are more easily retrieved than *you*, *won't* and *swim*). However, such a model would not be able to accommodate the finding that the processing advantage for high-frequency strings persists even when the token frequencies of component morphemes are kept constant (i.e., when strings are of different token frequencies but their component morphemes are equally frequent, e.g., *don't have to worry* vs. *don't have to wait*; Arnon & Snider, 2010).

A more plausible way of thinking about such models, therefore, is that they consider frequency to affect the connection weights between morphemes (possibly even beyond immediately adjacent morphemes), but not the morphemes themselves. On this view, morphemes represent the context-invariant and unconditional primitive building blocks of any transparent language sequence but are more or less easy to assemble depending on frequency (see Figure 6.2).

This chapter adopts a conservative approach in considering that studies that do not specifically test for chunk status only support the weaker view, that is, higher fluency of composition. The present section reviews such studies, whereas the next section is devoted to studies focusing on chunk status proper.

```
I ↔ don't ↔ know
You ↔ won't ↔ swim
```

Fig. 6.2: Syntagmatic connection weights between morphemes in high- versus low-frequency sequences. According to models assuming across-the-board bottom-up composition, the identity of morphemes is not affected by frequency.

6.3.2 A Few Words on Experimental Paradigms

This section offers some essential background knowledge on experimental techniques that have been used to explore the cognitive effects of string frequency and that will be taken for granted in the rest of this chapter (readers with prior knowledge in the field may safely skip this section).

In a typical self-paced reading experiment, subjects are asked to click their way through a sentence presented word by word, with response times (RTs) being recorded for each word. To keep attention constant and to ensure some processing depth, subjects are often asked to perform an additional task, such as responding to a yes–no comprehension question after each sentence. Likewise, in so-called decision tasks, subjects have to judge, as quickly as possible, whether a given word, phrase, or sentence is acceptable in their language. Decision tasks are often combined with priming, which measures the extent to which responses to target stimuli vary as a function of properties of other stimuli ("primes") presented in the course of the experiment. Responses are typically made via button press, and RTs as well as response accuracies are collected. In priming experiments, RTs are assumed to vary as a function of the degree of mental relatedness between prime and target such that more tightly associated stimuli yield lower RTs (Blumenthal-Dramé, 2012).

As valuable as these and many other traditional psycholinguistic paradigms have proven to be, they compress the results of complex and potentially interacting cognitive processes unfolding at the scale of milliseconds into a single behavioral output (typically, but not necessarily, reflecting the end state of some critical process; Siyanova-Chanturia, 2013; Stemmer & Connolly, 2011). By contrast, more recent and sophisticated tools make it possible to record language processing in real time. Thus, eye-trackers make it possible to monitor online the eye movements of subjects while they complete language-related tasks (e.g., reading or looking at pictures while listening to speech; see Günther, Müller, & Geyer, Chapter 13, this volume). Likewise, event-related brain potentials (ERPs) in electroencephalography (EEG) afford immediate insights into the action potentials generated by large populations of cortical neurons in response to stimuli of interest (Ingram, 2007, pp. 59–61). Besides their ability to track dynamic language processing in real time, ERPs and eye movements are also ecologically more valid than the earlier-mentioned paradigms to the extent that they do not require people to push buttons. On a more negative note, however, it must be acknowledged that completing a task with an electrode cap or an eye-tracker mounted on one's head is still anything but natural (even though techniques are constantly improving). Moreover, like purely behavioral experiments, such techniques typically require highly artificial stimuli and conditions for effects to be measurable.

Another noninvasive technique for measuring the neurophysiological correlates of language processing is fMRI. fMRI capitalizes on the fact that neural activity triggers local changes in cerebral blood oxygenation, thereby inducing minute changes in magnetic blood properties. These changes are captured by the so-called blood oxygen-level dependent (BOLD) signal. In other words, the BOLD signal tracks the hemodynamic (or metabolic) response that supplies neurons a few seconds after their activity, which has two important implications: first, the BOLD signal represents a much less direct reflection of neural activity than ERPs from EEG. Moreover, it offers comparatively weak temporal resolution, making it impossible to track how the brain dynamically reacts to stimuli in real time. However, because of its impressive spatial resolution, the fMRI BOLD response is useful to pinpoint brain areas whose activity changes during a specific linguistic task.

6.3.3 Testing Fluency of Composition

Several phrasal decision and self-paced reading experiments have shown that higher frequency sequences yield lower reaction times than matched lower frequency sequences. Thus, phrasal decision tasks by Bod (2001) show that native speakers of English react more quickly to high- than to low-frequency strings (e.g., *I like it* vs. *I keep it*). Likewise, on the basis of grammaticality judgment tasks, Jiang and Nekrasova (2007) demonstrated that both native and nonnative speakers of English respond significantly faster and more accurately to high- versus low-frequency multiword expressions (e.g., *to begin with* vs. *to dance with*). A similar point was made by Arnon and Snider (2010), who conducted phrasal decision experiments showing that the processing time for compositional four-word phrases (e.g., *don't have to worry*) correlates negatively with their string frequency in a fashion that is not reducible to the frequencies of individual component words or substrings.

In a similar vein, several self-paced reading experiments by Bannard (2006) revealed that high-frequency phrases are read significantly quicker than infrequent counterparts. This holds both for sequences that are identical except for the terminal word (e.g., *a state of pregnancy* vs. *a state of emergency*) and for sequences that merely share syntactic form but are matched in terms of length in letters, component word frequencies, and sequence-internal transitional probabilities (*from the point of view* vs. *about the role of taste*). Tremblay, Derwing, Libben, and Westbury (2011) found lower self-paced reading times as well as better recall accuracy for high- versus low-frequency strings (*in the middle of the* vs. *in the front of the*). Siyanova-Chanturia, Conklin, and van Heuven (2011) tracked eye movements while participants read so-called irreversible binomial expressions, that is, three-word-sequences consisting of two lexical items from the same part of speech connected by *and*, with one word order being more frequently attested than the reversed one (e.g., *bride and groom* vs. *groom and bride*; *east and west* vs. *west and east*). Among other things, the authors find that phrasal frequency significantly correlates with eye-tracking measures reflecting different stages of online reading, thereby attesting to the cognitive pervasiveness of frequency effects.

Converging evidence for the effect of string frequency comes from speech experiments. Arnon and Priva (2013) demonstrated that the frequency of multiword sequences correlates inversely with their phonetic duration in both elicited and spontaneous speech. More specifically, the phonetic duration of a sequence such as *a lot of* differs depending on whether it is embedded into a high-frequency (e.g., *a lot of work*) or low-frequency (e.g., *a lot of years*) sequence. This modulation occurs across the whole frequency spectrum and is not attributable to substring frequencies or other variables that might modulate phonetic durations. Tremblay and Tucker (2011) presented a speech experiment comparing the influence of different probabilistic measures on voice onset latency (thought to reflect the efficiency of sequence recognition) and sequence production duration. Participants were asked to read visually presented four-word sequences (e.g., *at the same time, this is not a*) appearing on a screen as quickly as possible. Measures related to logarithmic probability of occurrence turned out to be the most relevant predictors of voice onset latency. By contrast, frequency of whole-string occurrence was the best predictor for production durations, to the effect that higher frequencies correlated with lower durations.

Tremblay and Baayen (2010) compared ERPs and behavioral responses with regular four-word sequences of different usage frequencies (*in the middle of, becoming increasingly clear that*). Participants had to complete an immediate free recall task, which involved reproducing items from a previously memorized list in any order. Tremblay and Baayen found that the number of correctly recalled sequences varied as a function of whole-sequence probability of occurrence (more exactly, the logarithmic probability of obtaining the last word given the three initial words of the sequence), sequence-internal word frequencies, and trigram frequencies (i.e., the frequency of the two three-word substrings in a four-word-sequence). ERPs to correctly remembered sequences showed that whole-sequence probability modulates amplitudes at the early time window of about 110 to 150 ms after stimulus onset. On the basis of previous research linking this time window to frequency effects in single words, Tremblay and Baayen concluded that high-frequency four-word sequences must to some extent be represented in a wordlike (i.e., holistic) fashion. However, as Siyanova-Chanturia (2015) pointed out, this conclusion has to be taken with a grain of salt because the relevant amplitudes might just as well be taken to reflect language-independent attentional processes.

Blumenthal-Dramé (2012) and Blumenthal-Dramé et al. (2016) report a masked priming study involving bimorphemic derivatives of different usage frequencies (e.g., *kissable, worthless, settlement*). Their priming paradigm exploits the so-called sandwich technique (Forster & Davis, 1984), which consists in inserting a briefly displayed prime (60 ms) between a forward mask (a row of hash marks) and a target that functions as a backward mask that disrupts the initial prime processing stages. Because of the masks and the short prime presentation times, this paradigm provides a window into very early stages of word processing. Moreover, it has the advantage that primes are not available for report and that reactions to targets cannot be distorted by conscious strategies (even though certain participants perceive a kind of flash before the target).

Nineteen native speakers of English were asked to complete lexical decision on 612 targets from different prime–target conditions presented in randomly intermixed order. One of these conditions (108 prime–target pairs) examined part-to-whole priming. More specifically, this condition analyzed whether the extent to which derivatives (e.g., *paleness, worthless*) are preactivated by their bases (*pale, worth*) varies as a function of usage frequency. Different frequency measures relating to the bases, the derivatives, and their relationship (as well as further psycholinguistic metrics) were compared for their predictive power. Logarithmically transformed relative frequency (the usage frequency of the derivative relative to that of its base; henceforth LogRelFreq) surfaced as the best entrenchment predictor in terms of RTs. Applied to the condition at hand, this means that pairs such as *worth–worthless* (high LogRelFreq) elicit lower RTs than pairs such as *tear–tearless* (low LogRelFreq).

The fMRI correlate of reduced RTs in priming is the phenomenon of fMRI adaptation, which refers to increases or decreases in BOLD activity as a function of the degree of prime–target relatedness (for a review, see Segaert, Weber, de Lange, Petersson, & Hagoort, 2013). In line with this, the parametric whole-brain analysis carried out by Blumenthal-Dramé and colleagues identifies several brain clusters with a negative correlation between BOLD signal and LogRelFreq. In these clusters, prime–target pairs such as *prophet–prophetess* (low LogRelFreq) elicit more activity than pairs such as *agree–agreement* (high LogRelFreq). The largest of these clusters is located in left frontal regions and peaks in the *pars triangularis* (Brodmann's area [BA] 45), which is part of Broca's area, the classical language area. In addition, the analyses also reveal a few clusters displaying the reverse pattern, that is, a positive correlation between BOLD signal and LogRelFreq. In these regions (located around the right superior medial gyrus, the precunei, the middle cingulate cortices, and the right angular gyrus), prime–target pairs such as *doubt–doubtful* (high LogRelFreq) yield a stronger BOLD signal than pairs such as *soft–softish* (low LogRelFreq). A thorough interpretation of these localizations is beyond the scope of the present survey, but as Blumenthal-Dramé et al. (2016) show, they are perfectly in line with the view that higher degrees of entrenchment go along with tighter syntagmatic bonds between morphemes and accordingly lower cognitive demands in a priming direction that taps into our sequential experience with language.

6.4 Entrenchment and Chunk Status: Experimental Perspectives

6.4.1 Operationalizing Chunk Status

As stated earlier, although the findings reported in Section 6.3 are both suggestive and interesting in their own right, they do not conclusively demonstrate that the relevant sequences are represented in a holistic format because subjects may simply assemble them with greater ease and efficiency as a result of greater association strengths between morphemes. This section reviews studies confirming the usage-based view that the cognitive difference between high- and low-frequency sequences is not reducible to connection weights between fully independent and bottom-up accessed morphemes but that chunk status does indeed play a role.

Chunk status will be interpreted in terms of the notion of global precedence, which is familiar from the experimental literature on holistic Gestalt perception (see Gobet, Chapter 11, this volume) across different domains of cognition (e.g., face perception). According to this notion, a configuration of elements qualifies as a cognitive chunk, if the configuration as a whole is cognitively more prominent than its individual component parts. This view dovetails nicely with the usage-based tenet that chunk status is a gradient property that arises from the interplay between complex wholes and their component parts (Bybee, 2010; Hay & Baayen, 2005). Note, however, that it might not actually be in line with most people's phenomenal experience, where chunk status might rather feel like an all-or-nothing quality.

One common way of operationalizing cognitive precedence is in terms of greater ease of access to the whole than to its parts ("seeing the forest before the trees"; de-Wit & Wagemans, 2015; Poljac, de-Wit, & Wagemans, 2012; Pomerantz & Cragin, 2015). This criterion, which has been exploited by various psychological experiments tracking the relative time course of access to representation levels, can be illustrated by means of so-called Navon figures (Navon, 1977; see Figure 6.3): When confronted with complex hierarchical stimuli such as big letters made up of smaller letters, subjects with no mental disabilities will not systematically proceed from parts to wholes. Rather, as experiments have shown, the first and only necessary processing stage involves access to the global level (Kimchi, 2015).

A further way of operationalizing cognitive precedence is in terms of top-down effects of higher on lower levels (Engel, Fries, & Singer, 2001, p. 705). This implies the even stronger assumption that in chunks, the whole is not only accessed before its parts but also influences how these parts are interpreted or even perceived. Top-down effects have long been invoked by interactive activation models to account for well-known psycholinguistic phenomena such as the *word superiority effect* (i.e., the finding that letters are easier to recognize in real words such as FATHER than in nonwords like JBDVLM) or the *pseudohomophone effect* (pseudohomophones such as *taksi* are

```
AA              AA
AA              AA
AA              AA
AA              AA
AA              AA
AA              AA
AAAAAAAAAAAAAAAAAAAA
AAAAAAAAAAAAAAAAAAAA
AA              AA
AA              AA
AA              AA
AA              AA
AA              AA
AA              AA
```

Fig. 6.3: Illustrations of the principle of global precedence. When processing a typical Navon letter, people will access the global before the local level.

more difficult to identify as nonwords than strings not sounding like a real word, e.g., *tatsi*; Carreiras, Armstrong, Perea, & Frost, 2014; Twomey, Kawabata Duncan, Price, & Devlin, 2011). Interactive activation models interpret top-down effects in terms of bidirectional information flow between higher and lower levels. More specifically, they assume that partially resolved sensory input can offer a direct shortcut to high-level knowledge (broadly speaking, any information associated with a given stimulus on the basis of prior experience), which then top-down constrains how further incoming input is processed.

On a more general plane, the assumptions on global precedence presented in this section tie in perfectly with the much-debated hierarchical predictive coding paradigm in the cognitive neurosciences, which has recently been described as "a genuine departure from many of our previous ways of thinking about perception, cognition, and the human cognitive architecture" (Clark, 2013, p. 7; see also Günther, Müller, & Geyer, Chapter 13, this volume). One core tenet of this paradigm is that from the very first stages of processing, incoming sensory information is matched with and constrained by high-level representations, which play an active and driving role in generating the perceptions that we have (Bar & Bubic, 2013; Hohwy, 2013). In line with Gestalt theory, this paradigm thus turns standard bottom-up accounts of perception upside down because the brain need not extract and fully process all available input to arrive at a perceptual estimate of the world.

6.4.2 Testing Frequency-Induced Chunk Status

Experiments with an explicit focus on the relationship between chunking and frequency in compositional language sequences are admittedly still sparse. Caldwell-

Harris, Berant, and Edelman (2012) set out to test whether words really are "the privileged unit of mental representation of processing that all... scientific attention makes them out to be" (p. 166). They described several experiments exploiting the psycholinguistic technique of perceptual identification in which a linguistic stimulus is presented on a screen for less than 100 ms and then replaced by a visual mask (e.g., a row of hash marks) to disrupt the normal processing flow. Although subjects in such experiments tend to have the impression that they cannot read the stimuli, they are actually able to guess their identity above chance, especially when the stimuli are cognitively highly accessible, that is, strongly entrenched.

Caldwell-Harris et al.'s (2012) experiments demonstrated that such top-down effects also extend to multiword sequences and that strength of entrenchment need not always enhance identification accuracy but may also decrease it by inducing miscorrection. More specifically, they reported a statistical correlation between the purported degree of entrenchment of two-word sequences (gauged in terms of their log string frequencies across different corpora) and the probability of subjects perceiving them in their expected order even though they are actually displayed in sequentially reversed order (e.g., perceiving *next step* when presented with *step* followed by *next*). These "reversal errors" are strongest for high-frequency collocations (e.g., *zip code*, *fan club*, *health care*), second highest for lower frequency word combinations (e.g., *machine gun*), next for rare or unattested adjective–noun combinations (e.g., *huge church*), and lowest for random word pairs (e.g., *puppy hill*, *weep job*). This effect persisted even when subjects' attention was explicitly drawn to the fact that certain stimuli are presented in noncanonical order.

A few experiments have started to investigate the neurofunctional underpinnings of frequency-related chunking. Thus, the masked priming fMRI experiments by Blumenthal-Dramé and colleagues (Blumenthal-Dramé, 2012; Blumenthal-Dramé et al., 2016; see also Section 6.3.3) included a condition specifically designed to test the prediction that "chunkedness" varies as a function of usage frequency. More concretely, this condition examined whole-to-part priming (e.g., *gauntness–gaunt*), thereby reversing the stimulus order relative to the part-to-whole priming condition presented in Section 6.3.3. Starting from the assumptions that frequency correlates with chunk status and that chunk status implies greater ease of access to the whole than to its parts, Blumenthal-Dramé and colleagues predicted a negative correlation between the usage frequency of a derivative and the degree to which its morphemic component parts are coactivated in the early processing stages tracked by masked priming. In other words, they expected weaker priming for pairs such as *harmless–harm* than for pairs such as *gauntness–gaunt*. LogRelFreq turned out to correlate with chunk status in the predicted way.

The fMRI analysis identified several neuronal clusters where BOLD signal increases as a function of LogRelFreq (no effects were observed in the opposite direction). The largest activation cluster was located in left frontal regions around the left precentral gyrus (BA 6) and extended into the *pars opercularis* (BA 44), the Rolandic operculum and the *pars triangularis* (BA 45). Neurolinguistic research has related this area to morphological decomposition (Bozic, Marslen-Wilson, Stamatakis, Davis, & Tyler, 2007; Marslen-Wilson & Tyler, 2007; Pliatsikas, Wheeldon, Lahiri, & Hansen, 2014) and monomorphemic word retrieval alike (Buckner, Koutstaal, Schacter, & Rosen, 2000; Hauk, Davis, & Pulvermüller, 2008; Taylor, Rastle, & Davis, 2013). Blumenthal-Dramé et al.'s (Blumenthal-Dramé, 2012; Blumenthal-Dramé et al., 2016) results did not allow them to adjudicate between these interpretations. As a consequence, the left frontal activation observed in this experimental condition might either reflect difficulty of prime decomposition or difficulty retrieving the target, given a more or less closely connected prime. Importantly, however, both alternatives are in line with the assumption that parts of more frequent (and thus more entrenched) wholes are more difficult to activate.

It is interesting to note that compatible findings have been reported with regard to the submorphemic level. Thus, the ease of detecting nonmorphemic /ʌp/ in spoken sequences has been shown to correlate inversely with the frequency of the word in which this stimulus is embedded (e.g., *puppy, hiccups*; Kapatsinski & Radicke, 2009). Likewise, at the morphemic level, spoken *of* is more difficult to detect when it is part of extremely frequent (*lot of, kind of*) compared with lower frequency (*piece of, sense of*) combinations (Sosa & MacFarlane, 2002). By contrast, the detection of the particle /ʌp/ in verb-*up* combinations has been reported to be slowed down for both high- and low-frequency combinations relative to those in the middle range (Kapatsinski & Radicke, 2009). Initial neurophysiological findings are in line with the view that known verb–particle combinations can be stored in a holistic fashion and suggest no significant differences between semantically fully transparent (*rise up*) and metaphorical (*heat up*) combinations (Cappelle, Shtyrov, & Pulvermüller, 2010). However, the extent to which semantic transparency (e.g., *give up, look up,* and *go up*) interacts with frequency-induced entrenchment has not been systematically explored so far and remains an interesting topic for further research.

6.5 Outstanding Questions

As the last two sections have shown, usage-based entrenchment assumptions have received increasing experimental attention in recent years. As a result, the situation that "there was still very little investigation into the nature of the effects of repetition or frequency on the cognitive representation of language" (Bybee, 2007, pp. 6–7) has begun to be at least partially remedied. However, we are still a long way from fully understanding the intricate relationships among usage frequency, entrenchment, and others factors that might modulate the strength and autonomy of linguistic representations in our minds. The present section aims to sketch some questions that might drive the field forward in the not too distant future. Overall, it will be argued that empirical research should explore the boundaries of entrenchment along the schematic dimension by exploring representations that are not (or not entirely) lexically specific. Moreover, it would be fruitful to investigate in more detail how long-term entrenchment interacts with online processing and, finally, to find out more about the extent to which there might exist intersubjective differences in cognitive style that are relevant to entrenchment.

6.5.1 Entrenchment at Abstract Levels of Representation

In the usage-based view, the phenomenon of entrenchment is not restricted to lexically specific sentences but also applies to schemas (see Schmid, Chapter 1, this volume). Thus, Langacker (2009) claimed that "both specific expressions and abstracted schemas are capable of being entrenched psychologically and conventionalized in a speech community, in which case they constitute established linguistic units" (p. 2).

A schema is a more or less abstract pattern that captures the commonalities between all experienced exemplars that it subsumes, thereby imposing constraints on new exemplars (Langacker, 1987, p. 492). An example of a semiabstract schema is HAVE a Y, where Y represents a variable (or "open slot") that can be filled by a restricted range of lexical fillers (e.g., *drink, run, swim, jog, lie down*) and where the small caps in HAVE are supposed to indicate that different forms of this verb can be used (e.g., *had, will have, is having*). The degree of abstraction of a schema is thought to depend on the number and scope of variables it contains. The scope of a slot is determined by its type frequency (i.e., the number of distinct fillers that it covers) and by the degree of similarity between the attested slot-fillers (less similar fillers require higher level abstractions; Behrens, 2009; Bybee, 2010, p. 9; Croft, 2001, p. 28). The most general schemas are those in which all elements are lexically unspecific. A case in point is the so-called resultative construction consisting of a noun phrase (NP), a verb, a second NP, and an adjective (e.g., *The hammer pounded the metal flat*; Goldberg, 1995, p. 193).

In what way is the notion of entrenchment relevant to (semi-)abstract patterns? It is important to emphasize that the two most specific entrenchment criteria seem to have been proposed with lexically specific, compositional sequences in mind because they presuppose the existence of potentially autonomous subcomponents and of options. Thus, the chunking criterion is informative only to the extent that it is applied to sequences which could logically also be represented in a nonchunked format. Likewise, the fluency-of-composition criterion only makes sense when there is something to compose in the first place. However, the nature of schemas is precisely to unify autonomous units and to abstract from options.

Moreover, schemas are generally described as arbitrary form–meaning pairings that are simply more abstract than words or noncompositional idioms. As has been extensively discussed in the usage-based literature, there are good reasons to believe that abstract schemas carry meaning, independently of the meanings contributed by their specific lexical fillers (see Goldberg, 1995). This provides further support to the view that schemas must be seen as constituting single choices that represent chunks by definition. It also means that chunking and ease of composition seem unsuitable as a means of operationalizing entrenchment at the (semi-)schematic level.

As a result, the only entrenchment criterion that seems applicable to schemas is strength of representation, measured in terms of ease of activation. But what modulates the degree of accessibility of schemas? Let's discuss this on the basis of a concrete example, the schema for the double object dative construction NP1 – VERB – NP2 – NP3 (e.g., *Mary gave me a book*). On the usage-based account, the extent to which this schema is activated on any processing occasion where it is descriptively involved depends on the cognitive accessibility of competing representations. Under a maximally narrow interpretation, competing representations in language comprehension are all those that can be exploited to process a given lexically specific string. Remember from Section 6.2 that usage-based cognitive linguists assume that language users can draw on redundant levels of representation for one and the same string, with abstractions either being computed online (and thus only potentially available) or being stored in long-term memory (and thus always available and "waiting for" retrieval), depending on the specific version of usage-based linguistics adopted.

Whatever the specific account, the assumption is that the following representations are in some way available to process a string like *He gave me a book*:

- The maximally abstract schema (NP1 – VERB – NP2 – NP3), as well as its concrete slot-fillers (*He, gave, me, a, book*).
- The lexically specific representation stored as such (*He gave me a book*).
- A number of (more and less abstract) intermediate representations combining lexically concrete material with open slots (e.g., NP1 *gave me* NP3, *He gave me* NP3, etc.), as well as the fillers of these slots.

Note that especially the third option represents a gross oversimplification because it is plausible to assume that speakers' medium-level representations differ from maximally abstract schemas not only in terms of the number of open slots but also in their scope. Thus, although the notation NP1 in the third option suggests any subject semantically compatible with *giving* to be covered by the schema, it could also be the case that language users have at their disposal slots of smaller scope (e.g., subsuming only third-person personal pronouns).[1]

---

[1] A complete account of competition would, of course, need to take into account further representations posited to exist by usage-based construction grammars. These include potential argument-structure alternations (i.e., alternative schemas that are functionally broadly equivalent and allow for a common subset of lexical fillers, such as the prepositional dative construction NP1 VERB NP2 *to* NP3 [*He gave a book to me*] relative to the preceding double object construction), along with their different abstraction levels. Moreover, in the usage-based view, a given string may instantiate several schemas at the same time (e.g., *He didn't give me a book* instantiates not only the double object construction but also the negative construction; Croft, 2001, p. 25). Furthermore, a full and psycholinguistically informed account would also need to take into consideration nonconstructional (e.g., submorphemic) dimensions of competition, as well as the fact that competition varies as a function of task and modality.

It would be interesting to find out which of these competing levels is most entrenched (or, for that matter, separately represented), how these levels interact, and how this interaction can be captured in statistical terms. However, before sketching a few tentative thoughts on these questions, it is important to emphasize that claims pertaining to the entrenchment of schemas are inherently more general than those pertaining to the entrenchment of concrete strings: While statements about string entrenchment only generalize within and across subjects (a given string may be strongly entrenched in one subject, but less so in another subject, and a given subject may draw on more or less entrenched representations for one and the same string on different occasions), those about the entrenchment of a schema additionally abstract over all processing instances in which this schema is descriptively involved.

To put this in other words, if the notion of schema entrenchment is to have an added value over and above the notion of string entrenchment, the entrenchment of a schema must be seen as correlating inversely with the entrenchment of all its specific instantiations. This follows from the view that the activation of a schema in a single string processing instance essentially informs us about the entrenchment value of the relevant string (remember that low degrees of string entrenchment by definition involve high co-activation of schemas). Of course, such a result can also be taken to indicate that a certain level of abstraction has been reached by the cognitive system, but it does not tell us whether this level is representative or just a rarely reached maximal value.

To illustrate this on the basis of two made-up extreme scenarios, a schema that was exclusively realized by highly entrenched strings would be weakly entrenched or not cognitively represented at all because all its instantiations would be represented as self-contained units, with no links to descriptively related component parts and schemas. However, a schema that was only realized by weakly entrenched strings would be constantly activated and therefore highly entrenched. Importantly, this view implies that it is theoretically possible for a schema to be highly entrenched without being accessed in all circumstances.

A lot of interesting predictions follow from the redundancy and competition assumptions sketched here. One of these predictions is that strongly entrenched semiabstract representations should block the emergence and activation of maximally abstract representations in exactly the same way as strongly entrenched lexical strings do. This prediction also follows from the general "bottom-up orientation" of usage-based models, which propose that "lower-level schemas, expressing regularities of only limited scope, may in balance be more essential to language structure than high-level schemas representing the broadest generalizations" (Langacker, 2000, p. 118; see also Dąbrowska, 2004, p. 214). Maybe even more interesting is the prediction that identical string token frequencies should not mechanistically result in identical string entrenchment values. Rather, the degree of entrenchment of competing representations should play a role as well, to the extent that instances of more strongly entrenched schemas should require proportionally higher token frequencies to achieve the same entrenchment level.

An important question is how schema entrenchment can be empirically assessed. A rather indirect way of doing so would consist in measuring schema activation across a representative sample of strings. Here, the psycholinguistic method of choice would probably be structural priming, where subjects are presented with a prime sentence instantiating a certain schema (e.g., *He gave me a book*) and then prompted to read or produce a different target sentence. Structural priming occurs when subjects show a preference for the structure they have just experienced over functionally equivalent sentences with a different structure (e.g., *She sent him an e-mail* vs. *She sent an e-mail to him*). This difference can show up in terms of processing speed or, in production experiments, in terms of repetition, and can be interpreted as indicating the reactivation of a previously accessed schema.

Priming might also be the way to go to disentangle the representation and entrenchment of (semi-)abstract from totally abstract representations. It has often been documented that especially in language comprehension, the repetition of content words (especially the verb) or semantic features tends to significantly enhance structural priming (for reviews, see Pickering & Ferreira, 2008; Tooley, Swaab, Boudewyn, Zirnstein, & Traxler, 2014). This has been interpreted as showing that syntactic representations are not necessarily totally abstract but may also be associated with lexically specific items or featural constraints. From an entrenchment perspective, it would be fruitful to explore interactions between frequencies and priming effects at different levels of abstraction.

A more direct way of assessing schema entrenchment would be to measure its productivity (Croft, 2001, p. 28; for a somewhat different view, see Booij, 2013, p. 258). Productivity refers to language users' ability to creatively generalize from previously encountered to as yet unattested instances of a given schema, in both comprehension and production. Importantly, these productive extensions are not arbitrary but in line with top-down constraints that the schema imposes on its variables (e.g., **have an eat*, **He watched the TV broken*), indicating that language users actually represent these constraints and the relevant level of abstraction (Croft & Cruse, 2004, p. 243; Goldberg, 1995, p. 181).

In the long run, it would be interesting to find out how far the boundaries of entrenchment can be pushed in terms of complexity and abstractness. How complex and abstract can entrenched schemas be—for example, can schematic knowledge span several sentence boundaries?

6.5.2 Differences Between (and Within) Subjects

The usage-based framework assumes that our experience with language shapes its mental representation. This leads to the prediction that the entrenchment of linguistic sequences should vary between subjects as a function of their differential experience with language. Thus, Schmid (2014, p. 249) argues that the sequence *how can I help you today* is likely to be more strongly entrenched in hotline telephone counselors than other speakers of English. In line with this, Berant, Caldwell-Harris, and Edelman (2008) show that the entrenchment of liturgical Hebrew sequences varies depending on the prayer recitation habits of two groups of Israelis, observant and secular Jews. Likewise, Dąbrowska (2012) reviews several studies suggesting that adult native speakers of a language do not share the same language representations, a result shown to be at least partially attributable to differences in language experience. Günther (2016) shows by means of an eye-tracking experiment that in language-associated tasks involving the use of the same construction types, differences in the presumed entrenchment of constructions (as measured by linguistic usage preferences) correlate with differences in patterns of attention allocation to perceived referent scenes.

A different but related question is whether it is possible to identify intersubjective differences that are not due to differences in input, but to the existence of different cognitive styles. The language acquisition literature has long suggested a distinction between two types of language learners: *expressive* (or *holistic*) children, who tend to proceed from unitary chunks to words, and *referential* (or *analytic*) learners, who proceed the other way round (Nelson, 1981). Moreover, it has recently been suggested that at least in the domain of visual perception, the well-attested cognitive precedence of global over local patterns (as assessed by Navon letters, see Section 6.4.1) declines as a function of age (Staudinger, Fink, Mackay, & Lux, 2011). Other research suggests that local versus global bias might be culture-dependent, which opens up a host of exciting questions concerning potential interactions between (linguistic and nonlinguistic) experience, culture, and cognitive biases (Davidoff, Fonteneau, & Fagot, 2008). Besides the existence of more or less holistic cognitive styles, individuals may also vary in terms of their statistical learning capabilities, which might in turn give rise to differential language processing preferences (Misyak & Christiansen, 2012; see also Jost & Christiansen, Chapter 10, this volume).

All this suggests that generalizations pertaining to the linguistic knowledge of an idealized average language user may only be weakly informative of what goes on in the minds of actual language users and that cognitive linguistic research would gain new insights from investigating differences between groups of subjects and from modeling their interaction (Blumenthal-Dramé, 2012, Chapter 8).

6.5.3 Interaction Between Long-Term Entrenchment and Online Processing

A further question that remains to be addressed in a systematic way is how long-term entrenchment interacts with online processing. In the literature, it has been repeatedly suggested that the function that relates token frequency to entrenchment "is not linear but instead follows the power law of learning with the effects of practice being greatest at early stages of learning but eventually reaching asymptote" (Ellis, 2006,

p. 10). This implies that rarer events should have a stronger entrenchment impact than more frequent events (see Jost & Christiansen, Chapter 10, this volume). However, entrenchment research so far has mainly focused on comparing the processing of rare and frequent strings, without exploring the differential impact that these strings might have on short- and long-term language representations. Fortunately, the situation is starting to change, with at least one recent study confirming that unexpected structures have a stronger short-term impact on language representations than expected ones (Jaeger & Snider, 2013). It would be interesting to extend research in this spirit to other kinds of entrenchment levels (e.g., lexically specific strings), as well as to explore how long-lasting such updates are and to what extent they generalize to different experimental contexts.

6.6 Conclusion

As the present review has shown, different strands of psycholinguistic and neurolinguistic research are compatible with the view that the usage frequency of expressions correlates with their entrenchment in the minds of language users, to the effect that more frequent expressions are easier to process.

However, how this gain in processing ease should be modeled is still under debate. On the one hand, the cognitive and usage-based literature has described entrenchment as a multifaceted phenomenon comprising different cognitive dimensions (notably strength of representation, ease of activation, fluency of composition, and chunk status; Section 6.2). On the other hand, many definitions are unspecific as to the mental representation level supposed to be affected by individual entrenchment criteria. For example, it is usually not specified whether representation strength and activation ease affect the individual component morphemes of an expression, the expression as a whole, or the connection weights between its morphemes. Moreover, at least two criteria, fluency of composition and chunk status, are not straightforwardly intercompatible (in common understanding, if something can be retrieved as a holistic chunk, it need not be concatenated).

In addition—and despite claims to the contrary—most of the rich experimental literature on frequency effects does not provide conclusive support for the distinctively usage-based claim that high-frequency sequences are represented in a holistic fashion. Rather, most results are equally compatible with the weaker alternative interpretation that higher frequency strings are simply assembled with greater efficiency as a result of greater association strengths between morphemes (Section 6.3). Fortunately, the recent literature has started to operationalize and test frequency-induced chunk status, with results that support the usage-based view (Section 6.4).

As argued in Section 6.5, major issues that are likely to drive future research include how far the boundaries of entrenchment can be pushed in terms of abstractness and complexity, whether it makes sense to cling to the working hypothesis that all language users (including those of different languages) are equally responsive to frequency, and how our long-term experience with language interacts with new processing events.

Finally, it would be exciting to explore the extent to which psycholinguistic and neurolinguistic models of entrenchment could be integrated with more general cognitive neuroscience frameworks, such as hierarchical predictive coding (Section 6.4.1). At first sight, this paradigm, which has so far been applied mainly to nonlinguistic action and perception, seems perfectly compatible with the usage-based view that entrenchment is a gradient property resulting from the cognitive precedence of higher over lower levels in a hierarchically layered system.

References

Abbot-Smith, K., & Tomasello, M. (2006). Exemplar-learning and schematization in a usage-based account of syntactic acquisition. *The Linguistic Review, 23*, 275–290. http://dx.doi.org/10.1515/TLR.2006.011

Arnon, I., & Priva, U. C. (2013). More than words: The effect of multi-word frequency and constituency on phonetic duration. *Language and Speech, 56*, 349–371. http://dx.doi.org/10.1177/0023830913484891

Arnon, I., & Snider, N. (2010). More than words: Frequency effects for multi-word phrases. *Journal of Memory and Language, 62*, 67–82. http://dx.doi.org/10.1016/j.jml.2009.09.005

Bannard, C. (2006). *Acquiring phrasal lexicons from corpora* (Doctoral dissertation). University of Edinburgh, Scotland.

Bar, M., & Bubic, A. (2013). Top-down effects in visual perception. In K. N. Ochsner & S. Kosslyn (Eds.), *The Oxford handbook of cognitive neuroscience* (pp. 60–73). Oxford, England: Oxford University Press.

Behrens, H. (2009). Usage-based and emergentist approaches to language acquisition. *Linguistics, 47*, 383–411. http://dx.doi.org/10.1515/LING.2009.014

Berant, J., Caldwell-Harris, C., & Edelman, S. (2008, July). *Tracks in the mind: Differential entrenchment of common and rare liturgical and everyday multiword phrases in religious and secular Hebrew speakers*. Presented at the Annual Meeting of the Cognitive Science Society, Washington, DC. Retrieved from http://csjarchive.cogsci.rpi.edu/Proceedings/2008/pdfs/p869.pdf

Blumenthal-Dramé, A. (2012). *Entrenchment in usage-based theories: What corpus data do and do not reveal about the mind*. http://dx.doi.org/10.1515/9783110294002

Blumenthal-Dramé, A., Glauche, V., Bormann, T., Weiller, C., Musso, M., & Kortmann, B. (2016). *Frequency and chunking in derived words: A parametric fMRI study*. Unpublished manuscript.

Bod, R. (2001, January). *Sentence memory: Storage vs. computation of frequent sentences*. Presented at the CUNY Conference on Human Sentence Processing, Philadelphia, PA.

Booij, G. E. (2013). Morphology in construction grammar. In T. Hoffmann & G. Trousdale (Eds.), *The Oxford handbook of construction grammar* (pp. 255–273). Oxford, England: Oxford University Press.

Bozic, M., Marslen-Wilson, W. D., Stamatakis, E. A., Davis, M. H., & Tyler, L. K. (2007). Differentiating morphology, form, and meaning: Neural correlates of morphological complexity. *Journal of Cognitive Neuroscience, 19*, 1464–1475. http://dx.doi.org/10.1162/jocn.2007.19.9.1464

Buckner, R. L., Koutstaal, W., Schacter, D. L., & Rosen, B. R. (2000). Functional MRI evidence for a role of frontal and inferior temporal cortex in amodal components of priming. *Brain: A Journal of Neurology, 123*, 620–640. http://dx.doi.org/10.1093/brain/123.3.620

Bybee, J. L. (2007). *Frequency of use and the organization of language.* http://dx.doi.org/10.1093/acprof:oso/9780195301571.001.0001

Bybee, J. L. (2010). *Language, usage and cognition.* http://dx.doi.org/10.1017/CBO9780511750526

Bybee, J. L., & McClelland, J. L. (2005). Alternatives to the combinatorial paradigm of linguistic theory based on domain general principles of human cognition. *The Linguistic Review, 22*, 381–410. http://dx.doi.org/10.1515/tlir.2005.22.2-4.381

Bybee, J. L., & Torres Cacoullos, R. (2009). The role of prefabs in grammaticization: How the particular and the general interact in language change. In R. Corrigan, E. A. Moravcsik, H. Ouali, & K. Wheatley (Eds.), *Formulaic Language: Vol. 1. Distribution and historical change* (pp. 187–218). Amsterdam, the Netherlands: Benjamins.

Caldwell-Harris, C. L., Berant, J., & Edelman, S. (2012). Entrenchment of phrases with perceptual identification, familiarity ratings, and corpus frequency statistics. In D. Divjak & S. T. Gries (Eds.), *Frequency effects in language representation* (pp. 165–194). http://dx.doi.org/10.1515/9783110274073.165

Cappelle, B., Shtyrov, Y., & Pulvermüller, F. (2010). Heating up or cooling up the brain? MEG evidence that phrasal verbs are lexical units. *Brain and Language, 115*, 189–201. http://dx.doi.org/10.1016/j.bandl.2010.09.004

Carreiras, M., Armstrong, B. C., Perea, M., & Frost, R. (2014). The what, when, where, and how of visual word recognition. *Trends in Cognitive Sciences, 18*, 90–98. http://dx.doi.org/10.1016/j.tics.2013.11.005

Clark, A. (2013). Whatever next? Predictive brains, situated agents, and the future of cognitive science. *Behavioral and Brain Sciences, 36*, 181–204. http://dx.doi.org/10.1017/S0140525X12000477

Croft, W. (2001). *Radical construction grammar: Syntactic theory in typological perspective.* http://dx.doi.org/10.1093/acprof:oso/9780198299554.001.0001

Croft, W., & Cruse, D. A. (2004). *Cognitive linguistics.* http://dx.doi.org/10.1017/CBO9780511803864

Dąbrowska, E. (2004). *Language, mind and brain: Some psychological and neurological constraints on theories of grammar.* Edinburgh, Scotland: Edinburgh University Press.

Dąbrowska, E. (2012). Different speakers, different grammars: Individual differences in native language attainment. *Linguistic Approaches to Bilingualism, 2*, 219–253. http://dx.doi.org/10.1075/lab.2.3.01dab

Davidoff, J., Fonteneau, E., & Fagot, J. (2008). Local and global processing: Observations from a remote culture. *Cognition, 108*, 702–709. http://dx.doi.org/10.1016/j.cognition.2008.06.004

De Smet, H., & Cuyckens, H. (2007). Diachronic aspects of complementation: Constructions, entrenchment and the matching-problem. In C. M. Cain & G. Russom (Eds.), *Studies in the history of the English language III: Managing chaos: Strategies for identifying change in English* (pp. 1–37). http://dx.doi.org/10.1515/9783110198515.3.187

de-Wit, L., & Wagemans, J. (2015). Individual differences in local and global perceptual organization. In J. Wagemans (Ed.), *Oxford handbook of perceptual organization* (pp. 713–735). Oxford, England: Oxford University Press.

Docherty, G. J., & Foulkes, P. (2014). An evaluation of usage-based approaches to the modelling of sociophonetic variability. *Lingua, 142*, 42–56. http://dx.doi.org/10.1016/j.lingua.2013.01.011

Ellis, N. C. (2006). Language acquisition as rational contingency learning. *Applied Linguistics, 27*, 1–24. http://dx.doi.org/10.1093/applin/ami038

Engel, A. K., Fries, P., & Singer, W. (2001). Dynamic predictions: Oscillations and synchrony in top-down processing. *Nature Reviews Neuroscience, 2*, 704–716. http://dx.doi.org/10.1038/35094565

Forster, K. I., & Davis, C. (1984). Repetition priming and frequency attenuation in lexical access. *Journal of Experimental Psychology: Learning, Memory, and Cognition, 10*, 680–698. http://dx.doi.org/10.1037/0278-7393.10.4.680

Goldberg, A. E. (1995). *Constructions: A construction grammar approach to argument structure.* Chicago, IL: University of Chicago Press.

Günther, F. (2016). *Constructions in cognitive contexts: Why individuals matter in linguistic relativity research.* Berlin, Germany: De Gruyter Mouton.

Hauk, O., Davis, M. H., & Pulvermüller, F. (2008). Modulation of brain activity by multiple lexical and word form variables in visual word recognition: A parametric fMRI study. *NeuroImage, 42*, 1185–1195. http://dx.doi.org/10.1016/j.neuroimage.2008.05.054

Hay, J. B., & Baayen, R. H. (2005). Shifting paradigms: Gradient structure in morphology. *Trends in Cognitive Sciences, 9*, 342–348. http://dx.doi.org/10.1016/j.tics.2005.04.002

Hohwy, J. (2013). *The predictive mind.* http://dx.doi.org/10.1093/acprof:oso/9780199682737.001.0001

Ingram, J. C. L. (2007). *Neurolinguistics: An introduction to spoken language processing and its disorders.* http://dx.doi.org/10.1017/CBO9780511618963

Jaeger, T. F., & Snider, N. E. (2013). Alignment as a consequence of expectation adaptation: Syntactic priming is affected by the prime's prediction error given both prior and recent experience. *Cognition, 127*, 57–83. http://dx.doi.org/10.1016/j.cognition.2012.10.013

Jiang, N., & Nekrasova, T. M. (2007). The processing of formulaic sequences by second language speakers. *Modern Language Journal, 91*, 433–445. http://dx.doi.org/10.1111/j.1540-4781.2007.00589.x

Kapatsinski, V., & Radicke, J. (2009). Frequency and the emergence of prefabs: Evidence from monitoring. In R. Corrigan, E. A. Moravcsik, H. Ouali, & K. Wheatley (Eds.), *Formulaic language: Vol. 2. Acquisition, loss, psychological reality, and functional explanations* (pp. 499–520). Amsterdam, the Netherlands: Benjamins.

Kimchi, R. (2015). The perception of hierarchical structure. In J. Wagemans (Ed.), *The Oxford handbook of perceptual organization* (pp. 129–149). Oxford, England: Oxford University Press.

Langacker, R. W. (1987). *Foundations of cognitive grammar: Theoretical prerequisites.* Palo Alto, CA: Stanford University Press.

Langacker, R. W. (2000). *Grammar and conceptualization.* Berlin, Germany: Mouton de Gruyter.

Langacker, R. W. (2008). *Cognitive grammar: A basic introduction.* http://dx.doi.org/10.1093/acprof:oso/9780195331967.001.0001

Langacker, R. W. (2009). *Investigations in cognitive grammar.* http://dx.doi.org/10.1515/9783110214369

Lieven, E., & Tomasello, M. (2008). Children's first language acquisition from a usage-based perspective. In P. Robinson & N. C. Ellis (Eds.), *Handbook of cognitive linguistics and second language acquisition* (pp. 168–196). London, England: Routledge.

Marslen-Wilson, W. D., & Tyler, L. K. (2007). Morphology, language and the brain: The decompositional substrate for language comprehension. *Philosophical Transactions of the Royal Society of London: Series B. Biological Sciences, 362*, 823–836. http://dx.doi.org/10.1098/rstb.2007.2091

Misyak, J. B., & Christiansen, M. H. (2012). Statistical learning and language: An individual differences study. *Language Learning, 62*, 302–331. http://dx.doi.org/10.1111/j.1467-9922.2010.00626.x

Navon, D. (1977). Forest before trees: The precedence of global features in visual perception. *Cognitive Psychology*, *9*, 353–383. http://dx.doi.org/10.1016/0010-0285(77)90012-3

Nelson, K. (1981). Individual differences in language development: Implications for development and language. *Developmental Psychology*, *17*, 170–187. http://dx.doi.org/10.1037/0012-1649.17.2.170

O'Grady, W. (2008). The emergentist program. *Lingua*, *118*, 447–464. http://dx.doi.org/10.1016/j.lingua.2006.12.001

Pickering, M. J., & Ferreira, V. S. (2008). Structural priming: A critical review. *Psychological Bulletin*, *134*, 427–459. http://dx.doi.org/10.1037/0033-2909.134.3.427

Pliatsikas, C., Wheeldon, L., Lahiri, A., & Hansen, P. C. (2014). Processing of zero-derived words in English: An fMRI investigation. *Neuropsychologia*, *53*, 47–53. http://dx.doi.org/10.1016/j.neuropsychologia.2013.11.003

Poljac, E., de-Wit, L., & Wagemans, J. (2012). Perceptual wholes can reduce the conscious accessibility of their parts. *Cognition*, *123*, 308–312. http://dx.doi.org/10.1016/j.cognition.2012.01.001

Pomerantz, J. R., & Cragin, A. I. (2015). Emergent features and feature combination. In J. Wagemans (Ed.), *The Oxford handbook of perceptual organization* (pp. 88–107). Oxford, England: Oxford University Press.

Schmid, H.-J. (2014). Lexico-grammatical patterns, pragmatic associations and discourse frequency. In T. Herbst, H-J. Schmid, & S. Faulhaber, *Constructions Collocations Patterns* (pp. 239–293). http://dx.doi.org/10.1515/9783110356854.239

Segaert, K., Weber, K., de Lange, F. P., Petersson, K. M., & Hagoort, P. (2013). The suppression of repetition enhancement: A review of fMRI studies. *Neuropsychologia*, *51*, 59–66. http://dx.doi.org/10.1016/j.neuropsychologia.2012.11.006

Siyanova-Chanturia, A. (2013). Eye-tracking and ERPs in multi-word expression research: A state-of-the-art review of the method and findings. *The Mental Lexicon*, *8*, 245–268. http://dx.doi.org/10.1075/ml.8.2.06siy

Siyanova-Chanturia, A. (2015). On the "holistic" nature of formulaic language. *Corpus Linguistics and Linguistic Theory*, *11*, 285–301. http://dx.doi.org/10.1515/cllt-2014-0016

Siyanova-Chanturia, A., Conklin, K., & van Heuven, W. J. B. (2011). Seeing a phrase "time and again" matters: The role of phrasal frequency in the processing of multiword sequences. *Journal of Experimental Psychology: Learning, Memory, and Cognition*, *37*, 776–784. http://dx.doi.org/10.1037/a0022531

Sosa, A. V., & MacFarlane, J. (2002). Evidence for frequency-based constituents in the mental lexicon: Collocations involving the word *of*. *Brain and Language*, *83*, 227–236. http://dx.doi.org/10.1016/S0093-934X(02)00032-9

Staudinger, M. R., Fink, G. R., Mackay, C. E., & Lux, S. (2011). Gestalt perception and the decline of global precedence in older subjects. *Cortex*, *47*, 854–862. http://dx.doi.org/10.1016/j.cortex.2010.08.001

Stemmer, B., & Connolly, J. F. (2011). The EEG/ERP technologies in linguistic research: An essay on the advantages they offer and a survey of their purveyors. *The Mental Lexicon*, *6*, 141–170. http://dx.doi.org/10.1075/ml.6.1.06ste

Taylor, J. S. H., Rastle, K., & Davis, M. H. (2013). Can cognitive models explain brain activation during word and pseudoword reading? A meta-analysis of 36 neuroimaging studies. *Psychological Bulletin*, *139*, 766–791. http://dx.doi.org/10.1037/a0030266

Tooley, K. M., Swaab, T. Y., Boudewyn, M. A., Zirnstein, M., & Traxler, M. J. (2014). Evidence for priming across intervening sentences during on-line sentence comprehension. *Language, Cognition and Neuroscience*, *29*, 289–311. http://dx.doi.org/10.1080/01690965.2013.770892

Tremblay, A., & Baayen, R. H. (2010). Holistic processing of regular four-word sequences: A behavioral and ERP study of the effects of structure, frequency, and probability on immediate free recall. In D. Wood (Ed.), *Perspectives on formulaic language: Acquisition and communication* (pp. 151–173). London, England: Continuum.

Tremblay, A., Derwing, B., Libben, G., & Westbury, C. (2011). Processing advantages of lexical bundles: Evidence from self-paced reading and sentence recall tasks. *Language Learning*, *61*, 569–613. http://dx.doi.org/10.1111/j.1467-9922.2010.00622.x

Tremblay, A., & Tucker, B. V. (2011). The effects of N-gram probabilistic measures on the recognition and production of four-word sequences. *The Mental Lexicon*, *6*, 302–324. http://dx.doi.org/10.1075/ml.6.2.04tre

Twomey, T., Kawabata Duncan, K. J., Price, C. J., & Devlin, J. T. (2011). Top-down modulation of ventral occipito-temporal responses during visual word recognition. *NeuroImage*, *55*, 1242–1251. http://dx.doi.org/10.1016/j.neuroimage.2011.01.001

Dirk Geeraerts
7 Entrenchment as Onomasiological Salience

7.1 Introduction

The original model of entrenchment as introduced by Ronald Langacker (1987, pp. 59–60; see also Langacker, Chapter 2, this volume) evokes a double problem of logic: that of an infinite regress and that of a regression to infinity. In that original model, Langacker is concerned with the process of unit formation: a particular linguistic construct (e.g., a new compound, the use of a word in a new reading) may gradually transcend its initial incidental status by being used more often, until it is so firmly entrenched in the grammar or the lexicon that it has become a regular, well-established unit of the linguistic system. Such a process mediates between usage and system: An increased frequency of use strengthens the position of the construct in the system. Accordingly, the process of entrenchment involves the impact of language as a sociocommunicative event on language as a cognitive phenomenon: A well-entrenched construct is one that is more frequently used in actual communication, but at the same time (and precisely through its higher frequency of use), it becomes more firmly anchored in the language user's knowledge of the language.

The danger of an infinite regress emerges if we ask where the initial sociocommunicative frequencies come from. Constructs that are more highly entrenched in the mind of the language user will be used more often, but that degree of cognitive "wiring in" itself reflects the frequency with which the language user has encountered the expression in the usage of speakers in his or her communicative environment, and then that frequency itself derives from the cognitive entrenchment of the expression in the mind of those users, which they derived from the usage in their environment—and so on, ad infinitum. A regressing motion of this kind is not lethal, to the extent that it is typical of the historical sciences: We can think of the various groups of speakers as generations and accept that the description of human history inevitably has to assume an initial state of some kind beyond which further backward analysis is not relevant. Rather, the recognition of an infinite regress is important for another reason: It reflects on the proper treatment of entrenchment. Entrenchment is introduced as a primarily cognitive phenomenon, but that process assumes a sociocommunicative environment that is the product of a historical evolution. In line with the perspective of cognitive sociolinguistics (Geeraerts, Kristiansen, & Peirsman, 2010; Kristiansen & Dirven, 2008), then, an adequate treatment of entrenchment should embrace the social dimensions of language use, rather than relegating them to the background in favor of a dominant focus on psychological processes and cognitive representations.

DOI 10.1515/9783110341423-008

The danger of a regression to infinity looms on the other side of entrenchment as a process, that is, on the side of the outcome rather than that of the source. The simple model of entrenchment that we started with involves a positive feedback loop. Once the process is started, the frequency of a construct can only increase because the rising cognitive entrenchment in the individual will lead that individual to use the expression more often, which will cause the frequency in the collective behavior of the speech community to grow, which will lead to a further strengthening of the cognitive prominence in individuals—and so on, until the frequency of an expression reaches, well, not exactly infinity, but some maximum level. The conceptual flaw that is revealed by this reductio ad absurdum involves the absence of an explicitly comparative perspective: The increased frequency of an expression is only relevant if we think of it as a choice with regard to competing expressions. The initial relative frequency of the competitors will then undoubtedly influence the subsequent choices (just like the initial model of entrenchment suggests), but it will not be the only relevant factor: the existing position will clash or cooperate with other factors to determine the eventual selection among the competitors. Crucially within such a conception, the relevant set of competitors needs to be demarcated: What is the appropriate domain of variation, given that it would hardly make sense, for instance, to compare the frequency of *abide* with that of *zenith*? Expressions such as these do not contend with each other in any remotely pertinent sense. But ones that denote equivalent or similar concepts do, and so an onomasiological perspective—one that focuses on the relative frequency of alternative, competing expressions—is vital for a convincing model of entrenchment.

This chapter, then, presents the way in which the notion of entrenchment has been developed along the double dimension just highlighted: as a notion relying on the competition between alternatives and as a sociocommunicative and not just cognitive phenomenon. In more practical terms, the perspective defined by the combination of these two dimensions involves looking at entrenchment as a socially structured feature of observed language use (most often represented by corpus materials). To emphasize the distinction with "entrenchment" as the concept that triggered the discussion and the specification of dimensions, the term *onomasiological salience* is used. Section 7.2 introduces the various forms of onomasiological salience that may be usefully distinguished: formal, conceptual, and typological onomasiological salience. Sections 7.3 to 7.5 expand on each of these. Throughout, the focus lies on lexical phenomena because that is the field in which an onomasiological perspective was first developed and in which most of the contemporary advances are situated. This implies that there are two important restrictions on the scope of the chapter, that is, two research questions that are important for the study of entrenchment in the broader sense will only be marginally present in the following treatment of onomasiological salience. First, no systematic attempt will be made to show how the social perspective on onomasiological salience influences the study of entrenchment as a psychological process, even though there is increasing attention for the degree of correlation between corpus data and psychological observations (see, e.g., Gilquin & Gries, 2009; Schmid, 2010).

The overall message should be clear enough, however: Any study relying on raw frequencies or normalized text frequencies should be considered less sophisticated than a study incorporating relative frequencies of an onomasiological kind. Second, the extrapolation from the lexicon to other fields of linguistics, and specifically to the study of constructions, will not be systematically pursued here, although the concluding Section 7.6 takes a step in that direction. Needless to say, both extensions beyond the present scope of this chapter are imperative for the further study of entrenchment. The fact that they do not feature prominently in the following pages is the result of practical restrictions only.

7.2 Definition and Types of Onomasiological Salience

The distinction between onomasiology and semasiology is a fundamental one in the European tradition of lexicological research, invoking the Saussurean conception of the sign as consisting of a formal *signifiant* and a semantic *signifié*: Semasiology starts out from the signifiant and considers the various signifiés associated with it, whereas onomasiology takes the reverse perspective. Kurt Baldinger (1980), a prominent structuralist lexicologist, described the distinction as follows: "Semasiology . . . considers the isolated word and the way its meanings are manifested, while onomasiology looks at the designations of a particular concept, that is, at a multiplicity of expressions which form a whole" (p. 278). The distinction between semasiology and onomasiology, in other words, equals the distinction between meaning and naming: Semasiology takes its starting point in the word as a form and charts the meanings with which the word can occur; onomasiology takes its starting point in a concept and investigates by which different expressions the concept can be designated, or named. Between both, there is a difference of viewpoint: Semasiology starts from the expression and looks at its meanings; onomasiology starts from the meaning and looks at the different expressions with which it occurs. Onomasiological salience, however, is an eminently poststructuralist concept in two complementary ways: It focuses on usage rather than just structure, and it includes the referential level of language use.

In its simplest form, onomasiological salience is the relative frequency with which a *signifiant* is associated with a given *signifié*. Blue jeans may be referred to as *denims*, but *jeans* is probably the most common term—in other words, the onomasiological salience of *jeans* with regard to the concept "trousers made of denim or a denimlike fabric" is higher than that of *denims*. We may note now that the two descriptions of onomasiology that Baldinger (1980) mentioned are not exactly equivalent. On the one hand, studying "a multiplicity of expressions which form a whole" leads to the structuralist conception of onomasiology as the study of semantically related expressions—as in lexical field theory, or the study of the lexicon as a relational network of words interconnected by links of a hyponymous, antonymous, synonymous nature, and so on. On the other hand, studying "the designations of a particular concept" potentially opens the way to a contextualized, pragmatic conception of onomasiology, involving the actual choices made for a particular name as a designation of a particular concept or a particular referent. This distinction resembles the distinction between an investigation of structure and an investigation of use, or in Saussurean terms, between an investigation of *langue* and an investigation of *parole*. The structural perspective deals with sets of related expressions and basically asks the question: What are the relations among the alternative expressions? The pragmatic conception deals with the actual choices made from among a set of related expressions and basically asks the question: What factors determine the choice for one or the other alternative?

This straightforward distinction between a structural and a pragmatic conception of onomasiology (with salience effects belonging to the latter) is somewhat complicated by onomasiological salience as a typological phenomenon. Some languages have a different word for 'man in general' compared with 'male human being' or 'female human being.' English, for one, has just one word for 'human being in general' and 'human male': *man*; similarly, in French *homme*, Spanish *hombre*, or Italian *uomo*. German, however, makes a distinction between *Mann* 'human male' and *Mensch* 'human being,' as also in Dutch *man* versus *mens* or Danish *mand* versus *menneske*. It is an onomasiological question, then, whether the term for human beings in general is identical to the term for human males, and it is a matter of onomasiological salience how strong that pattern is—universally, within specific language families, or in given cultural or geographic areas. Such a typological interpretation of onomasiological salience is structural in the sense that it looks at individual languages as systems with specific features—namely, exhibiting specific onomasiological patterns—but at the same time, it resembles a pragmatic approach to the extent that it compares the frequency with which specific patterns are "chosen" by linguistic systems.

The picture is further complicated by a second major dimension in which the study of onomasiological salience moves beyond structuralism, that is, by the addition of a referential dimension to the study of meaning phenomena. Next to the layer of forms and the layer of senses, there is the layer of denotata: the real-world entities, states of affairs, processes, and so on that linguistic expressions may refer to, plus all the knowledge that language users associate with those denotata. Structuralist approaches far from deny the existence of this referential dimension and the associated "encyclopedic" concepts but argue that they do not belong to the system of the language. Poststructuralist approaches like cognitive semantics, by contrast, embrace the view that systematic attention for the referential layer is important to get a full understanding of how language works, and that linguistic meanings should in fact be thought of as concepts. This is the basic insight of prototype theory: beyond the recognition that *jeans* has the sense 'trousers made of denim,' it is important that that sense is typically, although not universally, represented by garments with reinforced seams, rivets, sewn-on back pockets, and a few other characteristic features. (For the full story of poststructuralist theories of semantics and the evolution of lexical semantics at large, see Geeraerts, 2010.) For the notion of onomasiological salience, taking into account the denotational level is interesting for three reasons.

First and foremost, it allows us to make a distinction between formal and conceptual onomasiology. Consider the following definitions, inspired by those in WordNet 3.0: 'a garment extending from the waist to the knee or ankle, covering each leg separately,' 'trousers ending just below the knee,' and 'underpants worn by women.' The first of these senses can be expressed by the word *trousers*, the second by *pants*, and the third by *breeches*. But *pants* is polysemous to the extent that it can also refer to trousers, and *breeches* has a synonym *knickers*, which is at the same time a synonym of *pants* in the reading 'underpants worn by women.' The overall situation is represented by Figure 7.1, which also includes, at the bottom level, an example of a real-world pair of breeches. Onomasiological variation now presents itself in two forms: There is the choice between synonyms for a given sense, such as *trousers* or *pants*, with regard to 'a garment extending from the waist to the knee or ankle, covering each leg separately,' and there is the choice between different senses that may be applied to a given denotatum. The item on the lowest level of the figure may be conceptualized as a pair of breeches, and then (disregarding synonyms not included in the example) the synonyms *breeches* and *knickers* are relevant expressions, but it may also be conceptualized on a higher, more general taxonomical level as a pair of trousers, and then *trousers* or *pants* would be the appropriate names. Terminologically, then, whereas conceptual onomasiological variation involves the choice of different conceptual categories for a denotatum, formal onomasiological variation involves the use of different names for the same conceptual category. Taking the terminology one step further, formal onomasiological salience involves the relative frequency with which either *trousers* or *pants* might be

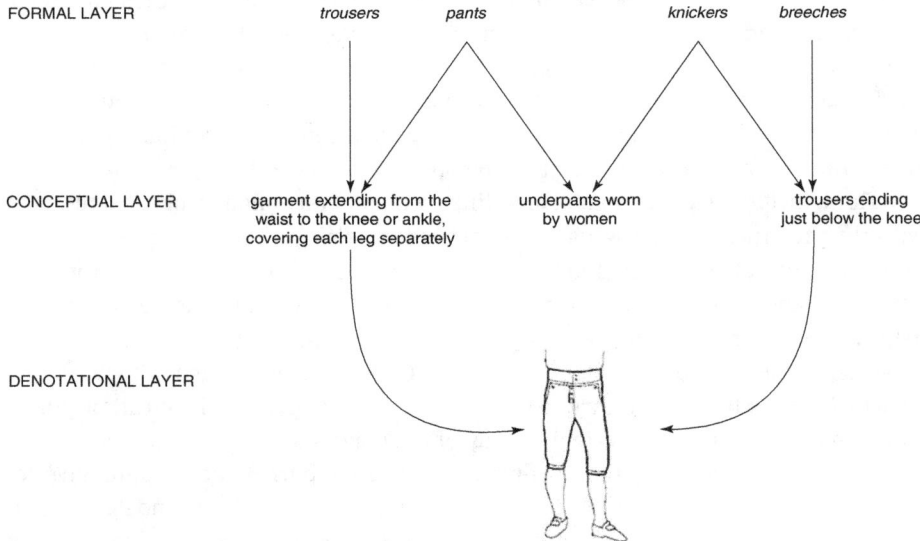

Fig. 7.1: The three layers of onomasiological structure.

used to express 'a garment extending from the waist to the knee or ankle, covering each leg separately,' whereas conceptual onomasiological salience involves the relative frequency with which a pair of breeches might be categorized as either *trousers/pants* or *breeches/knickers*.

Theoretically speaking, the distinction between formal and conceptual onomasiological salience as first formulated by Geeraerts, Grondelaers, and Bakema (1994) is a refinement of the original notion of entrenchment as introduced by Langacker discussed earlier. Specifically, it warns against the conflation of various frequency effects: the *experiential frequency* with which people encounter specific real-world phenomena, the *conceptual frequency* with which those phenomena are categorized in a specific way, and the *lexical frequency* with which those categories are expressed by specific forms. The frequency of occurrence of a linguistic construct results from these three types of frequency at the same time, and talking of entrenchment as a single, unitary phenomenon obscures those differences. The analytical apparatus introduced in this chapter and schematized in Figure 7.1 intends to bring more clarity into the notion of entrenchment.

Second, including the referential level helps us to see that looking at onomasiological salience (and particularly at conceptual onomasiological salience) is, despite being a relatively new perspective in semantics, an obvious thing to do given the mirroring relationship between a semasiological and an onomasiological perspective. Semasiological salience in fact only became a focus of semantic research by the introduction of prototype theory, that is, by the recognition that at the referential level, not all things are equal: Some of the referents representing a given sense may be more salient than others, for instance, in that a pair of blue jeans with reinforced seams, rivets, and sewn-on back pockets is more typical than one lacking those features. Looking at onomasiological salience extrapolates that interest in salience phenomena to the onomasiological perspective, and specifically, looking at conceptual onomasiological salience embodies the idea that not all ways of lexically categorizing phenomena are equally common. Onomasiological salience thus completes the poststructuralist turn toward a usage-based perspective on semantics.

Third, including the referential level links contemporary onomasiological research with the prestructuralist origins of the term *onomasiology*. The concept was in fact introduced by Adolf Zauner (1903) in his study on body-part terms in the Romance languages, and prestructuralist semantics harbored a referentially oriented onomasiological research tradition in the form of the *Wörter und Sachen* ("words and objects") movement inaugurated by Rudolf Meringer (1909) and Hugo Schuchardt (1912). The principal idea is that the study of words, whether etymological, historical, or purely variational, needs to incorporate the study of the objects denoted by those words. As Meringer (1912) noted in an article defining the scope and purpose of the journal *Wörter und Sachen* that he launched in 1909, "Bedeutungswandel ist Sachwandel . . . , und Sachwandel ist Kulturwandel [Semantic change is object change, and object change is cultural change]." The basic, characteristically onomasiological perspective is not

"What do words mean?" but "How are things named and classified through language?" Although the study of abstract concepts is not excluded, the emphasis in the *Wörter und Sachen* approach tended to fall almost exclusively on concrete objects, either natural kinds such as plants, animals, or body parts, or artifacts such as tools and all other elements of the material culture of a given language community or a historical period. For studying the language of an agricultural community, for instance, a good knowledge is required of its natural environment, farming techniques, customs, social organization, and the like. The whole approach has in fact a strong cultural orientation, which is translated methodologically in interdisciplinary links with archaeological and historical research. The *Wörter und Sachen* movement, and the onomasiological perspective in general, also had an important influence on the development of dialect geography, and specifically on the dialect atlases that were produced, or at least started, in the first decades of the twentieth century. In works like the *Atlas Linguistique de la France* edited by Jules Gilliéron, the *Sprach- und Sachatlas Italiens und der Südschweiz* by Karl Jaberg and Jakob Jud, or the *Deutscher Sprachatlas* by Ferdinand Wrede, onomasiological maps show the words used for a given concept in the geographic areas covered by the map.

From our contemporary perspective, the prestructuralist and the structuralist onomasiological traditions suffer from defects that mirror each other. The prestructuralist *Wörter und Sachen* approach privileges the referential level at the expense of the conceptual level, whereas the structuralist approach does exactly the opposite. By contrast, acknowledging both formal and conceptual onomasiological salience brings all relevant levels within the scope of the investigation. In the following pages, then, we go into detail about formal onomasiological salience and conceptual onomasiological salience, with a special focus on the onomasiological research lines developed in the Quantitative Lexicology and Variational Linguistics research team (QLVL) at the University of Leuven. The typological perspective is treated more summarily, as a reflection of the view that salience is primarily a frequency-based usage phenomenon. (The presentation is restricted to the lexicon, the original home ground of the semasiology/onomasiology distinction. However, the various forms of onomasiological analysis can be applied to any meaningful construct in the language: See Glynn, 2010, for a confrontation of lexical onomasiology and an onomasiological perspective on constructions and grammar.)

7.3 Formal Onomasiological Salience

A sociolinguistic variable in the sense of contemporary sociolinguistics is a set of alternative ways of expressing the same linguistic function or realizing the same linguistic element, where each of the alternatives has social significance: "Social and stylistic variation presuppose the option of saying 'the same thing' in several different ways: that is, the variants are identical in reference or truth value, but opposed in their social and/or stylistic significance" (Labov, 1972, p. 271). As such, a sociolinguistic variable is a linguistic element that is sensitive to a number of extralinguistic independent variables such as social class, age, sex, geographic group location, ethnic group, or contextual style and register. Formal onomasiology, then, amounts to treating lexical variation as a sociolinguistic variable, with sets of synonyms as different ways of expressing the same denotational content but with possibly diverging sociostylistic values. Studying the sociolinguistic distribution of the alternative expressions is therefore a natural ingredient of formal onomasiology: The question is not just whether some variants are selected more than others but also which factors (including influences of a social and stylistic nature) have an impact on those preferences.

The theoretical distinction among formal onomasiological, conceptual onomasiological, and semasiological variation was first formulated in Geeraerts et al. (1994), but the first full-fledged case study of a formal onomasiological nature was developed in Geeraerts, Grondelaers, and Speelman (1999), a monograph that investigates the convergence and divergence of the lexicon of Netherlandic Dutch and Belgian Dutch (for a summary presentation, see Speelman, Grondelaers, & Geeraerts, 2006). Methodologically speaking, the study of lexical variation as a sociolinguistic variable is coupled with a lectometrical perspective that quantifies the similarity between language varieties and the possible changes in those linguistic distances. Without going into the descriptive results of the study, the methodology may be introduced on the basis of the notions "onomasiological profile" and "uniformity."

The onomasiological profile of a concept in a particular source (like a collection of textual materials representing a language variety) is the set of synonymous names for that concept in that particular source, differentiated by their relative frequency. In this way, the onomasiological profile of a concept is a representation of the difference in salience of its competing expressions. Table 7.1, for instance, contains the onomasiological profiles for *shirt* in the Belgian and the Netherlandic data for 1990 in Geeraerts et al. (1999). Next, *uniformity* is a measure for the overlap between onomasiological profiles. In the extreme case, complete lexical uniformity in the naming of a concept obtains when two language varieties have a single identical name for that concept, or several names with identical frequencies in the two varieties. Much more common than complete uniformity, however, are partial correspondences as

Tab. 7.1: Onomasiological Profiles for *Shirt* in Belgian and Netherlandic Dutch

	Belgian Dutch	Netherlandic Dutch
hemd	31%	17%
overhemd	69%	46%
shirt	0%	37%

Note. Data (from 1990) are based on Geeraerts, Grondelaers, and Speelman (1999).

illustrated in Table 7.1. For the sake of illustration, we assume that the relative frequencies in Table 7.1 represent 100 actual naming instances in each of both profiles, rather than percentages. The partial overlap between the profiles in Table 7.1 is quantified by counting the naming instances for which there is a counterpart in the other profile. In Table 7.1, 14 instances of *hemd* in Belgian Dutch data have no counterpart in Netherlandic, 23 Belgian cases of *overhemd* have no Netherlandic counterpart, and there are no Belgian counterparts for the 37 Netherlandic *shirts*. On the grand total of 200 naming events in the two profiles, only $200 - (14 + 23 + 37) = 126$ instances have counterparts in the other profile, which yields a uniformity of $126/2 = 63\%$. If more than one concept is investigated, a uniformity index U may be defined as the average of the uniformity indexes of the separate concepts, whereas uniformity index U' may be defined as a weighted average, in which the relative frequency of each concept in the investigated samples is taken into account, such that high-frequency concepts have a more outspoken impact on the overall uniformity.

Building on this simple core idea, onomasiology-based lectometry has been developed in various directions. Methodological extensions are described in Peirsman, Geeraerts, and Speelman (2010, 2015); Ruette, Geeraerts, Peirsman, and Speelman (2014); Ruette, Speelman, and Geeraerts (2014); and Speelman, Grondelaers, and Geeraerts (2003). Descriptive extensions include applications to historical linguistics (Geeraerts, 1999), linguistic prescriptivism (Geeraerts & Grondelaers, 2000), the analysis of informal registers and computer mediated communication (Geeraerts, 2001; Grondelaers, Geeraerts, Speelman, & Tummers, 2001), dialectology (Geeraerts & Speelman, 2010; Speelman & Geeraerts, 2009), and contact linguistics and loan word research (Zenner, Speelman, & Geeraerts, 2012, 2014). Although these studies primarily use Dutch data, a case study involving European and Brazilian Portuguese may be found in Soares da Silva (2010).

7.4 Conceptual Onomasiological Salience

Possibly the major innovation introduced by the prototype-theoretical model of categorization is to give salience a place in the description of semasiological structure: Next to the qualitative relations among the elements in a semasiological structure (like metaphor and metonymy), a quantifiable center-periphery relationship is introduced as part of the semantic architecture. If we mirror the concept of conceptual salience in the onomasiological domain, the question becomes: Are there any dominant ways of conceptualizing and categorizing phenomena?

Studying how particular phenomena are conceptually categorized may take two forms, which we can roughly characterize as direct and indirect. In the direct approach, the focus lies on naming in its most straightforward guise: Which categorial label is used to refer to a given phenomenon? Is the pair of trousers in the lower part of Figure 7.1 categorized as "a garment extending from the waist to the knee or ankle, covering each leg separately" (in which case *trousers* or *pants* could be used), or is it categorized as "trousers ending just below the knee" (in which case *knickers* or *breeches* could be used)? But the way we think about things may also reveal itself in less categorial ways, for instance, through the words with which the immediate label is contextually associated. In Subsections 7.4.1 and 7.4.2, we will have a closer look at both perspectives.

7.4.1 Categorial Identification as Conceptual Onomasiology

In standard treatments of lexicology and cognitive semantics, the description of differences of onomasiological salience is mostly restricted to the *basic-level hypothesis* (although the concept *onomasiology* is seldom used). The hypothesis is based on the ethnolinguistic observation that folk classifications of biological domains usually conform to a general organizational principle, in the sense that they consist of five or six taxonomical levels (Berlin, 1978; Berlin, Breedlove, & Raven, 1973). Table 7.2 illustrates the idea with two sets of examples. The highest rank in the taxonomy is that of the "unique beginner," which names a major domain such as *plant* and *animal*. The domain of the unique beginner is subdivided by just a few general "life forms," which are in turn specified by "folk genera" such as *pine*, *oak*, *beech*, *ash*, *elm*, and *chestnut*. (The "intermediate" level is an optional one.) A folk genus may be further specified by "folk specifics" and "varietal taxa." To the extent that the generic level is the core of any folk biological category, it is the basic level: "Generic taxa are highly salient and are the first terms encountered in ethnobiological enquiry, presumably because they refer to the most commonly used, everyday categories of folk biological knowledge" (Berlin, 1978, p. 17). The generic level, in other words, is onomasiologically salient: Within the lexical field defined by the taxonomy, the generic level specifies a set of salient items. In this sense, the basic level embodies a set of naming preferences: Given a particular referent, the most likely name for that referent from among the alternatives provided by the taxonomy will be the name situated at the basic level. Apart from embodying a concept of onomasiological salience, basic-level

Tab. 7.2: Taxonomical Structures With Basic Levels

	Biological examples		Artifacts
kingdom	plant	animal	garment
life form	tree	fish	outer garment
intermediate	evergreen	freshwater fish	—
generic	pine	bass	trousers
specific	white pine	black bass	ski pants
varietal	western white pine	large-mouthed bass	stretch ski pants

categories are claimed to exhibit a number of other characteristics. From a psychological point of view, they are conceptualized as perceptual and functional gestalts. From a developmental point of view, they are early in acquisition, that is, they are the first terms of the taxonomy learned by the child. From a linguistic point of view, they are named by short, morphologically simple items. From a conceptual point of view, Rosch (1978) argued that the basic level constitutes the level where prototype effects are most outspoken, in the sense that they maximize the number of attributes shared by members of the category and minimize the number of attributes shared with members of other categories.

The basic-level model was developed for the description of the folk classification of natural kinds. It is an open question to what extent it may be generalized to all kinds of taxonomies, like the taxonomical classification of artifacts. If we apply the basic-level model to the lexical field of clothing terminology, items such as *trousers*, *skirt*, *sweater*, and *dress* are to be considered basic-level categories: Their overall frequency in actual language use is high, they are learned early in acquisition, and they typically have the monomorphemic form of basic-level categories. A further extrapolation yields the right-hand side of Table 7.2, in which *garment* is considered a unique beginner in contrast with, say, *utensil* or *toy*. If we extend the basic-level model to artifacts in this way, a crucial observation presents itself: Differences of onomasiological preference may also occur among categories on the same level in a taxonomical hierarchy. The basic-level model contains a hypothesis about alternative categorizations of referents: If a particular referent (a particular piece of clothing) can be alternatively categorized as a garment, a skirt, or a wraparound skirt, the choice will be preferentially made for the basic-level category *skirt*. Analogously, however, if a particular referent can be alternatively categorized as a wraparound skirt or a miniskirt, there could just as well be a preferential choice: When you encounter something that is both a wraparound skirt and a miniskirt, what is the most natural way of naming that referent? If, then, taxonomically speaking we have to reckon with intralevel differences of salience next to interlevel differences, the concept of onomasiological salience has to be generalized in such a way that it relates to individual categories at any level of the hierarchy. As introduced in Geeraerts et al. (1994), such a generalized concept of conceptual onomasiological salience is operationally defined as the ratio between the frequency with which the members of a lexical category are named with an item that is a unique name for that category, and the total frequency with which the category occurs in a corpus. For instance, the conceptual category *trousers ending just below the knee* can be considered highly entrenched if, of a total of 100 references to such garments, a majority occurs with the name *breeches* or *knickers* (or other synonyms, such as *knickerbockers*) rather than with hyperonyms such as *trousers* (and its synonyms).

To illustrate, we may have a look at some of the results obtained in Geeraerts et al. (1994). Let us note first that calculating conceptual onomasiological salience of this kind assumes that the referents of the expressions can be identified. In the

Tab. 7.3: Differences in Conceptual Onomasiological Salience Among Co-Hyponyms

Category	Conceptual onomasiological salience
broek ("trousers")	46.47
short-shorts	45.61
bermuda	50.88
legging-leggings-caleçon	45.50
jeans-jeansbroek-spijkerbroek	81.66

Note. Based on Geeraerts, Grondelaers, and Bakema (1994).

1994 study of clothing terms, this is achieved by using a "referentially enriched" corpus: Rather than using just a text corpus, the study uses illustrated magazines, so that the pictures accompanying the text provide independent access to the entities being named. This allows us, for instance, to spot cases in which *trousers* refers to a pair of breeches, even if they are not named as such—an indispensable piece of information for applying the definition of conceptual onomasiological salience. (A different type of referential enrichment is developed in Anishchanka, Speelman, & Geeraerts, 2014, where visual Internet data are used to study color terms.) Table 7.3, then, shows how the onomasiological salience of different categories on the same taxonomical level may differ considerably. For instance, in the upper part of the figure, *short*, *bermuda*, *legging*, and *jeans* are co-hyponyms because they all fall under the hyperonymous category *broek* ("trousers"). However, the onomasiological salience of the different concepts differs considerably: That of the concept *jeans*, for instance, doubles that of *legging*. This means that a potential member of the category *jeans* is twice as likely to be designated by an expression that names the category *jeans* than a member of the category *legging* would be likely to be designated by an expression that names the category *legging*.

7.4.2 Oblique Construal as Conceptual Onomasiology

Systematically speaking, indirect analyses of conceptual onomasiological salience come in two kinds. On the one hand, the textual context in which a topic appears may reveal aspects of how the topic is thought of. It would make a difference, for instance, whether *breeches* is dominantly accompanied by *uncomfortable* rather than *leisurely*. On the other hand, the categorial labels with which a phenomenon are named may themselves embody a specific way of looking: Although *skirt* does not express a specific perspective, *miniskirt* highlights the length of the garment, and *wraparound skirt* profiles the method of fastening. Specifically, when the designations have a figurative value, as with metaphors, looking for salient patterns in the semantic motifs expressed by the words used may show us something of how the phenomenon in question is conceptualized. Without in any way trying to be exhaustive, two illustrations may add some substance to this schematic characterization, while indicating how advanced corpus techniques can help give indirect onomasiological analyses a firm methodological footing. (Indirect approaches as meant here are quite popular in metaphor studies and critical discourse analysis, but their methods are predominantly qualitative. If salience, as a frequency phenomenon, is to be measured, some form of quantification on a broad observational basis is advisable.)

Peirsman, Heylen, and Geeraerts (2010) investigated the question whether the conceptualization of religions and the use of religious terms in Dutch have changed after the attacks of September 11, 2001. Using word space models (a family of approaches that were developed in the context of computational linguistics and cognitive science and that represent the meaning of a word in terms of its contexts in a large corpus; see Navigli, 2012), the words that are saliently associated with the concepts *islam* and *christianity* are charted, and comparing the degrees of association before and after 9/11 allows to track changes of conceptualization. Not surprisingly, the biggest climber in rank of relatedness for *islam* is *terrorisme* ("terrorism"). Among other things, the results further show a tighter link between *fundamentalisme* ("fundamentalism") and both religions after 9/11, and between *jihad* ("jihad") and *islam*. The other highest climbers are either more neutral in meaning or display an expected link with either of the two religions (as between *Koran* ["Quran"] and *islam*). Thus, there is indeed a notable increase in distributional relatedness between *islam* and a number of words related to terrorism, whereas this increase is far less clear with *christendom*.

Zhang, Geeraerts, and Speelman (2015) traced diachronic variation in the metonymic patterns with which target concepts like *woman*, *beautiful woman*, or *woman belonging to the imperial household* have been expressed throughout the history of Chinese. Linking up with the methodology sketched in Section 7.2, this article introduced *conceptual onomasiological profiles*, consisting of the relative frequency of different metonymical patterns (e.g., location for located or action for agent) in the total set of metonymic expressions that occur for a given target concept in a specific historical period. (See also Geeraerts & Gevaert, 2008, on the history of *anger* and the relative frequency of metaphorical, metonymical, literal construals of the concept.) Analogous to the uniformity measures for formal onomasiological variation, distance calculations across conceptual profiles allow identifying changes from one period to the other. For instance, changes in the metonymic patterns used for the expression of the target concept *beautiful woman* suggest a historical and cultural shift of the beauty ideal from intrinsic attributes to external decorative attributes.

7.5 Typological Onomasiological Salience

The two dimensions introduced earlier, that is, the distinction between formal and conceptual onomasiological salience and the distinction between a pragmatic and a typological view on salience, cross-classify: The pragmatic and the typological point of view can be taken within both the formal and the conceptual perspective. In practice, however, formal onomasiology hardly plays a role in a typological context. There is some similarity between formal onomasiological lectometry and the use of a Swadesh list in lexicostatistics and glottochronology (see McMahon & McMahon, 2005), but characteristically, the typological approaches are not profile-based. Extrapolating conceptual onomasiology to typology, then, involves the question: "Which conceptually different (types of) expressions do languages choose for designating specific phenomena?" As a first approximation, we can think about this in terms of preferred lexicogenetic mechanisms, that is, the mechanisms for introducing new pairs of word forms and word meanings into a language—all the traditional mechanisms, in other words, such as word formation, word creation, borrowing, blending, truncation, ellipsis, folk etymology and others, that introduce new items into the onomasiological inventory of a language. Within the set of lexicogenetic mechanisms, some could be more productive than others in a given language. Superficially, this could involve, for instance, an overall preference for borrowing rather than morphological productivity as mechanisms for introducing new words, but from a cognitive perspective, there are other, more subtle questions to ask: Do the ways in which novel words and expressions are being coined, reveal specific (and possibly preferred) ways of conceptualizing the onomasiological targets? An example of this type of research is Peter Koch and Andreas Blank's systematic exploration of the motivational preferences in the etymological inventory of the Romance languages (Blank & Koch, 2003). The approach takes the form of overviews like that in Table 7.4, adapted from Blank (2003). The table charts the different names for the target concept *match* in a number of European languages, as identified in the second row. Each of these names is itself derived from a source form, as may be found in the final row. Source form and target form are related in specific

Tab. 7.4: The Diachronic Onomasiology of *Match*

Target concept: 'match; short, slender piece of wood or other material tipped with a chemical substance which produces fire when rubbed against a rough or chemically prepared substance'		
Source form	**Process/relation**	**Target form**
English *match*, 'wick'	Semantic change based on metaphorical similarity	English *match*
French *allumette*, 'splinter for the transport of fire'	Semantic change based on taxonomical subordination	French *allumette*
German *streichen*, 'to rub,' *Holz*, 'wood'	Metonymical compound formation	German *Streichholz*
Old Greek *phosphóros*, 'fire-bringing'	Borrowing; metonymy-based conversion	Spanish *fósforo*
Spanish *cera*, 'wax,' diminutive suffix *-illa*	Semantic change based on metaphorical similarity	Spanish *cerilla*

Note. Based on Blank (2003).

ways, specified in the third row of the table. The relationship involves both a formal process and a semantic relation. The English target form *match*, for instance, is related by a process of semasiological change to the older reading *match* 'wick.' Semantically, the relationship between *wick* and 'short, slender piece of wood or other material tipped with a chemical substance which produces fire when rubbed on a rough or chemically prepared surface' is one of metaphorical similarity. German *Streichholz*, on the other hand, is related to the verb *streichen* and the noun *Holz* through a process of compounding; semantically, the relationship between target form and source form is metonymical. Needless to say, the source forms may often themselves be further analyzed as target forms: *allumette* 'splinter designated to transport fire,' for instance, is related by a process of suffixation and a semantic relationship of metonymy to the verb *allumer* ('to light') and the suffix *–ette*. If sufficient materials of the form illustrated in Table 7.4 are available, it is possible to compare the relative salience of different lexicogenetic mechanisms—not just on the abstract level where, for instance, the importance of metonymy in general would be gauged against the importance of metaphor in general, but more importantly, also on a more fine-grained level where the conceptualization of a specific target concept can be investigated: What kind of conceptual construal do various languages use for given targets?

If this type of reasoning is extended to the world's languages at large, questions of universality come to the fore: If typologically salient patterns can be detected in the onomasiological relationship between source and target concepts, and if those patterns occur in many genetically unrelated languages, they are good candidates for a universal mechanism. Then the further question arises regarding what factors of a cognitive or experiential nature might explain the salience of the association. This approach is well represented by the grammaticalization theory developed by Bernd Heine and his associates (see Heine, 1997; or Heine & Kuteva, 2002). The central question of the paradigm involves the motivation behind the creation of linguistic categories: Can we understand why particular ways of forming categories are cross-linguistically more common than others? A simple but telling example, taken from Heine (2004), may illustrate the perspective. Looking at cardinal numbers in a wide variety of languages, Heine made a number of observations. First, numeral systems having "5," "10," or "20" as the basis of their system are statistically predominant in the languages of the world, with systems based on "10" being most widespread. Second, the numerals for "5" and "10" often have nominal characteristics, whereas numerals from "6" to "9" often have a propositional, clauselike structure (e.g., a phrase meaning 'add the big finger' or 'jump from one hand to the other'). Third, expressions used for the mathematical operation of addition frequently find their source in function words with the meaning 'with' or 'on, upon.' These observations find a plausible explanation in human experience. The hands provide an obvious model for structuring a counting system, and so the most common structure in the world's languages is one in which the expression for "5" is derived from that for 'hand,' the expression for "10" from that for 'two hands,' and the expression for "20" from that for 'hands and feet' or 'whole person.'

Even when these numerals no longer have a nominal meaning but have become pure numerals, they may still have morphological and grammatical properties that show that they are relics from nouns. In a similar way, it seems plausible that the expression of an abstract mental operation like arithmetical addition finds its source in more concrete acts, like putting things together ('with') or on top of each other ('on, upon').

Typological semantic studies of the kind introduced in the preceding paragraph are enjoying an increasing popularity. Good places to start for a further acquaintance with this emerging addition are the overview by Koptjevskaja-Tamm, Rakhilina, and Vanhove (2015) and the collective volumes edited by Juvonen and Koptjevskaja-Tamm (in press) and Vanhove (2008).

7.6 Extending the Study of Onomasiological Salience

The study of onomasiological salience is relatively new, and it will be clear from the overview in this chapter that a number of open issues constitute a challenge that may guide the further development of the field. First, formal onomasiology relies on the identification of clearly demarcated senses that may be expressed by mutually competitive synonyms. Yet if senses themselves are intrinsically flexible and unstable (Geeraerts, 1993), we will have to move from a neat distinction between formal and conceptual onomasiology to more complicated models that combine semantic variability and variability of expression. Second, and somewhat similarly, conceptual onomasiology relies on the identification of referents: the extralinguistic things that are being talked about and that are being conceptualized in different ways. That kind of referential identification is sufficiently feasible when we have independent access to the referents (as with the visual information in our clothing terms study) or when we are dealing with relatively stable categories such as *woman*, but it constitutes a serious methodological problem when we try to go beyond such more-or-less clear cases. Third, the relationship between a typological and a usage-based pragmatic point of view needs to be further explored. Both were presented as highly parallel in the previous pages, but it needs to be established how far the parallelism actually extends and how the two levels interact.

Going beyond the lexical focus of the previous pages, onomasiological salience as investigated in the area of lexicology provides a point of comparison for the study of the entrenchment of constructions, specifically also because in construction grammar approaches, an onomasiological perspective is less well-entrenched than in lexical studies. The point may be illustrated along a methodological and a descriptive dimension. Methodologically speaking, the concept of onomasiological salience helps to see clearly in the diverse frequency phenomena with which a usage-based type of linguistics deals. The point was already made when we discussed Langacker's notion of entrenchment in the initial sections of the chapter, but it is important enough to reformulate it here. Consider the methodology of corpus linguistics. The raw frequencies and normalized text frequencies that are often used in corpus linguistics are not very informative: They are the combined result of the number of times a topic is discussed in a text, plus the number of times a certain conceptual construal is chosen to talk about that topic, plus the number of times a certain expression is used to verbalize that construal. Thinking analytically about types of entrenchment in this way cannot be restricted to lexical matters: Could similar distinctions be applied in construction grammar? An important step in that direction is the model developed by Schmid (2010, 2014), which introduces a principled and cognitively motivated distinction among various types of entrenchment, and accordingly critically scrutinizes popular methods of quantitative corpus linguistics (for a discussion of collostructional analysis, see Schmid & Küchenhoff, 2013). Schmid distinguishes among *cotext-free entrenchment* (the frequency of a construction relative to a collection of texts or an individual's production of language), *cotextual entrenchment* (the degree of syntagmatic association between expressions and the routinization of the composite construction), and *contextual entrenchment* (the relative frequency of identical or similar constructions with regard to a specific pragmatic context). Contextual entrenchment, then, is highly similar to onomasiological salience as explored in this chapter, except that Schmid refers to *pragmatic* contexts to signal that in the realm of constructional and syntactic analysis, identifying concepts is even less obvious than in the domain of lexical studies.

To illustrate the descriptive parallelism that may emerge between both fields, we can go back to the notion of conceptual onomasiological salience. Lexical research into conceptual onomasiological salience can in fact be extended in various directions; again, see Geeraerts et al. (1994). First, like formal onomasiological salience, conceptual salience may be context-dependent. Grondelaers and Geeraerts (1998), for instance, illustrated how shifting the taxonomical level of categorization is a register-dependent euphemistic strategy. Second, there is an interaction between semasiological and onomasiological salience (Geeraerts et al., 1994, pp. 156–176). The salience figures given in Table 7.3 represent the likelihood that one specific category, such as *legging* or *T-shirt* will be chosen to categorize and name a particular referent, in those cases where that referent is a potential member of the category. However, because the calculation is made for the category as a whole, an alternative calculation may take its starting point in a particular subset (or even a single member) of the entire range of application of the categories involved. The question asked so far boils down to this: What is the probability for the set of leggings as a whole that its members will be named with an expression that precisely identifies the category "legging"? The modified question would then read: Given a specific subtype of leggings (for instance, leggings that do not reach down to the ankles but are not longer than the calves), what is the likelihood that it will be named with the item *legging* or one of its synonyms? Obviously, the answer to the question will be determined by the overall salience of the category *legging* as calculated a moment ago, but it can be shown that it also depends on the structural position of the subset under investigation within the semasiological structure of *legging*: An expression will be used more often for naming a particular referent when that referent is a member of the prototypical core of that expression's range of application. When, for instance, a particular referent belongs to the core of item *x* but to the periphery of *y*, it is to be expected that *x* will be a more likely name for that referent than *y*. At the same time, of course, the choice for *x* will be a function of the global salience of the category represented by *x* in comparison to that of *y*. Categorization choices, in other words, result from various influences: the overall onomasiological salience of the competing concepts, the semasiological salience of the target within those concepts, and multiple contextual factors.

This lexical view on the interaction of onomasiological and semasiological salience may now be compared with Claes's (2015) recent study of constructional competition. Claes showed that the speakers of Dominican Spanish pluralize presentational *haber* under the influence of three factors: markedness of coding, statistical preemption, and structural priming. Although the terminology does not make the similarity apparent, this set of factors runs very much parallel to what we just described. Structural priming is a typically contextual factor; it involves the psycholinguistically well-studied phenomenon that an earlier occurrence of an expression in a stretch of discourse promotes the use of the same expression further on in the text (Pickering & Ferreira, 2008). Markedness of coding (Langacker, 1991, p. 298) relates to semasiological salience; it involves the expectation that a concept or denotatum that is more prototypical for a given expression will select that expression more readily than alternative expressions. And statistical preemption (Goldberg, 2006) links up with onomasiological salience; it involves the overall frequency of competing constructions relative to each other and the corresponding attraction of the more entrenched alternative.

The frameworks presented by Schmid and Claes are not standard in construction grammar, but the similarity with lexical studies is convincing enough to suggest a further confrontation. What would it involve, for instance, to distinguish between formal and conceptual onomasiological salience in constructional studies? Would it be methodologically feasible, and could it lead to lectometrical applications of the type developed in lexicology? And would it make sense to talk about indirect constructional construal, similar to the oblique conceptual construals discussed in this chapter? Because entrenchment is a cornerstone of the usage-based perspective that is dominant in construction grammar, it will be useful to explore how far the comparison between lexical and constructional approaches to corpus-based frequency phenomena can be carried.

In general, making onomasiological choices is an epistemologically fundamental feature of language, to the extent that it is a basic linguistic act—*the* basic act, in fact, on the side of language production. Hearers and readers may be focused on the interpretative, semasiological side of language, but for the speaker or writer, categorizing experience and putting that categorization into words is the primary linguistic activity. Language production takes the form of onomasiological choices of a formal and conceptual nature, and the concept of onomasiological salience involves the relative frequency with which such choices are made. As such, a focus on onomasiological salience is nothing else—but also nothing less—than a focus on what may well be the most fundamental feature of language production.

References

Anishchanka, A., Speelman, D., & Geeraerts, D. (2014). Referential meaning in basic and non-basic color terms. In W. Anderson, C. P. Biggam, C. Hough, & C. Kay (Eds.), *Colour studies: A broad spectrum* (pp. 323–338). http://dx.doi.org/10.1075/z.191.21ani

Baldinger, K. (1980). *Semantic theory*. Oxford, England: Blackwell.

Berlin, B. (1978). Ethnobiological classification. In E. Rosch & B. B. Lloyd (Eds.), *Cognition and categorization* (pp. 9–26). Hillsdale, NJ: Erlbaum.

Berlin, B., Breedlove, D. E., & Raven, P. H. (1973). General principles of classification and nomenclature in folk biology. *American Anthropologist*, *75*, 214–242. http://dx.doi.org/10.1525/aa.1973.75.1.02a00140

Blank, A. (2003). Words and concepts in time: Towards diachronic cognitive onomasiology. In R. Eckardt, K. von Heusinger, & C. Schwarze (Eds.), *Words in time: Diachronic semantics from different points of view* (pp. 37–65). http://dx.doi.org/10.1515/9783110899979.37

Blank, A., & Koch, P. (Eds.). (2003). *Kognitive romanische Onomasiologie und Semasiologie* [Cognitive onomasiology and semasiology of the Romance languages]. http://dx.doi.org/10.1515/9783110911626

Claes, J. (2015). Competing constructions: The pluralization of presentational *haber* in Dominican Spanish. *Cognitive Linguistics*, *26*, 1–30. http://dx.doi.org/10.1515/cog-2014-0006

Geeraerts, D. (1993). Vagueness's puzzles, polysemy's vagaries. *Cognitive Linguistics*, *4*, 223–272. http://dx.doi.org/10.1515/cogl.1993.4.3.223

Geeraerts, D. (1999). Vleeshouwers, beenhouwers en slagers: Het WNT als bron voor onomasiologisch onderzoek [Butchers, meat cutters, and slaughterers: The WNT as a source for onomasiological research]. *Nederlandse Taalkunde*, *4*, 34–46.

Geeraerts, D. (2001). Everyday language in the media: The case of Belgian Dutch soap series. In M. Kammerer, K.-P. Konerding, A. Lehr, A. Storrer, C. Thimm, & W. Wolski (Eds.), *Sprache im Alltag: Beiträge zu neuen Perspektiven in der Linguistik Herbert Ernst Wiegand zum 65: Geburtstag gewidmet* [Everyday language: Contributions to new perspectives in linguistics: Dedicated to Herbert Ernst Wiegand at the occasion of his 65th birthday] (pp. 281–291). http://dx.doi.org/10.1515/9783110880380.281

Geeraerts, D. (2010). *Theories of lexical semantics*. Oxford, England: Oxford University Press.

Geeraerts, D., & Gevaert, C. (2008). Hearts and (angry) minds in Old English. In F. Sharifian, R. Dirven, N. Yu, & S. Niemeier (Eds.), *Culture and language: Looking for the mind inside the body* (pp. 319–347). Berlin, Germany: Mouton de Gruyter.

Geeraerts, D., & Grondelaers, S. (2000). Purism and fashion: French influence on Belgian and Netherlandic Dutch. *Belgian Journal of Linguistics*, *13*, 53–68. http://dx.doi.org/10.1075/bjl.13.04gee

Geeraerts, D., Grondelaers, S., & Bakema, P. (1994). *The structure of lexical variation: Meaning, naming, and context*. Berlin, Germany: Mouton de Gruyter.

Geeraerts, D., Grondelaers, S., & Speelman, D. (1999). *Convergentie en divergentie in de Nederlandse woordenschat: Een onderzoek naar kleding- en voetbaltermen* [Convergence and divergence in the Dutch vocabulary: An investigation into clothing and football terms]. Amsterdam, the Netherlands: Meertens Instituut.

Geeraerts, D., Kristiansen, G., & Peirsman, Y. (Eds.). (2010). *Advances in cognitive sociolinguistics.* http://dx.doi.org/10.1515/9783110226461

Geeraerts, D., & Speelman, D. (2010). Heterodox concept features and onomasiological heterogeneity in dialects. In D. Geeraerts, G. Kristiansen, & Y. Peirsman (Eds.), *Advances in cognitive sociolinguistics* (pp. 23–40). http://dx.doi.org/10.1515/9783110226461.21

Gilquin, G., & Gries, S. (2009). Corpora and experimental methods: A state-of-the-art review. *Corpus Linguistics and Linguistic Theory, 5*, 1–26. http://dx.doi.org/10.1515/CLLT.2009.001

Glynn, D. (2010). Corpus-driven cognitive semantics: Introduction to the field. In D. Glynn & K. Fischer (Eds.), *Quantitative methods in cognitive semantics: Corpus-driven approaches* (pp. 1–41). Berlin, Germany: De Gruyter Mouton.

Goldberg, A. (2006). *Constructions at work: The nature of generalizations in language.* Oxford, England: Oxford University Press.

Grondelaers, S., & Geeraerts, D. (1998). Vagueness as a euphemistic strategy. In A. Athanasiadou & E. Tabakowska (Eds.), *Speaking of emotions: Conceptualisation and expression* (pp. 357–374). http://dx.doi.org/10.1515/9783110806007.357

Grondelaers, S., Geeraerts, D., Speelman, D., & Tummers, J. (2001). Lexical standardisation in internet conversations: Comparing Belgium and the Netherlands. In J. M. Fontana, L. McNally, M. T. Turell, & E. Vallduví (Eds.), *Proceedings of the First International Conference on Language Variation in Europe* (pp. 90–100). Barcelona, Spain: Universitat Pompeu Fabra, Institut Universitari de Lingüística Aplicada, Unitat de Investigació de Variació Lingüística.

Heine, B. (1997). *Cognitive foundations of grammar.* Oxford, England: Oxford University Press.

Heine, B. (2004). On genetic motivation in grammar. In G. Radden & K.-U. Panther (Eds.), *Studies in linguistic motivation* (pp. 103–120). Berlin, Germany: Mouton de Gruyter.

Heine, B., & Kuteva, T. (2002). *World lexicon of grammaticalization.* http://dx.doi.org/10.1017/CBO9780511613463

Juvonen, P., & Koptjevskaja-Tamm, M. (Eds.). (in press). *Lexico-typological approaches to semantic shifts and motivation patterns in the lexicon.* Berlin, Germany: De Gruyter Mouton.

Koptjevskaja-Tamm, M., Rakhilina, E., & Vanhove, M. (2015). The semantics of lexical typology. In N. Riemer (Ed.), *The Routledge handbook of semantics* (pp. 434–454). London, England: Routledge.

Kristiansen, G., & Dirven, R. (Eds.). (2008). *Cognitive sociolinguistics: Language variation, cultural models, social systems.* http://dx.doi.org/10.1515/9783110199154

Labov, W. (1972). *Sociolinguistic patterns.* Philadelphia: University of Pennsylvania Press.

Langacker, R. W. (1987). *Foundations of cognitive grammar: Vol. 1. Theoretical prerequisites.* Stanford, CA: Stanford University Press.

Langacker, R. W. (1991). *Foundations of cognitive grammar: Vol. 2. Descriptive application.* Stanford, CA: Stanford University Press.

McMahon, A., & McMahon, R. (2005). *Language classification by numbers.* Oxford, England: Oxford University Press.

Meringer, R. (1909). Wörter und sachen [Words and objects]. *Germanisch-Romanische Monatsschrift, 1*, 593–598.

Meringer, R. (1912). Zur Aufgabe und zum Namen unserer Zeitschrift [On the task and the name of our journal]. *Wörter und Sachen*, *3*, 22–56.

Navigli, R. (2012). A quick tour of word sense disambiguation, induction and related approaches. In M. Bieliková, G. Friedrich, G. Gottlob, S. Katzenbeisser, & G. Turán (Eds.), *Proceedings of the 38th Conference on Current Trends in Theory and Practice of Computer Science (SOFSEM)* (pp. 115–129). Heidelberg, Germany: Springer-Verlag.

Peirsman, Y., Geeraerts, D., & Speelman, D. (2010). The automatic identification of lexical variation between language varieties. *Natural Language Engineering*, *16*, 469–491. http://dx.doi.org/10.1017/S1351324910000161

Peirsman, Y., Geeraerts, D., & Speelman, D. (2015). The corpus-based identification of cross-lectal synonyms in pluricentric languages. *International Journal of Corpus Linguistics*, *20*, 54–80. http://dx.doi.org/10.1075/ijcl.20.1.03pei

Peirsman, Y., Heylen, K., & Geeraerts, D. (2010). Applying word space models to sociolinguistics. Religion names before and after 9/11. In D. Geeraerts, G. Kristiansen, & Y. Peirsman (Eds.), *Advances in cognitive sociolinguistics* (pp. 111–137). Berlin, Germany: de Gruyter Mouton.

Pickering, M. J., & Ferreira, V. S. (2008). Structural priming: A critical review. *Psychological Bulletin*, *134*, 427–459. http://dx.doi.org/10.1037/0033-2909.134.3.427

Rosch, E. (1978). Principles of categorization. In E. Rosch & B. B. Lloyd (Eds.), *Cognition and categorization* (pp. 27–48). Hillsdale, NJ: Erlbaum.

Ruette, T., Geeraerts, D., Peirsman, Y., & Speelman, D. (2014). Semantic weighting mechanisms in scalable lexical sociolectometry. In B. Wälchli & B. Szmrecsanyi (Eds.), *Aggregating dialectology, typology, and register analysis: Linguistic variation in text and speech* (pp. 205–230). http://dx.doi.org/10.1515/9783110317558.205

Ruette, T., Speelman, D., & Geeraerts, D. (2014). Lexical variation in aggregate perspective. In A. Soares da Silva (Ed.), *Pluricentricity: Language variation and sociocognitive dimensions* (pp. 227–241). Berlin, Germany: de Gruyter Mouton.

Schmid, H.-J. (2010). Does frequency in text really instantiate entrenchment in the cognitive system? In D. Glynn & K. Fischer (Eds.), *Quantitative methods in cognitive semantics: Corpus-driven approaches* (pp. 101–133). Berlin, Germany: de Gruyter Mouton.

Schmid, H.-J. (2014). Lexico-grammatical patterns, pragmatic associations and discourse frequency. In T. Herbst, H.-J. Schmid, & S. Faulhaber (Eds.), *Constructions collocations patterns* (pp. 239–293). http://dx.doi.org/10.1515/9783110356854.239

Schmid, H.-J., & Küchenhoff, H. (2013). Collostructional analysis and other ways of measuring lexicogrammatical attraction: Theoretical premises, practical problems and cognitive underpinnings. *Cognitive Linguistics*, *24*, 531–577. http://dx.doi.org/10.1515/cog-2013-0018

Schuchardt, H. (1912). Sachen und wörter [Objects and words]. *Anthropos: Internationale Zeitschrift für Völker- und Sprachenkunde*, *7*, 827–839.

Soares da Silva, A. (2010). Measuring and parameterizing lexical convergence and divergence between European and Brazilian Portuguese. In D. Geeraerts, G. Kristiansen, & Y. Peirsman (Eds.), *Advances in cognitive sociolinguistics* (pp. 41–83). http://dx.doi.org/10.1515/9783110226461.41

Speelman, D., & Geeraerts, D. (2009). The role of concept characteristics in lexical dialectometry. *International Journal of Humanities and Arts Computing*, *2*, 221–242. http://dx.doi.org/10.3366/E1753854809000408

Speelman, D., Grondelaers, S., & Geeraerts, D. (2003). Profile-based linguistic uniformity as a generic method for comparing language varieties. *Computers and the Humanities*, *37*, 317–337. http://dx.doi.org/10.1023/A:1025019216574

Speelman, D., Grondelaers, S., & Geeraerts, D. (2006). A profile-based calculation of region and register variation: The synchronic and diachronic status of the two main national varieties of Dutch. In A. Wilson, D. Archer, & P. Rayson (Eds.), *Corpus linguistics around the world* (pp. 195–202). Amsterdam, the Netherlands: Rodopi.

Vanhove, M. (Ed.). (2008). *From polysemy to semantic change: Towards a typology of lexical semantic associations*. http://dx.doi.org/10.1075/slcs.106

Zauner, A. (1903). Die romanischen namen der körperteile: Eine onomasiologische studie [The Romance names of body parts: An onomasiological study]. *Romanische Forschungen, 14*, 339–530.

Zenner, E., Speelman, D., & Geeraerts, D. (2012). Cognitive sociolinguistics meets loanword research: Measuring variation in the success of anglicisms in Dutch. *Cognitive Linguistics, 23*, 749–792. http://dx.doi.org/10.1515/cog-2012-0023

Zenner, E., Speelman, D., & Geeraerts, D. (2014). Core vocabulary, borrowability, and entrenchment: A usage-based onomasiological approach. *Diachronica, 31*, 74–105. http://dx.doi.org/10.1075/dia.31.1.03zen

Zhang, W., Geeraerts, D., & Speelman, D. (2015). Visualizing onomasiological change: Diachronic variation in metonymic patterns for "woman" in Chinese. *Cognitive Linguistics, 26*, 289–330. http://dx.doi.org/10.1515/cog-2014-0093

III Cognitive Foundations of Linguistic Entrenchment Processes

Atsuko Takashima and Iske Bakker
8 Memory Consolidation

8.1 Introduction

To make use of novel experiences and knowledge to guide our future behavior, we must keep large amounts of information accessible for retrieval. The memory system that stores this information needs to be flexible to rapidly incorporate incoming information but also requires that memory traces are stable and resistant to forgetting over a long period of time. More than a century of research on this topic has led to the insight that memory is not a unitary system but instead depends on a complex interaction between multiple memory systems that are subserved by different neural networks. The *complementary learning systems* (CLS) model, derived from the standard theory of systems-level memory consolidation, posits that a novel memory is initially encoded by the hippocampal memory system and subsequently undergoes a shift to the neocortical memory system. This process serves to stabilize and integrate novel information into persistent long-term memory without causing catastrophic interference to existing knowledge.

This chapter introduces the concept of multiple memory systems, which brain structures are engaged, and how they interact through the process of consolidation. Memory consolidation takes place both at the microscopic level, in the form of changes in synaptic strength, and at the whole-brain systems level, where it refers to a representational shift between different neural networks. We focus mainly on the systems level and discuss how the hippocampal (episodic and contextual) and neocortical (semantic and content) memory systems interact during specific stages of memory formation and consolidation.

Of particular relevance for the entrenchment of linguistic information is the idea that memory consolidation processes support qualitative changes in the representation of acquired information. For instance, consolidation is thought to underlie the generalization of overlapping information from multiple episodic memories into abstract representations and the integration of novel information with existing knowledge. We touch on the role of sleep in offline memory consolidation, which has been shown to boost memory stabilization as well as generalization and integration.

Linguistic information, like other memory representations, is thought to be acquired and retained in our memory system through the process of memory consolidation. The final section of the chapter focuses on recent findings related to linguistic memory consolidation, from word-form to semantics and syntax. These findings broadly support and add refinements to the CLS model of memory consolidation.

8.2 Memory Systems

Where did you buy this book? What does the word *book* mean? How do you make your fingers flip the pages? The answers to these questions draw on very different types of memory. Given the wide variety of experiences we encounter in daily life, and the multidimensionality of information that we need to extract from those experiences, it is perhaps unsurprising that these different types of memory are subserved by distinct neural systems (Eichenbaum & Cohen, 2001; Henke, 2010; Ullman, 2004).

8.2.1 Declarative and Procedural Memory

The main distinction that memory researchers generally make is between declarative, or explicit, memory and nondeclarative, or implicit, memory (Schacter, 1997; Squire, 1986; Squire & Knowlton, 1994; see Figure 8.1). *Declarative* memory can be consciously retrieved and contains our knowledge about events, such as buying a specific book at a bookstore, and facts, such as the meaning of words. *Nondeclarative* memory comprises motor and perceptual skills (known as procedural memory), conditioned reflexes, and other behaviors that you perform automatically without consciously knowing how you do them, such as flipping the pages of a book. It has been proposed that both memory systems contribute to language, with declarative memory providing a store for knowledge of words and sounds and procedural memory underlying the rules and patterns that govern the combination of these elements into complex structures (Ullman, 2004).

This division of memory into a declarative and a nondeclarative system finds neuropsychological support in the dissociation of impairments in patients with lesions to specific brain regions (e.g., Cohen & Squire, 1980). Studies in lesion patients and

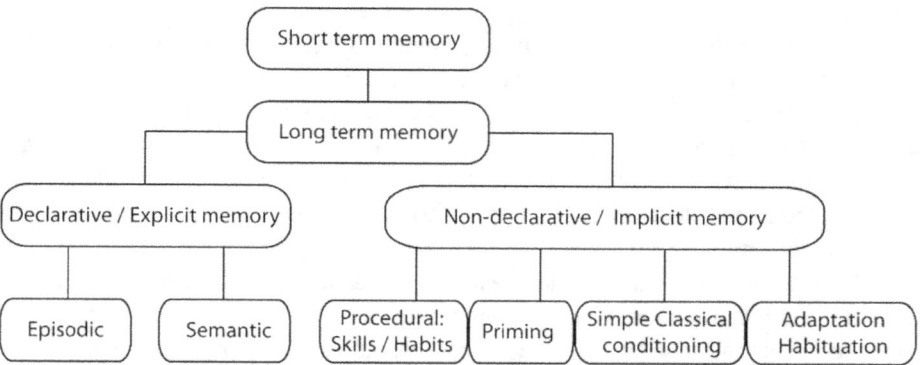

Fig. 8.1: The division of memory into multiple systems. From "The Medial Temporal Lobe Memory System," by L. R. Squire and S. Zola-Morgan, 1991, *Science, 253*, p. 1381. Copyright 1991 by American Association for the Advancement of Science. Adapted with permission.

animal models have suggested that the medial temporal lobe, including the hippocampus, is a critical region for the acquisition (encoding) of declarative memories (Alvarez & Squire, 1994; Eichenbaum, Sauvage, Fortin, Komorowski, & Lipton, 2012; Nadel & Moscovitch, 1997; Squire & Knowlton, 1994). The famous patient H. M., for instance, whose episodic memory was severely impaired after bilateral resection of parts of his medial temporal lobe, performed remarkably well on procedural tasks such as mirror drawing (Milner, 1962). Nondeclarative memory, in contrast, is thought to rely on a distinct network of structures including the basal ganglia, cerebellum, amygdala, and parts of frontal and parietal neocortex (Henke, 2010; Squire & Knowlton, 1994; Ullman, 2004). For example, patients with Parkinson disease who had damage to the striatum showed impaired acquisition of new implicit probabilistic associations but had no trouble remembering the learning event, again suggesting a dissociation of declarative and nondeclarative memory (Knowlton, Mangels, & Squire, 1996).

8.2.2 Episodic and Semantic Memory

Building on older philosophical observations, Tulving (1972, 2002) proposed that declarative memory can be further divided into two distinct neural systems, coding for episodic and semantic memory. *Episodic* memories refer to specific autobiographical events, whereas *semantic* memory concerns general world knowledge that is not linked to any spatiotemporal context. For instance, when you remember what you had for breakfast today, you are recalling an episodic memory, which probably contains a vivid, detailed representation of your surroundings, the sounds in the background and the taste of the food, for example. In contrast, when you read this sentence and retrieve the meaning of the word *breakfast*, you are activating your semantic knowledge about the concept of breakfast. (Note that *semantic* is used in a broader sense in the memory literature than it is in linguistics, and refers to both linguistic and nonlinguistic types of nonepisodic, generalized information.)

Again, the empirical basis for this distinction lies in case studies of patients with specific brain lesions. Starting with Scoville and Milner's (1957) description of the pattern of memory loss experienced by patient H. M., a long line of research has identified the hippocampus as a crucial contributor to episodic memory. After this structure and much of the surrounding tissue in the medial temporal lobe had been removed to relieve H. M. from his severe epilepsy, the previous 11 years of his life were erased from his memory (temporally graded *retrograde amnesia*). He was no longer able to form new memories (*anterograde amnesia*), and retained only a vague sense of what had occurred 15 minutes earlier—an experience that he described as continuously "waking from a dream" (Milner, Corkin, & Teuber, 1968). Remarkably, his semantic memory, in contrast, was almost completely intact: He still understood syntactically complex sentences, got the point of jokes, and even maintained his hobby of solving difficult crossword puzzles (Skotko et al., 2004). This dissociation of episodic and semantic memory has since been observed in many other patients with medial temporal lobe damage (e.g., Schmolck, Kensinger, Corkin, & Squire, 2002), suggesting that episodic and semantic memory are processed in different structures of the brain. The patterns of brain degeneration observed in dementia further support the idea that the hippocampus is a critical node for episodic memory, whereas neocortical areas, especially the lateral temporal cortex, are important for semantic memory. Alzheimer's dementia involves atrophy of the medial temporal lobe including the hippocampus in the early stages (Hampel et al., 2008; Mormino et al., 2009), and presents initially with impairments in episodic memory. Semantic dementia patients, in contrast, suffer from retrieval of semantic information and exhibit initial degeneration in the fronto-temporal aspect of the brain (Lambon Ralph & Patterson, 2008; Matthews, 2015; Patterson, Nestor, & Rogers, 2007; Snowden, 1999).

The episodic and semantic memory systems, however, do not act in isolation but interdependently (Greenberg & Verfaellie, 2010). Semantic knowledge is usually spared in hippocampally lesioned patients, both in developmental (Vargha-Khadem et al., 2003) and in adult-onset amnesics but adult-onset patients do have difficulties in acquiring novel semantic knowledge (Verfaellie, 2000). Although not impossible, the learning is slow, laborious, and requires that the input consists of many exemplars (Stark, Stark, & Gordon, 2005). In healthy participants, *deep encoding* strategies such as semantic elaboration enhance episodic memory for a list of words compared with *shallow encoding*, where participants attend to superficial elements of the word, such as in a letter monitoring task (Craik & Lockhart, 1972). Thus, episodic and semantic memories interact in that episodic memories help create new semantic memories, and associating semantic attributes with episodic memories aids the retention of encoded information. The precise way in which the two systems interact is still a matter of debate. Nonetheless, it can be argued that semantic memories are abstracted general features of overlapping characteristics across multiple episodes, devoid of specific contextual instances (Baddeley, 1988) and that we can comprehend and describe our experiences (episodes) using our semantic knowledge (Greenberg & Verfaellie, 2010; Reder, Park, & Kieffaber, 2009; Tulving, 2001).

8.3 Memory Consolidation

Memory traces are not static, but dynamic representations that change over time and influence other representations (Dudai, 2004, 2012). A newly encoded memory is still malleable and fragile and requires a gradual process of stabilization and integration into long-term memory to become resistant to forgetting. This process was termed *consolidation* by two pioneers of memory research, Müller and Pilzecker (1900). More than a century later, we are beginning to understand the central role that consolidation plays in various types of learning (McGaugh, 2000) and the neural mechanisms that underpin it.

8.3.1 Synaptic and Systems Consolidation

Contemporary memory research distinguishes between two levels of consolidation: consolidation on the molecular and cellular level and on the systems level (Josselyn, Köhler, & Frankland, 2015; Tonegawa, Liu, Ramirez, & Redondo, 2015). Consolidation at the cellular level occurs in the seconds to hours after initial learning, and refers to the cascade of processes that result in the formation of new synapses or the restructuring of existing synaptic connections. Since Hebb's (1949) seminal work, synaptic change has been viewed as the mechanism underlying long-term memory formation. The Hebbian principle states that simultaneous (or at least near-simultaneous) activation of multiple neuronal circuits promotes the formation of connections between them. From this point of view, consolidation constitutes reactivation and resulting stabilization of the newly formed synaptic structure. This mechanism appears to be universal across species and memory systems (Dudai, 2004). Systems consolidation, in contrast, involves brain regions rather than individual neurons and occurs on a time scale of hours to years. Because transfer of information between macrolevel memory systems is most relevant to the study of language acquisition, this chapter focuses on systems consolidation.

8.3.2 Models of Systems Consolidation

The widely accepted "standard model" of systems consolidation (Alvarez & Squire, 1994; Squire, Genzel, Wixted, & Morris, 2015) goes back to the ideas formulated by Marr (1970, 1971). In this view, the hippocampus, the core structure of the medial temporal lobe, serves to bind and integrate multiple components of a memory that are initially encoded in primary and associative neocortical areas. For instance, you might see a pile of round objects referred to as /æp.l/ and labeled *apple* in a market. The hippocampus binds together the multiple components of this experience, in this case, the groups of sensory neurons that were activated by the sound of the word and those that encoded the visual information. In another instance, you may see round objects on a tree in a park, again referred to as /æp.l/. This experience is encoded as a different episode by another set of hippocampal neurons, binding together sound and sensory-motor information experienced in the park (Figure 8.2, left-hand side, solid lines). Hippocampal–neocortical connections are assumed to be relatively fragile and transient, whereas cortico–cortical connections are considered to be more stable and long-lasting. Thus, hippocampal involvement gradually decreases over time while the novel memory becomes stabilized and integrated into the existing neocortical memory network (Figure 8.2, right-hand side, dashed lines between the hippocampus and the cortical nodes, and solid line between cortical nodes). The pattern of anterograde and temporally graded retrograde amnesia (i.e., more severe amnesia for recent than for remote episodes) observed in many hippocampal lesion patients and animal models follows naturally from this model: The older a memory

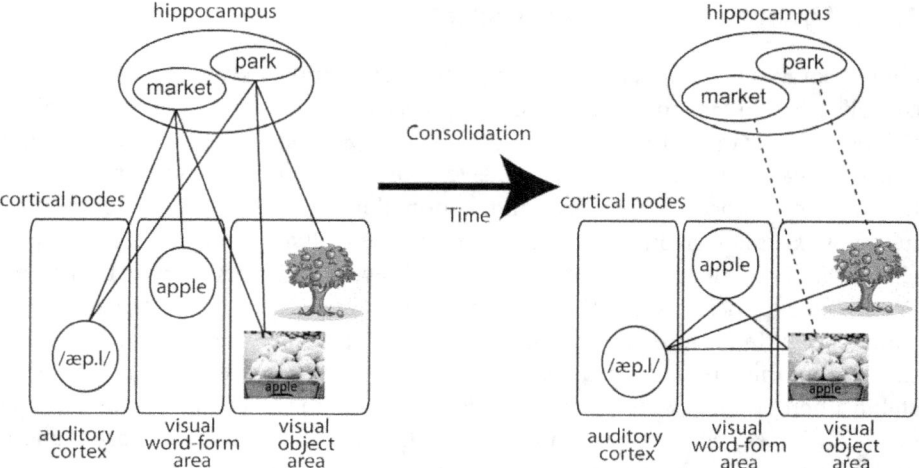

Fig. 8.2: Schematic view of systems consolidation. An apple experienced in a market and an experience of seeing an apple in a park are coded as separate episodes by different sets of hippocampal neurons (left-hand side: solid lines between cortical nodes and the hippocampus). Through systems consolidation, hippocampal–cortical connections decay (right-hand side: dashed line between the hippocampus and the cortical nodes), but cortico–cortical connections are strengthened (solid lines between the cortical nodes).

trace is, the more it has become independent of the hippocampus and the more likely it is to survive hippocampal lesioning (Frankland & Bontempi, 2005; Squire, Genzel, Wixted, & Morris, 2015). However, some salient experiences are never forgotten, such as your own wedding party or picking an apple from a tree in the park for the first time (Figure 8.2, right-hand side remaining connection between the hippocampus and the cortical nodes), and retrieving those memories may recruit the hippocampal episodic memory system even after the memory has become remote (Addis, Moscovitch, Crawley, & McAndrews, 2004; Bonnici et al., 2012; Gilboa, Winocur, Grady, Hevenor, & Moscovitch, 2004).

Building on these ideas, McClelland, McNaughton, and O'Reilly (1995) explored the computational properties of systems consolidation. According to their CLS account, the neocortical memory system can be viewed as a distributed connectionist network in which information is encoded by the connections between nodes. When new information is suddenly introduced, the rapid changes in connection weights can cause the network to "forget" previous information, a phenomenon known as catastrophic interference (McCloskey & Cohen, 1989). By temporarily storing new information in relative isolation in the hippocampus and only gradually interleaving it with existing knowledge in the neocortical network, systems consolidation circumvents this problem.

In contrast to the temporally graded amnesia predicted by the standard model, some hippocampal patients exhibit a much flatter gradient with impaired memory for both recent and remote events (Nadel & Moscovitch, 1997). Although patient H. M. appeared to retain some childhood memories, Corkin (2002) noted that many of these memories seemed to be semanticized and that he had difficulty relating the details of any specific events. To account for these findings, multiple trace theory (MTT) posits that episodic memories always remain dependent on the hippocampus for retrieval (Moscovitch, Nadel, Winocur, Gilboa, & Rosenbaum, 2006; Nadel & Moscovitch, 1997). Memory reactivation through retrieval leads to the formation of multiple traces between the hippocampus and the neocortex. Thus, in this view, autobiographical memories never become completely independent of the hippocampus. Whereas MTT focused primarily on autobiographical memory (thus episodic in nature), a follow-up theory termed trace-transfer theory agrees with the standard model of consolidation that semantic memory is independent of the hippocampal system (Winocur & Moscovitch, 2011). This is in line with the idea that through memory consolidation, some episodic memories are transformed to semantic memories and become encoded in the neocortical network. Because both the standard model and MTT/trace-transfer theory assume that semantic information is independent of the hippocampus, both views make the same prediction with regard to language learning: Hippocampal involvement in the storage of linguistic information will decrease over time until ultimately the new information is entirely neocortically integrated.

8.3.3 The Role of Sleep in Memory Consolidation

As early as 1924, Jenkins and Dallenbach reported that participants were better at recall if the period between learning and recall was spent asleep rather than awake. They concluded that the state of sleep passively protects the acquired information against interference from subsequent exposure to similar information (*retroactive interference*). Recent studies, however, have found that sleep not only passively protects memory from interference and decay but also enables active stabilization of the memory trace (Diekelmann & Born, 2010; Rasch & Born, 2013; Stickgold & Walker, 2007). The effect of this stabilization process can be observed in the form of increased resistance to interference (e.g., Ellenbogen, Hulbert, Stickgold, Dinges, & Thompson-Schill, 2006) as well as enhanced performance (Stickgold & Walker, 2007) after a consolidation period without any further training. Sleep consolidates both declarative and procedural knowledge, but different sleep stages or combinations of different sleep stages seem to selectively contribute to each type of memory (Stickgold & Walker, 2007), The deep-sleep stage, rich in slow waves, has been found to be important for consolidation of declarative memories in particular (Mölle & Born, 2011). Moreover, specific aspects of sleep physiology such as spindle density and the amount of slow-wave sleep have shown correlations with memory performance after sleep (Diekelmann & Born, 2010).

One of the possible mechanisms underlying active consolidation is the repeated reactivation of memory traces during sleep, which strengthens the newly formed neural circuits encoding the information. Spontaneous replay of novel memories during sleep has been shown directly in rats by comparing the firing patterns of single neurons while rats were exploring a maze with the firing patterns of the same cells during subsequent sleep (Louie & Wilson, 2001; Wilson & McNaughton, 1994). Specific firing sequences were replayed during sleep, as though the rats were "reliving" their spatial experience of the maze. Single cell firing patterns are difficult to measure in humans, but there is a growing body of evidence for memory reactivation at the whole-brain level using techniques such as electroencephalogram (EEG) and functional magnetic resonance imaging (fMRI). For example, Deuker et al. (2013) showed that patterns of brain activation associated with the processing of specific stimuli reoccurred spontaneously during postlearning sleep, and the amount of reactivation was correlated with participants' subsequent memory for those stimuli.

Furthermore, a number of studies have been able to demonstrate the causal role of reactivation by externally inducing increased levels of reactivation in the sleeping brain (Antony, Gobel, O'Hare, Reber, & Paller, 2012; Cairney, Durrant, Musgrove, & Lewis, 2011; Oudiette & Paller, 2013; Rasch, Büchel, Gais, & Born, 2007; Rudoy, Voss, Westerberg, & Paller, 2009). In a groundbreaking experiment, Rasch and colleagues (2007) taught participants pairings between objects and their locations on a grid while a rose odor was present in the room. One group of participants was exposed to the same odor during subsequent deep sleep, and another group was not. The group that was reexposed to the odor performed significantly better on a postsleep memory task, suggesting that the odor had cued reactivation of the newly learned object–place associations and stimulated their consolidation. A recent study revealed that induced reactivation can even improve consolidation of more complex material, such as novel words. Schreiner and Rasch (2015) trained German-speaking participants on Dutch–German translation pairs and exposed them during sleep with learned Dutch words. Sleep cueing improved subsequent translation performance, even though participants were completely unaware of the manipulation. Thus, spontaneous reactivation during postlearning rest and sleep is likely to be one of the mechanisms by which novel linguistic information, just like other types of memory, becomes stabilized and integrated. Through external stimulation, memory trace reactivation may further be induced to enhance consolidation.

8.3.4 Generalization, Integration, and the Role of Prior Knowledge

The term *consolidation* originally referred only to the strengthening and stabilization of memories, resulting in greater resistance to interference and forgetting (Frankland & Bontempi, 2005). However, today there is a general consensus that consolidation is more than just stabilization of the original memory trace (Dudai, 2012) and also entails processes related to abstraction of common features (i.e., generalization). The earlier-mentioned CLS model assumes that novel memories are integrated into existing knowledge through interleaved learning. This produces a qualitative change in the way the novel memory trace is stored: It is transformed from a single episodic memory into a generalized, semantic representation. Through experiencing multiple episodes that share common features, such as experiencing different kinds of objects that are always labelled *apple*, we are able to extract the core characteristics of apples, that they are a kind of round, sweet fruit with crispy texture (Figure 8.2, right-hand side). We may forget each and every individual instance of experiencing an apple, but we retain the knowledge of what an apple is (Baddeley, 1988). Similarly, we acquire the grammatical rules and patterns of our native language without remembering the actual input, and often without being able to explain those rules and patterns. This ability to generalize is what makes language such a powerful tool for efficient communication.

A number of studies have demonstrated the importance of offline consolidation, and in particular, sleep, in evoking such qualitative changes to the nature of new memories. Payne et al. (2009) examined the effect of sleep on the creation of false memories, induced by generalization across a set of exemplars. Participants studied a list of semantically related words, such as BED, REST, TIRED, which did not, however, include the word that binds them together: SLEEP. After having slept, participants were more likely to falsely remember having seen the word SLEEP, suggesting that they had extracted the gist from the multiple episodic memories they had encoded. Other studies have demonstrated that sleep promotes insight into logical problems (Wagner, Gais, Haider, Verleger, & Born, 2004) and drawing inferences about indirect associations (Ellenbogen, Hu, Payne, Titone, & Walker, 2007), suggesting that multiple individual item memories had become integrated into a coherent whole. It has been proposed that memory trace reactivation during sleep leads to strengthening of the neural activation patterns that are common across multiple episodes or tokens, resulting in generalization and abstraction (Lewis & Durrant, 2011). Memory replay during sleep may also contribute to interleaved learning, as the repeated reactivation of neural patterns related to novel experiences during sleep mimics reexperiencing, even if it occurs outside of our conscious awareness. In this way, integration of novel information into the existing knowledge network can be facilitated by sleep. In sum, postlearning rest and sleep not only stabilize novel memory traces but also produce qualitative changes in the form of increased generalization and integration.

The speed with which novel information is integrated with existing knowledge depends on many factors, including the nature of the learning material. If new information can be related to a coherent set of prior knowledge or a *schema*, memory consolidation has been shown to be accelerated and less hippocampus-dependent. For instance, if you already know what a book is (you have a "book" schema), it is easy to incorporate new information that shares some features with books, such as the concept of a magazine, or to learn the word for *book* in another language. In contrast, learning words or facts that are completely unrelated to your prior knowledge is much more challenging. Rapid neocortical integration in the presence of a schema has been demonstrated both in rodents (Tse et al., 2007) and humans (e.g., van Kesteren et al., 2013;

van Kesteren, Rijpkema, Ruiter, & Fernández, 2010; van Kesteren, Rijpkema, Ruiter, Morris, & Fernández, 2014; Zeithamova, Dominick, & Preston, 2012). Given that novel linguistic information is generally strongly related to existing linguistic knowledge, this discovery may prove to be especially relevant for our understanding of how the hippocampal and neocortical memory systems interact during language acquisition.

8.4 Memory Consolidation and Language Learning

8.4.1 Lexical Learning

A core feature shared by all modern psycholinguistic models is the ability of word representations in the mental lexicon to influence each other's activation levels. For example, efficient spoken-word recognition is believed to rely on a process of competition within the set of words that match the input (Gaskell & Marslen-Wilson, 1997; Marslen-Wilson, 1990; McClelland & Elman, 1986; Norris, 1994; Norris & McQueen, 2008). Learning a novel word therefore involves not only the formation of a new memory but, crucially, also its integration with the existing mental lexicon. As discussed in Section 8.3.4, integration is one of the main ways in which consolidation changes the nature of new memories. The CLS account of word learning outlined by Davis and Gaskell (2009) proposes that lexical integration is a result of systems consolidation and relies on the same process of hippocampal–neocortical transfer as nonlinguistic memories (see Figure 8.2). The hippocampus initially encodes an episodic representation of a novel word, which can be retrieved but does not yet interact with the existing mental lexicon. During the hours or days after learning, neocortical connections between the novel word's components (e.g., phonology and semantics) as well as connections between the novel word and related existing words are gradually strengthened, while hippocampal connections decay (see Figure 8.3).

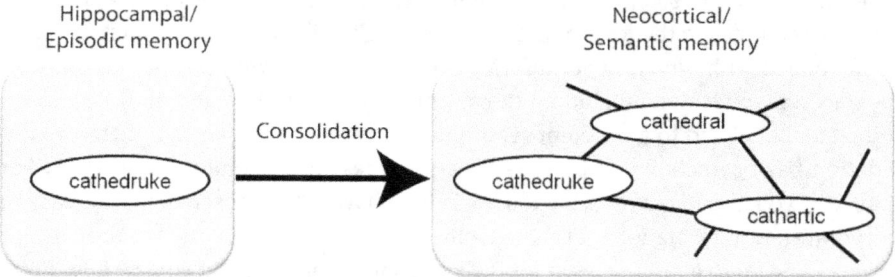

Fig. 8.3: Memory consolidation of novel words. A shift from an isolated episodic memory representation to an integrated neocortical representation with consolidation. Once integrated into the lexical network, the novel word interacts with its phonological, orthographic, and semantic neighbors.

Ultimately, the novel word is entirely neocortically represented and fully integrated into the existing mental lexicon, which allows it to interact with other lexical representations. Some episodic features—that is, the contextual memory of how the word was encountered (e.g., who said it, or how it was said)—may additionally remain in the episodic hippocampal system according to the MTT (Moscovitch et al., 2005).

The most frequently used method to test the effect of consolidation on a novel word's lexical status is to assess its influence on the recognition of related existing words. In the first study to use this approach, Gaskell and Dumay (2003) taught participants a set of novel words that overlapped phonologically with the initial portion of an existing word. Participants who had learned the novel word *cathedruke* became slower to respond to its existing neighbor *cathedral*, which, the authors argued, reflects increased lexical competition from the novel word. This effect only emerged after several days, suggesting that offline consolidation facilitated the integration of *cathedruke* into the mental lexicon. Similar patterns of competition after consolidation have been found with a variety of spoken-word recognition tasks (Davis, Di Betta, Macdonald, & Gaskell, 2009; Dumay & Gaskell, 2007, 2012; Tamminen, Payne, Stickgold, Wamsley, & Gaskell, 2010) as well as with written materials (Bowers, Davis, & Hanley, 2005). The effect also has been shown to generalize across different training and test modalities (Bakker, Takashima, van Hell, Janzen, & McQueen, 2014), confirming that it reflects activation of lexical rather than episodic information.

A second line of research has focused on the integration of novel word meanings with existing semantic knowledge. Two studies (Tamminen & Gaskell, 2013; van der Ven, Takashima, Segers, & Verhoeven, 2015) paired novel words with definitions and investigated the ability of those words to speed up recognition of semantically related existing words. This semantic priming effect was observed after a delay of 24 hours, again suggesting that offline consolidation aided integration. A somewhat different approach was taken by Clay, Bowers, Davis, and Hanley (2007). Their test task involved naming pictures of common objects, on which a distractor word was superimposed. Reaction times increased when the distractor word was a semantically related learned word, indicating that the novel meaning interfered with selection of the target, but this only occurred after a week. Tham, Lindsay, and Gaskell (2015) taught participants novel written names for familiar animals. After 12 hours, these words started to exhibit size–congruity effects similar to existing words: Participants were faster at indicating which item was printed in a larger font in pairs where the larger word referred to the larger animal, for example, "BEE–COW." The authors proposed that offline consolidation increased the automaticity of semantic access to novel words, enabling them to affect response times even in this nonsemantic, perceptual task. Thus, the research reviewed here suggests that newly encoded information about word forms and meanings undergoes a qualitative change in representation during offline consolidation. Only when novel word representations become embedded in the existing neocortical lexicon do they begin interacting with other representations and can they truly be said to function as words.

In apparent contrast to these observations of delayed consolidation-dependent lexicalization, however, several recent studies have reported immediate competition and priming effects. Borovsky, Elman, and Kutas (2012) observed a semantic priming effect from words that had just been trained, suggesting that these words had already been integrated sufficiently to interact with semantically related existing words. Competition effects have also been found immediately after training, for instance, in a visual world paradigm (Kapnoula, Packard, Gupta, & McMurray, 2015) and when training was implicit rather than explicit (Szmalec, Page, & Duyck, 2012). Even with a procedure similar to that used in the original study by Gaskell and Dumay (2003), Lindsay and Gaskell (2013) found that competition arose within a single day when novel and existing words were interleaved during the training phase. These findings of rapid lexicalization have been related to the ease with which novel information can be assimilated to a prior schema (see Section 8.3.4). It is possible that under circumstances in which schema integration is stimulated either by the nature of the material or the task, word learning may involve only a limited hippocampal contribution. This would explain why certain paradigms yield lexicalization effects that do not require offline consolidation.

8.4.2 The Neural Basis of Lexical Learning

Recent work has begun to explore the neural basis of lexicalization. Several studies provide support for the CLS claim that neocortical involvement in the representation of novel words increases over time. In an fMRI study by Takashima, Bakker, van Hell, Janzen, and McQueen (2014), participants learned novel neighbors of existing words (e.g., *cathedruke*). Their brain activity during spoken word recognition of the newly learned words was measured immediately after training, and again after a 24-hour consolidation period. Relative to the immediate test, increased activation was observed after 24 hours in the posterior middle temporal gyrus (pMTG). Furthermore, connectivity between the auditory cortex and the pMTG increased for those participants that showed behavioral effects of lexical competition between novel and existing words. The pMTG is believed to encode lexical information by mediating between phonological and semantic information stored in distributed parts of the cortex (Gow, 2012; Hickok & Poeppel, 2004, 2007). Increased involvement of this area therefore suggests that novel word retrieval became increasingly lexical in nature after the consolidation period.

Electrophysiological data provide further evidence that novel words start to function more like existing words after consolidation. One EEG study (Bakker, Takashima, van Hell, Janzen, & McQueen, 2015b) looked at the N400, an event-related potential that is generally larger for pseudo-words than existing words. Whereas novel words showed pseudo-wordlike N400 responses immediately after training, the N400 became significantly more wordlike after consolidation. Looking at the frequency domain of the EEG signal, Bakker, Takashima, van Hell, Janzen, and McQueen (2015a) showed that novel words initially elicited less power in the theta band (4–8 Hz) than existing words. This difference between novel and existing words decreased somewhat after participants acquired a meaning for the novel words but disappeared completely after 24 hours without further training. A recent MEG study localized the source of this consolidation effect to the pMTG (Bakker, Takashima, van Hell, Janzen, & McQueen, 2016), showing, in line with the fMRI data from Takashima et al. (2014), an increase in activation in that region. Together these data suggest that a lexical representation in the pMTG is gradually established during offline consolidation.

Although several studies have demonstrated a role for the hippocampus in the early stages of word learning (Breitenstein et al., 2005; Davis et al., 2009), there is little direct evidence so far that hippocampal involvement decreases after consolidation. Davis et al. (2009) reported that untrained words elicited more hippocampal activation than trained words, but failed to show a clear decrease after consolidation. Similarly, Takashima et al. (2014) found that the hippocampus still contributed to novel word form recognition after consolidation, especially for those word forms that were associated with a picture. It must be noted, however, that the time course tested for these laboratory studies are short (spanning 24 hours), and more time or repetition may be necessary for full consolidation and integration (see also Section 8.4.4). Thus, although current evidence strongly supports the gradual emergence of a neocortical lexical representation, future research will need to critically examine the CLS hypothesis of time-limited hippocampal involvement.

8.4.3 Grammar Learning

In addition to lexical learning, the extraction of generalized templates from exemplars is an essential component of language acquisition underlying, for instance, phonological, morphological, and syntactic learning. Although much less is known about the role of consolidation in grammar learning compared with lexical learning, several studies have provided evidence that the process of abstraction and generalization benefits greatly from offline consolidation and in particular, from sleep. Investigating the acquisition of phonotactic rules, Gaskell et al. (2014) asked participants to repeat syllable sequences in which the position of two specific phonemes within the syllable was determined by the adjacent vowel. Participants who napped, but not those who stayed awake, showed subsequent implicit knowledge of the rule and generalized it to untrained syllables. These data suggest that sleep consolidation aids the implicit extraction of linguistic rules (see Section 8.3.4 on generalization and abstraction of common features).

Results from studies looking at morphosyntactic rules corroborate this claim. Gómez, Bootzin, and Nadel (2006) demonstrated that 15-month-old infants became more sensitive to abstract rules after a nap but not after a similar time spent awake. In this study, children listened to sequences of three pseudo-words in which there was a sequential dependency between the first and third word. In a subsequent test with novel stimuli, the nap group showed sensitivity to sequences that followed the same rule as the first test trial (regardless of whether that rule had been presented in the exposure phase). The authors argue that sleep promoted sensitivity to abstract rules, which may underlie acquisition of linguistic long-distance dependencies such as subject–verb number agreement.

Nieuwenhuis, Folia, Forkstam, Jensen, and Petersson (2013) used a series of letter strings generated by a complex artificial grammar to investigate whether sleep benefits rule learning in adults. Different groups of participants were exposed to a set of grammatical strings and tested on their implicit knowledge of the underlying rules after various delays. Only those participants for whom the delay included sleep distinguished between new grammatical and ungrammatical sequences on a forced-choice test, again suggesting that sleep aided the extraction of a general rule. Crucially, this study controlled for the possibility of sleep's influence on strengthening the memory traces of particular "chunks" of letters rather than rule extraction (see Gobet, this volume, Chapter 11, on chunking). The authors reported that memory for high-frequency chunks were not modulated by sleep, suggesting that sleep indeed enhanced rule learning rather than stabilization of the exemplar specific memory (Nieuwenhuis et al., 2013).

Rule extraction can be seen as the formation of schemas or patterns that can be applied to multiple instances. In the context of language, this general template allows for the productive combination of words and phrases into sentences. Behavioral observations of implicit grammatical rule acquisition and pattern extraction through repeated exposure and sleep consolidation indicate that similar consolidation process may take place during grammatical and lexical learning, such as generalization and abstraction. However, if grammatical knowledge is viewed as a type of procedural memory (Ullman, 2004), we may expect syntactic acquisition to share some characteristics with procedural skill learning rather than declarative memory formation. It is possible that the neural structures involved in grammatical learning may differ from those underlying the consolidation of lexical representations, for instance, with a greater role for prefrontal areas that code for extracted patterns (Bahlmann, Schubotz, & Friederici, 2008; Uddén et al., 2008) or the left middle superior temporal cortex to retrieve rule-based inflectional morphology (Hultén, Karvonen, Laine, & Salmelin, 2014). It would also be illuminating to examine the effects of different sleep stages on lexical and syntactic consolidation effects within a single study. For instance, lexical consolidation may benefit more from deep sleep stages just like other declarative memories, whereas syntactic memories may rely more on shallow sleep stages (see Section 8.3.3).

8.4.4 Theoretical Implications

As the role of consolidation in lexical learning is currently much better understood than its involvement in grammatical learning, this section focuses on the CLS model of word learning. Nonetheless, many of the conclusions drawn from these data likely apply to grammar learning as well. The findings discussed earlier generally support Davis and Gaskell's (2009) CLS account of word learning in which hippocampal involvement decreases over time while neocortical integration gradually increases. At the same time, recent results suggest several refinements of the original model.

With regard to the first component, there is no direct evidence so far for a decrease in hippocampal involvement in word retrieval after consolidation. This may be due to laboratory studies generally using a relatively short delay of up to several days between training and test, whereas the hippocampus has been shown to remain involved in retrieval of certain types of memory for months to years (Moscovitch et al., 2005; Nadel & Moscovitch, 1997). Alternatively, the recent findings of rapid neocortical integration suggest that under certain circumstances, the hippocampus may play a more limited role than previously thought. To address this issue, McClelland (2013) showed that the CLS model is not computationally inconsistent with rapid neocortical integration of new information, if it is schema-consistent. Although the original simulations (McClelland et al., 1995) revealed catastrophic interference when novel information was suddenly introduced, McClelland (2013) pointed out that the information used in those simulations was unrelated to the network's prior knowledge by design. New simulations with schema-consistent information did produce successful learning and did not lead to interference. Thus, the interaction between the hippocampal and neocortical systems may be more flexible than suggested by the original CLS model, and the neocortex may need to be reconceptualized as a "prior knowledge-dependent" rather than a "slow-learning" system (McClelland, 2013).

The second main feature of the CLS model, gradual neocortical integration, finds strong support in the available data. A large body of behavioral evidence suggests that offline consolidation enhances the interaction between novel and existing words, both in terms of competition and priming (e.g., Bakker et al., 2014; Clay et al., 2007; Dumay & Gaskell, 2007, 2012; Gaskell & Dumay, 2003; Tamminen & Gaskell, 2013; Tham et al., 2015; van der Ven et al., 2015). Neuroimaging studies of word learning are now beginning to elucidate the exact neural underpinnings of this integration process, pointing specifically at an increase in activity in the left pMTG (Bakker et al., 2016; Takashima et al., 2014). This is in line with several models that assign a crucial role in lexical representation to this area (Gow, 2012; Hickok & Poeppel, 2004, 2007; Lau, Phillips, & Poeppel, 2008). These models view the pMTG as a lexical *association area*, serving as the interface among the various neocortical areas that code for phonological, orthographic, semantic, and syntactic information about words. Thus, the neural basis for lexical integration may be the formation and gradual strengthening of connections between each of these distributed neocortical areas and the pMTG, thereby creating a network that comprises the various types of information about a word.

The CLS model and the findings discussed here also make certain predictions with regard to more general theories of language and language learning. For example, the similarities between consolidation effects for linguistic and nonlinguistic information suggest that language learning depends to a large extent on domain-general mechanisms of memory formation and consolidation. This in turn implies that there is no fundamental difference between the neural underpinnings of first and second languages, although there may be quantitative differences in the degree to which these processes rely on the hippocampal and neocortical systems (Lindsay & Gaskell, 2010). If a second language is learned later in life (see MacWhinney, Chapter 15, this volume), its lexical representations may recruit the hippocampal system more strongly than those in the native language. This hypothesis is supported by data showing that, on the one hand, lexical competition occurs nonselectively between bilinguals' two languages (e.g., Marian, Spivey, & Hirsch, 2003) but that, on the other hand, the strength of competition from each language depends on proficiency (e.g., Blumenfeld & Marian, 2007). With respect to developmental aspects, a recent line of work by Henderson and colleagues suggests that consolidation and lexicalization follow similar patterns in children and adults (Henderson, Devine, Weighall, & Gaskell, 2015; Henderson, Weighall, Brown, & Gaskell, 2012, 2013; Henderson, Weighall, & Gaskell, 2013). Overall, the findings discussed here generally support a model in which all forms of language acquisition share a common neural mechanism involving an interaction between the hippocampus and distributed neocortical areas, but the relative contribution of these memory systems may vary depending on age, proficiency level, and other factors.

8.5 Concluding Remarks

Although memory consolidation has been studied experimentally for more than a century, it is only recently that psycholinguists have started to consider its relevance for understanding language acquisition. Language is one of our most complex cognitive abilities and naturally much remains to be explored about the precise ways in which consolidation processes operate on linguistic information. We are only beginning to investigate, for example, the precise time course of linguistic consolidation and the factors that influence it, as well as the similarities and differences among age groups, native and nonnative speakers, and so on. Second, an as yet underinvestigated issue is to what degree lexical learning and grammar learning share the same (neural) mechanisms of consolidation. Nonetheless, the picture that has emerged so far from the meeting of language and memory research is that most aspects of memory consolidation theories can be successfully applied to language learning. In agreement with the working definition of entrenchment as outlined in the introductory chapter of this volume, the data discussed here suggest that language acquisition (both lexical and grammatical) can be viewed as the product of domain-general consolidation processes acting on linguistic experience. Reactivation and rehearsal of multiple experiences not only strengthens individual memory traces but crucially also enables the consolidation of neocortical connections between representations. This integration process underlies the formation of generalized, abstract templates or schemas that generate productive language use. From the point of view of memory research, entrenchment can therefore be seen as the transformation of the episodic features of linguistic experiences into semanticized lexical and grammatical knowledge. This conceptualization of words and grammatical structures as dynamic memory representations that undergo processes of encoding, stabilization, generalization, and interaction with prior knowledge, just like nonlinguistic representations, has proven to be an extremely fruitful approach that will hopefully continue to inspire interdisciplinary work on memory and language acquisition.

References

Addis, D. R., Moscovitch, M., Crawley, A. P., & McAndrews, M. P. (2004). Recollective qualities modulate hippocampal activation during autobiographical memory retrieval. *Hippocampus*, *14*, 752–762. http://dx.doi.org/10.1002/hipo.10215

Alvarez, P., & Squire, L. R. (1994). Memory consolidation and the medial temporal lobe: A simple network model. *Proceedings of the National Academy of Sciences of the United States of America*, *91*, 7041–7045. http://dx.doi.org/10.1073/pnas.91.15.7041

Antony, J. W., Gobel, E. W., O'Hare, J. K., Reber, P. J., & Paller, K. A. (2012). Cued memory reactivation during sleep influences skill learning. *Nature Neuroscience*, *15*, 1114–1116. http://dx.doi.org/10.1038/nn.3152

Baddeley, A. (1988). Cognitive psychology and human memory. *Trends in Neurosciences*, *11*, 176–181. http://dx.doi.org/10.1016/0166-2236(88)90145-2

Bahlmann, J., Schubotz, R. I., & Friederici, A. D. (2008). Hierarchical artificial grammar processing engages Broca's area. *NeuroImage*, *42*, 525–534. http://dx.doi.org/10.1016/j.neuroimage.2008.04.249

Bakker, I., Takashima, A., van Hell, J. G., Janzen, G., & McQueen, J. M. (2014). Competition from unseen or unheard novel words: Lexical consolidation across modalities. *Journal of Memory and Language*, *73*, 116–130. http://dx.doi.org/10.1016/j.jml.2014.03.002

Bakker, I., Takashima, A., van Hell, J. G., Janzen, G., & McQueen, J. M. (2015a). Changes in theta and beta oscillations as signatures of novel word consolidation. *Journal of Cognitive Neuroscience*, *27*, 1286–1297. http://dx.doi.org/10.1162/jocn_a_00801

Bakker, I., Takashima, A., van Hell, J. G., Janzen, G., & McQueen, J. M. (2015b). Tracking lexical consolidation with ERPs: Lexical and semantic-priming effects on N400 and LPC responses to newly-learned words. *Neuropsychologia, 79, Part A*, 33–41. http://dx.doi.org/10.1016/j.neuropsychologia.2015.10.020

Bakker, I., Takashima, A., van Hell, J. G., Janzen, G., & McQueen, J. M. (2016). *Theta-band oscillations in the posterior MTG reflect novel word consolidation: An MEG study.* Manuscript in preparation.

Blumenfeld, H. K., & Marian, V. (2007). Constraints on parallel activation in bilingual spoken language processing: Examining proficiency and lexical status using eye-tracking. *Language and Cognitive Processes*, *22*, 633–660. http://dx.doi.org/10.1080/01690960601000746

Bonnici, H. M., Kumaran, D., Chadwick, M. J., Weiskopf, N., Hassabis, D., & Maguire, E. A. (2012). Decoding representations of scenes in the medial temporal lobes. *Hippocampus*, *22*, 1143–1153. http://dx.doi.org/10.1002/hipo.20960

Borovsky, A., Elman, J. L., & Kutas, M. (2012). Once is enough: N400 indexes semantic integration of novel word meanings from a single exposure in context. *Language Learning and Development*, *8*, 278–302. http://dx.doi.org/10.1080/15475441.2011.614893

Bowers, J. S., Davis, C. J., & Hanley, D. A. (2005). Interfering neighbours: The impact of novel word learning on the identification of visually similar words. *Cognition*, *97*, B45–B54. http://dx.doi.org/10.1016/j.cognition.2005.02.002

Breitenstein, C., Jansen, A., Deppe, M., Foerster, A.-F., Sommer, J., Wolbers, T., & Knecht, S. (2005). Hippocampus activity differentiates good from poor learners of a novel lexicon. *NeuroImage*, *25*, 958–968. http://dx.doi.org/10.1016/j.neuroimage.2004.12.019

Cairney, S. A., Durrant, S. J., Musgrove, H., & Lewis, P. A. (2011). Sleep and environmental context: Interactive effects for memory. *Experimental Brain Research*, *214*, 83–92. http://dx.doi.org/10.1007/s00221-011-2808-7

Clay, F., Bowers, J. S., Davis, C. J., & Hanley, D. A. (2007). Teaching adults new words: The role of practice and consolidation. *Journal of Experimental Psychology: Learning, Memory, and Cognition*, *33*, 970–976. http://dx.doi.org/10.1037/0278-7393.33.5.970

Cohen, N. J., & Squire, L. R. (1980). Preserved learning and retention of pattern-analyzing skill in amnesia: Dissociation of knowing how and knowing that. *Science*, *210*, 207–210. http://dx.doi.org/10.1126/science.7414331

Corkin, S. (2002). What's new with the amnesic patient H. M.? *Nature Reviews Neuroscience*, *3*, 153–160. http://dx.doi.org/10.1038/nrn726

Craik, F. I. M., & Lockhart, R. S. (1972). Levels of processing: A framework for memory research. *Journal of Verbal Learning & Verbal Behavior*, *11*, 671–684. http://dx.doi.org/10.1016/S0022-5371(72)80001-X

Davis, M. H., Di Betta, A. M., Macdonald, M. J. E., & Gaskell, M. G. (2009). Learning and consolidation of novel spoken words. *Journal of Cognitive Neuroscience*, *21*, 803–820. http://dx.doi.org/10.1162/jocn.2009.21059

Davis, M. H., & Gaskell, M. G. (2009). A complementary systems account of word learning: Neural and behavioural evidence. *Philosophical Transactions of the Royal Society of London. Series B. Biological Sciences*, *364*, 3773–3800. http://dx.doi.org/10.1098/rstb.2009.0111

Deuker, L., Olligs, J., Fell, J., Kranz, T. A., Mormann, F., Montag, C., . . . Axmacher, N. (2013). Memory consolidation by replay of stimulus-specific neural activity. *The Journal of Neuroscience*, *33*, 19373–19383. http://dx.doi.org/10.1523/JNEUROSCI.0414-13.2013

Diekelmann, S., & Born, J. (2010). The memory function of sleep. *Nature Reviews Neuroscience*, *11*, 114–126. http://dx.doi.org/10.1038/nrn2762

Dudai, Y. (2004). The neurobiology of consolidations, or, how stable is the engram? *Annual Review of Psychology*, *55*, 51–86. http://dx.doi.org/10.1146/annurev.psych.55.090902.142050

Dudai, Y. (2012). The restless engram: Consolidations never end. *Annual Review of Neuroscience*, *35*, 227–247. http://dx.doi.org/10.1146/annurev-neuro-062111-150500

Dumay, N., & Gaskell, M. G. (2007). Sleep-associated changes in the mental representation of spoken words. *Psychological Science*, *18*, 35–39. http://dx.doi.org/10.1111/j.1467-9280.2007.01845.x

Dumay, N., & Gaskell, M. G. (2012). Overnight lexical consolidation revealed by speech segmentation. *Cognition*, *123*, 119–132. http://dx.doi.org/10.1016/j.cognition.2011.12.009

Eichenbaum, H., & Cohen, N. J. (2001). *From conditioning to conscious recollection: Memory systems of the brain*. New York, NY: Oxford University Press.

Eichenbaum, H., Sauvage, M., Fortin, N., Komorowski, R., & Lipton, P. (2012). Towards a functional organization of episodic memory in the medial temporal lobe. *Neuroscience and Biobehavioral Reviews, 36*, 1597–1608. http://dx.doi.org/10.1016/j.neubiorev.2011.07.006

Ellenbogen, J. M., Hu, P. T., Payne, J. D., Titone, D., & Walker, M. P. (2007). Human relational memory requires time and sleep. *Proceedings of the National Academy of Sciences of the United States of America, 104*, 7723–7728. http://dx.doi.org/10.1073/pnas.0700094104

Ellenbogen, J. M., Hulbert, J. C., Stickgold, R., Dinges, D. F., & Thompson-Schill, S. L. (2006). Interfering with theories of sleep and memory: Sleep, declarative memory, and associative interference. *Current Biology, 16*, 1290–1294. http://dx.doi.org/10.1016/j.cub.2006.05.024

Frankland, P. W., & Bontempi, B. (2005). The organization of recent and remote memories. *Nature Reviews Neuroscience, 6*, 119–130. http://dx.doi.org/10.1038/nrn1607

Gaskell, M. G., & Dumay, N. (2003). Lexical competition and the acquisition of novel words. *Cognition, 89*, 105–132. http://dx.doi.org/10.1016/S0010-0277(03)00070-2

Gaskell, M. G., & Marslen-Wilson, W. D. (1997). Integrating form and meaning: A distributed model of speech perception. *Language and Cognitive Processes, 12*, 613–656. http://dx.doi.org/10.1080/016909697386646

Gaskell, M. G., Warker, J., Lindsay, S., Frost, R., Guest, J., Snowdon, R., & Stackhouse, A. (2014). Sleep underpins the plasticity of language production. *Psychological Science, 25*, 1457–1465. http://dx.doi.org/10.1177/0956797614535937

Gilboa, A., Winocur, G., Grady, C. L., Hevenor, S. J., & Moscovitch, M. (2004). Remembering our past: Functional neuroanatomy of recollection of recent and very remote personal events. *Cerebral Cortex, 14*, 1214–1225. http://dx.doi.org/10.1093/cercor/bhh082

Gómez, R. L., Bootzin, R. R., & Nadel, L. (2006). Naps promote abstraction in language-learning infants. *Psychological Science, 17*, 670–674. http://dx.doi.org/10.1111/j.1467-9280.2006.01764.x

Gow, D. W., Jr. (2012). The cortical organization of lexical knowledge: A dual lexicon model of spoken language processing. *Brain and Language, 121*, 273–288. http://dx.doi.org/10.1016/j.bandl.2012.03.005

Greenberg, D. L., & Verfaellie, M. (2010). Interdependence of episodic and semantic memory: Evidence from neuropsychology. *Journal of the International Neuropsychological Society, 16*, 748–753. http://dx.doi.org/10.1017/S1355617710000676

Hampel, H., Bürger, K., Teipel, S. J., Bokde, A. L. W., Zetterberg, H., & Blennow, K. (2008). Core candidate neurochemical and imaging biomarkers of Alzheimer's disease. *Alzheimer's & Dementia, 4*, 38–48. http://dx.doi.org/10.1016/j.jalz.2007.08.006

Hebb, D. O. (1949). *The organization of behavior*. New York, NY: Wiley.

Henderson, L. M., Devine, K., Weighall, A. R., & Gaskell, M. G. (2015). When the daffodat flew to the intergalactic zoo: Off-line consolidation is critical for word learning from stories. *Developmental Psychology, 51*, 406–417. http://dx.doi.org/10.1037/a0038786

Henderson, L. M., Weighall, A. R., Brown, H., & Gaskell, M. G. (2012). Consolidation of vocabulary is associated with sleep in children. *Developmental Science, 15*, 674–687. http://dx.doi.org/10.1111/j.1467-7687.2012.01172.x

Henderson, L. M., Weighall, A. R., Brown, H., & Gaskell, M. G. (2013). Online lexical competition during spoken word recognition and word learning in children and adults. *Child Development, 84*, 1668–1685. http://dx.doi.org/10.1111/cdev.12067

Henderson, L. M., Weighall, A. R., & Gaskell, M. G. (2013). Learning new vocabulary during childhood: Effects of semantic training on lexical consolidation and integration. *Journal of Experimental Child Psychology, 116*, 572–592. http://dx.doi.org/10.1016/j.jecp.2013.07.004

Henke, K. (2010). A model for memory systems based on processing modes rather than consciousness. *Nature Reviews Neuroscience*, *11*, 523–532. http://dx.doi.org/10.1038/nrn2850

Hickok, G., & Poeppel, D. (2004). Dorsal and ventral streams: A framework for understanding aspects of the functional anatomy of language. *Cognition*, *92*, 67–99. http://dx.doi.org/10.1016/j.cognition.2003.10.011

Hickok, G., & Poeppel, D. (2007). The cortical organization of speech processing. *Nature Reviews Neuroscience*, *8*, 393–402. http://dx.doi.org/10.1038/nrn2113

Hultén, A., Karvonen, L., Laine, M., & Salmelin, R. (2014). Producing speech with a newly learned morphosyntax and vocabulary: An magnetoencephalography study. *Journal of Cognitive Neuroscience*, *26*, 1721–1735. http://dx.doi.org/10.1162/jocn_a_00558

Jenkins, J. G., & Dallenbach, K. M. (1924). Oblivescence during sleep and waking. *The American Journal of Psychology*, *35*, 605–612. http://dx.doi.org/10.2307/1414040

Josselyn, S. A., Köhler, S., & Frankland, P. W. (2015). Finding the engram. *Nature Reviews Neuroscience*, *16*, 521–534. http://dx.doi.org/10.1038/nrn4000

Kapnoula, E. C., Packard, S., Gupta, P., & McMurray, B. (2015). Immediate lexical integration of novel word forms. *Cognition*, *134*, 85–99. http://dx.doi.org/10.1016/j.cognition.2014.09.007

Knowlton, B. J., Mangels, J. A., & Squire, L. R. (1996). A neostriatal habit learning system in humans. *Science*, *273*, 1399–1402. http://dx.doi.org/10.1126/science.273.5280.1399

Lambon Ralph, M. A., & Patterson, K. (2008). Generalization and differentiation in semantic memory: Insights from semantic dementia. *Annals of the New York Academy of Sciences*, *1124*, 61–76. http://dx.doi.org/10.1196/annals.1440.006

Lau, E. F., Phillips, C., & Poeppel, D. (2008). A cortical network for semantics: (De)constructing the N400. *Nature Reviews Neuroscience*, *9*, 920–933. http://dx.doi.org/10.1038/nrn2532

Lewis, P. A., & Durrant, S. J. (2011). Overlapping memory replay during sleep builds cognitive schemata. *Trends in Cognitive Sciences*, *15*, 343–351. http://dx.doi.org/10.1016/j.tics.2011.06.004

Lindsay, S., & Gaskell, M. G. (2010). A complementary systems account of word learning in L1 and L2. *Language Learning*, *60*, 45–63. http://dx.doi.org/10.1111/j.1467-9922.2010.00600.x

Lindsay, S., & Gaskell, M. G. (2013). Lexical integration of novel words without sleep. *Journal of Experimental Psychology: Learning, Memory, and Cognition*, *39*, 608–622. http://dx.doi.org/10.1037/a0029243

Louie, K., & Wilson, M. A. (2001). Temporally structured replay of awake hippocampal ensemble activity during rapid eye movement sleep. *Neuron*, *29*, 145–156. http://dx.doi.org/10.1016/S0896-6273(01)00186-6

Marian, V., Spivey, M., & Hirsch, J. (2003). Shared and separate systems in bilingual language processing: Converging evidence from eyetracking and brain imaging. *Brain and Language*, *86*, 70–82. http://dx.doi.org/10.1016/S0093-934X(02)00535-7

Marr, D. (1970). A theory for cerebral neocortex. *Proceedings of the Royal Society of London: Series B. Biological Sciences*, *176*, 161–234. http://dx.doi.org/10.1098/rspb.1970.0040

Marr, D. (1971). Simple memory: A theory for archicortex. *Philosophical Transactions of the Royal Society of London: Series B. Biological Sciences*, *262*, 23–81. http://dx.doi.org/10.1098/rstb.1971.0078

Marslen-Wilson, W. (1990). Activation, competition, and frequency in lexical access. In G. Altmann (Ed.), *Cognitive models of speech processing: Psycholinguistic and computational perspectives* (pp. 148–172). Cambridge, MA: MIT Press.

Matthews, B. R. (2015). Memory dysfunction. *Continuum: Behavioral Neurology and Neuropsychiatry*, *21*, 613–626. http://dx.doi.org/10.1212/01.con.0000466656.59413.29

McClelland, J. L. (2013). Incorporating rapid neocortical learning of new schema-consistent information into complementary learning systems theory. *Journal of Experimental Psychology: General*, *142*, 1190–1210. http://dx.doi.org/10.1037/a0033812

McClelland, J. L., & Elman, J. L. (1986). The TRACE model of speech perception. *Cognitive Psychology*, *18*, 1–86. http://dx.doi.org/10.1016/0010-0285(86)90015-0

McClelland, J. L., McNaughton, B. L., & O'Reilly, R. C. (1995). Why there are complementary learning systems in the hippocampus and neocortex: Insights from the successes and failures of connectionist models of learning and memory. *Psychological Review*, *102*, 419–457. http://dx.doi.org/10.1037/0033-295X.102.3.419

McCloskey, M., & Cohen, N. J. (1989). Catastrophic interference in connectionist networks: The sequential learning problem. In H. B. Gordon (Ed.), *Psychology of Learning and Motivation* (Vol. 24, pp. 109–165). http://dx.doi.org/10.1016/S0079-7421(08)60536-8

McGaugh, J. L. (2000). Memory—A century of consolidation. *Science*, *287*, 248–251. http://dx.doi.org/10.1126/science.287.5451.248

Milner, B. (1962). Les troubles de la memoire accompagnant des lesions hippocampiques bilaterales [Memory impairment accompanying bilateral hippocampal lesions]. In P. Passouant (Ed.), *Physiologie de l'hippocampe* (pp. 257–272). Paris, France: Centre National de la Recherche Scientifique.

Milner, B., Corkin, S., & Teuber, H.-L. (1968). Further analysis of the hippocampal amnesic syndrome: Fourteen-year follow-up study of HM. *Neuropsychologia*, *6*, 215–234. http://dx.doi.org/10.1016/0028-3932(68)90021-3

Mölle, M., & Born, J. (2011). Slow oscillations orchestrating fast oscillations and memory consolidation. *Progress in Brain Research*, *193*, 93–110. http://dx.doi.org/10.1016/B978-0-444-53839-0.00007-7

Mormino, E. C., Kluth, J. T., Madison, C. M., Rabinovici, G. D., Baker, S. L., Miller, B. L., . . . The Alzheimer's Disease Neuroimaging Initiative. (2009). Episodic memory loss is related to hippocampal-mediated β-amyloid deposition in elderly subjects. *Brain: A Journal of Neurology*, *132*, 1310–1323. http://dx.doi.org/10.1093/brain/awn320

Moscovitch, M., Nadel, L., Winocur, G., Gilboa, A., & Rosenbaum, R. S. (2006). The cognitive neuroscience of remote episodic, semantic and spatial memory. *Current Opinion in Neurobiology*, *16*, 179–190. http://dx.doi.org/10.1016/j.conb.2006.03.013

Moscovitch, M., Rosenbaum, R. S., Gilboa, A., Addis, D. R., Westmacott, R., Grady, C., . . . Nadel, L. (2005). Functional neuroanatomy of remote episodic, semantic and spatial memory: A unified account based on multiple trace theory. *Journal of Anatomy*, *207*, 35–66. http://dx.doi.org/10.1111/j.1469-7580.2005.00421.x

Müller, G. E., & Pilzecker, A. (1900). *Experimentelle beiträge zur lehre vom gedächtniss* [Experimental contributions to learning by memory] (Vol. 1). Leipzig, Germany: Barth.

Nadel, L., & Moscovitch, M. (1997). Memory consolidation, retrograde amnesia and the hippocampal complex. *Current Opinion in Neurobiology*, *7*, 217–227. http://dx.doi.org/10.1016/S0959-4388(97)80010-4

Nieuwenhuis, I. L. C., Folia, V., Forkstam, C., Jensen, O., & Petersson, K. M. (2013). Sleep promotes the extraction of grammatical rules. *PLoS ONE*, *8*, e65046. http://dx.doi.org/10.1371/journal.pone.0065046

Norris, D. (1994). Shortlist: A connectionist model of continuous speech recognition. *Cognition*, *52*, 189–234. http://dx.doi.org/10.1016/0010-0277(94)90043-4

Norris, D., & McQueen, J. M. (2008). Shortlist B: A Bayesian model of continuous speech recognition. *Psychological Review*, *115*, 357–395. http://dx.doi.org/10.1037/0033-295X.115.2.357

Oudiette, D., & Paller, K. A. (2013). Upgrading the sleeping brain with targeted memory reactivation. *Trends in Cognitive Sciences*, *17*, 142–149. http://dx.doi.org/10.1016/j.tics.2013.01.006

Patterson, K., Nestor, P. J., & Rogers, T. T. (2007). Where do you know what you know? The representation of semantic knowledge in the human brain. *Nature Reviews Neuroscience*, *8*, 976–987. http://dx.doi.org/10.1038/nrn2277

Payne, J. D., Schacter, D. L., Propper, R. E., Huang, L.-W., Wamsley, E. J., Tucker, M. A., . . . Stickgold, R. (2009). The role of sleep in false memory formation. *Neurobiology of Learning and Memory*, *92*, 327–334. http://dx.doi.org/10.1016/j.nlm.2009.03.007

Rasch, B., & Born, J. (2013). About sleep's role in memory. *Physiological Reviews*, *93*, 681–766. http://dx.doi.org/10.1152/physrev.00032.2012

Rasch, B., Büchel, C., Gais, S., & Born, J. (2007). Odor cues during slow-wave sleep prompt declarative memory consolidation. *Science*, *315*, 1426–1429. http://dx.doi.org/10.1126/science.1138581

Reder, L. M., Park, H., & Kieffaber, P. D. (2009). Memory systems do not divide on consciousness: Reinterpreting memory in terms of activation and binding. *Psychological Bulletin*, *135*, 23–49. http://dx.doi.org/10.1037/a0013974

Rudoy, J. D., Voss, J. L., Westerberg, C. E., & Paller, K. A. (2009). Strengthening individual memories by reactivating them during sleep. *Science*, *326*, 1079. http://dx.doi.org/10.1126/science.1179013

Schacter, D. L. (1997). The cognitive neuroscience of memory: Perspectives from neuroimaging research. *Philosophical Transactions of the Royal Society of London. Series B. Biological Sciences*, *352*, 1689–1695. http://dx.doi.org/10.1098/rstb.1997.0150

Schmolck, H., Kensinger, E. A., Corkin, S., & Squire, L. R. (2002). Semantic knowledge in patient H. M. and other patients with bilateral medial and lateral temporal lobe lesions. *Hippocampus*, *12*, 520–533. http://dx.doi.org/10.1002/hipo.10039

Schreiner, T., & Rasch, B. (2015). Boosting vocabulary learning by verbal cueing during sleep. *Cerebral Cortex*, *25*, 4169–4179. http://dx.doi.org/10.1093/cercor/bhu139

Scoville, W. B., & Milner, B. (1957). Loss of recent memory after bilateral hippocampal lesions. *Journal of Neurology, Neurosurgery, & Psychiatry*, *20*, 11–21. http://dx.doi.org/10.1136/jnnp.20.1.11

Skotko, B. G., Kensinger, E. A., Locascio, J. J., Einstein, G., Rubin, D. C., Tupler, L. A., . . . Corkin, S. (2004). Puzzling thoughts for H. M.: Can new semantic information be anchored to old semantic memories? *Neuropsychology*, *18*, 756–769. http://dx.doi.org/10.1037/0894-4105.18.4.756

Snowden, J. S. (1999). Semantic dysfunction in frontotemporal lobar degeneration. *Dementia and Geriatric Cognitive Disorders*, *10*(Suppl. 1), 33–36. http://dx.doi.org/10.1159/000051209

Squire, L. R. (1986). Mechanisms of memory. *Science*, *232*, 1612–1619. http://dx.doi.org/10.1126/science.3086978

Squire, L. R., Genzel, L., Wixted, J. T., & Morris, R. G. (2015). Memory consolidation. *Cold Spring Harbor Perspectives in Biology*, *7*, a021766. http://dx.doi.org/10.1101/cshperspect.a021766

Squire, L. R., & Knowlton, B. (1994). Memory, hippocampus, and brain systems. In M. Gazzinga (Ed.), *The cognitive neurosciences* (pp. 825–837). Cambridge, MA: MIT Press.

Squire, L. R., & Zola-Morgan, S. (1991). The medial temporal lobe memory system. *Science, 253*, 1380–1386. http://dx.doi.org/10.1126/science.1896849

Stark, C., Stark, S., & Gordon, B. (2005). New semantic learning and generalization in a patient with amnesia. *Neuropsychology, 19*, 139–151. http://dx.doi.org/10.1037/0894-4105.19.2.139

Stickgold, R., & Walker, M. P. (2007). Sleep-dependent memory consolidation and reconsolidation. *Sleep Medicine, 8*, 331–343. http://dx.doi.org/10.1016/j.sleep.2007.03.011

Szmalec, A., Page, M. P. A., & Duyck, W. (2012). The development of long-term lexical representations through Hebb repetition learning. *Journal of Memory and Language, 67*, 342–354. http://dx.doi.org/10.1016/j.jml.2012.07.001

Takashima, A., Bakker, I., van Hell, J. G., Janzen, G., & McQueen, J. M. (2014). Richness of information about novel words influences how episodic and semantic memory networks interact during lexicalization. *NeuroImage, 84*, 265–278. http://dx.doi.org/10.1016/j.neuroimage.2013.08.023

Tamminen, J., & Gaskell, M. G. (2013). Novel word integration in the mental lexicon: Evidence from unmasked and masked semantic priming. *Quarterly Journal of Experimental Psychology: Human Experimental Psychology, 66*, 1001–1025. http://dx.doi.org/10.1080/17470218.2012.724694

Tamminen, J., Payne, J. D., Stickgold, R., Wamsley, E. J., & Gaskell, M. G. (2010). Sleep spindle activity is associated with the integration of new memories and existing knowledge. *The Journal of Neuroscience, 30*, 14356–14360. http://dx.doi.org/10.1523/JNEUROSCI.3028-10.2010

Tham, E. K., Lindsay, S., & Gaskell, M. G. (2015). Markers of automaticity in sleep-associated consolidation of novel words. *Neuropsychologia, 71*, 146–157. http://dx.doi.org/10.1016/j.neuropsychologia.2015.03.025

Tonegawa, S., Liu, X., Ramirez, S., & Redondo, R. (2015). Memory engram cells have come of age. *Neuron, 87*, 918–931. http://dx.doi.org/10.1016/j.neuron.2015.08.002

Tse, D., Langston, R. F., Kakeyama, M., Bethus, I., Spooner, P. A., Wood, E. R., . . . Morris, R. G. (2007). Schemas and memory consolidation. *Science, 316*, 76–82. http://dx.doi.org/10.1126/science.1135935

Tulving, E. (1972). Episodic and semantic memory. In E. Tulving & W. Donaldson (Eds.), *Organization of Memory* (pp. 381–402). New York, NY: Academic Press.

Tulving, E. (2001). Episodic memory and common sense: How far apart? *Philosophical Transactions of the Royal Society of London. Series B. Biological Sciences, 356*, 1505–1515. http://dx.doi.org/10.1098/rstb.2001.0937

Tulving, E. (2002). Episodic memory: From mind to brain. *Annual Review of Psychology, 53*, 1–25. http://dx.doi.org/10.1146/annurev.psych.53.100901.135114

Uddén, J., Folia, V., Forkstam, C., Ingvar, M., Fernandez, G., Overeem, S., . . . Petersson, K. M. (2008). The inferior frontal cortex in artificial syntax processing: An rTMS study. *Brain Research, 1224*, 69–78. http://dx.doi.org/10.1016/j.brainres.2008.05.070

Ullman, M. T. (2004). Contributions of memory circuits to language: The declarative/procedural model. *Cognition, 92*, 231–270. http://dx.doi.org/10.1016/j.cognition.2003.10.008

van der Ven, F., Takashima, A., Segers, E., & Verhoeven, L. (2015). Learning word meanings: Overnight integration and study modality effects. *PLoS ONE, 10*, e0124926.

van Kesteren, M. T. R., Beul, S. F., Takashima, A., Henson, R. N., Ruiter, D. J., & Fernández, G. (2013). Differential roles for medial prefrontal and medial temporal cortices in schema-dependent encoding: From congruent to incongruent. *Neuropsychologia, 51*, 2352–2359. http://dx.doi.org/10.1016/j.neuropsychologia.2013.05.027

van Kesteren, M. T. R., Rijpkema, M., Ruiter, D. J., & Fernández, G. (2010). Retrieval of associative information congruent with prior knowledge is related to increased medial prefrontal activity and connectivity. *The Journal of Neuroscience, 30*, 15888–15894. http://dx.doi.org/10.1523/JNEUROSCI.2674-10.2010

van Kesteren, M. T. R., Rijpkema, M., Ruiter, D. J., Morris, R. G. M., & Fernández, G. (2014). Building on prior knowledge: Schema-dependent encoding processes relate to academic performance. *Journal of Cognitive Neuroscience, 26*, 2250–2261. http://dx.doi.org/10.1162/jocn_a_00630

Vargha-Khadem, F., Salmond, C. H., Watkins, K. E., Friston, K. J., Gadian, D. G., & Mishkin, M. (2003). Developmental amnesia: Effect of age at injury. *Proceedings of the National Academy of Sciences of the United States of America, 100*, 10055–10060. http://dx.doi.org/10.1073/pnas.1233756100

Verfaellie, M. (2000). Semantic learning in amnesia. In L. S. Cermak (Ed.), *Handbook of neuropsychology* (pp. 335–354). Amsterdam, the Netherlands: Elsevier Science.

Wagner, U., Gais, S., Haider, H., Verleger, R., & Born, J. (2004). Sleep inspires insight. *Nature, 427*, 352–355. http://dx.doi.org/10.1038/nature02223

Wilson, M. A., & McNaughton, B. L. (1994). Reactivation of hippocampal ensemble memories during sleep. *Science, 265*, 676–679. http://dx.doi.org/10.1126/science.8036517

Winocur, G., & Moscovitch, M. (2011). Memory transformation and systems consolidation. *Journal of the International Neuropsychological Society, 17*, 766–780. http://dx.doi.org/10.1017/S1355617711000683

Zeithamova, D., Dominick, A. L., & Preston, A. R. (2012). Hippocampal and ventral medial prefrontal activation during retrieval-mediated learning supports novel inference. *Neuron, 75*, 168–179. http://dx.doi.org/10.1016/j.neuron.2012.05.010

Robert J. Hartsuiker and Agnes Moors
9 On the Automaticity of Language Processing

9.1 Introduction

In *The Modularity of Mind*, Fodor's (1983) dedication quoted Merrill Garrett's view on the automaticity of sentence parsing during language comprehension: "What you have to remember about parsing is that basically it's a reflex." Around the same time, Levelt (1989) discussed the automaticity of language production. Whereas some language production processes, such as determining the message one wishes to convey and checking one's speech for errors and other problems were considered to be nonautomatic, all the other components were claimed to be largely automatic. According to both authors, some of the core processes in the comprehension and production of language basically run off by themselves, without control and without involvement of working memory. In this chapter, we ask to what extent such a view holds.

A priori, language processing seems to be an excellent candidate for a system of automatic processes. Speaking and listening are activities we engage in routinely and so are well-practiced. Language processing is difficult to counteract: It is difficult to listen to someone and deliberately not understand what they are saying. Much of language processing is *unconscious*. When we say a word, we retrieve and order its phonemes, but we are usually not aware of the details of phonological encoding. Additionally, language processing proceeds quickly and accurately: We can read about four words per second and speak at about half that rate, finding words from a lexicon containing at least 30,000 words, while producing speech errors at a rate of less than 1 per 1,000 words (e.g., Levelt, 1989). All of these properties (routinization, specialization, mandatory processing, unconscious processing, and speed) point to a strong degree of automaticity.

However, there are also indications that language processing is not completely automatic. For example, there is a long research tradition investigating the role of working memory in sentence understanding (e.g., Caplan & Waters, 1999; Gibson, 2000; Just & Carpenter, 1992). Although theoretical proposals differ, they have in common that understanding is constrained by a limited memory capacity. Furthermore, Garrett's reflex-like model of parsing breaks down when the reader encounters garden-path sentences such as Example 9.1.

Example 9.1 *The man accepted the prize was not for him.*

Preparation of this chapter was supported by the Research Foundation—Flanders (FWO; G.0223.13N) and the Research Fund of KU Leuven (GOA/15/003).

Arguably, to resolve a temporary structural ambiguity as in Example 9.1, processes concerned with error detection and revision need to be involved, which some authors view as nonautomatic (e.g., Hahne & Friederici, 1999). Furthermore, second-language learners often experience difficulties in the comprehension of complex sentences (e.g., Clahsen & Felser, 2006), which indicates that at least in some stages of language learning sentence comprehension is not fully automatic. In sum, sentence parsing seems to be constrained by working memory, regularly recruits control processes, and is less automatic for novices (L2 readers) than experts (L1 readers).

The aim of this chapter is to examine the automaticity of language production and comprehension processes, in light of three decades of research in the fields of psycholinguistics and attention and performance since Garrett (Fodor, 1983) and Levelt (1989) made their strong claims. Section 9.2 specifies what we mean with language processing by carving it into processes occurring in the individual listener and speaker (i.e., in monologue) as well as processes occurring in dialogue. Within each modality, we divide language processing into a conceptual level, a syntactic level, a lexical level, and a sound level. Section 9.3 describes the classic view of automaticity, and Section 9.4 describes how the classic view is applied to language processing. Section 9.5 spells out a contemporary view of automaticity (Moors, 2016), and Section 9.6 examines the implications of this contemporary view for language processing. We review evidence relevant for the question of which components of language processing can be considered to be more or less automatic. In Section 9.7, we explore the factors (repetition, complexity) and mechanisms (entrenchment, procedure strengthening) underlying automatization (i.e., the evolution of a process toward automaticity). The chapter closes with a discussion in Section 9.8.

9.2 Language Processing

In looking at automaticity on different levels of language processing, we rely here on the simple framework outlined in Exhibit 9.1, which divides language processing according to modality (production or comprehension), linguistic level, and social setting (monologue vs. dialogue).

Exhibit 9.1 reflects the dominant view in the field that the comprehension and production of language can be thought of as chains of processes through a hierarchy of levels. Thus, production typically begins with the intention to realize a particular communicative goal, and this next leads to the creation or activation of subsequent representations at a conceptual stratum, a lexical stratum, and a phonological stratum (Levelt, Roelofs, & Meyer, 1999; but see Pulvermüller, Shtyrov, & Hauk, 2009, for the alternative view that all such representations can be activated in parallel). Note that Exhibit 9.1 sketches these processes at a rather rough grain size: If we were to zoom in on a particular representational level, more fine-grained sets of representations and processing steps would appear, but these are outside of the scope of this chapter. It

Exhibit 9.1 Sketch of Representational Levels in Language Processing

I. Individual Level
    A. Comprehension
        1. Interpretation
        2. Syntactic level
        3. Lexical level
        4. Phonological/phonetic level
    B. Production
        1. Conceptualization
        2. Formulation: syntactic level
        3. Formulation: lexical level
        4. Phonological/phonetic/articulatory level
II. Social Level
    1. Conversation

is important to note, finally, that Exhibit 9.1 should be taken as a framework to organize our discussion of automaticity of different language processes; we do not commit to any notion that these levels are strictly hierarchically ordered or informationally encapsulated.

9.3 Classic View of Automaticity

Traditionally, cognitive psychology has made a binary dichotomy between automatic and nonautomatic processes. For example, several authors (e.g., Schneider & Shiffrin, 1977) characterized *automatic* processes as ones that are initiated by appropriate stimulus input, without the need for the subject's goal to engage in the process (*unintentional or uncontrolled in the promoting sense*), without demanding attentional capacity (*efficient*) or abundant time (*fast*), and without consciousness (*unconscious*), making it difficult to counteract the process (*uncontrollable in the counteracting sense*). Nonautomatic processes are the exact mirror image: They require the subject's goal to engage in the process (*intentional*), they demand attentional capacity (*nonefficient*) and abundant time (*slow*), they are *conscious*, and they are easy to counteract (*controllable in the counteracting sense*). Such a dichotomous view implies that there is coherence among the various features of automatic processes (a process that is unintentional is also efficient, fast, unconscious, and difficult to counteract) as well as among the various features of nonautomatic processes (a process that is intentional is also nonefficient, slow, conscious, and easy to counteract). From such a perspective, the job of evaluating the automaticity of language processing boils down to examining for each of the subprocesses of language whether one feature of automaticity applies (e.g., *unconscious*). The other features can then be inferred.

9.4 Application of the Classic View on Language Processing

In broad strokes, it is often assumed that the "higher" or "central" levels of processing (concerned with interpretation and conceptualization) are more capacity-demanding than the lower levels concerned with syntactic and lexical processing. In the case of dialogue, further capacity-demanding processes would come into play, such as modeling the perspective of one's interlocutor. These claims are based on both theoretical and empirical grounds. Thus, Levelt (1989) viewed conceptualization as a process that is constrained by working memory on the logical ground that it needs unrestricted access to semantic and episodic memory and representations of the current physical and social context as well as a record of the previous discourse. In contrast, subsequent processes of grammatical encoding and lexical retrieval execute well-defined tasks on the basis of limited and specialized sets of representations (i.e., the grammar and the lexicon). Thus, grammatical and lexical processes can be carried out by autonomous specialist systems that do not tap into central resources (and thus have a high degree of automaticity). In support of capacity-constrained conceptualization, Levelt cited the distribution of disfluencies ("uhs," "ums," repetitions, and the like) in spontaneous speech, which reflects phases of conceptualization (many disfluencies) followed by phases of formulation (few disfluencies).

For language comprehension, a similar argument can be made that lexical and syntactic processes can rely on restricted knowledge about words and rules, whereas processes such as mapping sentence structure on meaning and integrating it with discourse could be seen as more central processes. There is, however, considerable controversy in the literature about the degree of automaticity of syntactic and interpretation processes. For instance, Just and Carpenter (1992) proposed a working memory system that would be used for all verbal tasks. This system would be limited in capacity (with individuals varying in this capacity). Sentences would differ in their demand for capacity, with relatively simple sentences, such as ones with a subject-extracted relative clause (Example 9.2), demanding less capacity than more complex sentences, such as ones with an object-extracted relative clause (Example 9.3). If a sentence's demand for capacity would exceed a subject's available capacity, comprehension would break down, leading to increased reading times and errors of comprehension. As support for this theory, Just and Carpenter cited studies that considered effects of sentence complexity, working memory span, and extrinsic memory load.

Example 9.2 *The student that scolded the teacher got into trouble.*
Example 9.3 *The student that the teacher scolded got into trouble.*

Other authors (Caplan & Waters, 1999) agreed that sentence comprehension makes a demand on computational resources, but they rejected the notion of a general verbal working memory. These authors pointed out conceptual and empirical issues with measures of span and with memory load effects. Crucially, they also cited data from brain-damaged patients with spared sentence comprehension despite severe impairment of short-term memory. Rather than a general verbal working memory, these authors argued for a specific verbal memory for "sentence interpretation" processes that would comprise all comprehension processes including lexical and syntactic processing, assigning meaning, and integrating with the discourse. Importantly, so-called *post*-interpretive processes, such as using sentence meaning to draw an inference, or revising an initially incorrect interpretation (Example 9.4),[1] would not have access to this specialized resource. Thus, Caplan and Waters (1999) viewed all of the key processes in sentence comprehension as having a strong degree of automaticity: "Processors are thought to be obligatorily activated when their inputs are attended to. They generally operate unconsciously, and they usually operate quickly and remarkably accurately" (p. 93).

Example 9.4 *The defendant examined by the lawyer stuck with his story.*

One might argue that at the level of dialogue, processes related to audience design (i.e., tailoring one's utterances for the listener) are constrained by capacity because this would require some modeling of what the listener already knows. Assuming that language production (and in particular, conceptualization) itself already makes a demand on capacity, this predicts that speakers are often unsuccessful in audience design. Indeed, Lane, Groisman, and Ferreira (2006) observed that in a referential communication task, speakers sometimes "leaked" information that was relevant only for them and not for their interlocutor. Thus, if the speaker sees a big heart and a small heart and the listener can only see the big heart (because of an object occluding the small heart), an utterance such as *the big heart* is overspecified and potentially confusing. Nevertheless, speakers often produced such overspecifications and, when explicitly instructed to conceal the hidden information, were in fact *more* likely to overspecify. The latter suggests that keeping the instruction in mind overloaded the capacity for audience design.

To summarize the classic view, in language production, some processes, such as lexical access or phonological encoding are viewed as automatic, whereas other processes, such as conceptualization and audience design in the context of a dialogue, are seen as nonautomatic because they make a demand on central resources. In language comprehension, most processes are seen as automatic because many sentences can be understood quickly, efficiently, and obligatorily. Yet the observation that sentence comprehension suffers in the case of structural ambiguity or high complexity

---

[1] Many readers initially analyze the sentence as an active transitive with *the defendant* as the agent of *examine*, requiring them to revise their interpretation when encountering the *by*-phrase (Ferreira & Clifton, 1986).

has been taken to indicate that sentence comprehension is constrained by a limited capacity of working memory resources and thus is not so automatic after all.

9.5 Contemporary View of Automaticity

Contradicting the assumptions of the classic all-or-nothing view of automaticity, several authors (Bargh, 1992; Moors, 2016; Moors & De Houwer, 2006) have recently argued that the various automaticity features do not necessarily co-occur, and so particular processes should be considered as more or less automatic rather than fully automatic versus nonautomatic. This argument is based on studies that showed that automaticity features are often not necessary and sufficient for the presence of other features. With regard to the relation between goals and attentional capacity, for instance, in tasks involving the search for an object among many irrelevant objects, visual attention is often not solely dependent on the subject's goals (i.e., their task instructions) but also on visual properties of the display (e.g., the abrupt onset of a distractor stimulus or the presence of a distractor stimulus that shares a visual feature with the target; Theeuwes, 2010). Thus, having goals is not necessary for the allocation of attention. Similar conclusions can be drawn from studies with a paradigm that is often used in psycholinguistics: the visual world paradigm (e.g., Tanenhaus, Spivey-Knowlton, Eberhard, & Sedivy, 1995). In this paradigm, subjects view a display of objects and listen to speech while their eye movements are monitored. Subjects typically look at objects that are referred to in speech or objects that share properties with these objects. Importantly, overt visual attention (as indicated by eye movements) to objects that are named, or that are similar to named objects, happen irrespective of whether the subject has the goal to find the object (Huettig, Rommers, & Meyer, 2011). Thus, overt visual attention can be driven by high-level properties of a stimulus in the absence of the goal to direct attention to that stimulus.

In addition to the relation between goals and attention, Moors (2016) also analyzed the relation between attention and consciousness and concluded that attention is neither necessary nor sufficient for consciousness, citing studies showing that subjects become aware of unattended stimuli. Similarly, a stimulus does not need to be conscious for a goal-directed action to be applied on it. For example, Van Opstal, Gevers, Osman, and Verguts (2010) found that subjects applied the task (same–different judgments) to primes that were presented below the threshold of awareness.

On the basis of these data and considerations, Moors (2016) proposed an alternative view in which automaticity features are not seen as fixed properties of processes but rather as factors that jointly influence whether a process will occur.[2] The factors included

---

[2] Note that consciousness is not considered as a primary factor influencing the occurrence of processing, but it is shifted to the output side: The other factors determine whether the process will occur (unconsciously) and whether it will reach consciousness.

in the automaticity concept (goals, attentional capacity, and time or duration) are just a subset of many factors that can all jointly influence the occurrence of processes, next to factors such as the direction of attention, stimulus intensity, expectations, unexpectedness, novelty, goal relevance, recency, and frequency. Building on the assumption that processes require a minimal input for their occurrence, Moors proposed that all of the listed factors can influence the quality of representations that form the input of many processes. If this representational quality is high enough, it will trigger an (unconscious) process. If the representational quality is even higher, it will trigger a conscious process. Crucially, it is hypothesized that the listed factors influence the representational quality (and hence the occurrence of unconscious and conscious processes) in a compensatory way. For instance, stimulus intensity can trade off with stimulus duration, attention can trade off with stimulus repetition or training, and intention can trade off with recency. Empirical support comes from studies such as that of Tzur and Frost (2007). They manipulated both the luminance of a prime stimulus (i.e., a measure of intensity) and its duration and observed that an increase in luminance can compensate for a decrease in duration with respect to priming and vice versa. Factors that can influence representational quality can be divided into (a) factors related to the current stimulus itself (e.g., duration and intensity but also [un]expectedness, goal [in]congruence, and novelty), (b) factors related to prior stimuli (e.g., frequency and recency), and (c) factors related to prior stimulus representations (e.g., goals and expectations). The influences of some of these factors are moderated by attention.

What are the implications of this view for the diagnosis of a process as automatic? Moors and De Houwer (2006) recommended examining the presence or absence of each automaticity feature separately and not to draw conclusions about the presence of one feature based on the presence of another. Moreover, given the gradual nature of automaticity, only relative conclusions can be drawn: Rather than classifying a process as automatic or not, a process can be evaluated as being more or less automatic than another one. Moors (2016) went one step further, however, arguing that because of the compensatory relation of the factors influencing representational quality (and hence the occurrence of processes), it is not informative to compare processes with regard to a single feature of automaticity. If a process is found to operate with a smaller amount of attentional capacity than another process, this may indicate that the former process requires less representational quality than the latter, that the stimulus input of the first process happened to be more intense, or that their representations were preactivated by an intention, an expectation, or any other type of prior stimulus presentation. Thus, studying the amount of attentional capacity required by a process is not very informative unless all other factors are kept equal. If that is not possible, it is best to map a large network of factors required for processes to operate. In what follows, we adopt Moors's (2016) framework: Thus, we (a) see automaticity as gradual rather than all or none, (b) see automaticity features as a subset of many factors affecting language processes, and (c) assume that such factors can compensate for each other and that it is insightful to consider the joint effect of these many factors on the quality of an input representation.

9.6 Application of the Contemporary View on Language Processing

In this section, we recast the issue of automaticity of language processes in terms of the view that the occurrence of processes is a function of many driving factors, including but not limited to the factors implied in automaticity features (Moors, 2016). Mapping out the network of these factors can be called a *componential analysis*. Rather than attempting to be exhaustive in this analysis, we present a selected number of examples, with the aim of demonstrating that such an analysis is possible and potentially fruitful. Once again, we divide our discussion according to modality (i.e., comprehension, production, and dialogue).

9.6.1 Comprehension

In this section, we review studies that pertain to the features *efficient* and *uncontrolled*.

9.6.1.1 Is Comprehension Efficient?

As we have thus far sketched, the theory of a limited capacity for sentence comprehension has had much influence in the field. However, many authors have criticized this view. Thus, tests of verbal working memory capacity, like the reading span test, turn out to be unreliable (Waters & Caplan, 1996). Strikingly, there are patients with severe limitations of working memory capacity with spared sentence comprehension (Caplan & Hildebrandt, 1988). Several authors have further argued that the concept of *resources* is poorly defined and that a resource theory is impossible to falsify. For instance, Christiansen and MacDonald (1999) argued for a connectionist theory in which sentence comprehension is determined by the network architecture and the rate of activation spreading but not by any working memory system.

On the basis of these arguments, one can question whether a sentence comprehension system that is not capacity constrained can still account for phenomena that seemingly suggest such constraints. For instance, Examples 9.5 and 9.6 (taken from Van Dyke & Johns, 2012) illustrate that sentences are more difficult to understand if there is more material intervening between what Van Dyke and Johns dub a head (*the man*) and its dependents (*was afraid*).

> Example 9.5 *The boy understood the man was afraid.*
> Example 9.6 *The boy understood the man who was swimming near the dock was afraid.*
> Example 9.7 *It was Tony that Joey liked before the argument began.*
> Example 9.8 *It was the dancer that the fireman liked before the argument began.*

Example 9.9 *It was the boat that the guy who lived by the sea sailed / fixed after 2 days.*

This is at first glance compatible with a capacity-constrained system, suggesting that there is not enough capacity to hold *the man* active and process the further information, so that the representation of *the man* has decayed by the time *was afraid* needs to be linked to it. However, Van Dyke and Johns (2012) argued that such findings can be explained equally well by the concept of interference. In particular, they argued that the content of an extrinsic memory load affects the quality of sentence processing. For instance, Gordon, Hendrick, and Levine (2002) showed that a memory load consisting of three names (e.g., JOEL—GREG—ANDY) interfered with the processing of a sentence with matched content (Example 9.7) more strongly than a sentence with mismatched content (Example 9.8). This suggests that the semantic overlap between memory load and sentence created interference. Van Dyke and McElree (2006) further claimed that interference takes place at the moment when an antecedent is sought for a dependent. These authors presented memory lists such as TABLE—SINK—TRUCK while sentences such as Example 9.9 were presented, in which the verb (*fixed* or *sailed*) was separated from the antecedent (*boat*) by several words. All items on the memory list can be fixed (as is true of a boat), but in contrast to a boat, none of them can be sailed. If there is interference from memory at the moment an antecedent is sought for the verb, this would predict processing difficulty for *fixed* as compared to *sailed*. This is exactly what was found. On the basis of these and other findings, van Dyke and Johns proposed an account of sentence comprehension that is not constrained by capacity but that is constrained by stimulus factors (e.g., the presence or absence of multiple potential antecedents for a dependent and cues for retrieval) and person factors (e.g., the ability to exploit retrieval cues).

9.6.1.2 Is Comprehension Difficult to Control?

Provided we master a language, it seems impossible not to process an attended word or sentence in that language. A striking example is the well-known Stroop effect (e.g., MacLeod, 1991): Speakers are slower to name the ink color of a written word if that word is an incongruent color name (*green* written in red) compared with a congruent color name (*red* written in red) or a baseline (a series of X's or a noncolor word). The Stroop effect demonstrates that the subject comprehends a word even though he or she did not intend to comprehend it and even though comprehension actually hinders the task at hand, which suggests that the subject tried to counteract comprehension (but did not succeed). These arguments plead for the unintentional nature of comprehension processes, as well as for the idea that they are uncontrolled in the counteracting sense, either in the weak sense of being difficult to counteract or in the stronger sense of being impossible to counteract (i.e., obligatory).

Studies showing that comprehension breaks down when the stimulus is severely degraded do not support the strong view that comprehension is obligatory, however. This is illustrated by research on the perception of sine-wave speech (Remez, Rubin, Pisoni, & Carrell, 1981). Sine-wave speech is artificially synthesized speech consisting of a small number of sine waves with frequencies that are based on the formants of a real utterance. When listeners are not informed that they will hear speech, they typically classify this stimulus as "science fiction sounds," "computer bleeps," "music," and, in a minority of cases, as "human speech." Strikingly, when subjects are informed that they will listen to speech, they indeed perceive the sounds as speech, and they can successfully transcribe a sentence. If they are told they will hear speech and are informed about the sentence, they report hearing each word of that sentence clearly. This fits a view according to which a stimulus of sufficient quality (and which is attended to) will trigger comprehension. However, a stimulus of poor quality, even if it is attended to, further requires that the listener has *an expectation* to hear speech. Thus, expectation can compensate for a lack of stimulus quality with respect to whether comprehension takes place. It is interesting to note that Wiese, Wykowska, Zwickel, and Müller (2012) reported an analogous finding in the domain of gaze: Children and adults followed the gaze of people but not of robots, suggesting that an automatic behavior can be contingent on assumptions about the stimulus or situation.

9.6.1.3 Summary of Studies on Comprehension

The studies discussed in this section evaluated language comprehension in terms of two automaticity features. With respect to the feature *efficient*, we provided an alternative to the classic, resource-constrained view. With respect to the feature *uncontrolled* we showed that language is not always obligatorily processed: An attended stimulus of poor quality (as in sine wave speech) is not perceived as speech unless the listener *expects* speech.

9.6.2 Production

Most people find it difficult to give a speech, and many academics struggle with writing papers, suggesting that at least in some situations and especially in the written mode, language production is far from automatic. The question to what extent language production is automatic has been studied not only from a theoretical but also from an applied perspective. After all, the question of whether talking on the phone (even with a hands-free kit) affects driving has obvious implications for road safety. Bock, Dell, Garnsey, Kramer, and Kubose (2007) had subjects produce and comprehend language while maneuvering a car in a virtual environment in a driving simulator. Content and difficulty of production and comprehension were carefully matched. Both comprehension and production interfered with driving performance to a similar extent, suggesting that neither modality runs off fully automatically.

Theoretical approaches have focused most on verbal working memory and how this should be carved up. Just and Carpenter (1992) reported that working memory span tasks for comprehension (the reading span task) and for production (the speaking span task) correlated only moderately, and therefore suggested a fractionation of verbal working memory into separate resource pools for production and comprehension. We also note that Martin (2005) made an even more fine-grained division into a semantic short-term memory and a phonological short-term memory. This view is mainly based on studies of patients with dissociable impairments in the retention of semantic and phonological information. For now, we set aside the issue of fractionating memory systems and engage in a componential analysis of the automaticity of language production, as we did for comprehension. We review research pertaining to the features *efficient* (capacity unconstrained), *unintentional* (controlled in the promoting sense), and *unconscious*.

9.6.2.1 Is Language Production Efficient?

Relatively few studies have studied language production while imposing a secondary task. Bock et al. (2007) had people talk and drive but focused on the effect on driving parameters rather than speech production parameters. Kemper, Herman, and Lian (2003) did the reverse: Older and younger adults talked while performing one of several dual tasks (walking, finger tapping, ignoring irrelevant sounds). The two groups differed in their strategies to deal with the dual tasks: Younger speakers simplified and shortened the sentences, whereas older speakers spoke more slowly. Both strategies indicate that language production is not fully automatic but at least partly constrained by capacity limitations.

Other studies attempted to isolate specific processes in language production such as syntactic planning and lexical access. One strand of research investigated the production of number agreement between subject and verb in language production. Bock and Miller (1991) had speakers complete sentence fragments like Example 9.10 and showed that the speakers sometimes produced agreement errors, as in Example 9.11, especially when a plural noun occurred between a singular subject and the verb. Hartsuiker and Barkhuysen (2006) presented this task either with or without a three-word load. They found an interaction between load and (speaking) span, so that by far the most agreement errors were produced by low-span speakers under load. More recently, Allen et al. (2015) presented similar stimuli to diabetics and nondiabetics while their blood glucose level was manipulated with an insulin clamp. Hypoglycemia resulted in a significant reduction of reading span and a significant loss of accuracy on the agreement production task. Finally, Fayol, Largy, and Lemaire (1994) conducted a dictation version of the task in French, exploiting the fact that singular and plural verbs are often homophones in that language but differ in orthography (e.g., *arrive* vs. *arrivent*, 'arrive, first or third person singular' vs. 'arrive, third person plural'). Thus, when the participants hear Example 9.12, they need to produce correct agreement on the basis of the subject's number because the verb's auditory form provides no information. Fayol et al. observed that sentences like Example 9.12 elicited many agreement errors; these errors were more frequent when there was a secondary task (either click counting or a word load).

Example 9.10 *The letter from the lawyers . . .*
Example 9.11 **The letter from the lawyers <u>were</u> carefully written.*
Example 9.12 *Le chien des voisins arrive.* ('The dog of the neighbors arrives.')

Summarizing, this line of research suggests that the production of agreement is capacity constrained. Note, however, that it is not yet clear whether this capacity is needed for the core process of determining the number of the verb or whether it is needed for a subsequent checking or conflict-resolution process (Hartsuiker & Barkhuysen, 2006).

A further line of research asked whether the scope of planning in production is constrained by capacity. Consider an utterance such as Example 9.13.

Example 9.13 *The hat is next to the scooter.*

One possibility is that speakers fully plan the utterance before articulation. But it is also possible that they only plan the initial part of this utterance (e.g., *the hat is next*) and then start to articulate it (perhaps while planning the second part). A crucial difference between these accounts is whether the second noun (*scooter*) is part of the initial plan. To test this, Meyer (1996) and Wagner, Jescheniak, and Schriefers (2010) had people name two-object scenes with sentences such as Example 9.13 while presenting an auditory distractor word that was related to the first noun (e.g., *cap*), the second noun (e.g., *bike*), or unrelated to either (e.g., *dog*). Consistent with a broad planning scope, sentence naming onset was delayed both with a distractor related to the first and second noun. However, it has been suggested that there are individual differences in planning scope (Schriefers & Teruel, 1999), and it is possible that these differences are caused by capacity differences. In a follow-up study, Wagner et al. (2010) replicated Meyer's study but now with or without a secondary task. In one experiment, load was induced by having the speakers remember a word list. A probe word was presented after sentence production, and speakers indicated whether the probe had occurred in the list. The authors found no load effect on the scope of planning, which seems to argue against a capacity-constrained view of planning. However, when load was increased by increasing the complexity of the sentence (e.g., by adding adjectives) or by adding a further conceptual decision task, the interference effect increased for the first noun but decreased for the second noun, indicating a narrowing of the scope. These findings suggest that planning scope is flexible and dependent on available capacity. Note that the planning scope presumably also depends on the stimuli. Whereas the tested combinations were novel for all subjects, it is conceivable that frequently co-occurring combinations (e.g., *the bow and arrow*) would be planned simultaneously, as assumed by views relying on the idea of entrenchment.

A further dual-task study asked whether the production of single words is constrained by central capacity, and if so, for which stage(s) of word production this is the case. Ferreira and Pashler (2002) had participants simultaneously produce words and discriminate tones. They manipulated the difficulty of word production by manipulating aspects of the task and stimuli that arguably tap into early or late stages of word production. They reasoned that if a particular stage makes a demand on a central capacity, making this stage more difficult should delay performance on the secondary, tone-discrimination task. Manipulations related to lexical access (i.e., picture frequency, predictability, semantic overlap between picture and distractor word) all slowed down performance on the concurrent tone task. In contrast, a manipulation related to phonological encoding (i.e., phonological overlap between picture and distractor word) had no effect on the tone task. Thus, these findings suggest that only early stages of word production are constrained by a central capacity. However, Cook and Meyer (2008) provided some evidence that even the late stage of phoneme selection is capacity constrained. They conducted a version of Ferreira and Pashler's (2002) paradigm in which a picture was named in the presence of either another picture with a phonologically similar or dissimilar name, a phonologically similar or dissimilar word, or a *masked* phonologically similar or dissimilar word. When the distractor was a picture or masked word, phonological relatedness sped up both picture naming and tone discrimination, suggesting that phoneme selection does make a demand on a central capacity. No such effect was found when the word was visible, which the authors attributed to the additive effects of faster phoneme selection but slower self-monitoring processes.

In sum, studies on agreement production, planning scope, and single-word production all suggest that language formulation is capacity constrained (i.e., nonefficient) and thus not as automatic as often thought. We now turn to the automaticity features *unintentional* and *unconscious*.

9.6.2.2 Can Parts of Language Production Be Unintentional?

The subtitle of Levelt's (1989) book, *From Intention to Articulation*, suggests commitment to a view of speaking as a process with strong top-down control. The speaker begins with a communicative intention given the situation at hand and then sets into motion a chain of processes that translate this intention into speech motor activity. Thus, Levelt committed to a nonautomatic view in which information is only expressed when there is a goal to do so (the automaticity feature *intentional*; see Section 9.3). If language production is indeed fully driven by the speaker's goals, then productions should only contain information that realizes the goal and not unnecessary information that happens to be available. In contrast, the study of Lane et al. (2006) discussed earlier showed that speakers "leak" privileged information (i.e., that they can see both a small and a big heart) even when it is their explicit goal not to convey this information to the interlocutor. Thus, the authors concluded that "being part of a communicative intention is not a necessary condition for an accessible conceptual feature to influence grammatical encoding." (Lane et al., 2006, p. 276).

This conclusion resonates well with Vigliocco and Hartsuiker's (2002) review of the modularity of language production processes. These authors asked, for each of several interfaces in language production (e.g., between the message and grammatical encoding), whether processing at level n was affected by information at level $n + 1$ that was not part of its core input. Consistent with Lane et al. (2006), they cited numerous studies in which accessible but irrelevant conceptual features affected grammatical processing. For instance, even though the notional number of the head noun's referent in a distributive sentence such as Example 9.14 is not relevant for determining the verb's number, numerous studies have shown that agreement errors are much more likely with distributive rather than nondistributive sentences such as Example 9.15 (e.g., Vigliocco, Hartsuiker, Jarema, & Kolk, 1996). In a similar vein, studies such as Cook and Meyer (2008), discussed earlier, demonstrate that a picture one does not intend to name still leads to activation of its phonology and can therefore facilitate the production of another picture that one does intend to name. Together, these studies show that conceptual information outside of the speaker's (conscious) goals can still influence production, in contrast to the view that production is always intentional and thus nonautomatic in this sense.

>Example 9.14 *The label on the bottles is green.*
>Example 9.15 *The baby on the blankets is cute.*

However, Strijkers, Holcomb, and Costa (2011) argued that (conscious) intention matters for the time course of the naming process. They presented pictures of common objects with low- and high-frequency names and measured brain activity with electroencephalograms. In one condition, subjects were instructed to name the pictures. In another condition, they performed a nonverbal categorization task on the pictures. Event-related brain potentials were sensitive to the frequency manipulation in both tasks, suggesting that the pictures triggered production processes in both cases. However, in the naming task, such frequency effects began already after 152 ms, whereas they began 200 ms later in the categorization task. Thus, although intentions are not necessary to set production into motion, having such an intention speeds up that process considerably.

Of further relevance to the issue of intentionality, Lind, Hall, Breidegard, Balkenius, and Johansson (2014) argued that speakers sometimes have no clear "preview" of what they are about to say and rather infer this on the basis of auditory feedback.

They reported a study in which participants engaged in a Stroop task but in which auditory feedback was occasionally manipulated. For instance, when a speaker correctly named the color (gray) of the word *green* printed in gray, auditory feedback would sometimes be replaced, in real time, with a recording of that same speaker saying *green* (the recording was made in an earlier phase of the experiment). On such occasions, speakers often accepted the feedback as if they had produced that speech themselves. From this, the authors concluded that speakers often underspecify their intentions and construct them on the basis of feedback. Therefore, the sense of authorship of one's speech act would be reconstructive rather than predictive.

9.6.2.3 Can Unconscious Stimuli Influence Language Production?

Stimuli do not need to be conscious to influence language production. Earlier we gave an example (Cook & Meyer, 2008) of a study in which masked presentation of a word that was phonologically similar to a target picture facilitated naming of that picture. Several studies have also shown semantic effects of masked word primes (Dhooge & Hartsuiker, 2010; Finkbeiner & Caramazza, 2006). In contrast to tasks with visible primes (which typically show semantic interference), masking the distractor leads to semantic facilitation. Finkbeiner and Caramazza (2006) accounted for this in terms of multiple loci at which a semantic relationship plays a role. Masked distractors would lead to facilitation because they would activate their corresponding concept, which would spread activation to the target concept. Visible distractors would do the same but would further occupy a response output buffer. A semantic relationship would render the distractor difficult to exclude (as it resembles the target) from that buffer, slowing down the process.

9.6.2.4 Summary of Studies on Production

This review of production processes focused on three features of automaticity: *efficient*, *unintentional*, and *unconscious*. Studies considering efficiency indicate that language production is constrained by a central capacity. This holds not only for the higher level processes involved in conceptualization but also for lower level processes that deal with syntactic and lexical aspects of formulation. These data contradict the classical view that only higher level production processes are capacity demanding. With respect to the feature *unintentional*, we have seen that language production is not exclusively driven by (conscious) goals. Speakers are affected by information at the conceptual level that is irrelevant to their current goals and even detrimental to the realization of these goals. At the same time, having the conscious intention to name an object drastically reduces the time required for production processes. This is in line with the hypothesis that factors implied in automaticity (and beyond) can compensate for each other in their influence on the occurrence of processes. A final finding is that masked priming studies show that unconscious stimuli can influence language production.

9.6.3 Dialogue

Most research in psycholinguistics has studied the case of monologue; in typical studies, participants listen to sentences from a tape recording or speak the words labeling pictures of objects into a voice key. This is obviously quite different from the way language is typically used in the real word, namely, in dialogues in which an interlocutor interacts with another person and alternates between speaking and listening and communicative goals arise naturally in the context rather than as the result of an experimenter's instruction. At first glance, dialogue involves complex interactions among individuals. First, dialogue involves the coordination of turn taking. Analyses of the timing of turn taking (Wilson & Wilson, 2005) show that pauses between turns are often shorter than 200 ms and sometimes even 0 ms. This implies that speakers do not wait for the end of the previous speaker's turn to plan their utterance; rather, they must predict when the other speaker will end and plan their own turn so that it seamlessly continues the previous turn.

Second, successful dialogue arguably requires each participant to take into account the cognitive state of the other participant. After all, it makes little sense to state something that the other person already knows (e.g., because it was said just before or because it is blatantly obvious given that both dialogue partners share a common perceptual context) or that is impossible to understand for the other person given that she lacks an essential piece of information. Thus, interlocutors need to have a representation of what is in the *common ground* for both and what information related to the current topic is known or unknown by the other person. However, as the study of Lane et al. (2006) discussed earlier shows, speakers do not always successfully tailor their utterances to the listener's perspective and seem to be worse at this when they are provided with a further task (namely, to conceal information from the listener). This suggests that these complex processes are capacity limited, but it may also be the case that interlocutors do not always engage in them.

Finally, dialogue increases demands on monitoring systems (Postma, 2000). This involves self-monitoring for appropriateness and well-formedness but also for communicative success ("Has my interlocutor understood me?"). Furthermore, it involves monitoring the other person's productions ("Have they made a speech error or did they mean that? Have I heard this correctly or have I misperceived this?"). According to an influential view (Levelt, 1989), monitoring is a nonautomatic process, although it should be noted that this argument seems to be solely supported by introspection "self-corrections are hardly ever made without a touch of awareness" (p. 21).

Given the complex set of demands dialogue seems to make on functions such as memory, inference making, monitoring, and prediction, Garrod and Pickering (2004) asked, "Why is conversation so easy?" They proposed a theory that views dialogue as a joint action in which two actors collaborate to achieve a common goal (like a pair of ballroom dancers or, more mundane, two people carrying away a table). In such joint actions, there are usually no explicit negotiations (e.g., a countdown before lifting up the table); rather, the two actors interactively coordinate by mutually adapting their action to the perception of the other person's actions (i.e., interactive alignment). Similarly, two interlocutors have a joint goal, which Pickering and Garrod (2004) defined as aligning their "situation models." These are "multi-dimensional representations containing information about space, time, causality, intentionality, and currently relevant individuals" (Pickering & Garrod, 2004, p. 8). To converge on overlapping situation models, interlocutors would not use explicit negotiation, nor would they engage much in creating models of each other's mental states. Rather, dialogue partners would align in an interactive way (similar to the example of lifting up the table), and they would do so by mutual priming (i.e., preactivation) of representations at each linguistic level. Because representations from comprehension would prime representations in production, dialogue partners tend to converge on the same realization of speech sounds, the same words, and the same syntactic choices. Indeed, there is much evidence for priming from comprehension to production at many levels (see Pickering & Garrod, 2004, for a review).

To summarize, at first glance there seem to be many reasons why dialogue might be nonautomatic: It is hard to estimate when to take turns, to model the state of mind of the other person, and to tailor one's utterance to the social and dialogue context. In other words, the processes involved in dialogue are deemed too complex to be automatic. However, introspection tells us that dialogue is actually really easy, especially compared with holding a monologue. Part of the solution may lie in the consideration that the processes involved in dialogue are less complex than they seem. This aligns with the explanations for automatization discussed in the next section.

9.7 How to Explain Automatization?

In this section, we consider first the factors (repetition, complexity) and then the mechanisms (entrenchment, procedure strengthening) that influence automatization (i.e., the evolution of a process toward automaticity).

9.7.1 Factors Influencing Automatization

A well-established observation is that processes and behavior become more automatic as a result of practice (also called *repetition, training, frequency*) and that the complexity of a process is a factor that can impede automatization. We illustrate the role of complexity in the context of sentence comprehension. The question of how much complexity is involved in sentence comprehension in fact has been the topic of a theoretical divide in the field. On the one hand, modular models (Frazier, 1987) hold that the initial analysis of a sentence is determined only by the syntactic categories (e.g., noun, verb, preposition) of the input words. The parsing mechanism builds up a single analysis on the basis of a few syntactic principles (e.g., build a structure that is as simple as possible). Thus, when the listener hears something such as *put the apple on the towel*, the parsing system will build up an analysis in which *on the towel* is an argument of the verb *put* (it is the target location of the apple) rather than a modifier of *apple*. This is because the latter structure requires a more complex structure (i.e., it would be a reduced relative clause).

On the other hand, constraint-based models would argue that the parsing system uses all potential sources of information right away, including properties of the lexical items and their frequency of co-occurrence with particular structures, information about prior discourse, and knowledge of the world. Such accounts predict that *on the towel* can be interpreted as either an argument of the verb or a modifier of the noun, depending on the situation. Consistent with this latter view, Tanenhaus et al. (1995) demonstrated that if a display contained an apple on a towel, a box, an empty towel, and an irrelevant object, participants hearing *put the apple on the towel* would first look at the apple and then at the empty towel. When the sentence was then disambiguated (*in the box*), they quickly moved the eyes to the box, the actual target location. However, when the display was changed so that the irrelevant object was replaced by an apple on a napkin, participants no longer misanalyzed the sentence: When hearing *apple* they alternated between both apples, but when hearing *towel*, they looked at the apple on the towel and not at the empty towel. Thus, if the parser has a choice between two analyses, this choice is not exclusively driven by only the strictly necessary input, as modularist accounts would have it. Rather, the choice is determined by the input in conjunction with a host of other factors, which includes the visual context.

9.7.2 Mechanisms Underlying Automatization

In addition to asking which factors can influence automatization, researchers have asked which learning mechanisms (situated on a lower level of analysis) could be responsible for the automatization of a process (situated on a higher level of analysis). According to Logan (1988), automatization is explained by a shift from algorithm computation (or multistep memory retrieval) to direct (or single-step) memory retrieval. Children who learn to add pairs of digits initially count the units of both digits, but once a sufficiently strong association is formed in memory between the pair of digits and their sum, they retrieve this sum from memory, thereby circumventing the counting of units.

As an alternative to the shift to direct memory retrieval, Anderson (1992; see also Tzelgov, Yehene, Kotler, & Alon, 2000) argued that automatization can also be explained by the learning mechanism of procedure strengthening. Repetition of the same procedure (applied to the same or different stimuli) results in the storage of this procedure in procedural memory, which can be retrieved and applied faster and more efficiently thereafter.

Both learning mechanisms of direct memory retrieval and procedure strengthening seem to be covered in the language domain by the notion of entrenchment,[3] a set of mechanisms through which existing representations are strengthened or previously serially activated knowledge becomes clustered in a holistic unit or chunk. An equivalent of Logan's direct memory retrieval in the language is provided by Arnon and Snider's (2010) demonstration that speakers produce multiword phrases (e.g., *don't have to worry*) more quickly when these phrases appear more frequently (and that this cannot be reduced to the frequency of the individual words outside of these phrases). This suggests that an association is formed between the words within the phrases (*don't have* and *worry*) just like digits are associated with their sum (1 + 2 and 3). An equivalent of procedure strengthening in the language domain is proposed in models of syntactic processing in which repeated exposure to a syntactic structure results in the strengthening of the network connections needed for the production of that structure (Chang, Dell, & Bock, 2006).

Pickering and Garrod (2004) argued for entrenchment as an important explanation for the increasing fluency or automaticity of dialogue. They explicitly challenged the view that during each production, the speaker moves through all levels of processing as in Exhibit 9.1. Whenever they can, speakers will skip production levels, specifically when they produce a series of words that has become a *routine*. Indeed, casual speech contains many chunks of words that are recycled from the past, including, but certainly not limited to, idioms, and stock phrases. Thus, when a speaker produces "thank you very much" in a conversation, he might retrieve this in one go rather than going through the "normal" stages of conceptually driven word retrieval and combination. Such a view nicely fits with Arnon and Snider's (2010) finding that the frequency of multiword utterances predicts their production latencies. But what is more, Pickering and Garrod argued that routinization does not only happen at the level of the language but also in the much more restricted situation of single conversations. Thus, one can easily imagine a conversation in which a speaker introduces a novel multiword utterance that is repeated several times (because it is the topic of conversation and because of massive priming). As a result, this utterance would become entrenched (or routinized) on the fly, allowing the conversation partners to reuse it in one go, just like routines that are more fixed in the language. Garrod and Pickering (2004) argued that

---

3 The notion of entrenchment has been defined in various ways. Sometimes it is defined as a factor (i.e., repetition). At other times it is defined as a lower level process or mechanism (i.e., the creation of a holistic unit or chunk). At still other times, it is defined as an effect (i.e., the holistic unit, or the automaticity of a process). We argue for the clear separation of factors, effects, and mechanisms and propose using *entrenchment* in the sense of "mechanism."

an architecture in which there is massive priming and routinization on the fly solves many of the "problems" of dialogue. For instance, because interlocutors would, in the course of dialogue, converge on a shared set of aligned representations (an "implicit common ground"), there is no need to infer each other's state of mind. Furthermore, because entrenchment takes place within the time frame of a single dialogue, speakers can short-circuit some of the complex production processes and instead retrieve longer utterances directly.

9.8 Discussion

Is parsing basically a reflex? Does language formulation proceed largely automatically? There are no simple yes-or-no answers to such questions because automaticity features do not form coherent sets. Thus, a process can be more automatic with respect to one feature while being less automatic with respect to another. In our discussion of language *comprehension*, we examined the features *efficient* and *uncontrolled*. Regarding efficiency, there is an extensive literature that has argued for a capacity-constrained (less automatic) language comprehension system, while at the same time debating the nature of this capacity. Yet it is possible that effects that seem to imply a limited capacity can be explained by other factors, such as interference during retrieval operations. Another automaticity feature is *uncontrolled* in the promoting sense (i.e., *unintentional*). Certain stimuli, even when the person has the goal to comprehend them, do not trigger comprehension by themselves but only when the perceiver explicitly expects speech.

Language production can similarly be seen as a collection of more and less automatic processes depending on the specific automaticity features considered. Regarding the feature *efficient*, language production, like comprehension, often has been viewed as constrained by a capacity. In contrast to the classic view of automatic lower level processes in production, there is evidence supporting capacity limitations for lexical access and grammatical encoding. However, consideration of the feature *unintentional* shows that language production is not a fully nonautomatic process either. Even though the (conscious) intention to name an object speeds up production processes, it may not be needed to trigger it. Furthermore, if feedback is distorted, speakers sometimes claim agency for the production of words they did not intend to say and in fact did not say. Finally, with respect to the feature *unconscious*, we have seen that information does not need not to be conscious to affect production.

Dialogue, at first glance, appears to make a demand on highly nonautomatic processes such as making predictions about when it would be a good moment to take turns or reasoning about the mental states of the other person. In contrast, the interactive alignment theory of Pickering and Garrod (2004) claims that dialogue relies on less complex processes than is usually assumed and hence that less demand is needed than sometimes thought.

It thus appears that none of the language processes we have considered can easily be characterized as fully (or even largely) automatic versus fully (or largely) non-automatic. This is consistent with Moors's (2016) argument that automaticity features do not form coherent sets. Instead, it may be more fruitful to consider automaticity features as a subset of many mutually compensatory factors that jointly influence whether and how a particular process will be carried out. Thus, an attended sentence will elicit comprehension processes unless its quality is subthreshold. Poor stimulus quality can be compensated for by expectations, however. Similarly, an intention to speak is not necessary to trigger production processes but does affect the speed of such processes. Such a framework, in which automaticity features are only a subset of a legion of factors driving (or blocking) cognitive processes and in which these features do not necessarily covary, does raise the question of whether the automaticity concept still adds anything to the analysis of cognitive processes. Navon (1984) famously compared the concept of resources to a "soup stone."[4] Perhaps automaticity is a soup stone, too.

With regard to the explanation of automatization, we pointed at factors such as repetition, recency (or priming), and complexity. We also discussed entrenchment as a set of learning mechanism (especially direct memory retrieval) that can render a production or comprehension process more automatic. Entrenchment plays a major role in Pickering and Garrod's (2004) mechanistic theory of dialogue, both in the sense of having entrenched, long-term memory representations of units in one's language (e.g., a commonly used four-word combination) and in the sense of creating entrenched units on the fly during a dialogue (e.g., a particular referring expression that one of the interlocutors introduces in the dialogue and which is then repeated). Entrenchment (in both of these senses) creates subroutines that alleviate the burden of processing and thereby increase automaticity.

We end this chapter with a discussion of two theoretical issues that deserve further scrutiny in the future. First, one can make a theoretical distinction between core language processes and secondary language processes. Blurring of this distinction can have repercussions for the assignment of automaticity features to these core processes. With *core processes*, we mean processes that translate a linguistic representation at level n in a hierarchically organized sequence of processes to a representation at level $n + 1$: for instance, the process of retrieving a word on the basis of a concept. Secondary processes are processes that oversee core processes and intervene. For instance, if the core process of word retrieval makes a mistake (e.g., retrieving *dog* instead of *cat*), a self-monitoring system may detect this and set into motion processes of interruption and correction (e.g., Hartsuiker & Kolk, 2001). Similarly, if the parser has produced an initial analysis that turns out to be incorrect, a revision

---

4 Navon (1984) described a Jewish legend about a magical stone that was claimed to result in soup when added to boiling water. However, the soup would be better when vegetables were also added, and even better if you put in meat as well.

system might abandon the initial analysis and replace it with an alternative analysis. Detailed assessment of automaticity needs to find a way of distinguishing whether a given automaticity feature applies to the relevant core process itself or to a secondary process operating on it. For instance, Hartsuiker and Barkhuysen (2006) argued that effects of extrinsic memory load on agreement production did not affect the core processes that determine the number of the verb but rather a checking process, which, given enough capacity, would weed out incorrect number markings.

Second, the concept of automaticity is separate from but related to the issue of modularity because cognitive modules would have many of the features of automatic processes. The issue of modularity has had a profound influence on the literature for many decades. Many studies on the modularity of language processes have focused on information encapsulation. Thus, if a language processing level is a module, it responds only to its strictly necessary input and does not take into account other information. Much work in language comprehension and production has provided evidence against information encapsulation: Thus, parsing decisions are affected by information in the visual context, and language production decisions are affected by accessible but irrelevant conceptual features.

This chapter has reviewed a subset of the language-processing literature and interpreted the findings in terms of a componential view of automaticity. An obvious caveat is that our selection of the literature is not exhaustive but exemplary. Thus, a more ambitious goal would be to try to map out the interrelations between many more factors (related to automaticity and beyond) for the complete set of core cognitive processes involved in production and comprehension, in monologue and dialogue, while taking into account the possible influences of secondary processes such as checking and revising.

References

Allen, K. V., Pickering, M. J., Zammitt, N. N., Hartsuiker, R. J., Traxler, M. J., Frier, B. M., & Deary, I. J. (2015). Effects of acute hypoglycemia on working memory and language processing in adults with and without Type 1 diabetes. *Diabetes Care, 38*, 1108–1115. http://dx.doi.org/10.2337/dc14-1657

Anderson, J. R. (1992). Automaticity and the ACT* theory. *The American Journal of Psychology, 105*, 165–180. http://dx.doi.org/10.2307/1423026

Arnon, I., & Snider, N. (2010). More than words: Frequency effects for multi-word phrases. *Journal of Memory and Language, 62*, 67–82. http://dx.doi.org/10.1016/j.jml.2009.09.005

Bargh, J. A. (1992). The ecology of automaticity: Toward establishing the conditions needed to produce automatic processing effects. *The American Journal of Psychology, 105*, 181–199. http://dx.doi.org/10.2307/1423027

Bock, K., Dell, G. S., Garnsey, S., Kramer, A. F., & Kubose, T. T. (2007). Car talk, car listen. In A. Meyer, L. Wheeldon, & A. Krott (Eds.), *Automaticity and control in language production* (pp. 21–42). Hove, England: Psychology Press.

Bock, K., & Miller, C. A. (1991). Broken agreement. *Cognitive Psychology*, *23*, 45–93. http://dx.doi.org/10.1016/0010-0285(91)90003-7

Caplan, D., & Hildebrandt, N. (1988). *Disorders of syntactic comprehension*. Cambridge, MA: MIT Press.

Caplan, D., & Waters, G. S. (1999). Verbal working memory and sentence comprehension. *Behavioral and Brain Sciences*, *22*, 77–94. http://dx.doi.org/10.1017/S0140525X99001788

Chang, F., Dell, G. S., & Bock, K. (2006). Becoming syntactic. *Psychological Review*, *113*, 234–272. http://dx.doi.org/10.1037/0033-295X.113.2.234

Christiansen, M. H., & MacDonald, M. C. (1999). Fractionated working memory: Even in pebbles, it's still a soup stone. *Behavioral and Brain Sciences*, *22*, 97–98. http://dx.doi.org/10.1017/S0140525X99251783

Clahsen, H., & Felser, C. (2006). How native-like is non-native language processing? *Trends in Cognitive Sciences*, *10*, 564–570. http://dx.doi.org/10.1016/j.tics.2006.10.002

Cook, A. E., & Meyer, A. S. (2008). Capacity demands of phoneme selection in word production: New evidence from dual-task experiments. *Journal of Experimental Psychology: Learning, Memory, and Cognition*, *34*, 886–899. http://dx.doi.org/10.1037/0278-7393.34.4.886

Dhooge, E., & Hartsuiker, R. J. (2010). The distractor frequency effect in picture-word interference: Evidence for response exclusion. *Journal of Experimental Psychology: Learning, Memory, and Cognition*, *36*, 878–891. http://dx.doi.org/10.1037/a0019128

Fayol, M., Largy, P., & Lemaire, P. (1994). Cognitive overload and orthographic errors: When cognitive overload enhances subject–verb agreement errors. A study in French written language. *Quarterly Journal of Experimental Psychology*, *47*, 437–464. http://dx.doi.org/10.1080/14640749408401119

Ferreira, F., & Clifton, C., Jr. (1986). The independence of syntactic processing. *Journal of Memory and Language*, *25*, 348–368. http://dx.doi.org/10.1016/0749-596X(86)90006-9

Ferreira, V. S., & Pashler, H. (2002). Central bottleneck influences on the processing stages of word production. *Journal of Experimental Psychology: Learning, Memory, and Cognition*, *28*, 1187–1199. http://dx.doi.org/10.1037/0278-7393.28.6.1187

Finkbeiner, M., & Caramazza, A. (2006). Now you see it, now you don't: On turning semantic interference into facilitation in a Stroop-like task. *Cortex*, *42*, 790–796. http://dx.doi.org/10.1016/S0010-9452(08)70419-2

Fodor, J. A. (1983). *The modularity of mind*. Cambridge, MA: MIT Press.

Frazier, L. (1987). Sentence processing: A tutorial review. In M. Coltheart (Ed.), *Attention and performance XII: The psychology of reading* (pp. 559–586). Hillsdale, NJ: Erlbaum.

Garrod, S., & Pickering, M. J. (2004). Why is conversation so easy? *Trends in Cognitive Sciences*, *8*, 8–11. http://dx.doi.org/10.1016/j.tics.2003.10.016

Gibson, E. (2000). The dependency locality theory: A distance-based theory of linguistic complexity. In Y. Miyashita, A. Marantz, & W. O'Neil (Eds.), *Image, language, brain* (pp. 95–126). Cambridge, MA: MIT Press.

Gordon, P. C., Hendrick, R., & Levine, W. H. (2002). Memory-load interference in syntactic processing. *Psychological Science*, *13*, 425–430. http://dx.doi.org/10.1111/1467-9280.00475

Hahne, A., & Friederici, A. D. (1999). Electrophysiological evidence for two steps in syntactic analysis: Early automatic and late controlled processes. *Journal of Cognitive Neuroscience*, *11*, 194–205. http://dx.doi.org/10.1162/089892999563328

Hartsuiker, R. J., & Barkhuysen, P. N. (2006). Language production and working memory: The case of subject–verb agreement. *Language and Cognitive Processes*, *21*, 181–204. http://dx.doi.org/10.1080/01690960400002117

Hartsuiker, R. J., & Kolk, H. H. J. (2001). Error monitoring in speech production: A computational test of the perceptual loop theory. *Cognitive Psychology, 42*, 113–157. http://dx.doi.org/10.1006/cogp.2000.0744

Huettig, F., Rommers, J., & Meyer, A. S. (2011). Using the visual world paradigm to study language processing: A review and critical evaluation. *Acta Psychologica, 137*, 151–171. http://dx.doi.org/10.1016/j.actpsy.2010.11.003

Just, M. A., & Carpenter, P. A. (1992). A capacity theory of comprehension: Individual differences in working memory. *Psychological Review, 99*, 122–149. http://dx.doi.org/10.1037/0033-295X.99.1.122

Kemper, S., Herman, R. E., & Lian, C. H. T. (2003). The costs of doing two things at once for young and older adults: Talking while walking, finger tapping, and ignoring speech or noise. *Psychology and Aging, 18*, 181–192. http://dx.doi.org/10.1037/0882-7974.18.2.181

Lane, L. W., Groisman, M., & Ferreira, V. S. (2006). Don't talk about pink elephants! Speaker's control over leaking private information during language production. *Psychological Science, 17*, 273–277. http://dx.doi.org/10.1111/j.1467-9280.2006.01697.x

Levelt, W. J. M. (1989). *Speaking: From intention to articulation*. Cambridge, MA: MIT Press.

Levelt, W. J. M., Roelofs, A., & Meyer, A. S. (1999). A theory of lexical access in speech production. *Behavioral and Brain Sciences, 22*, 1–38. http://dx.doi.org/10.1017/S0140525X99001776

Lind, A., Hall, L., Breidegard, B., Balkenius, C., & Johansson, P. (2014). Speakers' acceptance of real-time speech exchange indicates that we use auditory feedback to specify the meaning of what we say. *Psychological Science, 25*, 1198–1205. http://dx.doi.org/10.1177/0956797614529797

Logan, G. D. (1988). Toward an instance theory of automatization. *Psychological Review, 95*, 492–527. http://dx.doi.org/10.1037/0033-295X.95.4.492

MacLeod, C. M. (1991). Half a century of research on the Stroop effect: An integrative review. *Psychological Bulletin, 109*, 163–203. http://dx.doi.org/10.1037/0033-2909.109.2.163

Martin, R. C. (2005). Components of short-term memory and their relation to language processing. Evidence from neuropsychology and neuroimaging. *Current Directions in Psychological Science, 14*, 204–208. http://dx.doi.org/10.1111/j.0963-7214.2005.00365.x

Meyer, A. S. (1996). Lexical access in phrase and sentence production: Results from picture–word interference experiments. *Journal of Memory and Language, 35*, 477–496. http://dx.doi.org/10.1006/jmla.1996.0026

Moors, A. (2016). Automaticity: Componential, causal, and mechanistic explanations. *Annual Review of Psychology, 67*, 263–287. http://dx.doi.org/10.1146/annurev-psych-122414-033550

Moors, A., & De Houwer, J. (2006). Automaticity: A theoretical and conceptual analysis. *Psychological Bulletin, 132*, 297–326. http://dx.doi.org/10.1037/0033-2909.132.2.297

Navon, D. (1984). Resources. A theoretical soup stone? *Psychological Review, 91*, 216–234. http://dx.doi.org/10.1037/0033-295X.91.2.216

Pickering, M. J., & Garrod, S. (2004). Toward a mechanistic psychology of dialogue. *Behavioral and Brain Sciences, 27*, 169–190. http://dx.doi.org/10.1017/S0140525X04000056

Postma, A. (2000). Detection of errors during speech production: A review of speech monitoring models. *Cognition, 77*, 97–132. http://dx.doi.org/10.1016/S0010-0277(00)00090-1

Pulvermüller, F., Shtyrov, Y., & Hauk, O. (2009). Understanding in an instant: Neurophysiological evidence for mechanistic language circuits in the brain. *Brain and Language, 110*, 81–94. http://dx.doi.org/10.1016/j.bandl.2008.12.001

Remez, R. E., Rubin, P. E., Pisoni, D. B., & Carrell, T. D. (1981). Speech perception without traditional speech cues. *Science, 212*, 947–949. http://dx.doi.org/10.1126/science.7233191

Schneider, W., & Shiffrin, R. M. (1977). Controlled and automatic human information processing: I. Detection, search, and attention. *Psychological Review, 84*, 1–66. http://dx.doi.org/10.1037/0033-295X.84.1.1

Schriefers, H., & Teruel, E. (1999). Phonological facilitation in the production of two-word utterances. *European Journal of Cognitive Psychology, 11*, 17–50. http://dx.doi.org/10.1080/713752301

Strijkers, K., Holcomb, P. J., & Costa, A. (2011). Conscious intention to speak proactively facilitates lexical access during overt object naming. *Journal of Memory and Language, 65*, 345–362. http://dx.doi.org/10.1016/j.jml.2011.06.002

Tanenhaus, M. K., Spivey-Knowlton, M. J., Eberhard, K. M., & Sedivy, J. C. (1995). Integration of visual and linguistic information in spoken language comprehension. *Science, 268*, 1632–1634. http://dx.doi.org/10.1126/science.7777863

Theeuwes, J. (2010). Top-down and bottom-up control of visual selection. *Acta Psychologica, 135*, 77–99. http://dx.doi.org/10.1016/j.actpsy.2010.02.006

Tzelgov, J., Yehene, V., Kotler, L., & Alon, A. (2000). Automatic comparisons of artificial digits never compared: Learning linear ordering relations. *Journal of Experimental Psychology: Learning, Memory, and Cognition, 26*, 103–120. http://dx.doi.org/10.1037/0278-7393.26.1.103

Tzur, B., & Frost, R. (2007). SOA does not reveal the absolute time course of cognitive processing in fast priming experiments. *Journal of Memory and Language, 56*, 321–335. http://dx.doi.org/10.1016/j.jml.2006.11.007

Van Dyke, J. A., & Johns, C. L. (2012). Memory interference as a determinant of language comprehension. *Language and Linguistics Compass, 6*, 193–211. http://dx.doi.org/10.1002/lnc3.330

Van Dyke, J. A., & McElree, B. (2006). Retrieval interference in sentence comprehension. *Journal of Memory and Language, 55*, 157–166. http://dx.doi.org/10.1016/j.jml.2006.03.007

Van Opstal, F., Gevers, W., Osman, M., & Verguts, T. (2010). Unconscious task application. *Consciousness and Cognition, 19*, 999–1006. http://dx.doi.org/10.1016/j.concog.2010.05.002

Vigliocco, G., & Hartsuiker, R. J. (2002). The interplay of meaning, sound, and syntax in sentence production. *Psychological Bulletin, 128*, 442–472. http://dx.doi.org/10.1037/0033-2909.128.3.442

Vigliocco, G., Hartsuiker, R. J., Jarema, G., & Kolk, H. H. J. (1996). One or more labels on the bottles? Notional concord in Dutch and French. *Language and Cognitive Processes, 11*, 407–442. http://dx.doi.org/10.1080/016909696387169

Wagner, V., Jescheniak, J. D., & Schriefers, H. (2010). On the flexibility of grammatical advance planning during sentence production: Effects of cognitive load on multiple lexical access. *Journal of Experimental Psychology: Learning, Memory, and Cognition, 36*, 423–440. http://dx.doi.org/10.1037/a0018619

Waters, G. S., & Caplan, D. (1996). The measurement of verbal working memory capacity and its relation to reading comprehension. *The Quarterly Journal of Experimental Psychology, 49*, 51–75. http://dx.doi.org/10.1080/713755607

Wiese, E., Wykowska, A., Zwickel, J., & Müller, H. J. (2012). I see what you mean: How attentional selection is shaped by ascribing intentions to others. *PLoS ONE, 7*, e45391. http://dx.doi.org/10.1371/journal.pone.0045391

Wilson, M., & Wilson, T. P. (2005). An oscillator model of the timing of turn-taking. *Psychonomic Bulletin & Review, 12*, 957–968. http://dx.doi.org/10.3758/BF03206432

Ethan Jost and Morten H. Christiansen
10 Statistical Learning as a Domain-General Mechanism of Entrenchment

10.1 Introduction

The birth of the statistical learning literature is often traced back to Reber's (1967) seminal study on implicit learning using an artificial grammar learning paradigm. However, to fully understand the relationship between such early implicit learning studies and the current notion of statistical learning, it is important also to consider its conception. The theory of perceptual learning by J. J. Gibson and Gibson (1955) paved the way for accounts of learning with a basis in sensory experience. In the Gibsons' theory of perceptual learning, which has close parallels to current ideas about entrenchment (Schmid, 2007), repeated experience with a percept enhances one's ability to discriminate between it and other percepts. This chapter argues that a communicative system characterized by entrenchment, as posited in this volume, likely relies to a considerable extent on the ability to track, learn, and use underlying associative relationships between linguistic elements and structures in comprehension and production.

When considering the origin of statistical learning as a theoretical construct, it is also important to consider the early work of Miller and Selfridge (1950), who thought that a reliance on transitional probabilities may be similar to the way in which grammar is learned. Other research informed by both Miller's work and the theory of perceptual learning espoused by J. J. Gibson and Gibson (1955) demonstrated that frequent co-occurrence due to underlying structure improved participants' recall of letter sequences (Miller, 1958) and that learning the positional relationships between linguistic units (i.e., morphemes) occurs as an experiential process of familiarization with the temporal positions in which such units are frequently encountered (Braine, 1963). This laid the foundation for future research investigating the close relationship between frequent co-occurrence and the strength and automaticity of recall at various levels of linguistic analysis.

From the beginning, research on implicit learning related to language was focused on the way(s) in which units of linguistic information are formed. Some of the early explanations for the ways in which this learning happened relied on experience-based accounts, as just described. However, experience-independent theories of language acquisition quickly became the dominant perspective primarily because of the widespread acceptance of the "poverty of the stimulus" argument (Chomsky, 1965; Crain, 1991). Saffran, Aslin, and Newport's (1996) research gave the psychology of language an experience-dependent statistical learning mechanism by which at least one aspect of linguistic knowledge (words) could be learned and demonstrated that this could be accomplished fairly rapidly even at an early stage in development; statistical learning can thus be thought of as the acquisition of distributional information from perceptual input.

Although the exact nature of the distributional information learners are thought to be sensitive to varies from study to study, this chapter aims to bring together research from multiple perspectives to provide a thorough overview of the field. The kinds of statistics that learners are using in each task and study are highlighted and contrasted, particularly when such differences are important from a theoretical standpoint. With the uncovering of this learning mechanism and the increased weight given to connectionist ideas about how the items and structure of language can emerge from the input (Elman, 1990), experience-dependent accounts of language learning and processing have again become central to the psychology of language. Building on these ideas, we define *statistical learning*[1] for the purpose of this chapter as the process through which learners uncover the structure of the input from its distributional properties (Frost, Armstrong, Siegelman, & Christiansen, 2015).

10.1.1 Implicit Learning Meets Statistical Learning

Since the resurgence of experience-dependent accounts of language in the 1990s, attempts have been made to synthesize the original implicit learning literature with the newer research on statistical learning (e.g., Conway & Christiansen, 2006; Perruchet & Pacton, 2006). Researchers have begun to question the "implicitness" of statistical learning, and the related artificial grammar paradigms that are common within the implicit learning literature. This is particularly relevant to discussions of entrenchment processes, as automaticity—or unconscious activation—is usually considered a feature of entrenchment (Schmid, 2007; for more details, see Hartsuiker & Moors, Chapter 9, this volume); the naming of an entrenched visual stimulus (i.e., an apple) does not require conscious processing in healthy adults. However, considering the manner in which most statistical learning paradigms are designed, with explicit familiarity judgments used at test, the relative amount of conscious processing that learners rely on has been debated.

---

[1] Note that the term *statistical learning* means something quite different in psychology than it does in the field of mathematics and machine learning (Vapnik, 1999). Also, there are a number of other learning theories within psychology that are neither at odds with statistical learning nor do they necessarily fall under the same umbrella, such as discriminative learning (Baayen, 2010). Such ideas about contextual learning can rather be thought of as parallel processes that also help to explain the way that learners gain knowledge from input, in conjunction with cognitive mechanisms such as statistical learning.

Within most statistical learning studies, self-report data and the mere fact that the instructions are incidental are used as evidence for implicit processing. Recent work has put this to the test, with evidence both for (Kim, Seitz, Feenstra, & Shams, 2009) and against (Bertels, Franco, & Destrebecqz, 2012) implicit interpretations of statistical learning. Further research has shown that access to the statistical relationships within two artificial languages can be consciously controlled, demonstrating that at least some aspects of the learned relationships are available for explicit processing (Franco, Cleeremans, & Destrebecqz, 2011). Early artificial grammar learning research pointed toward diminished performance when participants were given explicit instructions (Reber, 1976), although newer research suggests that the duration of stimulus presentation may modulate this relationship, with longer presentations leading to an improvement in learning when instructions are explicit, at least in the visual domain (Arciuli, Torkildsen, Stevens, & Simpson, 2014). There appears to be a strong argument for the implicit and incidental nature of statistical learning, but some room for explicit processing should be built into accounts of statistical learning. Some of the issues in understanding the implicit nature of statistical learning are due to the lack of coherence between the implicit and statistical learning literatures but may be resolved in time as the two become more closely integrated.

Perruchet and Pacton (2006) claimed that although the two literatures have grown increasingly similar in terms of methodology, implicit learning relies more on the process of chunking as an explanation of learning (see Gobet, Chapter 11, this volume), whereas the statistical learning literature is primarily interested in exploring the role of distributional information. However, these computations do not need to be interpreted as dichotomous; depending on the properties of the input, they could both occur in what we think of as statistical learning (Franco & Destrebecqz, 2012).

Tracking conditional probabilities may lead to the formation of chunks at later stages of learning, which then become elements themselves between which conditional probabilities may be tracked. In fact, recent models of language acquisition have demonstrated the feasibility of such a process (McCauley & Christiansen, 2014; Monaghan & Christiansen, 2010). Thinking of chunks as the outcome of statistical learning provides a direct connection with entrenchment: Throughout learning, frequently co-occurring elements and structures become more deeply entrenched, strengthening such representations.

10.1.2 Statistical Learning as a Mechanism of Entrenchment

This perspective fits in nicely with the notion of entrenchment in language and promotes the idea of statistical learning as a mechanism of entrenchment. Entrenchment itself is often thought of as a process, but it can also be viewed as an effect. In this way, statistical learning can itself be thought of as part of the process by which entrenchment can occur. The well-established effect of frequency on processing linguistic elements and structures (Oldfield & Wingfield, 1965) can be viewed as a measure of entrenchment in language, although new, more sensitive measures such as meaning-dependent phonetic duration and reading time effects may lead to a more nuanced view of the entrenchment process (Jolsvai, McCauley, & Christiansen, 2013). Therefore, a continuously updated relationship due to the tracking of distributional information and associated formation of meaningful units can lead to varying degrees of entrenchment for any particular element. This interpretation of entrenchment would relate to the learning of a word from a continuous stream of speech (Saffran, Aslin, & Newport, 1996) and to the formation of chunks including frequently co-occurring nonadjacent morphemes (Gómez, 2002), along with other linguistic structures.

However, statistical learning is not a mechanism of entrenchment solely in the linguistic domain. In the auditory domain, it may also pertain to the learning of tone sequences (Saffran, Johnson, Aslin, & Newport, 1999), whereas in the visual domain, it may relate to the extraction of probabilistic information and structure from visual scenes (Fiser & Aslin, 2002). This points to another key aspect of statistical learning—specifically, its domain-general nature. Statistical learning can take place between stimuli within various sensory modalities (Conway & Christiansen, 2005), and statistical relationships between actions, labels, and referents can be tracked across situations (Yu & Smith, 2007). Along with other domain-general cognitive processes, including attention, memory, communicative inference, and general world knowledge, we can understand language as being built on a foundation that is not specific to language (for a detailed overview of this perspective, see Christiansen & Chater, 2008). Understanding statistical learning as domain-general is also important for considering the ways in which language and statistical learning interact with other aspects of cognition.

10.2 Statistical Learning in Multiple Domains

The domain-generality of statistical learning has been extensively studied since the advent of the modern statistical learning literature. This aspect of the statistical learning mechanism is important for a number of reasons. To begin with, it tied into assumptions about implicit learning, proposed by Reber (1993), who hypothesized that implicit learning was a phylogenetically ancient and conserved cognitive ability. Given that other species possess complex communication but not language, this meant that artificial grammars with nonlinguistic elements ought to be learnable by humans and likely some other extant species. However, strong theories of cognitive modularity argue that the cognitive architecture is built out of domain-specific modules (Fodor, 1983). Thus, experimental findings in which similar cognitive processes were used by different hypothesized modules (e.g., between vision and language) provided counterevidence to such claims. Due primarily to these theoretical motivations, a number of researchers have attempted to elucidate the extent of the generality of this mechanism.

10.2.1 Statistical Learning at Multiple Levels of Linguistic Processing

The first studies of statistical learning focused on the learnability of wordlike units from a continuous stream of syllables based solely on the different transitional probabilities within versus between "words" in infants (Saffran, Aslin, & Newport, 1996) and adults (Saffran, Newport, & Aslin, 1996). In adults, it was found that additional prosodic cues at word boundaries facilitated learning.

Within the statistical learning literature, this type of relationship between syllables would come to be defined as an adjacent dependency (e.g., /tu-pi-ro/da-pu-ki/). It was suggested to be analogous to the type of statistical relationship formed between syllables within words versus between words in terms of lexical processing; the syllable transitions that are found within words (*pi-ro*) have higher transitional probabilities than the syllable transitions that exist between words (*ro-da*). The conditional probabilities that are tracked between adjacent items in a sequence lead to the learning of these frequently co-occurring items.

Another type of dependency that has become part of statistical learning parlance is the nonadjacency (e.g., *a/X/d* where *a* predicts *d* with various random intervening elements instantiating *X*; Gómez, 2002). The nonadjacent dependency in statistical learning paradigms was argued to be similar to the type of relationship found between auxiliaries and inflectional morphemes (e.g., *was running*; *had beaten*) and number agreement across multiple words (e.g., *the dogs out in the yard are howling*).

These studies, when combined with the research on adjacent dependencies, point to powerful learning mechanisms that may underlie entrenchment across a variety of linguistic domains. That is, learners seem to be sensitive to continuously updated statistical–probabilistic relationships not only between items that are temporally adjacent but also across intervening items, so long as the intervening items are sufficiently variable. Additional evidence from the event-related potentials literature has demonstrated that the brain processes syllable-to-syllable transitions in Saffran-style statistical learning paradigms differently within versus between words, as greater N100 amplitudes were found at between-word syllable boundaries than at within-word syllable boundaries (Sanders, Newport, & Neville, 2002). The N100 is often thought to reflect early bottom-up sensory processing (van den Brink, Brown, & Hagoort, 2001).

10.2.2 Statistical Learning in Different Domains

It is important to note that the basic units of learning (syllables) in these statistical learning paradigms are the same as what are thought of as one of the most basic units of language; thus, these nonword stimuli are typically described as linguistic in nature (Newport & Aslin, 2004). However, the stimuli used in statistical learning paradigms are not limited to language-like items. Statistical learning has been studied in a number of other domains, including audition, vision, and touch.

10.2.2.1 Audition

If statistical learning was domain-specific and only related to the way in which language is learned and processed, then statistical relationships among nonlinguistic elements should not be learnable. This appears not to be the case, because the ability to learn from the transitional probabilities in sequences of auditory tones has been well described in the literature. Saffran and colleagues (1999) first reported the sensitivity of adults and infants to the underlying statistical relationships between tones, using the same type of dependency previously investigated using syllables (Saffran, Aslin, & Newport, 1996; Saffran, Newport, & Aslin, 1996). The ability of participants to track adjacent dependencies between tones that are inherently nonlinguistic indicates that statistical learning is likely a domain-general mechanism.

Other kinds of acoustic information have also been used in statistical learning studies, with varying results depending on the properties of the acoustic stimuli (Creel, Newport, & Aslin, 2004). Interestingly, certain aspects of the stimulus (e.g., pitch register, timbre) led to different patterns of sensitivity in learning nonadjacency versus adjacency structure in the stimulus stream, suggesting that Gestalt-like properties of the stimulus may shape learning in different ways. Other reports of statistical learning have relied on artificial grammars using musical stimuli, further demonstrating the domain-general nature of statistical learning (e.g., Bly, Carrión, & Rasch, 2009). This domain-generality indicates that language is subserved by neural mechanisms that are used for processing a variety of input, and/or that the same general computational principle operates across perceptual and cognitive domains.

10.2.2.2 Vision

Auditory input is still somewhat language-like, as in that sensory modality is also used for listening to speech. Vision is a sensory domain further removed from language processing, and to find that statistical learning of visual sequences is possible would strengthen claims about this mechanism's domain-general nature. Evidence of visual statistical learning began with a study examining infant looking times to statistically determined patterns of shapes, finding differences in looking times between familiar and unfamiliar patterns (Kirkham, Slemmer, & Johnson, 2002; Fiser & Aslin, 2002). The statistical coherence between elements within these visual scenes led to their entrenchment as higher order representations. The features of visual stimuli often consist of color, shape, and positional information with various types of biases existing between learning these features versus objects (Turk-Browne, Isola, Scholl, & Treat, 2008), similar to the effect of the stimulus-level differences noted in auditory statistical learning. For example, when two features, such as color and shape, perfectly covary within each object in a triplet, participants struggle to identify acceptable triplets when tested on only one of the two features (either color or shape). However, when shape and color are decoupled during training and vary across objects, the underlying pattern for each feature can be learned independently. In terms of development, adults and children seem to show similar underlying neural processes when learning sequential information in the visual domain, with stable P300 responses across age groups to visual stimuli that are highly predictive of a target stimulus (Jost, Conway, Purdy, Walk, & Hendricks, 2015).

10.2.2.3 Touch and Other Domains

Touch is another modality in which statistical learning has been studied. Conway and Christiansen (2005) investigated whether statistical structure could be learned purely from tactile input. They found that performance with tactile input is similar to performance in the visual modality, although auditory learning was superior to both when the same artificial grammar was used in each modality. Further theories point toward the use of a statistical learning mechanism as a basis for social understanding (Lieberman, 2000; Ruffman, Taumoepeau, & Perkins, 2012) and motor skill learning (Robertson, 2007).

These findings lead to interesting questions about what kinds of constraints are placed on learning due to the nature of stimuli in different sensory modalities. For example, auditory information is usually encountered in rapid succession and is quite transient in nature. Thus, basic sensory processing mechanisms for auditory input are tuned to this bias in presentation. Visual input varies across time as well, but is much more stable, and thus statistical learning studies incorporating visual stimuli require longer interstimulus intervals to achieve the same levels of learning as in audition (Emberson, Conway, & Christiansen, 2011). One possible explanation for the patterns of similarity and differences in statistical learning across domains is the existence of multiple modality-specific mechanisms, each using the same underlying computational principles but subject to different modality-specific constraints (Frost et al., 2015).

The evidence of statistical learning across different modalities and domains suggests that entrenchment might not be a language-specific phenomenon. Examples such as the incidental categorization of single tones into triplets due to frequent co-occurrence in a continuous stream (e.g., Saffran et al., 1999) and the extraction of statistical structure from visual scenes (e.g., Fiser & Aslin, 2002, Kirkham et al., 2002) provide compelling arguments for statistical learning as a domain-general process of entrenchment. The construction of holistic units out of basic elements is a hallmark of entrenchment. Building tone triplets out of a sequence of single tones based on co-occurrence may not be perfectly analogous to the process by which linguistic structures are thought to be entrenched, but it does capture the basic properties of a process that, as described earlier, may operate at various levels of linguistic processing as a foundation for the formation of such associations.

10.3 Statistical Learning in Development

This section focuses on developmental changes in statistical learning abilities, and how such changes may affect language development (for an extended review, see Misyak, Goldstein, & Christiansen, 2012). The human infant is born into a world full of input from which it must extract structure (Goldstein et al., 2010; James, 1890). Although this may seem to be a difficult task, the infant's environment, experience, and biology constrain the kinds of input to which it is sensitive (Elman et al., 1996). However, actually extracting structure from the input requires some kind of learning mechanism; this is where statistical learning comes into play.

Reber (1993) hypothesized that implicit learning was developmentally invariant due to its basic adaptive value and ancient phylogenetic roots. Therefore, if Reber were correct, robust statistical learning mechanisms should be present from an early age. Indeed, infant studies formed the foundation for modern research on statistical learning, as humans seem to possess powerful statistical learning abilities from infancy (Saffran, Aslin, & Newport, 1996; Saffran et al., 1999). By at least 8 months, infants can track an aspect of the speech stream that allows them to learn words, and they appear to do so in a way similar to adults (Saffran, Newport, & Aslin, 1996). In the domain of vision, older children from ages 6 to 12 years have been found to possess neural correlates of learning similar to adults in a simple sequential learning paradigm, giving credence to Reber's claim in a nonlinguistic task (Jost et al., 2015). Amso and Davidow (2012) have also provided compelling evidence for developmental invariance in statistical learning of environmental regularity by examining saccadic eye movements and reaction times to probabilistically determined object relationships in infants and adults.

Deeper investigation into the developmental invariance of statistical learning has provided some counterevidence, forcing a reappraisal of Reber's original position. From birth, infants have the ability to segment continuous speech using statistical information, as evidenced by event-related potentials (Teinonen, Fellman, Näätänen, Alku, & Huotilainen, 2009). However, infants may be sensitive to different components of auditory information than adults because infants do not track statistical relationships defined by relative pitch whereas adults do (Saffran & Griepentrog, 2001). In another study by Saffran (2001), adults and children both performed above chance on measures of learning following exposure to an artificial grammar containing predictive dependencies, but adults consistently outperformed children. Although this may have been due to differences in memory ability, given that children consistently performed worse on longer strings while adults did not show the same effect, the influence of other cognitive processes on statistical learning ability along with widely varying amounts of experience with stimuli in various domains (i.e., sensitivity to relative pitch) may contribute to developmental differences in statistical learning abilities.

The first study of nonadjacency learning in adults and infants also found that infants possess adultlike abilities to track such dependencies (Gómez, 2002). However, developmental differences in the ability to learn from nonadjacent dependencies have also been found (Gómez & Maye, 2005). Twelve-month-old infants were unable to learn the predictive relationship between nonadjacent elements in a task that infants aged 15 months and older were able to perform. At this point, it seems likely that true developmental invariance is not a characteristic of statistical learning and that studies reporting such findings do not include a sufficient range of ages across development.

This growing literature on statistical learning in development not only demonstrates the existence of statistical learning abilities at early stages of development but also provides a window into the interaction between experience and cognitive development. It seems clear that infants have access to cognitive mechanisms that contribute to the entrenchment of lexical items as well as certain aspects of linguistic structure. However, sensitivity to certain statistical properties of speech from the very onset of development as opposed to others may bias the types of language learning we see in development. Considering that neonates have the ability to learn syllable chunks by tracking adjacent dependencies, a mechanism for the construction of lexical items seems to exist very early in development (Teinonen et al., 2009).

The idea that humans, and infants in particular, are guided by statistical structure when learning, due to a fundamental attempt to reduce uncertainty (E. J. Gibson, 1991; Gómez, 2002), provides an explanation for the way in which language develops. Sensitivity to the adjacent structures in language provides quite a bit of information and allows for syllables to become associated with one another to form words, and for words to become associated with one another, forming chunks; sensitivity to the nonadjacent structures in language provides a means through which more complex associations required for learning certain aspects of morphology and syntax, for example, constructional schemas, are developed. In this way, statistical learning contributes to entrenchment of both linguistic elements and linguistic structures.

10.4 Individual Differences in Statistical Learning and Language

Reber (1993) stated that because of the fundamentally ancient nature of implicit learning, it was unlikely that there would be profound individual variation in related abilities. Although he later reconsidered this claim (Reber & Allen, 2000), his initial hypothesis has had a great deal of influence on the field of statistical learning. However, recent evidence has pointed toward individual variation in statistical learning abilities, and studies of this evidence have also attempted to elucidate how these individual differences contribute to differences in language abilities (see for a discussion, Frost et al., 2015).

Shafto, Conway, Field, and Houston (2012) provided developmental evidence for direct links between individual differences in statistical learning and language abilities. Prelinguistic infants aged 8.5 months had their learning abilities evaluated on a visuospatial statistical learning task and then were assessed 5 months later for their early language skills using the MacArthur–Bates Communicative Development Inventory. Early statistical learning abilities were found to predict language development: Infants who were able to track the statistical relationships in the visual learning paradigm showed better language outcomes than those who did not. More longitudinal studies investigating the relationship between statistical learning and language would greatly benefit our understanding of their relationship (Arciuli & Torkildsen, 2012).

Other individual differences studies with adult participants have demonstrated covariation between statistical learning and language abilities. One study found that individuals' performance on a visual statistical learning task was correlated with performance on a task designed to test linguistic knowledge by querying whether they were able to decipher a predictable word in degraded auditory conditions (Conway, Bauernschmidt, Huang, & Pisoni, 2010). Individuals' statistical learning scores have also been found to be a better predictor of language comprehension than performance on a verbal working memory task (Misyak & Christiansen, 2012). Another study in which implicit learning was identified as a distinct cognitive ability found it to be associated with verbal analogical reasoning (Kaufman et al., 2010).

The previous discussion of adjacency and nonadjacency learning has painted a picture of two similar computations performed over the same kinds of stimuli but with varying spatiotemporal signatures. It seems plausible that they contribute to the entrenchment of linguistic features at multiple levels of processing and are recruited preferentially depending on the structure of the statistical relationships between stimuli. Misyak, Christiansen, and Tomblin (2010) found an association between statistical learning ability and reading time at the main verb in a sentence containing an object-relative clause (e.g., *the reporter that the senator attacked admitted* the error). Individuals who were better at learning the nonadjacent dependencies in the statistical learning task also processed the long-distance dependency between the head noun and main verb more efficiently in a self-paced reading paradigm. Importantly, the better learners did not show significantly faster reading times when reading the main verb in subject-relative clauses (e.g., *the reporter that attacked the senator admitted the error*).

A similar reading-time effect exists for individuals who are more sensitive to a grammar relying on the learners' ability to track adjacent dependencies (Misyak & Christiansen, 2010). The better an individual was at learning the adjacent dependencies in a statistical learning task, the more interference they experienced when processing subject–verb number agreement with conflicting local information (e.g., *the* key to the cabinets *was* rusty). This suggests that such learners are hypersensitive to adjacent relations even when it was misleading, as all sentences of this type were grammatical. Of note, individual differences in adjacent and nonadjacent statistical learning ability are not correlated with one another (Misyak & Christiansen, 2010).

The individual differences literature on statistical learning further clarifies the relationship between statistical learning and language. Findings demonstrating that better statistical learning abilities are related to greater language skill validate the idea that statistical learning itself is a contributing factor in language learning and processing, although a direct causal link cannot be inferred because of the correlational nature of these findings. The nuanced literature surrounding the relationships among adjacent statistical learning, nonadjacent statistical learning, and language also contributes to the idea that this domain-general process plays an important role in language. It remains to be seen whether the same underlying neural circuitry subserves adjacent and nonadjacent statistical learning, although some recent findings suggest that both can be tracked simultaneously under certain conditions (Vuong, Meyer, & Christiansen, 2016).

Individuals with greater experience tracking the types of relationships involved in processing sentences with nonadjacent dependencies should not only show higher performance on language tasks involving such dependencies, they should also show similar performance on tasks that rely on the same types of structure in other domains. This is consistent with other evidence pointing toward the effect that frequency has on processing (e.g., Reali & Christiansen, 2007; Wells, Christiansen, Race, Acheson, & MacDonald, 2009). As individuals track the same types of relationships over and over in language, we would expect them to learn the underlying associations between elements that reduce uncertainty if they possess a mechanism for extracting such patterns. Wells et al. (2009) demonstrated that experience with the reading of relative clause sentences facilitates object-relative clause reading times in adults, demonstrating the importance of experience for language processing and also providing compelling evidence for the plasticity of entrenchment throughout development. Learners track relationships between linguistic elements over the course of experience and use the information in these relationships to continuously update their expectations and representations: Statistical learning abilities can be thought of as mediating the effect of linguistic experience. Thus, even adults can become better at processing complex linguistic structures once those structures have become entrenched through experience-dependent learning mechanisms, indicating that it is a continuous, lifelong process of learning in language use (for a discussion, see Christiansen & Chater, 2016a).

The individual differences literature shows that there is variation across individuals in how good they are at picking up regularities given their linguistic experience. These differences highlight the importance of statistical learning in the entrenchment of linguistic structures, and linguistic relationships more generally; increased experience with certain structures leads to more automatic processing of those structures.

10.5 Statistical Learning in Models and Theories of Language Learning and Processing

Statistical learning is clearly related to some aspects of language learning and processing. Can models and theories of language learning and processing incorporate this mechanism and show that it helps to explain linguistic development?

Usage-based approaches to language (e.g., Goldberg, 2003; Tomasello, 2003) argue that grammatical knowledge is learned through the chunking and entrenchment of multiword utterances, rather than relying on innate language-specific knowledge (e.g., Pinker, 1999). Language users have since been shown to rely on such chunks when processing language (for a review, see Arnon & Christiansen, 2016). For example, young children are able to repeat words in highly frequent nonidiomatic chunks more rapidly and accurately than when the same words form lower frequency chunks (Bannard & Matthews, 2008). Adults have also been found to have a processing advantage for high-frequency multiword chunks (Arnon & Snider, 2010; Janssen & Barber, 2012), an effect that is modulated by the meaningfulness of the utterance (Jolsvai et al., 2013). This set of findings indicates the importance of entrenchment to language processing and also highlights the importance of conventionalized form–meaning mappings, supporting construction grammar approaches to language (e.g., Goldberg, 2003). Language users seem to chunk multiple words together in ways that improve processing; these constructions are best understood as entrenched linguistic elements.

How might statistical learning operate as a mechanism for the construction of such chunks? Sensitivity to statistical relationships, such as the backward transitional probabilities that infants as young as 8 months are capable of tracking (Pelucchi, Hay, & Saffran, 2009), has been built into certain models attempting to understand how children might form their early lexicon through the construction of these entrenched chunks. The peaks and dips in forward transitional probability have also been identified as potential cues for placing phrasal boundaries when computed over word classes (Thompson & Newport, 2007).

McCauley and Christiansen (2011) created a model that is capable of tracking the statistical relationships between single words and, based on these relationships, forming chunks. The model is trained on corpora of child-directed speech from the CHILDES (Child Language Data Exchange System) database (MacWhinney, 2000), giving it a naturalistic input from which to learn. The model is able to accurately place boundaries between phrases and also outperforms competing models when attempting to reproduce the utterances of the children in the corpora. In addition, the model parallels child performance in an artificial grammar learning paradigm (Saffran, 2002) when the learning takes place over individual items, rather than classes of items, mirroring its relative performance in the analyses of language production and comprehension, contradicting the findings of Thompson and Newport

(2007). This model demonstrates that entrenched units can be formed on the basis of distributional information alone, identifying statistical learning as a mechanism of entrenchment in the contexts of both natural and artificial language.

10.6 Conclusion

The ability to track and learn probabilistic dependencies between elements seems to be a property of the way that humans learn in multiple domains. Whether the elements are tones (Saffran et al., 1999), syllables (Saffran, Aslin, & Newport, 1996; Saffran, Newport, & Aslin, 1996), wordlike units (Gómez, 2002), visual scenes (Fiser & Aslin, 2002), or complex audiovisual stimuli (Mitchel, Christiansen, & Weiss, 2014; van den Bos, Christiansen, & Misyak, 2012), humans are able to learn about the statistical structure underlying their co-occurrence. This evidence points toward statistical learning as a robust, domain-general process (Saffran & Thiessen, 2007), likely implemented in separate modality-specific neural networks relying on similar computational principles (Frost et al., 2015).

The manner in which statistical learning operates, by tracking relational and distributional information for items across space and time, leads to the entrenchment of learned relationships. The degree of entrenchment varies among items as a function of frequency (Reali & Christiansen, 2007), meaningfulness (Jolsvai et al., 2013), and predictability (Aslin, Saffran, & Newport, 1998) and is fundamentally plastic throughout the lifespan (Wells et al., 2009). This general understanding of how statistical learning leads to the construction of units that contain meaning fits well into emergent, experience-based theories about language (i.e., Bybee, 2006; Christiansen & Chater, 2016a, 2016b; Elman et al., 1996; Goldberg, 2003) and identifies it as integral to theories postulating that language learning and processing rely on sensitivity to multiple cues in the input (Christiansen, Allen, & Seidenberg, 1998). Highly entrenched items can be stored as chunks, which can become the building blocks of language in development (McCauley & Christiansen, 2011) and which can also affect language processing (Bannard & Matthews, 2008). These entrenched representations are built up over the course of development as a result of statistical learning, allowing higher level linguistic features to be learned.

References

Amso, D., & Davidow, J. (2012). The development of implicit learning from infancy to adulthood: Item frequencies, relations, and cognitive flexibility. *Developmental Psychobiology, 54*, 664–673. http://dx.doi.org/10.1002/dev.20587

Arciuli, J., & Torkildsen, J. V. K. (2012, August). Advancing our understanding of the link between statistical learning and language acquisition: The need for longitudinal data. *Frontiers in Psychology, 3*, 324.

Arciuli, J., Torkildsen, J. V. K., Stevens, D. J., & Simpson, I. C. (2014, July). Statistical learning under incidental versus intentional conditions. *Frontiers in Psychology, 5*, 747.

Arnon, I., & Christiansen, M. H. (2016). *Multiword units as building blocks for language.* Manuscript submitted for publication.

Arnon, I., & Snider, N. (2010). More than words: Frequency effects for multi-word phrases. *Journal of Memory and Language, 62*, 67–82. http://dx.doi.org/10.1016/j.jml.2009.09.005

Aslin, R. N., Saffran, J. N., & Newport, E. L. (1998). Computation of conditional probability statistics by 8-month-old infants. *Psychological Science, 9*, 321–324. http://dx.doi.org/10.1111/1467-9280.00063

Baayen, R. H. (2010). Demythologizing the word frequency effect: A discriminative learning perspective. *The Mental Lexicon, 5*, 436–461. http://dx.doi.org/10.1075/ml.5.3.10baa

Bannard, C., & Matthews, D. (2008). Stored word sequences in language learning: The effect of familiarity on children's repetition of four-word combinations. *Psychological Science, 19*, 241–248. http://dx.doi.org/10.1111/j.1467-9280.2008.02075.x

Bertels, J., Franco, A., & Destrebecqz, A. (2012). How implicit is visual statistical learning? *Journal of Experimental Psychology: Learning, Memory, and Cognition, 38*, 1425–1431. http://dx.doi.org/10.1037/a0027210

Bly, B. M., Carrión, R. E., & Rasch, B. (2009). Domain-specific learning of grammatical structure in musical and phonological sequences. *Memory & Cognition, 37*, 10–20. http://dx.doi.org/10.3758/MC.37.1.10

Braine, M. D. S. (1963). On learning the grammatical order of words. *Psychological Review, 70*, 323–348. http://dx.doi.org/10.1037/h0047696

Bybee, J. (2006). From usage to grammar: The mind's response to repetition. *Language, 82*, 711–733. http://dx.doi.org/10.1353/lan.2006.0186

Chomsky, N. (1965). *Aspects of the theory of syntax.* Cambridge, MA: MIT Press.

Christiansen, M. H., Allen, J., & Seidenberg, M. S. (1998). Learning to segment speech using multiple cues: A connectionist model. *Language and Cognitive Processes, 13*, 221–268. http://dx.doi.org/10.1080/016909698386528

Christiansen, M. H., & Chater, N. (2008). Language as shaped by the brain. *Behavioral and Brain Sciences, 31*, 489–508. http://dx.doi.org/10.1017/S0140525X08004998

Christiansen, M. H., & Chater, N. (2016a). *Creating language: Integrating evolution, acquisition, and processing.* Cambridge, MA: MIT Press.

Christiansen, M. H., & Chater, N. (2016b). The Now-or-Never bottleneck: A fundamental constraint on language. *Behavioral and Brain Sciences, 39*, e62. http://dx.doi.org/10.1017/S0140525X1500031X

Conway, C. M., Bauernschmidt, A., Huang, S. S., & Pisoni, D. B. (2010). Implicit statistical learning in language processing: Word predictability is the key. *Cognition, 114*, 356–371. http://dx.doi.org/10.1016/j.cognition.2009.10.009

Conway, C. M., & Christiansen, M. H. (2005). Modality-constrained statistical learning of tactile, visual, and auditory sequences. *Journal of Experimental Psychology: Learning, Memory, and Cognition, 31*, 24–39. http://dx.doi.org/10.1037/0278-7393.31.1.24

Conway, C. M., & Christiansen, M. H. (2006). Statistical learning within and between modalities: Pitting abstract against stimulus-specific representations. *Psychological Science, 17*, 905–912. http://dx.doi.org/10.1111/j.1467-9280.2006.01801.x

Crain, S. (1991). Language acquisition in the absence of experience. *Behavioral and Brain Sciences*, *14*, 597–612. http://dx.doi.org/10.1017/S0140525X00071491

Creel, S. C., Newport, E. L., & Aslin, R. N. (2004). Distant melodies: Statistical learning of nonadjacent dependencies in tone sequences. *Journal of Experimental Psychology: Learning, Memory, and Cognition*, *30*, 1119–1130. http://dx.doi.org/10.1037/0278-7393.30.5.1119

Elman, J. L. (1990). Finding structure in time. *Cognitive Science*, *14*, 179–211. http://dx.doi.org/10.1207/s15516709cog1402_1

Elman, J. L., Bates, E. A., Johnson, M. H., Karmiloff-Smith, A., Parisi, D., & Plunkett, K. (1996). *Rethinking innateness: A connectionist perspective on development*. Cambridge, MA: MIT Press.

Emberson, L. L., Conway, C. M., & Christiansen, M. H. (2011). Timing is everything: Changes in presentation rate have opposite effects on auditory and visual implicit statistical learning. *The Quarterly Journal of Experimental Psychology: Human Experimental Psychology*, *64*, 1021–1040. http://dx.doi.org/10.1080/17470218.2010.538972

Fiser, J., & Aslin, R. N. (2002). Statistical learning of new visual feature combinations by infants. *Proceedings of the National Academy of Sciences of the United States of America*, *99*, 15822–15826. http://dx.doi.org/10.1073/pnas.232472899

Franco, A., Cleeremans, A., & Destrebecqz, A. (2011). Statistical learning of two artificial languages presented successively: How conscious? *Frontiers in Psychology*, *2*, 229. http://dx.doi.org/10.3389/fpsyg.2011.00229

Franco, A., & Destrebecqz, A. (2012). Chunking or not chunking? How do we find words in artificial language learning? *Advances in Cognitive Psychology*, *8*, 144–154. http://dx.doi.org/10.5709/acp-0111-3

Frost, R., Armstrong, B. C., Siegelman, N., & Christiansen, M. H. (2015). Domain generality versus modality specificity: The paradox of statistical learning. *Trends in Cognitive Sciences*, *19*, 117–125. http://dx.doi.org/10.1016/j.tics.2014.12.010

Fodor, J. A. (1983). *The modularity of mind*. Cambridge, MA: MIT Press.

Gibson, E. J. (1991). *An odyssey in learning and perception*. Cambridge, MA: MIT Press.

Gibson, J. J., & Gibson, E. J. (1955). Perceptual learning: Differentiation or enrichment? *Psychological Review*, *62*, 32–41. http://dx.doi.org/10.1037/h0048826

Goldberg, A. E. (2003). Constructions: A new theoretical approach to language. *Trends in Cognitive Sciences*, *7*, 219–224. http://dx.doi.org/10.1016/S1364-6613(03)00080-9

Goldstein, M. H., Waterfall, H. R., Lotem, A., Halpern, J. Y., Schwade, J. A., Onnis, L., & Edelman, S. (2010). General cognitive principles for learning structure in time and space. *Trends in Cognitive Sciences*, *14*, 249–258. http://dx.doi.org/10.1016/j.tics.2010.02.004

Gómez, R. L. (2002). Variability and detection of invariant structure. *Psychological Science*, *13*, 431–436. http://dx.doi.org/10.1111/1467-9280.00476

Gómez, R. L., & Maye, J. (2005). The developmental trajectory of nonadjacent dependency learning. *Infancy*, *7*, 183–206. http://dx.doi.org/10.1207/s15327078in0702_4

James, W. (1890). *The principles of psychology*. New York, NY: Holt. http://dx.doi.org/10.1037/11059-000

Janssen, N., & Barber, H. A. (2012). Phrase frequency effects in language production. *PLoS ONE*, *7*, e33202. http://dx.doi.org/10.1371/journal.pone.0033202

Jolsvai, H., McCauley, S. M., & Christiansen, M. H. (2013). Meaning overrides frequency in idiomatic and compositional multiword chunks. In M. Knauff, M. Pauen, N. Sebanz, & I. Wachsmuth (Eds.),

Proceedings of the 35th Annual Conference of the Cognitive Science Society. Austin, TX: Cognitive Science Society.

Jost, E., Conway, C. M., Purdy, J. D., Walk, A. M., & Hendricks, M. A. (2015). Exploring the neurodevelopment of visual statistical learning using event-related brain potentials. *Brain Research*, *1597*, 95–107. http://dx.doi.org/10.1016/j.brainres.2014.10.017

Kaufman, S. B., Deyoung, C. G., Gray, J. R., Jiménez, L., Brown, J., & Mackintosh, N. (2010). Implicit learning as an ability. *Cognition*, *116*, 321–340. http://dx.doi.org/10.1016/j.cognition.2010.05.011

Kim, R., Seitz, A., Feenstra, H., & Shams, L. (2009). Testing assumptions of statistical learning: Is it long-term and implicit? *Neuroscience Letters*, *461*, 145–149. http://dx.doi.org/10.1016/j.neulet.2009.06.030

Kirkham, N. Z., Slemmer, J. A., & Johnson, S. P. (2002). Visual statistical learning in infancy: Evidence for a domain general learning mechanism. *Cognition*, *83*, B35–B42. http://dx.doi.org/10.1016/S0010-0277(02)00004-5

Lieberman, M. D. (2000). Intuition: A social cognitive neuroscience approach. *Psychological Bulletin*, *126*, 109–137.

MacWhinney, B. (2000). *The CHILDES project: Tools for analyzing talk: Vol. 2. The database*. Mahwah, NJ: Erlbaum.

McCauley, S. M., & Christiansen, M. H. (2011). Learning simple statistics for language comprehension and production: The CAPPUCCINO model. In L. Carlson, C. Hölscher, & T. Shipley (Eds.), *Proceedings of the 33rd Annual Conference of the Cognitive Science Society* (pp. 1619–1624). Austin, TX: Cognitive Science Society.

McCauley, S. M., & Christiansen, M. H. (2014). Acquiring formulaic language: A computational model. *Mental Lexicon*, *9*, 419–436. http://dx.doi.org/10.1075/ml.9.3.03mcc

Miller, G. A. (1958). Free recall of redundant strings of letters. *Journal of Experimental Psychology*, *56*, 485–491. http://dx.doi.org/10.1037/h0044933

Miller, G. A., & Selfridge, J. A. (1950). Verbal context and the recall of meaningful material. *The American Journal of Psychology*, *63*, 176–185. http://dx.doi.org/10.2307/1418920

Misyak, J. B., & Christiansen, M. H. (2010). When "more" in statistical learning means "less" in language: Individual differences in predictive processing of adjacent dependencies. In R. Catrambone & S. Ohlsson (Eds.), *Proceedings of the 32nd Annual Conference of the Cognitive Science Society* (pp. 2686–2691). Austin, TX: Cognitive Science Society.

Misyak, J. B., & Christiansen, M. H. (2012). Statistical learning and language: An individual differences study. *Language Learning*, *62*, 302–331. http://dx.doi.org/10.1111/j.1467-9922.2010.00626.x

Misyak, J. B., Christiansen, M. H., & Tomblin, J. B. (2010). Sequential expectations: The role of prediction-based learning in language. *Topics in Cognitive Science*, *2*, 138–153. http://dx.doi.org/10.1111/j.1756-8765.2009.01072.x

Misyak, J. B., Goldstein, M. H., & Christiansen, M. H. (2012). Statistical-sequential learning in development. In P. Rebuschat & J. Williams (Eds.), *Statistical learning and language acquisition* (pp. 13–54). Berlin, Germany: Mouton de Gruyter.

Mitchel, A. D., Christiansen, M. H., & Weiss, D. J. (2014). Multimodal integration in statistical learning: Evidence from the McGurk illusion. *Frontiers in Psychology*, *5*, 407. http://dx.doi.org/10.3389/fpsyg.2014.00407

Monaghan, P., & Christiansen, M. H. (2010). Words in puddles of sound: Modelling psycholinguistic effects in speech segmentation. *Journal of Child Language*, *37*, 545–564. http://dx.doi.org/10.1017/S0305000909990511

Newport, E. L., & Aslin, R. N. (2004). Learning at a distance I: Statistical learning of non-adjacent dependencies. *Cognitive Psychology, 48*, 127–162. http://dx.doi.org/10.1016/S0010-0285(03)00128-2

Oldfield, R. C., & Wingfield, A. (1965). Response latencies in naming objects. *The Quarterly Journal of Experimental Psychology, 17*, 273–281. http://dx.doi.org/10.1080/17470216508416445

Pelucchi, B., Hay, J. F., & Saffran, J. R. (2009). Learning in reverse: Eight-month-old infants track backward transitional probabilities. *Cognition, 113*, 244–247. http://dx.doi.org/10.1016/j.cognition.2009.07.011

Perruchet, P., & Pacton, S. (2006). Implicit learning and statistical learning: One phenomenon, two approaches. *Trends in Cognitive Sciences, 10*, 233–238. http://dx.doi.org/10.1016/j.tics.2006.03.006

Pinker, S. (1999). *Words and rules: The ingredients of language.* New York, NY: HarperCollins.

Reali, F., & Christiansen, M. H. (2007). Processing of relative clauses is made easier by frequency of occurrence. *Journal of Memory and Language, 57*, 1–23. http://dx.doi.org/10.1016/j.jml.2006.08.014

Reber, A. S. (1967). Implicit learning of artificial grammars. *Journal of Verbal Learning & Verbal Behavior, 6*, 855–863. http://dx.doi.org/10.1016/S0022-5371(67)80149-X

Reber, A. S. (1976). Implicit learning of synthetic languages: The role of instructional set. *Journal of Experimental Psychology: Human Learning and Memory, 2*, 88–94. http://dx.doi.org/10.1037/0278-7393.2.1.88

Reber, A. S. (1993). *Implicit learning and tacit knowledge: An essay on the cognitive unconscious.* New York, NY: Oxford University Press.

Reber, A. S., & Allen, R. (2000). Individual differences in implicit learning. In R. G. Kunzendorf & B. Wallace (Eds.), *Individual differences in conscious experience* (pp. 227–248). http://dx.doi.org/10.1075/aicr.20.11reb

Robertson, E. M. (2007). The serial reaction time task: Implicit motor skill learning? *The Journal of Neuroscience, 27*, 10073–10075. http://dx.doi.org/10.1523/JNEUROSCI.2747-07.2007

Ruffman, T., Taumoepeau, M., & Perkins, C. (2012). Statistical learning as a basis for social understanding in children. *British Journal of Developmental Psychology, 30*, 87–104. http://dx.doi.org/10.1111/j.2044-835X.2011.02045.x

Saffran, J. R. (2001). The use of predictive dependencies in language learning. *Journal of Memory and Language, 44*, 493–515. http://dx.doi.org/10.1006/jmla.2000.2759

Saffran, J. (2002). Constraints on statistical language learning. *Journal of Memory and Language, 47*, 172–196. http://dx.doi.org/10.1006/jmla.2001.2839

Saffran, J. R., Aslin, R. N., & Newport, E. L. (1996). Statistical learning by 8-month-old infants. *Science, 274*, 1926–1928. http://dx.doi.org/10.1126/science.274.5294.1926

Saffran, J. R., & Griepentrog, G. J. (2001). Absolute pitch in infant auditory learning: Evidence for developmental reorganization. *Developmental Psychology, 37*, 74–85.

Saffran, J. R., Johnson, E. K., Aslin, R. N., & Newport, E. L. (1999). Statistical learning of tone sequences by human infants and adults. *Cognition, 70*, 27–52. http://dx.doi.org/10.1016/S0010-0277(98)00075-4

Saffran, J. R., Newport, E. L., & Aslin, R. N. (1996). Word segmentation: The role of distributional cues. *Journal of Memory and Language, 35*, 606–621. http://dx.doi.org/10.1006/jmla.1996.0032

Saffran, J. R., & Thiessen, E. D. (2007). Domain-general learning capacities. In E. Hoff & M. Shatz (Eds.), *Handbook of language development* (pp. 68–86). Cambridge, England: Blackwell.

Sanders, L. D., Newport, E. L., & Neville, H. J. (2002). Segmenting nonsense: An event-related potential index of perceived onsets in continuous speech. *Nature Neuroscience, 5,* 700–703. http://dx.doi.org/10.1038/nn873

Schmid, H. J. (2007). Entrenchment, salience, and basic levels. In D. Geeraerts & H. Cuyckens (Eds.), *The Oxford Handbook of cognitive linguistics* (pp. 117–138). Oxford, England: Oxford University Press.

Shafto, C. L., Conway, C. M., Field, S. L., & Houston, D. M. (2012). Visual sequence learning in infancy: Domain-general and domain-specific associations with language. *Infancy, 17,* 247–271. http://dx.doi.org/10.1111/j.1532-7078.2011.00085.x

Teinonen, T., Fellman, V., Näätänen, R., Alku, P., & Huotilainen, M. (2009). Statistical language learning in neonates revealed by event-related brain potentials. *BMC Neuroscience, 10,* 21. http://dx.doi.org/10.1186/1471-2202-10-21

Thompson, S. P., & Newport, E. L. (2007). Statistical learning of syntax: The role of transitional probability. *Language Learning and Development, 3,* 1–42. http://dx.doi.org/10.1080/15475440709336999

Tomasello, M. (2003). *Constructing a language: A usage-based theory of language acquisition.* Cambridge, MA: Harvard University Press.

Turk-Browne, N. B., Isola, P. J., Scholl, B. J., & Treat, T. A. (2008). Multidimensional visual statistical learning. *Journal of Experimental Psychology: Learning, Memory, and Cognition, 34,* 399–407. http://dx.doi.org/10.1037/0278-7393.34.2.399

van den Bos, E., Christiansen, M. H., & Misyak, J. B. (2012). Statistical learning of probabilistic nonadjacent dependencies by multiple-cue integration. *Journal of Memory and Language, 67,* 507–520. http://dx.doi.org/10.1016/j.jml.2012.07.008

van den Brink, D., Brown, C. M., & Hagoort, P. (2001). Electrophysiological evidence for early contextual influences during spoken-word recognition: N200 versus N400 effects. *Journal of Cognitive Neuroscience, 13,* 967–985. http://dx.doi.org/10.1162/089892901753165872

Vapnik, V. N. (1999). An overview of statistical learning theory. *Neural Networks. IEEE Transactions on, 10,* 988–999.

Vuong, L. C., Meyer, A. S., & Christiansen, M. H. (2016). Concurrent statistical learning of adjacent and nonadjacent dependencies. *Language Learning, 66,* 8–30. http://dx.doi.org/10.1111/lang.12137

Wells, J. B., Christiansen, M. H., Race, D. S., Acheson, D. J., & MacDonald, M. C. (2009). Experience and sentence processing: Statistical learning and relative clause comprehension. *Cognitive Psychology, 58,* 250–271. http://dx.doi.org/10.1016/j.cogpsych.2008.08.002

Yu, C., & Smith, L. B. (2007). Rapid word learning under uncertainty via cross-situational statistics. *Psychological Science, 18,* 414–420. http://dx.doi.org/10.1111/j.1467-9280.2007.01915.x

Fernand Gobet
11 Entrenchment, Gestalt Formation, and Chunking

11.1 Introduction

Since one often-quoted conception of entrenchment (Langacker, 1987, p. 59) is based on the idea of unit-formation and the gradual strengthening of units, the ideas of cognitive organization, unit, and grouping are central to the notion of entrenchment. In cognitive psychology, grouping has been mainly studied by two traditions: (a) Gestalt psychology, which focused on perception, although other aspects of cognition such as problem solving were considered as well; and (b) the line of research interested in chunking, which focuses on memory, although aspects of perception and problem solving have been studied as well. This chapter first reviews these two traditions of research, highlighting both the phenomena studied and the mechanisms proposed to explain them. Following a historical order, it first discusses Gestalt psychology and then research on chunking. The final part of the chapter considers how the notions of Gestalt and chunking help understand some key aspects of language.

11.2 Gestalt Formation

The motivation behind Gestalt psychology was von Ehrenfels's (1890) observation that a melody is recognized even when it is played in different keys. Thus, although each component (note) is different, the musical pattern is the same. As von Ehrenfels famously put it, "the whole is more than the sum of its parts". He called this phenomenon a *Gestalt* ("form" in German). How can such a surprising phenomenon be explained? Does it apply to other aspects of the mind? These are some of the questions that Gestalt psychology, which was active from the 1890s to the 1930s, set out to answer. According to this school, which was in stark opposition to the reductionist approach of structuralism, perception is a process characterized by the self-organization of basic elements.

Dmitry Bennett and Arnaud Rey provided useful comments on an earlier draft of this paper. I'm also particularly grateful to Hans-Jörg Schmid for many pointers to the linguistics literature.

11.2.1 Perception

A first major contribution of Gestalt psychology is to have uncovered numerous perceptual phenomena to which the concept of Gestalt applied. For example, Wertheimer described the optical illusion known as the *phi phenomenon*, in which stationary stimuli presented in rapid succession are perceived as moving continuously.

In a second key contribution, Gestalt psychologists proposed principles of perceptual organization to explain these phenomena. The central principle is the *principle of Prägnanz* (in German, *Prägnanz* means "succinctness" or "simplicity"). This principle states that the perceptual input is organized so that what is perceived is the simplest and most stable form. Based on this principle, Gestalt psychologists derived six laws of perception.

According to the *law of proximity*, objects are clustered together based on their proximity (see Figure 11.1, Panel A). Thus, objects that are close to each other are perceived as an independent group separated from other objects. The *law of similarity* states that objects that look similar are grouped together. For example, in Panel B, circles and triangles are perceived as four horizontal rows in the left-hand drawing, and four vertical columns in the right-hand drawing. The *law of closure* asserts that perception often adds information to objects so that they are perceived as wholes. For example, in Panel C, most people see a large circle consisting of small circles, although there are gaps between those.

According to the *law of symmetry*, objects are perceived as if they are organized around symmetrical axes or centers (see Panel D). The *law of continuity* stipulates that objects tend to be perceived as using smooth continuous shapes. For example, in Panel E, most people see two oblique lines partly hidden by a horizontal rectangle. The disconnected parts of the lines are automatically inferred to belong to the same line. (In fact, the two segments of each "line" are offset and thus do not form a line; this illusion illustrates the power of the Gestalt laws).

Finally, according to the *law of figure-ground segregation*, visual scenes tend to be divided into two parts: a figure and a ground. For example, the panel at the bottom of Figure 11.1 illustrates figure-ground segregation. The drawing is perceived either as two opposing faces or as a goblet. In the first case, the faces are the focus of attention and constitute the figure while the goblet recedes to the back of attention and forms the ground; in the second case, the goblet is perceived as the figure and the faces as the ground. People normally can switch which part of the drawing is perceived as the figure and which part is perceived as the ground; however, when one object is perceived as the figure, the other is automatically perceived as the ground. Note that the drawing is an example of a *bistable percept*.

11.2.2 Problem Solving

A third important contribution of Gestalt psychology is to have shown that perception, and thus Gestalt concepts, also applied to thinking and, in particular, to prob-

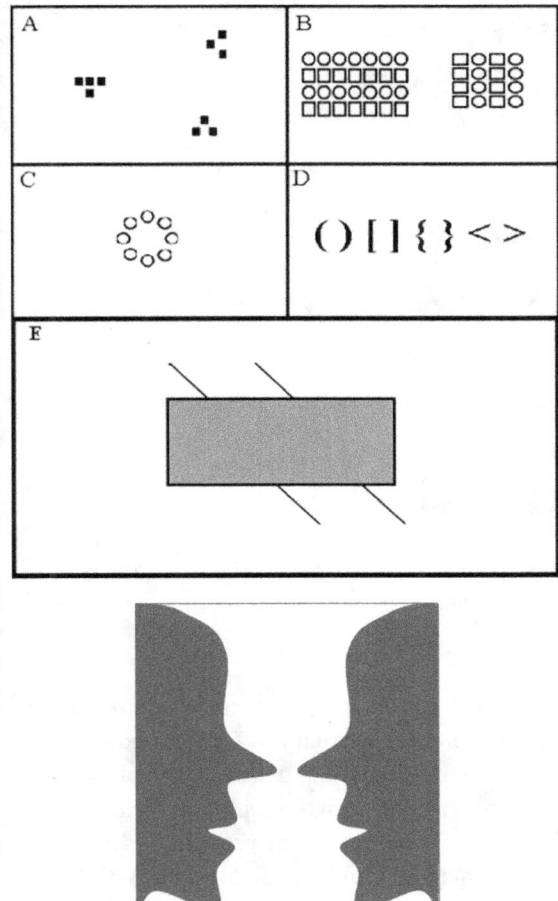

Fig. 11.1: Gestalt laws. Upper panel from *Foundations of Cognitive Psychology* (p. 56), by F. Gobet, P. Chassy, and M. Bilalić, 2011, London, England: McGraw Hill. Copyright 2011 by McGraw Hill. Adapted with permission.

lem solving. In a series of ingenious experiments, Gestalt psychologists showed that some problems are solved not by incremental thinking processes, but by an abrupt reorganization of thought, which they called *insight*. For example, consider the nine-dot problem (Maier, 1930) shown in Figure 11.2.

The task is to connect the nine dots without lifting the pen. Most participants act as if they are "fixated" on the square formed by the dots and assume that the lines must be inside this shape. The problem cannot be solved until it is realized that (some of) the lines must go beyond the perceptual squares suggested by the nine dots (see the solution in Figure 11.3). This problem illustrates that perceptual organization imposes constraints on possible solutions, even though these constraints might not be part of the original problem formulation.

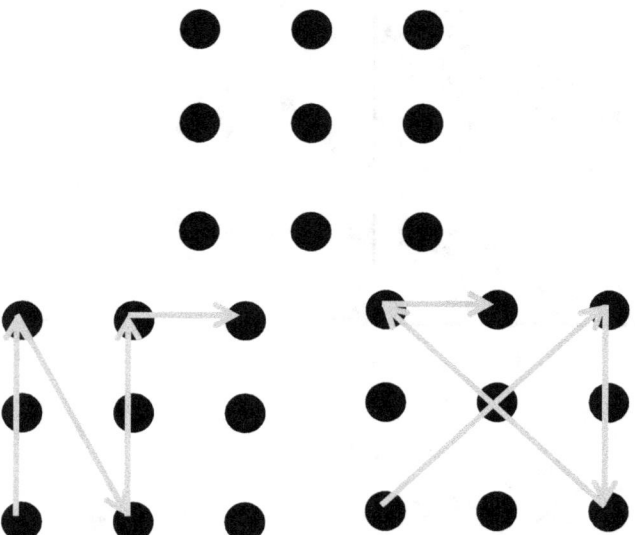

Fig. 11.2: Top: The nine-dot problem. Join all nine dots by drawing four continuous straight lines without lifting the pencil. Bottom: Two incorrect solutions. (A correct solution is given in Figure 11.3.)

With respect to entrenchment, if taken as referring to degrees of strengths of knowledge representations, Gestalt psychologists carried out striking experiments showing that previous knowledge sometimes hinders the discovery of solutions. In Maier's (1931) two-string problem, two strings hang from the ceiling and the task is to tie them together. Unfortunately, they are too far apart for the participants to be able to hold one string in each hand. Most participants find it difficult to solve the problem, and pay little attention to a number of objects, including pliers, that lie on the

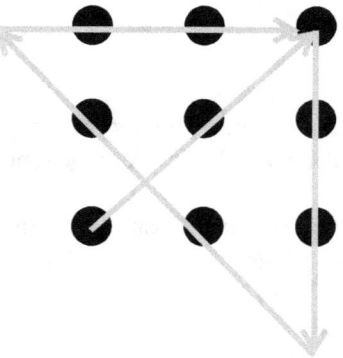

Fig. 11.3: Solution to the nine-dot problem.

floor. The solution is actually to use the pliers as a pendulum. Then, when one string is set in motion, one grasps the other string and waits that the first one swings back. Most participants fail to solve this problem. Providing subtle hints such as inadvertently brushing one string helps some but not all participants. According to Maier (1931), perception of the solution is sudden, and the insight of the solution involves unconsciously restructuring the problem, rather than using associations acquired through trials and errors. The two-string problem also illustrates what Duncker (1945) called "functional fixedness": Our mind is blinded by prior knowledge of objects and their usage so that we cannot see that they can be used in a different way.

Birch and Rabinowitz (1951) extended Maier's (1931) experiment by manipulating the function of objects. They first instructed participants to complete an electrical circuit by using either a relay or a switch. In the second task, participants faced the two-string problem and could use several objects, including relays and switches. The key result was that participants who repaired the circuit with a relay in the first task tended to choose the switch in the two-string problem, whereas those who used a switch in the first task tended to choose a relay in the second. As in Maier's (1931) experiment, knowledge of how an object is used reduces the likelihood of using it in a different way.

Perhaps the most spectacular example of how entrenched knowledge can block new solutions and can be induced experimentally was provided by Luchins (1942) in his experiment on the *Einstellung effect* (or *set effect*). Participants had to solve arithmetic problems, presented as water-jug problems, where one has to fill one jug with the right amount of water by using jugs of different capacities. The first five problems could be solved with the same solution. Problems 6 and 7, called *critical problems*, could be solved both by the same solution and a shorter solution. Eighty percent of the participants used the familiar solution and failed to see the shorter one. Finally, Problem 8, called the *extinction problem*, could be solved only with the short solution. Surprisingly, nearly two thirds of the participants could not solve the problem. This level of failure cannot be explained by the difficulty of the extinction problem because it was solved by 95% of the participants in a control group that did not receive the first five problems. Luchins's study illustrates how entrenchment and the automatization of thought might lead to unsuccessful problem solving.

The participants in Luchins's (1942) experiment were novices, and an important question is whether experts fall prey to the *Einstellung* effect as well. This is certainly what several influential authors have proposed in the literature: Experts, who have acquired considerable knowledge and have automatized their skills, have a more rigid mode of thinking and are actually more prone to the *Einstellung* effect than novices. For example, Sternberg (1996) argued that "there are costs as well as benefits to expertise. One such cost is increased rigidity: The expert can become so entrenched in a point of view or a way of doing things that it becomes hard to see things differently" (p. 347). Researchers on creativity have come to the same conclusion (e.g., Csikszentmihalyi, 1996).

Bilalić, McLeod, and Gobet (2008a) tackled this question with chess, a game that has been extensively studied in expertise research. They designed two kinds of chess positions. The first had two solutions: a familiar solution that was not optimal and an unfamiliar solution that was optimal. The results mirrored those found in Luchins's (1942) experiment: Chess players tended to go for the familiar solution even though it was not optimal. In fact, when they were asked to find a better solution than the familiar one, most failed. This could not be due to the difficulty of the problem because players who faced the second kind of positions, which had only the unfamiliar solution, could find it easily. Critically, the strength of the *Einstellung* effect decreased as the skill level increased and reached the level of grandmasters. This suggests that expertise, at least to some extent and from a certain level of proficiency upwards, protects against the deleterious *Einstellung* effect. Thus, *pace* Sternberg (1996), expertise does not make thinking more rigid, it makes it less rigid.

In another experiment (Bilalić, McLeod, & Gobet, 2008b), eye-movement recordings showed that while candidate masters thought that they were trying to find a better solution after having selected the familiar one, they actually continued to fixate on the squares that were critical for the familiar solution. In spite of the players' good intentions, their attention was controlled by schemata associated with the familiar solution that they had found first. It is likely that a similar mechanism occurs in other examples of entrenchment, such as the confirmation bias and scientists' tendency to neglect empirical results that do not fit the predictions of their own theories.

11.2.3 Gestalt Formation: Discussion

Although Gestalt psychologists described important principles that organize perception and uncovered important and sometimes spectacular phenomena, the explanations they proposed (e.g., Gestalt, restructuring) were ill-specified and thus weaker. When they offered more detailed physiological explanations, these turned out to be wrong. For example, Köhler and Held (1949) proposed that percepts were caused by electric fields in the brain. This hypothesis of isomorphism between percepts and neural mechanisms was tested by Lashley, Chow, and Semmes (1951). Inserting gold foils in large areas of the visual cortex of monkeys should have interfered with the electric fields and thus the perception of visual patterns. However, the results showed that this was not the case.

As with perception, Gestalt research on problem solving revealed stunning phenomena but lacked precise mechanisms. Terms such as *insight, restructuring,* and *Einstellung* were more labels to describe phenomena than genuine mechanisms. Nevertheless, the Gestalt approach predicts some aspects related to linguistic entrenchment that play a role in current theorizing and empirical findings. For one thing, the *Einstellung* effect finds a correlate in the phenomena of preemption and blocking in language acquisition (see Theakston, Chapter 14, this volume) and morphology

(Aronoff, 1976, p. 43). The Gestalt psychologists' insight that it can sometimes have negative consequences shows in second-language acquisition when learners have to combat (see MacWhinney, Chapter 15, this volume) strongly entrenched first-language knowledge. In Cognitive Grammar (see Langacker, 1987), the principle of figure–ground segregation has been transferred to syntax and seen as a cognitive force motivating the separation of simple sentences in syntactic figure (i.e., subject) and ground (i.e., objects and other complements).

11.3 Chunking

Whilst Gestalt psychologists paid little attention to memory and learning, the tradition of research on chunking has addressed questions that are focused primarily on these cognitive faculties. Cognitive psychologists often distinguish between short-term memory (STM—a temporary buffer where information accessible to consciousness is stored briefly) and long-term memory (LTM—a permanent structure where information, not accessible to consciousness, is stored permanently; see Takashima & Bakker, Chapter 8, this volume), and both kinds of memory have led to research on chunking. The interest centers on how information can be grouped in STM to make recall easier, and how learning leads to the formation of LTM structures that group information together.

To organize the literature, it is useful to consider how and when chunking is thought to occur and to distinguish between deliberate chunking and automatic chunking (Gobet et al., 2001). *Deliberate chunking* concerns chunking processes that are controlled, goal-oriented, strategic, and conscious. *Automatic chunking* concerns chunking processes that are noncontrolled, implicit, continuous, and unconscious; these processes typically occur during perception (perceptual chunking). Research on the first type of chunking tends to focus on STM, whereas research on the second type of chunking occurs more often in the framework of LTM. Despite this important distinction, Gobet et al. (2001) offer a general definition of a chunk as a "collection of elements having strong associations with one another, but weak associations with elements within other chunks" (p. 236).

11.3.1 Deliberate Chunking

Research into deliberate chunking has focused on the means used by humans to circumvent the limits of memory. The first line of research has studied the extent to which stimuli to memorize can be compressed by taking advantage of redundancies. The interest is in STM tasks where little LTM knowledge can be used. The second line of research concerns the use of mnemonics, where the emphasis is on the use of conscious strategies to rapidly encode information in LTM.

11.3.1.1 STM Tasks

Considerable research in psychology has been devoted to measuring the capacity of STM. A milestone was the realization that the correct measure for this capacity is not the amount of information, as expressed by measures proposed by information theory such as bits (Shannon, 1948), but the number of chunks. In a classic paper, Miller (1956) proposed that the capacity of STM was limited to 7 ± 2 chunks. More recent research puts the estimate to 3 ± 1 chunks (Cowan, 2001; Gobet & Clarkson, 2004).

In computer science, coding theory studies how it is possible to take advantage of redundancies for encoding and storing information more efficiently. Compression techniques are now central in many technological applications—think of the ZIP format for compressing documents. Recent research (Mathy & Feldman, 2012; Robinet, Lemaire, & Gordon, 2011) has studied the role of redundancies in the material to memorize, whilst trying to minimize the role of prior knowledge. When presented with a list of digits to memorize (e.g., a phone number), a powerful strategy is to find patterns in the items. For example, one can identify repeating patterns (1 2 1 2 1 2), increasing (1 2 3 4) or decreasing (6 5 4 3) patterns, or symmetries (2 3 3 2). As we shall see below, some mnemonics use such strategies.

Mathy and Feldman (2012) investigated the extent to which humans exploit redundancies to memorize information in STM tasks by manipulating the compressibility of lists of digits. They asked participants to memorize lists consisting of increasing and decreasing series. For example, the list (1 2 3 4 8 6 4) consists of two runs: an increasing series (start at 1 and increase by 1 three times) and a decreasing series (start at 8 and decrease by 2 twice). They found that the best predictor of STM capacity was the length of the lists after compression and that the best estimate of this capacity was about three to four chunks. Interestingly, with lists of typical compressibility, the estimate was seven uncompressed digits, which is in line with Miller's estimate. On the basis of these results, and Kolmogorov's (1965) mathematical measure of complexity and compressibility, Mathy and Feldman (2012) defined a chunk as a unit obtained with an optimally compressed code.

Robinet, Lemaire, and Gordon (2011) were also interested in the way redundant information can be compressed. They used the minimum description length (MDL) principle (Rissanen, 1978). MDL can be seen as an application of Occam's razor principle, which states that one should choose the hypothesis that makes the fewest assumptions. Applied to information science, this amounts to choosing the model that provides the greatest compression of the data. More specifically, MDL is defined as the length of the shortest program that can reproduce a given input. Robinet et al. assumed that humans follow the *principle of simplicity*, which states that the simplest structures are chosen whenever possible. The model they developed, called MDLCHUNKER, addresses both working memory tasks and LTM tasks, and uses a hierarchy of chunks. It dynamically decides whether to build a new chunk using MDL and thus to recode the data more efficiently. High-frequency chunks enable greater compression of the data and thus are predicted to make recall easier. To test the model, Lemaire, Robinet, and Portrat (2012) carried out an experiment in which chunk frequency was systematically manipulated. Prior knowledge was controlled for by using a visuospatial task in which the participants were required to memorize a sequence of locations presented on a computer screen. In line with the model's predictions, recall performance was superior with sequences consisting of high-frequency chunks compared with sequences consisting of low-frequency chunks.

11.3.1.2 Mnemonics

An important source of information on the role of chunking in memory is provided by mnemonics (i.e., procedures for improving one's memory), which are learnt deliberately and consciously. Methods for recoding information to make it more memorable have been known since Greek antiquity. A wide range of mnemonics were developed and used by orators, who did not have access to paper or computers for writing their speeches (Yates, 1966).

The mechanisms underpinning mnemonics are well understood and take advantage of basic principles of human memory. It has been shown experimentally that mnemonics, which often can be mastered relatively quickly, can improve memory significantly (Atkinson & Raugh, 1975). In general, mnemonics enable a more rapid encoding into LTM than would have been the case otherwise. The likelihood of remembering information is increased by (a) making associations, either with other items to remember or with prior knowledge; (b) elaborating information by processing it at a deep level, for example by making semantic associations; (c) recoding, where information is represented in a different and hopefully more efficient way; (d) creating *retrieval structures* (LTM items that are organized in such a way that encoding and retrieving new information are optimized); and (e) grouping information (i.e., chunking). Note that mnemonics nearly always use LTM.

A powerful method, commonly used by memory experts, is the *method of loci*, also called the *memory palace* (Yates, 1966). First, one learns a list of locations (e.g., garage, bedroom, kitchen, and so on). Then, one associates the material to memorize with each location in this list, as bizarrely and vividly as possible. For example, if the word to memorize is "car" and the current location "kitchen," one imagines a car being cooked in a pot in the kitchen. To some extent, the association forms a unit and could be considered as a chunk.

Recoding information using prior knowledge is also an efficient technique for remembering information. In his famous paper, Miller (1956) discussed recoding binary digits into decimal digits. (While the decimal system expresses numbers using digits from 0 to 9, the binary system uses only 0 and 1. For example, 101, or $1 \times 2^2 + 0 \times 2^1 + 1 \times 2^0$, is the binary equivalent of 5 in the decimal system.) A long sequence of binary digits can be efficiently recoded by using the decimal system. For example, 10001000111110 (14 digits) can be recoded as 8766 (four digits). Similarly, letters can be recoded as known acronyms. For example, (I B M U S A) can be recoded as two chunks: IBM and USA.

The research by Ericsson, Chase, and Faloon (1980) and Ericsson and Staszewski (1989) on the digit span task has shed considerable light on the use of chunking and other methods in expert memory. In this task, which we have already met above, digits are dictated rapidly, 1 second each. While most of us cannot remember more than about seven digits (Miller, 1956), Ericsson and colleagues trained two students, SF and DD, who had a normal memory capacity at the beginning of the experiment, to correctly memorize up 84 and 106 digits, respectively. At the time, this was comparable to the performance of the best mnemonists in the world. Practice was intensive but did not last particularly long (SF trained for about 250 hours in 2 years, and DD trained for about 800 hours in just above 3 years).

Two main factors account for SF and DD's performance. First, they made extensive use of chunking. Being keen amateur runners, both had acquired a large knowledge of running times (e.g., world record for the 10,000 meters). Like average students, they also knew many numbers (e.g., arithmetic results, historical dates). With training, they were able to use this knowledge to chunk digits into groups of three or four quickly and without much effort. Ericsson and Staszewski (1989) give the example of the sequence 3492, which DD would encode as "3 minutes, 49.2 seconds," a time close to the mile world record. The hypothesis that SF and DD used LTM chunks to encode digits was supported by free recall tests carried out at the end of a session; when several lists had been memorized during a session, they were able to recall the chunks that they had employed to encode each of these lists.

The second factor behind SF and DD's extraordinary memory performance was their use of retrieval structures. Retrieval structures use prior knowledge to organize the material to memorize. While most top mnemonists use the method of loci for this task, supplemented by techniques for recoding digits into words, SF and DD developed their own coding scheme, which was optimized for the digit-span task. The structure used by the two students was hierarchical: the bottom level encoded digits; the second level stored mnemonic codes (i.e., chunks such as running times); the third level was made of super-groups, which encoded several chunks of digits of equal size; finally, the fourth level consisted of super-group clusters, which joined several super-groups. This hierarchical structure was inferred from the two students' verbal comments and was corroborated by the pattern of pauses during recall (Richman, Staszewski, & Simon, 1995).

The learning and behavior of one of the two students, DD, was simulated in detail by Richman and colleagues (1995). Their model, the Elementary Perceiver and Memorizer, Model IV (EPAM-IV), is based on EPAM (Feigenbaum & Simon, 1962, 1984), which used a chunking mechanism for learning (see Section 11.3.2.2 below). An important addition is that EPAM-IV implements the idea of retrieval structures, which are learned deliberately.

EPAM-IV comprises a visual STM, an auditory STM, and an LTM. Visual STM consists of two subsystems that work in tandem: One subsystem stores four chunks for a limited amount of time, and the other uses the information contained in these chunks to construct a visuospatial representation. Auditory STM has a similar bipartite structure, with one subsystem maintaining a limited number of verbal chunks and another subsystem rehearsing the information contained in the chunks. LTM is divided into a semantic component and a procedural component.

The advantage of using a computer program to implement the theory is that one can specify in great detail the way chunks and retrieval structures are acquired, and how they are used in the digit-span task to store and retrieve digits. Since all cognitive processes have a time parameter, it is possible to simulate the time course of behavior in this task, both at the micro-level (recall of one list) and the macro-level (acquisition of skill over 3 years). EPAM-IV successfully simulated DD's behavior at both levels, quantitatively and qualitatively.

11.3.2 Automatic Chunking

This sort of chunking is the most interesting from the point of view of linguistic entrenchment and especially language acquisition, as children do not go about intending to memorize information using strategies, but learn implicitly. Automatic chunking is also directly related to the issue of entrenchment, since most of the proposed mechanisms assume some kind of grouping and are interested in the role of frequency on the way information is learned.

11.3.2.1 Alphabet Recitation

When the alphabet is recited back, people recall letters in a burst of activity followed by a pause. More specifically, letters are grouped in chunks, and chunks are grouped in super-chunks (Klahr, Chase, & Lovelace, 1983). This structure is reflected in the speed with which letters are accessed when participants have to name the letter in the alphabet preceding or following a probe letter. Klahr and colleagues (1983) developed a model using a two-level hierarchical structure, which consisted of six chunks containing from two to seven letters. The model accounted for 80% of the variance of the data on alphabet recitation. In a similar line of research, McLean and Gregg (1967) asked participants to learn lists made of scrambled orders of the English alphabet. The letters were presented with different groupings (either one, three, four, six, or eight letters). When participants had successfully learned the list, they were asked to recite it backwards. The time intervals between the letters, both for forward and backward recitations, provided support for the hypothesis that letters were chunked as induced by the experimental manipulation.

11.3.2.2 Verbal Learning

This field of research, which was very influential in the first half of the 20th century, studies the mechanisms underpinning the learning of verbal material, such as letters and words. Whilst participants have the intention to learn, they do not specifically choose strategies on the basis of chunking and are not aware that the cognitive processes they use might be based on chunking.

Considerable research has been carried out using the paired-associate paradigm. In a typical experiment, participants learn pairs of nonsense trigrams, such as XIR-BOJ. When presented with the stimulus (here, XIR), they have to produce the response (here, BOJ). This paradigm provides two important advantages. First, participants have to learn both the items and the association between the items; therefore, it provides data for testing both the creation of chunks and the way chunks are linked. Second, it offers a simplified environment for studying explicit strategies. This tradition of research has used a very tight methodology to systematically investigate the role of numerous variables on verbal learning. This makes it a particularly rich source of data to model, and several models have simulated experiments from paired-associate learning. We discuss EPAM (Feigenbaum & Simon, 1984) at some length, as it proposes mechanisms for (unconsciously) creating and using chunks.

EPAM stores chunks as nodes within a *discrimination network*, also known as a *chunking network*, which is a network of nodes linked by tests. This network makes it possible to store and retrieve information in LTM. Information is encoded in a hierarchical way; at the lowest level, there are primitives (i.e., the letters of the English alphabet). At higher levels, primitives are grouped and form sequences of letters. The tests in the discrimination network check for the presence of individual primitives. There are two learning mechanisms: *discrimination* and *familiarization*. Discrimination adds a new node to the network. This occurs when the information retrieved after sorting the input through the network is inconsistent with the information provided by the input. Familiarization adds information to an existing node. This occurs when the information in the chunk under-represents, but is consistent with, the information held in the input. Attention mechanisms determine which aspect of the input will be learned; for example, EPAM tends to focus on the beginning and end of the trigrams. In the simulations, EPAM receives the same input (in our case paired-associates) as human participants. EPAM has accounted for numerous phenomena in the verbal learning literature, such as the effect of stimulus and response similarity, retroactive inhibition and the von Restorff effect (the fact that stimuli that are perceptually salient tend to be learned faster than other stimuli; see Günther, Müller, & Geyer, Chapter 13, this volume, on salience). In general, EPAM illustrates the power of chunking as a psychologically plausible learning mechanism but also indicates that other factors are important to understand the participants' behavior, notably the strategies they use and the role of attention.

11.3.2.3 Expertise

Research into expertise has produced some key contributions to the study of chunking. Already De Groot (1965; De Groot, Gobet, & Jongman, 1996) had noted that chess experts perceived pieces not individually but as groups, in which perceptual and dynamic facets are interleaved. But the key study on chunking was carried out by Simon and Chase (1973) and led to two major contributions: first, a method for identifying chunks and second, a theory proposing mechanisms explaining how chunks are used in memory and problem solving tasks.

Simon and Chase (1973) used two tasks. In the recall task, a chess position was presented for 5 seconds and players had to reconstruct it afterward. In the copy task, players had to copy a chess position that remained in view on a second board. According to Simon and Chase, the advantage of the copy task is that it made it possible, by observing when players glance at the stimulus position, to infer the boundaries between chunks. The results showed that most of the piece placements within a glance were separated by less than 2 seconds, whilst most the piece placements between two glances were separated by more than 2 seconds. The distributions of latencies between the placement of two pieces was similar in the copy and recall tasks, which suggests that the same processes were implicated. Finally, an analysis of the number of relations shared between successively placed pieces (proximity, kind, color, attack, and defense) showed that the number of relations negatively correlated with the latencies in placement, both in the copy and the recall task. Thus, within-chunk relations are much stronger than between-chunk relations. Based on these results, Simon and Chase proposed to use the 2-second boundary as an operational definition for a chunk.

Further research (Gobet & Clarkson, 2004; Gobet & Simon, 1998) replicated these key findings with a larger sample—the original study had only three subjects. It also resolved a double anomaly in Simon and Chase's (1973) data. First, the size of the chunks was relatively small (at most five to six pieces), which conflicts with chess experts' comments when they analyze games; second, more chunks were replaced by the better players. While the number of chunks was within the postulated limit of 7 ± 2 chunks, this result was at variance with the hypothesis that all players had the same STM capacity. It turned out that these inconsistencies were due to the experiment being carried out with a standard physical chess board and players using their hand to replace pieces. In the replications, the experiment was carried out with a computer, which removed the limitations imposed by the capacity of the hand. Additional data on chess and other domains of expertise have been collected, and alternative ways to operationalize a chunk developed. In general, these studies support Simon and Chase's claim that chunks play a central role in expert behavior (see Gobet, 2015, for a discussion of this research).

In addition to their remarkable memory for material taken from their field, experts can solve problems rapidly and successfully. Simon and Chase (1973) developed a theory, known as *chunking theory*, that accounted for both phenomena. The theory makes several assumptions for which the idea of pattern recognition is central. First, LTM information is stored as chunks, which are units both of perception and meaning. Chunks are organized by a discrimination network. Second, STM capacity does not differ between novices and experts and is limited to around seven items. Third, learning is relatively slow: Creating a new chunk (discrimination) takes about 8 seconds and adding information to an existing chunk takes 2 seconds (Simon, 1969). Fourth, the key difference between experts and novices is that the former have acquired, during the long years of study and practice it takes to become an expert, both more chunks and larger chunks. Simon and Gilmartin (1973) combined computer simulations and mathematical analysis to estimate the number of chunks that a chess master has stored and reached the number 50,000 (more or less equivalent to the number of words known by the average American college student). Fifth, chunks provide access to relevant actions and information (e.g., in chess, what move to play). In other words, they act as the *conditions* of *actions*, thus forming *productions* (Newell & Simon, 1972). During look-ahead search, which is carried out in the mind's eye, players recursively apply pattern recognition. Thus, moves and plans are suggested by chunks not only in the problem situation but also in the positions that are imagined during search.

Template theory (Gobet & Simon, 1996, 2000) extended chunking theory, in particular by showing how perception, learning, and problem solving are closely intertwined and by providing mechanisms explaining how schemata (called *templates*) are created from chunks. Templates comprise two parts: the core and the slots. The core consists of a chunk and is thus stable information. The slots encode variable information and are particularly useful when there is variation in the kind of information that occurs in a domain. Template theory is implemented in a chunking-network model (CHREST; Chunk Hierarchy and REtrieval STructures), which has carried out detailed simulations in a number of domains, including expertise, implicit learning, language acquisition, and concept formation (Gobet et al., 2001). A great strength of the model is to make detailed and correct predictions about how information is chunked. As examples, a model of chess expertise successfully simulated the number and size of the chunks recalled at different levels of skills (Gobet & Simon, 2000), and a model of diagrammatic reasoning reproduced how physics novices acquire chunks for diagrams of electric circuits (Lane, Cheng, & Gobet, 2001).

11.3.2.4 Implicit Learning

The properties of implicit learning have been extensively studied in controlled laboratory experiments. Four experimental paradigms have received particular attention: the learning of artificial grammars, the learning of sequential material, the learning of complex, dynamic systems, and the serial reaction time task (Berry, 1997; Cleeremans,

1993). In all these domains, unbeknown to the participants, the stimuli to learn are generated by a set of well-defined rules—sometimes with the addition of noise. Questions of interest include the level of awareness of what is learnt, the form of representation used (rules, fragments, graded representations), the rate of learning, the effect of interfering tasks, the role of attention, and the possibility of transfer to situations in which the surface structure of the material is changed while the deep structure is left unaltered.

Where early debates centered on questions regarding the abstractness of participants' representations, it is now mostly accepted that participants increasingly respond on the basis of recognized fragments or chunks (bigrams or trigrams) that were present in the training materials (Perruchet & Pacteau, 1990). Some of these fragments are more perceptually salient than others and may recruit special (explicit) attention from participants.

Several computational models based on chunking have been developed to account for implicit-learning data. Three of them are briefly reviewed here. With Competitive Chunker (Servan-Schreiber & Anderson, 1990), a chunk is a hierarchical structure consisting of (sub-) chunks; some of the chunks (primitives) are supposed to be known to the program at the beginning of a simulation. Each chunk has a strength parameter, which depends on its frequency and recency of use, and which decays as a function of time. Another parameter is support, which is the average strength of the sub-chunks of a chunk. When simulating an artificial grammar learning task where strings of letters are presented, each stimulus is decomposed as chunks; in case of multiple possible decompositions, one is chosen probabilistically. The model was able to successfully simulate sensitivity to chunk violations.

The aim of PARSER (Perruchet & Vinter, 1998) was to show that words can be extracted from continuous sequences using statistical regularities only. PARSER uses a hierarchy of chunks built on primitive chunks. Chunks are created when a percept is not known but when its constituting elements are known. Thus, like EPAM and CHREST, PARSER selects the information to learn by using mismatches between a percept and currently known information. Chunks have a weight which indicates familiarity with a percept. Due to a time-based forgetting mechanism that decreases weight, chunks that are infrequent have a low weight. When this weight falls below a threshold, chunks are deleted. An interference mechanism penalizes short chunks when they are included in longer chunks (see Giroux & Rey, 2009, for empirical support for this assumption). Finally, the mechanism of *perception shaping* uses known chunks to guide the segmentation of the sequence of syllables. PARSER successfully simulated the results of Saffran, Aslin, and Newport's (1996) experiment. In that experiment, six trisyllabic artificial words (*babupu, bupada, dutaba, patubi, pidabu,* and *tutibu*) were presented repeatedly and continuously, in random order, to 8-month-old infants, who were able to segment the words.

Given that there is strong evidence that participants use fragments or chunks in implicit-learning tasks, CHREST is a natural candidate for modeling such data. CHREST learns through the nonconscious, automatic acquisition of perceptual chunks; thus, its basic learning mechanisms, as well as the information learnt, are implicit. What is accessible to consciousness, and thus explicit, is the contents of the chunks placed in STM. Consistent with this analysis, Lane and Gobet (2012) showed that when receiving the same artificial-grammar stimuli as human participants, CHREST was able to closely simulate their behavior.

11.3.3 Interim Discussion

Chunking illustrates the power of grouping information in human cognition. With deliberate chunking, grouping is carried out consciously; with automatic chunking, it is carried out unconsciously. However, chunking is more than grouping. As noted by Miller (1956) and Simon (1974), using chunking amounts to recoding a set of elements into a single chunk or symbol; it is therefore a form of information compression. In recent years, there has been considerable interest in formalizing this notion of compression with new formalisms from computer science.

Research on chunking has shed important light on the question of *rationality*—the extent to which humans act optimally when they try to achieve a goal—and clearly supports Simon's (1957) notion of bounded rationality: Humans cannot achieve full rationality. This is because their cognition is characterized by several important restrictions: limited-capacity STM, small attention span, and slow learning rates. These constraints have been captured in computational models such as PARSER, Competitive Chunker, and in particular, EPAM and CHREST (MDLCHUNKER, which optimizes chunking, is an exception in this respect). By storing information in LTM so that it will be rapidly available for future use, chunking can be seen as an important way to alleviate the limits imposed by bounded rationality. Note that, in most models, learning is incremental, with only little information being learned at each point in time. In addition to being plausible psychologically, as information decays rapidly from sensory memory and STM, this permits flexibility in learning and avoids being committed too early to a specific representation (a form of negative entrenchment). The small chunks that are learned early on impose few constraints, which means that their recoding ability is limited but also that they can be used often. In particular, they can flexibly be used to accommodate changes in the input. By contrast, large chunks can compress much information, but they can be used rarely because they impose many constraints, and their learning occurs only after considerable exposure to stimuli that are highly frequent. They are also brittle in the sense that small changes in the input can make them inaccessible and thus useless. Thus, there is here a trade-off between how much information can be captured by a chunk and how often it can be used, and chunking uses frequency to find a good balance. Incremental chunk-based learning also has the consequence that learning will speed up with experience in a domain: Because chunks—the building blocks of further knowledge—get increasingly larger, later learning becomes quicker. Thus, while learning as formalized by most models of chunking is not optimal, it is highly adaptive.

There are several open issues in research into chunking. First, identifying what forms a chunk is not always easy. While the methods developed by Simon and Chase (1973) for chess are reasonably successful, their application to other domains is sometimes problematic. For example, one can plan one's behavior in advance, so that independent chunks are produced continuously and appear as a single chunk (Gobet et al., 2001). Second, defining primitive chunks might be difficult and arbitrary in some domains, although the use of computational models for explaining the empirical data ensures a fair amount of coherence and objectivity. A related problem concerns identifying chunks that have already been learnt, a problem that is particularly acute when the aim is to estimate STM capacity à la Miller (Miller, 1956). For example, previous knowledge of number sequences will facilitate, through the use of chunks, the recall of digits (Gobet, 2015; Jones & Macken, 2015). Again, using computer models partly addresses this issue. Third, with the exception of EPAM-IV and CHREST, no model links deliberate chunking and the use of explicit strategies with automatic chunking. Finally, a recent debate is whether chunks are the proper measure of STM capacity. Whilst some of the theories discussed in this section (e.g., EPAM, CHREST) argue that this is the case, others suggest that measures based on complexity and information theory are better estimates (e.g., MDLCHUNKER).

11.4 What Do Gestalt and Chunking Explanations Tell Us About Language?

Gestalt psychologists had very little to say about language. The exception is Karl Bühler's (1934/1990) book, although his approach was more influenced by semiotics and cybernetics than by Gestalt theory. However, as pointed out in Section 11.2.3, some concepts from Gestalt had an enduring legacy on the study of language. The effect of *Einstellung* shows when strongly entrenched structures inhibit the emergence of novel structures (Langacker, 1991). The so-called *mutual-exclusivity* constraint (Golinkoff, Mervis, & Hirsh-Pasek, 1994) in word learning in language acquisition, which keeps children from accepting that several words (e.g., synonyms, hyponyms) can refer to the same (type of) entity, can also be traced back to something like *Einstellung*. The concepts of figure and ground have been used in the study of language, for example for describing degrees of salience of the constituents of grammatical structures and relational configurations with prepositions (Schmid, 2007). Further controversial but potentially strong effects of Gestalt principles reside in the concept-forming or hypostatizing power of words, that is, the impression that words, especially nouns, stand for neatly delimited Gestalt-like conceptual entities (Leech, 1981, p. 32; Leisi, 1952/1975, p. 26; see also Schmid, 2008), and in the claim that word-meanings are stored and processed holistically rather than in an analytical, feature-like fashion (Ungerer & Schmid, 2006, pp. 34–43).

The links between chunking and language are stronger. An obvious source of evidence, mentioned by Simon (1969), concerns the hierarchical nature of language: Letters are grouped into words, words into sentences, and sentences into paragraphs. Another source concerns the important role of collocations and idioms in adult language (Schmid, 2007) and their development across decades and even centuries, as studied by historical linguistics (Bybee, 2003). Processes involved in grammaticalization and language change such as fusion, reduction, and coalescence have been linked to chunking (Bybee, 2015). Similarly, the substantial presence of rote-learned formulae in child language is strong support for chunking mechanisms (Pine & Lieven, 1993). If chunking operates over associations, as the general definition of chunking given at the outset of Section 11.3 above suggests, then linguistic chunking can indeed be seen as being based on the strengthening of syntagmatic associations (see Schmid, 2014, 2015). Furthermore, if it is true that specific functions tend to be involved in the formation of chunks, as the psychological models discussed above suggest, then this ties in nicely with claims that communicative intentions and pragmatic associations play a role in the emergence of linguistic chunks.

Building on this evidence, some of the chunking models discussed above have been used to simulate aspects of language directly. PARSER carries out word segmentation in its simulations of artificial-language learning. It was also used to model how a first language affects the segmentation of a second language (Perruchet, Poulin-Charronnat, Tillmann, & Peereman, 2014). Two chunking networks based on CHREST have successfully simulated a number of empirical results on the acquisition of language. MOSAIC accounts for developmental patterns in the acquisition of syntactic structure, in particular, related to the "optional-infinitive" phenomenon, in six different languages (Freudenthal, Pine, Aguado-Orea, & Gobet, 2007; Freudenthal, Pine, Jones, & Gobet, 2015). EPAM-VOC simulates detailed aspects of the nonword repetition task, including the pattern of phonological errors within syllables (Jones, Gobet, & Pine, 2007; Tamburelli, Jones, Gobet, & Pine, 2012); an interesting aspect of this model is that it provides mechanisms linking phonological working memory and LTM. Note that these two models were not aimed at explaining chunking phenomena per se but at how chunking helps explain key phenomena in language acquisition.

11.5 Conclusion

This chapter has presented key empirical results and theoretical ideas related to the concepts of Gestalt formation and chunking.

A key claim of Gestalt theory was that the whole is more than the sum of the parts. This is correct, but when it is realized that the whole is equal to the sum of the parts *plus their relations*, the Gestalt dictum loses some of its magic. Relations between constituents are, of course, central to language. Another idea that has relevance to language and, in particular, entrenchment, is the notion of *Einstellung*. Despite these ideas, it is fair to say that the contribution of Gestalt psychology to the study of language has been limited.

By comparison, the research on chunking has had considerable impact on the study of language. First, a number of empirical phenomena are well described by the notion of chunking. Then, several computational models have successfully addressed issues linked to language acquisition. In general, a strength of chunking theories is that they provide mechanisms explaining how the human cognitive system is able to pick up the statistical structure of the linguistic environment. In particular, chunking networks have offered detailed simulations of empirical data and have contributed to our understanding of language acquisition at several levels, including the phonemic, lexical, and syntactic ones.

Chunking mechanisms have been proposed either as a general cognitive mechanism (e.g., EPAM, CHREST) or a mechanism accounting for language acquisition (e.g., PARSER). It is noteworthy that chunking networks have been used for modelling both the acquisition of expertise and the acquisition of language, with essentially the same learning mechanisms. Thus, they make the controversial claim, especially when contrasted with innatist approaches, that language acquisition is a form of expertise acquisition.

References

Aronoff, M. (1976). *Word formation in generative grammar*. Cambridge, MA: MIT Press.
Atkinson, R. C., & Raugh, M. R. (1975). An application of the mnemonic keyword method to the acquisition of Russian vocabulary. *Journal of Experimental Psychology: Human Learning and Memory, 1*, 126–133. http://dx.doi.org/10.1037/0278-7393.1.2.126
Berry, D. C. (Ed.). (1997). *How implicit is implicit learning?* http://dx.doi.org/10.1093/acprof:oso/9780198523512.001.0001
Bilalić, M., McLeod, P., & Gobet, F. (2008a). Inflexibility of experts—reality or myth? Quantifying the Einstellung effect in chess masters. *Cognitive Psychology, 56*, 73–102. http://dx.doi.org/10.1016/j.cogpsych.2007.02.001
Bilalić, M., McLeod, P., & Gobet, F. (2008b). Why good thoughts block better ones: The mechanism of the pernicious Einstellung (set) effect. *Cognition, 108*, 652–661. http://dx.doi.org/10.1016/j.cognition.2008.05.005
Birch, H. G., & Rabinowitz, H. S. (1951). The negative effect of previous experience on productive thinking. *Journal of Experimental Psychology, 41*, 121–125. http://dx.doi.org/10.1037/h0062635
Bühler, K. (1990). *The theory of language: The representational function of language* (D. F. Goodwin, Trans.). http://dx.doi.org/10.1075/fos.25 (Original work published 1934)
Bybee, J. (2003). Mechanisms of change in grammaticization: The role of frequency. In B. D. Joseph & R. D. Janda (Eds.), *The handbook of historical linguistics* (pp. 602–623). http://dx.doi.org/10.1002/9780470756393.ch19
Bybee, J. (2015). *Language change*. Cambridge, MA: Cambridge University Press.

Cleeremans, A. (1993). *Mechanisms of implicit learning*. Cambridge, MA: The MIT Press.
Cowan, N. (2001). The magical number 4 in short-term memory: A reconsideration of mental storage capacity. *Behavioral and Brain Sciences, 24*, 87–114. http://dx.doi.org/10.1017/S0140525X01003922
Csikszentmihalyi, M. (1996). *Creativity: Flow and the psychology of discovery and invention*. New York, NY: Harper Collins.
De Groot, A. D. (1965). *Thought and choice in chess*. The Hague, the Netherlands: Mouton Publishers.
De Groot, A. D., Gobet, F., & Jongman, R. W. (1996). *Perception and memory in chess: Studies in the heuristic of the professional eye*. Assen, the Netherlands: Van Gorcum.
Duncker, K. (1945). On problem-solving. *Psychological Monographs, 58*, i–113.
Ericsson, K. A., Chase, W. G., & Faloon, S. (1980). Acquisition of a memory skill. *Science, 208*, 1181–1182. http://dx.doi.org/10.1126/science.7375930
Ericsson, K. A., & Staszewski, J. J. (1989). Skilled memory and expertise: Mechanisms of exceptional performance. In D. Klahr & K. Kotovski (Eds.), *Complex information processing: The impact of Herbert A. Simon* (pp. 235–267). Hillsdale, NJ: Erlbaum.
Feigenbaum, E. A., & Simon, H. A. (1962). A theory of the serial position effect. *British Journal of Psychology, 53*, 307–320. http://dx.doi.org/10.1111/j.2044-8295.1962.tb00836.x
Feigenbaum, E. A., & Simon, H. A. (1984). EPAM-like models of recognition and learning. *Cognitive Science, 8*, 305–336. http://dx.doi.org/10.1207/s15516709cog0804_1
Freudenthal, D., Pine, J. M., Aguado-Orea, J., & Gobet, F. (2007). Modeling the developmental patterning of finiteness marking in English, Dutch, German, and Spanish using MOSAIC. *Cognitive Science, 31*, 311–341.
Freudenthal, D., Pine, J. M., Jones, G., & Gobet, F. (2015). Simulating the cross-linguistic pattern of optional infinitive errors in children's declaratives and Wh- questions. *Cognition, 143*, 61–76. http://dx.doi.org/10.1016/j.cognition.2015.05.027
Giroux, I., & Rey, A. (2009). Lexical and sublexical units in speech perception. *Cognitive Science, 33*, 260–272. http://dx.doi.org/10.1111/j.1551-6709.2009.01012.x
Gobet, F. (2015). *Understanding expertise: A multidisciplinary approach*. London, England: Palgrave.
Gobet, F., Chassy, P., & Bilalić, M. (2011). *Foundations of cognitive psychology*. London, England: McGraw Hill.
Gobet, F., & Clarkson, G. (2004). Chunks in expert memory: Evidence for the magical number four... or is it two? *Memory, 12*, 732–747. http://dx.doi.org/10.1080/09658210344000530
Gobet, F., Lane, P. C. R., Croker, S., Cheng, P. C. H., Jones, G., Oliver, I., & Pine, J. M. (2001). Chunking mechanisms in human learning. *Trends in Cognitive Sciences, 5*, 236–243. http://dx.doi.org/10.1016/S1364-6613(00)01662-4
Gobet, F., & Simon, H. A. (1996). Templates in chess memory: A mechanism for recalling several boards. *Cognitive Psychology, 31*, 1–40. http://dx.doi.org/10.1006/cogp.1996.0011
Gobet, F., & Simon, H. A. (1998). Expert chess memory: Revisiting the chunking hypothesis. *Memory, 6*, 225–255. http://dx.doi.org/10.1080/741942359
Gobet, F., & Simon, H. A. (2000). Five seconds or sixty? Presentation time in expert memory. *Cognitive Science, 24*, 651–682. http://dx.doi.org/10.1207/s15516709cog2404_4
Golinkoff, R. M., Mervis, C. B., & Hirsh-Pasek, K. (1994). Early object labels: The case for a developmental lexical principles framework. *Journal of Child Language, 21*, 125–155. http://dx.doi.org/10.1017/S0305000900008692

Jones, G., Gobet, F., & Pine, J. M. (2007). Linking working memory and long-term memory: A computational model of the learning of new words. *Developmental Science, 10*, 853–873. http://dx.doi.org/10.1111/j.1467-7687.2007.00638.x

Jones, G., & Macken, B. (2015). Questioning short-term memory and its measurement: Why digit span measures long-term associative learning. *Cognition, 144*, 1–13. http://dx.doi.org/10.1016/j.cognition.2015.07.009

Klahr, D., Chase, W. G., & Lovelace, E. A. (1983). Structure and process in alphabetic retrieval. *Journal of Experimental Psychology: Learning, Memory, and Cognition, 9*, 462–477. http://dx.doi.org/10.1037/0278-7393.9.3.462

Köhler, W., & Held, R. (1949). The cortical correlate of pattern vision. *Science, 110*, 414–419. http://dx.doi.org/10.1126/science.110.2860.414

Kolmogorov, A. N. (1965). Three approaches to the quantitative definition of information. *Problems of Information Transmission, 1*, 1–7.

Lane, P. C. R., Cheng, P. C. H., & Gobet, F. (2001). Learning perceptual chunks for problem decomposition. In *Proceedings of the 23rd Meeting of the Cognitive Science Society* (pp. 528–533). Mahwah, NJ: Erlbaum.

Lane, P. C. R., & Gobet, F. (2012). CHREST models of implicit learning and board game interpretation. *Lecture Notes in Computer Science*, 148–157.

Langacker, R. W. (1987). *Foundations of cognitive grammar: Vol. 1. Theoretical prerequisites.* Stanford, CA: Stanford University Press.

Langacker, R. W. (1991). *Foundations of cognitive grammar: Vol. 2. Descriptive application.* Stanford, CA: Stanford University Press.

Lashley, K. S., Chow, K. L., & Semmes, J. (1951). An examination of the electrical field theory of cerebral integration. *Psychological Review, 58*, 123–136. http://dx.doi.org/10.1037/h0056603

Leech, G. (1981). *Semantics: The study of meaning* (2nd ed.). Harmondsworth, England: Penguin Books Ltd.

Leisi, E. (1975). *Der Wortinhalt: Seine Struktur im Deutschen und Englischen* [The word content: Its structure in German and English; 5th ed.]. Heidelberg, Germany: Winter. (Original work published 1952)

Lemaire, B., Robinet, V., & Portrat, S. (2012). Compression mechanisms in working memory. *Mathematical Social Sciences, 199*, 71–84.

Luchins, A. S. (1942). Mechanization in problem solving: The effect of Einstellung. *Psychological Monographs, 54*, i–95. http://dx.doi.org/10.1037/h0093502

Maier, N. R. F. (1930). Reasoning in humans. I. On direction. *Journal of Comparative Psychology, 10*, 115–143. http://dx.doi.org/10.1037/h0073232

Maier, N. R. F. (1931). Reasoning in humans. II. The solution of a problem and its appearance in consciousness. *Journal of Comparative Psychology, 12*, 181–194. http://dx.doi.org/10.1037/h0071361

Mathy, F., & Feldman, J. (2012). What's magic about magic numbers? Chunking and data compression in short-term memory. *Cognition, 122*, 346–362. http://dx.doi.org/10.1016/j.cognition.2011.11.003

McLean, R. S., & Gregg, L. W. (1967). Effects of induced chunking on temporal aspects of serial recitation. *Journal of Experimental Psychology, 74*, 455–459. http://dx.doi.org/10.1037/h0024785

Miller, G. A. (1956). The magical number seven, plus or minus two: Some limits on our capacity for processing information. *Psychological Review, 63*, 81–97. http://dx.doi.org/10.1037/h0043158

Newell, A., & Simon, H. A. (1972). *Human problem solving.* Englewood Cliffs, NJ: Prentice-Hall.

Perruchet, P., & Pacteau, C. (1990). Synthetic grammar learning: Implicit rule abstraction or explicit fragmentary knowledge? *Journal of Experimental Psychology: General, 119*, 264–275. http://dx.doi.org/10.1037/0096-3445.119.3.264

Perruchet, P., Poulin-Charronnat, B., Tillmann, B., & Peereman, R. (2014). New evidence for chunk-based models in word segmentation. *Acta Psychologica, 149*, 1–8. http://dx.doi.org/10.1016/j.actpsy.2014.01.015

Perruchet, P., & Vinter, A. (1998). PARSER: A model for word segmentation. *Journal of Memory and Language, 39*, 246–263. http://dx.doi.org/10.1006/jmla.1998.2576

Pine, J. M., & Lieven, E. V. (1993). Reanalysing rote-learned phrases: Individual differences in the transition to multi-word speech. *Journal of Child Language, 20*, 551–571.

Richman, H. B., Staszewski, J. J., & Simon, H. A. (1995). Simulation of expert memory using EPAM IV. *Psychological Review, 102*, 305–330. http://dx.doi.org/10.1037/0033-295X.102.2.305

Rissanen, J. (1978). Modeling by shortest data description. *Automatica, 14*, 465–471. http://dx.doi.org/10.1016/0005-1098(78)90005-5

Robinet, V., Lemaire, B., & Gordon, M. B. (2011). MDLChunker: A MDL-based cognitive model of inductive learning. *Cognitive Science, 35*, 1352–1389. http://dx.doi.org/10.1111/j.1551-6709.2011.01188.x

Saffran, J. R., Aslin, R. N., & Newport, E. L. (1996). Statistical learning by 8-month-old infants. *Science, 274*, 1926–1928. http://dx.doi.org/10.1126/science.274.5294.1926

Schmid, H.-J. (2007). Entrenchment, salience, and basic levels. In D. Geeraerts & H. Cuyckens (Eds.), *The Oxford handbook of cognitive linguistics* (pp. 117–138). Oxford, England: Oxford University Press.

Schmid, H.-J. (2008). New words in the mind: Concept-formation and entrenchment of neologisms. *Anglia, 126*, 1–36. http://dx.doi.org/10.1515/angl.2008.002

Schmid, H.-J. (2014). Lexico-grammatical patterns, pragmatic associations and discourse frequency. In T. Herbst, H.-J. Schmid, & S. Faulhaber (Eds.), *Constructions Collocations Patterns* (pp. 239–293). http://dx.doi.org/10.1515/9783110356854.239

Schmid, H.-J. (2015). A blueprint of the entrenchment-and-conventionalization model. *Yearbook of the German Cognitive Linguistics Association, 3*, 3–26. http://dx.doi.org/10.1515/gcla-2015-0002

Servan-Schreiber, E., & Anderson, J. R. (1990). Learning artificial grammars with competitive chunking. *Journal of Experimental Psychology: Learning, Memory, and Cognition, 16*, 592–608. http://dx.doi.org/10.1037/0278-7393.16.4.592

Shannon, C. E. (1948). A mathematical theory of communication. *The Bell System Technical Journal, 27*, 379–423. http://dx.doi.org/10.1002/j.1538-7305.1948.tb01338.x

Simon, H. A. (1957). *Models of man: Social and rational.* New York, NY: John Wiley and Sons, Inc.

Simon, H. A. (1969). *The sciences of the artificial.* Cambridge, MA: The MIT Press.

Simon, H. A. (1974). How big is a chunk? *Science, 183*, 482–488. http://dx.doi.org/10.1126/science.183.4124.482

Simon, H. A., & Chase, W. G. (1973). Skill in chess. *American Scientist, 61*, 394–403.

Simon, H. A., & Gilmartin, K. (1973). A simulation of memory for chess positions. *Cognitive Psychology, 5*, 29–46. http://dx.doi.org/10.1016/0010-0285(73)90024-8

Sternberg, R. J. (1996). Costs of expertise. In K. A. Ericsson (Ed.), *The road to excellence* (pp. 347–354). Mahwah, NJ: Erlbaum.

Tamburelli, M., Jones, G., Gobet, F., & Pine, J. M. (2012). Computational modelling of phonological acquisition: Simulating error patterns in nonword repetition tasks. *Language and Cognitive Processes, 27*, 901–946. http://dx.doi.org/10.1080/01690965.2011.583510

Ungerer, F., & Schmid, H.-J. (2006). *An introduction to cognitive linguistics* (2nd ed.). London, England: Pearson Longman.

Von Ehrenfels, C. (1890). Über "Gestaltqualitäten" [About "Gestalt qualities"]. *Vierteljahrsschrift für wissenschaftliche Philosophie, 14,* 249–292.

Yates, F. A. (1966). *The art of memory.* Chicago, IL: University of Chicago Press.

Anne-Kristin Cordes
12 The Roles of Analogy, Categorization, and Generalization in Entrenchment

12.1 Introduction

According to Schmid (Chapter 1, this volume), *entrenchment* is the lifelong cognitive reorganization and adaptation process of linguistic knowledge in the individual speaker. Entrenchment is dependent on language exposure, afforded by domain-general cognitive processes and embedded in the social and pragmatic context. Schmid distinguishes cognitive processes underlying entrenchment, determinants, and predictors as well as cognitive and linguistic effects of entrenchment. He proposes several facets of entrenchment that create the generativity of linguistic competence: (a) the strength of representation of linguistic elements and structures, (b) chunking and the holistic representation of linguistic elements and structures, and (c) the emergence and reorganization of variable schemas. In contrast to established accounts using the concept of constructions (e.g., cognitive grammar, construction grammar, see Croft, 2001; Goldberg, 1995, 2006; Langacker, 1987, 2000a), Schmid suggests that all linguistic knowledge is available in the format of associations. Consequently, entrenchment processes operate over associations rather than constructions. He considers relatively stable pairings of linguistic forms and meanings (e.g., words, fixed strings) to be *symbolic associations*. Associations between forms and meanings that occur sequentially in language use are referred to as *syntagmatic associations*. Further associations are *paradigmatic associations* that link associations that compete with each other in language use and *pragmatic associations* that link any association to contextual and situational input (see Schmid, 2015, for more details).

"Entrenchment is brought about by the routinization effected by the repeated processing of identical or similar stimuli" (Schmid, Chapter 1, this volume, Section 1.5) and is thought to affect all these different types of associations. The psychological affordances vary depending on the type of association involved (see Schmid, Chapter 1, this volume). This chapter sets out to provide a proposal of how the psychological processes of analogy, categorization, and generalization may be involved in

---

DOI 10.1515/9783110341423-013

entrenching associations of different types. First, it is briefly sketched which role analogy formation, categorization, and generalization play in the entrenchment of associations. Subsequently, the psychological background of analogical reasoning and categorization processes is presented and the processes are applied to language use in more detail (using examples from first language acquisition). Finally, the part played by analogy and categorization for the entrenchment of different types of associations is reassessed.

12.2 Sketching the Role of Analogy Formation, Categorization, and Generalization in Entrenching Associations

Language is a system with relational structure. The formation, use, and constant reorganization of this system require the use of domain-general cognitive processes and sociocultural skills (Tomasello, 2000, 2003). The sociocultural skills essentially entail intention-reading and theory of mind, that is, understanding that people's actions and utterances are performed with an intention and reflect their knowledge and view of the extralinguistic world. The domain-general cognitive processes can be summarized as pattern-finding—the ability to detect patterns in the linguistic input. The domain-general processes of analogy formation, categorization, and generalization make this possible. I propose they apply to the formation, use, and organization (and reorganization) of individuals' linguistic systems and the entrenchment of linguistic associations in the following way: Analogical reasoning entails a structural mapping process in which parallel structures are aligned in order for inferences about the less familiar structure to be drawn based on knowledge about the more familiar one. The relational nature of language allows the alignment and mapping of identical or similar linguistic material to which speakers are exposed. Following the alignment, an abstraction (or generalization) of the commonalities of the two structures may be formed and retained (Holyoak, 2012, p. 234). This more abstract representation and the examples that brought it about may be thought of as an exemplar-abstraction category (Abbot-Smith & Tomasello, 2006; Ross & Makin, 1999). Input frequencies determine how well it is retained, that is, how deeply it becomes entrenched. Following Langacker (2000a, p. 7) new examples may be added to the category by being captured by an attractor, which would be a category member or a prototype. Again, it is possible to think of this capture in terms of a structure alignment and mapping. The inclusion of a new member based on such an analogical comparison as well as the production of a new example using the same process may also be termed *generalization*.

12.3 Psychological Background

12.3.1 Analogy Formation

The concept of analogies originates from the psychological field of reasoning and was not initially used as the fundamental principle to describe language use or learning in the individual[1] (for a more detailed account see Cordes, 2014, pp. 46–54). A classical task in analogy research is the "fictive radiation problem." In a first step, participants were introduced to the so-called tumor problem (Gick & Holyoak, 1980):

> Suppose you are a doctor faced with a patient who has a malignant tumor in his stomach. It is impossible to operate on the patient, but unless the tumor is destroyed the patient will die. There is a kind of ray that can be used to destroy the tumor. If the rays reach the tumor all at once at a sufficiently high intensity, the tumor will be destroyed. Unfortunately, at this intensity the healthy tissue that the rays pass through on the way to the tumor will also be destroyed. At lower intensities the rays are harmless to the healthy tissue, but they will not affect the tumor either. What type of procedure might be used to destroy the tumor with the rays, and at the same time avoid destroying the healthy tissue? (pp. 307–308)

Participants considered this task difficult, with a mere 10% spontaneously proposing a successful, feasible solution. In a second step, participants were told the fortress story, which significantly affected the number of correct responses (Gick & Holyoak, 1980):

> A small country fell under the iron rule of a dictator. The dictator ruled the country from a strong fortress. The fortress was situated in the middle of the country, surrounded by farms and villages. Many roads radiated outward from the fortress like spokes on a wheel. A great general arose who raised a large army at the border and vowed to capture the fortress and free the country of the dictator. The general knew that if his entire army could attack the fortress at once it could be captured. His troops were poised at the head of one of the roads leading to the fortress, ready to attack. However, a spy brought the general a disturbing report. The ruthless dictator had planted mines on each of the roads. The mines were set so that small bodies of men could pass over them safely, since the dictator needed to be able to move troops and workers to and from the fortress. However, any large force would detonate the mines. Not only would this blow up the road and render it impassable, but the dictator would then destroy many villages in retaliation. A full-scale direct attack on the fortress therefore appeared impossible. The general, however, knew what to do. He divided his army up into small groups and dispatched each group to the head

---

[1] Paul (1975, pp. 107, 112–116), however, used proportional analogies of the form *Tag: Tages: Tage = Arm: Armes: Arme = Hund: Hundes: Hunde* [day: day's: days = arm: arm's: arms = dog: dog's: dogs], resembling mathematical equations, to describe the language system and language change (i.e., mechanisms of conventionalization in Schmid's terminology), which may be instigated by the individual speaker. In traditional grammar, analogy primarily served to account for pattern extensions that were not warranted by more general rules.

of a different road. When all was ready he gave the signal, and each group marched down a different road. Each group continued down its road to the fortress, so that the entire army finally arrived together at the fortress at the same time. In this way, the general was able to capture the fortress, and thus overthrow the dictator. (p. 352)

After hearing this story and being encouraged to use it to solve the tumor problem, 75% of participants suggested that the doctor should administer low-intensity rays from different angles at the same time, so that they all meet on the tumor resulting in high-intensity treatment of the tumor without harming adjacent healthy tissue due to the low intensity of individual rays (Holyoak & Thagard, 1995, pp. 112–114).

Developing this solution involved a comparison of the two stories such that the fortress was linked to the tumor, the army to the rays, and the general to the doctor. The tumor and the fortress with the dictator were the respective problems. The general was unable to send his entire army down one single route because the mines would have exploded, just as the doctor was unable to send all rays down the same way for danger of damaging healthy tissue. Initially, the analogy remains incomplete, since only the fortress story has different routes leading to the point of danger. But if the comparison highlights the similar relations between the other components, participants can fill in the missing part of the analogy and thus solve the tumor problem: By sending rays down different routes, damage to the healthy tissue is avoided and the malignant tumor can be treated successfully.

The tumor problem can be described using Holyoak's (2012) definition of *analogies*, which conceives of the compared entities in terms of *source* and *target*. The latter refers to the representation of a new situation, the former to the representation of a well-known situation.

> Two situations are analogous if they share a common pattern of relationships among their constituent elements even though the elements themselves differ across the two situations. Typically... the source or base is more familiar or better understood than the ... target. ... This asymmetry in initial knowledge provides the basis for analogical transfer—using the source to generate inferences about the target. (p. 234)

Encountering the target usually triggers the retrieval of the source from memory (the experimental example is an exception, since the source was introduced only after the presentation of the target). Objects and relations of the source and the target situations are aligned and mapped to each other. This *structure-mapping* process is crucial to the analogy, because commonalities and differences between the two situations become apparent when the best "structurally consistent match" is determined (Gentner, 2003, p. 201). This matching process follows three principles: (a) *one-to-one mappings*: each element in one situation corresponds to one element in the second situation; (b) *parallel connectivity*: when two elements correspond, the elements they govern correspond as well, for example, the doctor corresponds to the general, the general commands the army, the doctor commands the rays; and (c) *systematicity*: there is a preference for the deepest and richest match over more superficial ones.

A successful mapping allows inferences about the target based on more profound knowledge about the source. The tumor problem is solved in this way. It is possible for inferences to be more extensive than the original source, to evoke a restructuring of the source or to result in the abstraction (i.e., generalization) of a schema based on both source and target. For the tumor example, a potential abstraction would be that "a central danger can be controlled by applying moderate forces that converge on the danger from different directions." Analogy is thus both a powerful mechanism for the acquisition of new knowledge and for the reorganization of knowledge into a more abstract format (Gentner, 2003, pp. 203–204).[2]

Similarity is a prerequisite for the formation of analogies (i.e., structure alignment and mapping) in children and adults. Mapping source and target was found to be easiest and most feasible in cases of *literal similarity*, where source and target are identical, and in cases of *high-concrete similarity*, where source and target are only minimally different from each other (Gentner, 2003; Gentner & Kurtz, 2006, p. 636). Rich matches are perceived as more similar than sparse matches. For example, two identical dachshunds are considered more similar than two identical circles (Gentner, 2003, p. 200). The importance of similarity between relations increases in the course of children's development. Young children holistically compare two situations. Later, children direct their attention toward particular objects that are present in both situations. Finally, they focus on *relational similarity* between the two situations. Shifting attention from object to relational similarity has been termed *relational-shift hypothesis* (Gentner, 1988, 2003; Gentner & Rattermann, 1991; Kotovsky & Gentner, 1996; Markman & Gentner, 1993; Rattermann & Gentner, 1998). Children further move their attention away from mere perceptual towards functional and conceptual commonalities. A study illustrating the relational shift explored how children and adults interpret metaphors (Gentner, 1988). Metaphors were either attributional, requiring responses based on perceptual-object similarity, or relational, calling for relational interpretations. *A snake is like a hose* would be an attributional metaphor since snakes and hoses share perceptual attributes—both are long and wiggly. *A cloud is like a sponge* would be a relational metaphor, because they are functionally similar—both hold and give off water. Gentner found that the number of attributional responses to attributional metaphors was stable across preschoolers, primary-school children, and adults, while relational responses to relational metaphors increased with age. The relational shift proved to be a more profound consideration of relations rather than a simple

---

[2] It is a bone of contention whether it is possible to acquire new knowledge by analogy. Gentner, in agreement with numerous colleagues working on analogy in psychology, does not assume that the *tertium comparationis* (i.e., the point of comparison) and the potential abstractions are known before the analogy is formed (2003, p. 203). Nevertheless, it has been claimed that similarities between situations cannot be recognized unless the relevant dimension of similarity and the abstractions are known a priori ("problem of inductive reasoning"; Chomsky, 1988, p. 147). It is, however, impossible to test this hypothesis or refute it on logical grounds (Tomasello, 2000, p. 241).

move away from object similarity (Kotovsky & Gentner, 1996). The relational shift in ontogenesis is also present in children's and adults' information processing, where object similarities are processed before relational ones. Nevertheless, the relational shift allows for structural alignments and mappings in the absence of supporting object similarity.

Object and relational similarity also cooperate. In fact, object similarity facilitates the recognition of relational similarity in situations where object similarity is in line with relational commonalities (DeLoache, 1990; Gentner & Markman, 1997; Gentner & Medina, 1998; Gentner & Toupin, 1986; Holyoak & Thagard, 1995, pp. 83–84; Keane, 1987). Younger children often require object similarity to lead them to relational commonalities, while older children form analogies based on relational similarity alone. However, even adults profit from supporting object similarity and form analogies more readily with this extra support (Keane, 1987). Furthermore, it proved easier for young children to detect higher-order similarity after repeated exposure to examples with object similarity (*progressive-alignment hypothesis*; Kotovsky & Gentner, 1996).

If object and relational similarity clash, certain factors determine which mapping is formed. Cross-mapping studies are used to explore this issue. Cross-mapping tasks allow an object match and a relational match. One task uses two pictures (Markman & Gentner, 1993). On the first task, a woman is handed food in a paper bag by a delivery man, and on the second one, a woman feeds nuts to a squirrel. If the focus is on object similarity, the two women are matched. If the focus is on relational similarity, the two givers of food, the two receivers of food, and the food in the two scenes are matched (delivery man–woman, woman–squirrel, food in a paper bag–nuts). As soon as participants are asked to form more than one match or rate the similarity between the two scenes before making their matches, relational matching (i.e., analogies) prevails. The reason is that the need to form several matches as well as similarity ratings brings similarity (both object and relational similarity) to participants' attention, and they consequently follow the systematicity principle: they prefer the deeper, richer, and more powerful relational matches. Accordingly, situations are judged as more similar if they are based on relational rather than object similarity (Goldstone, Medin, & Gentner, 1991; Markman & Gentner, 1993). Certain manipulations can, nevertheless, guide participants toward object matches, such as decreases in the coherence of a relational match or the enrichment of object attributes (Markman & Gentner, 1993).

In summary, relational similarity is, by definition, a prerequisite for analogy formation. Structure alignment and mapping promote "relational commonalities over common object properties" and thus analogy formation over alternative mappings, such as mere object matches (Gentner, 2003, p. 201). Supporting object similarity is not required but facilitates the process and possibly initiates it in young children. Figure 12.1 illustrates the roles of object and relational similarity in analogy formation. Structure alignment and mapping are easiest and the most straightforward if source and target are identical, that is, literal similarity is given (a). Here,

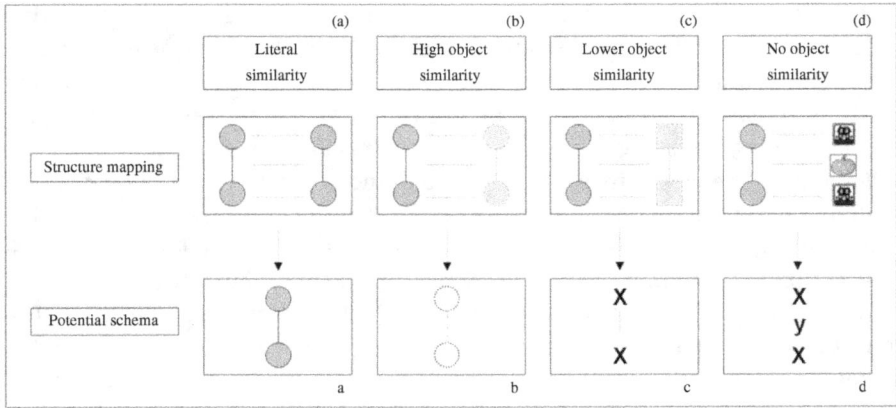

Fig. 12.1: The role of supporting object similarity in analogy formation. Object similarity decreases from left (a) to right (d), whereas relational similarity is given in all four cases. From *The Role of Frequency in Children's Learning of Morphological Constructions* (p. 53), by A.-K. Cordes, 2014, Tübingen, Germany: Narr Francke Attempto. Copyright 2014 by Narr Francke Attempto. Reprinted with permission.

object and relational similarity maximally support each other and only one mapping is possible. If object similarity is high, it supports relational alignment (b). Object similarity is lower but still facilitative in (c), whereas mapping must rely on similar relations alone in (d). The potentially abstracted schema becomes increasingly abstract from (a) through (d), as object similarity of source and target decreases and mapping comes to rely on relational similarity alone.

12.3.2 Categorization

Categorization is a means of making sense of the world (Cordes, 2014, p. 38). It is such an automatic and natural process that it goes unnoticed, unless it is disturbed. In Jorge Luis Borges' (1964) novel *Labyrinths*, the character Funes is a fictional example of somebody who lacks the ability to categorize the world.

> Funes remembered not only every leaf of every tree of every wood, but also every one of the times he had perceived or imagined it.... He was, let us not forget, almost incapable of ideas of a general, Platonic sort. Not only was it difficult for him to comprehend that the generic symbol *dog* embraces so many unlike individuals of diverse size and form; it bothered him that the dog at three fourteen (seen from the side) should have the same name as the dog at three fifteen (seen from the front). His own face in the mirror, his own hands, surprised him every time he saw them. (p. 68)

Funes's inability reveals that categorization entails a comparison in which elements that are "judged equivalent for some purpose" (Langacker, 2000a, p. 17) are grouped together, thereby facilitating the understanding of new situations based on previously experienced similar situations. Categories are thus a means of acquiring new knowledge, just like analogies, and, at the same time, they are a means of retaining and representing previously learned knowledge (Kruschke, 2005). Ramscar and Port (2015) consider concept learning and categorization as the discriminative processes of learning and using systems of alternative responses in context.[3]

For a long time, it was thought that language determines mental categories and therefore the way we perceive the extralinguistic world.[4] "All observers are not led by the same physical evidence to the same picture of the universe, unless their linguistic backgrounds are similar" (Whorf, 1956, p. 214). The Whorfian linguistic-relativity view was initially supported and later challenged by research in color naming. The finding that color terms themselves, and the number of color terms, vary considerably between languages seemed to be in line with linguistic relativity (Brown & Lenneberg, 1954; Lenneberg, 1967). It was when Berlin and Kay (1969; see also Kay & McDaniel, 1978) discovered that speakers of 20 different languages converge on the same reference points for each color for which their language had a name that linguistic relativity was disputed. Participants' preference for what Berlin and Kay called *focal colors* suggests that categorization is ingrained in human perception.

Berlin and Kay's (1969) results further questioned the classical Aristotelian theory of categories. It was impossible to retain the concept of categories as abstract containers with distinct boundaries when participants consistently judged some color shades as more typical and others as less typical. Category membership could no longer be determined by the presence or absence of necessary and sufficient characteristics, as category members did not appear to be equally representative of the category.

Rosch (1973, 1975; Rosch & Mervis, 1975; Rosch, Mervis, Gray, Johnson, & Boyes-Braem, 1976) and Labov (1973) extended Berlin and Kay's (1969) findings and Rosch developed the so-called prototype theory of categories. In Rosch's goodness-of-example ratings, participants judged potential members for how good they were as examples of a certain category (e.g., How good an example of the category FRUIT is apple/banana/date?). Rosch's results revealed that category membership is graded from best examples to less typical to debatable ones (Rosch & Mervis, 1975). Categories are structured around a perceptually salient prototype or best example, which is acquired earlier, remembered more accurately, and produced more rapidly than other examples. Labov's study (1973) inquired into the naming of drinking vessels in relation to several characteristics including their height-width ratio, the presence or absence of a handle, their content, etc. Labov's findings also reflected graded-category structure and further illustrated the fuzziness of category boundaries, where participants' judgments were less unanimous.

---

[3] Ramscar and Port (2015) understand "concepts as emergent aspects of systems" (p. 76) rather than discrete mental tokens.

[4] The philosophical debate on this issue, in particular, the dispute between realists and nominalists on universals and particulars, is not discussed here.

Wittgenstein's (1958) analysis of the various members of the category GAMES revealed new means of category coherence. He discerned that each member shares certain attributes with some other members and other attributes with others. For example, some but not all games involve winning and losing, the role skill and luck play varies considerably between games, and competition may or may not be a driving force behind playing a certain game. Wittgenstein observed, however, that there is not a single attribute that is common to all members. Instead, the category is held together by a "network of overlapping similarities" (Ungerer & Schmid, 2006, p. 29). Good or prototypical category members share high numbers of attributes with other category members, whereas bad examples share only a few (Rosch & Mervis, 1975). An advantage of this view is that damaged examples can be categorized as well. For example, a bird with a broken wing is still considered a BIRD, even though a necessary feature (i.e., the ability to fly) in Aristotelian terms is violated.

There are different views of what a category's *prototype* ultimately is. It may be an *actual category member*: the most-typical member (Langacker, 1987, p. 371), the most-salient member, the most-frequent member, or the member that unites the most-frequent attributes. It may be an *idealized member*: a central tendency, the average, or an idealization that is as distinctive as possible from adjacent categories (Kruschke, 2005). It may be an *abstraction*: an integrated structure bearing the commonalities of all distinct members and disregarding their differences, a *schema* in Langacker's terms (Langacker, 2000a, p. 4). Or it may be *internal theories* people hold, comprising cultural and common knowledge, experience, assumptions, observations, and beliefs (Aitchison, 2003, p. 70; Croft & Cruse, 2004, pp. 95–105; Langacker, 1987, p. 147; Taylor, 2009, pp. 87–91; Ungerer & Schmid, 2006, pp. 47–59). While basic level and subordinate categories typically have prototypes, it is impossible to determine a perceptually stable prototype for superordinate (e.g., FURNITURE) and functional (e.g., THINGS TO TAKE TO A DESERT ISLAND) categories. They might, however, have a schematic prototype.

The differences between the conceptions of what a prototype is are mirrored in the question of how categories are represented (i.e., how category knowledge is retained). Essentially, discussion revolves around the issue of whether more than mere exemplars is stored—whether knowledge is retained in a more abstract format (see Baayen & Ramscar, 2015, for a detailed account of advantages and drawbacks of abstractionist, exemplar-based, hybrid, and discriminative categorization models). What is considered "pure" exemplar theory holds that no abstractions are formed based on exposure to examples, neither in terms of a prototype or a schema nor in the form of necessary and sufficient features. Only exemplars are stored (or, more accurately, entrenched; see Chandler, 2002, for a review). Differences in frequencies and interrelations between members are thought to be responsible for differences in centrality. However, as Ross and Makin (1999, p. 215) pointed out, this conception takes away "the 'categoriness' of categories." The mere assumption that frequencies and interrelations are reflected in some way suggests that at least some more knowledge than just the instances is retained. Moreover, it is unclear how a category could be perceived as such and how category membership would be determined. Even labelling the category would be problematic if no abstractions of any kind were formed and available. These objections are supported by findings from Ross, Perkins, and Tenpenny (1990). Their study revealed that adults learn more general aspects about a category, even if the experimental design forces them to resort exclusively to exemplar-based comparisons. It seems inevitable to form certain abstractions (generalizations) or schematizations in the comparison process that categorization entails. Based on this evidence Abbot-Smith and Tomasello (2006) and Ross and Makin (1999) argued that it is impossible to conceive of a category as such without any more abstract representation of the commonalities that its members share. In their *exemplar-abstraction model* they propose that both individual exemplars and abstractions are retained and represented in the mind (Abbot-Smith & Tomasello, 2006). Consequently, both examples and abstractions might be used in the comparison necessary to categorize new input.

There is further debate on exactly how this categorization of new potential members is performed. Following Langacker (1987), new "elements are assimilated to the category on the basis of their perceived resemblance" to the prototype, which he defined as a typical example or a schema (p. 371). Langacker assumed that the new stimulus activates several established categories—their schema or most-typical member. These serve as potential standards in the comparison, to which the new material is compared. The standard that is most-strongly activated is selected and serves to categorize the new stimulus. The new material is thus "captured" by the most activated "attractor" (Langacker, 2000a, p. 7). Connectionist models propose detailed accounts of how learning via activation spreading can be envisioned (e.g., Elman et al., 1996; McClelland, Rumelhart, & PDP Research Group, 1986; Rumelhart, McClelland, & PDP Research Group, 1986). Langacker (1987, pp. 371–372) called categorization where the new member fulfills all specifications of the standard of the most highly activated category *instantiation* or *elaboration*. He theorized that in this case the standard of comparison is a schema. The new member differs from the schema only in that it is more specific and more detailed. If there are more discrepancies between the most highly activated standard and the new material, Langacker referred to the process as *extension*, since the category is broadened in that way. He assumed that the standard is an exemplar rather than the schema in the case of extension. However, Langacker did not elaborate on how the two types of comparison (by a typical member or by a schema) can be differentiated in practice. In fact, he admitted that "the two modes are sometimes difficult to distinguish in practice." He did not, however, consider this missing discriminability a "matter of concern" (1987, p. 372). Langacker's account is one example of a similarity-based approach.[5]

---

[5] Similarity-based views of categorization are common in psychology as well, where similarity is often modelled in terms of spatial distance between exemplars (Nosofsky, 1986; Shepard, 1962a, 1962b; Tversky, 1977; Tversky & Gati, 1978).

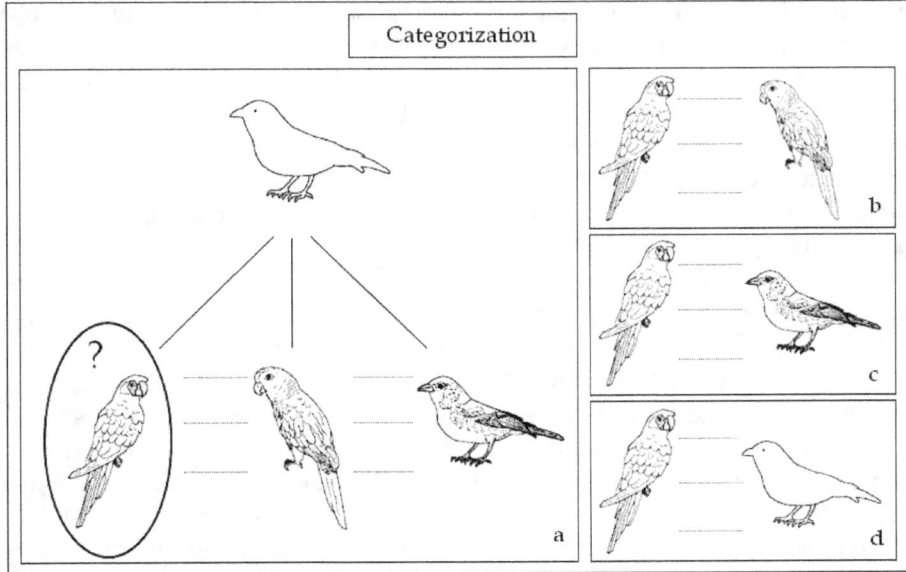

Fig. 12.2: The categorization process. From *The Role of Frequency in Children's Learning of Morphological Constructions* (p. 44), by A.-K. Cordes, 2014, Tübingen, Germany: Narr Francke Attempto. Copyright 2014 by Narr Francke Attempto. Reprinted with permission.

Figure 12.2 provides an illustration[6] of how categorization by comparison can be envisioned. A new stimulus (the bird circled in [a]) activates the relevant structures of several categories and is then compared to a highly similar exemplar (b), a highly frequent or particularly salient member (c), or a more abstract, schematic representation of category commonalities (d) of the most strongly activated category.

12.4 Application to Language

The previous sections illustrated the background of analogy and categorization. Regardless of their different origins and terminology, they are surprisingly similar, in that both processes involve a comparison whose outcome is determined by similarity (Cordes, 2014, p. 55). One might argue that the standard of comparison is the major difference between analogy formation and categorization, seeing that analogies usually involve a comparison to another example whereas categorization might be based

---

[6] This figure is solely for illustration. Since it is a drawing, it is limited to the expression of visual attributes. This is not to imply that all or even the majority of attributes are of visual nature.

on a comparison to either an example or a more abstract, schematic entity (possibly named prototype). It is, however, very difficult to determine the exact standard of comparison in individual instances and at least the earliest comparisons formed to create a "new" category must be based on two examples, thus resembling analogies more. In fact, several authors use the terms *analogy* and *categorization* interchangeably at times (Gentner & Namy, 1999; Kotovsky & Gentner, 1996; Tomasello, 2003, p. 4). The question is what exactly the circumstances are that allow this interchangeability (see Cordes, 2014, pp. 54–57, for a more detailed account).

Analogies are usually phrased as *A is like B in way C*.[7] For instance, an atom is like the solar system with respect to its configuration. The center of the atom, the nucleus, is mapped to the sun as the center of the solar system. The electrons are mapped to the planets. The relation between nucleus and electrons is mapped to that between sun and planets. Categorizations are ordinarily phrased as *an A is a C* (and so is *a B*). For example, a retriever is a DOG (and so is an Alsatian). The term C is the hyperonym and linguistic label of the respective category, whereas A and B are in a way both hyponyms (i.e., subcategories), and exemplars of the category. If it is indeed possible to interchangeably use the terms *analogy formation* and *categorization*, then the atom-solar system example must be describable as a categorization and it must be feasible to put the dog example as an analogy. An atom is a PHYSICAL MODEL INVOLVING ORBITAL STRUCTURE (which most people who are not physicists are certainly unlikely to have hypostatized as a concept) and so is the solar system. Conversely, a retriever is like an Alsatian in that their attributes, builds, and characteristics can be mapped, such as they are both quadrupeds, have tails, and bark (see Cordes, 2014, pp. 54–57, for more details). This change in perspective works well for basic-level and subordinate categories but it runs into difficulties when superordinate (e.g., FURNITURE) or functional categories (e.g., THINGS TO TAKE TO A DESERT ISLAND) are considered. The reason Cordes (2014, p. 57) proposed is that the attempt to align the examples of such categories structurally fails. Consequently, the terms *analogy formation* and *categorization* may be used interchangeably if the comparison at hand involves the structural alignment of parallel relations. The term *analogy* is probably preferred when the comparison process and the standard of comparison are in focus; the term *categorization* is more likely used when shared commonalities or a more abstract representation (e.g., schema, abstraction, generalization; Langacker, 2000a) are supposed to be highlighted. *Generalization* may refer to the formation of a more

---

7 Alternatively, they may be phrased as *a is to b as c is to d* (*a:b::c:d*). Strictly speaking, this alternative is a mere reformulation, where the dimension of relational similarity (i.e., *with respect to their configuration*) remains implicit, cf. nucleus:electrons::sun:planets. Proportional analogies of this format are also found in Paul's (1975) account of language change. Paul's analogies resemble the linguistic analogies described below to some degree, but are more restricted in both their scope (referring to inflection and word formation in language change rather than the process of building a repertoire of associations in individuals) and nature (meaning the potential dimensions of similarity).

abstract representation, that is, a schema (Langacker, 1987, p. 437), as a consequence of a comparison (be it named *analogy* or *categorization*) as well as to the extension of a category to new exemplars (Cordes, 2014, p. 59).

Bearing these similarities in mind, looking at children's language development provides a number of insights that help with understanding the role of analogies, categorization, and generalization in entrenchment processes in language use in general. The idea is that children form analogies in each area of their lives from infancy on (Gentner, 2003, pp. 200–201). Gentner (2003) proposed that experiencing temporally close repetitions of the same action or event highlights very small differences between them and results in ever-so-slightly more abstract representations of the relevant action or event. Progressively larger differences are tolerated and lead to increasingly abstract representations of the respective action or event.

If the same is true for language learning, symbolic associations (Schmid, Chapter 1, this volume) may be formed and entrenched this way. Tokens of the same word form + meaning (e.g., *mommie* – 'mother') or of a fixed string + communicative function (e.g., *bye-bye* – 'farewell') are produced by different speakers in slightly varying contexts and provide children's input. If their processing is conceptualized in terms of analogy and categorization, the repetition of tokens of words and fixed-word strings entails the repeated alignment of parallel structures. This recurrent-structural alignment is facilitated by the high degree of (object) similarity that is present in the individual realizations of the same word or word string. The constant analogical comparisons result in the formation of an abstraction of what all examples share. Following Gentner's nonlinguistic examples (2003), this must be true even for words and fixed strings due to slight variations found in the input (e.g., due to different speakers). The repeated analogies *increase the representational strength* of the respective abstracted association (between word form + meaning or fixed string + function) and thus cause its successive entrenchment. Tomasello (2003, p. 124) used Langacker's (2000b, pp. 214–215) transparency metaphor to illustrate this process. Comparing minimally distinct examples is likened to stacking highly similar, but not identical, overhead transparencies on top of each other. A slightly more abstract representation, disregarding minimal differences, is formed and becomes progressively entrenched.

It is possible to conceptualize how children acquire schemas in the same manner: they learn associations between word strings with type variation in at least one position and their meaning or communicative function (e.g., *Let's [verb phrase]* – 'invitation to joint activity'; *[noun phrase] hugs [noun phrase]* – 'hugging action involving agent and patient'). Lieven, Behrens, Speares, and Tomasello (2003), and Lieven, Salomo, and Tomasello (2009), among others, provide corpus evidence that shows that children do seem to gradually build more abstract associations. Again, token and type repetition may be envisioned as repeated analogical structural-alignment processes of individual examples. However, in this case, through type variation the symbolic stacking of transparencies on top of each other makes apparent where slot positions are. The repeated analogies thus allow the abstraction of the slot positions and the formation of a more abstract association that becomes progressively entrenched as do the individual examples. Structural alignment is still facilitated by the high degree of object similarity between instances, that is, the stable part of the word string, which makes it easier to perceive higher-order similarity (see also Section 12.3.1, as well as Cordes, 2014, p. 65; Kotovsky & Gentner, 1996), or the relational similarity between the aligned structures.

Supporting object similarity further decreases as the number of open slot positions rises and form-meaning associations of schemas become increasingly abstract (e.g., *[noun phrase] [verb phrase] [noun phrase] [noun phrase]* – "transfer"). Relational similarity between the instantiations persists and so encourages speakers to form structural alignments over different examples. Transparency stacking would yield a very blurry picture but categories of abstract form and meaning associations may be formed based on commonalities emerging in the analogical comparison of relationally similar instances as well as semantic and/or functional similarities.

During this process children also start grouping together words and expressions that may be used interchangeably in certain positions, developing paradigmatic associations and, eventually, categories. For instance, the structural alignment of fixed strings with one variable slot may yield categories of different word classes as Figure 12.3 illustrates. Members of such categories with similar meanings or functions compete for selection in particular slot positions.

In short, it is possible to conceptualize generalizations to new cases in terms of analogies to patterns of associations that are already entrenched to a certain degree. In comprehension, new input is aligned to more entrenched associations that are relationally (and, sometimes, literally) similar. By aligning the form and function sides of an association in context in such a manner, the unfamiliar utterance becomes

| Give me *a* BOOK | Give me *some* CARs | Give me *the* DOGGIE |
| Give me *a* TOY | Give me *some* BOOKs | Give me *the* BOOK |

Give me *a* HUG　　Give me *some* TOYs　　Give me *the* BABY

Give me *a* BREAK　　Give me *some* GRAPEs　　Give me *the* TOY

Fig. 12.3: The formation of grammatical categories. Lexemes with similar communicative functions, which recur in similar positions (in capitals) and with similar linguistic material (underlined), are grouped together in paradigmatic categories. From *The Role of Frequency in Children's Learning of Morphological Constructions* (p. 65), by A.-K. Cordes, 2014, Tübingen, Germany: Narr Francke Attempto. Copyright 2014 by Narr Francke Attempto. Reprinted with permission.

intelligible. Existent categories can be extended by such new members the more entrenched the new exemplars become. At the same time the category's prototype (if it is conceptualized in that way) can be adapted to include potential innovations. If patterns of associations are seen as categories that are formed based on analogical comparison, production is the formation of a new association on the basis of more entrenched examples or a prototypical example and the function that the speaker wishes to express in a given context.

12.5 Reassessing the Role of Analogy Formation, Categorization, and Generalization in Association Entrenchment

According to Schmid (Chapter 1, this volume), "linguistic knowledge is available in one format only, namely...symbolic, syntagmatic, paradigmatic, and pragmatic" (Section 1.5) associations. Entrenchment processes operate over these associations. This terminology bears the advantage that the gradualness and dynamicity of entrenchment is reflected more clearly than when the term *construction* is used, since the latter implies an all-or-nothing mechanism of memory retention. In accord with Schmid's perspective, the use of the term *category* in the preceding section needs to be qualified. Though it might be misleading to use the term at all, the term is useful to conceptualize the (potential) organization of associations. Additionally, the terms *category formation*, *categorization*, or *generalization* can serve as tools to express how categories are formed and modified through usage over time.

Schmid proposes that entrenchment is "brought about by the routinization effected by the repeated processing of identical or similar stimuli" (Chapter 1, this volume, Section 1.5). The ideas presented in the previous sections elaborate on how entrenchment is induced. It is suggested that entrenchment is more specifically caused by the repeated alignment of structurally parallel (i.e., relationally similar) associations in an analogical comparison process. The results of this process are the deeper entrenchment of the experienced association and, potentially, the progressive entrenchment of a more abstract association that reflects the commonalities of the encountered examples of the respective association. Examples of an association and an abstraction of the commonalities might be entrenched as a category.

Therefore, it is possible to specify the cognitive entrenchment processes presented in Schmid's Table 1.1 (Chapter 1, this volume): Analogy, categorization, and generalization processes involving the structural alignment detailed above are at work even in the entrenchment of symbolic associations at the level of words and fixed strings and in the entrenchment of syntagmatic associations in the form of identical sequences. The reason is that even in these cases, mere *token repetition* causes the analogical comparisons guided by both literal and relational similarity and yields abstractions of the relevant associations. Literal object similarity decreases, while relational similarity gains significance, when *type repetition* is the determinant of entrenchment. The emergence of variable slots in shorter and longer sequences is the result of repeated alignment of parallel structures where certain positions are filled by varying types. The associations that are formed and progressively entrenched are necessarily more abstract in nature. They are either *symbolic* or *syntagmatic* according to Schmid's classification, depending on the number of open slots. The more abstract associations might form a category together with the individual realizations that allowed their entrenchment in the first place. *Paradigmatic associations* are built as by-products of the comparisons formed to establish symbolic and syntagmatic associations through token repetition and type repetition. *Pragmatic associations* are listed separately by Schmid (Chapter 1, this volume). However, contextual and situational information should facilitate the alignment of structures in any comparison since they enrich the functional side of the form-function association (see also Ramscar & Port, 2015). Pragmatic associations are thus an integral part of the entrenchment process of all other types of associations described here in terms of analogies, categorization, and generalization.

Apart from similarity (literal, relational, and contextual) further forces affect attention and perception in the previously described comparison process. The concept of *salience* (see Günther, Müller, & Geyer, Chapter 13, this volume) captures many of them. Schmid (2007, pp. 119–120) distinguished cognitive and ontological salience. *Cognitive salience* refers to the activation of concepts in the mind during processing and is achieved by selective attention or spreading activation from related concepts (Deane, 1992, pp. 34–35). *Ontological salience* refers to the relatively stable property of entities in the world to attract attention (Schmid, 2007, p. 120). *Situational salience* relates to both these definitions. It defines salience as "the degree of relative prominence of a unit of information, at a specific point in time, in comparison to other units of information" (Chiarcos, Claus, & Grabski, 2011, p. 2). Whatever stands out in a particular situation is salient. If a man in a suit is pushing a toddler in a stroller, the man's formal clothing stands out at a nursery-school picnic, whereas the child in the stroller stands out at a business lunch (Smith & Mackie, 2000, pp. 67–68). The respective salient aspect causes extra activation in the mind (cognitive salience). In this manner, any aspect that stands out situationally, contextually, or linguistically affects the analogies being formed. This may include the most recent information, which is retained particularly well, likely because it is still activated in the mind (recency effects, Ebbinghaus, 1913, pp. 90–113, e.g., in priming, see Pickering & Ferreira, 2008, for a review), prototypical character, which is the fact that typical examples stand out (Rosch, 1975), prior knowledge, or novelty. It might be possible to understand similarity in terms of salience, since it likely also causes this extra activation, but it is probably more useful to keep the two concepts apart so as to maintain more specificity.

12.6 Conclusion

Structural alignment and mapping based on similarity of relations and, if present, more literal similarity provide a useful conceptualization of the entrenchment of associations that are more or less general/abstract. The mechanisms of analogy and categorization help conceptualize how speakers' linguistic systems are built, used, and (constantly re-)organized. More detailed, evidence-based accounts of how categories are selected and extended in comprehension and production are still needed, as are theories predicting the impact of and interactions between contributing factors including frequency, similarity, and salience among others.

References

Abbot-Smith, K., & Tomasello, M. (2006). Exemplar-learning and schematization in a usage-based account of syntactic acquisition. *The Linguistic Review, 23*, 275–290. http://dx.doi.org/10.1515/TLR.2006.011

Aitchison, J. (2003). *Words in the mind. An introduction to the mental lexicon.* Oxford, England: Blackwell.

Baayen, H., & Ramscar, M. (2015). Abstraction, storage and naive discriminative learning. In E. Dąbrowska & D. Divjak (Eds.), *Handbook of cognitive linguistics* (pp. 99–120). http://dx.doi.org/10.1515/9783110292022-006

Berlin, B., & Kay, P. (1969). *Basic color terms: Their universality and evolution.* Berkeley: University of California Press.

Borges, J. L. (1964). *Labyrinths.* London, England: New Directions.

Brown, R. W., & Lenneberg, E. H. (1954). A study in language and cognition. *The Journal of Abnormal and Social Psychology, 49*, 454–462. http://dx.doi.org/10.1037/h0057814

Chandler, S. (2002). Skousen's analogical approach as an exemplar-based model of categorization. In R. Skousen, D. Lonsdale, & D. B. Parkinson (Eds.), *Analogical modeling* (pp. 51–105). http://dx.doi.org/10.1075/hcp.10.07cha

Chiarcos, C., Claus, B., & Grabski, M. (2011). Introduction: Salience in linguistics and beyond. In C. Chiarcos, B. Claus, & M. Grabski (Eds.), *Salience: Multidisciplinary perspectives on its function in discourse* (pp. 1–28). http://dx.doi.org/10.1515/9783110241020.1

Chomsky, N. (1988). *Language and problems of knowledge: The Managua lectures.* Cambridge, MA: MIT Press.

Cordes, A.-K. (2014). *The role of frequency in children's learning of morphological constructions.* Tübingen, Germany: Narr Francke Attempto.

Croft, W. (2001). *Radical construction grammar.* http://dx.doi.org/10.1093/acprof:oso/9780198299554.001.0001

Croft, W., & Cruse, D. A. (2004). *Cognitive linguistics.* http://dx.doi.org/10.1017/CBO9780511803864

Deane, P. D. (1992). *Grammar in mind and brain: Explorations in cognitive syntax.* http://dx.doi.org/10.1515/9783110886535

DeLoache, J. S. (1990). Young children's understanding of models. In R. Fivush & J. A. Hudson (Eds.), *Knowing and remembering in young children* (pp. 94–126). Cambridge, England: Cambridge University Press.

Ebbinghaus, H. (1913). *Memory: A contribution to experimental psychology.* http://dx.doi.org/10.1037/10011-000

Elman, J. L., Bates, E. A., Johnson, M. H., Karmiloff-Smith, A., Parisi, D., & Plunkett, K. (1996). *Rethinking innateness: A connectionist perspective on development.* Cambridge, MA: MIT Press.

Gentner, D. (1988). Metaphor as structure mapping: The relational shift. *Child Development, 59,* 47–59. http://dx.doi.org/10.2307/1130388

Gentner, D. (2003). Why we're so smart. In D. Gentner & S. Goldin-Meadow (Eds.), *Language in mind: Advances in the study of language and thought* (pp. 195–235). Cambridge, MA: MIT Press.

Gentner, D., & Kurtz, K. J. (2006). Relations, objects, and the composition of analogies. *Cognitive Science, 30,* 609–642. http://dx.doi.org/10.1207/s15516709cog0000_60

Gentner, D., & Markman, A. B. (1997). Structure mapping in analogy and similarity. *American Psychologist, 52,* 45–56. http://dx.doi.org/10.1037/0003-066X.52.1.45

Gentner, D., & Medina, J. (1998). Similarity and the development of rules. *Cognition, 65,* 263–297. http://dx.doi.org/10.1016/S0010-0277(98)00002-X

Gentner, D., & Namy, L. L. (1999). Comparison in the development of categories. *Cognitive Development, 14,* 487–513. http://dx.doi.org/10.1016/S0885-2014(99)00016-7

Gentner, D., & Rattermann, M. J. (1991). Language and the career of similarity. In S. A. Gelman & J. P. Byrnes (Eds.), *Perspectives on language and thought: Interrelations in development* (pp. 225–277). http://dx.doi.org/10.1017/CBO9780511983689.008

Gentner, D., & Toupin, C. (1986). Systematicity and surface similarity in the development of analogy. *Cognitive Science, 10,* 277–300. http://dx.doi.org/10.1207/s15516709cog1003_2

Gick, M. L., & Holyoak, K. J. (1980). Analogical problem solving. *Cognitive Psychology, 12,* 306–355. http://dx.doi.org/10.1016/0010-0285(80)90013-4

Goldberg, A. E. (1995). *Constructions: A construction grammar approach to argument structure.* Chicago, IL: University of Chicago Press.

Goldberg, A. E. (2006). *Constructions at work: The nature of generalization in language.* Oxford, England: Oxford University Press.

Goldstone, R. L., Medin, D. L., & Gentner, D. (1991). Relational similarity and the nonindependence of features in similarity judgments. *Cognitive Psychology, 23,* 222–262. http://dx.doi.org/10.1016/0010-0285(91)90010-L

Holyoak, K. J. (2012). Analogy and relational reasoning. In K. J. Holyoak & R. G. Morrison (Eds.), *The Oxford handbook of thinking and reasoning* (pp. 234–259). http://dx.doi.org/10.1093/oxfordhb/9780199734689.013.0013

Holyoak, K. J., & Thagard, P. (1995). *Mental leaps: Analogy in creative thought.* Cambridge, MA: MIT Press.

Kay, P., & McDaniel, C. K. (1978). The linguistic significance of the meanings of basic color terms. *Language, 54,* 610–646. http://dx.doi.org/10.1353/lan.1978.0035

Keane, M. (1987). On retrieving analogues when solving problems. *The Quarterly Journal of Experimental Psychology Section A, 39,* 29–41. http://dx.doi.org/10.1080/02724988743000015

Kotovsky, L., & Gentner, D. (1996). Comparison and categorization in the development of relational similarity. *Child Development, 67,* 2797–2822. http://dx.doi.org/10.2307/1131753

Kruschke, J. K. (2005). Category learning. In K. Lamberts & R. L. Goldstone (Eds.), *Handbook of cognition* (pp. 184–201). http://dx.doi.org/10.4135/9781848608177.n7

Labov, W. (1973). The boundaries of words and their meaning. In C.-J. Bailey & R. W. Shuy (Eds.), *New ways of analyzing variation in English* (pp. 340–373). Washington, DC: Georgetown University Press.

Langacker, R. W. (1987). *Foundations of cognitive grammar: Vol. 1. Theoretical prerequisites.* Stanford, CA: Stanford University Press.

Langacker, R. W. (2000a). A dynamic usage-based model. In M. Barlow & S. Kemmer (Eds.), *Usage-based models of language* (pp. 1–63). Stanford, CA: CSLI.

Langacker, R. W. (2000b). *Grammar and conceptualization.* New York, NY: Mouton De Gruyter.

Lenneberg, E. H. (1967). *Biological foundations of language.* New York, NY: Wiley.

Lieven, E., Behrens, H., Speares, J., & Tomasello, M. (2003). Early syntactic creativity: A usage-based approach. *Journal of Child Language, 30,* 333–370. http://dx.doi.org/10.1017/S0305000903005592

Lieven, E., Salomo, D., & Tomasello, M. (2009). Two-year-old children's production of multiword utterances: A usage-based analysis. *Cognitive Linguistics, 20,* 481–507. http://dx.doi.org/10.1515/COGL.2009.022

Markman, A. B., & Gentner, D. (1993). Structural alignment during similarity comparisons. *Cognitive Psychology, 25,* 431–467. http://dx.doi.org/10.1006/cogp.1993.1011

McClelland, J. L., Rumelhart, D. E., & PDP Research Group. (1986). *Parallel distributed processing: Vol. 2. Explorations in the microstructure of cognition: Psychological and biological models.* Cambridge, MA: MIT Press.

Nosofsky, R. M. (1986). Attention, similarity, and the identification–categorization relationship. *Journal of Experimental Psychology: General, 115,* 39–57. http://dx.doi.org/10.1037/0096-3445.115.1.39

Paul, H. (1975). *Prinzipien der Sprachgeschichte* [Principles of language history]. Tübingen, Germany: Niemeyer.

Pickering, M. J., & Ferreira, V. S. (2008). Structural priming: A critical review. *Psychological Bulletin, 134,* 427–459. http://dx.doi.org/10.1037/0033-2909.134.3.427

Ramscar, M., & Port, R. (2015). Categorization (without categories). In E. Dąbrowska & D. Divjak (Eds.), *Handbook of cognitive linguistics* (pp. 75–99). Berlin, Germany: De Gruyter Mouton.

Rattermann, M. J., & Gentner, D. (1998). More evidence for a relational shift in the development of analogy: Children's performance on a causal-mapping task. *Cognitive Development, 13,* 453–478. http://dx.doi.org/10.1016/S0885-2014(98)90003-X

Rosch, E. (1973). On the internal structure of perceptual and semantic categories. In T. E. Moore (Ed.), *Cognitive development and the acquisition of language* (pp. 111–144). New York, NY: Academic Press.

Rosch, E. (1975). Cognitive representation of semantic categories. *Journal of Experimental Psychology: General, 104,* 192–233. http://dx.doi.org/10.1037/0096-3445.104.3.192

Rosch, E., & Mervis, C. B. (1975). Family resemblances: Studies in the internal structure of categories. *Cognitive Psychology, 7,* 573–605. http://dx.doi.org/10.1016/0010-0285(75)90024-9

Rosch, E., Mervis, C. B., Gray, W. D., Johnson, D. M., & Boyes-Braem, P. (1976). Basic objects in natural categories. *Cognitive Psychology, 8,* 382–439. http://dx.doi.org/10.1016/0010-0285(76)90013-X

Ross, B. H., & Makin, V. S. (1999). Prototype versus exemplar models in cognition. In R. J. Sternberg (Ed.), *The nature of cognition* (pp. 205–241). Cambridge, MA: MIT Press.

Ross, B. H., Perkins, S. J., & Tenpenny, P. L. (1990). Reminding-based category learning. *Cognitive Psychology, 22,* 460–492. http://dx.doi.org/10.1016/0010-0285(90)90010-2

Rumelhart, D. E., McClelland, J. L., & PDP Research Group. (1986). *Parallel distributed processing: Vol. 1. Explorations in the microstructure of cognition: Foundations.* Cambridge, MA: MIT Press.

Schmid, H.-J. (2007). Entrenchment, salience, and basic levels. In D. Geeraerts & H. Cuyckens (Eds.), *The Oxford handbook of cognitive linguistics* (pp. 117–138). Oxford, England: Oxford University Press.

Schmid, H.-J. (2015). A blueprint of the entrenchment-and-conventionalization model. *Yearbook of the German Cognitive Linguistics Association, 3*, 3–26. http://dx.doi.org/10.1515/gcla-2015-0002

Shepard, R. N. (1962a). The analysis of proximities: Multidimensional scaling with an unknown distance function. Part I. *Psychometrika, 27*, 125–140. http://dx.doi.org/10.1007/BF02289630

Shepard, R. N. (1962b). The analysis of proximities: Multidimensional scaling with an unknown distance function. Part II. *Psychometrika, 27*, 219–246. http://dx.doi.org/10.1007/BF02289621

Smith, E. R., & Mackie, D. M. (2000). *Social psychology.* Philadelphia, PA: Taylor & Francis.

Taylor, J. R. (2009). *Linguistic categorization.* Oxford, England: Oxford University Press.

Tomasello, M. (2000). Do young children have adult syntactic competence? *Cognition, 74*, 209–253. http://dx.doi.org/10.1016/S0010-0277(99)00069-4

Tomasello, M. (2003). *Constructing a language: A usage-based theory of language acquisition.* Cambridge, MA: Harvard University Press.

Tversky, A. (1977). Features of similarity. *Psychological Review, 84*, 327–352. http://dx.doi.org/10.1037/0033-295X.84.4.327

Tversky, A., & Gati, I. (1978). Studies of similarity. In E. Rosch & B. B. Lloyd (Eds.), *Cognition and categorization* (pp. 79–98). Hillsdale, NJ: Erlbaum.

Ungerer, F., & Schmid, H.-J. (2006). *Introduction to cognitive linguistics* (2nd ed.). London, England: Pearson Education.

Whorf, B. L. (1956). *Language, thought, and reality.* Cambridge, MA: MIT Press.

Wittgenstein, L. (1958). *Philosophical investigations.* Oxford, England: Blackwell.

Franziska Günther, Hermann J. Müller, and Thomas Geyer
13 Salience, Attention, and Perception

13.1 Introduction

Humans are continuously encountering a myriad of events in their environments at any given time. Processing these various inputs, linking them to representations stored in memory, and organizing appropriate linguistic and nonlinguistic responses to all or some of them imposes a huge load on their brains. However, while the human brain has an impressive capability of parallel processing, its capacity is strongly limited. Thus, humans cannot consciously represent all the information available to them at any one time, and they cannot simultaneously initiate more than a few different actions. In order to overcome these limitations, humans have to select a limited subset of the sensory input to which they are exposed for perception, action, and interaction. The neurocognitive mechanisms that mediate this selection are referred to as *attention*.

In the past decades, attention—and the role it plays in perception, cognition, and action—has become one of the most extensively investigated issues in cognitive/neurocognitive psychology. One main line of research in this field concerns the control of attention based on *salience*, which can, in very general terms, be defined as the conspicuity of a stimulus relative to its surrounding items. Salience also figures centrally in several theories and fields of research in linguistics and psycholinguistics. Attention and salience thus constitute major points of contact between linguistics and psychology, and, as such, could provide a solid basis for interdisciplinary research.

What is, however, in the way of joint research activities is that *salience* has been defined, used, and operationalized in many different ways. This marks a considerable source of division between disciplines, as well as among subdisciplines. A precondition for salience to function as a bridge between linguistics and psychology therefore consists in arriving at an understanding of salience that is valid and interdisciplinarily accepted, and, ideally, can be readily operationalized for empirical investigation. As a first step, this requires that researchers become aware of the diversity of approaches to salience in their own as well as in other disciplines.

This chapter makes a contribution to this first step. It provides a selective overview of some of the main lines of current research on salience and salience-related phenomena in cognitive and neurocognitive psychology, linguistics, and psycholinguistics and takes this as a basis for illustrating and discussing different approaches to and definitions of salience. This overview culminates in a discussion of whether the different ways in which salience has been defined and used can be covered by one general concept of *salience* ("SALIENCE"), or whether it is necessary to differentiate between several *types of salience* ("saliences"). In addition, the relation of salience to other concepts, in particular, entrenchment, is discussed. Based on this, ideas for future—and joint—psychological-linguistic research are proposed. This also includes research that might contribute to a better understanding of what renders salience, attention, and perception major determinants of entrenchment processes.

13.2 Salience in (Visual) Perception and Salience in Language

The major and most obvious difference between research on salience in experimental psychology and linguistics consists in whether the *carriers* of salience are linguistic or nonlinguistic in nature. Apart from that, these two strands of research address markedly similar research questions. If one focuses on a relatively general level, many of the psychological, linguistic, and psycholinguistic research projects presented and discussed in the following sections centrally investigate what renders an item salient (relative to its surroundings), that is, they try to identify the *sources* of salience. This necessarily also involves taking into account the possible *effects* of salience, as well as the *contextual conditions* under which processes of salience ascription occur.

13.2.1 Salience in Experimental Psychology

One highly influential "test bed" for elucidating which factors influence visual attention allocation, and, accordingly, what the sources of salience are, is a paradigm much used in current cognitive-neuroscientific research (including our own): *visual search*.

In visual-search paradigms, ecological situations (e.g., finding a goal-relevant object in a cluttered, resource-limited environment, such as an edible berry among inedible leaves or toxic berries) are recreated in the laboratory by presenting to the participants an array of stimuli, one set of which is defined as *target*, the others as *nontargets*. The set of possible actions is usually restricted to pressing one of several alternative-response buttons (e.g., to indicate target presence) or to moving the hand or the eyes to the location of the target.

What causes an item to be salient during visual search is one of the central questions addressed by research in this field. Current theories of visual search (and also selective attention in general) usually assume the existence of two major salience mechanisms: *bottom-up salience* and *top-down salience*. Visual search is said to be driven by bottom-up mechanisms when attention selects an item in the field because this item displays certain inherent features or properties that mark it as different from (and thus salient relative to) its surroundings. Bottom-up salience mechanisms are, accordingly, stimulus-driven. Top-down mechanisms, on the other hand, ensure that attention is deployed to items that match observers' expectations. That is, they are driven by the current goals of the observer that are mapped onto the observed scene or situation. Thus, bottom-up salience defines *externally* provided, stimulus-inherent information as the major source of salience, while the main source of top-down salience is *internally* (pre)activated information, whose activation can be triggered by various factors of influence, such as task instructions, action intentions, or memory of previous stimulus and task attributes or of the actions performed in the previous trial(s).

One major point of debate relates to how these potential sources of perceptual salience interrelate. Views range from the suggestion that bottom-up salience governs visual selection (Belopolsky, Schreij, & Theeuwes, 2010; Theeuwes, 1991) to the opposing view that bottom-up sensory signals capture attention only when they match observers' top-down expectations (Bacon & Egeth, 1994; Folk, Remington, & Johnston, 1992). This issue is the focus of this section. The studies reviewed are representative of a whole set of recent investigations that suggest an integrative position, providing evidence that top-down factors have a corrective influence on bottom-up salience. The projects presented differ, however, with respect to which top-down sources of salience, and thus which potential complements of bottom-up salience, they focus on: task instructions, intended actions, visual memory, or social interaction.

That task instructions can modulate bottom-up triggered attentional processes is indicated, for example, by findings from a recent eye-tracking study by Paoletti, Weaver, Braun, and van Zoest (2015). Paoletti and collaborators showed that observers' saccadic target responses were more accurate when they had previously been instructed to be "accurate" than when they had been instructed to be "fast." Note that in Paoletti et al. (2015) the search displays contained two singletons,[1] one target and one distractor, with the target being, in terms of its bottom-up characteristics, less salient than the additional, task-irrelevant distractor. The authors also demonstrated that this was the case even when saccadic reaction times were matched between the accurate- and the fast-instruction conditions. This suggests that task instructions alter the initial bottom-up sweep of information prior to deployments of overt, that is, saccadic, attention.

Similar effects have also been observed with intended actions, which may or may not be task-induced. There is plenty of evidence indicating that goal-directed actions can boost the sensory processing of information related to them. One central and robust finding obtained in investigations that make use of visual cues to direct observer-actors' attention is that discrimination performance is improved at the location of an intended motor, for example, saccadic, reaching action, including

---

[1] In visual search, the term *singleton* refers to an item that can be differentiated by the surrounding items by a single property (e.g., color, size, motion, orientation).

sequential movements (e.g., Baldauf & Deubel, 2010). Findings along these lines indicate that intended movements are preceded by covert shifts of visual attention to the movement target.

A study by Wykowska, Schubö, and Hommel (2009) indicated in addition that such effects are sensitive to the type of action that is planned. In this study, observers had to prepare a movement (grasping vs. pointing) and subsequently performed a visual-search task for size- versus luminance-defined targets. It was found that action planning primes the perceptual dimensions that provide information for the open parameters of the intended action; preparing for grasping facilitated detection of size targets, while preparing for pointing facilitated detection of luminance targets. This indicates that action-induced salience can *selectively* apply to specific scene dimensions, and can, in this way, modulate bottom-up attention.

Memory-based information relating to the frequency structure of visual input plays a role in a series of studies conducted by Töllner, Müller, and Zehetleitner (2012). Töllner et al. found that the latency of a specific waveform of the event-related potential of the EEG signal which indexes the operation of focal attention towards peripheral targets was reduced when task-irrelevant distractors were frequent and thus expected (i.e., suppressed). This lines up well with the findings revealed by other (oculomotor) studies by Müller and collaborators (Geyer, Müller, & Krummenacher, 2008; Müller, Geyer, Zehetleitner, & Krummenacher, 2009), in which a variant of the additional singleton paradigm was used to investigate in more detail how different sources of salience interrelate. What is characteristic of this paradigm is that the most bottom-up salient item is not the target but a distracting nontarget that has to be ignored (Theeuwes, 1991). When reaction times (RTs) are measured in this task, behavioral and oculomotor responses to the target are typically slower in the presence compared with the absence of the distractor (an effect referred to as *distractor interference*). Müller and collaborators demonstrated that this effect is sensitive to variation in the proportions of distractor to no-distractor trials. Variably using distractors in 20%, 50%, or 80% of the trials, they observed a linear trend in distractor interference: the interference effect decreased relative to an increase in distractor frequency. Moreover, initial training with distractors also led to a reduction of the interference effect. The effect was overall smaller in "test" blocks—containing 20%, 50%, or 80% distractors—when observers had previously been presented with distractors in an initial "training" block. Taken together, these findings indicate that bottom-up driven visual behavior can be modulated by expectations generated based on recent experiences of frequency distribution patterns in the situational environment; or, put differently, it indicates that recent experiences, including both short- and long-term memory influences, can act as primes to subsequent visual-search behavior.

Müller and colleagues interpret these findings in terms of their dimension-weighting account (DWA) of perceptual selection (Found & Müller, 1996; Müller, Heller, & Ziegler, 1995). They assume that (a) stimulus salience is represented in individual, dimension-specific salience representations; (b) attentional selection is driven by an overall salience- or master-map of the visual array; and (c) attention prioritizes those stimuli that achieve the highest activation on this cognitively represented map. The findings just reported strongly suggest that this map is not simply computed in a bottom-up, stimulus-driven manner but that salience computations may be biased in a spatially parallel manner by top-down signals that reflect the observers' expectations of particular stimulus attributes (see also Zehetleitner, Koch, Goschy, & Müller, 2013, for a formal implementation of this idea). Therefore, according to DWA, the visual selection operates via an overall salience map, which represents the integrated effects of bottom-up and top-down salience signals (see also Bisley & Goldberg, 2010; Zhaoping, 2014).

A study by Gökce, Geyer, Finke, Müller, and Töllner (2014) complemented this view by addressing an issue relating to the processes and brain mechanisms involved in the memory-based guidance of visual search, namely position priming. Gökce et al. combined reaction time (RT) measures with specific sensory- and motor-driven event-related lateralizations (ERLs) to investigate whether intertrial priming facilitates *early sensory* processes (*preselective view*), or whether it instead facilitates processes of response selection/execution that take place after target selection (*postselective view*). The results showed that these two views are not mutually exclusive; instead, both types of influence can variably occur under different conditions. The appearance of a target at a previous distractor location (relative to targets at previous target and neutral, that is, empty positions) was associated with a delayed buildup of the sensory-driven ERL, indicating that distractor positions are suppressed at *early* stages of visual processing. The re-presentation of a target at a previous target location (relative to neutral and distractor locations), by contrast, modulated the elicitation of the subsequent motor-driven ERL, which indicates that *later*, postselective response selection is facilitated if the target occurred at the same position as in the previous trial. These findings indicate that top-down memory can influence multiple stages in the visual-processing hierarchy, including the bottom-up computation of stimulus salience.

In the examples presented so far, what is rendered top-down salient is what is expected to occur in the very near future. However, other studies have found the opposite effects, providing evidence indicating that observers are more sensitive to sensory input, such as perceived direction of motion, which *deviates* from their intended actions (see, e.g., Müsseler & Hommel, 1997; Zwickel, Grosjean, & Prinz, 2010). For instance, Gozli and Pratt (2011) showed that target discrimination is normally superior at a spatially cued relative to an uncued location, but that this changes when observers had to execute a movement (i.e., respond to the target) along the same axis as the movement cue; under these conditions, the difference between cued and uncued locations disappeared.

Such findings are usually explained on the basis of predictive coding theories, which hold that observers continuously predict the sensory consequences of goal-directed actions (or perception in general; see, e.g., A. Clark, 2013; Friston, 2010) and compare these predictions with the actual sensory input from the movement. In the case of a match, sensory information is attenuated because it does not add significantly to what is already known and currently cognitively activated. Since self-generated sensations can be predicted very accurately by individuals, this would explain why sensory suppression is particularly strong for self-generated movements. On this view, what is salient are those parts of the input that have *not* been predicted (or expected to be relevant) and thus come as a surprise (in the following referred to as *surprisal-induced* salience; see A. Clark, 2013; Tribus, 1961). As indicated by the findings of Gozli and Pratt (2011), whether salience results from surprisal seems to depend, among other things, on the kind of task performed, for example, on whether or not self-generated motion was involved, as well as on the type of cue used (e.g., spatial cue vs. movement cue), that is, on what functions as the specific source or trigger of top-down salience. Furthermore, findings from developmental studies (e.g., Houston-Price & Nakai, 2004) indicate that whether expected or surprising information attracts attention might depend on how much an observer already knows about an item or context, with surprisal-based salience effects increasing with rising expertise. If considered from this perspective, systematic investigations of the relations between these two types of salience-inducing mechanisms might also prove highly relevant for defining more clearly the relation(s) between salience and entrenchment (see Section 13.3).

Findings from research on social-interactive forms of behavior in interactive-situational environments suggest similar conclusions. A top-down factor widely investigated in this context is gaze direction. In gaze-cueing experiments, faces with eyes gazing to the left or to the right, and thus either into the direction in which a to-be-detected item (target) will appear (valid trials) or into the opposite direction (invalid trials) are used as cues, and thus form a potential source of visual salience. A general finding in experiments employing this method (e.g., Müller & Rabbitt, 1989; Posner, 1980) is that responses on valid trials are faster, and/or more accurate, than responses on invalid trials, that is, that gaze direction can function as an efficient attentional cue.

However, there is evidence indicating that face cues differ considerably from other types of cues because they do not automatically attract attention. Instead, their effects are dependent on specific social-cognitive abilities, such as attributing intention to the face cue (see, e.g., Teufel et al., 2009; Wiese, Wykowska, Zwickel, & Müller, 2012; Wykowska, Wiese, Prosser, & Müller, 2014).

In one study, Wykowska and collaborators (Wiese et al., 2012) used pictures of a human and a robot face as gaze cues and manipulated observers' beliefs about whether or not the human or robot has a mind (intentional stance). Across conditions, participants were variably told that they were observing (a) a human and (b) a robot, or (c) a human-like mannequin and (d) a robot whose eyes are controlled by a human being. They found that gaze-cuing effects were significantly larger when participants thought that the eye movements were the result of human intentional behavior (conditions [a] and [d]) than when they believed that the observed faces were parts of an automatically operating machine (conditions [b] and [c]). That is, gaze only functioned as a social salience cue in the cases in which participants thought they were observing an intentional being. This indicates that top-down expectations relating to the social importance of a face cue can modulate the bottom-up salience signal associated with a particular cue. On more general grounds, it may suggest that intentionality attribution (in Dennett's, 1989, terms: "adopting the intentional stance") is an essential precondition for gaze to function as a source of visual salience. It also appears as a precondition for individuals to enter into a state of joint attention—and, thus, an essential precondition for joint action, likely including the use of language[2] (see also Tomasello, 2003, 2009).

In sum, the above studies yield a picture of salience as a complex and multifaceted phenomenon that is governed by a range of different sources. The findings reported do not only indicate that bottom-up and top-down salience mechanisms work together in complex ways, and do so variably depending on the specific situational, in particular social, context. They also reveal a picture of considerable variation with respect to at least three issues:

- There are multiple *carriers* of salience. Attentional selection can variably be object-centered, such as the selection of target objects as compared with distractor objects in Paoletti et al. (2015); space-centered, as in Gökce et al.'s (2014) investigation of position priming; or feature/dimension-centered, as is the case with the selection of size- versus luminance-defined targets in Wykowska et al.'s (2009) investigation of action-induced attentional selection.
- There are multiple *sources* of salience. On a general level, one can differentiate between bottom-up versus top-down salience. On a more specific level, it is also useful to distinguish different top-down factors like task instruction, action intention, visual memory, and situational (social) context.
- Concerning the *manifestations* of salience, or *mechanisms* of salience ascription, items can either be salient because they are expected (i.e., they meet observers' goals) or because they are unexpected (i.e., they are novel and/or induce a surprise response).

As will become clear from the discussion in the next section, this picture of considerable diversity is also characteristic of the ways salience has been approached in linguistics. What will be shown as well is that linguistic investigations and theories of

---

[2] Whether and to what extent other-modelling really plays a role during communicative interaction constitutes a much debated issue in alignment research (see, e.g., Garrod & Pickering, 2007), discussion of which is beyond the scope of this chapter. For an overview with a focus on the possible role of common-ground establishment and other-modelling see, for example, Günther (2016).

salience display many parallels with the psychological perspective just illustrated, but do not simply mirror it. Instead, the special characteristics of language as a conventional system of signs or constructions, that is, form–meaning pairs, and as a medium of communicative interaction, add even more complexity to the picture of salience sketched so far.

13.2.2 Salience in Linguistics

The major characteristics of language just referred to—its composition of form–meaning pairs, its conventional nature, and its symbolic and communicative-interactive functions—provide a good basis for illustrating both the parallels and the differences between approaches to salience in experimental psychology and in linguistics.

Given that linguistic forms (either visually or auditorily) usually take perceptible shape, form-focused linguistic salience research provides particularly clear and strong points of contact between the disciplines. Such approaches to linguistic salience are, for instance, widespread in particular strands of sociolinguistic and sociophonetic research, on which the following discussion exemplarily focuses. Researchers in these fields are concerned with the following salience-related questions: Which features of a local or social accent are perceived as salient and are thus categorized as typical of this variety by its speakers and/or by outsiders? Which features of an accent, or of a variety more generally, that is not their own do speakers adapt to (*accommodation*)? And, of course, why is this the case?

Form-focused (socio)linguistic investigations largely parallel the psychological research sketched in Section 13.2.1 in that they display a major interest in identifying the different bottom-up and top-down sources of salience of particular linguistic forms, or of some of their characteristic features. However, findings from corpus-based and field studies (e.g., Auer, Barden, & Grosskopf, 1998; Honeybone & Watson, 2013; see also references below) have triggered a major shift in focus in the tradition of sociolinguistic salience research and have increased the distance between bottom-up focused psychological approaches and sociolinguistic approaches to salience. These findings indicate that socio-affective top-down factors are by far more dominant than stimulus-inherent or structure-related bottom-up factors in rendering linguistic items subject to salience-induced processes such as accommodation. As a consequence, many current sociolinguistic theories (e.g., Docherty & Foulkes, 2014; Kerswill & Williams, 2002; Lenz, 2010; Purschke, 2014; Rácz, 2013) define salience as a *primarily* or even *exclusively* social-affective/evaluative phenomenon, and thus propose a concept of salience that is specific to sociolinguistics in many respects (see Auer, 2014). However, many recent sociolinguistic investigations strongly draw on predictive coding models (see, e.g., Rácz, 2013), which indicates that the developments just sketched do not so much mark a complete break of sociolinguistics with the psychological tradition, but rather a reorientation relative to it.

If considered from a more global perspective, this tendency in sociolinguistics casts a fresh light on differences concerning (a) which possible *effects* of salience are of interest in sociolinguistics, and (b) what are the major *loci* of salience-related processes. As indicated above, much of sociolinguistic research draws on salience as an explanatory concept in investigating phenomena like dialect accommodation (e.g., Giles, Coupland, & Coupland, 1991; Labov, 1972; Trudgill, 1986; Yaeger-Dror, 1993) or contact-induced language change (e.g., Auer, 2014; Honeybone & Watson, 2013; Kerswill & Williams, 2002; Trudgill, 1986), and thus phenomena of conventionalization that occur within or across whole speech communities (see also Labov, 2014). Issues that centrally occupy linguists (also beyond sociolinguistics) are the following: How can attentional behavior—which is performed by *individual* language users in *specific* contexts and which, presumably, has effects on their *individual* knowledge structures—trigger effects on the level of whole speech communities? In particular, how and to what extent are forms of individual behavior and individual experiences of the same external input similar across individual speakers? And, given that bottom-up factors only seem to play a minor role, what causes this similarity, that is, how are behavior and experiences synchronized?

Paradoxical as it may seem given the discussion so far, these questions explain another major difference between linguistic and psychological research on salience. Many linguistic approaches to salience focus even more strongly, or more exclusively, on the dimension of cognition, in particular, on knowledge representation. To understand this, the perspective has to be extended from form-focused to meaning-focused approaches to salience in linguistics. More specifically, the following issues have to be taken into account: What is linguistic meaning? How are linguistic forms and linguistic meanings related? How does meaning become manifest during communicative interactions?

In the following, these issues are approached from a usage-based cognitive linguistic perspective (e.g., Barlow & Kemmer, 2000; Langacker, 1987, 2008; Schmid, 2014), where it is assumed that

- language is an integral part of general cognition; therefore, what is understood as the meaning of linguistic forms/constructions is a network of units of knowledge that have become associated with the respective forms;
- all linguistic forms/constructions carry meaning, that is, meaning is not exclusively a feature of words or of what is traditionally considered lexical items;
- meaning emerges from use, and this entails that
  - forms become associated with meanings throughout lifelong experience with language in use, and
  - what is understood to be the meaning of a form depends on the context of use of this form. This context can further be differentiated into the dimensions of external (social and situational) context, (preceding, discourse-specific)

linguistic context (i.e., cotext), and internal/cognitive context, that is, patterns of form-associated knowledge structures in individual language-users' minds whose degree of activation depends on previous experience and/or (current) external contextual conditions.

On this view, form–meaning associations are complex in nature, as can be seen from phenomena like polysemy, synonymy, or prototypicality, and are highly likely to vary between contexts and individuals. This means that on each occasion of active or passive use of a particular form, the language user has to construct meaning by selecting some knowledge structures for active processing. These knowledge structures can either be the result of earlier experiences (entrenchment in the more narrow sense) or of the very recent or current experience of contextually situated language use (i.e., can be part of the current discourse model or *situation model*; see, e.g., van Dijk & Kintsch, 1983). It is these processes of form-triggered selection of knowledge structures for current use that many linguists—in particular, but not exclusively from the cognitive-linguistic camp—primarily refer to when using the term *salience*. What is salient is what is readily accessible and, eventually, "loaded . . . into current working memory" (Schmid, 2007, p. 119). In line with Schmid (2007, 2014), this subtype of salience is referred to as *cognitive salience* in the following.

Across theories and approaches, cognitive salience has been accessed in a fairly strong context- or discourse-dependent manner. At the largely context-detached end of this scale are approaches like the one proposed by Geeraerts (2000), who draws on salience in modelling lexical relations from an onomasiological perspective. He defines salience in entrenchment-based terms and independently of external/situational contextual conditions as a function of the relative frequency with which speakers have experienced a particular association between a concept (*signifié*) and a linguistic form (*signifiant*) (see Geeraerts, Chapter 7, this volume). At the more strongly context-focused end are text- and discourse-focused approaches, among which, however, salience definitions still vary markedly in their degrees of context-dependence.

Text- and discourse-focused approaches start from the basic assumption that comprehenders have to construct meaning in a way that allows for the current discourse to be perceived as coherent. They assume that language-users have to draw on and/or establish connections between many knowledge resources in order to achieve this: the experienced forms, their background knowledge about these forms and their meanings, and their knowledge about the nonlinguistic information they have recently received and/or are currently receiving from external (situational and social) context. Cognitive salience comes into this picture in the form of the following central question: What determines which among the many knowledge structures associated with a particular form are salient (i.e., accessible) enough to eventually become selected for processing?

Current theories suggest the following: A knowledge structure is the more likely to become activated, and thus the more cognitively salient, (a) the more deeply entrenched it is (independently of specific context), and (b) the more compatible it is with the current discourse context. One major point of debate across approaches is how these two potential sources of cognitive salience are related and which of the two, if any, has priority. This is also the main cause of divergences in the use of the term *salience*. Across theories and investigations, salience is variably used for referring to the accessibility of either context-independent, entrenchment-based knowledge structures (e.g., Giora, 2003; Giora, Raphaely, Fein, & Livnat, 2014) or context-dependent knowledge structures, that is, memory traces from the currently ongoing discourse (e.g., Ariel, 1990; Chiarcos, Claus, & Grabski, 2011; Gundel, Hedberg, & Zacharski, 1993; Jaszczolt & Allan, 2011). However, findings from experimental research (e.g., Brown-Schmidt, Byron, & Tanenhaus, 2005; Kaiser & Trueswell, 2008) call these opposing positions into question by identifying in particular those definitions of salience that focus exclusively on the current discourse context as too narrow.

How context-dependent and context-independent factors interact in rendering knowledge structures cognitively salient has yet to be clarified by future research (see Jaeger & Weatherholtz, 2016; Schmid & Günther, 2016). Such research will also have to address an issue that has emerged as central from the discussion of sociolinguistic approaches to salience provided above: To what extent is salience-induced attentional behavior driven by individual-specific relative to interindividually valid factors and principles?

This issue is highly relevant for explaining how interlocutors can communicate successfully at all, that is, arrive at sufficiently similar discourse models despite the fact that they construe meaning based on their own, individual knowledge structures. One way in which this might be achieved is that interlocutors (a) exchange salience-inducing signals through their choice of particular linguistic constructions; and (b) send out or draw on other, nonlinguistic signals in situational and social context.

Functional approaches to linguistics (e.g., Givón, 1983, 2001)—including many of the discourse approaches referred to above—embrace the idea that the choice of a particular linguistic structure for expressing a certain thought or making a reference to a particular item or event is associated with structuring the content to be expressed in terms of the prominence, relevance, or salience of its components. This idea is captured by the concept of information structure. In addition, it is a core idea in cognitive linguistics, in particular, Cognitive Grammar, in which it is enshrined in the concept of *construal* (e.g., Langacker, 2008, pp. 66–73; Verhagen, 2007).

What these theories have in common is, first, that what functions as main-salience markers are not lexical items, but what is in traditional terms classified as grammatical structures. In line with cognitive linguistic theories, this identifies these structures as meaningful. Second, members of both theoretical camps at least tacitly seem to assume that speakers agree relatively strongly as to which structural variant realizes which salience pattern. This entails the assumption that the precondition for linguistic salience signals to work—a high degree of conventionalization—is fulfilled. This idea of a one-to-one mapping between particular linguistic forms and particular salience patterns might be seen supported by evidence from alignment research (e.g., H. H. Clark & Wilkes-Gibbs, 1986; Garrod & Pickering, 2004, 2007), which suggests that interlocutors tend to adapt to each other's choice of (grammatical) constructions. This presumably renders communication more efficient, making it easier to arrive at a joint focus of attention when asked to solve a communicative task that requires interaction with items in the situational context, such as identifying, moving around, or sorting objects (see, e.g., Barr & Keysar, 2002; Metzing & Brennan, 2003).

Such contexts of situated referential language use, that is, of the use of language for referring to an item that is currently visually accessible to the language user(s), also constitute the major area in which external nonlinguistic salience signals, and their interaction with linguistic signals, have been investigated. With such research, two central salience-associated functions of language have been accorded particular attention: first, the function of language as an attention-directing device, that is, as a *source* of (visual-perceptual) salience (language-to-perception effects); and, second, the function of language as an indicator of a speakers' current attentional state, and thus as a *carrier* of salience (perception-to-language effects).

Evidence in support of perception-to-language effects has been provided by research that demonstrates the following: Visual items that have been rendered top-down salient by means of overt (e.g., Tomlin, 1995, 1997) or covert/subliminal (e.g., Gleitman, January, Nappa, & Trueswell, 2007) visual cueing are mentioned earlier in referential utterances than their less salient competitors, and/or occupy more prominent functional slots, such as the subject slot, in sentence-level constructions (see also Tomlin & Myachykov, 2015). In addition, there is even evidence indicating that the salience structure of the visual input can induce speakers to make use of disfavored linguistic constructions (Gleitman et al., 2007), which are constructions that are not as deeply entrenched in these speakers' minds as their functionally and largely equivalent alternatives. Such findings suggest that speakers indeed often make use of external salience signals in selecting linguistic constructions for use. That they are flexible in doing so is, among other things, indicated by evidence in support of reverse, language-to-perception effects.

Such evidence has recently been provided by studies that make use of variants of the *visual world* paradigm. What is characteristic of this paradigm is that language users' eye movements are recorded while they listen to or produce language that refers to a currently perceived scene (see, for example, Hartsuiker, Huettig, & Olivers, 2011; Huettig, Rommers, & Meyer, 2011; Salverda, Brown, & Tanenhaus, 2011). Studies of this type have demonstrated that eye movements to a visual item are time-locked to the active or passive use of its linguistic label (e.g., Altmann & Kamide, 2004; Cooper, 1974; Griffin & Bock, 2000; Tanenhaus, Spivey-Knowlton, Eberhard, & Sedivy, 1995). In addition, they have provided relatively robust evidence indicating that specific perceptual-attentional effects can differentially be triggered by the (current)[3] use of

---

[3] The highly controversial issue of more permanent/pervasive "Whorfian" effects will not be discussed here. For a discussion and overview, see, for example, Wolff and Holmes (2011) and Günther (2016).

particular grammatical patterns (e.g., Altmann & Kamide, 2004, 2007; Flecken, von Stutterheim, & Carroll, 2014) or (complex) construction types (Günther, 2016; Papafragou, Hulbert, & Trueswell, 2008).

There is, however, evidence which indicates that language hardly ever interacts exclusively with visual perception (e.g., Bock, Irwin, & Davidson, 2004) and that language-to-perception effects of the type just reported can become subject to considerable modulation by influences from other potential top-down sources of salience in external and/or internal contexts. Among those count, for example, nonverbal signals (e.g., Hanna & Brennan, 2007), explicit or implicit communicative tasks (Montag & MacDonald, 2014; Salverda et al., 2011), a speaker's "individual-focusing history" (Strohner, Sichelschmidt, Duwe, & Kessler, 2000, p. 510), a speaker's language (e.g., Bock, Irwin, Davidson, & Levelt, 2003), or a speaker's individual patterns of entrenched linguistic knowledge (Günther, 2016; Schmid & Günther, 2016).

On the one hand, such findings indicate that we are still far away from fully understanding how—if at all—interlocutors can arrive at discourse models that are similar in content and salience structure. However, since they have emerged from investigations of the interactions and interrelations between language in use and visual perception, these findings, on the other hand, open up further perspectives for future joint linguistic-psychological research that can build on an already existing tradition of empirical research at the boundary between these two disciplines. Concrete proposals for such research will be provided in Section 13.3.3, together with further ideas for future interdisciplinary cooperation.

This is, however, not the only reason why the findings from language-perception research just reported are highly relevant to the present discussion. They also have theoretical implications that can centrally contribute to reconciling the different approaches to salience just introduced and discussed. This issue is addressed in Section 13.3.2. Prior to this, an overview of the picture of salience that has emerged so far is provided in Section 13.3.1.

13.3 Discussion

13.3.1 Defining Salience I: Dimensions of Variation

Considered together, the psychological and linguistic approaches to salience presented in this chapter suggest that the following dimensions of variation are centrally relevant for modelling salience:

- *Dimension 1. Sources* of salience—salience can be triggered by a range of different bottom-up/stimulus-inherent or top-down factors.
- *Dimension 2. Carriers* of salience—salience can variably be associated with linguistic or nonlinguistic items, as well as with different features of these items such as color, shape, or location in the visual domain, or form versus meaning,

and sounds versus words versus complex "grammatical" constructions in the linguistic domain.
- *Dimension 3. Domains* of salience—salience can be defined as the distinctiveness of an item relative to its surrounding items (and thus as a phenomenon that is located in the perceptual domain[4]) or with regard to the accessibility of a stimulus in long-term memory (and thus relative to the cognitive domain).
- *Dimension 4. Loci* of salience—salience can be defined relative to individuals (individual perspective) or relative to the collective of a society or speech community (social perspective).
- *Dimension 5. Manifestations* of salience—an item can be rendered salient because it meets or collides with observers'/language-users' perceptual, cognitive, or action-related expectations.

As has been shown above, these dimensions, first, interrelate and/or cross-cut each other in multiple ways, and, second, are differently central to psychological and linguistic research and theory formation. The dimension of *sources* is, for instance, extremely central to experimental psychology, whereas the dimensions of *domains* and *loci* constitute major issues in linguistics, or, rather, across different linguistic approaches.

This finding of discipline-internal and interdisciplinary variation gives rise to the following questions: Given the diversity of salience approaches, is it still possible and indeed useful to postulate one unified meta-concept of SALIENCE, or would it instead be more adequate to speak of different "saliences," or even resort to different terms altogether for the different phenomena? And, given the main focus of this volume: How does entrenchment fit into this picture? These issues are addressed in Section 13.3.2.

13.3.2 Defining Salience II: SALIENCE or Saliences

At first sight, at least some of the approaches to salience presented in this chapter seem considerably remote from each other. However, based on the following observations and considerations a holistic meta-concept of SALIENCE might still be applicable even cross-disciplinarily (see also Jaeger & Weatherholtz, 2016; Schmid & Günther, 2016).

Differentiating between several clearly delimited *source*-defined saliences (Dimension 1) appears problematic given that most of the research reported above (Section 13.2) found that there is hardly ever one single source of salience. Instead, what was hypothesized to be this source is revealed to interact in complex ways with other contextual factors. Not drawing a clear-cut dividing line between different source-defined saliences seems even more justified if one takes into account

---

[4] Note, however, that this form of salience is not equivalent to physical salience, as it includes contributions from top-down/contextual factors.

that what is (in specific studies) taken to be the *major* source of salience and what is defined as *contextual factors* that modulate the effects of this source might to a considerable extent be an artifact of the specific research questions asked, the corresponding choice of design, and the theoretical perspectives taken during data interpretation (see also Anderson, Chiu, Huette, & Spivey, 2011, p. 182).

An integrative perspective on variation along Dimensions 2 and 3, that is, on different views of what are the *carriers* and *domains* of salience, is suggested by the findings reported above that language can influence perception and vice versa (see Section 13.2.2). These findings lend very strong support to theories of embodied cognition, in particular simulation-based ones (e.g., Barsalou, 1999, 2008; Glenberg, de Vega, & Graesser, 2008; Meteyard, Cuadrado, Bahrami, & Vigliocco, 2012; Pecher & Zwaan, 2005). These theories hold that perception, action, and language operate on analogous formats of knowledge representation and are controlled by the same sets of general cognitive mechanisms, including attention (see also Anderson et al., 2011; Thompson-Schill, 2003). This entails, first, that a multimodal experience, such as the experience of situated referential language use, results in the formation of one joint cognitive representation of the (referential) situation (see, for example, Huettig, Olivers, & Hartsuiker, 2011). Second, it indicates that attentional processes can act on this representation just as they can act on the external information that feeds into it. Since the same accounts for information stored in long-term memory, embodied-cognition models also provide a basis for accommodating in one framework contextual and context-detached salience mechanisms. On such a strongly cognition-focused, representation-based view, attentional processes occurring in the cognitive domain thus emerge as a necessary consequence of attentional processes in the external/perceptual domain, and consequently, as the processes that should be the major focus of interest and investigation (see, for example, Altmann & Kamide, 2007; Iani, Nicoletti, Rubichi, & Umiltà, 2001; Theeuwes, Kramer, & Irwin, 2011; Vecera & Farah, 1994). Accepting this, it becomes possible to accommodate under one general, primarily cognitively defined SALIENCE-concept even seemingly very distant approaches such as bottom-up-driven perceptual views and accessibility-focused linguistic theories.

What, at first sight, proves more difficult to accommodate under this strongly cognition-focused view is variation along Dimension 4 (i.e., variation in focus on either the *individual* or the *collective* perspective). This is due to the fact that a focus on cognitive representations naturally correlates with a focus on the individual. From a simulation-based embodied perspective, this does not, however, result in an exclusion of the collective perspective. Instead, by modelling knowledge as derived from perceptual interaction with the environment and as represented in such perceptual terms, embodied-cognition approaches provide a framework in which social-interactive components of experiences can become part of general knowledge. Although existing models do not (yet) provide a complete solution to the question of how the individual and the collective interact exactly, they at least provide a framework in which learning from and about social context could readily be integrated.

This learning-related issue also proves central to addressing the following questions: First, (how) can variation along Dimension 5 (*expectation-driven* vs. *surprisal-driven salience*) be reconciled? And, second, which role does entrenchment play in this context, as well as in the more general context of defining salience and salience-driven mechanisms? These questions are closely interrelated. On the one hand, the formation of expectations (as top-down sources of salience) presupposes the availability and accessibility of stored/entrenched knowledge (cognitive salience). On the other hand, what is rendered salient and thus attended to either because it is in line with top-down expectations, or because it violates these expectations, or because it displays certain highly conspicuous inherent features (bottom-up salience), is most likely to become entrenched and be used as a basis for expectation-formation in the future. This indicates that understanding the role of entrenchment relative to salience is strongly intertwined with understanding the interplay between (different forms of) top-down and bottom-up salience.

It is assumed here that entrenchment, top-down salience, and bottom-up salience interact in a complex manner that can perhaps best be described as a *feedback loop* (see Günther, 2016). First, cognitive salience constitutes the precondition for top-down salience, and thus also the starting point of any top-down/expectation-driven forms of attentional behavior. Second, if one accepts that becoming cognitively represented and thus actively processed in current working memory constitutes the major purpose (or effect) of attention allocation (see, e.g., Desimone & Duncan, 1995; Iani et al., 2001), cognitive salience also constitutes the end-stage of attentional processes driven by top-down/surprisal-induced and bottom-up salience mechanisms. As a consequence, processes of *salience transfer* from bottom-up and surprisal-induced salience to expectation-driven salience are likely to occur as a result of bottom-up and surprisal-induced attentional events, in particular, repeated ones. Initially bottom-up salient or surprising information is likely to become entrenched and thus to be used for making predictions, that is, to become cognitively salient on later occasions. In addition, it might also be the case that pre-activated knowledge structures (expectations) gain even more representational strength if they match the experienced information, that is, (further) entrenchment might occur as an effect of the repeated confirmation of predictions. On this view, entrenchment can variably be driven by bottom-up salient, surprising, and/or expected and thus already deeply entrenched information. This in turn indicates that high frequency of experience can, but does not always have to be a central entrenchment-relevant factor. Furthermore, it reveals that attention (as a salience-driven process) both contributes to modulating the patterns of entrenched knowledge in an individual and, at the same time, is at least partly controlled by the current state of entrenched knowledge in this same individual.

For our understanding of how salience and entrenchment interact it seems essential to take into account (a) when, that is, under what conditions, salience is driven by stimulus-inherent properties, by surprisal, or by the confirmation of expectations; and (b) what are the cognitive/memory-related effects of attentional behavior triggered by these different mechanisms. And, very crucially for the present discussion, throwing light on these issues also proves central to defining more clearly a general metaconcept of SALIENCE because their cognitive/memory-effects constitute the major level on which these different *source-* and *manifestations*-defined salience types can become related and eventually integrated (see also Schmid & Günther, 2016).

Taking for granted that this constitutes a challenge still to be met by future research, only a very provisional sketch of what might become a definition of the metaconcept of SALIENCE can be provided here. In light of what has been discussed in this section, SALIENCE could provisionally be defined as a multidimensional set of processes which effect that cognitively represented information (variably originating from sensory input or long-term memory) becomes selected for current processing by a particular individual at a particular point in time in a particular constellation of external (social and situational) and internal (cognitive) contexts.

Although this idea of SALIENCE is still very general, aiming toward an integrative view of SALIENCE is still considered here a theoretically more useful and sound approach than opting for several saliences. The reasons for this are as follows. First, as has just been shown, a clear-cut differentiation between salience types is hardly possible within each of the proposed dimensions. That is, speaking of different saliences on a dimension-internal level does not seem appropriate. Second, as regards the option of differentiating between dimension-specific saliences, the psychological and the linguistic research presented in Section 13.2 clearly indicate that unidimensional saliences are not suited for capturing salience-induced attentional phenomena and their effects in a cognitively realistic manner. Third, different discipline-specific saliences constitute a major obstacle to interdisciplinary research, whereas the modelling of SALIENCE as a multidimensional but holistic concept allows for the identification of many points of contact between disciplines. In particular, it allows for identifying different approaches to salience as resulting from differences in emphasis on some dimensions (or factors within these dimensions) rather than others. This difference in emphasis, again, largely corresponds to different selective perspectives on the same general phenomenon. On this view, interdisciplinary research, as well as better inner- and cross-disciplinary communication and cooperation, would open up a major chance of arriving at a more holistic and thus more cognitively realistic picture of salience, as well as of salience-related processes and their effects. Some concrete research questions that derive from this view, and that could be addressed by future joint psychological-linguistic research are proposed in the following Section.

13.4 Some Perspectives on Future (Joint) Research

Future joint research could add on to the already existing tradition of language-perception research (see Section 13.2.2). Questions to be addressed could be: What is the exact mixture of sources of salience on particular occasions of situated referential language use? Do the different sources interact, and how so? Or, on even more general grounds: What are apt measures for language-induced visual perception? Is language indeed fully comparable to other sources and/or carriers of salience, or is it still "special" in certain respects, and if so, in which?

A second major area of fresh interdisciplinary research could derive from what is discussed in Section 13.3.2. One aim of future cooperations could be to explore in detail the interrelations between learning/entrenchment and the different dimensions of salience, in particular, the different manifestations of salience (Dimension 5). Concrete questions that could be asked in this context include: (What determines) which aspects of attended information do indeed add onto and/or modulate patterns of entrenched knowledge, that is, under what conditions does cognitive salience trigger entrenchment processes? (In how far) does this relate to or even depend on whether salience was triggered by the confirmation of expectations or by surprisal? Which information units really become reactivated from long-term memory or influence future attentional behavior, and why? And, finally, can these questions be answered in similar ways for linguistic and nonlinguistic units of information and types of behavior?

References

Altmann, G. T. M., & Kamide, Y. (2004). Now you see it, now you don't: Mediating the mapping between language and the visual world. In J. M. Henderson & F. Ferreira (Eds.), *The interface of language, vision, and action* (pp. 347–387). New York, NY: Psychology Press.

Altmann, G. T. M., & Kamide, Y. (2007). The real-time mediation of visual attention by language and world knowledge: Linking anticipatory (and other) eye movements to linguistic processing. *Journal of Memory and Language, 57*, 502–518. http://dx.doi.org/10.1016/j.jml.2006.12.004

Anderson, S. E., Chiu, E., Huette, S., & Spivey, M. J. (2011). On the temporal dynamics of language-mediated vision and vision-mediated language. *Acta Psychologica, 137*, 181–189. http://dx.doi.org/10.1016/j.actpsy.2010.09.008

Ariel, M. (1990). *Accessing noun phase antecedents*. London, England: Routledge.

Auer, P. (2014). Anmerkungen zum Salienzbegriff in der Soziolinguistik [Notes on the notion of salience in sociolinguistics]. *Linguistik Online, 66*. Retrieved from http://www.bop.unibe.ch/linguistik-online/issue/view/388

Auer, P., Barden, B., & Grosskopf, B. (1998). Subjective and objective parameters determining 'salience' in long-term dialect accommodation. *Journal of Sociolinguistics, 2*, 163–187. http://dx.doi.org/10.1111/1467-9481.00039

Bacon, W. F., & Egeth, H. E. (1994). Overriding stimulus-driven attentional capture. *Perception & Psychophysics, 55*, 485–496. http://dx.doi.org/10.3758/BF03205306

Baldauf, D., & Deubel, H. (2010). Attentional landscapes in reaching and grasping. *Vision Research, 50*, 999–1013. http://dx.doi.org/10.1016/j.visres.2010.02.008

Barlow, M., & Kemmer, S. (Eds.). (2000). *Usage-based models of language*. Stanford, CA: CSLI.

Barr, D. J., & Keysar, B. (2002). Anchoring comprehension in linguistic precedents. *Journal of Memory and Language, 46*, 391–418. http://dx.doi.org/10.1006/jmla.2001.2815

Barsalou, L. W. (1999). Perceptual symbol systems. *Behavioral and Brain Sciences, 22*, 577–609.
Barsalou, L. W. (2008). Grounded cognition. *Annual Review of Psychology, 59*, 617–645. http://dx.doi.org/10.1146/annurev.psych.59.103006.093639
Belopolsky, A. V., Schreij, D., & Theeuwes, J. (2010). What is top-down about contingent capture? *Attention, Perception, & Psychophysics, 72*, 326–341. http://dx.doi.org/10.3758/APP.72.2.326
Bisley, J. W., & Goldberg, M. E. (2010). Attention, intention, and priority in the parietal lobe. *Annual Review of Neuroscience, 33*, 1–21. http://dx.doi.org/10.1146/annurev-neuro-060909-152823
Bock, J. K., Irwin, D. E., & Davidson, D. J. (2004). Putting first things first. In J. M. Henderson & F. Ferreira (Eds.), *The interface of language, vision, and action* (pp. 249–278). New York, NY: Psychology Press.
Bock, J. K., Irwin, D. E., Davidson, D. J., & Levelt, W. J. M. (2003). Minding the clock. *Journal of Memory and Language, 48*, 653–685. http://dx.doi.org/10.1016/S0749-596X(03)00007-X
Brown-Schmidt, S., Byron, D. K., & Tanenhaus, M. K. (2005). Beyond salience: Interpretation of personal and demonstrative pronouns. *Journal of Memory and Language, 53*, 292–313. http://dx.doi.org/10.1016/j.jml.2005.03.003
Chiarcos, C., Claus, B., & Grabski, M. (Eds.). (2011). *Salience: Multidisciplinary perspectives on its function in discourse.* http://dx.doi.org/10.1515/9783110241020
Clark, A. (2013). Whatever next? Predictive brains, situated agents, and the future of cognitive science. *Behavioral and Brain Sciences, 36*, 181–204. http://dx.doi.org/10.1017/S0140525X12000477
Clark, H. H., & Wilkes-Gibbs, D. (1986). Referring as a collaborative process. *Cognition, 22*, 1–39. http://dx.doi.org/10.1016/0010-0277(86)90010-7
Cooper, R. M. (1974). The control of eye fixation by the meaning of spoken language: A new methodology for the real-time investigation of speech perception, memory, and language processing. *Cognitive Psychology, 6*, 84–107. http://dx.doi.org/10.1016/0010-0285(74)90005-X
Dennett, D. C. (1989). *The intentional stance.* Cambridge, MA: MIT Press.
Desimone, R., & Duncan, J. (1995). Neural mechanisms of selective visual attention. *Annual Review of Neuroscience, 18*, 193–222. http://dx.doi.org/10.1146/annurev.ne.18.030195.001205
Docherty, G. J., & Foulkes, P. (2014). An evaluation of usage-based approaches to the modelling of sociophonetic variability. *Lingua, 142*, 42–56. http://dx.doi.org/10.1016/j.lingua.2013.01.011
Flecken, M., von Stutterheim, C., & Carroll, M. (2014). Grammatical aspect influences motion event perception: Findings from a cross-linguistic non-verbal recognition task. *Language and Cognition, 6*, 45–78. http://dx.doi.org/10.1017/langcog.2013.2
Folk, C. L., Remington, R. W., & Johnston, J. C. (1992). Involuntary covert orienting is contingent on attentional control settings. *Journal of Experimental Psychology: Human Perception and Performance, 18*, 1030–1044. http://dx.doi.org/10.1037/0096-1523.18.4.1030
Found, A., & Müller, H. J. (1996). Searching for unknown feature targets on more than one dimension: Investigating a "dimension-weighting" account. *Perception & Psychophysics, 58*, 88–101. http://dx.doi.org/10.3758/BF03205479
Friston, K. (2010). The free-energy principle: A unified brain theory? *Nature Reviews Neuroscience, 11*, 127–138. http://dx.doi.org/10.1038/nrn2787
Garrod, S., & Pickering, M. J. (2004). Why is conversation so easy? *Trends in Cognitive Sciences, 8*, 8–11. http://dx.doi.org/10.1016/j.tics.2003.10.016
Garrod, S., & Pickering, M. J. (2007). Alignment in dialogue. In G. Gaskell (Ed.), *Oxford handbook of psycholinguistics* (pp. 443–451). Oxford, England: Oxford University Press.

Geeraerts, D. (2000). Salience phenomena in the lexicon: A typology. In L. Albertazzi (Ed.), *Meaning and cognition: A multidisciplinary approach* (pp. 79–101). http://dx.doi.org/10.1075/celcr.2.05gee

Geyer, T., Müller, H. J., & Krummenacher, J. (2008). Expectancies modulate attentional capture by salient color singletons. *Vision Research, 48,* 1315–1326. http://dx.doi.org/10.1016/j.visres.2008.02.006

Giles, H., Coupland, N., & Coupland, J. (1991). Accommodation theory: Communication, context, and consequence. In H. Giles, J. Coupland, & N. Coupland (Eds.), *Contexts of accommodation: Developments in applied sociolinguistics* (pp. 1–68). http://dx.doi.org/10.1017/CBO9780511663673.001

Giora, R. (2003). *On our mind: Salience, context, and figurative language.* http://dx.doi.org/10.1093/acprof:oso/9780195136166.001.0001

Giora, R., Raphaely, M., Fein, O., & Livnat, E. (2014). Resonating with contextually inappropriate interpretations in production: The case of irony. *Cognitive Linguistics, 25,* 443–455. http://dx.doi.org/10.1515/cog-2014-0026

Givón, T. (1983). Introduction. In T. Givón (Ed.), *Topic continuity in discourse: A quantitative cross-language study* (pp. 5–41). http://dx.doi.org/10.1075/tsl.3

Givón, T. (2001). *Syntax* (2nd ed.). Amsterdam, the Netherlands: Benjamins.

Gleitman, L. R., January, D., Nappa, R., & Trueswell, J. C. (2007). On the give and take between event apprehension and utterance formulation. *Journal of Memory and Language, 57,* 544–569. http://dx.doi.org/10.1016/j.jml.2007.01.007

Glenberg, A. M., de Vega, M., & Graesser, A. C. (2008). Framing the debate. In M. de Vega, A. M. Glenberg, & A. C. Graesser (Eds.), *Symbols and embodiment: Debates on meaning and cognition* (pp. 1–10). http://dx.doi.org/10.1093/acprof:oso/9780199217274.003.0001

Gökce, A., Geyer, T., Finke, K., Müller, H. J., & Töllner, T. (2014). What pops out in positional priming of pop-out: Insights from event-related EEG lateralizations. *Frontiers in Psychology, 5,* 688. http://dx.doi.org/10.3389/fpsyg.2014.00688

Gozli, D. G., & Pratt, J. (2011). Seeing while acting: Hand movements can modulate attentional capture by motion onset. *Attention, Perception, & Psychophysics, 73,* 2448–2456. http://dx.doi.org/10.3758/s13414-011-0203-x

Griffin, Z. M., & Bock, K. (2000). What the eyes say about speaking. *Psychological Science, 11,* 274–279. http://dx.doi.org/10.1111/1467-9280.00255

Gundel, J. K., Hedberg, N., & Zacharski, R. (1993). Cognitive status and the form of referring expressions in discourse. *Language, 69,* 274–307. http://dx.doi.org/10.2307/416535

Günther, F. (2016). *Constructions in cognitive contexts: Why individuals matter in linguistic relativity research.* Berlin, Germany: De Gruyter Mouton.

Hanna, J. E., & Brennan, S. E. (2007). Speakers' eye gaze disambiguates referring expressions early during face-to-face conversation. *Journal of Memory and Language, 57,* 596–615. http://dx.doi.org/10.1016/j.jml.2007.01.008

Hartsuiker, R. J., Huettig, F., & Olivers, C. N. L. (2011). Visual search and visual world: Interactions among visual attention, language, and working memory (introduction to the special issue). *Acta Psychologica, 137,* 135–137. http://dx.doi.org/10.1016/j.actpsy.2011.01.005

Honeybone, P., & Watson, K. (2013). Salience and the sociolinguistics of Scouse spelling: Exploring the phonology of the contemporary humorous localised dialect literature of Liverpool. *English World-Wide, 34,* 305–340. http://dx.doi.org/10.1075/eww.34.3.03hon

Houston-Price, C., & Nakai, S. (2004). Distinguishing novelty and familiarity effects in infant preference procedures. *Infant and Child Development, 13*, 341–348. http://dx.doi.org/10.1002/icd.364

Huettig, F., Olivers, C. N. L., & Hartsuiker, R. J. (2011). Looking, language, and memory: Bridging research from the visual world and visual search paradigms. *Acta Psychologica, 137*, 138–150. http://dx.doi.org/10.1016/j.actpsy.2010.07.013

Huettig, F., Rommers, J., & Meyer, A. S. (2011). Using the visual world paradigm to study language processing: A review and critical evaluation. *Acta Psychologica, 137*, 151–171. http://dx.doi.org/10.1016/j.actpsy.2010.11.003

Iani, C., Nicoletti, R., Rubichi, S., & Umiltà, C. (2001). Shifting attention between objects. *Cognitive Brain Research, 11*, 157–164. http://dx.doi.org/10.1016/S0926-6410(00)00076-8

Jaeger, T. F., & Weatherholtz, K. (2016). What the heck is salience? How predictive language processing contributes to sociolinguistic perception. *Frontiers in Psychology, 7*. http://dx.doi.org/10.3389/fpsyg.2016.01115

Jaszczolt, K. M., & Allan, K. (Eds.). (2011). *Salience and defaults in utterance processing.* http://dx.doi.org/10.1515/9783110270679

Kaiser, E., & Trueswell, J. C. (2008). Interpreting pronouns and demonstratives in Finnish: Evidence for a form-specific approach to reference resolution. *Language and Cognitive Processes, 23*, 709–748. http://dx.doi.org/10.1080/01690960701771220

Kerswill, P., & Williams, A. (2002). 'Salience' as an explanatory factor in language change: Evidence from dialect levelling in urban England. In M. C. Jones, & E. Esch (Eds.), *Language change: The interplay of internal, external and extra-linguistic factors* (pp. 81–110). Berlin, Germany: De Gruyter Mouton.

Labov, W. (1972). *Sociolinguistic patterns.* Philadelphia: University of Pennsylvania Press.

Labov, W. (2014). The sociophonetic orientation of the language learner. In C. Celata & S. Calamai (Eds.), *Advances in sociophonetics* (pp. 17–28). http://dx.doi.org/10.1075/silv.15.01lab

Langacker, R. W. (1987). *Foundations of cognitive grammar: Vol. 1. Theoretical prerequisites.* Stanford, CA: Stanford University Press.

Langacker, R. W. (2008). *Cognitive grammar: A basic introduction.* http://dx.doi.org/10.1093/acprof:oso/9780195331967.001.0001

Lenz, A. N. (2010). Zum Salienzbegriff und zum Nachweis Salienter Merkmale [On the concept of salience and on providing evidence of salient features]. In A. C. Anders, M. Hundt, & A. Lasch (Eds.), *Perceptual Dialectology: Neue Wege der Dialektologie* [Perceptual Dialectology: New Directions in Dialectology] (pp. 89–110). Berlin, Germany: De Gruyter Mouton.

Meteyard, L., Cuadrado, S. R., Bahrami, B., & Vigliocco, G. (2012). Coming of age: A review of embodiment and the neuroscience of semantics. *Cortex, 48*, 788–804. http://dx.doi.org/10.1016/j.cortex.2010.11.002

Metzing, C., & Brennan, S. E. (2003). When conceptual pacts are broken: Partner-specific effects on the comprehension of referring expressions. *Journal of Memory and Language, 49*, 201–213. http://dx.doi.org/10.1016/S0749-596X(03)00028-7

Montag, J. L., & MacDonald, M. C. (2014). Visual salience modulates structure choice in relative clause production. *Language and Speech, 57*, 163–180. http://dx.doi.org/10.1177/0023830913495656

Müller, H. J., Geyer, T., Zehetleitner, M., & Krummenacher, J. (2009). Attentional capture by salient color singleton distractors is modulated by top-down dimensional set. *Journal of Experimental*

Psychology: Human Perception and Performance, 35, 1–16. http://dx.doi.org/10.1037/0096-1523.35.1.1

Müller, H. J., Heller, D., & Ziegler, J. (1995). Visual search for singleton feature targets within and across feature dimensions. *Perception & Psychophysics, 57*, 1–17. http://dx.doi.org/10.3758/BF03211845

Müller, H. J., & Rabbitt, P. M. (1989). Reflexive and voluntary orienting of visual attention: Time course of activation and resistance to interruption. *Journal of Experimental Psychology: Human Perception and Performance, 15*, 315–330. http://dx.doi.org/10.1037/0096-1523.15.2.315

Müsseler, J., & Hommel, B. (1997). Blindness to response-compatible stimuli. *Journal of Experimental Psychology: Human Perception and Performance, 23*, 861–872. http://dx.doi.org/10.1037/0096-1523.23.3.861

Paoletti, D., Weaver, M. D., Braun, C., & van Zoest, W. (2015). Trading off stimulus salience for identity: A cueing approach to disentangle visual selection strategies. *Vision Research, 113*, 116–124. http://dx.doi.org/10.1016/j.visres.2014.08.003

Papafragou, A., Hulbert, J., & Trueswell, J. (2008). Does language guide event perception? Evidence from eye movements. *Cognition, 108*, 155–184. http://dx.doi.org/10.1016/j.cognition.2008.02.007

Pecher, D., & Zwaan, R. (Eds.). (2005). *Grounding cognition: The role of perception and action in memory, language, and thinking.* http://dx.doi.org/10.1017/CBO9780511499968

Posner, M. I. (1980). Orienting of attention. *Quarterly Journal of Experimental Psychology, 32*, 3–25. http://dx.doi.org/10.1080/00335558008248231

Purschke, C. (2014). "I remember it like it was interesting." Zur Theorie von Salienz und Pertinenz [On the theory of salience and pertinence]. *Linguistik Online* [Linguistics Online], *66*, 31–50. Retrieved from http://www.bop.unibe.ch/linguistik-online/issue/view/388

Rácz, P. (2013). *Salience in sociolinguistics.* http://dx.doi.org/10.1515/9783110305395

Salverda, A. P., Brown, M., & Tanenhaus, M. K. (2011). A goal-based perspective on eye movements in visual world studies. *Acta Psychologica, 137*, 172–180. http://dx.doi.org/10.1016/j.actpsy.2010.09.010

Schmid, H.-J. (2007). Entrenchment, salience, and basic levels. In D. Geeraerts & H. Cuyckens (Eds.), *The Oxford handbook of cognitive linguistics* (pp. 117–138). Oxford, England: Oxford University Press.

Schmid, H.-J. (2014). Lexico-grammatical patterns, pragmatic associations and discourse frequency. In T. Herbst, H.-J. Schmid, & S. Faulhaber (Eds.), *Constructions Collocations Patterns* (pp. 239–294). http://dx.doi.org/10.1515/9783110356854.239

Schmid, H.-J., & Günther, F. (2016). Toward a unified socio-cognitive framework for salience in language. *Frontiers in Psychology, 7*. http://dx.doi.org/10.3389/fpsyg.2016.01110

Strohner, H., Sichelschmidt, L., Duwe, I., & Kessler, K. (2000). Discourse focus and conceptual relations in resolving referential ambiguity. *Journal of Psycholinguistic Research, 29*, 497–516. http://dx.doi.org/10.1023/A:1005172126134

Tanenhaus, M. K., Spivey-Knowlton, M. J., Eberhard, K. M., & Sedivy, J. C. (1995). Integration of visual and linguistic information in spoken language comprehension. *Science, 268*, 1632–1634. http://dx.doi.org/10.1126/science.7777863

Teufel, C., Alexis, D. M., Todd, H., Lawrance-Owen, A. J., Clayton, N. S., & Davis, G. (2009). Social cognition modulates the sensory coding of observed gaze direction. *Current Biology, 19*, 1274–1277. http://dx.doi.org/10.1016/j.cub.2009.05.069

Theeuwes, J. (1991). Cross-dimensional perceptual selectivity. *Perception & Psychophysics*, *50*, 184–193. http://dx.doi.org/10.3758/BF03212219

Theeuwes, J., Kramer, A. F., & Irwin, D. E. (2011). Attention on our mind: The role of spatial attention in visual working memory. *Acta Psychologica*, *137*, 248–251. http://dx.doi.org/10.1016/j.actpsy.2010.06.011

Thompson-Schill, S. L. (2003). Neuroimaging studies of semantic memory: Inferring "how" from "where." *Neuropsychologia*, *41*, 280–292. http://dx.doi.org/10.1016/S0028-3932(02)00161-6

Töllner, T., Müller, H. J., & Zehetleitner, M. (2012). Top-down dimensional weight set determines the capture of visual attention: Evidence from the PCN component. *Cerebral Cortex*, *22*, 1554–1563. http://dx.doi.org/10.1093/cercor/bhr231

Tomasello, M. (2003). The key is social cognition. In D. Gentner & S. Goldin-Meadow (Eds.), *Language in mind: Advances in the study of language and thought* (pp. 47–57). Cambridge, MA: MIT Press.

Tomasello, M. (2009). The usage-based theory of language acquisition. In E. L. Bavin (Ed.), *The Cambridge handbook of child language* (pp. 69–88). http://dx.doi.org/10.1017/CBO9780511576164.005

Tomlin, R. S. (1995). Focal attention, voice, and word order. In P. Downing & M. Noonan (Eds.), *Word order in discourse* (pp. 517–554). http://dx.doi.org/10.1075/tsl.30.18tom

Tomlin, R. S. (1997). Mapping conceptual representations into linguistic representations: The role of attention in grammar. In J. Nuyts & E. Pederson (Eds.), *Language and conceptualization* (pp. 162–189). http://dx.doi.org/10.1017/CBO9781139086677.007

Tomlin, R. S., & Myachykov, A. (2015). Attention and salience. In E. Dąbrowska & D. Divjak (Eds.), *Handbook of cognitive linguistics* (pp. 31–52). http://dx.doi.org/10.1515/9783110292022-003

Tribus, M. (1961). *Thermostatics and thermodynamics: An introduction to energy, information and states of matter, with engineering applications.* New York, NY: Van Nostrand.

Trudgill, P. (1986). *Dialects in contact.* Oxford, England: Blackwell.

Van Dijk, T. A., & Kintsch, W. (1983). *Strategies of discourse comprehension.* New York, NY: Academic Press.

Vecera, S. P., & Farah, M. J. (1994). Does visual attention select objects or locations? *Journal of Experimental Psychology: General*, *123*, 146–160. http://dx.doi.org/10.1037/0096-3445.123.2.146

Verhagen, A. (2007). Construal and perspectivization. In D. Geeraerts & H. Cuyckens (Eds.), *The Oxford handbook of cognitive linguistics* (pp. 48–81). Oxford, England: Oxford University Press.

Wiese, E., Wykowska, A., Zwickel, J., & Müller, H. J. (2012). I see what you mean: How attentional selection is shaped by ascribing intentions to others. *PLoS ONE*, *7*, e45391. http://dx.doi.org/10.1371/journal.pone.0045391

Wolff, P., & Holmes, K. J. (2011). Linguistic relativity. *Wiley Interdisciplinary Reviews: Cognitive Science*, *2*, 253–265. http://dx.doi.org/10.1002/wcs.104

Wykowska, A., Schubö, A., & Hommel, B. (2009). How you move is what you see: Action planning biases selection in visual search. *Journal of Experimental Psychology: Human Perception and Performance*, *35*, 1755–1769. http://dx.doi.org/10.1037/a0016798

Wykowska, A., Wiese, E., Prosser, A., & Müller, H. J. (2014). Beliefs about the minds of others influence how we process sensory information. *PLoS ONE*, *9*, e94339. http://dx.doi.org/10.1371/journal.pone.0094339

Yaeger-Dror, M. (1993). Linguistic analysis of dialect "correction" and its interaction with cognitive salience. *Language Variation and Change*, *5*, 189–224. http://dx.doi.org/10.1017/S0954394500001460

Zehetleitner, M., Koch, A. I., Goschy, H., & Müller, H. J. (2013). Salience-based selection: Attentional capture by distractors less salient than the target. *PLoS ONE, 8*, e52595. http://dx.doi.org/10.1371/journal.pone.0052595

Zhaoping, L. (2014). *Understanding vision: Theory, models, and data.* http://dx.doi.org/10.1093/acprof:oso/9780199564668.001.0001

Zwickel, J., Grosjean, M., & Prinz, W. (2010). On interference effects in concurrent perception and action. *Psychological Research, 74*, 152–171. http://dx.doi.org/10.1007/s00426-009-0226-2

IV Entrenchment in Language Learning and Language Attrition

Anna L. Theakston
14 Entrenchment in First Language Learning

14.1 Introduction

The majority of researchers working in the domain of children's language acquisition acknowledge the existence of frequency or entrenchment effects. However, their significance in terms of the underlying learning mechanism remains the subject of debate (see Ambridge, Kidd, Rowland, & Theakston, 2015, for a review and commentaries). In this chapter, the ways in which entrenchment might operate in children's early language use over the course of acquisition are examined. First, the role of item-based collocations in children's early language is considered with respect to the processes of entrenchment and abstraction. Then the relation between the language children hear and what they learn is explored, with a particular focus on type and token frequencies. Next, the ways in which entrenchment and abstraction operate to influence children's production of grammatical errors are examined. Finally, the ways in which semantics, context, perceptual salience, and pragmatics interact with the learning of language, and work to support the entrenchment of forms, are considered from a developmental perspective, in which the shifting nature of linguistic representations is most evident. Throughout this chapter, the theoretical difficulties in defining entrenchment and abstraction will become apparent. On the one hand, entrenchment and abstraction are sometimes conceived of as opposing forces, with entrenched forms seen to inhibit the process of abstraction. On the other hand, the process of abstraction is thought to underlie the acquisition and entrenchment of more adultlike linguistic representations. Thus, one of the most critical questions for language-acquisition researchers is to determine precisely how the two processes interact to support children's comprehension and production of language across development.

14.2 Lexical Strings in Early Child Language

As evidenced elsewhere in this volume, in adult language the existence of frequent collocations or recurring strings in both written and spoken language is well established (Biber, Johansson, Leech, Conrad, & Finegan, 1999), most notably in the speech of sports commentators, auctioneers, and the like who are required to quickly and accurately convey information from scratch with little time to plan utterances (Kuiper, 1996). The use of collocations, varying in their degrees of specificity from the relatively

DOI 10.1515/9783110341423-015

fully specified (e.g., *How are you? X kicked the bucket*) to the relatively more flexible (e.g., *X found X's way PP, X let alone Y*) to the fully abstract (e.g., *X Verb Y*), is observed in normal everyday speech as well, and there is ample evidence that there are processing advantages associated with producing and interpreting frequently occurring strings (see Conklin & Schmitt, 2012, for an overview, and Schmid's introduction to this volume for further references).

In the language-acquisition field, researchers have sought to understand whether the speech addressed to children also exhibits these same distributional properties. A high degree of repetition in the input would provide children with exposure to high-frequency collocations which could then be used to support the child's initial learning of the grammar. Cameron-Faulkner, Lieven, and Tomasello (2003) carried out an extensive analysis of the speech addressed to 12 English-learning children between the ages of 2 to 3 years. They found that half of the maternal utterances addressed to the children could be characterized by 52 item-based frames, with 45% beginning with one of just 17 different words. Although other languages are not so consistent in their word order, analyses of languages such as German and Russian have revealed similar results (Stoll, Abbot-Smith, & Lieven, 2009), suggesting that even in so-called free(er) word-order languages, there is still a degree of repetition in the input that could facilitate the early acquisition of low-scope frames. Cameron-Faulkner et al. (2003) therefore argued that the distributional properties of the input were conducive to children's acquisition of lexical frames, and that entrenchment of these frames could provide a route into the more abstract linguistic system: "Whatever else it is, the acquisition of a language is the acquisition of a skill, and skills are crucially dependent on repetition and repetition with variation" (p. 868). In other work, researchers have demonstrated that computational models can derive grammatical-class information from child-directed speech (CDS) across a variety of languages (e.g., Croatian, English, Estonian, Dutch, French, Hebrew, Hungarian, Japanese, Sesotho) using a combination of distributional (overall word order and adjacency statistics; Chang, Lieven, & Tomasello, 2008) and phonological information (Monaghan, Christiansen, & Chater, 2007), with the different cues playing a greater or lesser role according to the typology of the language. Localized slot-and-frame patterns have also been used, with variable success depending on the precise distributional information made available (e.g., trigram vs. bigram frequencies in fixed or variable frames), to derive grammatical-category membership (Mintz, 2003; St. Clair, Monaghan, & Christiansen, 2010). Taken together, these different strands of work demonstrate that the kinds of distributional information found in the input, particularly where there are converging sources of evidence, can cross-linguistically support the acquisition of lexical strings and grammatical categories.

A wealth of evidence demonstrates that young children's early utterances are relatively less complex and abstract than those of their adult counterparts. Extending back to the early work of Braine and Bowerman (1976) and continuing into more recent work across a wide range of linguistic domains, the observed patterning of children's early multiword utterances has led researchers to posit the existence of low-scope formulae or frames as a means of characterizing children's underlying linguistic representations. Some suggest that rather than operating with the kinds of abstract schemas or rules for combining words into utterances that underpin the adult linguistic system, children rely more heavily on lexically specific formulae, that is, rules for combining words that are based around a particular word or phrase with a variable slot into which a range of different items can be inserted. For example, Braine and Bowerman (1976) described children's early utterances in terms of a pivot grammar, in which individual "pivot" words were used in combination with a range of other words to create high-frequency lexical frames (e.g., *more X*). Later work demonstrated that a large proportion of children's early utterances can be accounted for by a small number of high-frequency frames based around specific lexical items or multiword chunks (e.g., *It's a X, Where's X? What can X? I'm V-ing it*; Lieven, Pine, & Baldwin, 1997; Pine, Lieven, & Rowland, 1998). Frames have been posited to explain children's early use of determiners (Pine & Lieven, 1997), questions (Rowland & Pine, 2000), and auxiliary verbs (Theakston, Lieven, Pine, & Rowland, 2005), as well as early instances of grammatical constructions such as the transitive (Childers & Tomasello, 2001; Theakston, Maslen, Lieven, & Tomasello, 2012). Many of these frames show considerable overlap with the high-frequency collocations identified in CDS (Cameron-Faulkner et al., 2003).

Further studies found that these frames in early child language show relatively little overlap in their content, for example, with respect to the nouns produced with particular determiners (e.g., *a X* vs. *the Y*), and the main verbs used with particular auxiliaries (e.g., *can't X* vs. *don't Y*; Pine & Lieven, 1997; Pine et al., 1998). This apparent lack of overlap lends some support to the idea that the frames are individually learned from the input and, initially at least, contain lexically and/or semantically restricted slots. More direct evidence that children store multiword sequences comes from the finding that children are better able to repeat four-word sequences found frequently in CDS than less frequent four-word sequences, even when the frequency of the individual items and bigrams is carefully controlled (e.g., compare *a cup of tea* with *a cup of milk*; Bannard & Matthews, 2008). These frames are often described as being relatively "entrenched" in the child's system, that is, well-known enough to afford some degree of productivity on the part of the child but lacking full flexibility in use. Finally, there is also evidence that children (and sometimes adults) appear to rely on lexically based frames in the production of complex utterances. Diessel and Tomasello (2001) reported that children's earliest complement clauses are organized around only a small number of main verbs, while Dąbrowska, Rowland, and Theakston (2009) found that both children and adults were better able to repeat questions with long-distance dependencies (e.g., *What do you think the old man really likes?*) if the question began with a high-frequency collocation (e.g., *What do you think...?*) compared to questions taking the same grammatical form, but a less frequent collocation (e.g., *What does the old man think...?*).

14.3 The Role of Lexical Frames in the Abstraction of Grammatical Knowledge

That formulaic and semiformulaic utterances exist in children's early language is clear. However, their theoretical importance is subject to debate. Some researchers have argued that these low-scope frames are rote-learned and as such are not a direct reflection of the child's underlying linguistic system (e.g., Pinker, 1984; Radford, 1990). Others argue that they simply reflect the distributional properties of the input and the pragmatic contexts of use, as similar patterns of repetition are seen in adult language (Yang, 2013). Given that adults are clearly capable of producing more varied and abstract utterances should the situation demand it, some argue that this same knowledge should be attributed to children as well. Yet another perspective is to argue that children are capable of making linguistic abstractions but are also conservative learners, sticking close to the input in order to determine the particular combinatorial properties of individual lexical items (e.g., Fisher, 2002; Naigles, 2002). On the other hand, although it is obviously true that children's language use is likely to resemble that of an adult speaker as all human language is subject to the same general constraints (e.g., the perceptual system, memory, processing limitations), researchers working within a usage-based perspective argue that these frames form the starting point in the language-acquisition process. These frames are thought to allow children to gradually dissect and recombine linguistic elements to arrive at the degree of linguistic flexibility seen in adult speakers (e.g., Lieven, Salomo, & Tomasello, 2009; Tomasello, 1992).

From a usage-based perspective, early collocations are not seen as simply a dead end in language learning, used early on to bypass the communicative problems of operating with an immature grammar and/or limited vocabulary. Nor are they solely a reflection of extralinguistic and speaker-internal pressures on an adultlike linguistic system. Rather, they are viewed as the starting point from which children can begin to build a more abstract grammar. From these high-frequency strings, children are thought to generalize across lexical items to create more abstract frames, which eventually link up to create an adultlike grammar. For example, a child may group together lexical items that share similar distributional characteristics and form-function mappings to build categories (e.g., the utterances *I can't see it* and *I can't do it* combine to form a schema *I can't PROCESS it*; Lieven et al., 2009). Researchers have begun to demonstrate how children might use these entrenched high-frequency collocations and low-scope schemas as the building blocks from which to create longer, more complex utterances. In his diary data, Tomasello (1992) observed that for one child, there was added value in her use of individual verbs from her earlier productions with those same verbs, reflecting their cumulative frequency of use:

> In general, by far the best predictor of this child's use of a given verb on a given day was not her use of other verbs on that same day, but rather her use of that same verb on the immediately preceding days. (Tomasello, 2003, pp. 117–118)

This claim has been tested more widely using naturalistic data from 12 English-speaking children. McClure, Pine, and Lieven (2006) demonstrated that verb utterances produced at Stage 2 (mean length of utterance [MLU] 2.0–2.49) were more complex for verbs that had been acquired at Stage 1 (MLU < 2.0) and consequently had a higher cumulative frequency of use, than for verbs newly acquired at Stage 2 (see also Theakston et al., 2012, for a dense data analysis). One possibility is that entrenched items function to free up the child's processing resources as a result of automatization of chunking in memory or greater ease of retrieval (Logan, 1988), enabling them to extend their earlier productions. Computational modelling provides some support for the role of chunking in the gradual generation of more abstract utterances. Using a connectionist model exposed to CDS that encoded words from the ends of utterances and built up longer strings in a frequency-sensitive manner, Freudenthal, Pine, and Gobet (2007) replicated English-speaking children's changing rates of subject omission over development, demonstrating that the developmental pattern could be explained in terms of increasing exposure to repeated lexical forms and collocations.

Further evidence for the process of chunking comes from a series of studies that attempted to derive later utterances from those heard or produced earlier in development. At 2 years of age, it is possible to derive many of a child's apparently novel utterances by characterizing their earlier speech in terms of low-scope schemas (e.g., *a baby REFERENT*), motivated by their frequency of use, and making only very minor changes to them (substituting or adding items in a semantically constrained way, e.g., *a baby dragon*; Lieven et al., 2009). In a more robust test of this process, frequency-driven grammars of this type derived from child speech using a Bayesian computational model (Bannard, Lieven, & Tomasello, 2009) have been demonstrated to provide a better fit to children's early utterances than a more abstract grammar incorporating broad categories such as *noun* and *verb*. Thus, prior entrenchment of use of particular lexical collocations and low-scope variable frames appears to provide a plausible route into more abstract grammatical representations.

The process of abstraction and its relation to distributional patterns in the input can also be seen in studies comparing child productivity with patterns of use in adult speech. A recent study applying a number of novel analyses of early productivity with a number of important controls to children's use of nouns with transitive verbs demonstrates in detail the similarities and differences between children's early language and that of their caregivers (Theakston, Ibbotson, Freudenthal, Lieven, & Tomasello, 2015). Using densely collected naturalistic data from three children between the ages of 2 and 3 years, the authors showed that the relative degrees of flexibility evidenced in the children's use of different subjects and objects with their transitive verbs can be predicted by their caregivers' use of those same verbs, reflecting both input-based learning and the semantic affordances of the verbs in question. However, the analyses also revealed that the children's flexibility in the use of subjects and objects varied, with objects reaching adultlike flexibility earlier than subjects. This is thought to reflect the distributional properties of subject and object use in the input, namely, that the object slot typically has higher type frequency (and perhaps also greater semantic heterogeneity) than the subject slot. Moreover, as flexibility increased, both the degree of lexical overlap with the caregivers and the degree of unique items attested in the children's speech increased. Together, these analyses reveal that children's developing knowledge of how to produce transitive verbs relies on the entrenchment of frequent collocations from the input but also on the gradual abstraction of variable slots, defined in terms of their semantic affordances and variability in the input.

Although there is a growing body of evidence to suggest that children's ability to produce a range of sentence types develops only gradually toward adultlike levels of flexibility, much more work is needed to identify the precise conditions under which the kinds of "similarities" that lead to abstraction are registered. One possibility is that distributional co-occurrences can be used as a proxy for semantic similarity in the tradition of lexical semantic analysis (LSA), and there is evidence that this kind of approach can be effective in determining the scope of children's productivity (e.g., Matthews & Bannard, 2010).

Another suggestion is that the process of gradual abstraction may be particularly facilitated by the presence of variation sets in the input. In variation sets, successive utterances contain partial lexical overlap (e.g., *You got to push them to school, push them, push them to school, take them to school*; Onnis, Waterfall, & Edelman, 2008, p. 424), highlighting both how parts of speech can be combined together, and also the kinds of lexical items which can be substituted for each other within a particular construction slot. Around 20% of utterances in child-language corpora occur within variation sets (e.g., Küntay & Slobin, 1996), leading to the suggestion that they may facilitate the acquisition of phrase structure. Indeed, in adults acquiring an artificial language, phrase and constituent learning is facilitated by input-containing variation sets (Onnis et al., 2008). Overlap in terms of which items occur in which sentence positions has also been shown to be important in children's differentiation of causal versus unspecified object verbs, both of which can appear in transitive and intransitive constructions. Critically, these two verb groups differ in CDS in the relative frequency with which both the intransitive subject is animate, and the nouns used as subjects versus objects overlap. Children taught a novel verb in variation sets mimicking this input distribution were able to associate the verb with the correct event type (Scott & Fisher, 2009). Direct contrast of forms has also been suggested to play a role in children's acquisition of verbal morphology, with children receiving input of irregular verb forms in response to their own overregularization errors learning better than those who received input in noncontrastive contexts (Saxton, 1997).

On the other hand, across a variety of domains including the acquisition of complex-sentence constructions (Ambridge, Theakston, Lieven, & Tomasello, 2006), learning and abstraction are enhanced when the learning exemplars are presented at different times (distributed), rather than in quick succession (massed). Furthermore, overlap in lexical items across constructions has been observed to both support and hinder the subsequent acquisition of other-related forms. Abbot-Smith and Behrens

(2006) argued that the acquisition of two German-passive constructions was differentially influenced by the presence of lexical and semantic overlap with earlier-learned constructions, suggesting that overlap is not always conducive to the acquisition process. Links to work on attention (see Günther, Müller, & Geyer, Chapter 13, this volume) and its role in memory formation and subsequent consolidation will be needed to explain when and how lexical overlap and immediate contrast versus distributed learning facilitates the process of abstraction in language acquisition. In addition, links to work in the domains of nonlinguistic analogy and categorization (see Cordes, Chapter 12, this volume) and memory (see Takashima & Bakker, Chapter 8, this volume) will be needed to improve our understanding of how these processes might operate in the linguistic domain.

So far, evidence concerning the nature of children's early combinatorial speech and the kinds of lexical frames that might underlie these early uses has been presented, noting the similar occurrence of such frames in CDS and touching on how these frames might be acquired. But while the child's frequency of use is an important determinant of entrenchment, in acquisition it is necessary to consider in more detail the origins of these early acquired forms. Here, evidence that children's acquisition of grammatical forms is linked more directly to frequency of use in the input will now be reviewed.

14.4 Type and Token Frequency Effects

The processes of entrenchment and abstraction work together in language acquisition, and are likely to be underpinned by two different kinds of frequency effects. On the one hand, *token frequency* can serve to entrench a specific form, making it resistant to both internal analysis (Gathercole, 1986), and interference from competitors (Marslen-Wilson, 1990). On the other hand, *type frequency* is thought to promote abstraction by allowing the process of schematization to take place (e.g., Bybee, 1995). To determine the roles of these two frequency processes in acquisition, we need evidence that the frequency of occurrence of specific lexical items, collocations, and frames in the input relates to children's acquisition of these same forms.

Taking token-frequency effects first, there is evidence that children's order of acquisition of verbs is predicted by the verb's overall frequency, its relative frequency of occurrence in competing constructions (e.g., transitive vs. intransitive, Ninio, 1999; Theakston, Lieven, Pine, & Rowland, 2001), the relative frequency of its different senses (Theakston, Lieven, Pine, & Rowland, 2002), and its frequency in utterance-final position (Naigles & Hoff-Ginsberg, 1998). Verb frequency is also a good predictor of children's ability to correct word order errors. In so-called weird word order studies (e.g., Akhtar, 1999) children are exposed to novel verbs or known verbs of varying frequencies, modelled in an ungrammatical word order. Children are then questioned to elicit spontaneous uses of these verbs to determine whether they will change the word order to the dominant order for their language. The main finding is that children are more likely to correct the word order for higher frequency familiar verbs than for lower frequency or novel verbs. This has been taken as evidence that knowledge of how to produce verb-argument structure correctly accumulates gradually as a function of frequency of exposure.

Pronouns have also been observed to play a privileged role in the process of language acquisition, reflecting their frequency of use and, in particular, their combinatorial properties in the input (Lieven et al., 1997). In general, children's acquisition of specific pronoun + auxiliary combinations is predicted by their frequency of occurrence in the input (Theakston et al., 2005). However, not only are pronouns frequent in the input allowing entrenchment in the child's linguistic system, they also provide stable anchors for the acquisition of constructions due to their propensity to combine with a variety of different verbs. For example, pronouns account for over 80% of transitive subjects in the input to young English-speaking children (Cameron-Faulkner et al., 2003), and therefore may support the acquisition of lexically specific frames such as *He's V-ing it*, into which new verbs can be inserted. There is some evidence to support this claim. In the weird word order studies described above, when children corrected the weird word orders, roughly half of the time they did so by using pronouns rather than lexical nouns for the subjects and objects of the verbs (Akhtar, 1999). Further evidence demonstrates that in a densely collected corpus, proper-name subjects along with the object pronoun *it* formed the basis for one child's early transitive utterances (Theakston et al., 2012). In addition, children can generalize the transitive subject-verb-object construction to a novel verb when exposed to hundreds of transitive sentences with known verbs, but generalization is better if these models include a mixture of pronominal and lexical subjects and objects rather than lexical forms only (Childers & Tomasello, 2001). Also, syntactic priming for the active/passive transitive construction is facilitated by overlap in lexical items, specifically pronominal forms (Savage, Lieven, Theakston, & Tomasello, 2003), and even 19-month-olds are able to map a transitive sentence including a novel verb onto a causal scene if the verb has previously been modelled with pronoun subjects and objects (Yuan, Fisher, & Snedeker, 2012), although only older children can do so if the sentences contain full lexical nouns.

Computational models provide another means of investigating the role of entrenched lexical forms in the acquisition of abstract grammatical knowledge. For example, a computational model of early language exposed to CDS spontaneously generated pronoun islands of organization based on frequency of exposure (Jones, Gobet, & Pine, 2000), and other computational modelling work suggests that high-frequency frames such as [*you__it*] may provide a useful means of categorizing words into grammatical categories, in this case the subgroup of transitive verbs (Mintz, 2003; but see St. Clair et al., 2010, for the limitations of this approach). Taken together, the behavioral and modelling evidence suggests that the entrenchment of pronouns and the abstraction of frames based around them may play a central role in children's acquisition of more abstract-grammatical representations.

However, as we would expect, such entrenchment and abstraction effects can only be observed when the frequency distribution of pronouns in the input lends itself to their early acquisition. To illustrate, consider a weird word order study with French-speaking children (Matthews, Lieven, Theakston, & Tomasello, 2007). When correcting weird word orders to subject-verb-object (SVO) word order, in contrast with English-speaking children, French-speaking children rarely produced pronominal objects. But word order in French is more variable than in English and differs according to whether lexical or pronominal forms are produced. Thus, object-clitic pronouns are used pre-verbally (SOV: *Il **la** pousse* "he pushes her"), whereas lexical noun objects occur after the verb (SVO: *Il pousse **Mary*** "he pushes Mary"). This lack of structural overlap may mean that the form-function mappings which underpin French-speaking children's acquisition of the transitive construction are initially more fragmented than those of English-speaking children, and learned more slowly due to the lower individual frequency of the two-word orders. Moreover, object clitics are generally lacking in phonological salience, resulting in lower perceptual frequency, are identical to forms used as definite articles (*le, la, les*—competing form-function mappings), and are used less frequently to express objects than the corresponding-pronominal forms in English, at least with some verbs. Together, these factors suggest that the pronominal-transitive construction is likely to be less well entrenched for French-speaking children than for English-speaking children, leading to the later acquisition of the various forms of object expression in French. However, further behavioral and modelling work is needed across a variety of other languages to pin down the precise relation between input frequency and the child's acquisition of, and reliance on, lexical frames of different kinds.

Turning to type-frequency effects and their role in schematization, in order to understand how entrenchment operates in acquisition, we need to understand how type and token frequencies interact. The process of language development represents the linguistic system in its greatest state of flux, with the relative reliance on token frequencies versus type-frequency variation and schematization shifting over a relatively short period of time. In the learning of morphological regularities, patterns in which a large number of different verbs participate are expected to be more readily generalized to new forms than patterns with lower type frequency (Bybee, 1995). For example, overregularization of the past tense "ed" inflection in English is well evidenced in children's early speech (e.g., *runned, comed, swimmed*), and only later in development are other kinds of overgeneralization errors seen, where children extend a pattern with lower type frequency, but one that provides a better phonological match to the target (e.g., *sing-sang > bring/*brang* vs. **bringed* or *brought*; see, e.g., Marchman, 1997). On the other hand, the precise patterns of learning observed vary as a function of the language being learned with the effects of type frequency mediated by factors such as phonology and segmentability (Kirjavainen, Nikolaev, & Kidd, 2012).

In terms of construction learning, young infants are better able to detect nonadjacent patterns in strings of syllables if there is sufficient variation in an intervening element (Gómez, 2002), and in older children there is some evidence that higher verb-type frequency promotes greater generalization of constructions to new verbs (Savage, Lieven, Theakston, & Tomasello, 2006; Wonnacott, Boyd, Thomson, & Goldberg, 2012).

Type- and token-frequency distributions interact in complex ways to support the acquisition process. Goldberg, Casenhiser, and Sethuraman (2004) argued that the type/token frequency distributions of particular verbs in particular constructions in CDS facilitate the acquisition of grammatical constructions. For most basic-level constructions, they reported that there is typically only one or a handful of verbs which account for the lion's share of verb tokens for a particular construction. For example, the verb *go* accounted for 39% of uses of the intransitive-motion construction, even though 39 different verbs were attested in the construction overall. They argued that this skewed distribution makes it easier for children to learn grammatical constructions because initially the form-function mapping for the construction is synonymous with the meaning of the verb with which it most often occurs (see Casenhiser & Goldberg, 2005, for experimental evidence, and Ellis & Ferreira-Junior, 2009, for evidence from second-language learners). For 5-year-olds, generalization of a novel argument-structure construction may be affected by the precise distributional properties of the input such that overlap in the lexical nouns used in the training and test sentences is required to support generalization (Boyd & Goldberg, 2012), but this effect seems very sensitive to the particular-input characteristics and disappears when the training set of nouns is more varied (Wonnacott et al., 2012). However, there is some suggestion that the learning of morphological patterns may be facilitated by a more even distributional spread of tokens across types (e.g., Siebenborn, Krajewski, & Lieven, 2016). Thus, the exact way in which the entrenchment of individual forms might serve to facilitate or inhibit the process of abstraction is not fully understood.

Another possibility is that differences in the type frequency of verbs appearing in particular constructions may determine children's learning and generalization of those constructions. For example, in CDS the simple-transitive construction is roughly three times as frequent as the simple-intransitive construction (Cameron-Faulkner et al., 2003) and might thus be earlier acquired and generalized. Indeed, studies of children's spontaneous argument-structure overgeneralization errors suggest that children are more likely to extend intransitive verbs into the transitive frame (e.g., *He disappeared it*) than vice versa (e.g., Bowerman, 1988). However, verb-type frequency and the semantic affordances of the constructions in question are likely to be conflated, making it difficult to disentangle the relative contribution of each factor to abstraction.

Although we currently do not know enough about how the distributional properties of particular constructions facilitate the process of abstraction in children's speech, studies of artificial-language learning can provide some insights into the learning process. Wonnacott, Newport, and Tanenhaus (2008) systematically manipulated the frequency with which individual verbs were modelled in one or both of two novel transitive-like constructions, and the number of verbs that appeared in both constructions. They then tested learners' willingness to generalize verbs to a nonattested construction. They found that verb-specific and verb-general statistics interacted to determine behavior. Verb-general information was more influential for low-frequency verbs, whereas verb-specific information determined performance with high-frequency verbs, a finding mirrored in work on German children's comprehension of the passive construction where children were initially poorer at comprehending known than novel verbs because of their frequent association with and entrenchment in the competing-active construction (Dittmar, Abbot-Smith, Lieven, & Tomasello, 2014).

Taken together, these various lines of research demonstrate that both type- and token-frequency effects operate during the language-acquisition process, but the critical question concerns the precise ways in which they interact over development, as the child's linguistic system becomes increasingly abstract. However, language-acquisition researchers face a challenging problem in determining exactly how the kinds of frequency information thought to have an impact on acquisition should be measured.

14.5 Measuring Type and Token Frequencies

One question that has challenged language-acquisition researchers interested in determining how entrenchment and abstraction might operate over the course of acquisition relates to what kinds of frequency information are most critical, and how these different sources of information interact over the course of acquisition. This is most clearly seen in work within a competition-model framework (Bates & MacWhinney, 1987) as applied to children's acquisition of the transitive construction cross-linguistically. Specifically, the issue concerns the relative importance of linguistic devices such as word order, case marking and agreement, in addition to nonlinguistic properties such as the animacy of the participants, to indicate who did what to whom in a causal action. In principle at least, it should be possible to predict which cues children will be most sensitive to from their relative frequencies in the input as a function of the typology of the language being learned: Cues that are both more available (frequent) and more reliable (demonstrating a systematic relation between form and function) should become entrenched in the child's system earliest and therefore used more consistently in sentence comprehension. For example, in languages in which both word order is relatively fixed and argument omissions largely infelicitous (e.g., English), the word order cue is much more frequent and reliable than in languages where word order can vary (e.g., Finnish, German, Polish) and/or arguments can be omitted (e.g., Cantonese). We would predict therefore that in languages such as English, word order will quickly become entrenched in the child's linguistic system, leading to earlier comprehension of sentences relying on this cue.

A number of studies across a number of different languages suggest that children are best able to interpret frequently occurring "prototype" sentences in which multiple cues operate to indicate the same interpretation versus lower frequency sentences in which there is either only a single cue to meaning, or cues give rise to conflicting interpretations (Candan, Küntay, Yeh, Cheung, Wagner, & Naigles, 2012; Chan, Lieven, & Tomasello, 2009; Dittmar, Abbot-Smith, Lieven, & Tomasello, 2008; Ibbotson, Theakston, Lieven, & Tomasello, 2011). Moreover, as predicted, in languages in which word order is largely fixed, children show earlier adultlike performance with this cue in isolation, reflecting its stronger entrenchment relative to languages in which other cues carry greater predictive weight (e.g., Chan et al., 2009). However, although there is general support for the process of entrenchment in determining cue strength, researchers do not have a detailed understanding of exactly what determines the patterns of acquisition observed. For example, the scope over which cue frequency should be measured is unclear and is likely to change over development as the child's linguistic system becomes more interconnected (e.g., frequency within or across constructions; including or excluding sentences with omitted arguments; separating or combining different lexical forms; see Dittmar et al., 2008, for a discussion, and Diessel & Tomasello, 2005, for a consideration of cross-construction frequency effects in relative-clause acquisition).

14.6 Children's Grammatical Errors

Children's grammatical errors provide a particularly rich source of evidence regarding the processes of entrenchment and abstraction in their developing linguistic systems, as well as provide insights into the kinds of frequency information feeding into the acquisition system at any given point in development. As argued by Ambridge et al. (2015), the entrenchment of particular linguistic forms can both protect against and promote error, such that high-frequency forms are produced correctly but may also be substituted incorrectly for lower frequency forms leading to errors. The patterning of any such substitution errors provides evidence regarding the existing links in the child's system.

The concept of entrenchment has been widely applied to children's argument-structure overgeneralization errors (Braine & Brooks, 1995), but it is equally applicable to many other kinds of errors. It is well established that children are less likely to produce higher frequency verbs in an erroneous argument-structure construction than lower frequency verbs (e.g., *I disappeared/vanished the rabbit*; Brooks, Tomasello, Dodson, & Lewis, 1999), and both children and adults judge instances of argument-structure errors to be more acceptable, across a range of grammatical constructions, with lower than higher frequency verbs (Theakston, 2004; see Ambridge, Pine, Rowland, Chang, & Bidgood, 2012, for an overview). These findings are assumed to reflect the speaker's greater knowledge of the appropriate verb-construction mappings for familiar verbs which effectively wins out over low-level activation of their use in competing constructions. Similar effects have been observed in children's production of morphological (Räsänen, Ambridge, & Pine, 2014) and agreement errors (Theakston & Rowland, 2009), as well as in the repetition of complex sentences (Kidd, Lieven, & Tomasello, 2010) in which high-frequency forms are correctly produced but also substituted for lower frequency forms. Here, the assumption is that high-frequency forms are sufficiently well entrenched to support correct use but also more easily retrieved and hence substituted for lower frequency forms with which the child is less familiar. Interestingly, these substitution errors are not random but rather reflect some cross-activation of forms indicating some degree of abstractness in the linguistic system, for example, the use of high-frequency forms of auxiliary BE in place of low-frequency forms.

The entrenchment of lexical strings is another source of children's errors, and a means of protecting from error. For example, in *wh-* and *yes-no-*question production, children have been observed to produce fewer uninversion errors (e.g., **What he can do?*) and fewer double marking errors (e.g., **Can he can't go to the park?*) for questions where the corresponding *wh* + auxiliary or auxiliary + pronoun combination is frequent in the input, providing children with an entrenched frame around which to base their question (Ambridge & Rowland, 2009; Rowland & Pine, 2000). Even complex questions with long-distance dependencies appear to be subject to the same protective influence of high-frequency strings in children and in adults (Dąbrowska et al., 2009). It is important to note, however, that some error types are more frequent than would be predicted directly by input frequency alone (e.g., double marking in negative questions, errors with auxiliary *do*), demonstrating the need for more complex models of acquisition in which entrenchment is explicitly driven by multiple factors.

In some situations, the differential activation of competing forms via a priming mechanism can be the cause of grammatical errors. For example, hearing syntactic constructions in which no overt person/tense marker appeared between the subject and the verb (e.g., *Will it mib/Are you mibbing*) resulted in lower levels of third-person singular-verb marking and increased auxiliary-verb omissions in declaratives (*it mib/you mibbing*) in typically developing children's speech (Theakston & Lieven, 2008; Theakston, Lieven, & Tomasello, 2003), and in language-impaired populations (Finneran & Leonard, 2010; Leonard & Deevy, 2011). One argument is that children are learning strings from a number of linguistic structures in the input, leading to omissions when these strings are used in inappropriate contexts.

Further studies have shown that the forms that compete are related to the input children hear, suggesting that relative levels of entrenchment are responsible, in part, for children's errors. Kirjavainen, Theakston, and Lieven (2009) showed that 2- to 3-year-old children who produced a higher proportion of *me-for-I* errors (e.g., **me do it*) had caregivers who produced a relatively high proportion of complex sentences in which the accusative pronoun *me* appeared preverbally (e.g., *Let me do it*) compared with utterances in which the nominative pronoun *I* appeared preverbally (e.g., *I'll do it*). The authors suggested that children acquire both a *me-verb* and an *I-verb* frame from the input which compete for activation in a frequency-sensitive manner.

Similarly, competing representations at different levels of abstraction may in part explain children's *to*-infinitive omission errors (e.g., **I want (to) go there*; Kirjavainen & Theakston, 2011). Children ages 2 to 3 years produced infinitival *to* more frequently after hearing target verbs combined with infinitival *to* (e.g., *want to go*, a *want-to* frame) than after sentences modelling a competing frame (e.g., *want a drink*: want-NP frame derived as a function of its higher type frequency in the input). Again, the children's rates of *to*-infinitive omissions reflected the relative distribution of these two constructions in their input. However, the majority of the children went on to produce errors that could not have been modelled directly on the input. For example, the errors **me can't do it*, **me goes there* suggest that they had abstracted a **me-verb* frame which they then productively used. In addition, the priming effect of the two *want* constructions changed over development. The assumption is that these errors are gradually eradicated as children build up representations of the appropriate complex-sentence structures, thus reducing the activation of erroneous competing forms for simple sentences.

One possibility is that learning from the ends of utterances (representing a recency effect in memory) may provide a possible mechanism by which competing constructions are acquired across languages. Cross-linguistic computational-modelling work demonstrates how this process might operate, in this case resulting in various tense-omission errors (Freudenthal, Pine, Aguado-Orea, & Gobet, 2007). Errors reduce over time as a result of exposure to increasing amounts of input, which allows the model to chunk co-occurring units together and consequently learn longer and more complex linguistic units.

14.7 The Learning Mechanism

A number of studies illustrate the fact that children's language productions are influenced not only by the global statistics of the input but also by local-discourse properties. Children show priming effects for a number of grammatical constructions such that they are more likely to produce a particular construction if it has recently been heard and/or produced (e.g., Rowland, Chang, Ambridge, Pine, & Lieven, 2012; Savage et al., 2003; Shimpi, Gámez, Huttenlocher, & Vasilyeva, 2007), and for a variety of error types, such that hearing particular strings either promotes or inhibits errors (Kirjavainen & Theakston, 2011; Kirjavainen et al., 2009; Theakston & Lieven, 2008). A number of researchers have argued that language acquisition is a form of implicit, error-based learning (e.g., Chang, Dell, & Bock, 2006; Rowland et al., 2012; Savage et al., 2006), such that weighted connections between parts of the system change as a function of each input exemplar, resulting in the entrenchment and abstraction effects seen in children's language. Although the adult-language system is assumed to be sensitive to changes in the language statistics at both a local and global level, evidenced by syntactic-priming phenomenon (see, e.g., Pickering & Ferreira, 2008, for a review) and differences in linguistic expertise in adult speakers as a function of levels of exposure to complex sentence types (Dąbrowska & Street, 2006), the developing system is particularly sensitive to the properties of the input. Each utterance the child hears constitutes a larger proportion of the total input to the system than in the older child or adult, and can thus change the child's representations significantly, especially if that input mismatches what the child was expecting to hear (Chang et al., 2006). Therefore, to fully understand how entrenchment might operate in the developing system, we need theoretical and computational models that allow for the changing influence over development of both the global statistics of the language, and the in-the-moment information provided by the prior discourse. However, it is likely that any such models will need to incorporate not only form frequency distributional information but also important semantic, pragmatic, and contextual information, as all of these factors influence the prediction mechanism.

14.8 Entrenchment of Form Frequency in Interaction

A lot of work in language-acquisition research has focused primarily on the type and token frequencies of forms in the input, and how this impacts on the acquisition of particular-grammatical constructions. At the same time, the language-acquisition process is often conceptualized as the learning of form-function mappings (e.g., Goldberg, 1995; Tomasello, 2003), leading to the inevitable conclusion that to understand the effects of entrenchment and the process of abstraction in the acquisition process, it is necessary to examine how the frequency of specific-sentence types interacts with the meanings and functions they are used to encode. In adult language, there is ample evidence that semantic/thematic and lexical statistics influence performance on a range of tasks, demonstrating that contextual information is stored alongside grammatical structure (e.g., Hare, McRae, & Elman, 2004; Trueswell & Tanenhaus, 1994). Here, the role of contextual information in children's developing representations is considered.

Taking the entrenchment of individual words first, in some languages researchers have suggested that pure token frequency is not particularly helpful in guiding children's acquisition of verb meaning. In Tzeltal, for instance, children apparently acquire some lower frequency transitive-verb meanings first (Brown, 2008). However, as Brown (2008) pointed out, the form-function mapping for these verbs may be more transparent than for higher frequency but semantically more general verbs. Tzeltal allows considerable object ellipsis, and it is easier to recover the object when the verb meaning restricts the range of possible referents. In other work, the role of perceptual salience is invoked to explain why highly frequent items are not acquired early. For instance, children fail to both perceive and produce sentence-medial third-person singular-verb marking in English, despite showing higher levels of perception and provision in utterance-final position (Sundara, Demuth, & Kuhl, 2011). In some cases, perceptual salience may interact with pragmatic factors governing what children choose to attend to and to talk about. Theakston et al. (2005) noted that although the frequency of individual pronoun + auxiliary combinations in the input predicted their order of emergence and, to some extent, their levels of provision in children's speech, this was not true of the highly frequent form *you're*. This form was acquired later, and levels of omission of third-person-plural auxiliary *are* were higher than for third-person singular *is* even when children knew both forms, especially in sentence-medial position in declaratives and wh-questions (Theakston & Rowland, 2009). These findings reveal the need for predictive accounts of acquisition to incorporate perceptual salience and the influence of pragmatic motivation (children prefer to talk about themselves) on attention as filters on the input to which children are exposed.

In the abstraction of constructions, semantics and pragmatic function also play an important role. Many discussions of slot-and-frame patterns in acquisition are predicated on the assumption that the linguistic items that can be inserted into any variable slot or construction must be constrained in some way, reflected in the choice of terminology (e.g., *I process thing*; Lieven et al., 2009), and there is some evidence that slot-and-frame patterns in CDS may be functionally restricted (Cameron-Faulkner & Hickey, 2011). A challenge for language-acquisition researchers is to establish the nature of the constraints that operate on particular constructions, their origins, and how they change over development as a function of the child's current representations and the variability present in the input. One study that provides some insight into this process found that children were better able to repeat a novel four-word sequence (e.g., *a piece of [brick]*) if the fourth word was not easily predicted from the preceding sequence (high-slot entropy) but the items that typically followed that sequence were distributionally and/or semantically similar (Matthews & Bannard, 2010). This suggests that low predictability of the form combined with high predictability of the semantic scope may provide an optimum context for generalization, illustrating the tensions between entrenchment and abstraction. However, there are still many open questions concerning how children come to recognize semantic similarity. Infancy research examining the formation of object categories provides useful insights into the role of perceptual versus linguistic cues in determining similarity (see Westermann & Mareschal, 2014, for a recent overview), whereas work on older children's ability to reason analogically provides insights into the roles of perceptual versus relational similarity (Gentner, 1988), working memory (Halford, 1993) and inhibitory control (Morrison, Holyoak, & Truong, 2001) in determining children's abilities to recognize relations between similar items or events. It is likely that bidirectional influences between children's developing knowledge of categorization and ability to make analogies of different kinds, and the distributional properties of the input, will drive categorization and abstraction within the linguistic system. However, a great deal more work is needed to tie together work across these domains.

Linguistic creativity poses another challenge to researchers wishing to understand how entrenchment and abstraction might operate in acquisition, and requires a focus on communicative function. For example, Cameron-Faulkner, Lieven, and Theakston (2007) examined in detail one child's early use of negation in utterances with simple, uninflected-verb forms. They reported that the child initially used *no-verb* (largely ungrammatical in English), later progressing to *not-verb*, and finally to a range of negated auxiliaries (*can't, don't-verb*) used to express different functions. Although the child's uses did not directly mirror patterns in the input, there was a relationship between input and output which changed over development: *no* was the most frequent single-word negator in the input and was used earliest by the child, *not* was the most frequent form used in multiword utterances in the input and was later adopted for use across the board in neg-V utterances by the child, and the negated auxiliaries were used with differing frequencies to encode different functions in the input, a pattern that the child acquired late but in a function-specific manner. The authors argued that the pattern of development was motivated by a need to communicate in the absence of the appropriate linguistic knowledge, resulting in the creative use of the most-entrenched forms available at any given developmental point. Similar findings have been reported for children's use of double-marked questions (e.g., *Why do you don't like cake?*), such that, in the absence of a suitable negative-question frame (*Don't you...?*) children may resort to combining a well-known question frame (*Do you...?*) with an entrenched-declarative form (*You don't like cake*; Ambridge & Rowland, 2009). Thus, there is an interaction between the meaning that the child wishes to convey and the linguistic tools available to them, leading to instances in which the use of highly entrenched forms leads to error.

Turning to sentence-level constructions, there are many instances in which the semantic and/or pragmatic properties of the constructions themselves influence children's performance in comprehension and production tasks. This variability reveals insights into the nature of children's underlying representations, and in turn to the processes of entrenchment and abstraction. For example, children's ability to comprehend the double-object dative (DOD) construction is enhanced if the two postverbal nouns are differentiated by the use of a proper name and a lexical noun (e.g., *I gave Frog the bunny*) rather than having two lexical nouns (Rowland & Noble, 2010). Although it is well established that processing two consecutive-undifferentiated nouns is difficult (Bever, 1974), it is also the case that the DOD typically occurs with an animate postverbal pronoun or proper noun-indirect object, and an inanimate utterance-final lexical-noun direct object. Thus, it appears that children's ability to comprehend this construction is influenced by the level of entrenchment of the construction and its semantic and pragmatic components. Similar evidence can be seen in children's comprehension of object relative clauses in which the animacy and linguistic form of the object determines children's level of performance (Brandt, Kidd, Lieven, & Tomasello, 2009). Again, children's performance increases when the constructions they are exposed to map onto the prototypical form of the construction in the input in terms of both form and function. On the other hand, the prototypical mapping of form and function can interfere with children's ability to identify the precise relation between them. For example, pragmatic factors influence the choice of referring expressions for subjects and objects in the transitive construction. According to patterns of preferred-argument structure (Du Bois, 1987), which are mirrored in CDS (Clancy, 2003) and appear to be motivated by processing considerations, the subject of a transitive typically encodes accessible information, and therefore can be omitted or realized pronominally, whereas the object typically encodes new information and consequently is realized lexically. There is evidence that very young children show some sensitivity to the accessibility of referents, selecting appropriately informative referring expressions in ways which resemble their input (see Allen, Skarabela, & Hughes, 2008, for an overview). However, even 5-year-olds apparently struggle to isolate the pragmatic determinants of pronominal selection, erroneously producing pronoun subjects, in line with the prototypical-transitive sentence, to refer to inaccessible agents of transitive-causal actions (Theakston, 2012). These studies illustrate the need to consider children's developing linguistic representations in terms of the entrenchment of forms and functions, and how this coupling both facilitates and impedes the process of abstraction.

In other lines of research, the semantics of constructions as a whole have been shown to interact with form frequency to impact on children's ability to avoid errors and to create abstractions. For example, an interaction between form frequency and meaning is required to explain how children learn to avoid making argument structure-overgeneralization errors. If verb frequency was the sole factor (entrenchment), then any novel verb, having no prior use, should be equally acceptable in a given construction. However, Ambridge and colleagues, following Goldberg (1995), have argued that the verb slot in any given grammatical construction is associated with particular semantic properties that determine its compatibility with the meaning of any new verb (Ambridge et al., 2012). In a number of studies, Ambridge and colleagues have demonstrated that verbs are judged to exhibit different degrees of compatibility with the semantics of particular argument-structure constructions, and that this measure is a good predictor of children's and adults' judgments of verb acceptability in those same constructions. They have argued that entrenchment operates not at the level of verb frequency per se but rather that every instance of hearing a verb entrenches its meaning, resulting in more frequent verbs being judged as less compatible with unattested argument-structure constructions. At the same time, even newly acquired verbs, provided they are associated with some meaning, can be more or less compatible with the meaning of a particular construction, accounting for the variable performance seen with novel verbs. Finally, the process of abstracting argument-structure constructions may also be influenced by the semantic heterogeneity of the verbs with which they occur. For example, there is some evidence that despite learning to comprehend some instances of the transitive construction around 2 years of age, 5-year-old children may operate with less joined-up representations of this semantically wide-ranging constructions than adults. After exposing participants to a series of transitive sentences, none of which exemplified all of the semantic properties prototypically associated with this construction, adults and children were asked to rate a series of sentences according to whether they had been heard before. Whereas the adults falsely thought they had already heard sentences exemplifying prototypical-transitive semantics, the children identified these as new sentences (Ibbotson, Theakston, Lieven, & Tomasello, 2012). The authors argued that in adults, hearing sentences containing some of the prototypical characteristics of the transitive served to prime the entrenched-prototype representation, leading to false recall of new-prototypical sentences. One possible explanation for the children's behavior is that a weaker priming effect for the prototype occurred, suggesting that the process of abstraction takes considerable developmental time, especially for constructions allowing semantic variability.

14.9 Summary

In this chapter, we have considered the evidence for the processes of entrenchment and abstraction in language acquisition with respect to the development of grammatical representations. We could summarize thus: Children first learn high-frequency items or collocations from the input; they then notice similarities between the early-learned items in terms of their forms and functions; where there is overlap in form and function coupled with variation, this leads to the abstraction of linguistic constructions around fixed anchors which themselves gradually become more abstract; along the way, some of these abstractions turn out to be wrong and lead to errors, but in the end repeated exposure to adultlike input reinforces only the acceptable, grammatical representations, driving out the rest.

But of course, the devil is in the detail, and here we are only starting to make small inroads into the complexity of the problem. Although there is a wealth of evidence pertaining to both entrenchment and abstraction, only some of which is covered here, it is clear that there are many gaps in our understanding that will require careful work. For example, we know that children learn high-frequency words and longer linguistic chunks based on their token frequency in the input. But we cannot yet be precise about exactly which chunks will be learned early and which will not: This depends on the child's focus of attention, their communicative requirements, the perceptual salience of the items, their overlap with other, already-acquired constructions, and so on. Similarly, we know that in production children appear to build up linguistic knowledge from earlier-acquired simpler sentences. But we are not able to predict with any great certainty which early-learned chunks will recombine with which others—to some extent this appears to be a question of communicative necessity which sometimes leads to errors. We are only really beginning to work out the optimum conditions for abstraction. For example, we know that the spaced-temporal distribution of items can be important, but in other work contrast of forms within the immediate discourse appears beneficial. The frequency distribution of different forms within a construction may also be important, but whether a skewed or even distribution is optimum may depend on the nature of what is being learned. All of these processes may have a role to play, but they may facilitate different types of learning (e.g., implicit vs. explicit), or be suited to the registering of different kinds of distributional statistics. Computational models have an important contribution to make in narrowing down and pinpointing precisely how and where abstraction occurs across the system. However, these models to date have made relatively little progress toward implementing realistic semantic representations, or encoding the pragmatic information that influences comprehension and production. So while we can gain significant insights into how learning might take place from these models, it will be necessary to move beyond simple form frequency information to a richer representation of the role of semantic and pragmatic information to tease apart the relative contributions of different kinds of input to the learning process.

Finally, greater integration is needed between work in language acquisition and that in other developmental domains, for example, on children's attentional mechanisms, the formation of categories, analogical reasoning, and memory, to fully understand how children arrive at an adultlike linguistic system. Many researchers are beginning to make more explicit connections between children's linguistic abilities and their abilities in other, nonlinguistic cognitive domains (e.g., statistical learning, pattern finding, implicit/explicit memory), but research-intensive longitudinal studies will be needed to gain real insights into the relations between these domains. The potential benefits of understanding the processes of entrenchment and abstraction in language acquisition, however, cannot be overstated. Only with this knowledge can we really hope to understand when, why, and how these processes fail in language-impaired populations, allowing interventions to be developed in ways that optimize learning.

References

Abbot-Smith, K., & Behrens, H. (2006). How known constructions influence the acquisition of other constructions: The German passive and future constructions. *Cognitive Science, 30*, 995–1026. http://dx.doi.org/10.1207/s15516709cog0000_61

Akhtar, N. (1999). Acquiring basic word order: Evidence for data-driven learning of syntactic structure. *Journal of Child Language, 26*, 339–356. http://dx.doi.org/10.1017/S030500099900375X

Allen, S. E. M., Skarabela, B., & Hughes, M. (2008). Using corpora to examine discourse effects in syntax. In H. Behrens (Ed.), *Corpora in language acquisition research: History, methods, perspectives* (pp. 99–137). http://dx.doi.org/10.1075/tilar.6.07all

Ambridge, B., Kidd, E., Rowland, C. F., & Theakston, A. L. (2015). The ubiquity of frequency effects in first language acquisition. *Journal of Child Language, 42*, 239–273. http://dx.doi.org/10.1017/S030500091400049X

Ambridge, B., Pine, J. M., Rowland, C. F., Chang, F., & Bidgood, A. (2012). The retreat from over-generalization in child language acquisition: Word learning, morphology, and verb argument structure. Advance online publication. *WIREs Cognitive Science, 4*, 47–62. http://dx.doi.org/10.1002/wcs.1207

Ambridge, B., & Rowland, C. F. (2009). Predicting children's errors with negative questions: Testing a schema-combination account. *Cognitive Linguistics, 20*, 225–266. http://dx.doi.org/10.1515/COGL.2009.014

Ambridge, B., Theakston, A. L., Lieven, E. V. M., & Tomasello, M. (2006). The distributed learning effect for children's acquisition of an abstract syntactic construction. *Cognitive Development, 21*, 174–193. http://dx.doi.org/10.1016/j.cogdev.2005.09.003

Bannard, C., Lieven, E., & Tomasello, M. (2009). Modeling children's early grammatical knowledge. *Proceedings of the National Academy of Sciences of the United States of America, 106*, 17284–17289. http://dx.doi.org/10.1073/pnas.0905638106

Bannard, C., & Matthews, D. (2008). Stored word sequences in language learning: The effect of familiarity on children's repetition of four-word combinations. *Psychological Science, 19*, 241–248. http://dx.doi.org/10.1111/j.1467-9280.2008.02075.x

Bates, E., & MacWhinney, B. (1987). Competition, variation, and language learning. In B. MacWhinney (Ed.), *Mechanisms of language acquisition* (pp. 157–193). Hillsdale, NJ: Erlbaum.

Bever, T. G. (1974). The ascent of the specious, or there's a lot we don't know about mirrors. In D. Cohen (Ed.), *Explaining linguistic phenomena* (pp. 173–200). Washington, DC: Hemisphere.

Biber, D., Johansson, S., Leech, G., Conrad, S., & Finegan, E. (1999). *Longman grammar of spoken and written English*. London, England: Longman.

Bowerman, M. (1988). The "no negative evidence" problem: How do children avoid constructing an overgeneral grammar? In J. A. Hawkins (Ed.), *Explaining language universals* (pp. 73–101). Oxford, England: Blackwell.

Boyd, J. K., & Goldberg, A. E. (2012). Young children fail to fully generalize a novel argument structure construction when exposed to the same input as older learners. *Journal of Child Language, 39*, 457–481. http://dx.doi.org/10.1017/S0305000911000079

Braine, M. D. S., & Bowerman, M. (1976). Children's first word combinations. *Monographs of the Society for Research in Child Development, 41*, 1–104. http://dx.doi.org/10.2307/1165959

Braine, M. D. S., & Brooks, P. J. (1995). Verb argument structure and the problem of avoiding an overgeneral grammar. In M. Tomasello & W. E. Merriman (Eds.), *Beyond names for things: Young children's acquisition of verbs* (pp. 353–376). Hillsdale, NJ: Erlbaum.

Brandt, S., Kidd, E., Lieven, E., & Tomasello, M. (2009). The discourse bases of relativization: An investigation of young German and English-speaking children's comprehension of relative clauses. *Cognitive Linguistics, 20*, 539–570. http://dx.doi.org/10.1515/COGL.2009.024

Brooks, P. J., Tomasello, M., Dodson, K., & Lewis, L. B. (1999). Young children's overgeneralizations with fixed transitivity verbs. *Child Development, 70*, 1325–1337. http://dx.doi.org/10.1111/1467-8624.00097

Brown, P. (2008). Verb specificity and argument realization in Tzeltal child language. In M. Bowerman & P. Brown (Eds.), *Crosslinguistic perspectives on argument structure. Implications for learnability* (pp. 167–189). Mahwah, NJ: Erlbaum.

Bybee, J. (1995). Regular morphology and the lexicon. *Language and Cognitive Processes, 10*, 425–455. http://dx.doi.org/10.1080/01690969508407111

Cameron-Faulkner, T., & Hickey, T. (2011). Form and function in Irish child directed speech. *Cognitive Linguistics, 22*, 569–594. http://dx.doi.org/10.1515/cogl.2011.022

Cameron-Faulkner, T., Lieven, E., & Theakston, A. (2007). What part of *no* do children not understand? A usage-based account of multiword negation. *Journal of Child Language*, *34*, 251–282. http://dx.doi.org/10.1017/S0305000906007884

Cameron-Faulkner, T., Lieven, E., & Tomasello, M. (2003). A construction based analysis of child directed speech. *Cognitive Science*, *27*, 843–873. http://dx.doi.org/10.1207/s15516709cog2706_2

Candan, A., Küntay, A. C., Yeh, Y. C., Cheung, H., Wagner, L., & Naigles, L. R. (2012). Language and age effects in children's processing of word order. *Cognitive Development*, *27*, 205–221. http://dx.doi.org/10.1016/j.cogdev.2011.12.001

Casenhiser, D., & Goldberg, A. E. (2005). Fast mapping between a phrasal form and meaning. *Developmental Science*, *8*, 500–508. http://dx.doi.org/10.1111/j.1467-7687.2005.00441.x

Chan, A., Lieven, E., & Tomasello, M. (2009). Children's understanding of the agent-patient relations in the transitive construction: Cross-linguistic comparison between Cantonese, German, and English. *Cognitive Linguistics*, *20*, 267–300. http://dx.doi.org/10.1515/COGL.2009.015

Chang, F., Dell, G. S., & Bock, K. (2006). Becoming syntactic. *Psychological Review*, *113*, 234–272. http://dx.doi.org/10.1037/0033-295X.113.2.234

Chang, F., Lieven, E., & Tomasello, M. (2008). Automatic evaluation of syntactic learners in typologically different languages. *Cognitive Systems Research*, *9*, 198–213. http://dx.doi.org/10.1016/j.cogsys.2007.10.002

Childers, J. B., & Tomasello, M. (2001). The role of pronouns in young children's acquisition of the English transitive construction. *Developmental Psychology*, *37*, 739–748. http://dx.doi.org/10.1037/0012-1649.37.6.739

Clancy, P. M. (2003). The lexicon in interaction: Developmental origins of preferred argument structure in Korean. In J. W. Du Bois, L. E. Kumpf, & W. J. Ashby (Eds.), *Preferred argument structure: Grammar as architecture for function* (pp. 81–108). http://dx.doi.org/10.1075/sidag.14.06cla

Conklin, K., & Schmitt, N. (2012). The processing of formulaic language. *Annual Review of Applied Linguistics*, *32*, 45–61. http://dx.doi.org/10.1017/S0267190512000074

Dąbrowska, E., Rowland, C., & Theakston, A. (2009). The acquisition of questions with long-distance dependencies. *Cognitive Linguistics*, *20*, 571–597. http://dx.doi.org/10.1515/COGL.2009.025

Dąbrowska, E., & Street, J. (2006). Individual differences in language attainment: Comprehension of passive sentences by native and non-native English speakers. *Language Sciences*, *28*, 604–615. http://dx.doi.org/10.1016/j.langsci.2005.11.014

Diessel, H., & Tomasello, M. (2001). The acquisition of finite complement clauses in English: A corpus-based analysis. *Cognitive Linguistics*, *12*, 97–142. http://dx.doi.org/10.1515/cogl.12.2.97

Diessel, H., & Tomasello, M. (2005). A new look at the acquisition of relative clauses. *Language*, *81*, 882–906. http://dx.doi.org/10.1353/lan.2005.0169

Dittmar, M., Abbot-Smith, K., Lieven, E., & Tomasello, M. (2008). German children's comprehension of word order and case marking in causative sentences. *Child Development*, *79*, 1152–1167. http://dx.doi.org/10.1111/j.1467-8624.2008.01181.x

Dittmar, M., Abbot-Smith, K., Lieven, E., & Tomasello, M. (2014). Familiar verbs are not always easier than novel verbs: How German preschool children comprehend active and passive sentences. *Cognitive Science*, *38*, 128–151. http://dx.doi.org/10.1111/cogs.12066

Du Bois, J. W. (1987). The discourse basis of ergativity. *Language*, *63*, 805–855. http://dx.doi.org/10.2307/415719

Ellis, N. C., & Ferreira-Junior, F. (2009). Construction learning as a function of frequency, frequency distribution, and function. *The Modern Language Journal*, *93*, 370–385. http://dx.doi.org/10.1111/j.1540-4781.2009.00896.x

Finneran, D. A., & Leonard, L. B. (2010). Role of linguistic input in third person singular -s use in the speech of young children. *Journal of Speech, Language, and Hearing Research, 53*, 1065–1074. http://dx.doi.org/10.1044/1092-4388(2009/09-0056)

Fisher, C. (2002). The role of abstract syntactic knowledge in language acquisition: A reply to Tomasello (2000). *Cognition, 82*, 259–278. http://dx.doi.org/10.1016/S0010-0277(01)00159-7

Freudenthal, D., Pine, J. M., Aguado-Orea, J., & Gobet, F. (2007). Modeling the developmental pattern of finiteness marking in English, Dutch, German and Spanish using MOSAIC. *Cognitive Science, 31*, 311–341. http://dx.doi.org/10.1207/s15516709cog0000_47

Freudenthal, D., Pine, J. M., & Gobet, F. (2007). Understanding the developmental dynamics of subject omission: The role of processing limitations in learning. *Journal of Child Language, 34*, 83–110. http://dx.doi.org/10.1017/S0305000906007719

Gathercole, V. C. (1986). The acquisition of the present perfect: Explaining differences in the speech of Scottish and American children. *Journal of Child Language, 13*, 537–560. http://dx.doi.org/10.1017/S0305000900006875

Gentner, D. (1988). Analogical inference and analogical access. In A. Prieditis (Ed.), *Analogica* (pp. 63–88). Los Altos, CA: Morgan Kaufmann.

Goldberg, A. E. (1995). *Constructions: A construction grammar approach to argument structure.* Chicago, IL: University of Chicago Press.

Goldberg, A. E., Casenhiser, D. M., & Sethuraman, N. (2004). Learning argument structure generalizations. *Cognitive Linguistics, 15*, 289–316. http://dx.doi.org/10.1515/cogl.2004.011

Gómez, R. L. (2002). Variability and detection of invariant structure. *Psychological Science, 13*, 431–436. http://dx.doi.org/10.1111/1467-9280.00476

Halford, G. S. (1993). *Children's understanding: The development of mental models.* Hillsdale, NJ: Erlbaum.

Hare, M., McRae, K., & Elman, J. (2004). Admitting that admitting verb sense into corpus analyses makes sense. *Language and Cognitive Processes, 19*, 181–224. http://dx.doi.org/10.1080/01690960344000152

Ibbotson, P., Theakston, A. L., Lieven, E. V. M., & Tomasello, M. (2011). The role of pronoun frames in early comprehension of transitive constructions in English. *Language Learning and Development, 7*, 24–39. http://dx.doi.org/10.1080/15475441003732914

Ibbotson, P., Theakston, A. L., Lieven, E. V. M., & Tomasello, M. (2012). Semantics of the transitive construction: Prototype effects and developmental comparisons. *Cognitive Science, 36*, 1268–1288. http://dx.doi.org/10.1111/j.1551-6709.2012.01249.x

Jones, G., Gobet, F., & Pine, J. M. (2000). A process model of children's early verb use. In L. R. Gleitman & A. K. Joshi (Eds.), *Proceedings of the 22nd Annual Meeting of the Cognitive Science Society* (pp. 723–728). Mahwah, NJ: Erlbaum.

Kidd, E., Lieven, E. V. M., & Tomasello, M. (2010). Lexical frequency and exemplar-based learning effects in language acquisition: Evidence from sentential complements. *Language Sciences, 32*, 132–142. http://dx.doi.org/10.1016/j.langsci.2009.05.002

Kirjavainen, M., Nikolaev, A., & Kidd, E. (2012). The effect of frequency and phonological neighbourhood density on the acquisition of past tense verbs by Finnish children. *Cognitive Linguistics, 23*(2). Advance online publication. http://dx.doi.org/10.1515/cog-2012-0009

Kirjavainen, M., & Theakston, A. (2011). Are infinitival *to* omission errors primed by prior discourse? The case of WANT constructions. *Cognitive Linguistics, 22*, 629–657. http://dx.doi.org/10.1515/cogl.2011.024

Kirjavainen, M., Theakston, A., & Lieven, E. (2009). Can input explain children's me-for-I errors? *Journal of Child Language, 36*, 1091–1114. http://dx.doi.org/10.1017/S0305000909009350

Kuiper, K. (1996). *Smooth talkers: The linguistic performance of auctioneers and sportscasters.* Mahwah, NJ: Erlbaum.

Küntay, A., & Slobin, D. I. (1996). Listening to a Turkish mother: Some puzzles for acquisition. In D. I. Slobin, J. Gerhardt, A. Kyratzis, & J. Guo (Eds.), *Social interaction, social context, and language: Essays in honor of Susan Ervin-Tripp* (pp. 265–286). Mahwah, NJ: Lawrence Erlbaum.

Leonard, L. B., & Deevy, P. (2011). Input distribution influences degree of auxiliary use by children with specific language impairment. *Cognitive Linguistics, 22*, 247–273. http://dx.doi.org/10.1515/cogl.2011.010

Lieven, E. V. M., Pine, J. M., & Baldwin, G. (1997). Lexically-based learning and early grammatical development. *Journal of Child Language, 24*, 187–219. http://dx.doi.org/10.1017/S0305000996002930

Lieven, E. V. M., Salomo, D., & Tomasello, M. (2009). Two-year-old children's production of multiword utterances: A usage-based analysis. *Cognitive Linguistics, 20*, 481–507. http://dx.doi.org/10.1515/COGL.2009.022

Logan, G. D. (1988). Toward an instance theory of automatization. *Psychological Review, 95*, 492–527. http://dx.doi.org/10.1037/0033-295X.95.4.492

Marchman, V. A. (1997). Children's productivity in the English past tense: The role of frequency, phonology, and neighborhood structure. *Cognitive Science, 21*, 283–304. http://dx.doi.org/10.1207/s15516709cog2103_2

Marslen-Wilson, W. (1990). Activation, competition, and frequency in lexical access. In G. T. M. Altmann (Ed.), *Cognitive models of speech processing: Psycholinguistic and computational perspectives* (pp. 148–172). Hove, England: Erlbaum.

Matthews, D., & Bannard, C. (2010). Children's production of unfamiliar word sequences is predicted by positional variability and latent classes in a large sample of child-directed speech. *Cognitive Science, 34*, 465–488. http://dx.doi.org/10.1111/j.1551-6709.2009.01091.x

Matthews, D., Lieven, E., Theakston, A., & Tomasello, M. (2007). French children's use and correction of weird word orders: A constructivist account. *Journal of Child Language, 34*, 381–409. http://dx.doi.org/10.1017/S030500090600794X

McClure, K., Pine, J. M., & Lieven, E. V. M. (2006). Investigating the abstractness of children's early knowledge of argument structure. *Journal of Child Language, 33*, 693–720. http://dx.doi.org/10.1017/S0305000906007525

Mintz, T. H. (2003). Frequent frames as a cue for grammatical categories in child directed speech. *Cognition, 90*, 91–117. http://dx.doi.org/10.1016/S0010-0277(03)00140-9

Monaghan, P., Christiansen, M. H., & Chater, N. (2007). The phonological-distributional coherence hypothesis: Cross-linguistic evidence in language acquisition. *Cognitive Psychology, 55*, 259–305. http://dx.doi.org/10.1016/j.cogpsych.2006.12.001

Morrison, R. G., Holyoak, K. J., & Truong, B. (2001). Working memory modularity in analogical reasoning. In J. D. Moore & K. Stenning (Eds.), *Proceedings of the Twenty-Third Annual Conference of the Cognitive Science Society* (pp. 663–668). Mahwah, NJ: Erlbaum.

Naigles, L. R. (2002). Form is easy, meaning is hard: Resolving a paradox in early child language. *Cognition, 86*, 157–199. http://dx.doi.org/10.1016/S0010-0277(02)00177-4

Naigles, L. R., & Hoff-Ginsberg, E. (1998). Why are some verbs learned before other verbs? Effects of input frequency and structure on children's early verb use. *Journal of Child Language, 25*, 95–120. http://dx.doi.org/10.1017/S0305000997003358

Ninio, A. (1999). Pathbreaking verbs in syntactic development and the question of prototypical transitivity. *Journal of Child Language*, 26, 619–653. http://dx.doi.org/10.1017/S0305000999003931

Onnis, L., Waterfall, H. R., & Edelman, S. (2008). Learn locally, act globally: Learning language from variation set cues. *Cognition*, 109, 423–430. http://dx.doi.org/10.1016/j.cognition.2008.10.004

Pickering, M. J., & Ferreira, V. S. (2008). Structural priming: A critical review. *Psychological Bulletin*, 134, 427–459. http://dx.doi.org/10.1037/0033-2909.134.3.427

Pine, J. M., & Lieven, E. V. M. (1997). Slot and frame patterns and the development of the determiner category. *Applied Psycholinguistics*, 18, 123–138. http://dx.doi.org/10.1017/S0142716400009930

Pine, J. M., Lieven, E. V. M., & Rowland, C. F. (1998). Comparing different models of the development of the English verb category. *Linguistics*, 36, 807–830. http://dx.doi.org/10.1515/ling.1998.36.4.807

Pinker, S. (1984). *Language learnability and language development*. Cambridge, MA: Harvard University Press.

Radford, A. (1990). *Syntactic theory and the acquisition of English syntax*. Oxford, England: Blackwell.

Räsänen, S. H. M., Ambridge, B., & Pine, J. M. (2014). Infinitives or bare stems? Are English-speaking children defaulting to the highest-frequency form? *Journal of Child Language*, 41, 756–779. http://dx.doi.org/10.1017/S0305000913000159

Rowland, C. F., Chang, F., Ambridge, B., Pine, J. M., & Lieven, E. V. M. (2012). The development of abstract syntax: Evidence from structural priming and the lexical boost. *Cognition*, 125, 49–63. http://dx.doi.org/10.1016/j.cognition.2012.06.008

Rowland, C. F., & Noble, C. L. (2010). The role of syntactic structure in children's sentence comprehension: Evidence from the dative. *Language Learning and Development*, 7, 55–75. http://dx.doi.org/10.1080/15475441003769411

Rowland, C. F., & Pine, J. M. (2000). Subject–auxiliary inversion errors and wh-question acquisition: "What children do know?" *Journal of Child Language*, 27, 157–181. http://dx.doi.org/10.1017/S0305000999004055

Savage, C., Lieven, E., Theakston, A., & Tomasello, M. (2003). Testing the abstractness of children's linguistic representations: Lexical and structural priming of syntactic constructions in young children. *Developmental Science*, 6, 557–567. http://dx.doi.org/10.1111/1467-7687.00312

Savage, C., Lieven, E., Theakston, A., & Tomasello, M. (2006). Structural priming as implicit learning in language acquisition: The persistence of lexical and structural priming in 4-year-olds. *Language Learning and Development*, 2, 27–49. http://dx.doi.org/10.1207/s15473341lld0201_2

Saxton, M. (1997). The contrast theory of negative input. *Journal of Child Language*, 24, 139–161. http://dx.doi.org/10.1017/S030500099600298X

Scott, R. M., & Fisher, C. (2009). Two-year-olds use distributional cues to interpret transitivity-alternating verbs. *Language and Cognitive Processes*, 24, 777–803. http://dx.doi.org/10.1080/01690960802573236

Shimpi, P. M., Gámez, P. B., Huttenlocher, J., & Vasilyeva, M. (2007). Syntactic priming in 3- and 4-year-old children: Evidence for abstract representations of transitive and dative forms. *Developmental Psychology*, 43, 1334–1346. http://dx.doi.org/10.1037/0012-1649.43.6.1334

Siebenborn, A., Krajewski, G., & Lieven, E. (2016). *Frequency distribution and the learning of novel morphological constructions*. Manuscript in preparation.

St. Clair, M. C., Monaghan, P., & Christiansen, M. H. (2010). Learning grammatical categories from distributional cues: Flexible frames for language acquisition. *Cognition, 116*, 341–360. http://dx.doi.org/10.1016/j.cognition.2010.05.012

Stoll, S., Abbot-Smith, K., & Lieven, E. (2009). Lexically restricted utterances in Russian, German, and English child-directed speech. *Cognitive Science, 33*, 75–103. http://dx.doi.org/10.1111/j.1551-6709.2008.01004.x

Sundara, M., Demuth, K., & Kuhl, P. K. (2011). Sentence-position effects on children's perception and production of English third person singular -s. *Journal of Speech, Language, and Hearing Research, 54*, 55–71. http://dx.doi.org/10.1044/1092-4388(2010/10-0056)

Theakston, A. L. (2004). The role of entrenchment in children's and adults' performance on grammaticality judgment tasks. *Cognitive Development, 19*, 1534.

Theakston, A. L. (2012). "The spotty cow tickled the pig with a curly tail": How do sentence position, preferred argument structure, and referential complexity affect children's and adults' choice of referring expression? *Applied Psycholinguistics, 33*, 691–724. http://dx.doi.org/10.1017/S0142716411000531

Theakston, A. L., Ibbotson, P., Freudenthal, D., Lieven, E. V. M., & Tomasello, M. (2015). Productivity of noun slots in verb frames. *Cognitive Science, 39*, 1369–1395. http://dx.doi.org/10.1111/cogs.12216

Theakston, A. L., & Lieven, E. V. M. (2008). The influence of discourse context on children's provision of auxiliary BE. *Journal of Child Language, 35*, 129–158. http://dx.doi.org/10.1017/S0305000907008306

Theakston, A. L., Lieven, E. V. M., Pine, J. M., & Rowland, C. F. (2001). The role of performance limitations in the acquisition of verb-argument structure: An alternative account. *Journal of Child Language, 28*, 127–152. http://dx.doi.org/10.1017/S0305000900004608

Theakston, A. L., Lieven, E. V. M., Pine, J. M., & Rowland, C. F. (2002). Going, going, gone: The acquisition of the verb 'go'. *Journal of Child Language, 29*, 783–811. http://dx.doi.org/10.1017/S030500090200538X

Theakston, A. L., Lieven, E. V. M., Pine, J. M., & Rowland, C. F. (2005). The acquisition of auxiliary syntax: BE and HAVE. *Cognitive Linguistics, 16*, 247–277. http://dx.doi.org/10.1515/cogl.2005.16.1.247

Theakston, A. L., Lieven, E. V. M., & Tomasello, M. (2003). The role of the input in the acquisition of third person singular verbs in English. *Journal of Speech, Language, and Hearing Research, 46*, 863–877. http://dx.doi.org/10.1044/1092-4388(2003/067)

Theakston, A. L., Maslen, R., Lieven, E. V. M., & Tomasello, M. (2012). The acquisition of the active transitive construction in English: A detailed case study. *Cognitive Linguistics, 23*, 91–128. http://dx.doi.org/10.1515/cog-2012-0004

Theakston, A. L., & Rowland, C. F. (2009). The acquisition of auxiliary syntax: A longitudinal elicitation study. Part 1: Auxiliary BE. *Journal of Speech, Language, and Hearing Research, 52*, 1449–1470. http://dx.doi.org/10.1044/1092-4388(2009/08-0037)

Tomasello, M. (1992). *First verbs: A case study of early grammatical development*. http://dx.doi.org/10.1017/CBO9780511527678

Tomasello, M. (2003). *Constructing a language: A usage-based theory of language acquisition*. Cambridge, MA: Harvard University Press.

Trueswell, J. C., & Tanenhaus, M. K. (1994). Toward a lexicalist framework of constraint-based syntactic ambiguity resolution. In C. Clifton, L. Frazier, & K. Rayner (Eds.), *Perspectives in sentence processing* (pp. 155–180). Hillsdale, NJ: Lawrence Erlbaum.

Westermann, G., & Mareschal, D. (2014). From perceptual to language-mediated categorization. *Philosophical Transactions of the Royal Society of London: Series B. Biological Sciences*, *369*, 20120391. http://dx.doi.org/10.1098/rstb.2012.0391

Wonnacott, E., Boyd, J. K., Thomson, J., & Goldberg, A. E. (2012). Input effects on the acquisition of a novel phrasal construction in 5 year olds. *Journal of Memory and Language*, *66*, 458–478. http://dx.doi.org/10.1016/j.jml.2011.11.004

Wonnacott, E., Newport, E. L., & Tanenhaus, M. K. (2008). Acquiring and processing verb argument structure: Distributional learning in a miniature language. *Cognitive Psychology*, *56*, 165–209. http://dx.doi.org/10.1016/j.cogpsych.2007.04.002

Yang, C. (2013). Who's afraid of George Kingsley Zipf? Or: Do children and chimps have language? *Significance*, *10*, 29–34. http://dx.doi.org/10.1111/j.1740-9713.2013.00708.x

Yuan, S., Fisher, C., & Snedeker, J. (2012). Counting the nouns: Simple structural cues to verb meaning. *Child Development*, *83*, 1382–1399. http://dx.doi.org/10.1111/j.1467-8624.2012.01783.x

Brian MacWhinney
15 Entrenchment in Second-Language Learning

15.1 Introduction

This chapter examines the role of entrenchment in second-language (L2) learning. It is generally recognized that language learning success declines with age. However, the exact nature and causes of this decline are not yet clear. The earliest accounts of age-related effects in L2 learning were based on the critical period concept derived from embryology and ethology. However, the gradual nature of declines in L2 learning outcomes, along with evidence of successful learning during adulthood, do not correspond well to this model. Neural network models succeed in simulating the gradual decline of language learning abilities by focusing on the role of entrenchment. However, these models also predict catastrophic interference during the learning of L2. To resolve this paradox, the unified competition model (UCM) reformulates the issue in terms of the interplay of four risk factors (entrenchment, transfer, overanalysis, and isolation) with four support or protective factors (resonance, decoupling, chunking, and participation). This model provides a more complete account of age-related declines in L2 learning and ways in which they can be mitigated.

15.2 Critical Periods

In his landmark study of the biological foundations of language, Lenneberg (1967) postulated a critical period for the acquisition of language that terminates as a result of the onset of cerebral lateralization at puberty. Lenneberg thought of this critical period as applying to the learning of both the first language (L1) and a second language (L2). He attributed the loss of cerebral equipotentiality to the factors of myelination and neuronal commitment. Subsequent research (Feldman, MacWhinney, & Sacco, 2002) has supported Lenneberg's ideas about early cerebral equipotentiality and plasticity. Using fMRI scanning, Booth et al. (2000) showed that children who had left hemisphere brain lesions during gestation and infancy developed language by relying on right hemisphere regions such as the inferior frontal gyrus that correspond to damaged regions on the left. Moreover, when these children reached ages 6 to 8, both the functional use of language and basic information processing skills underlying language use (Feldman et al., 2002) ended up being generally well within the normal range. Interestingly, this pattern of nearly optimal recovery of language despite often massive brain injury does not extend to other cognitive skills. In particular, damage to right hemisphere areas from early focal lesions can result in major spatial deficits (Stiles, Trauner, Engel, & Nass, 1997), and there is a general tendency for language to be better preserved than other cognitive skills (Aram & Eisele, 1994). This pattern has been called *cognitive crowding* because it indicates that the development of successful language skills can come at the expense of other skills such as math or reading that might be acquired later in development.

Lenneberg's (1967) proposal corresponds well with some facts about early equipotentiality. However, his reliance on lateralization as the mechanism underlying the termination of the critical period suffers from two basic problems. The first is that lateralization is present well before age 13. Anatomical and neuroimaging work has shown that lateralization is already present at birth (Molfese, Freeman, & Palermo, 1975) and that it increases during the first two years (Mills, Coffey-Corina, & Neville, 1997). A second problem is that Lenneberg's analysis relied on hemispherectomy data from Basser (1962) to support the idea that equipotentiality terminates at age 13. However, the cases reported by Basser involved confounds with ongoing epileptic status, size of epileptic focus, and language measurement that make it impossible to establish any close link between the onset of puberty and the loss of a right hemisphere ability to reacquire the first language.

Lenneberg (1967) also suggested that myelination could be a mechanism underlying a critical period transition at puberty. We know that there is progressive myelination throughout children's development (Gao et al., 2009) and that this myelination largely culminates by puberty. However, there are two problems with attempts to rely on myelination as an explanation for termination of a critical period for L2 acquisition. The first is that, even during adulthood, focused cognitive training can lead to measurable changes in white matter mass through myelination (Engvig et al., 2012; Posner, Tang, & Lynch, 2014; Sampaio-Baptista et al., 2013; Takeuchi et al., 2010), indicating that this form of neuronal plasticity extends well past the postulated critical period of childhood. Second, myelination is a process that affects all major fiber tracts, not just those supporting language skills. However, no one would want to argue that all aspects of adult behavior are locked in by critical period effects.

More generally, it is questionable whether age-related decreases in L2 learning outcomes qualify as a critical period in the sense used in embryology (Browman, 1989) or ethology (Lorenz, 1958). In these areas, critical periods are defined by radical stimulus deprivation, such as blindness (Hubel & Wiesel, 1963), deafness (Kral & Sharma, 2012), or social isolation (Marler, 1991). For second-language learning, we are not talking about massive deprivation during infancy but about the ability to modify an already intact system across the lifespan. Moreover, the critical periods studied in animals are not shaped by some specific single neural process, such as lateralization, synaptic pruning, myelination, metabolic decline, or increases in estrogen. Instead, they arise from a complex set of interactions and modulations between cortical structures and basal ganglia involving various neural transmitters, and these modularity developmental effects work differentially in particular areas of structures, such as segments of the auditory cortex (Kral & Sharma, 2012) or motor cortex (Yamamoto, Hoffman, & Strick, 2006).

Johnson and Newport (1989) conducted the first psycholinguistic test of Lenneberg's (1967) critical period analysis. They examined grammaticality judgments from 46 participants whose first languages were Chinese or Korean and who had arrived in the United States at various ages from 3 to 39. They observed a significant correlation between age of arrival and success in grammaticality judgments, but only for early arrivers. However, in his review of additional studies replicating and extending this initial study, Birdsong (2005) concluded that the accuracy of grammaticality judgments shows a continuous linear decline for older ages of arrival, even in the data from Johnson and Newport. This conclusion suggests that the decline is not linked to a critical or even sensitive period, but simply to decreasing plasticity. Further evidence for this conclusion comes from a large census-based study (Hakuta, Bialystok, & Wiley, 2003; Wiley, Bialystok, & Hakuta, 2005) showing that the gap in L2 attainment resulting from later age of arrival is equal in size to the gap caused by lower levels of education.

15.3 Entrenchment

A contrasting approach attributes age-related L2 learning effects to basic properties of learning in neural nets. Rather than referring to specific biological processes such as lateralization, myelination, synaptic pruning, or gene expression, this account attributes age-related effects to entrenchment, which is viewed as the emergent result of network computation (Zevin, 2012). Once a network has been trained to respond to a large variety of stimuli, it settles into an attractor state that is very difficult to modify. When such states are reached, the relevant patterns apply quickly and uniformly during processing (Segalowitz, Segalowitz, & Wood, 1998) and are difficult to modify developmentally (Brooks & Tomasello, 1999).

Entrenchment has been demonstrated both for parallel distributed processing networks (Seidenberg & Zevin, 2006) and for self-organizing feature maps (Li, Farkas, & MacWhinney, 2004). The nature of this effect in the emergence of word classes can be demonstrated graphically in self-organizing feature maps for lexical development of the type created by the DevLex simulation (Li et al., 2004). After 50 cycles of learning, these maps have a rather loose and unstable organization of lexical items by part of speech. However, as learning progresses, more items are added to the map, and the boundaries of the different parts of speech categories become sharper. Moreover, during the first stages of L1 learning, the categories migrate around the map. During later stages there is no more movement of category boundaries, because the shape of the parts of speech and the location of particular items on the feature map have become entrenched.

These neural network simulations of the entrenchment process represent existence proofs showing that critical periods can arise from the strengthening of organized connections between units. On the neuronal level, this effect would be based on the strengthening of synaptic connections according to the Hebbian rule (Pulvermüller, 2003) that "neurons that fire together, wire together." Entrenchment is further supported by synaptic pruning, which can disallow certain patterns that are not needed for first-language functioning. Myelination, hormonal changes, and lateralization can play further secondary roles in terms of locking in patterns of connection between major brain areas. Neural network simulations have not yet been configured to represent the interactions between these various physiological changes. Rather, current simulations capture only the overall trajectory of entrenchment.

The computational account of entrenchment can be used to account for critical period effects in L2 learning of audition, articulation, syntax, and morphology. Such accounts do not need to postulate any sudden or sharp end to the critical period. In that way, they provide a satisfying account for the observed window of decreasing plasticity that slowly closes over a long period of time.

Entrenchment can also account for findings regarding articulatory development. A study of Italian immigrants to Canada (Munro, Flege, & Mackay, 1996) found that unless these participants had arrived before age 6, it was possible to detect some features of an Italian accent in their English. However, it is possible that these effects arose not so much from entrenchment as from the fact that immigrants who arrived at a later age tended to interact more frequently with the local Italian community, thereby maintaining an Italian accent in English. An interesting feature of this study is the suggestion that entrenchment could close off a critical period for articulation well before the onset of puberty. However, it is possible to modify L1 influences on articulation in adults through concentrated training (Flege, 1995).

Even earlier entrenchment effects have been postulated for the development of auditory perception. Studies by Werker and Tees (2005) and Kuhl (2004) have demonstrated a loss of certain perceptual contrasts during the first year of life. These effects led Kuhl to formulate the perceptual magnet hypothesis, according to which a child loses the ability to make discriminations between sounds that are not contrastive in the native language. According to this hypothesis, the loss arises because sounds that vary in perceptual detail are assimilated to the core of a given phonemic category. This account attributes age-related changes in perception to the entrenchment of the perceptual magnet. Although this model works well for many empirical results, there are several phenomena that it cannot handle. One problem is that certain sounds, such as clicks and nasals, are reliably detected at all ages (Werker, 1995). Another problem involves the fact that after age 3, children begin to improve in their ability to detect certain contrasts (Werker, 1995). Moreover, deficits in perceptual accuracy in adult bilinguals do not link up directly to the age at which they began learning a second language during childhood, instead showing wide individual variation (Flege & MacKay, 2004).

The most intensely studied auditory entrenchment effect involves the inability of many Japanese speakers to discriminate English /r/ and /l/. This inability may stem from the fact that discrimination of phonemic contrasts in Japanese does not require attention to the third formant, although the distinction between English /r/ and /l/ is made clearest through processing of the third formant. Several studies have succeeded in training perception of this contrast using artificial stimuli (Bradlow, Akahane-Yamada, Pisoni, & Tohkura, 1999; Ingvalson, Holt, & McClelland, 2012; McCandliss, Fiez, Protopapas, Conway, & McClelland, 2002). However, generalization to speech stimuli has been limited, suggesting that more work is needed using real speech as training materials.

Entrenchment can also be used to account for the problems that L2 learners have with the learning and usage of grammatical morphology. It is often observed that learners of languages such as German or Spanish fail to acquire full control over grammatical markings for noun declension or verb inflection (Sagarra & Herschensohn, 2010, 2011; VanPatten, Keating, & Leeser, 2012). VanPatten and colleagues (2012) argued that this deficit is attributable to the termination of a critical period for the use of universal grammar. Approaching this issue from a rather different perspective, Newport (1990) hypothesized that children are better able to learn grammar because they start with small chunks. However, initial evidence supporting this idea from Elman (1993) failed later replication (Rohde & Plaut, 1997). In fact, it seems that, if anything, children store larger units than do adults (McCauley, Monaghan, & Christiansen, 2014).

Another explanation for adult problems with morphology comes from Ullman (2004), who argued that increased estrogen levels at puberty lead to weakening of the procedural learning system involved in combinatorial morphology and compensatory strengthening of declarative memory. This hypothesis predicts stronger learning of irregular morphology in adulthood and weaker learning of regular morphology. However, studies of the training of grammatical morphology in adult L2 learners (Presson, Sagarra, MacWhinney, & Kowalski, 2013) and experiments with artificial grammars (Kürten, De Vries, Kowal, Zwitserlood, & Flöel, 2012) have demonstrated exactly the opposite effect, indicating that there is no obvious procedural learning deficit in adults. Together, these results indicate that a more likely account is that adults seek to learn lexical stems in a highly analytic manner that reduces concomitant acquisition of attached grammatical markers. Thus, this is a problem with learning style, rather than a basic maturational limitation.

We have seen that the timing and nature of the age-related effects attributed to the operation of entrenchment vary markedly across the domains of audition, articulation, syntax, and morphology. Moreover, when we look in greater detail at each of these areas, we find additional variation across structures and processes. If entrenchment is to work as an account for all of their effects, we need to understand how it can be that some neural networks entrench much more rapidly than others. In large part, these variations in entrenchment speed and rigidity can be explained by the fact that some skills are learned before others. For example, the child works on the distinction between /p/ and /b/ long before learning to produce *wh* questions in English or mark the subjunctive in Spanish. However, we may also need to refine the theory of entrenchment to account for differential entrenchment in various cortical areas. Clear evidence of such differences comes from work on plasticity in motor cortex. Studies using infection with rabies virus (Yamamoto et al., 2006) have revealed one network of neurons capable of ongoing developmental plasticity along with another network that is no longer plastic during adult development. It is likely that local variations in plasticity during adulthood can be triggered by interactions between cortical areas, particularly in the highly interactive areas subserving higher language functions.

Apart from the need to consider complex patterns of neuronal variation, the entrenchment hypothesis suffers from two other problems. The first involves the phenomenon of catastrophic interference (McCloskey & Cohen, 1989). When a neural net that has been trained on one set of inputs is suddenly shifted to a new set of inputs, the weights derived from the earlier training set are overwritten. For second-language learning, this would mean that learning of a second language erases memory of the first language. Such effects may occur when a child is adopted into a new language community and not given any opportunity to continue use of the first language (Pallier et al., 2003). However, for older children and adults, the termination of use of a first language leads not to total forgetting but rather to gradual attrition (Steinkrauss & Schmid, Chapter 16, this volume). One could argue that maintenance of the first language in older learners reflects a higher level of entrenchment. However, explaining how entrenchment or stability can exist alongside plasticity has been a problem for neural network modeling.

Although a variety of technical solutions to this problem have been explored (Hamker, 2001; McClelland, McNaughton, & O'Reilly, 1995; Richardson & Thomas, 2008), it appears that successful learning must treat the learning of L2 as a separate task encoded in a partially separate network (Carpenter, Grossberg, & Reynolds, 1991). Achieving this separation requires control from attentional areas, and it is reasonable to assume that this separation between languages occurs in real-life second-language learning.

The obverse of catastrophic interference is irreversible entrenchment. If networks are configured in ways that maximize the increase of stability or entrenchment over time, they become incapable of new learning. In the extreme, the entrenchment account predicts that adults should be nearly incapable of learning second languages. In fact, some adults are able to learn second languages quite well, often to the level of native speaker competence (Birdsong, 2005; Bongaerts, 1999). For audition, we know that adults can acquire an ability to respond quickly to second-language auditory contrasts as reflected in the early mismatch negativity component of the EEG (Winkler et al., 1999) after even just 6 hours of training (Kraus et al., 1995). Moreover, in adult rats, noise exposure can reinstate critical period plasticity, demonstrating that at least some of the effects of entrenchment are reversible (Zhou, Panizzutti, de Villers-Sidani, Madeira, & Merzenich, 2011). Thus, although entrenchment provides a reasonable account for a decline in learning abilities, it overestimates the extent to which the brain loses plasticity.

We can summarize this brief review in terms of three major points:

1. The linkage of age-related effects in language learning directly to the onset of lateralization, increases in estrogen, or the effects of myelination has not been supported.
2. Age-related effects in L2 learning can be partially attributed to entrenchment in neural nets. However, learning of a second language must involve control processes that avoid triggering of catastrophic interference effects through construction of partially separate systems.
3. Patterns of plasticity, early canalization, and later learning vary markedly across individuals, language domains, and specific target structures. This indicates that entrenchment is not a uniform process across cortical areas, but rather a feature that varies markedly in onset, duration, and tenacity, depending on additional neurodevelopmental interactions.

Together, these results point to the need for a model that treats entrenchment as only one component of a more complex account of age-related effects in second-language learning. In other words, entrenchment alone cannot explain age-related effects in L2 acquisition.

15.4 Unified Competition Model

The UCM (MacWhinney, 2012) seeks to address the issue of age-related variation in L2 learning by highlighting the interplay between risk factors and support processes. For L2 learning past early childhood, the model postulates the four risk factors of entrenchment, transfer, overanalysis, and isolation. To overcome these four risk factors, adults can rely on the support processes of resonance, decoupling, chunking, and participation. These processes are described in detail in Sections 15.5 to 15.8. This analysis is similar to that presented in MacWhinney (2012) with three important modifications. First, the risk factor of parasitism is treated here as a logical consequence of transfer, rather than as a separate process. Second, the earlier account discussed misconnection between cortical areas as a risk factor. Because the exact neurological basis of misconnection between cortical areas is still unclear, reference to that risk factor is now removed from the model and left as a topic for future research. Third, the current version places a stronger emphasis on the risk factor of overanalysis. Other aspects of the previous analysis remain the same.

The UCM holds that all of these risk factors and support processes are available to both children and adults. In that sense, there is no fundamental difference (Bley-Vroman, 2009) between children and adults as language learners. What differs between language learning in childhood and adulthood is the way in which risk and support processes are configured and the need for explicit invocation of support processes by adult learners.

There are four obvious differences between child and adult language learners. First, during the process of first-language learning, infants are also engaged in learning about how the world works. In contrast, adult second-language learners already have a basic understanding of the world and human society. Second, infants are able to rely on a brain that has not yet undergone entrenchment. In contrast, adult second-language learners have to deal with a brain that has already been dynamically configured for the task of processing the first language. Third, infants can rely on an intense system of social support from their caregivers (Snow, 1999). In contrast, adult second-language learners are often heavily involved in L1 social and business commitments that distract them from L2 interactions. Fourth, children have not yet developed adult-like methods for executive control of attention. Although the executive control areas of the brain are active at birth (Doria et al., 2010), they continue to develop through childhood and adolescence (Asato, Terwilliger, Woo, & Luna, 2010; Casey, Giedd, & Thomas, 2000). Regularity and inhibitory control over behavior increases in complexity and refinement across the whole period of childhood and adolescence (Munakata, McClelland, Johnson, & Siegler, 1997). To the degree that language and language learning depend on executive control, we can expect differences between adults and children from these sources, although there is no sharp transition point.

Along with these four areas of difference, there are many shared features between L1 and L2 learners. Both groups are trying to learn the same target language, both need to segment speech into words, both need to learn the meanings of these words, both need to figure out the patterns that govern word combination in syntactic constructions, and both have to interleave their growing lexical and syntactic systems to achieve fluency. Thus, both the overall goal and the specific subgoals involved in reaching that goal are the same for both L1 and L2 learners. In addition, the neurocognitive mechanisms available to solve these problems are the same for the two groups. Both rely on episodic memory to encode new forms and chunks, both have access to embodied encodings of actions and objects, both use statistical learning (see Jost & Christiansen, Chapter 10, this volume) and generalization (see Cordes, Chapter 12, this volume) to extract linguistic patterns, and both solidify knowledge and procedures through routine and practice. Both groups are enmeshed in social situations that require a continued back and forth of communication, imitation, and learning, as well as understandings regarding shared intentions and common ground.

One could recognize the shared nature of all those mechanisms and processes but still claim that the remaining differences are the ones that are fundamental (Bley-Vroman, 2009). The question is whether those remaining differences are great enough to motivate two separate theories for learning and processing. The thesis of the UCM is that the inclusion of L1 and L2 learning in a single unified model produces a more coherent and insightful analysis. The fact that L2 learning is so heavily influenced by transfer from L1 means that it would be impossible to construct a model of L2 learning that did not take into account the structure of the first language. Unless the two types of learning and processing share virtually no important commonalities, it is conceptually simpler to formulate a unified model within which the specific areas of divergence can be clearly distinguished from the numerous commonalities.

15.5 Entrenchment and Resonance

As long as a neural network continues to receive input in the first language, entrenched first-language patterns will block learning of conflicting second-language patterns. However, if input from the first language tapers off or stops, the network will undergo catastrophic interference leading to loss of the first language. In real L2 learning, this is not what we observe. Thus, the computational mechanism of entrenchment can be used only as an account of age-related effects in the case of ongoing use of L1 during learning of L2.

As noted earlier, the effects of entrenchment in neural network models vary markedly across language processing levels. The detailed operation of entrenchment in self-organizing feature maps has been modeled most explicitly for lexical and phonological structure using the DevLex model (Li, Zhao, & MacWhinney, 2007) and auditory structure using the DIVA model (Guenther & Gjaja, 1996). However, the UCM holds that cortical maps exist for each of the structural levels recognized by traditional linguistics, including syntax (Pulvermüller, 2003), mental models (MacWhinney, 2008), and discourse patterning (Koechlin & Summerfield, 2007) as given in Table 15.1.

Table 15.1 presents the major brain areas involved in each level of language processing, some of the processes involved, and the theories that have been developed to account for each type of processing. For audition, auditory cortex is the focus of initial processing. However, according to Hickok and Poeppel (2004), additional areas are

Tab. 15.1: Levels of Linguistic Processing

Map	Brain area	Processes	Theory
Audition	Auditory cortex	Extracting units	Statistical learning
Articulation	Inferior frontal gyrus, motor cortex	Targets, timing	Gating
Lexicon	Superior temporal gyrus, anterior temporal lobe	Sound to meaning	DevLex
Syntax	Inferior frontal gyrus	Slots, sequences	Item-based patterns
Mental models	Dorsal lateral prefrontal cortex	Deixis, perspective	Perspective, roles
Discourse	Frontal cortex	Conversation	Conversation analysis, pragmatics

involved in linking auditory patterns to lexical items. Studies of statistical learning focus on the ways in which these patterns become encoded in auditory and lexical cortex. Articulation involves communication between gestural patterns in the *pars opercularis* of the inferior frontal gyrus and detailed activation of patterns in motor cortex. The actual firing of these patterns is gated by a monitor (Roelofs, 2011) that checks to see if output patterns align with lexical targets. In the DevLex framework, lexical patterns are organized phonologically in the superior temporal gyrus and conceptually in the anterior temporal lobe. Syntactic processing involves communication between general constructions involving the *pars triangularis* of the inferior frontal gyrus and the anterior temporal lobe in accord with the theory of item-based patterns (MacWhinney, 2014). Mental model construction relies on frontal areas such as the dorsal lateral prefrontal cortex to assign case roles and track perspectives. Additional frontal areas are involved in tracking the overall pragmatic flow and sequencing of conversation.

Entrenchment in cortical maps is the strongest risk factor for auditory phonology (Kuhl, Conboy, Padden, Nelson, & Pruitt, 2005), articulatory phonology (Major, 1987), and syntax (DeKeyser, 2000). For audition and articulation, the power of entrenchment arises from the fact that myriads of detailed coordinations are involved in attaining nativelike proficiency. For articulation, there are many muscles to be controlled, and the ways in which these must be sequenced in words to achieve fluency are numerous and require frequent practice. Moreover, many of the connections between motor cortex and the spinal cord are fixed early in development. For audition, learning of L1 involves adjustment to a wide range of speaker variations, as well as the ability to use top-down information to reconstruct sounds in noise. On the lexical level, interference between L1 and L2 leads to fewer direct clashes. As a result, L2 learning of new words suffers minimal age-related declines. In fact, adults can acquire new L2 vocabulary more efficiently than children (Snow & Hoefnagel-Hohle, 1978).

In a thorough review of studies comparing L1 and L2 learning of syntax, Clahsen and Felser (2006) found no significant differences for the majority of morphological and syntactic processes. This finding is in line with the claim of the UCM regarding the fundamental similarity of L1 and L2 learning. However, Clahsen and Felser also noted that L2 learners often encounter problems in their processing of complex syntactic patterns involving discontinuities and gaps. Based on these data, they formulated the shallow structure hypothesis, which holds that L2 learners are not able to extract deeper, more abstract levels of syntactic structure, whereas L1 learners eventually acquire this ability. However, it is possible that the movement and gapping structures in question may present challenges to learners because of interference from entrenched L1 processes, particularly in Asian languages.

The risk factor of entrenchment can be counteracted during L2 learning by explicit reliance on the support factor of resonance. *Resonance* can be defined as the consolidation of new linguistic patterns through support from existing relations. It provides new encoding dimensions to reconfigure old neuronal territory, permitting the successful encoding of L2 patterns. Because this encoding must operate against the underlying forces of entrenchment, special configurations are needed to support resonance. Resonance can be illustrated most easily in the domain of lexical learning. Since the days of Ebbinghaus (1885), we have understood that the learning of the associations between words requires repeated practice. However, a single repetition of a new vocabulary pair such as *mesa–table* is not enough to guarantee robust learning. Instead, it is important that initial exposure be followed by additional test repetitions timed to provide correct retrieval before forgetting prevents efficient resonance from occurring (Pavlik & Anderson, 2005). Because robustness accumulates with practice, later retrieval trials can be spaced further and further apart. This is the principle of graduated interval recall that was formulated for second-language learning by Pimsleur (1967).

The success of graduated interval recall can be attributed, in part, to its use of resonant neural connections between cortical areas. When two cortical areas are coactive, the hippocampus can store their relation long enough to create an initial memory consolidation (see Takashima & Bakker, Chapter 8, this volume). Repeated hippocampal access to this trace (Wittenberg, Sullivan, & Tsien, 2002) can further consolidate the memory. Once initial consolidation has been achieved, maintenance requires only occasional reactivation of the relevant retrieval pathway (Nadel, Samsonovich, Ryan, & Moscovitch, 2000). This type of resonance can be used to consolidate new forms on the phonological, lexical (Gupta & MacWhinney, 1997), and construction levels.

The success of graduated interval recall also depends on correctly diagnosing the point at which a new memory trace is still available, albeit slightly weakened. At this point, when a learner attempts to remember a new word, sound, or phrase, some additional work will be needed to generate a retrieval cue. This retrieval cue then establishes a resonance with the form being retrieved. This resonant cue may involve lexical analysis, onomatopoeia, imagery, physical responses, or some other relational pattern. Because there is no fixed set of resonant connections (Ellis & Beaton, 1995), we cannot use group data to demonstrate the use of specific connections in lexical learning. However, we do know that felicitous mnemonics provided by the experimenter (Atkinson, 1975) can greatly facilitate learning.

Orthography provides a major support for resonance in L2 learning. During reading, one can activate the sounds of words (Perfetti, Bell, & Delaney, 1988), and the sounds of words can activate their orthographies (Share, 1995). When an L2 learner of German encounters the word *Wasser*, the regularity of German spelling makes it easy to map the sounds of the word directly to the image of the letters. However, when the L2 learner is illiterate, or when the L2 orthography is unlike the L1 orthography, this backup orthographic system is not available to support resonance. Delays in L2 learning of Chinese by speakers of languages with Roman scripts illustrate this problem.

15.6 Transfer and Decoupling

The UCM holds that L2 learners will attempt transfer whenever they can perceive a match between an item in L1 and a corresponding item in L2. If the match between L1 and L2 is close enough, the result is positive transfer, which is not a risk factor. For example, it is often easy to transfer the basic pragmatic functions (Bardovi-Harlig, 2013) that help structure conversations and the construction of mental models. Transfer is also easy enough for the semantics of lexical items (Kroll & Tokowicz, 2005), for which transfer is often largely positive, particularly between languages with similar linguistic and cultural patterns. In the initial stages of L2 word learning, this type of transfer requires very little reorganization, because L2 forms are initially parasitic upon L1 forms (Kroll, Van Hell, Tokowicz, & Green, 2010). However, apart from the issue of lexical parasitism, transfer can encounter some mismatches in meaning (Dong, Gui, & MacWhinney, 2005) and translation ambiguities (Prior, MacWhinney, & Kroll, 2007).

There is also a great deal of transfer from L1 to L2 in terms of patterns on both auditory and articulatory maps. It is reasonable enough to map a Chinese /p/ to an English /p/, even though the Chinese sound has a different time of voicing onset and no aspiration. The result of this type of imperfect transfer is what leads to the establishment of a foreign accent in L2 learners.

However, transfer is difficult or impossible for item-based syntactic patterns (MacWhinney, 2005) because these patterns cannot be readily matched across languages. For the same reason, transfer is unlikely for the formal aspects of conjugational or declensional patterns and classes. The fact that transfer is difficult for these systems does not mean that they are easy for L2 learners, but rather that they must be learned from the bottom up without any support from the L1. Apart from these formal aspects, the semantic distinctions involved in grammatical structures can readily transfer from L1 to L2. For example, the conceptual notion of an indirect object can transfer from English to German, although the actual use of the dative case in German involves many additional complexities not found in English.

When learners have several possible L1 forms that they can transfer to L2, they tend to prefer to transfer the least marked forms (Eckman, 1977; Major & Faudree, 1996). For example, as Pienemann, Di Biase, Kawaguchi, and Håkansson (2005) noted, Swedish learners of German prefer to transfer to German the unmarked Swedish word order that places the subject before the tense marker in the German equivalent of sentences such as *Peter likes milk today*. Although Swedish has a pattern that allows the order *Today likes Peter milk*, learners tend not to transfer this pattern initially, because it is the more marked alternative.

To correct the errors produced by transfer, learners must construct an independent L2 lexicon, phonology, and syntax. We can refer to this process of creating this independent system as *decoupling*. Decoupling involves creating new L2 forms and patterns and linking them not to L1 items, but to each other in the emerging separate grammar. To strengthen links between L2 items, learners must use the language either in real conversations or for inner speech (Vygotsky, 1934). Because items that fire together wire together, this use creates new connections within the emerging L2 system. This type of coactivation can help us understand the growth of the ability to engage in code-switching. If a language is being repeatedly accessed, it will be in a highly resonant state. Although another language will be passively accessible, it may take a second or two before the resonant activation of that language can be triggered by a task (Grosjean, 1997). Thus, a speaker may not immediately recognize a sentence in a language that has not been spoken in the recent context. In contrast, a simultaneous interpreter maintains both languages in continual receptive activation, while trying to minimize resonant activations in the output system of the source language.

Decoupling can be further promoted by invoking resonance to link up forms and meanings. For example, if I hear the phrase *ins Mittelalter* ("into the Middle Ages") in German, I can think to myself that this means that the stem *Alter* must be neuter gender—that is, *das Alter*. This means that the dative must take the form *in welchem Alter* ("in which [dative] age") or *in meinem Alter* ("in my [dative] age"). These form-related exercises can be conducted in parallel with more expressive exercises in which I simply try to talk to myself about things around me in German, or whatever language I happen to be learning. Even young children engage in practice of this type (Berk, 1994; Nelson, 1998).

15.7 Overanalysis, Proceduralization, and Chunking

Adult L2 learners excel in the learning of new vocabulary items (Folse, 2004; Nation, 2001). Language textbooks encourage this process by introducing new lexical items in terms of their basic stems, sometimes along with annotations regarding additional morphological forms, such as plurals or case markers. However, learners often just ignore these additional markings—an example of what we can call *overanalysis*. Children who are learning L1, on the other hand, have to discover the relations between alternative forms of words on their own. Although this would seem to impose an additional burden on the child learner, it ends up conferring them with an advantage, because they pick up words in a fuller context that helps them link into patterns of declension, conjugation, and collocation. In effect, children learn chunks from which they then extract items, whereas adults learn items from which they must then reconstruct larger patterns, often without having the contextual context needed for the reconstruction.

For example, adult L2 learners of German often learn the word *Mann* in isolation as the translation for English *man*. If, instead, they would learn phrases such as *der alte Mann* ('the old man'), *meines Mannes* ('my [genitive] man [genitive],' 'of my man'), *den jungen Männern* ('the [dative, plural] young [dative, plural] men [dative]'), and *ein guter Mann* ('a good man'), they would have a good basis for acquiring the declensional paradigm for both the noun and its modifiers. If learners were to store larger chunks of this type, then the rules of grammar could emerge from analogic processing of the chunks stored in feature maps (Bybee & Hopper, 2001; Ellis, 2002; MacWhinney, 1982; Tomasello, 2003). However, if learners analyze a phrase like *der alte Mann* into the literal string "the + old + man" and throw away all of the details of the inflections on *der* and *alte*, then they will lose an opportunity to induce the grammar from implicit generalization across stored chunks.

There is an understandable confusion in the literature regarding the relations between entrenchment, chunking, and proceduralization. Proceduralization involves taking two or more items or patterns that are initially separate and joining them together into a unified whole. Often, the resultant procedure is referred to as a *chunk* (Newell, 1990; see also Gobet, Chapter 11, this volume). However, it would be less confusing to refer to the process as *proceduralization* and to the result as a *procedure*. Once pieces are unitized, they tend to dominate over analytic alternatives. In other words, the stronger the whole, the weaker the parts (Bybee & Brewer, 1980; Hadley & Healy, 1991; Kapatsinski & Radicke, 2009; Sosa & MacFarlane, 2002).

Chunks are created through a very different noncombinatorial process in which a series of items is pulled out of the speech stream as a whole. For example, children may learn *do you want any more* as a chunk, at least receptively. Later on, they may learn the sequence *any more* and use that to further analyze the larger chunk. Adult L2 learners are likely to avoid chunk acquisition in the first place, moving directly to analysis of the phrase into separate lexical items. To distinguish these two processes, we could use *proceduralization* to refer to the first and *chunk extraction* to refer to the second. Proceduralization operates most obviously in terms of production, whereas chunk extraction is a perceptual process. Neither of these processes should be confused with entrenchment, as it is understood here, which can operate equally well on analyzed or unanalyzed items.

To compensate for the risk factor of overanalysis, L2 learners can rely on explicit invocation of the protective processes of chunking and proceduralization. To the degree that L2 learners can focus their attention on larger input strings, such as full preposition phrases or verb–particle combinations, they will be able to pick up chunks corresponding to the forms learned by the child. However, they can also rely on overt control of proceduralization by combining known pieces. For example, a Spanish phrase such as *quisiera comprar* ("I would like to buy") can be used with any manner of noun to talk about things one would like to buy. In each of these cases, producing one initial combination, such as *quisiera comprar una cerveza* ("I would like to buy a beer") may be halting at first. However, soon the result of the proceduralization process can be stored as a unit. In this case, it is not the actual phrase that is stored, but rather the process of activating the predicate combination (*quisiera comprar*) and then going ahead and filling the argument. In other words, we develop fluency by repeated practice in making combinations.

Once learners have developed fluency in the combination of well-learned words, they can still experience disfluency when trying to integrate newly learned words into established constructions. For example, even if we have learned to use the frame *quisiera comprar* fluently with words such as *una cerveza* ("a beer") or *un reloj* ("a clock"), we may still experience difficulties when we need to talk about buying "a round-trip ticket to Salamanca" (*un billete de ida y vuelta para Salamanca*). In this selection, we might have particular problems when we hit the word *para* since the English concept of "for, to" can be expressed in Spanish using either *por* or *para*, and our uncertainty regarding the choice between these two forms can slow us down and cause disfluency or error. In general, for both L1 and L2 learners, disfluencies arise from delays in lexical access, misordering of constituents, and selection of agreement markings. Fluency arises through the practicing of argument filling and improvements in the speed of lexical access and the selections between competitors.

Paradis (2004) argued that L2 learners cannot proceduralize their second language. Ullman (2004) agreed that L2 learners have problems with proceduralization, but he believed that L2 proceduralization is possible, albeit difficult and delayed. As a result, L2 productions may remain forever slow and nonfluent. We can refer to the Paradis–Ullman position as the *proceduralization deficit hypothesis* (PDH). In support of this idea, a study by Hahne and Friederici (2001) indicated that, even after 5 or more years learning German, native Russian and Japanese speakers failed to show rapid early left anterior negativity (ELAN) responses to grammaticality violations in German sentences. These results suggested that, after the end of the critical period, comprehension could not be automated or proceduralized. However, further studies using artificial language systems (Friederici, Steinhauer, & Pfeifer, 2002; Mueller, Hahne, Fujii, & Friederici, 2005) have shown that, if the rules of the target language are simple and consistent, L2 learners can develop proceduralization, as measured by ELAN, within a couple of months of training. Thus, it appears that proceduralization can be successful in adult learners, as long as cues are consistent, simple, and reliable (MacWhinney, 1997; Tokowicz & MacWhinney, 2005). This finding is in accord with the UCM analysis, rather than the PDH analysis, because it shows that the crucial factor is not the age of the learner but the reliability of the patterns in the input.

Crucially, proceduralization relies on the ability of the basal ganglia to form new connections between preexisting cortical patterns (Dominey & Boussaoud, 1997; Graybiel, 1995, 1998). The fact that this system is designed to create sequential recombinations of patterns encoded in cortical areas provides us with a fundamental understanding of how decoupling can occur and how catastrophic interference can be avoided. For articulation, the basal ganglia, including striate cortex, work to recombine L1 patterns stored in motor cortex into new chains for use in L2. For audition, this can be done by acquiring new sequential regularities based on statistical learning and new phonotactic patterns. For grammar, this involves new constructions of sentential patterns (Hinaut & Dominey, 2013), again through the action of corticostriatal projections and reinforcement learning in the basal ganglia.

15.8 Isolation and Participation

The fourth risk factor for older L2 learners is social isolation. As we get older, full integration into a second language community becomes increasingly difficult. There are at least three reasons for this. First, as we age, it can become increasingly difficult to set aside L1 allegiances and responsibilities. Second, L2 communities tend to be more immediately supportive of younger L2 learners. As children get older, peer groups become increasingly critical of participants who fail to communicate in accepted ways. Third, as we age, we may develop images regarding our social status that make it difficult to accept corrective feedback, teasing, or verbal challenges, even if these are excellent sources of language input. The cumulative effect of these social factors is that positive support for language learning can decrease markedly across the lifespan. Unless older learners focus directly on making friends in the new community and developing a full L2 persona (Pavlenko & Lantolf, 2000), they can become isolated and cut off.

The support factor that can counter isolation is participation. Older learners can increase their participation (Pavlenko & Lantolf, 2000) in the L2 community in a variety of ways. They can join religious groups, athletic teams, or work groups. Often these groups are highly motivated to improve the language abilities of new members so that they can function smoothly within the group. Older learners can also engage in formal study and expose themselves to L2 input through books, films, and music.

15.9 Conclusion

Explanations of age-related declines in L2 learning outcomes have often focused on the notion of a critical period shaped by a small set of biological mechanisms. These accounts postulate a rapid termination of language learning ability that is not observed in real learners. Accounts based on gradual entrenchment in neural nets fare a bit better but run into problems accounting for the lack of catastrophic interference effects in real learners. Entrenchment alone cannot explain age-related effects in L2 acquisition.

The UCM provides an alternative account of declines in L2 learning outcomes that focuses on the interplay between the risk factors (entrenchment, transfer, overanalysis, and isolation) and support factors (resonance, decoupling, chunking, and participation). The basal ganglia can recombine entrenched cortical patterns to form new L2 structures, thereby permitting decoupling of L2 from L1 and a gradual escape from L1 entrenchment.

The successful application of each of the support factors requires conscious manipulation of input, metalinguistic reflection, good linguistic and pedagogical analysis, study of L2 materials, and ongoing spoken interactions in the new language.

To facilitate this process, L2 instruction can provide focused instruction on basic language skills using online learning tutors (see, e.g., http://www.talkbank.org) along with community support for "language learning in the wild" (Clark, Wagner, Lindemalm, & Bendt, 2011) based on language learning tours, QR [quick response] codes, translator apps, and on-site recordings, all blended with and linked to support from classroom instruction (MacWhinney, 2015).

References

Aram, D. M., & Eisele, J. A. (1994). Intellectual stability in children with unilateral brain lesions. *Neuropsychologia, 32*, 85–95. http://dx.doi.org/10.1016/0028-3932(94)90071-X

Asato, M. R., Terwilliger, R., Woo, J., & Luna, B. (2010). White matter development in adolescence: A DTI study. *Cerebral Cortex, 20*, 2122–2131. http://dx.doi.org/10.1093/cercor/bhp282

Atkinson, R. (1975). Mnemotechnics in second-language learning. *American Psychologist, 30*, 821–828. http://dx.doi.org/10.1037/h0077029

Bardovi-Harlig, K. (2013). Developing L2 pragmatics. *Language Learning, 63*(Suppl. 1), 68–86. http://dx.doi.org/10.1111/j.1467-9922.2012.00738.x

Basser, L. S. (1962). Hemiplegia of early onset and the faculty of speech with special reference to the effects of hemispherectomy. *Brain, 85*, 427–460. http://dx.doi.org/10.1093/brain/85.3.427

Berk, L. E. (1994). Why children talk to themselves. *Scientific American, 271*, 78–83. http://dx.doi.org/10.1038/scientificamerican1194-78

Birdsong, D. (2005). Interpreting age effects in second language acquisition. In J. F. Kroll & A. M. B. DeGroot (Eds.), *Handbook of bilingualism: Psycholinguistic approaches* (pp. 105–127). New York, NY: Oxford University Press.

Bley-Vroman, R. (2009). The evolving context of the fundamental difference hypothesis. *Studies in Second Language Acquisition, 31*, 175–198. http://dx.doi.org/10.1017/S0272263109090275

Bongaerts, T. (1999). Ultimate attainment in L2 pronunciation: The case of very advanced late L2 learners. In D. Birdsong (Ed.), *Second language acquisition and the critical period hypothesis* (pp. 133–159). Mahwah, NJ: Lawrence Erlbaum.

Booth, J. R., MacWhinney, B., Thulborn, K. R., Sacco, K., Voyvodic, J. T., & Feldman, H. M. (2000). Developmental and lesion effects in brain activation during sentence comprehension and mental rotation. *Developmental Neuropsychology, 18*, 139–169. http://dx.doi.org/10.1207/S15326942DN1802_1

Bradlow, A. R., Akahane-Yamada, R., Pisoni, D. B., & Tohkura, Y. (1999). Training Japanese listeners to identify English /r/ and /l/: Long-term retention of learning in perception and production. *Perception & Psychophysics, 61*, 977–985. http://dx.doi.org/10.3758/BF03206911

Brooks, P. J., & Tomasello, M. (1999). How children constrain their argument structure constructions. *Language, 75*, 720–738. http://dx.doi.org/10.2307/417731

Browman, H. I. (1989). Embryology, ethology and ecology of ontogenetic critical periods in fish. *Brain, Behavior and Evolution, 34*, 5–12. http://dx.doi.org/10.1159/000116486

Bybee, J., & Brewer, M. (1980). Explanation in morphophonemics: Changes in Provençal and Spanish preterite forms. *Lingua, 52*, 201–242. http://dx.doi.org/10.1016/0024-3841(80)90035-2

Bybee, J., & Hopper, P. (Eds.). (2001). *Frequency and the emergence of linguistic structure.* http://dx.doi.org/10.1075/tsl.45

Carpenter, G., Grossberg, S., & Reynolds, J. (1991). ARTMAP: Supervised real-time learning and classification of nonstationary data by a self-organizing neural network. *Neural Networks*, *4*, 565–588. http://dx.doi.org/10.1016/0893-6080(91)90012-T

Casey, B. J., Giedd, J. N., & Thomas, K. M. (2000). Structural and functional brain development and its relation to cognitive development. *Biological Psychology*, *54*, 241–257. http://dx.doi.org/10.1016/S0301-0511(00)00058-2

Clahsen, H., & Felser, C. (2006). Grammatical processing in language learners. *Applied Psycholinguistics*, *27*, 3–42. http://dx.doi.org/10.1017/S0142716406060024

Clark, B., Wagner, J., Lindemalm, K., & Bendt, O. (2011, April). *Språkskap: Supporting second language learning "in the wild."* Paper presented at the conference of INCLUDE, London.

DeKeyser, R. (2000). The robustness of critical period effects in second language acquisition studies. *Studies in Second Language Acquisition*, *22*, 499–533.

Dominey, P. F., & Boussaoud, D. (1997). Encoding behavioral context in recurrent networks of the fronto-striatal system: A simulation study. *Cognitive Brain Research*, *6*, 53–65. http://dx.doi.org/10.1016/S0926-6410(97)00015-3

Dong, Y.-P., Gui, S.-C., & MacWhinney, B. (2005). Shared and separate meanings in the bilingual mental lexicon. *Bilingualism: Language and Cognition*, *8*, 221–238. http://dx.doi.org/10.1017/S1366728905002270

Doria, V., Beckmann, C. F., Arichi, T., Merchant, N., Groppo, M., Turkheimer, F. E., . . . Edwards, A. D. (2010). Emergence of resting state networks in the preterm human brain. *Proceedings of the National Academy of Sciences of the United States of America*, *107*, 20015–20020. http://dx.doi.org/10.1073/pnas.1007921107

Ebbinghaus, H. (1885). *Über das Gedächtnis* [On memory]. Leipzig, Germany: Duncker.

Eckman, F. R. (1977). Markedness and the contrastive analysis hypothesis. *Language Learning*, *27*, 315–330. http://dx.doi.org/10.1111/j.1467-1770.1977.tb00124.x

Ellis, N. (2002). Frequency effects in language processing. *Studies in Second Language Acquisition*, *24*, 143–188.

Ellis, N., & Beaton, A. (1995). Psycholinguistic determinants of foreign language vocabulary learning. In B. Harley (Ed.), *Lexical issues in language learning* (pp. 107–165). Philadelphia, PA: Benjamins.

Elman, J. L. (1993). Learning and development in neural networks: The importance of starting small. *Cognition*, *48*, 71–99. http://dx.doi.org/10.1016/0010-0277(93)90058-4

Engvig, A., Fjell, A. M., Westlye, L. T., Moberget, T., Sundseth, Ø., Larsen, V. A., & Walhovd, K. B. (2012). Memory training impacts short-term changes in aging white matter: A longitudinal diffusion tensor imaging study. *Human Brain Mapping*, *33*, 2390–2406. http://dx.doi.org/10.1002/hbm.21370

Feldman, H. M., MacWhinney, B., & Sacco, K. (2002). Sentence processing in children with early unilateral brain injury. *Brain and Language*, *83*, 335–352. http://dx.doi.org/10.1016/S0093-934X(02)00037-8

Flege, J. E. (1995). Second language speech learning: Theory, findings, and problems. In W. Strange (Ed.), *Speech perception and linguistic experience: Theoretical and methodological issues* (pp. 229–273). Baltimore, MD: York Press.

Flege, J. E., & MacKay, I. R. A. (2004). Perceiving vowels in a second language. *Studies in Second Language Acquisition*, *26*, 1–34. http://dx.doi.org/10.1017/S0272263104261010

Folse, K. S. (2004). *Vocabulary myths: Applying second language research to classroom teaching*. Ann Arbor, MI: University of Michigan Press.

Friederici, A. D., Steinhauer, K., & Pfeifer, E. (2002). Brain signatures of artificial language processing: Evidence challenging the critical period hypothesis. *Proceedings of the National Academy of Sciences of the United States of America, 99*, 529–534. http://dx.doi.org/10.1073/pnas.012611199

Gao, W., Lin, W., Chen, Y., Gerig, G., Smith, J. K., Jewells, V., & Gilmore, J. H. (2009). Temporal and spatial development of axonal maturation and myelination of white matter in the developing brain. *American Journal of Neuroradiology, 30*, 290–296. http://dx.doi.org/10.3174/ajnr.A1363

Graybiel, A. M. (1995). Building action repertoires: Memory and learning functions of the basal ganglia. *Current Opinion in Neurobiology, 5*, 733–741. http://dx.doi.org/10.1016/0959-4388(95)80100-6

Graybiel, A. M. (1998). The basal ganglia and chunking of action repertoires. *Neurobiology of Learning and Memory, 70*(1–2), 119–136. http://dx.doi.org/10.1006/nlme.1998.3843

Grosjean, F. (1997). Processing mixed languages: Issues, findings and models. In A. M. B. de Groot & J. F. Kroll (Eds.), *Tutorials in bilingualism: Psycholinguistic perspectives* (pp. 225–254). Mahwah, NJ: Lawrence Erlbaum.

Guenther, F. H., & Gjaja, M. N. (1996). The perceptual magnet effect as an emergent property of neural map formation. *The Journal of the Acoustical Society of America, 100*, 1111–1121. http://dx.doi.org/10.1121/1.416296

Gupta, P., & MacWhinney, B. (1997). Vocabulary acquisition and verbal short-term memory: Computational and neural bases. *Brain and Language, 59*, 267–333. http://dx.doi.org/10.1006/brln.1997.1819

Hadley, J., & Healy, A. (1991). When are reading units larger than the letter? Refinement of the unitization reading model. *Journal of Experimental Psychology: Learning, Memory, and Cognition, 17*, 1062–1073. http://dx.doi.org/10.1037/0278-7393.17.6.1062

Hahne, A., & Friederici, A. (2001). Processing a second language: Late learners' comprehension mechanisms as revealed by event-related brain potentials. *Bilingualism: Language and Cognition, 4*, 123–141. http://dx.doi.org/10.1017/S1366728901000232

Hakuta, K., Bialystok, E., & Wiley, E. (2003). Critical evidence: A test of the critical-period hypothesis for second-language acquisition. *Psychological Science, 14*, 31–38. http://dx.doi.org/10.1111/1467-9280.01415

Hamker, F. H. (2001). Life-long learning cell structures—Continuously learning without catastrophic interference. *Neural Networks, 14*, 551–573. http://dx.doi.org/10.1016/S0893-6080(01)00018-1

Hickok, G., & Poeppel, D. (2004). Dorsal and ventral streams: A framework for understanding aspects of the functional anatomy of language. *Cognition, 92*, 67–99. http://dx.doi.org/10.1016/j.cognition.2003.10.011

Hinaut, X., & Dominey, P. F. (2013). Real-time parallel processing of grammatical structure in the fronto-striatal system: A recurrent network simulation study using reservoir computing. *PLoS ONE, 8*(2), e52946.

Hubel, D. H., & Wiesel, T. N. (1963). Receptive fields of cells in striate cortex of very young, visually inexperienced kittens. *Journal of Neurophysiology, 26*, 994–1002.

Ingvalson, E. M., Holt, L. L., & McClelland, J. L. (2012). Can native Japanese listeners learn to differentiate /r–l/ on the basis of F3 onset frequency? *Bilingualism: Language and Cognition, 15*, 434–435. http://dx.doi.org/10.1017/S1366728912000041

Johnson, J. S., & Newport, E. L. (1989). Critical period effects in second language learning: The influence of maturational state on the acquisition of English as a second language. *Cognitive Psychology, 21*, 60–99. http://dx.doi.org/10.1016/0010-0285(89)90003-0

Kapatsinski, V., & Radicke, J. (2009). Frequency and the emergence of prefabs: Evidence from monitoring. In R. Corrigan, E. Moravcsik, H. Ouali, & K. Wheatley (Eds.), *Formulaic language: Vol. 2. Acquisition, loss, psychological reality, and functional explanations* (pp. 499–522). Amsterdam, the Netherlands: Benjamins.

Koechlin, E., & Summerfield, C. (2007). An information theoretical approach to prefrontal executive function. *Trends in Cognitive Sciences, 11*, 229–235. http://dx.doi.org/10.1016/j.tics.2007.04.005

Kral, A., & Sharma, A. (2012). Developmental neuroplasticity after cochlear implantation. *Trends in Neurosciences, 35*, 111–122. http://dx.doi.org/10.1016/j.tins.2011.09.004

Kraus, N., McGee, T., Carrell, T. D., King, C., Tremblay, K., & Nicol, T. (1995). Central auditory system plasticity associated with speech discrimination training. *Journal of Cognitive Neuroscience, 7*, 25–32. http://dx.doi.org/10.1162/jocn.1995.7.1.25

Kroll, J. F., & Tokowicz, N. (2005). Models of bilingual representation and processing: Looking back and to the future. In J. F. Kroll & A. M. B. de Groot (Eds.), *Handbook of bilingualism: Psycholinguistic approaches* (pp. 531–553). New York, NY: Oxford University Press.

Kroll, J. F., Van Hell, J. G., Tokowicz, N., & Green, D. W. (2010). The revised hierarchical model: A critical review and assessment. *Bilingualism: Language and Cognition, 13*, 373–381.

Kuhl, P. K. (2004). Early language acquisition: Cracking the speech code. *Nature Reviews Neuroscience, 5*, 831–843. http://dx.doi.org/10.1038/nrn1533

Kuhl, P. K., Conboy, B., Padden, D., Nelson, T., & Pruitt, J. (2005). Early speech perception and later language development: Implications for the "critical period." *Language Learning and Development, 1*, 237–264. http://dx.doi.org/10.1080/15475441.2005.9671948

Kürten, J., De Vries, M. H., Kowal, K., Zwitserlood, P., & Flöel, A. (2012). Age affects chunk-based, but not rule-based learning in artificial grammar acquisition. *Neurobiology of Aging, 33*, 1311–1317. http://dx.doi.org/10.1016/j.neurobiolaging.2010.10.008

Lenneberg, E. (1967). *Biological foundations of language*. New York, NY: Wiley.

Li, P., Farkas, I., & MacWhinney, B. (2004). Early lexical development in a self-organizing neural network. *Neural Networks, 17*, 1345–1362. http://dx.doi.org/10.1016/j.neunet.2004.07.004

Li, P., Zhao, X., & MacWhinney, B. (2007). Dynamic self-organization and early lexical development in children. *Cognitive Science, 31*, 581–612. http://dx.doi.org/10.1080/15326900701399905

Lorenz, K. Z. (1958). The evolution of behavior. *Scientific American, 199*, 67–78. http://dx.doi.org/10.1038/scientificamerican1258-67

MacWhinney, B. (1982). Basic syntactic processes. In S. Kuczaj (Ed.), *Syntax and semantics: Vol. 1. Language acquisition* (pp. 73–136). Hillsdale, NJ: Lawrence Erlbaum.

MacWhinney, B. (1997). Implicit and explicit processes. *Studies in Second Language Acquisition, 19*, 277–281. http://dx.doi.org/10.1017/S0272263197002076

MacWhinney, B. (2005). Item-based constructions and the logical problem. *Association for Computational Linguistics, 2005*, 46–54.

MacWhinney, B. (2008). How mental models encode embodied linguistic perspectives. In R. Klatzky, B. MacWhinney, & M. Behrmann (Eds.), *Embodiment, ego-space, and action* (pp. 369–410). Mahwah, NJ: Lawrence Erlbaum.

MacWhinney, B. (2012). The logic of the unified model. In S. Gass & A. Mackey (Eds.), *The Routledge handbook of second language acquisition* (pp. 211–227). New York, NY: Routledge.

MacWhinney, B. (2014). Item-based patterns in early syntactic development. In T. Herbst, H.-J. Schmid, & S. Faulhaber (Eds.), *Constructions collocations patterns* (pp. 33–70). http://dx.doi.org/10.1515/9783110356854.33

MacWhinney, B. (2015). Multidimensional SLA. In S. Eskilde & T. Cadierno (Eds.), *Usage-based perspectives on second language learning* (pp. 22–45). http://dx.doi.org/10.1515/9783110378528-004
Major, R. (1987). The natural phonology of second language acquisition. In A. James & J. Leather (Eds.), *Sound patterns in second language acquisition* (pp. 207–224). Dordrecht, Germany: Foris.
Major, R., & Faudree, M. (1996). Markedness universals and the acquisition of voicing contrasts by Korean speakers of English. *Studies in Second Language Acquisition*, *18*, 69–90. http://dx.doi.org/10.1017/S0272263100014686
Marler, P. (1991). Song-learning behavior: The interface with neuroethology. *Trends in Neurosciences*, *14*, 199–206. http://dx.doi.org/10.1016/0166-2236(91)90106-5
McCandliss, B. D., Fiez, J. A., Protopapas, A., Conway, M., & McClelland, J. L. (2002). Success and failure in teaching the [r]–[l] contrast to Japanese adults: Tests of a Hebbian model of plasticity and stabilization in spoken language perception. *Cognitive, Affective & Behavioral Neuroscience*, *2*, 89–108. http://dx.doi.org/10.3758/CABN.2.2.89
McCauley, S., Monaghan, P., & Christiansen, M. (2014). Language emergence in development: A computational perspective. In B. MacWhinney & W. O'Grady (Eds.), *Handbook of language emergence* (pp. 415–436). New York, NY: Wiley.
McClelland, J. L., McNaughton, B. L., & O'Reilly, R. C. (1995). Why there are complementary learning systems in the hippocampus and neocortex: Insights from the successes and failures of connectionist models of learning and memory. *Psychological Review*, *102*, 419–457. http://dx.doi.org/10.1037/0033-295X.102.3.419
McCloskey, M., & Cohen, N. (1989). Catastrophic interference in connectionist networks: The sequential learning problem. In G. Bower (Ed.), *The psychology of learning and motivation* (Vol. 24, pp. 109–165). http://dx.doi.org/10.1016/S0079-7421(08)60536-8
Mills, D., Coffey-Corina, S., & Neville, H. (1997). Language comprehension and cerebral specialization from 13 to 20 months. *Developmental Neuropsychology*, *13*, 397–445. http://dx.doi.org/10.1080/87565649709540685
Molfese, D. L., Freeman, R. B., Jr., & Palermo, D. S. (1975). The ontogeny of brain lateralization for speech and nonspeech stimuli. *Brain and Language*, *2*, 356–368. http://dx.doi.org/10.1016/S0093-934X(75)80076-9
Mueller, J. L., Hahne, A., Fujii, Y., & Friederici, A. D. (2005). Native and nonnative speakers' processing of a miniature version of Japanese as revealed by ERPs. *Journal of Cognitive Neuroscience*, *17*, 1229–1244. http://dx.doi.org/10.1162/0898929055002463
Munakata, Y., McClelland, J. L., Johnson, M. H., & Siegler, R. S. (1997). Rethinking infant knowledge: Toward an adaptive process account of successes and failures in object permanence tasks. *Psychological Review*, *104*, 686–713. http://dx.doi.org/10.1037/0033-295X.104.4.686
Munro, M. J., Flege, J. E., & Mackay, I. R. A. (1996). The effects of age of second language learning on the production of English vowels. *Applied Psycholinguistics*, *17*, 313–334. http://dx.doi.org/10.1017/S0142716400007967
Nadel, L., Samsonovich, A., Ryan, L., & Moscovitch, M. (2000). Multiple trace theory of human memory: Computational, neuroimaging, and neuropsychological results. *Hippocampus*, *10*, 352–368. http://dx.doi.org/10.1002/1098-1063(2000)10:4<352::AID-HIPO2>3.0.CO;2-D
Nation, P. (2001). *Learning vocabulary in another language*. http://dx.doi.org/10.1017/CBO9781139524759
Nelson, K. (1998). *Language in cognitive development: The emergence of the mediated mind*. New York, NY: Cambridge University Press.
Newell, A. (1990). *A unified theory of cognition*. Cambridge, MA: Harvard University Press.

Newport, E. (1990). Maturational constraints on language learning. *Cognitive Science, 14,* 11–28. http://dx.doi.org/10.1207/s15516709cog1401_2

Pallier, C., Dehaene, S., Poline, J. B., LeBihan, D., Argenti, A. M., Dupoux, E., & Mehler, J. (2003). Brain imaging of language plasticity in adopted adults: Can a second language replace the first? *Cerebral Cortex, 13,* 155–161. http://dx.doi.org/10.1093/cercor/13.2.155

Paradis, M. (2004). *A neurolinguistic theory of bilingualism.* http://dx.doi.org/10.1075/sibil.18

Pavlenko, A., & Lantolf, J. (2000). Second language learning as participation and the (re)construction of selves. In A. Pavlenko & J. Lantolf (Eds.), *Sociocultural theory and second language learning* (pp. 155–178). Oxford, England: Oxford University Press.

Pavlik, P. I., Jr., & Anderson, J. R. (2005). Practice and forgetting effects on vocabulary memory: An activation-based model of the spacing effect. *Cognitive Science, 29,* 559–586. http://dx.doi.org/10.1207/s15516709cog0000_14

Perfetti, C. A., Bell, L. C., & Delaney, S. M. (1988). Automatic (prelexical) phonetic activation in silent word reading: Evidence from backward masking. *Journal of Memory and Language, 27,* 59–70. http://dx.doi.org/10.1016/0749-596X(88)90048-4

Pienemann, M., Di Biase, B., Kawaguchi, S., & Håkansson, G. (2005). Processing constraints on L1 transfer. In J. F. Kroll & A. M. B. de Groot (Eds.), *Handbook of bilingualism: Psycholinguistic approaches* (pp. 128–153). New York, NY: Oxford University Press.

Pimsleur, P. (1967). A memory schedule. *Modern Language Journal, 51,* 73–75. http://dx.doi.org/10.1111/j.1540-4781.1967.tb06700.x

Posner, M. I., Tang, Y.-Y., & Lynch, G. (2014). Mechanisms of white matter change induced by meditation training. *Frontiers in Psychology, 5,* 1220. http://dx.doi.org/10.3389/fpsyg.2014.01220

Presson, N., Sagarra, N., MacWhinney, B., & Kowalski, J. (2013). Compositional production in Spanish second language conjugation. *Bilingualism: Language and Cognition, 16,* 808–828. http://dx.doi.org/10.1017/S136672891200065X

Prior, A., MacWhinney, B., & Kroll, J. F. (2007). Translation norms for English and Spanish: The role of lexical variables, word class, and L2 proficiency in negotiating translation ambiguity. *Behavior Research Methods, 39,* 1029–1038. http://dx.doi.org/10.3758/BF03193001

Pulvermüller, F. (2003). *The neuroscience of language.* http://dx.doi.org/10.1017/CBO9780511615528

Richardson, F. M., & Thomas, M. S. (2008). Critical periods and catastrophic interference effects in the development of self-organizing feature maps. *Developmental Science, 11,* 371–389. http://dx.doi.org/10.1111/j.1467-7687.2008.00682.x

Roelofs, A. (2011). Modeling the attentional control of vocal utterances: From Wernicke to WEAVER. In J. Guendozi, F. Loncke, & M. Williams (Eds.), *The handbook of psycholinguistic and cognitive processes: Perspectives in communication disorders* (pp. 189–208). http://dx.doi.org/10.4324/9780203848005.ch9

Rohde, D. C., & Plaut, D. (1997). Simple recurrent networks and natural language: How important is starting small? In *Proceedings of the 19th Annual Conference of the Cognitive Science Society* (pp. 656–661). Hillsdale, NJ: Lawrence Erlbaum.

Sagarra, N., & Herschensohn, J. (2010). The role of proficiency and working memory in gender and number agreement processing in L1 and L2 Spanish. *Lingua, 120,* 2022–2039. http://dx.doi.org/10.1016/j.lingua.2010.02.004

Sagarra, N., & Herschensohn, J. (2011). Proficiency and animacy effects on L2 gender agreement processes during comprehension. *Language Learning, 61,* 80–116. http://dx.doi.org/10.1111/j.1467-9922.2010.00588.x

Sampaio-Baptista, C., Khrapitchev, A. A., Foxley, S., Schlagheck, T., Scholz, J., Jbabdi, S., ... Johansen-Berg, H. (2013). Motor skill learning induces changes in white matter microstructure and myelination. *The Journal of Neuroscience, 33,* 19,499–19,503.

Segalowitz, S., Segalowitz, N., & Wood, A. (1998). Assessing the development of automaticity in second language word recognition. *Applied Psycholinguistics, 19,* 53–67. http://dx.doi.org/10.1017/S0142716400010572

Seidenberg, M. S., & Zevin, J. D. (2006). Connectionist models in developmental cognitive neuroscience: Critical periods and the paradox of success. In Y. Munakata & M. Johnson (Eds.), *Processes of change in brain and cognitive development: Attention and performance XXI* (pp. 585–612). Oxford, England: Oxford University Press.

Share, D. L. (1995). Phonological recoding and self-teaching: Sine qua non of reading acquisition. *Cognition, 55,* 151–218. http://dx.doi.org/10.1016/0010-0277(94)00645-2

Snow, C. E. (1999). Social perspectives on the emergence of language. In B. MacWhinney (Ed.), *The emergence of language* (pp. 257–276). Mahwah, NJ: Lawrence Erlbaum.

Snow, C. E., & Hoefnagel-Hohle, M. (1978). The critical period for language acquisition: Evidence from second language learning. *Child Development, 49,* 1114–1128. http://dx.doi.org/10.2307/1128751

Sosa, A. V., & MacFarlane, J. (2002). Evidence for frequency-based constituents in the mental lexicon: Collocations involving the word *of*. *Brain and Language, 83,* 227–236. http://dx.doi.org/10.1016/S0093-934X(02)00032-9

Stiles, J., Trauner, D., Engel, M., & Nass, R. (1997). The development of drawing in children with congenital focal brain injury: Evidence for limited functional recovery. *Neuropsychologia, 35,* 299–312. http://dx.doi.org/10.1016/S0028-3932(96)00088-7

Takeuchi, H., Sekiguchi, A., Taki, Y., Yokoyama, S., Yomogida, Y., Komuro, N., ... Kawashima, R. (2010). Training of working memory impacts structural connectivity. *The Journal of Neuroscience, 30,* 3297–3303. http://dx.doi.org/10.1523/JNEUROSCI.4611-09.2010

Tokowicz, N., & MacWhinney, B. (2005). Implicit and explicit measures of sensitivity to violations in second language grammar: An event-related potential investigation. *Studies in Second Language Acquisition, 27,* 173–204. http://dx.doi.org/10.1017/S0272263105050102

Tomasello, M. (2003). *Constructing a first language: A usage-based theory of language acquisition.* Cambridge, MA: Harvard University Press.

Ullman, M. T. (2004). Contributions of memory circuits to language: The declarative/procedural model. *Cognition, 92,* 231–270. http://dx.doi.org/10.1016/j.cognition.2003.10.008

VanPatten, B., Keating, G. D., & Leeser, M. J. (2012). Missing verbal inflections as a representational problem: Evidence from self-paced reading. *Linguistic Approaches to Bilingualism, 2,* 109–140. http://dx.doi.org/10.1075/lab.2.2.01pat

Vygotsky, L. S. (1934). *Thought and language.* Cambridge, MA: MIT Press.

Werker, J. F. (1995). Exploring developmental changes in cross-language speech perception. In L. Gleitman & M. Liberman (Eds.), *An invitation to cognitive science: Language* (Vol. 1, pp. 87–106). Cambridge, MA: MIT Press.

Werker, J. F., & Tees, R. C. (2005). Speech perception as a window for understanding plasticity and commitment in language systems of the brain. *Developmental Psychobiology, 46,* 233–251. http://dx.doi.org/10.1002/dev.20060

Wiley, E. W., Bialystok, E., & Hakuta, K. (2005). New approaches to using census data to test the critical-period hypothesis for second-language acquisition. *Psychological Science, 16,* 341–343. http://dx.doi.org/10.1111/j.0956-7976.2005.01537.x

Winkler, I., Kujala, T., Tiitinen, H., Sivonen, P., Alku, P., Lehtokoski, A., ... Näätänen, R. (1999). Brain responses reveal the learning of foreign language phonemes. *Psychophysiology, 36,* 638–642. http://dx.doi.org/10.1111/1469-8986.3650638

Wittenberg, G. M., Sullivan, M. R., & Tsien, J. Z. (2002). Synaptic reentry reinforcement based network model for long-term memory consolidation. *Hippocampus, 12,* 637–647. http://dx.doi.org/10.1002/hipo.10102

Yamamoto, K., Hoffman, D. S., & Strick, P. L. (2006). Rapid and long-lasting plasticity of input–output mapping. *Journal of Neurophysiology, 96,* 2797–2801. http://dx.doi.org/10.1152/jn.00209.2006

Zevin, J. D. (2012). A sensitive period for shibboleths: The long tail and changing goals of speech perception over the course of development. *Developmental Psychobiology, 54,* 632–642. http://dx.doi.org/10.1002/dev.20611

Zhou, X., Panizzutti, R., de Villers-Sidani, E., Madeira, C., & Merzenich, M. M. (2011). Natural restoration of critical period plasticity in the juvenile and adult primary auditory cortex. *The Journal of Neuroscience, 31,* 5625–5634. http://dx.doi.org/10.1523/JNEUROSCI.6470-10.2011

Rasmus Steinkrauss and Monika S. Schmid
16 Entrenchment and Language Attrition

16.1 Introduction

The term *language attrition* refers to the process of change, reduced accessibility, or deterioration of linguistic knowledge of an individual speaker who had demonstrably acquired this knowledge at some earlier point in time. This process occurs when the language in question has come to be used less frequently or not at all, in favor of some other, later-learned language. This link between the reversal of development of linguistic knowledge on the one hand and the frequency of use of the language on the other makes attrition an ideal field to investigate from a cognitive linguistic point of view.

Despite this connection between entrenchment and language attrition, there have been no cognitive linguistic studies or theoretical models explicitly focusing on language attrition so far. In addition, previous research on language attrition has suggested that factors other than frequency of use might play a part in the attrition process. The current chapter is an attempt to bridge the gap between theories of entrenchment and research on language attrition. We first discuss entrenchment from a cognitive linguistic point of view and formulate entrenchment-related hypotheses for the process of language attrition. Thereafter, we review previous attrition research in light of these hypotheses before turning to another factor in language processing that seems to influence language attrition, namely, inhibition. We argue that it is an interaction of the forces of entrenchment and inhibition that ultimately appears to have the potential to shed light on the process of language attrition.

16.2 Cognitive Linguistics and Language Attrition

In cognitive linguistics, frequency of use is viewed as a fundamental factor driving individual linguistic development. Foundational to this assumption is the idea that learning a language makes use of the same cognitive processes that underlie other types of learning and that linguistic knowledge is thus acquired with the help of domain-general learning mechanisms. Factors such as the recency, frequency, or context of stimuli (e.g., Anderson, 2014) play a role in the construction of linguistic knowledge by each individual speaker, just as they do in other learning situations.

One central concept in this regard is entrenchment. Applied to individual linguistic development, *entrenchment* refers to the process (and the result; see Schmid, Chapter 1, this volume) of strengthening a speaker's representation of linguistic knowledge through repeated processing, in comprehension as well as production. Importantly, this development operates on the level of specific instances of language use that a speaker takes part in. Every time a speaker processes (i.e., interprets or produces) a linguistic structure, this adds to earlier memories of linguistic events and strengthens the representation of what is shared among these instances of language use. When the different instances share specific linguistic constructions such as words or idioms, this will entrench lexically specific representations, whereas more abstract overlap in linguistic form or function will lead to more schematic representations. Building up linguistic knowledge is thus seen as a usage-based, bottom-up process: Abstract linguistic knowledge, such as knowledge of thematic roles, word classes, or syntactic patterns, is based on the knowledge of specific constructions and emerges from the commonalities between these (Langacker, 1988, 2000).

In first-language (L1) acquisition, this process has the effect that children tend to start out with fixed word combinations and use grammatical constructions that are tied to specific lexical material (item-based constructions; see the overview in Tomasello, 2003). A child who can use different verb forms in one linguistic context might not yet be able to use the same forms in other contexts (e.g., Pine, Lieven, & Rowland, 1998; Pizzuto & Caselli, 1992; Tomasello, 1992). Which constructions are used in that way is closely related to the frequency of the constructions and the form in which they occur in the input (e.g., Rubino & Pine, 1998). Similar frequency-based effects that can be explained with different degrees of entrenchment have also been observed in second-language (L2) learning (see the overview in Ellis, 2013). The concept of entrenchment, in cognitive linguistics, is thus closely linked to frequency, and constructions "are variably entrenched depending on the frequency of occurrence" (Langacker, 1987, p. 59).

Because language attrition is the result of a substantial decrease in the frequency of use of a language (in production as well as comprehension), entrenchment—understood as both the process and the result—is a potentially powerful concept for predicting and explaining its cause and development. Even more importantly, attrition could provide an additional perspective for verifying and validating the hypotheses that cognitive linguistics in general makes about linguistic knowledge and about the role of entrenchment. These hypotheses should hold true for contexts not only of acquisition and use but also of maintenance and deterioration in the face of nonproduction and the absence of input. In spite of this need, there are to date no studies taking an explicitly cognitive linguistic approach to language attrition. This lack is particularly surprising because the prediction that the disuse of linguistic structures will have a negative impact on their degree of entrenchment (and consequently on linguistic knowledge) was already expressed in early and foundational texts for cognitive linguistic approaches, such as Langacker (1987, pp. 59, 100). Studying language attrition should thus be an integral part of the cognitive linguistic endeavor.

At the same time, it is clear that frequency of use is not the only factor at work in language attrition. Language attrition occurs when a speaker uses the language undergoing attrition less often because of shifting to another language (e.g., as an effect of emigration to a different linguistic environment). Often, attrition also entails a change of the dominant language from the L1 to the L2. The age at which the use of the L1 was reduced and the presence of a competing L2 system in the speaker's mind therefore play important roles in attrition as well. Language attrition is thus a process that is inextricably linked with bilingualism and involves a complex interplay of different factors, which makes it difficult to assess the exact role these aspects play in language attrition. However, it was recently proposed that a comparison of L1 attriters with monolingual native speakers and advanced L2 users could have the potential of disentangling the relative contributions made by factors such as frequency and contexts of use, age at learning, and competition between languages (Schmid, 2014). In such an approach, bilingual development is seen as a holistic process involving all linguistic knowledge and not isolated to either the acquisition (and limits thereof) of L2 knowledge on the one hand, or the deterioration or maintenance of the L1, on the other.

As mentioned above, so far there has not been any research on language attrition taking an explicit cognitive linguistic approach. Applying the concept of entrenchment to previous research and interpreting the results from a cognitive linguistic point of view therefore require some caution. In the context of attrition, entrenchment can most directly be operationalized as frequency of (reported) productive and receptive language use (often assessed for different contexts and situational settings) or as external corpus frequency, for example, in assessments of lexical diversity. The first thus refers to the activation and ongoing entrenchment of the attriting language as a whole, and the latter is a proxy for the relative degree of entrenchment of specific words (requiring the methodological leap discussed by Schmid, Chapter 1, this volume, Section 1.3.1). With few exceptions (e.g., Pavlenko's studies of semantic fields; Pavlenko, 2004, 2010), attrition studies have not looked into lexically specific constructions and have confined themselves to measuring overall vocabulary size and diversity, whereas for grammar, abstract categories and general word order phenomena have generally been the focus of the investigations.

Specific hypotheses from a cognitive linguistic point of view regarding the effect of entrenchment in language attrition are therefore difficult to formulate, apart from the prediction that frequency of use will play a role for the amount of attrition if the fact that the attriting L1 has been entrenched from birth does not supersede effects of decreasing frequency of use. A model of linguistic processing that draws on the concept of entrenchment and possibly allows more specific hypotheses about attrition is MacWhinney's (2008, 2011; Chapter 15, this volume) unified model, which has its roots in the competition model (Bates & MacWhinney, 1982; MacWhinney, 1987). Although originally aiming at explaining the acquisition of linguistic knowledge, for hypotheses about attrition the model has the advantage that it takes into account both L1 and L2 development and allows for linguistic transfer in both directions (MacWhinney, 2008, p. 351).

In this model, because the L1 is acquired first, L1 knowledge is assumed to be deeply entrenched and represented in local cortical maps (MacWhinney, 2011, p. 215). This local organization is "more and more difficult to reverse or modify" (MacWhinney, 2008, p. 344) with increasing age and decreasing plasticity of the brain. As the robustness of L1 knowledge accumulates with use, "later retrievals can be spaced farther and farther apart" (MacWhinney, 2011, p. 216). This means that attrition effects should be stronger the earlier the switch from the L1 to the L2, and minimal when the L1 has been spoken for a long time and is still occasionally being used. In cases in which the switch from L1 to L2 started early enough, however, at a point before L1 knowledge had "'crystallized' in the brain" (Hernandez, Li, & MacWhinney, 2005, p. 224), even a complete forgetting of the L1 is possible. An fMRI study by Pallier et al. (2003), who found exactly this pattern in Korean children adopted in France when they were between 3 and 8 years old, is cited as supporting evidence (Hernandez et al., 2005, pp. 223–224).

The latest versions of the unified competition model (MacWhinney, 2011; Chapter 15, this volume) list several factors supporting and endangering the acquisition, development, and maintenance of linguistic knowledge. They are originally formulated with L1 and L2 acquisition in mind but may be applied to the context of L1 attrition as well. The most important risk factors (i.e., factors contributing to L1 attrition) seem to be disentrenchment, negative transfer, and isolation. *Disentrenchment* refers to the fact that the neural connections storing L1 knowledge may be weakened as a consequence of disuse, and *negative transfer* refers to possible negative L2 influences on the L1. The third factor, isolation, is a social factor: The less contact there is with the language community in question, in this case the L1 community, the more strongly this factor favors attrition.

At the same time, support factors may counter L1 attrition. Isolation may be prevented by participation in the (local) L1 community or by distance communication (to which there were considerable financial obstacles in the communities most often studied in the context of attrition—speakers who emigrated in the 1950s, 1960s, and 1970s—but which in this age of e-mail, Skype, and budget flights is cheap and easy). Negative transfer may be counteracted by positive transfer—that is, transfer from an L2 that is similar to the L1 and in this way supports L1 maintenance. Finally, the central risk of disentrenchment can be warded off by resonance. When an L1 word is activated, its activation spreads to other L1 words and thus strengthens the connections between L1 forms, making it more robust against intrusion from the L2. This mutual activation is inherent when processing input (Hernandez et al., 2005, pp. 221–222), but it also occurs in the active use of language.

Taken together, these factors mean that L1 attrition should be weakest for speakers who emigrated late in life, speak an L2 that is similar to the L1 (supporting positive transfer), still use the L1 occasionally (in reception or production, leading to resonance and entrenchment), and are active in their L1 community (preventing isolation). Specific factors supporting entrenchment and local organization—and thus

L1 maintenance—explicitly mentioned are reading (if the writing system reflects the phonology of the language), inner speech, and thinking in the language in question (*internalization*; Hernandez et al., 2005, p. 222; MacWhinney, 2008, p. 362; 2011, p. 221). Speakers with these characteristics should thus experience comparatively less attrition.

What kinds of error can be expected in L1 attriters? Generally speaking, linguistic transfer is expected to happen on the level of individual constructions, not across the board (MacWhinney, 2008, p. 352). Also, in L2 learning, transfer is initially expected for unmarked forms and only later also for forms that are marked in the L1. In language attrition, because the attriting language is deeply entrenched, once attrition starts, marked forms should be affected first. Starting from these assumptions, the following development might be expected: In the area of the lexicon, which is the least entrenched (MacWhinney, 2008, p. 363) and thus the most prone to attrition, words with specialist meanings such as subordinates should show transfer first (MacWhinney, 2008, p. 349). In syntax, occasional L1 word order violations in some constructions may be expected, but no wholesale transfer of L2 sentence patterns, and here also the process starts with marked syntactic alternatives such as topicalization constructions (MacWhinney, 2008, p. 352). The area of morphosyntax is generally less prone to transfer (MacWhinney, 2008, p. 352–353), as those features often do not have direct correlates in the other language. For example, the gender system of German should remain intact in L1 German attriters with an L2 that does not morphologically encode gender (MacWhinney, 2008, p. 353). Finally, phonology is the most entrenched of all linguistic areas, and transfer should be marginal (MacWhinney, 2008, p. 363).

With this background in mind, we now turn to the findings from investigations of language attrition. Going into all of the areas mentioned above is beyond the scope of this chapter, and testing the hypotheses is made difficult by the fact that L1 attrition studies have been carried out on the basis of theoretical assumptions that differ from those presented above. Also, not all of the topics above have been researched equally well. Therefore, we restrict ourselves to two key areas that might tell us something about the role of entrenchment: (a) the impact of frequency and context of L1 use and (b) the impact of the frequency of lexical items versus similarity of items in L1 and L2.

16.3 Use It or Lose It? The Impact of Frequency and Context of L1 Use

The prediction that "continued experience with L1 keeps the language entrenched" (Paradis, 2009, p. 134)—that is, that language attrition is the result of language disuse and that continued exposure and use will lead to language maintenance—is one of the most basic and prevalent assumptions underlying attrition research. At first glance, there seems to be a solid underpinning of this idea in research on memory and accessibility that is closely linked to the notion of entrenchment: We know that in order to activate any given memory trace, a certain amount of neural energy is needed. This variable has been referred to as the *activation threshold* (AT; Paradis, 1993, 2004), and its value is determined by two factors: frequency and recency. Every time an item of information is retrieved from memory, this process of access causes a reduction in the AT, making it easier to access again the next time. Items that are used or encountered frequently consequently have a lower AT than rare ones. Over periods of disuse, the AT gradually increases, so that even items that had been very frequent at some time, but have not been activated over a long period, will require more energy to access again (Paradis, 2004). Note that this is the exact neurolinguistic correlate of cognitive linguistic statements on entrenchment such as the ones by Langacker (1987) quoted above and is compatible with the memory processes assumed by the unified model. Also, effects of an interplay between frequency and recency of use have been reported repeatedly (see the overviews in Ellis, 2012, and Pfänder & Behrens, 2016). The idea of an AT therefore predicts a straightforward and more or less linear impact of factors such as the amount of L1 use in the emigration situation and the length of residence on the degree of attrition an individual experienced, modulated only by the frequency of the linguistic item or structure affected by the attritional process.

It is probably because this hypothesis is so apparently straightforward and so intuitively evident that for many years it was assumed to be virtually axiomatic. As a consequence, frequency of use was very rarely included as a predictor in attrition studies. This lack is partly attributable to the inherent difficulties of measuring this construct: Unlike other factors involved in the attritional process, such as length of residence or age at emigration, language use cannot be observed independently and objectively but has to be measured based on self-assessments. Early studies attempted to do this by means of a single, binary, or scaled variable, but they failed to identify any clear-cut effects on the outcome variables (e.g., De Bot, Gommans, & Rossing, 1991; Jaspaert & Kroon, 1989; Köpke, 1999).

These findings led to the assumption (Köpke & Schmid, 2004) that an experiential factor as complex as that of language use (often called *language exposure* in these studies but usually referring to both productive and receptive language use) could not meaningfully be reduced to a single variable, such as the percentage of time that speakers estimate spending on using L1 versus L2 (Köpke, 1999) or a Likert-scale frequency estimate (De Bot et al., 1991), let alone a binary predictor such as the native language of the spouse (Jaspaert & Kroon, 1989) or the question "Do you speak language X?" answered with a yes–no answer (Ammerlaan, 1996). The Language Attrition Test Battery (Schmid, 2011) was thus developed to provide a multifactorial questionnaire for the assessment of linguistic habits across a range of interlocutors and contexts.[1] The items included in the questionnaire cover different modalities (speaking and listening, reading and writing, inner language in a variety

---

[1] The questionnaire is available online in several languages (http://www.languageattrition.org/resources-for-researchers/experiment-materials/sociolinguistic-questionnaires/).

of contexts such as counting, praying, and cursing) and language modes (bilingual, intermediate, monolingual). Schmid and Dusseldorp (2010) reported a multifactorial analysis of data obtained by this instrument, which resulted in a range of subscales or compound predictors with good internal validity. These compound predictors have since been replicated and applied in a number of investigations of the attrition of various languages and fall into clusters related to language mode in interactive contexts on the one hand and passive exposure, inner language, and attitudinal factors on the other.

The principal component analysis (PCA) conducted by Schmid and Dusseldorp (2010) revealed three subsets of variables related to the frequency of use of the L1 in informal, everyday settings with other bilingual speakers: use of the L1 (a) with the partner or spouse, (b) with children (or grandchildren), and (c) with friends. Although there was no strong internal correlation between these factors (probably attributable to the fact that they were dependent on the presence of suitable bilingual speakers across the three settings, a factor that is largely outside the control of the individual speaker), it was hypothesized that they would all pertain to a similar kind of speech setting—crucially, one that corresponds to the description of "bilingual mode" in Grosjean's (2001) model of bilingual interaction, a context where both languages are highly active and code-switching is frequent and situation appropriate.

A second cluster of factors pertains to interactions in contexts where code-switching is not appropriate, namely, the use of the language in L1 institutions such as churches and clubs (where the mixing of languages is often frowned upon) or with friends or family members in the country of origin. Thirdly, the use of the L1 for professional purposes—that is, in what Grosjean (2001) termed the *intermediate mode*, a formal setting where external stimuli keep the L2 at an extremely high level of activation but where code-switching is situationally inappropriate—remained separate in the analysis from any of the other interactional variables. Two more largely attitudinal sets of predictors emerged, one of which also encompasses receptive language use through reading, music, TV, and so on, and the other associated with feelings toward both languages and cultures and toward language maintenance and transmission (Schmid & Dusseldorp, 2010, pp. 139–142).

Schmid and Dusseldorp (2010) then explored the predictive power of the compound factors calculated on the basis of the PCA for the scores that 106 L1 attriters of German achieved on a range of formal linguistic tasks as well as for lexical diversity, accuracy, and fluency in free speech (when background factors such as age, length of residence, and education were controlled for). Interestingly, the only factor that emerged as significant was the use of the L1 for professional purposes. This finding corresponds to an analysis that Schmid (2007) conducted on the same data before, in which the language use variables had been clustered exclusively on the basis of Grosjean's (2001) language mode model: Here, too, L1 use in settings where both languages are highly active but code-switching is situationally inappropriate emerged as the only significant predictor. In particular, both of these studies suggest that the type of L1 use that arguably makes up the largest proportion of overall use—informal conversations within the family or with friends—does not play any role whatsoever in diversity, accuracy, or fluency in L1 attrition.

This result is so unexpected that one might be tempted to ascribe it to some kind of quirk in the data at hand. Note, however, that the investigation comprised what can be considered a fairly large sample of 106 bilingual speakers who were shown to differ significantly from a monolingual reference group—matched for age, sex, and education—across all of the outcome variables considered. What's more, the design used in these two studies has been replicated in a number of PhD investigations in various linguistic settings (Cherciov, 2011, on Romanian–English bilinguals; Dostert, 2009, on English–German bilinguals; Keijzer, 2007, on Dutch–English bilinguals; Lubińska, 2011, on Polish–Swedish bilinguals; Varga, 2012, on Hungarian–Danish bilinguals; and Yilmaz & Schmid, 2012, on Turkish–Dutch bilinguals). None of these investigations found an impact of predictors related to amount or type of language use. Professional L1 use was again the exception, but not all of the studies had large enough numbers of speakers to whom this factor applied (professional opportunities, for example, for which Hungarian is required being rather limited in Denmark). The only investigation that found a significant correlation is Opitz (2011), who calculated one compound attrition measure composed of the z-scores across all her tasks and one overall compound measure of L1 use. Although these two variables correlated moderately ($r = .545$; Opitz, 2011, p. 300), no other background variables were partialled out in this analysis, and the differential impact of different types of exposure and use was not assessed. So this particular finding is somewhat difficult to interpret.

All in all, it therefore seems that the notion that there should be a straightforward correspondence between frequency of L1 use on the one hand and amount of L1 attrition on the other, as has often been suggested, is too simplistic. Schmid (2007) suggested that there may be a kind of saturation threshold in the development of the monolingual native speaker: The linguistic experience of someone who has been immersed in the L1 environment up to adolescence or adulthood (as was the case for the participants in all of the investigations listed above) is much more intensive than that in any other system of knowledge that we possess, as we arguably engage with it in some form or other at every waking moment (and a good deal of the time when we are asleep). Once the saturation threshold has been reached, further exposure and use (refreshment of the neural trace) may therefore no longer be necessary to maintain knowledge. This assumption is in line with the predictions made by MacWhinney (2011) and Hernandez and colleagues (2005), and it also receives support from several of the speakers in Schmid's sample who stated not to have used their first language at all for several decades but still retained native or near-native fluency, accuracy, and lexical diversity (see also Schmid, 2009, for an extreme case).

It thus seems that the simple frequency of L1 use by itself is not a sufficient explanatory concept for the degree of L1 attrition and that L1 knowledge may possibly stay entrenched regardless of the amount of L1 use. Instead, it might rather be the type and quality of L1 use that can partially account for the differences between L1 attriters. Accordingly, Schmid (2007) proposed an alternative explanation that is based not on activation frequency but on inhibitory mechanisms (see Section 16.4, this chapter).

16.4 Frequency of Lexical Items and Cross-Linguistic Similarity

A second entrenchment-related prediction for language attrition is that less frequent items should be prone to attrition effects and accessibility problems earlier than more frequent ones (e.g., Paradis, 2007, p. 121). From a cognitive linguistic point of view, this prediction should apply to both lexically specific items and more abstract constructions; L1 attrition studies, however, have applied this hypothesis most often to lexical knowledge.

The lexicon is often assumed to be the most vulnerable part of the linguistic repertoire—that is, the part that will be affected first, fastest, and most dramatically by any attritional process (see Schmid & Jarvis, 2014, p. 729, for an overview). These predictions are in accord with MacWhinney's (2008, 2011) unified model. There are solid theoretical and empirical grounds from other fields of linguistic investigation underpinning the a priori assumption that the lexicon is more prone to change in a language contact situation than other aspects of linguistic knowledge and that nonuse will lead to loss. For example, Paradis (2007) related the lexicon's presumed vulnerability to characteristics of different memory systems and their role for language: Declarative memory (which is assumed to underlie semantic knowledge and to be non-modality-specific) is thought to be more susceptible to L2 transfer and to forgetting in general than procedural memory (on which, in Paradis's framework, grammatical knowledge and other predominantly or fully automatized processes are based; Paradis, 2007, p. 127; see Takashima & Bakker, Chapter 8, and Hartsuiker & Moors, Chapter 9, this volume).

Schmid and Köpke (2008) furthermore referred to volume, frequency, and interconnectedness effects: The mental lexicon contains more information and fewer connections than, for example, the phoneme inventory, which typically consists of a limited number of items that are used extremely frequently and exist in a densely connected network. This assumption implies that, although small changes in a closed-class system will quickly ramify across the entire network, the lexicon can tolerate and absorb a certain number of changes. This process is mirrored in the resilience found in models of the self-organizing cortical maps assumed by the unified model that still responded properly even when a particular unit in the map was destroyed (MacWhinney, 2008, p. 344). Findings from language shift and language death also indicate that lexical borrowings from the surrounding language and loss or inaccessibility of items in the disappearing one are among the most common phenomena (e.g., Dorian, 1973, 1978).

Although existing findings, interpretations, claims, and assumptions regarding the lexicon's elevated susceptibility to cross-linguistic interference, nonuse, and attrition are interesting, the difficulty of establishing a common basis of comparison between different linguistic levels makes it very difficult to evaluate predictions that refer to differential attrition rates and effects (Schmid & Köpke, 2008). For example, is it really possible to make a meaningful comparison of the number of words a person might have "lost" and the amount of phonetic drift that has taken place in their linguistic repertoire? A well-designed longitudinal investigation across the first few years of the incubation period might conceivably be able to demonstrate that an individual attriter is experiencing attrition effects in the lexicon at a stage at which other linguistic levels are, as yet, unaffected. To date, there are no such studies charting the earliest years of attrition.

However, recent findings demonstrating phonetic drift in the L1 of beginning L2 learners within the first 6 weeks of an intensive language course (Chang, 2012) make it unlikely that lexical attrition should indeed be the primary phenomenon: Just like later L2 learners (in whom this has been demonstrated repeatedly, starting with Flege, 1987), they showed a drift of voice onset times and formant frequency in their L1 toward the L2 norms in some sounds. This finding is surprising from the point of view of the unified model, in which the L1 phonology is viewed as the most entrenched of all linguistic areas (MacWhinney, 2008, p. 363), and no phonetic attrition other than possibly a loss of fluency or a change in pausing patterns (as in Schmid & Fägersten, 2010) would be expected.

Notwithstanding, the lexicon can potentially offer interesting insights into the role of frequency of reinforcement for the maintenance or attrition of linguistic knowledge. In this context, two hypotheses formulated by Andersen (1982) remain valid:

> An LA [language attriter] will have a smaller number and a smaller variety of lexical items available to him than a comparable LC [linguistically competent individual] in the same language. . . . An LA's lexical repertoire will match his recent (and prior) experience with different domains of use and semantic areas. His lexicon will be most impoverished in those areas where he has had little or no experience. He will exhibit greater numbers of gaps in those areas where he has no recent experience in comparison with other areas where he has had recent experience using the language. . . . What lexicon the LA has retained will be of common, highly-frequent, unmarked lexical items; the gaps will be of less-common, low-frequency, highly-marked items. (p. 94)

Again, this prediction tallies perfectly with entrenchment approaches such as the unified model and the activation threshold hypothesis.

To test and evaluate these predictions, a number of studies (comprising the same set of PhD theses quoted above: Cherciov, 2011; Dostert, 2009; Keijzer, 2007; Lubińska, 2011; Opitz, 2011; Varga, 2012; Yilmaz & Schmid, 2012) assessed global attrition effects. Both formal tasks (e.g., verbal fluency of picture naming) and lexical diversity in free speech were investigated in these studies, with somewhat varying findings. Schmid and Jarvis (2014, p. 732) pointed out a pattern in the results: Significant differences between attriters and controls consistently emerged only in populations larger than 25 speakers (whereas the increase of disfluency phenomena in free speech, which may also be an indication of lexical access problems, appears to be somewhat more robust in smaller sample sizes). They concluded that the lack of a significant difference in those studies investigating smaller populations may be a Type II error because of the relative subtlety of the process of change (in itself an argument against the pervasive notion that the lexicon is the part of the linguistic repertoire that is most vulnerable to attrition).

Schmid and Jarvis (2014) then attempted to assess the impact of corpus frequency on lexical attrition in order to test the hypothesis that attriters retain only "common, highly-frequent, unmarked lexical items" and show gaps where "less-common, low-frequency, highly-marked items" are concerned, as predicted by Andersen (1982, p. 94). In two speech samples from a population of 106 attriters of German (who had been residing in an L2 English or L2 Dutch environment for an average of 37 and 34 years, respectively) and 53 monolingual controls, they investigated the distribution of more and less frequent lexical items (based on their distribution in both the speech samples at hand and the COSMAS II corpus[2]). For lexical frequencies based exclusively on their own corpus, the authors found a slight but significant tendency of attriters to overuse more frequent and underuse less frequent items. This tendency, however, all but disappeared when lexical frequency is based on the much larger COSMAS II corpus. For L1 attriters immersed in an English-speaking environment, there was still a significant difference, but effect sizes were extremely weak (η^2 between .04 and .01; Schmid & Jarvis, 2014, p. 739), whereas for L1 attriters in a Dutch environment there were no significant differences from the controls at all. Extralinguistic factors, such as frequency of use of the L1, played no significant role for any of these frequency measures.

The finding that the attriters with Dutch as L2 showed no difference from the controls but the attriters with English as L2 did is interesting because it suggests that the large proportion of cognates that the Dutch and the German language share may make it easier for the Dutch L2 speakers to maintain their lexicon. Indeed, the authors also demonstrated that these speakers, but not the L2 English speakers, overused lexical items that are similar in their two languages as compared with the monolingual controls (Schmid & Jarvis, 2014, p. 740). This finding tallies with the predictions made on the basis of the unified model, as positive transfer is one of the factors proposed to support the maintenance of linguistic knowledge. From a cognitive linguistic point of view, such a positive effect should also occur with larger and less lexically specific constructions such as idioms or grammatical constructions (e.g., word order). To date, there are no attrition studies specifically investigating this; however, in a review of several studies on errors in attriters, Schmid (2013) compared the number of syntactic errors in L1 German attriters with Dutch or English as L2. Although both

---

[2] Corpus Search Management and Analysis is maintained by the Institut für Deutsche Sprache at Mannheim and is based on approximately 5.4 billion word forms.

languages are closely related to German, the similarities shared with Dutch in the syntactic domain are far greater than those shared with English. In spite of this, both groups of attriters showed the same amount of syntactic errors in their L1 in their free speech (Schmid, 2013, p. 101). This finding runs against the expectations formulated above. However, further studies looking into the effects of positive transfer for other constructions than words are needed to allow firm conclusions.

Taken together, the findings suggest that there may indeed be a slight role of frequency of reinforcement for lexical attrition. However, it is clear that predictions such as the one by Andersen (1982) quoted above strongly overstate the case: Although the use of very low frequency words by the attriters in the studies above was slightly reduced overall compared with the controls, they still did avail themselves of that part of their linguistic repertoire.

16.5 Entrenchment, Inhibition, and Cognitive Control

Investigations of L1 attrition often express the authors' surprise at the degree to which the native language of migrants can be maintained, apparently largely intact, over many decades, and the findings reported above show that this maintenance is not influenced dramatically by the amount to which the language remains in use. This stability contrasts starkly with findings of first-language maintenance and loss among younger migrants or heritage speakers, who often possess a knowledge of their first language that is dramatically impoverished and more similar to that of foreign language speakers than of natives (see, e.g., Montrul, 2008; Schmid, 2013). In particular, findings from international adoptees have shown that the birth language can be forgotten almost entirely, and that whatever traces of the linguistic experience are retained in memory are likely confined to the phonological level and do not extend to, for example, syntax or the lexicon (Hyltenstam, Bylund, Abrahamsson, & Park, 2009; Oh, Au, & Jun, 2010; Pallier et al., 2003; Pierce, Klein, Chen, Delcenserie, & Genesee, 2014; Schmid, 2012; Zhou & Broersma, 2014).

These findings suggest that there is a point in linguistic development, situated substantially later than the age at which individual grammatical features are usually taken to become targetlike (typically between ages 2 and 6), at which the memory for the native language becomes in some way consolidated or "crystallized" (Hernandez et al., 2005, p. 224). Before this age, it is susceptible to change under conditions of massive input from another language and to erosion because of reduced input, whereas afterward it becomes largely impervious to such matters. This conclusion suggests an important role for entrenchment not only for language acquisition but also for the consolidation of linguistic memory.

After this age, it appears that rehearsal is no longer required to maintain native linguistic knowledge and keep it accessible. What appears to be more important is the online competition between a bilingual's different language systems. The mechanism invoked by Schmid (2007) to account for the protective function that L1 use for professional purposes has for L1 maintenance thus relies not so much on the activation but on the inhibition of knowledge: Migrants who use their L1 for work-related purposes (e.g., language teachers, secretaries or administrators in businesses with international links, translators, and interpreters, but also staff members in restaurants or shops catering to certain cuisines or backgrounds) do so in a setting in which all kinds of stimuli keep the second language at a very highly active level. They usually have to use both languages frequently in the course of their working day, but also to keep them separate and avoid mixing, involuntary switching, and cross-linguistic interference. The massive practice they have at this inhibitory mechanism (for both their languages) may make it easier for them to perform the tasks usually used in attrition investigations.

Interestingly, this suggestion, first made by Schmid in 2007, is very much in line with recent work in the context of what has been termed the "bilingual advantage"—the finding that long-term bilinguals often outperform monolinguals when it comes to tasks measuring executive function and cognitive control. This finding is usually ascribed to the fact that the effort that goes toward both maintaining and keeping separate more than one linguistic system in daily life can result in enhanced domain-general cognitive control and executive function (for recent overviews, see Baum & Titone, 2014; Bialystok, Craik, Green, & Gollan, 2009; Valian, 2015). However, the bilingual advantage appears to be modulated by many factors, and it is, as yet, unclear which specific phenomena linked with the bilingual experience are conducive to its formation.

One factor that has been mentioned in this context is the extent to which individual bilinguals separate their languages in daily use: There is substantial research demonstrating that all of a bilingual's languages are active at any given point in time during speech production, but that the activation of the language not currently in use can vary from minimal (single-language/monolingual mode) to very high (dense code-switching situation/bilingual mode; e.g., Green & Abutalebi, 2013; Grosjean, 2001). It has been assumed for some time that bilinguals who rarely code-switch, or *nonswitchers*, benefit more in terms of cognitive control and executive function than *fluent* or *dense switchers* (Green, 2011) because nonswitchers have more practice in exerting language control in order to minimize the activation of the nontarget language and so prevent switches or interference between their languages (Green, 2014). This assumption suggests that patterns of language use and language mixing not only may have an impact on the maintenance or attrition of the first language but also may have wider implications for overall mechanisms of domain-general cognitive control.

16.6 Conclusion

This chapter has attempted to show ways in which current investigations and findings from the area of first-language attrition can benefit cognitive linguistic approaches and theories of entrenchment. We have argued that the loss, deterioration, or change of linguistic knowledge is the other side of the coin of its acquisition, establishment, and entrenchment and that, as such, the study of attrition should form an integral part of the cognitive linguistic endeavor. However, although it is often implicitly or explicitly evoked in theoretical treatments, language attrition has never yet been explicitly addressed within the empirical work on usage-based and entrenchment-oriented approaches. Investigating attrition has the potential to elucidate the importance of factors such as the frequency of overall use and the frequency of items or constructions in memory consolidation, as well as the development of domain-general cognitive functions. We have shown that the entrenchment of L1 skills and the related processes of retention or forgetting of linguistic items do not depend in a straightforward or linear way on frequency-related predictors, but on a complex interaction of factors, including age and patterns of language use. More specifically, the process of attrition might be affected not only by the entrenchment of the L1 knowledge, but also by the ability of the speaker to inhibit the L2 knowledge.

References

Ammerlaan, T. (1996). *You get a bit wobbly: Exploring bilingual lexical retrieval processes in the context of first language attrition* (Unpublished doctoral dissertation). Katholieke Universiteit Nijmegen, Nijmegen, the Netherlands.

Andersen, R. W. (1982). Determining the linguistic attributes of language attrition. In R. D. Lambert & B. F. Freed (Eds.), *The loss of language skills* (pp. 83–118). Rowley, MA: Newbury House.

Anderson, J. R. (2014). *Cognitive psychology and its implications* (8th ed.). New York, NY: Worth Publishers.

Bates, E., & MacWhinney, B. (1982). Functionalist approaches to grammar. In E. Wanner & L. Gleitman (Eds.), *Language acquisition: The state of the art* (pp. 173–218). New York, NY: Cambridge University Press.

Baum, S., & Titone, D. (2014). Moving toward a neuroplasticity view of bilingualism, executive control, and aging. *Applied Psycholinguistics, 35*, 857–894. http://dx.doi.org/10.1017/S0142716414000174

Bialystok, E., Craik, F. I. M., Green, D. W., & Gollan, T. H. (2009). Bilingual minds. *Psychological Science in the Public Interest, 10*(3), 89–129. http://dx.doi.org/10.1177/1529100610387084

Chang, C. B. (2012). Rapid and multifaceted effects of second-language learning on first-language speech production. *Journal of Phonetics, 40*, 249–268. http://dx.doi.org/10.1016/j.wocn.2011.10.007

Cherciov, M. (2011). *Between attrition and acquisition: The case of Romanian in immigrant contexts* (Unpublished doctoral dissertation). University of Toronto, Toronto, Ontario, Canada.

De Bot, K., Gommans, P., & Rossing, C. (1991). L1 loss in an L2 environment: Dutch immigrants in France. In H. W. Seliger & R. M. Vago (Eds.), *First language attrition* (pp. 87–98). http://dx.doi.org/10.1017/CBO9780511620720.006

Dorian, N. (1973). Grammatical change in a dying dialect. *Language, 49*, 413–438. http://dx.doi.org/10.2307/412461

Dorian, N. (1978). Fate of morphological complexity in language death: Evidence from East Sutherland Gaelic. *Language, 54*, 590–609. http://dx.doi.org/10.1353/lan.1978.0024

Dostert, S. (2009). *Multilingualism, L1 attrition and the concept of "native speaker"* (Unpublished doctoral dissertation). Heinrich-Heine-Universität Düsseldorf, Düsseldorf, Germany.

Ellis, N. C. (2012). What can we count in language, and what counts in language acquisition, cognition, and use? In S. T. Gries & D. S. Divjak (Eds.), *Frequency effects in cognitive linguistics: Vol. 1. Statistical effects in learnability, processing and change* (pp. 7–34). http://dx.doi.org/10.1515/9783110274059.7

Ellis, N. C. (2013). Second language acquisition. In G. Trousdale & T. Hoffmann (Eds.), *Oxford handbook of construction grammar* (pp. 365–378). Oxford, England: Oxford University Press.

Flege, J. E. (1987). The production of "new" and "similar" phones in a foreign language: Evidence for the effect of equivalence classification. *Journal of Phonetics*, *15*, 47–65.

Green, D. W. (2011). Language control in different contexts: The behavioral ecology of bilingual speakers. *Frontiers in Psychology*, *2*, 103. http://dx.doi.org/10.3389/fpsyg.2011.00103

Green, D. W. (2014). Individual variability and neuroplastic changes. *Applied Psycholinguistics*, *35*, 910–912. http://dx.doi.org/10.1017/S0142716414000228

Green, D. W., & Abutalebi, J. (2013). Language control in bilinguals: The adaptive control hypothesis. *Journal of Cognitive Psychology*, *25*, 515–530. http://dx.doi.org/10.1080/20445911.2013.796377

Grosjean, F. (2001). The bilingual's language modes. In J. Nicol (Ed.), *One mind, two languages: Bilingual language processing* (pp. 1–22). Oxford, England: Blackwell.

Hernandez, A., Li, P., & MacWhinney, B. (2005). The emergence of competing modules in bilingualism. *Trends in Cognitive Sciences*, *9*, 220–225. http://dx.doi.org/10.1016/j.tics.2005.03.003

Hyltenstam, K., Bylund, E., Abrahamsson, N., & Park, H.-S. (2009). Dominant language replacement: The case of international adoptees. *Bilingualism: Language and Cognition*, *12*, 121–140. http://dx.doi.org/10.1017/S1366728908004008

Jaspaert, K., & Kroon, S. (1989). Social determinants of language loss. *ITL: Review of Applied Linguistics*, *83–84*, 75–98.

Keijzer, M. (2007). *First language attrition: A crosslinguistic investigation of Jakobson's regression hypothesis* (Unpublished doctoral dissertation). Vrije Universiteit Amsterdam, Amsterdam, the Netherlands.

Köpke, B. (1999). *L'attrition de la première language chez le bilingue tardif: Implications pour l'étude psycholinguistique du bilinguisme* [First language attrition in late bilinguals: Implications for the psycholinguistic study of bilingualism] (Unpublished doctoral dissertation). Université de Toulouse–Le Mirail, Toulouse, France.

Köpke, B., & Schmid, M. S. (2004). First language attrition: The next phase. In M. S. Schmid, B. Köpke, M. Keijzer, & L. Weilemar (Eds.), *First language attrition: Interdisciplinary perspectives on methodological issues* (pp. 1–45). http://dx.doi.org/10.1075/sibil.28.02kop

Langacker, R. W. (1987). *Foundations of cognitive grammar: Vol. 1. Theoretical prerequisites.* Stanford, CA: Stanford University Press.

Langacker, R. W. (1988). A usage-based model. In B. Rudzka-Ostyn (Ed.), *Topics in cognitive linguistics* (pp. 127–161). http://dx.doi.org/10.1075/cilt.50.06lan

Langacker, R. W. (2000). A dynamic usage-based model. In S. Kemmer & M. Barlow (Eds.), *Usage-based models of language* (pp. 1–63). Stanford, CA: Center for the Study of Language and Information.

Lubińska, D. (2011). *Förstaspråksattrition hos vuxna: Exemplet polsktalande i Sverige* [Adult first language attrition: The case of Polish speakers in Sweden] (Unpublished doctoral dissertation). University of Stockholm, Stockholm, Sweden.

MacWhinney, B. (1987). The competition model. In B. MacWhinney (Ed.), *Mechanisms of language acquisition* (pp. 249–308). Hillsdale, NJ: Erlbaum.

MacWhinney, B. (2008). A unified model. In N. Ellis & P. Robinson (Eds.), *Handbook of cognitive linguistics and second language acquisition* (pp. 341–372). Mahwah, NJ: Erlbaum.

MacWhinney, B. (2011). The logic of the unified model. In S. M. Gass & A. Mackey (Eds.), *The Routledge handbook of second language acquisition* (pp. 211–227). New York, NY: Routledge.

Montrul, S. (2008). *Incomplete acquisition in bilingualism: Re-examining the age factor.* http://dx.doi.org/10.1075/sibil.39

Oh, J. S., Au, T. K. F., & Jun, S. A. (2010). Early childhood language memory in the speech perception of international adoptees. *Journal of Child Language, 37*, 1123–1132. http://dx.doi.org/10.1017/S0305000909990286

Opitz, C. (2011). *First language attrition and second language acquisition in a second-language environment* (Unpublished doctoral dissertation). Trinity College, Dublin, Dublin, Ireland.

Pallier, C., Dehaene, S., Poline, J.-B., LeBihan, D., Argenti, A.-M., Dupoux, E., & Mehler, J. (2003). Brain imaging of language plasticity in adopted adults: Can a second language replace the first? *Cerebral Cortex, 13*, 155–161. http://dx.doi.org/10.1093/cercor/13.2.155

Paradis, M. (1993). Linguistic, psycholinguistic, and neurolinguistic aspects of interference in bilingual speakers: The activation threshold hypothesis. *International Journal of Psycholinguistics, 9*, 133–145.

Paradis, M. (2004). *A neurolinguistic theory of bilingualism.* http://dx.doi.org/10.1075/sibil.18

Paradis, M. (2007). L1 attrition features predicted by a neurolinguistic theory of bilingualism. In B. Köpke, M. S. Schmid, M. Keijzer, & S. Dostert (Eds.), *Language attrition: Theoretical perspectives* (pp. 121–133). http://dx.doi.org/10.1075/sibil.33.09par

Paradis, M. (2009). *Declarative and procedural determinants of second languages.* http://dx.doi.org/10.1075/sibil.40

Pavlenko, A. (2004). L2 influence and L1 attrition in adult bilingualism. In M. S. Schmid, B. Köpke, M. Keijzer, & L. Weilemar (Eds.), *First language attrition: Interdisciplinary perspectives on methodological issues* (pp. 47–59). http://dx.doi.org/10.1075/sibil.28.04pav

Pavlenko, A. (2010). Verbs of motion in L1 Russian of Russian–English bilinguals. *Bilingualism: Language and Cognition, 13*, 49–62. http://dx.doi.org/10.1017/S1366728909990198

Pfänder, S., & Behrens, H. (2016). Experience counts: An introduction to frequency effects in language. In H. Behrens & S. Pfänder (Eds.), *Experience counts: Frequency effects in language* (pp. 1–20). Berlin, Germany: de Gruyter.

Pierce, L. J., Klein, D., Chen, J. K., Delcenserie, A., & Genesee, F. (2014). Mapping the unconscious maintenance of a lost first language. *Proceedings of the National Academy of Sciences of the United States of America, 111*, 17314–17319. http://dx.doi.org/10.1073/pnas.1409411111

Pine, J. M., Lieven, E. V. M., & Rowland, C. F. (1998). Comparing different models of the development of the English verb category. *Linguistics, 36*, 807–830. http://dx.doi.org/10.1515/ling.1998.36.4.807

Pizzuto, E., & Caselli, M. C. (1992). The acquisition of Italian morphology: Implications for models of language development. *Journal of Child Language, 19*, 491–557. http://dx.doi.org/10.1017/S0305000900011557

Rubino, R. B., & Pine, J. M. (1998). Subject–verb agreement in Brazilian Portuguese: What low error rates hide. *Journal of Child Language, 25*, 35–59. http://dx.doi.org/10.1017/S0305000997003310

Schmid, M. S. (2007). The role of L1 use for L1 attrition. In B. Köpke, M. S. Schmid, M. Keijzer, & S. Dostert (Eds.), *Language attrition: Theoretical perspectives* (pp. 135–153). http://dx.doi.org/10.1075/sibil.33.10sch

Schmid, M. S. (2009). On L1 attrition and the linguistic system. *EuroSLA Yearbook, 9*, 212–244.

Schmid, M. S. (2011). *Language attrition*. http://dx.doi.org/10.1017/CBO9780511852046

Schmid, M. S. (2012). The impact of age and exposure on bilingual development in international adoptees and family migrants: A perspective from Holocaust survivors. *Linguistic Approaches to Bilingualism*, 2, 177–208. http://dx.doi.org/10.1075/lab.2.2.03sch

Schmid, M. S. (2013). First language attrition: State of the discipline and future directions. *Linguistic Approaches to Bilingualism*, 3, 94–115. http://dx.doi.org/10.1075/lab.3.1.05sch

Schmid, M. S. (2014). The debate on maturational constraints in bilingual development: A perspective from first language attrition. *Language Acquisition*, 21, 386–410. http://dx.doi.org/10.1080/10489223.2014.892947

Schmid, M. S., & Dusseldorp, E. (2010). Quantitative analyses in a multivariate study of language attrition: The impact of extralinguistic factors. *Second Language Research*, 26, 125–160. http://dx.doi.org/10.1177/0267658309337641

Schmid, M. S., & Fägersten, K. B. (2010). Fluency and language attrition. *Language Learning*, 60, 753–791. http://dx.doi.org/10.1111/j.1467-9922.2010.00575.x

Schmid, M. S., & Jarvis, S. (2014). Lexical access and lexical diversity in first language attrition. *Bilingualism: Language and Cognition*, 17, 729–748. http://dx.doi.org/10.1017/S1366728913000771

Schmid, M. S., & Köpke, B. (2008). L1 attrition and the mental lexicon. In A. Pavlenko (Ed.), *The bilingual mental lexicon: Interdisciplinary approaches* (pp. 209–238). Bristol, England: Multilingual Matters.

Tomasello, M. (1992). *First verbs: A case study of early grammatical development*. http://dx.doi.org/10.1017/CBO9780511527678

Tomasello, M. (2003). *Constructing a language: A usage-based theory of language acquisition*. Cambridge, MA: Harvard University Press.

Valian, V. (2015). Bilingualism and cognition. *Bilingualism: Language and Cognition*, 18, 3–24. http://dx.doi.org/10.1017/S1366728914000522

Varga, Z. (2012). *First language attrition and maintenance among Hungarian speakers in Denmark* (Unpublished doctoral dissertation). Aarhus University, Aarhus, Denmark.

Yilmaz, G., & Schmid, M. S. (2012). L1 accessibility among Turkish–Dutch bilinguals. *The Mental Lexicon*, 7, 249–274. http://dx.doi.org/10.1075/ml.7.3.01yil

Zhou, W., & Broersma, M. (2014). Perception of birth language tone contrasts by adopted Chinese children. In C. Gussenhoven, Y. Chen, & D. Dediu (Eds.), *Proceedings of the 4th International Symposium on Tonal Aspects of Language* (pp. 63–66). Baixas, France: International Speech Communication Association.

V Deconstructing Entrenchment

Philip Herdina
17 Entrenchment, Embeddedness, and Entanglement: A Dynamic Complexity View

> Comme les choses aussi ont souvent de la ressemblance entre elles, il est difficile quelquesfois de designer les differences precises [Because things themselves also frequently resemble one another, it is sometimes difficult to determine the precise differences].
> —Gottfried Wilhelm Leibniz, *De l'imperfection des mots* [The imperfection of words]

17.1 Introduction

In *dynamic complexity theory* (DCT), complex systems are represented in terms of interacting subsystems resulting in emergent properties that cannot be attributed to the individual subsystems or units. Properties of the system are therefore conceived of as dynamic results of systemic interaction and as functions rather than inherent properties of units. It is further assumed that identifiable relations behave in a nonlinear way—that is, the relationships are always codetermined by the specific context in which they occur—which renders it impossible to establish invariable relations between two factors in isolation. Finally, DCT adopts a holistic approach, questioning the fundamental assumptions of established analytical and reductionist procedures. This approach is best summed up in the claim that there is no point in looking for system properties in the units that make up the system and that many supposed unit properties will prove to be system properties.

This chapter suggests that many of the apparent perplexities incurred by frequentist approaches dissolve once the concept of frequency and associated terms are reanalyzed in line with fundamental ideas of DCT. Its aim is to outline how DCT can contribute to the goal discussed by Schmid (Chapter 1, this volume):

> ... to show that the large diversity of entrenchment processes can be reconciled in a unified framework if types of inputs to entrenchment processes, types of determinants, and types of effects of entrenchment are systematically distinguished. (Section 1.5)

This goal will be achieved by highlighting specific core issues in entrenchment research and sketching the DCT approach to the respective problem.

17.2 Frequency Hypothesis

> Corpus-based studies of frequency effects have tested the assumption that the frequencies of occurrence of lexical elements and syntactic constructions in large corpora mirror degrees of entrenchment and strengths of representation. (Schmid, Chapter 1, this volume, Section 1.3.1)

There appears to be general agreement that frequency has an influence on features such as entrenchment, automatization, and embeddedness (see Ellis, 2002, p. 178; Ellis, 2012; Ellis & Ogden, 2015). The basic version of the frequency hypothesis claims that there is some linear correlation between frequency and entrenchment. The higher the frequency of a language unit (lingueme or chunk), the more entrenched it is. The assumed connection between frequency and entrenchment seems at first to be a plausible and accepted hypothesis.

This frequency hypothesis is also closely associated with the usage-based theory of language championed inter alia by Bybee, Perkins, and Paglivia (1994; see also Bybee, 2007, 2008, 2011; Bybee & Hopper, 2001). Its origins can be traced back to Halliday (1994) and Langacker (1987):

> Every use of a structure has a positive impact on its degree of entrenchment, whereas extended periods of disuse have a negative impact. With repeated use, a novel structure becomes progressively entrenched, to the point of becoming a unit; moreover, units are variably entrenched depending on the frequency of their occurrence. (p. 59)

Furthermore, a focus on frequency at the expense of other linguistic features suggests a commitment to the quantitative paradigm (see Bayley, 2013). This paradigm makes the following assumptions: Linguistic data can be broken down into language units (see Ellis, 2002, p. 164), and the frequency data obtained allow us to make quantitative claims concerning these relationships. It is tacitly assumed that the relationship between unit frequency and the effect it has on any language variable will turn out to be a linear one, which is why linguistic research tends to ask questions concerning the effect of frequency on entrenchment. Underlying the frequency hypothesis is also an inductive assumption of the following nature: By adding the results for individual features, we can obtain results applicable to all features. Such an approach does not allow for the existence of emergent properties in language.

Yet, such a decontextualized focus on frequency as a quantitative and cumulative variable does not appear to provide satisfactory answers to the correlations between unit frequency and other factors associated with it. As stated by Schmid, there seems to be some limitation to conventional analysis:

> Frequency as such is no more than an idealized and mechanical approximation of repeated use and exposure by individual speakers taking place in concrete situations. What pure frequency counts can certainly not inform us about are the manifold ways in which repeated exposure can affect the cognitive and linguistic system depending on the linguistic, situational, and social contexts of specific usage events. (Schmid, Chapter 1, this volume, Section 1.3.3)

As is suggested in this chapter, the assumption of a linear correlation between frequency and entrenchment cannot be shared by DCT. The frequency hypothesis lends itself to a more differentiated set of interpretations, as outlined below. It can be read to imply the following positive correlations with embeddedness, routinization, and automatization (see Hartsuiker & Moors, Chapter 9, this volume), as well as with memory and retention (see Takashima & Bakker, Chapter 8, this volume):

- The more frequent a language unit, chunk, or pattern is, the more entrenched it is.
- The more frequent a language unit, chunk, or pattern is, the more embedded it is.
- The more entrenched a language unit, chunk, or pattern is, the more embedded it is, and vice versa.
- The more frequent a language unit, chunk, or pattern is, the more automatized it is.
- The more frequently a language unit, chunk, or pattern is used, the more likely it is to be retained.

However, if there is a positive correlation between frequency and more than one other factor cited, then these factors must themselves relate to each other in some way that is compatible with the frequency assumptions. This observation explains why it is useful to discuss frequency and entrenchment in the context of all these other processes.

- DCT: Complex dynamic systems properties are emergent and result from the incremental effect of frequencies of occurrence. The mode of occurrence is contextualized: Effects of frequency contain traces of previous occurrences. So the distribution patterns of language units are not equiprobable, and context of use must not be ignored.

17.2.1 Type Frequency and Token Frequency

> A fundamental insight . . . is that the repetition of identical tokens in the input (known as *token frequency*) results in increased entrenchment in terms of the strength of the corresponding specific representation, whereas repetition of varied items sharing commonalities of form or meaning (*type frequency*) facilitates categorization, abstraction, generalization, and the emergence of variable schemas. (Schmid, Chapter 1, this volume, Section 1.3.1; emphasis in original)

Significant frequency in language is interpreted as the frequency of occurrence of a language feature, unit, or pattern. It is generally acknowledged (see Schmid, Chapter 1, this volume, Section 1.3.1) that there is a need to distinguish at least two different types of frequency: type frequency and token frequency. *Tokens* are realizations of paradigmatic or syntagmatic patterns, whereas *types* are conventionally considered paradigmatic or syntagmatic patterns. For the distinction to be meaningful and to achieve the desired level of complexity reduction, it has to be assumed that there must be more tokens than types or fewer types than tokens. The type–token distinction was originally introduced by Peirce (1906):

> In another sense of the word "word," however, there is but one word "the" in the English language.... Such a... form I propose to term a Type.... In order that a Type may be used, it has to be embodied in a Token which shall be a sign of the Type, and thereby of the object the Type signifies. (p. 537)

The type frequency–token frequency relationship defined here suggests that there is a precisely determinable relation between types and tokens and that the respective sets of tokens therefore define a type. Even if we consider tokens as exemplifications of types or assume that types represent natural kinds, the type–token ratio is always expressed as a set-theoretical relation (Biber, Johansson, Leech, Conrad, & Finegan, 1999; Bybee, 2008; Quine, 1987). A set-theoretical interpretation does not admit of the nontypical occurrences of tokens that will initially form clusters from which, as these clusters stabilize, new types will emerge. If high-frequency elements result in entrenchment, established types will always be more entrenched than emergent types and typological change in language would be impossible. The dominant interpretation of type–token relationships and their conditions cannot explain the process of systematic change.

As Milicka (2009) observed, "If we consider type–token relation to be a feature of text and not of language, we can approach a theoretically based and precise description of this relation" (p. 99). Type–token relations can take the simple pattern suggested by Peirce (1906), such as the occurrence of *I* representing the word *I*, but similarly *I* can be considered an occurrence of the first-person singular pronoun in English. So *I* can be a token of the word *I* or a token of the pronoun *I*, and so forth.

Within complex dynamic systems, we are interested in the dynamic relationship between type and token. The relative values of type frequency and token frequency can accordingly vary. So within a dynamic system, we shall have to accept the possibility of a token without a type as an instance of type emergence; otherwise, we would not be able to observe processes of change such as grammaticalization, as exemplified by the emergence of auxiliary constructions or the *to* infinitive in early English. The emergence of the auxiliary use of *be*, *have*, and even *going to* from Anglo-Saxon full verbs *beon*, *habban*, and *gan*, plus the emergence of an identifiable infinitive, would result in what is defined as a token of aux + *to* infinitive. The occurrence of *to* + infinitive was originally restricted to substantival uses of the verb, and the verbs used to express intention slowly extended their meaning to express futurity.

The use of the type–token relationship in the context of corpus analysis does not appear to generate a problem because every occurrence of a unit can be classified as a token of a type. The units are assumed to be clearly defined and easily identifiable. If we see language as an open and dynamic system, then frequency has a significant role in identifying type. Any regular recurrence of a unit or a pattern can be assumed to be indicative of the existence of a potential type. Within DCT, the identification of a type–token relationship is the result of a creative process of tokenization. So tokenization, as defined by Peirce (1906) can be interpreted in two different ways: (a) as an issue of classification in which the type is assumed to be given (see Fasold & Connor-Linton, 2014, p. 479, on tokenization) or (b) as the creative use of tokenization to generate new types.

The dynamic relationship between token and type in language as a dynamic system generates competing negentropic and entropic tendencies incompatible with the conventional interpretation of type–token relationships generally determined by corpus-based research. The most conventional phenomenon is the emergence of grammatical or morphological type. As already suggested, a principle observed by Hopper and Traugott (2003) is that of *grammaticalization*, in which individual tokens represent emergent types and the token precedes the type. The emergence of a new type appears to be frequency based. At some stage, for instance, a second use of frequent main verbs must have occurred leading to the function of subsidiary or auxiliary verbs, such as *wyllan* and *sculan*, expressing futurity as well as intention or obligation.

The identification of frequency as a prerequisite for type emergence cannot, however, be considered a sufficient condition because the frequent inflected Germanic verbs appear to have survived in present-day English (PDE) only because they have been lexicalized and no longer represent a conjugational type. We might suggest that the irregular verbs survive only by being lexicalized and no longer being perceived as representing a verb class but rather an individual verb form similar to the anomalous verbs *beon* and *gan*. A more extreme case is the survival of Anglo-Saxon dative plural *whilom*, which appears to be the only extant case of the use of the dative plural ending in *-om*. *Seldom* might seem to be another instance but is derived from the adverb *seldan*.

A further conundrum is generated by the existence of *kennings*, which are distinguished from compounds by being nonce or quasi-nonce formations. There is no semantic or morphological difference between the kenning *hron rad* ('whaleroad'; see Marsden, 2015, p. 33) and the compound *hring iren* ('ring iron'; see Grein, 1912). The sole distinction appears to lie in frequency of occurrence, the nonce or near-nonce formations being classified as kennings. The necessary condition for the token representing this morphological type (i.e., metaphorical compound for poetic use) is the low or nonce frequency of occurrence. The type–token relationship has to admit of the emergence of types or the generation of tokens. Type–token relationships in DCT are essentially dynamic.

In addition, in a learner system the token–type ratio is variable, not constant. As the system develops, the type–token ratio changes over time. Young learners develop their own classification types and their own regularization patterns presupposing the emergence of an idiolectal type (e.g., German *gesingt* ['singed,' past participle] vs. *gesungen* ['sung'] vs. dialectal *gemolden* [ablaut past participle of *melden*, 'to report'] vs. *gemeldet* ['reported,' past participle]).

- DCT: The type–token relationship is not merely a part–whole or unit–system relation. It is dynamic, permitting the emergence of new types and new tokens, in which types generate new tokens and tokens generate new types.

17.2.2 Frequency Paradox

> The models would predict that the most productive of these irregular patterns would have high frequency values. However, we also found little support for the ability of frequency factors to account for differences in the productivity of the past tense alternations. There was no relationship between overall token frequency, average token frequency, or the ratio of past to base frequency and productivity of the past tense alternations. There was no relationship between overall token frequency, average token frequency, or the ratio of past to base frequency and productivity.... This result may be surprising given the general assumption that high frequency forms resist change. (Moder, 1992, p. 189)

If we assume a positive correlation between frequency and factors such as entrenchment, we are confronted with the fact that the empirical data do not appear to bear this out, or at least not in the way we would expect (as in Moder, 1992). The findings can best be described as paradoxical because the frequency hypothesis claims that the more frequent a token or type is, the more entrenched it is. The historical data we have suggest the opposite claim to be equally valid: The less frequent a type or token is, the more entrenched it is, and the less likely it is to change as evidenced by the PDE survival of low-frequency common words such as *hale, lank, lithe, brine,* and *hythe* in their Anglo-Saxon form.

Frequent activation appears to have two possible consequences: First, the more frequently a type or token is used, the more entrenched a pattern will become. This is illustrated by the existence of clichéd or formulaic expressions. Conversely, the more frequent a type or token is, the more likely it is to be subject to attrition or bleaching (see Hopper & Traugott, 2003), a phenomenon we can observe in the use of boosters and intensifiers (see Quirk, Greenbaum, Leech, & Svartvik, 1972, pp. 439–452). The clichéd or formulaic use of euphemisms, exemplified by expressions used for *dying* (e.g., *passing away*) or for *lavatory* (e.g., *washroom*), however, can also lead to semantic contamination rather than bleaching as an originally neutral term is increasingly loaded with undesired semantic associations resulting in its displacement by another euphemism. We can term this process *semantic accretion* and regard it as being opposed to bleaching.

We would therefore expect frequency of use to result in a strengthening of type and reduction of variation and, at least when grammaticalized, of semantic strength or phonetic strength—that is, semantic bleaching and phonetic attrition (see Bybee, 2010, p. 112). If there is a development toward a more grammatical function, strengthening of type should be accompanied by both bleaching and attrition. Without grammaticalization, no such effect will be observed. According to this principle, we would expect phonetic attrition in so-called *wh* words, which does not occur, so that we still retain a phonetic distinction between the aspirated *where* and the nonaspirated *were*. The *wh* + vowel sequences are still phonetically distinct from the *w* + vowel sequences (see Jones, 1979). In contrast, prepositional *through* is subject to a degree of orthographic and phonetic variation in Middle English that is incompatible with the grammaticalization hypothesis (see, e.g., *through, thrugh, thurg*).

Although we can observe bleaching or attrition in the adverbial *very* (from Old French *vraie*, 'true'), known to be an unusually high frequency non-Germanic word, we obtain exactly the opposite effect when lack of use results in a strengthening of type, such as prepositional stranding in French and German (e.g., *la fille que je suis sorti avec*) or the use of binomials in English (e.g., *hale and hearty*, *hither and thither*). We suggest that grammaticalization leads to a strengthening of type providing it restricts the context of use, as in the case of auxiliaries and semiauxiliaries in PDE or limited constructions like *tough movement* (see Schmid, 2007, p. 118). We can further assume that restricted use does indeed lead to a strengthening of type, whereas frequency alone does not. Alternatively, frequency combined with *scatter*—that is, use of different patterns in different contexts—leads to a weakening of type (i.e., type attrition). This is a necessary precondition of language change and the emergence of new types.

All this suggests that the relationship between frequency and entrenchment has to be viewed as nonlinear, rather than linear. This nonlinear relationship has some significant consequences: First, the effect of frequency has to be interpreted as variable and can therefore take the form of an (inverted) U-curve. So the frequency effect cannot be represented as a power relationship: As frequency of occurrence increases, the effect of frequency changes. Thus, the minimal distinction we have to make is between low frequency, average frequency, and high frequency, and we must assume that these frequencies have differing effects.

Furthermore, the effect frequency has will depend on the system it is applied to: High frequency in a learner-speaker system will have a different effect from high frequency in a user-speaker system. As observed in child learners, a high level of repetition or frequency of occurrence has a useful function (see Theakston, Chapter 14, this volume, for more details). So high frequency for a learner-speaker has a corroborating effect, whereas for a proficient speaker the same high-frequency phenomenon will appear repetitive and thus generate greater variation. If we compare child language with adult language, we observe a frequency difference. Use of the same term or type for different objects is characteristic of early learner language, whereas use of different terms or types for the same object is a feature of native adult language in a nondialogue context. Thus, the relationship between the size of the lexical repertoire and the frequency of the use of the elements available is inversely proportional. Frequency effects are therefore functions of the respective interacting systems. Language as an ideal type (see Weber, 1904/1988) is based on the identification of high-frequency collocations and collostructions as language norms, whereas low frequency and nonce occurrences tend to be identified as noise (see Biber et al., 1999, pp. 38–46). Finally, the effect of frequency depends on context of use, differing contexts resulting in scatter and similar contexts resulting in convergence.

Although we obviously have to attribute a linguistic significance to frequency, the effect of frequency appears to be variable or nonlinear—that is, its effect keeps changing over time. The nonlinearity of the frequency effect can be attributed to the fact that it depends on an interacting variable we can call *markedness*, which is the extent to which a systemic feature is likely to attract attention depending on the heuristic procedure applied by the language user. This assumption is compatible with what is known as the *noticing hypothesis* (Schmidt, 2010) but is not restricted to language learners. If we relate frequency to markedness, we suggest that markedness is a function of frequency and frequency is a function of markedness. This complex interaction is best likened to the predator–prey relationship in ecosystems; markedness preys upon frequency and vice versa. Although we accept that frequency can result in markedness, we also have to accept that too high a frequency will result in loss of markedness through accommodation and that too low a frequency will be devoid of markedness and not result in the emergence of a new type. Markedness defines a relational property in second order complex systems.

- DCT: Frequency effects are nonlinear, and there can therefore be no invariable correlation between the frequency of a language unit and a linguistic effect. Different frequencies have different effects. Frequencies covary with other factors such as markedness to produce varied results.

17.2.3 Bounded Frequency

> What pure frequency counts can certainly not inform us about are the manifold ways in which repeated exposure can affect the cognitive and linguistic system depending on the linguistic, situational, and social contexts of specific usage events. . . . Frequency counts also overlook the fact that entrenchment as a repetition-conditioned cognitive process can only become effective if the traces of processing events "survive." (Schmid, Chapter 1, this volume, Section 1.3.3)

Although the distinction between absolute frequency (overall count) and relative frequency (comparative frequency values) is clearly defined and determinable in closed systems such as linguistic corpora, for real language use a different measure is required. The base rate problem (e.g., recent frequency distorting overall frequency judgments; see Bar-Hillel, 1980) proves that language users do not use absolute frequencies but work with frequency scopes. In fact, language users generally work with frequency intuitions that are distorted by priming or recency effects. The respective scope identifies what counts when we consider frequencies. In complex dynamic systems, the relevant criterion applied is neither absolute nor relative frequency, but what is known as *bounded frequency* (see Doyle, 2011; Seiffert, 2001). This means that the same unit can be ascribed different frequency values depending on the context of occurrence. So the significance of frequency in language use is not homogeneous, but is best viewed as being cumulative or incremental. The difference between additive and incremental frequency can best be shown by a simple illustration. In the case of additive frequency, $1+2+3+4+5$ equals 15; in the case of cumulative frequency, $1+2+3+4+5 \rightarrow 1+3+6+10+15$ equals 35, as the subsequent figure consistently represents a resultant value. The more recent unit in a series (i.e., the more proximal unit) therefore has greater weight, although it is part of the same series (see recency priming in McClelland & Rumelhart, 1988), whereas standard frequency measures assume the equidistribution of weight (i.e., each item in a series is attributed equal weight).

The salience of the item whose frequency is determined is initial-state dependent, and the chain of repeated occurrences of which the unit is part therefore forms a non-Markov chain. In contrast to Markov chains (see Ellis, 2002, p. 156), non-Markov chains retain traces of previous occurrences and thus have a memory function. This clearly indicates that we cannot establish the effect of frequency without including both the system in which unit frequency occurs and the effect of type or token frequency on this system. The question of whether frequency has a positive effect on entrenchment cannot be answered without inclusion of relevant system parameters. This requires us to rethink the question of the role of frequency in nonlinear and in complex terms.

- DCT: The determination of frequency has to be bounded and incremental. When determining frequency effects, we have to specify the range or scope of frequency and the recency of occurrence of the units contributing to the frequency count.

17.3 Complexities

> The study of language change is another field in which entrenchment has been tied to discourse frequency. . . . Again, this is despite the fact that there is a considerable methodological gap between collective language change (i.e., conventionalization), which provides the data and explananda, on the one hand, and individual entrenchment, on the other hand. (Schmid, Chapter 1, this volume, Section 1.3.1)

Complexity theory attempts to bridge the gap between entrenched collective language use, individual entrenchment in the language user, and last but not least, entrenchment as reflected in the system of language as social fact (see de Saussure, 1974, p. 9). Language must therefore be seen as a complex system consisting of interacting subsystems rather than a unitary system. Neither can we understand language learner patterns if we do not interpret these as results of interaction between the learner system, the language users, and the ideal representation of language (use). Linguistic features seem to be unique in requiring us to learn to think in terms of higher order complex systems. A reductionist approach is obviously intent on getting rid of complexity as noise and will certainly consider higher order complexities superfluous.

First order complexity is based on the realization that a complex system consists of a number of subsystems and that the relationships between the subsystems and the (meta-) systems themselves are nonadditive. Language properties are therefore emergent. The language system has to include language as an ideal type, as well as language as a system of use as employed by the language community and language as a system in the process of being acquired by a language learner.

A hypercomplex system is hypercomplex in the sense that it includes the linguist as a language researcher, as someone who is both an investigator of language as an object of research and a language user at the same time. The linguist partakes in his or her own object of research and thus influences the object in the process of use and as the object of research. Research in linguistics is therefore both observation and practice at the same time. This is significant as the frequency judgments of the speaker, the learner, and the linguist, and therefore also the effects of frequency on the speaker and learner system and the ideal type, will differ (see Herdina, 2015a).

- DCT: Language is not a homogeneous system but consists of at least three identifiable and interacting subsystems—the ideal type representation of language, learner systems, and speaker systems—in which differing effects of frequency of occurrence of a language unit will be observed in the respective language system.

17.4 Entrenchment and Variation

The understanding in terms of strength of representation evokes a purely quantitative, gradual, potentially asymptotic trajectory, whereas the understanding in terms of a holistic chunk promotes the picture that a qualitative change from analytic and declarative to holistic and procedural processing takes place at some point. (Schmid, Chapter 1, this volume, Section 1.2)

At first sight, change appears to be the opposite of entrenchment, reflecting the complex interaction among the language unit, the language user, and the language system. This interaction inevitably causes variation, which can affect both the unit and the system. This poses the question of whether there can be unit change without corresponding system change and vice versa. In other words, do we have to distinguish between drift (i.e., variation in individual units, but not in the system as a whole) and shift (i.e., a change in an individual unit that affects language as a system)? Both types of variation exist: Drift represents a gradual approximation of value *a* to *b*. A shift occurs when the drifting item latches onto a new attractor (see Bybee, 2010, pp. 198–199; van Geert & Verspoor, 2015, p. 548). Drift results in variation, as in phonetic variation, or the emergence of allophones without phonemic consequences, such as intervocalic voicing of fricatives in Anglo-Saxon or the original graphemic representation of phonetic *v* and *u* as allographs, making the initial prevocalic and central intervocalic realizations allophonetic, as in *haue* ('have') and *loued* ('loved') versus *vs* ('us') in 15th-century English. Distality requirements would lead to a split resulting in the graphemic distinction between *v* and *u* (e.g., *vase* vs. *uva* ['bearberry']).

When does a drift effect a shift? Systemic stability relies on the retention of distality requirements (i.e., semantic, phonetic, graphemic, syntactic differentiability). If these requirements are not maintained, system stability is endangered and the system is restructured, as observed in the Anglo-Saxon vowel shift (i.e., palatalization in Old

English), the Great English Vowel Shift, the loss of inflections, and the attrition of prefixation in Middle English. The existence of drift without shift in language allows us to assume that all phonetic values are approximations expressing dynamic variation in the phonetic system. The shift identifies a change in the phonemic system, in which a value merges or splits (i.e., values *a* and *b* converging to form *c*, or value *a* splitting to form *b* and *c*).

The result of semantic drift, for example, can be observed when we look for cognates in related languages. Cognates do not give an accurate representation of related terms, suggesting that we are looking at a semantic web rather than semantic sets. As use changes, some units experience a semantic drift, as illustrated by the following cognates suggesting a common origin: *et* (French), *and* (English), *og* (Danish), *und* (German) (cf. *auch*, German), and so forth; *animal* (French), *animal* (English), *dyr* (Danish), *Tier* (German) (cf. *deer*, English); *cendre* (French), *ashes* (English), *aske* (Danish), *Asche* (German) (cf. *cinder*, English, *Zunder*, German); *parceque* (French), *because* (English), *fordi* (Danish), *weil* (German) (cf. *while, for which*, English) (cf. Barber, Beal, & Shaw, 2009, p. 71).

- DCT: Language units can show a degree of variation (drift) without resulting systemic effects (shift). When investigating frequency effects, we have to distinguish between effects on the unit and effects on the system, as these cannot be coextensive.

17.5 Anchoring and Priming

> If entrenchment relates to the minds of individual speakers, it is . . . subject to individual speaker-related differences. . . . Most of these are hard to grasp and control methodologically. (Schmid, Chapter 1, this volume, Section 1.3.4)

Whereas usage-based accounts typically focus on the effect of priming, non-Markov chain models used by DCT (see Smyth, 1999) require initial-state determination by a procedure we shall call *anchoring*. To be able to specify individual differences in the respective systems and their interactions, we have to determine the respective initial state. Frequency effects must be modified by the application of a heuristic to determine whether the item identified is bound or governed (see Chomsky, 1981). To establish whether an item is entrenched, we need to determine whether it is bound—that is, whether it is determined by a preceding unit or by a subsequent element (i.e., anaphoric or cataphoric determination). In English, binding shows directionality and is also specified by proximity, generally expressed as contiguity in collocations and collostructions. Discontinuous units are comparatively rare. In DCT we have to assume that binding is initial-state dependent. *Anchoring* refers to initial-state determination, which is essentially unmotivated and tendentially defines a nonce type.

The significance of anchoring in determining units or tokens is best illustrated by the patterning of Old English alliterative verse, in which the determination of assonance and alliteration relies on the identification of the anchoring initial consonant or vowel. For instance, in *Hynthu ond hrafyl ic thaes hrothgar maeg* (Beowulf, line 277, in Porter, 1975; "scathe and slaughter I for that Hrothgar wanted"), preliquid *h* forms the *hw, hl, hr* consonant cluster. *Hrothgar* and *hrafyl* have to be the alliterative stressed consonants. As *hrafyl* forms a binomial with *hynthu*, we can assume that these would be bound by alliteration or assonance, again an indication of the phonemic value of *h*. The leading consonant or vowel is determined by the first lexeme, which determines the subsequent alliterative pattern. It is evident that Anglo-Saxon verse does not rely merely on alliteration but also assonance. So we observe a second pattern in the assonance of *thaes* and *maeg*. The subsequent patterns are therefore defined by initial choice, and although we can determine the prevalence of certain fricatives, liquids, or vowels in the alliterative patterns, the initial anchor is not predetermined but subject to (poetic) choice. The anchor is essentially arbitrary and generates an unstable token whose recurrence generates an emergent type.

The arbitrariness of anchoring can also be observed in the misappropriation of the Arabic article as prefix in *algebra* and *algorithm* in contrast to *chemist* and *gazelle* rather than *alchemist* and *algazel(le)* and the *el* in *elixir* in contrast to *giraffe* or *tariff*. In some instances the article of the Arabic loanword is assimilated as prefix, and in other cases it is ignored for no grammatical or phonetic reason, as illustrated by original co-occurrence of *ghazal, gazelle*, and *algazel* in early Elizabethan English.

- DCT: In order to be able to specify the effects of frequency, we have to be able to determine the initial state of the affected system. The initial state is specified by a process called *anchoring*.

17.6 Embeddedness and Isolation

> The present proposal ... rejects the distinction between constructions serving as nodes in the network and relations between nodes and instead assumes that linguistic knowledge is available in one format only, namely associations. ... associations come in four different types: symbolic, syntagmatic, paradigmatic, and pragmatic. (Schmid, Chapter 1, this volume, Section 1.5)

One implication of Schmid's associative claim is that there is a danger of entrenchment being topicalized at the expense of what is known as *embeddedness* in DCT. The focus on individual language units or chunks tends to decontextualize the object of investigation. A DCT approach envisages language units as linked to other dimensions or systems of language that constantly interact with and affect the unit under scrutiny. This network of associations and links is referred to as *embedding*. This is a function of the cotext or context of use or both. To simplify, the nature and type of embeddedness that characterizes a unit is reflected inter alia in the number and types of pragmatic, paradigmatic, and syntagmatic relationships contracted by the unit. The paradigmatic aspect of embeddedness can be captured in terms of similarity sets based on interchangeability in context. The degree of embeddedness is based on the number of items the individual unit is linked to. Significantly, embeddedness is not an inherent feature of a unit, but rather a relational property depending on the language environment and its systemic features. Embeddedness is not coupled with entrenchment, as units might be entrenched but not embedded, as in the persistence of island phenomena reflecting resistance to change without being functionally central, such as *and* (Old English *and/ond*), *I* (Old English *ic*), and *be* (Old English *beon*) vs. *whilom* (Old English *hwilum*), *quondam* (Latin *quondam*), and *seldom* (Old English *seldan*) and even *seldseen* (Old English *seldsiene*), the first three examples being central and frequent, and the other examples being peripheral and infrequent.

The degree of semantic, symbolic, or pragmatic embedding is defined by the linguistic environment. As mentioned above, embeddedness must at least be taken to include syntagmatic and paradigmatic relationships. It must, however, be considered that embeddedness is not restricted to these clearly definable relationships; rather, embeddedness is a function of proximity relations as they might be defined by the user and learner. These proximity relationships are more likely to define an amorphous linguistic space corresponding to clusters or clouds. Lexical clustering is conventionally provided by unspecified proximity, as illustrated by the thesaurus entry (Rodale, 1978) for *celebrated*: *famous, famed, renowned, well-known, prominent, big-name, respected, venerable, distinguished, distingué, eminent, pre-eminent, notable, noted, illustrious, great, glorious, radiant, lustrous, honored, exalted, acclaimed, much-touted, popular, well-liked, immortal, fabled, legendary, historical*, and so on. Depending on the heuristics applied, we can obtain differing proximity sets from this cluster such as a set of hyphenated compounds expressing similar meanings, including *well-known, much-touted, well-liked*, and so forth. Different morphological, phonetic, or grammatical criteria will result in different sets (e.g., *-ed* participle).

- DCT: Because the frequency effect is nonlinear, entrenchment can be a result of both high-frequency associations, and therefore a high degree of embeddedness, or low-frequency associations, resulting in a low degree of embeddedness or type or token isolation.

17.7 Entanglement

> Entrenchment processes are seen as operating over these four types of associations in the network rather than over constructions. (Schmid, this volume, Section 1.5)

In the attempt to classify the types of associative relations defining linguistic systems, it is easy to overlook the fact that these associations are cross-categorical: They transcend the conventional linguistic subdivisions into semantic, morphological, phonetic, or grammatical features. If a language unit does not behave as we would expect, this may well be because of the entanglement of its features. The notion of entanglement is derived from quantum physics. In language systems, entanglement describes a situation in which two seemingly distant or independent units are somehow connected and therefore covary or correlate without being evidently close.

Entanglement thus refers to another type of proximity relation. For instance, whereas the definition of a phoneme is based on the principle of binary opposition, and binding is based on concatenation principles, entanglement is based on a perceived similarity or association not based on semantic, phonetic, syntactic, or graphemic proximity alone. We can observe a large number of instances of entanglement in speaker-user systems and in learner systems. For instance, the origin of *ye* as a lexical alternative to the definite article *the* is attributable to the graphemic similarity of the *eth* and *yogh* rune in Early English. Phonetically, *ye* cannot be derived from the Anglo-Saxon demonstrative *se/thaet* ("the"). Entanglement can be observed as an interlingual and intralingual phenomenon. Well-known examples are the /v/–/w/ confusions and the /l/–/r/ confusions observed respectively in German and Japanese learners of English resulting from different graphemic and phonemic distribution patterns in the respective primary languages.

Entanglement can be defined as cross-dimensional and cross-categorical embedding. It should have become evident that entrenchment cannot be attributed to embeddedness alone but has to take factors like function, weight, value, and entanglement into consideration.

- DCT: Language units are subject not merely to systematic associations (embedding) but also to idiosyncratic and unsystematic associations. The principle of entanglement identifies the possibility of cross-categorical and cross-linguistic associations.

17.8 Stability or Entrenchment

> *Entrenchment* refers to the ongoing reorganization and adaptation of individual communicative knowledge, which is subject to exposure to language and language use and to the exigencies of domain-general cognitive processes and the social environment. (Schmid, Chapter 1, this volume, Section 1.5; emphasis in original)

The definition of entrenchment provided by Schmid at first appears paradoxical if we assume that entrenched language units should be considered invariable when the term is applied to the language system rather than the language user (see Schmid, 2007, p. 118). We have to hypothesize that entrenchment can occur in all dimensions of the language system and that it cannot merely be seen as a psycholinguistic category because degrees of entrenchment in psycholinguistic terms are reflected both in language use and the language system. The notion of entrenchment as an explanatory category was originally introduced by Goodman (1954) in addressing problems of induction most frequency models are confronted with. It is only when we contextualize entrenchment that we obtain an essentially dynamic concept, which replaces entrenchment in terms of invariability of the language unit by the notion of stability within a specific language system and its use by learners and speakers.

A language unit is described as *entrenched* if it appears to be invariable over time and stable. A language unit is entrenched when it is sufficiently automated and autonomous to persist in use despite change. The establishment of a degree of entrenchment is based on linguistic factors: the language system and also the language environment (i.e., the speaker system and the position of the learner-speaker system). The degree of entrenchment cannot be established on individual systemic principles alone. It has to be based on processes of intralinguistic interaction and cross-linguistic interaction in language contact situations as evidenced by the history of English as a mixed language and the emergence of plurilingualism as the norm (see Herdina & Jessner, 2002).

Within DCT, entrenchment of a unit can be expressed in terms of its degree of stability. The stability of the language unit is relative and not absolute. Unit stability can be attained by seemingly conflicting means: Stability can be achieved by regularization, on the one hand, and by lexicalization, on the other, for instance. Significantly, the stability of irregular verbs in PDE is the result of lexicalization, such that the general inflectional principles applied to the different conjugations are lexicalized, the pattern being linked to individual units rather than applied as general principles. The regular Anglo-Saxon strong verb patterns (conjugations) associated with frequent verbs—that is, the vocalic types (*writan, creopan, findan, beran, brecan*) that used to be paradigmatic—have increasingly been ousted by the regular weak forms. These strong forms have evidently achieved a new level of stability through the process of lexicalization. The original grammaticalized patterns were increasingly marginalized and threatened by the new regular patterns, which would have led to regularization as observed in *dive/dived* versus *dive/dove*, *hang/hanged* versus *hang/hung*, and so forth. Through the process of lexicalization, the strong forms have achieved a new level of stability as they no longer compete with the regularized patterns (see MacWhinney, 2001). These changes cannot be attributed solely to differences in frequency of use.

If the variety of lexicalized patterns is excessive, however, the pattern will be regularized, resulting in a reduction of memory load. So irregular plurals (cf. Greek plural *phenomenon/phenomena*) and Latin neuter plurals (*datum/data*) are also subject to likely regularization through recategorization. This process is evident in the morphological rule applied to *ize/ise* suffixization, originally subject to the distinction between Greek and Latin etymology. In these instances stability is achieved by regularization of a morphological rule, as the need to retain individual lexical information leads to an unnecessary complexification of the language system. Only a few lexicalized units are considered invariable (e.g., *compromise*).

- DCT: The definition of entrenchment in a dynamic system is based on stability rather than invariability. Stability can be achieved by a process of adaptation to the language environment (lexicalization or regularization).

17.9 Retention and Interaction

> This takes us to a higher, interactional level of situational aspects of entrenchment, where imitation, emulation, and joint activity come into play as determinants of repetition and memory consolidation. (Schmid, Chapter 1, this volume, Section 1.3.3)

Absolute frequency presupposes absolute memory. Just as the learner's and competent language user's knowledge is bounded, so is their memory. As memory fades, the distality requirements fail, distinctness fades, and separate language units begin to merge. This is illustrated by recall failure and word selection errors as in *deputize/jeopardize* or *affect/effect*. Members of a language community have not only individual but also collective memories based on the process of linguistic interaction. The regeneration of memory is illustrated by the processes of reanalysis (*a nappe plié* reanalyzed as *an apple pie* as in *apple pie order/bed*), which allows the unit to be retained in collective memory by making it meaningful, as opaque language units are more difficult to memorize. So entrenchment must also be a function of retention.

As suggested by the dynamic model of multilingualism (Herdina & Jessner, 2002), DCT requires a dynamic model of memory. Language attrition phenomena presuppose the malleability of linguistic memory. The retention of linguistic knowledge is dependent on language use and frequency criteria, and forgetting is a result of lack of use. As a use factor, language memory cannot be attributed merely to the individual speaker or learner but also to the language community. The retention of specific language units or features is dependent on the continued activation by the speakers of a language (cf. priming effects), and these language units therefore form part of dynamic collective memory. The death of a language is coextensive with the demise of the language community. The stability of retention is assisted by the degree of embeddedness, type conformity, and also analyzability of an expression. Chunking combined with opacity results in a restriction of contexts and frequency of use. So retention is also a function of entrenchment.

- DCT: Language memory is dynamic and interactive and results from interaction between individual memory and collective memory. Language retention is autopoietic and pragmatic as frequency of use results in retention and retention results in frequency of use. Linguistic memory is therefore not restricted to the individual language user.

17.10 Frequency as a Complex Function

> The relation between attention, salience, and entrenchment is far from trivial. . . . On the one hand, because salient forms and referents are more likely to attract attention and therefore invite repeated processing, they are also more likely to become entrenched. . . . On the other hand, while entrenched form–meaning pairings are unlikely to attract attention, less entrenched constructions, such as rare words, are highly salient. (Schmid, Chapter 1, this volume, Section 1.3.4)

If we assume that frequency is a complex function, this means that there is no direct correlation between frequency and a factor x, such as learnability. Therefore, the frequency function is not a constant simple function. This means that though we attribute some significance to frequency that can be expressed as a function, this function has to be defined as complex—that is, as containing more than one interacting variable. The effect of the frequency function will therefore vary according to the value obtained by the function.

Thus, a high-frequency element will be marked for the language learner until it has been acquired. When it has been acquired, the occurrence of further tokens will have a conservative effect and will therefore not promote change but rather consolidation. A high-frequency effect in a language learner system can lead to overgeneralization of type followed by type diversification. High frequency within a stable system will lead to variation. We could assume that frequency of occurrence is an expression of a balance of entropic and negentropic tendencies in language.

If a function is initial-state dependent and the system is dynamic, the function will change over time. If it changes over time, the function will be a differential one. The frequency function represents such an exemplary differential function in the following respect: As the learner's knowledge of language and vocabulary increases, the function of frequency will change. We may define such a function expressed as the number of words or language units of a type acquired in relation to the frequency of occurrence of a new token. So the effect attributed to frequency must be a result of markedness generated by frequency (see Günther, Müller, & Geyer, Chapter 13, this volume, on attention and salience). The effect of frequency in generating markedness will depend on whether the frequent unit or type is given or new in relation to the system, and on whether the learner-user system is stable or not. In order to determine the effect of frequency, we have to determine how it covaries with markedness.

Markedness cannot be a function of units but must be expressed as a unit–system function, as the markedness of a unit will also depend on the state of the (learner or user) system at any specific point of time. It is therefore a relational term expressing an emergent property. The frequency function will also have to take into account the degree of scatter observed, as mentioned above (see Chesley, 2011).

Nonlinear functions are generally complex, because they include the initial state of the system and the state of the system after the effect and thus include feedback loops. A common system effect observed is therefore system saturation or exhaustion of embedded units.

- DCT: The variable effect of frequency is to be attributed to the fact that the frequency effect is a complex function (containing more than one interacting variable) and not a unit property. The interacting and interdependent variables have a dynamic effect.

17.11 Attractors and Final Causes

> Once entrenched, these routines are activated more quickly and with less effort and are therefore more likely to be repeated. Obviously, this gives rise to a feedback loop in which frequency comes to serve as both a cause and an effect of entrenchment. (Schmid, Chapter 1, this volume, Section 1.3.4)

As indicated in the introductions both to this volume and to this chapter, the issue of frequency and entrenchment represents a challenge to conventional methodology. Both analytical procedures that require a degree of decontextualization and conventional causal correlations appear to provide an inadequate analysis of the interrelationships that actually exist and occur. The methodological challenge lies in the ability to develop sound procedures that include contextual information and provide more powerful explanations than conventional causal analysis. Within DCT it has proved useful to work with emergent properties and emergent goals, or *attractors*. As new patterns and types emerge, they form attractors for existing patterns.

How can we, for example, explain the change of the high-frequency *th* from Anglo-Saxon initial voiceless *th* (thorn), as in *thing, thanc*, and *thyncan*, to initial voiced *th* (eth), as in pronominal *they, them*, and *there*, which is both grammaticalized and not subject to attrition? According to Anglo-Saxon usage, voicing is normally restricted to intervocalic fricatives. The transition from initial voiceless to initial voiced fricatives can be determined by identifying the isoglosses as resulting from the transition from the Anglo-Saxon paradigmatic initial voiceless fricative to the Norse pattern of initial voiced fricative realization of thorn (see Herdina, 2015b). This agrees with the covariation of *eth/thorn* and the digraph *th* and the replacement of the traditional Anglo-Saxon pronominal *hie/hiera* by *they, them*, and so forth. Frequency of occurrence has therefore to be complemented by the determination of attractors as patterns of distribution providing paradigms of use.

Does the failure of the frequency hypothesis imply the general failure of inductive principles? Does frequency not count at all? Complex frequency does attribute a role and significance to frequency effects but accepts that frequency effects are conditional and bounded. The realization of the limits to the validity of inductive principles, generally attributed to Hume and redefined by Goodman (1954), implies that there can be no universal grammatical significance attributable to frequency effects and that linear relations are not universally valid. In complex systems, frequency effects will be limited to subsystems and states of systems at a particular point in time and system interaction. Frequency effects are therefore by necessity conditional and bounded, and the ability to determine system bounds and the emergence of critical states form a necessary precondition of complexity methodology.

- DCT: Explanations of frequency effects and language change have to complement efficient cause explanations by final cause explanations using attractors and attractor states to identify converging patterns.

17.12 Conclusion

By adopting DCT principles in explaining language change and entrenchment, what has hitherto appeared to be a linguistic conundrum resolves itself. Nonlinear relationships imply that equal causes can have different effects, and different causes can have equal effects. These are the principles of equicausality and equifinality originally defined by Bertalanffy (1971). Entrenchment can therefore be a result of embeddedness or isolation. Entrenchment can take the form of invariability or retention through adaptation to a changing linguistic environment, as observed in the persistence of Anglo-Saxon verb patterns in present-day English. The process of retention must be located not in language, but rather in the respective subsystems and their interaction so that language units (from phonemes to chunks) are retained in individual and collective memory and represented in the language system.

What we generally refer to as *language* is in effect a result of the complex interaction between learner systems (e.g., the effect of Norse on Anglo-Saxon), speaker systems (language as used by the community), and an ideal type (the linguist's construction of historical English or PDE). The language units linguists analyze always form part of a tangled web of meaning and significance, reflecting the principles of entanglement and embeddedness. The frequencies we observe in language are in fact traces of the movement of language through time, resulting in the death or attrition of old patterns and the emergence of the new. As new patterns emerge, they form attractors upon which the old patterns converge, effecting change.

References

Barber, C., Beal, J., & Shaw, P. (2009). *The English Language: A historical introduction.* http://dx.doi.org/10.1017/CBO9780511817601

Bar-Hillel, M. (1980). The base rate fallacy in probability judgements. *Acta Psychologica, 44,* 211–233. http://dx.doi.org/10.1016/0001-6918(80)90046-3

Bayley, R. (2013). The quantitative paradigm. In J. K. Chambers & N. Schilling (Eds.), *The handbook of language variation and change* (pp. 85–108). http://dx.doi.org/10.1002/9781118335598.ch4

Bertalanffy, L. (1971). *General system theory: Foundations, development, applications*. Harmondsworth, England: Penguin University Books.

Biber, D., Johansson, S., Leech, G., Conrad, S., & Finegan, E. (1999). *Longman grammar of spoken and written English*. Harlow, England: Pearson.

Bybee, J. (2007). *Frequency of use and the organization of language*. http://dx.doi.org/10.1093/acprof:oso/9780195301571.001.0001

Bybee, J. (2008). Usage based grammar and second language acquisition. In P. Robinson & N. Ellis (Eds.), *Handbook of cognitive linguistics and second language acquisition* (pp. 216–236). London, England: Routledge.

Bybee, J. (2010). *Language, usage and cognition*. http://dx.doi.org/10.1017/CBO9780511750526

Bybee, J. (2011). Usage based grammar and grammaticization. In H. Narrog & B. Heine (Eds.), *The Oxford handbook of grammaticalization* (pp. 69–79). Oxford, England: Oxford University Press.

Bybee, J., & Hopper, P. (Eds.). (2001). *Frequency and the emergence of linguistic structure*. http://dx.doi.org/10.1075/tsl.45

Bybee, J., Perkins, R., & Paglivia, W. (1994). *The evolution of grammar: Tense, aspect, and modality in the languages of the world*. Chicago, IL: University of Chicago Press.

Chesley, P. (2011). *Linguistic, cognitive, and social constraints on lexical entrenchment* (doctoral dissertation). Retrieved from ERIC (ED534336).

Chomsky, N. (1981). *Lectures on government and binding: The Pisa lectures*. Dordrecht, Germany: Foris.

de Saussure, F. (1974). *Course in general linguistics* (C. Bally & A. Sechehaye, Eds.; W. Baskin, Trans.). Bungay, England: Fontana.

Doyle, J. (2011). Bounded rationality. In R. Wilson & F. Keil (Eds.), *The MIT encyclopedia of cognitive sciences* (pp. 94–95). Cambridge, MA: MIT Press.

Ellis, N. (2002). Frequency effects in language processing: A review with implications for theories of implicit and explicit language acquisition. *Studies in Second Language Acquisition, 24*, 143–188.

Ellis, N. (2012). What can we count in language, and what counts in language acquisition, cognition and use? In S. Gries & D. Divjak (Eds.), *Frequency effects in language learning and processing* (Vol. 1, pp. 7–34). http://dx.doi.org/10.1515/9783110274059.7

Ellis, N., & Ogden, D. (2015). Language cognition: Comments on Ambridge, Kidd, Rowland, and Theakston "The ubiquity of frequency effects in first language." *Journal of Child Language, 42*, 282–286. http://dx.doi.org/10.1017/S0305000914000646

Fasold, R., & Connor-Linton, J. (2014). *An introduction to language and linguistics*. Cambridge, England: Cambridge University Press.

Goodman, N. (1954). *Fact, fiction, forecast*. Cambridge, MA: Harvard University Press.

Grein, C. (1912). *Sprachschatz der angelsächsischen Dichter* [Word hoard of the Anglo-Saxon poets] (J. Köhler, Ed.). Heidelberg, Germany: Karl Winter.

Halliday, M. A. K. (1994). *An introduction to functional grammar* (2nd ed.). London, England: Edward Arnold.

Herdina, P. (2015a). First, second, third order complexity and the hypercomplex. In J. Müller & J. Zelger (Eds.), *Gabek als Lernverfahren für Organisationen* [Gabek as an organizational learning strategy] (pp. 71–86). Innsbruck, Austria: Studia.

Herdina, P. (2015b). Historical multilingualism as a linguistic challenge. In S. Fink, M. Lang, & M. Schretter (Eds.), *Sprachsituation und Sprachpolitik. Mehrsprachigkeit im Altertum* [Language situation and language policy: Multilingualism in antiquity]. Münster, Germany: Ugarit Verlag.

Herdina, P., & Jessner, U. (2002). *The dynamic model of multilingualism: Perspectives of change in psycholinguistics*. Bristol, England: Multilingual Matters.
Hopper, P., & Traugott, E. (2003). *Grammaticalization*. http://dx.doi.org/10.1017/CBO9781139165525
Jones, D. (1979). *Everyman's English pronouncing dictionary* (14th ed.). London, England: Dent & Sons.
Langacker, R. (1987). *Foundations of cognitive grammar: Vol. 1. Theoretical prerequisites*. Stanford, CA: Stanford University Press.
MacWhinney, B. (2001). The competition model: The input, the context, and the brain. In P. Robinson (Ed.), *Cognition and second language instruction* (pp. 69–90). http://dx.doi.org/10.1017/CBO9781139524780.005
Marsden, R. (2015). *The Cambridge Old English reader*. Cambridge, England: Cambridge University Press.
McClelland, J., & Rumelhart, D. (1988). *Explorations in parallel distributed processing: A handbook of models, programs and exercises*. Cambridge, MA: MIT Press.
Milicka, J. (2009). Type token and hapax token relation: A combinatorial model. *Glottotheory: International Journal of Theoretical Linguistics*, *2*(1), 99–110.
Moder, C. (1992). Rules and analogy. In G. Davis & G. Iverson (Eds.), *Explanation in historical linguistics* (pp. 179–192). http://dx.doi.org/10.1075/cilt.84.12mod
Peirce, C. (1906). Prolegomena to an apology for pragmatism. *The Monist*, *16*, 492–546. http://dx.doi.org/10.5840/monist190616436
Porter, J. (1975). *Beowulf: Text and translation*. Pinner, England: Anglo-Saxon Books.
Quine, W. O. (1987). *Quiddities: An intermittently philosophical dictionary*. Cambridge, MA: Harvard University Press.
Quirk, R., Greenbaum, S., Leech, G., & Svartvik, J. (1972). *A comprehensive English grammar*. Cambridge, England: Cambridge University Press.
Rodale, J. (1978). *The synonym finder*. New York, NY: Warner Books.
Schmid, H.-J. (2007). Entrenchment, salience, and basic levels. In D. Geeraerts & H. Cuyckens (Eds.), *The Oxford handbook of cognitive linguistics* (pp. 117–139). Oxford, England: Oxford University Press.
Schmidt, R. (2010). Attention, awareness, and individual differences in language learning. In W. Chan, S. Chi, K. N. Cin, J. Istanto, M. Nagami, J. W. Sew, . . . I. Walker (Eds.), *Proceedings of CLaSIC* (pp. 721–737). Singapore: Centre for Language Studies, National University of Singapore.
Seiffert, C. (2001). Situated cognition and learning. In R. Wilson & F. Keil (Eds.), *The MIT encyclopedia of cognitive sciences* (pp. 767–768). Cambridge, MA: MIT Press.
Smyth, P. (1999). Hidden Markov models. In R. Wilson & F. Keil (Eds.), *The MIT encyclopedia of cognitive sciences* (pp. 373–374). Cambridge, MA: MIT Press.
van Geert, P., & Verspoor, M. (2015). Dynamic systems and language development. In B. MacWhinney & W. O'Grady (Eds.), *The handbook of language emergence* (pp. 537–554). New York, NY: Wiley-Blackwell.
Weber, M. (1988). Die "Objektivität" sozialwissenschaftlicher und sozialpolitischer Erkenntnis [The "objectivity" of sociological and sociopolitical knowledge]. In J. Winckelmann (Ed.), *Gesammelte Aufsätze zur Wissenschaftslehre* [Collected papers on the theory of science] (pp. 146–214). Tübingen, Germany: Mohr. (Original work published 1904)

Stephen J. Cowley
18 Entrenchment: A View From Radical Embodied Cognitive Science

18.1 Introduction

This chapter denies explanatory value to *entrenchment*[1] by taking what Shapiro (2010) treated as a strong view of embodied cognition. Accordingly, I argue that action and perception characterize all species that depend on a central nervous system (CNS) or are "embrained." Although all such systems possess primitive sensing (Keijzer, 2015), brains permit the entrenching of distinctions used by the organism. Yet, "choices" animate even brainless organisms. Nonetheless, the seminal case remains "what the frog's eye tells the frog's brain" (Lettvin, Maturana, McCulloch, & Pitts, 1959, p. 1940). In experimental work, the authors explored how frogs can—and fail to—discriminate between pellets and flies. As one of the coauthors later realized, the result draws, first, on a history of how aspects of the environment (the medium) trigger the frog's action. Second, and crucially, it depends on a human observer. For Maturana, the coauthor in question, judgment depends on languaging in a world where things can be "said."[2] Crucially, anything that is said is said by someone: Observing presupposes human practices or, for Maturana (1978), a consensual domain (see Raimondi, 2014).

Below, I pursue how humans link entrenching to practices—and pragmatics—as they master languages. My claim is that this is irreducible to the entrenching that occurs in pigeons and rats (operant conditioning). Such animals rely on not just physical distinctions but on using these to act and perceive (as can be described by an observer). As intelligent species, they grant some distinctions functional value or, in

---

[1] The claim is that (the concept of) entrenchment is a measure, and measures, in themselves, cannot explain anything at all. To think otherwise confuses what can be measured with what the measure describes (i.e., a history of acting–perceiving that draws on growing familiarity with speech in a particular language).

[2] Raimondi (2014) defined *languaging* as "a process based on recursive consensual coordination of individuals' interrelated operations, taking place in the interindividual relational domain" (p. 307). Provided wordings are defined as nonce events that arise from reiterations, it becomes nonritualized face-to-face "activity in which wordings play a part" (Cowley, 2014, p. 1085).

First of all, I thank Hans-Jörg Schmid for his kind words of encouragement and valuable editorial advice. Second, I thank John Collier for inspiring me to engage with how physical information can contribute to the domain of the living. Third, many thanks to Christian Mosbæk Johannessen for help with the diagram in Figure 18.1. Finally, I thank Robert Port for his concise review and Matthew Harvey for his serious challenge to so many of the wordings that I had proposed. As a result of all that, the reader and I find ourselves faced by escapees from an enormous can of worms.

terms from ecological tradition, they treat them as affordances (see Chemero, 2003; Gibson, 1979). Humans, too, use action and perception in evaluating a changing world as, over time, they learn to behave. In an example pursued later in this chapter, a person who leaves her house can turn left or right; as she goes right more often than left, the choice can be said to be entrenched. Although rats act similarly in a maze, measures of maze running frequency differ from applications to either a person's turning right or the use made of linguistic phenomena. The contrast arises because, unlike rats, humans observe. A living person's acting and perceiving is supplemented by functional information that, given experience with language, can be used in more or less willful ways. Human choices reflect on verbal patterns (and a history of languaging) to connect historically derived traditions with speaking and acting.

This history of doing things with language, I suggest, drives the re-entrenching of acting and perceiving as people master routines and practices (e.g., saying "how do you do" or making a presentation). Skills with what are loosely called *words*, *sentences*, and *utterances* transform human ways of living. Although based on distinctions of functional value, humans also use a community's norms to reorganize their practical and vocal behavior. Entrenching has a major role in learning to utter, attend to, and interpret *phonetic gestures*—speech activity that, in literate traditions, is described in terms of words, sentences, utterances, and so forth. Indeed, with literacy, communities formalize phonetic gestures (by using, above all, ideographic and alphabetic writing systems) and use the results to ground new practices.[3] As they master routines, entrenching grants people new skills and, of course, routines that can be described by measures of entrenchment.

18.2 Overview

A radical embodied view of cognitive science traces flexible and adaptive behavior (including language) to a history of interactions (Chemero, 2011). Rather than attribute cognition to the CNS, the agency of living systems is traced to a history of action and perception or, in ecological tradition, to using affordances. The CNS self-organizes and thus enables a baby to become a person who inhabits a social world. Human agency depends on interactions that transform neural systems as bodies increasingly attune to a local history. Far from pertaining to a person, mind, or brain, language is distributed in time and space (see Cowley, 2011, 2014). Not only is it nonlocalizable, but it is also integrated with artifacts, media, and institutions. Language is extended by the use of books, legal systems, technologies, and the like. Far from reducing to a synchronic (or diachronic) "system," language unites material and organizational

---

[3] Following Fowler (2010) and others, I assume that speech depends, in part, on making and tracking phonetic gestures.

factors such as neural modulations, gestural movements, human situation awareness, and, of course, a person's developmental, historical, and evolutionary past: In this sense, language is multiscalar.

In cognitive science, the approach is connected with what is called *radical embodiment* (see Shapiro, 2010; Wilson & Golonka, 2013). Its hallmark lies in replacing the view that brains depend on representations (or entrenched forms) with the methodological premise that cognition must derive from agent–environment relations. Humans, I add, use language to link these relations with the CNS's self-organizing powers. As observers, individuals have no need to construct language systems or to identify, store, and manipulate linguistic types. Rather, human forms of life can build on ways of reconnecting functional information. In defending the view, I present the following case:

- Entrenching is not to be confused with measures of entrenchment. Although robots use entrenching to simulate language learning, they cannot use the functional information of the kind that is captured in measures of entrenchment.
- Complex action arises as individuals come to control how they act and perceive and, in humans, was extended as communities came to combine historical practices (based on language and culture) with individual habits (based on languaging).
- Measures of linguistic entrenchment pick out delicate phenomena; they identify not neural mechanisms but pragmatic routines and practices. These ensure that language can be distributed, as a history of entrenching and re-entrenching enables people to perform as linguistic actors.

Using cognitive science, I now draw distinctions between applications of "information." Then, I return to a radical embodied view of entrenching, language, and what measures of entrenchment can—and cannot—be used to show.

18.3 Radical Embodied Cognitive Science and Linguistic Entrenchment

Radical embodied cognitive science avoids the computer metaphor, methodological solipsism, and philosophical commitments to what is called "original intentionality." The agenda arises from taking the methodological position that cognition is likely to derive from a history of coordination between biological systems and the world. Rather than focus on individuals, minds, or brains, agency arises in *being with* the world. Whether one focuses on cells, bacteria, rats, people, or human populations, agency emerges from a lineage of similar individuals and species. Their capacities reflect on a heritage that coevolved with life worlds, and for this reason, it is unsurprising that humans are genetically similar to chimpanzees or share genes with *Drosophila*.

Because the life world is as important as the body, one seeks not knowledge of an objective world but ways of understanding how people coordinate.[4] In this view, language is fundamentally pragmatic (a part of complex social action). What people call *knowledge* draws on not representational content but bodies whose modes of action and perception are coupled with doing things while using language (and languaging). Although space permits only a sketch of the view, its roots lie in asking how human cognition builds on evolutionary history.

Cognitive science uses mathematics in making models. In relation to a measure of entrenchment, therefore, it is not enough to establish facts about the relevant frequency of events. Rather, a key question concerns the status of the information adduced. In an attempt to clear up this difficult question, I use Collier's (2011) considered view of how the term *information* is applied. In science, a frequent usage is computational; drawing on algorithms, computational information has no value for the machines themselves. It is physical, can use probabilities, and can simulate material structures (it can be organized hierarchically). Collier deemed such information *substantive*. In cognitive science, all concur that substantive information is never encountered but, rather, must be measured. This applies, for example, when the Hubble constructs pictures of deep space or in claiming that the poverty of the stimulus is compatible with treating language as "input" (Chomsky, 1965). Generally, substantive information is indifferent to the entities that it also constitutes and, in this sense, is disembodied. The description applies to aspects of language such as lexis, grammatical patterns, and probabilistic facts about language activity.[5] To grasp how these can be more than patterns, one needs other applications of the term *information*.

All substantive information can be measured because, in both microphysics and macrophysics, it depends on laws (see Pattee & Rączaszek-Leonardi, 2012). However, the evolution of living systems marks a discontinuity in nature. While constituted of substantive information, they also depend on organizational aspects of, in the first place, DNA. Although this can be described as biochemistry, it functions as RNA acts as a measuring system, folds onto the transcribed DNA, and synthesizes proteins. For Pattee (2012), the workings of DNA are thus irreducible to processing because the selections of RNA measuring systems exploit how substantive distinctions can be used by the cell. They act as differences *for* a system. For Collier (2011), the domain of the living is a domain of *functional information*, or, in Bateson's (1979) phrase, one where differences make a difference. Most people working in theoretical biology acknowledge that living systems use functional information. Similar claims grounded

---

4 The insight that language is coordination is widespread (see, e.g., Rączaszek-Leonardi & Kelso, 2008).
5 Crucially, this does *not* make these patterns negentropic—although statistical measures can be applied to arrangements of digits and alphabetic or ideographic characters, it is unclear whether this applies to affect-laden talk, listening, or, indeed, to the exercise of literacies (reviewing papers, writing poetry, or performing religious chanting).

Gibson's (1979) views of affordances, work in code biology, and biosemiotics; Varela's (1979) view of autonomy; and, crucially, Maturana's (1978) insight that only observers can willfully make distinctions (or judgments derived from languaging). Crucially, a central nervous system links substantive information, how this is rendered functional, and above all a history of using both to coordinate action and perception. Far from "representing" content, the CNS can fine-tune bodily activity to meet the needs of communities, organisms, and persons.

Most functional information is encountered directly—an object may seem "inviting" or feel "hot." However, this fails to capture how disembodied aspects of language contribute to judgments as simple as, for example, saying, "This is my right hand."[6] To come to terms with how judgments draw on language, one thus needs to account for two transitions. First, one must show how a living being organizes substantive information to ensure that it is functional. Second, one must account for how a living being's functional information can be given a sense in a wider community such that, using language (and languaging), it enables action by human observers.

In studying measures of entrenchment, one must ask how the results bear on the world. Are the facts related to substantive, functional, or observer-relevant applications of information? In other terms, do the measures have any explanatory value? In pursuing how entrenchment bears on measures-as-information, I offer an imaginary case in which, in leaving her house, a woman called Sally turns right or left (houses opposite prevent her going straight ahead). In a substantial sample of cases, she turns right 70% of the time, and in 28% of cases, she goes left (2% of the time, she returns inside). Although the measure establishes facts, it shows nothing about Sally or her world and, thus, captures no one application of *information*. Now let us consider the entrenchment of her decisions. For example, we might compare the total data set with when Sally leaves the house between 7 and 8 a.m. on weekdays. Now, we find that she goes right 90% of the time, goes left 6%, and returns home 4%. By taking an observer's perspective, the measures reveal trends that can be described as conditional probabilities. Early on weekdays, there is a 20% higher chance that she will choose to turn right and, strikingly, a 100% increase in the frequency of returning home. Because the "information" is likely to be unknown to Sally and her brain, there is no support for the view that it identifies a "mechanism."

The measures (the changing frequency effects) are valuable for observers. This is because, in observing, one combines functional and substantive applications of information. In the example, distinctions and differences matter to Sally—at least indirectly. From an observer's view, the facts can be used, for example, in betting on Sally's movements. Given the measures, it is rational to predict that, especially on weekdays, she will turn right. In such cases, she is seen as a moving object in space,

---

[6] I follow Wittgenstein (1980) in using the example to illustrate certainties or the capacity to reach "agreement in judgments."

and the measure refers to substantive information. However, I may also ask why she turns right or left: In generating hypotheses, I can appeal to functional information. Does she turn right on the way to the bus stop or the office? Is Sally forgetful in the morning? In such cases, I postulate information that, at time t, may (or may not) matter to Sally. Inevitably, I appeal to the social and physical world, and as an observer, I rely on language (and languaging). Accordingly, the measures themselves are uninformative about Sally's action.

Their indirectness, moreover, applies to all measures of entrenchment. No measure can show, for example, that Sally has a regular rendezvous with a lover. Their indirectness arises because, as a person, Sally observes actions that others can also observe (she may want spies to believe that she has a lover). Given an observation history, she exerts some control over her action. Naturally enough, this complicates how the frequency attributed to biological functions relates to measures (as types and subtypes) and how information (i.e., the measured) functions for a person or organism. Leaving aside issues of control, the argument can be simply stated. My claim is that, in measuring entrenchment (as with, say, habits of turning right), one learns nothing about the nature of the information (or the mix of information) that is measured. Emphatically, there is no evidence for (or against) any mechanism. In this sense, measures of entrenchment lack explanatory value. Nonetheless, it is still of considerable interest to ask about the extent to which brains represent any given mix of information and the extent to which the measures depend on observers. Before turning to that issue, I summarize as follows:

- To say that X is entrenched is to identify a measure of frequency differences (e.g., *and* is more frequent than *but*).
- It says nothing about the data that are actually measured (e.g., actual uses of *and* and *but*).
- To understand an observer's "information" (e.g., that *and* is more frequent than *but*), one must consider what the statistics measure (complex action) and not the measures themselves (e.g., differences in frequencies).

18.4 Entrenchment: Information, Brains, and Language

In bringing radical embodied science to linguistic entrenchment, I have one reservation about the following: "As a first rough approximation, ... entrenchment can be understood as referring to a set of cognitive processes—mainly memory consolidation, chunking, and automatization—taking place in the minds of individual speakers" (Schmid, Chapter 1, this volume, Section 1.2). While concurring that the phenomena bear on memory consolidation, chunking, and automatization, I see no reason to posit minds (whatever those are taken to be). Rather, I trace the facts to observation by coordinating bodies. Specifically, Sally shows why entrenchment differs from learning: She has not learned to turn right early on weekdays, and for this reason, in the 6% of occasions when she turns left, she does not make an error. Rather, even if reliant on continuous neural modulation and reorganization, Sally exerts delicate control over actions. She is an observer and an actor: She lives in a language-saturated world.

Once generalized, the argument shows the importance of delicacy. Measures of entrenchment pinpoint subtle behavior—how we present ourselves through routines. Accordingly, they bear only indirectly on the measured. So, even if we think that we know what language is (a dubious assumption), entrenchment is no proxy for a mechanism. Yet, chunking has been described as a "natural and unavoidable way of perceiving language" (Sinclair & Mauranen, 2006, p. 20). But are perceivers the persons, organisms, brains, or some kind of extended system? If the claim is that persons can use chunks and tend to use certain chunks, it is merely overstated (because it is neither natural nor unavoidable). But if its allegedly unavoidable nature is taken seriously, the claim erroneously implies that there is an underlying mechanism. It confuses a fact with how this is interpreted in relation to "representations." It is false that, in any sense, brains (or minds) perceive language: Rather, they sensitize to physical distinctions (and substantive information) while also using embodiment to self-organize in ways granting information functional value.

Although this applies to all creatures, humans also draw on social practices to use the world as observers. They depend on other people to connect functional information with language as, over time, they learn how to coordinate. They gradually gain skills in connecting functional information to language and languaging. As they become observers, they can ascribe value to aspects of the world (they make up and detect affordances and "signs"). Thus, statistics capture facts about behavioral probability that lack explanatory value—as applied to living agents. Further, what applies to behavior may well also apply at other time scales. There is no evidence for a chunking mechanism, let alone that such an entity applies in different scales. Quite different factors may undergird measures of reaction time, discourse frequency, grammatical constructions, and historical change.

For example, imagine a measure of a set of women who act like Sally. Not inconceivably, a population might turn right slightly more often than left. However, this would tell us nothing about what the women do in the morning. Simply, the brain is a way station in entrenching—a self-organizing component in human action.[7] Given its stunning capacities for reuse, it grants flexibility in rather the same way as does the road outside Sally's front door.

---

[7] Radical embodied cognitive science stresses that the brain evolved by drawing on principles of reuse (see Anderson, 2010). In appeal to entrenching and re-entrenching, I also posit that this occurs during enculturation.

18.5 Robots Against Cognitivist Views of Entrenchment

It is all too easy to conflate measures with a mechanism. Given that minds cannot be observed, this is a perennial problem faced by mentalism. It appears in Chomsky's (1965) claim that a mind uses environmental structure to discover structure in form–meaning mappings.[8] In positing that individuals "contain" a language faculty, he posited that, like a von Neumann machine, brains use "representations." Because input is deemed to be disembodied (or "formal"), language is localized "in the head."

In defense of cognitivism, others invoked methodological solipsism by placing language between perception and action. Linguistic behavior ("performance") was said to arise as brains generate intentional states by processing input for an autonomous individual (with "competence").[9] When language reduces to forms and use, brains are bound to deduce or construct knowledge about frequencies. Indeed, Chomsky's program was historically based in his challenge to his supervisor's view that learning to talk could be explained by human sensitivity to the distribution of substantive information (Harris, 1998).

First, there is no "processing" between perception and action: As Noë (2004) rediscovered, we act as we perceive, and, inseparably, perceiving is action. Second, it is unlikely that brains detect linguistic forms, let alone verbal patterns. Indeed, to think otherwise is to make what Bennett and Hacker (2003) called a *mereological error*: People, not brains, detect linguistic forms, and for this reason, language does not reduce to message-sending by a "form"-producing or -processing neural machine.[10] Further, because both living systems and robots use bodies to coordinate in ways that mimic language, the embodied view is simpler. Together, people use coordination in what an observer sees as learning—or entrenching—as they pick up physical distinctions.

Language can be traced to substantive information (not formal input) because it is part of the social world (even Chomsky acknowledged the existence of what he called "E-language"). Arnon (2015) is likely to be mistaken to assert that a brain can "extract distributional regularities" or "store" the results. Like robots, the CNS is likely to rely on physical distinctions. Before pursuing this alternative, I stress the bizarre nature of positing that input is both stored and reconstructed within the organism; see the inner block in Figure 18.1. In this view, brains use entrenching (E in Figure 18.1) or,

---

[8] For example, Saffran (2009) claims, "To the extent that structure in the environment is patterned, learners with appropriate learning mechanisms can make use of that patterning to discover underlying structures" (p. 180). She fails to note that the mechanisms are posited because she forgets that (inner) language draws on bodies that are "exposed" to situated gesturing and its physical effects—the data are not intrinsically verbal.

[9] Enactivists regard language as participatory sense-making used in coping with perturbances (De Jaegher & Di Paolo, 2007; for a critique, see Cowley & Gahrn-Andersen, 2015).

[10] Classic challenges of encodingism appear in Bickhard (1992) and code views of language in Love (2004) and Kravchenko (2007).

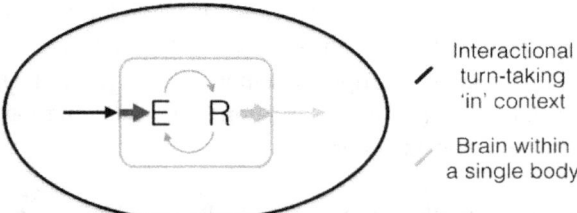

Fig. 18.1: A cognitivist model. Interaction provides input that gives rise to the recognition and reading of intentional states (R) that allegedly suffice to construct (E) or entrench knowledge (in the brain).

in other words, a history of input to construct representations (R). Not only are these mysterious entities posited to drive production, but input (whatever that is) is said to be processed such that the results trigger the identification (and/or construction) of forms. Linguistic knowledge drives brains that extract, process, store, and use. Whether in entrenched or representational guise, linguistic items link predictive uses to action–language production. A classic exposition is Tomasello's (2003) claim that children "construct" a language by linking input, statistical learning, and recognitions and readings of intentional states (as shown by R in Figure 18.1).

The representational model of entrenchment can be summarized as follows:

- Brains extract distributional information from input.
- Brains identify linguistic patterns and use entrenching to construct stores of linguistic "data."
- By linking stores based in entrenching to speech production, brains repeat the cycle.
- Iterated cycles give rise to entrenched mechanisms that self-construct new forms of (predictive) mechanisms and ways of producing linguistic output.
- Constructions enable a person to conform to local practices by linking speaking and hearing to other mechanisms (e.g., systems for intention identification and recognition).

Arnon (2015) suggested that children learn to talk by using mechanisms of this kind. Her evidence is that, based on measuring differences between frequencies, common items "tend to be acquired earlier" and shape both "correct production" and "error patterns." Such evidence, she believes, must be used in modeling acquisition (challenging the Skinner–Chomsky view that language consists in forms).[11] This is because, for Arnon, speech is also statistical (for a brain). Thus, brains use frequency

---

[11] For Skinner (1957), forms are "stimuli" and, for Chomsky (1965), "input." Both concur that they set off processes in the organism (i.e., learning and encoding, respectively). For Chomsky, forms are too impoverished to be learned, and thus he replaced learning by appeal to universal grammar. If brains extract or calculate their statistical properties, a language faculty must couple with a universal calculating machine. The alternative, of course, is to grant a role of linguistic embodiment.

to formulate and identify chunks of speech (or what observers also see as information). Without argument, these are taken to self-configure by using statistics to identify and categorize language (i.e., to use measures that correspond to hers). It is as if Sally's actions and beliefs depended on frequency observations about turning left and right. In this view, frequency measures pick out what Sally uses as "information" when she decides where to turn.

The radical embodied view offers a simple alternative. It posits that, like robots, brains identify substantive information—distinctions that exist in the world. Second, using embodiment, children, not brains, gain skills with linguistic categories. Before pursuing this view, however, I stress that artificial agents use substantive information in ways that, for an observer, seem stunningly languagelike.

In tackling the symbol grounding problem (see Belpaeme, Cowley, & MacDorman, 2009; Harnad, 1990), robots learn to map language-type "symbols" onto "meanings." In saying this, I put "symbol" and "meaning" in quotation marks to stress the observer's perspective and the observer's semantics (a third-person view of symbol grounding leaves aside how systems master language). In seminal work, robots were designed to use formal types (symbols) to act "about" the world. Steels and Belpaeme's (2005) robots used coordination games to discriminate invariances observers see as colors (e.g., red, blue, green). Each robot developed categories that, given a history of correction, triggered symbol-based routines. Thus, using hardware, a well-structured environment, errors, and statistical learning, robots mapped symbols onto referents, and each robot developed its own "categories." However, internal structures do not map onto "measures" (as history weights their neural networks). Indeed, because each robot perceived a different "world," the design would fail. Although "identical" machines were used in the same environment, their *partly* overlapping categories drew on interaction history. Categories converged only if a "coordination game" enabled robots to use linguistic routines. Just as for humans, a perceptual history enabled robots to perform (normative) action.

Belpaeme and Bleys (2005) thus saw color perception and language as uniting cultural and universal constraints (i.e., physical and pseudophysiological ones). Elsewhere, the approach is applied to grammars (Steels & De Beule, 2006) and to how the physics of human vision changes robot categorization (Baronchelli, Gong, Puglisi, & Loreto, 2010). Although not called *entrenching*, in these experiments robots used substantive information to manage social interactions and act "about" the world. They formed network-style representations that mimicked memory consolidation, chunking, and the automatic use of form–meaning pairs.

Robots build routines that permit linguistic description (by a human observer). Seen as a result of entrenching, they resemble the cognitivist's hypothetical brains in two senses. First, they extract distributional information from substantive information, and second, they use stores of (what an observer regards as) linguistic data to produce linguistic output. However, robots lack the agency required to self-construct (predictive) mechanisms that grant flexibility to their units of speech (constructions).

Robots cannot link utterances to local practices by binding speaking and hearing with, say, intention identification and recognition.[12] Quite simply, autonomous systems can make no use of functional information and, thus, lack the adaptivity of even a single-celled organism. Indeed, although robot learning uses a history of body–world encounters, the machines lack the flexibility of bacteria, let alone rats, pigeons, or babies. In using statistics to manage arbitrary symbol strings, they rely on digital values. Unlike even Lettvin et al.'s (1959) frogs, they cannot recognize "sames," and in this sense, their "linguistic" information is not functional. While using body–world coordination to develop routines, the "symbols" mean nothing for robots. Artificial agents lack values, do not orient, and cannot refine their acting and perceiving: They rely on hardware and central control. Robot moves are meaningless to the agents, and in this sense, living systems (and people) are quite different.

Later I trace this to how substantive information takes on functional potential through the development of robust and situation-sensitive skills. In terms derived from Bernstein's (1967) work, they bind action with perception such that partial repetitions of situations prompt anticipatory modes of action. However, before turning to flexibility, it is of value to consider what we can learn from artificial agents who explore entrenching in a social context.

18.6 Entrenching in an Artificial Social World

Robots simulate how substantive information can be used to mimic linguistic function. However, what observers see as "linguistic" is, for robots, substantive information. Unlike persons, they lack any way of connecting with the said (or a history of languaging that coevolves with social practices). In turning to how the entrenching of substantive social information mimics changes in form (and, by implication, use) of formal patterns, I turn to other artificial agents. These evolve in a setting like a video game in which software agents use learning to simulate phonetic change.

Stanford and Kenny (2013) used agent-based modeling to simulate how child-based phonetic knowledge changes faster than that of adults. Inspired by work on the Northern vowel shift (Labov, 2007), they replicated the effects in a simple model. In their work, artificial agents interact as they meet in a virtual Chicago, a virtual St. Louis, and on a virtual highway between cities. At each meeting, agents mimic one another's vowel utterances, and if deemed phonetically similar, the agent's algorithm classifies them as sames. The system then records not the match but a digital version of the partner's token (scored as a numerical value). In later encounters, each agent aggregates its records (i.e., digitally close matches) in self-presenting and producing (or

---

[12] Tomasello (2003) replaced linguistic universals with universals for recognizing and identifying intentions (for a critique, see Cowley, 2007).

failing to produce) potential matches. In effect, vowel production is distributed across a population through feedback between interactions and individual exemplar-based memory.

Given rich memory systems (i.e., an ability to detect substantive information), the agents' vowels can be shown to covary with sociolinguistic observations. Over time, effects of utterance frequency show up as changes in global vowel averages and do so, of course, without any change in the agents (or mechanism). Unlike the autonomous players of coordination games, the agents maintain sound structure through interaction. Thus, whereas Labov (2007) ascribed children's pronunciations to something like Chomsky's (1965) language acquisition device, the model uses entrenching to simulate interaction-driven change. Quite simply, "learning" about vowel change links interactions with a population's rich phonetic memory. Not only are learning and vowel change free of any language acquisition device (for detail, see Cowley, 2016), but the indirect effects of an interaction history enable artificial child-agents to "speak" in ways that mimic ongoing phonetic change.

Using substantive information, these artificial agents learn like robots. Unsurprisingly, they too build routines that permit linguistic description (by a human observer) that draw on entrenching. Further, like the cognitivist's brains, they not only extract distributional information but also develop stores of "linguistic" data that serve in producing linguistic patterns. However, they go further than the robots. Because they simulate, not knowledge systems, but interactions, they show how agents can conform to local practices by linking "speaking and hearing" with rich memory (given systems for intention identification and recognition). They show that formal aspects of language can evolve independently of bodies and modes of life.

Nonetheless, they face the same critique as do the robots. As artificial agents, they lack functional information, and for this reason, their doings mean nothing to the agents. Like the robots, they fail to link linguistic "data" to surrogates of action and perception and, for this reason, cannot construct "mechanisms": Nothing could induce predictive ways of making (or identifying) linguistic units of variable value. Strikingly, this applies in spite of their pragmatic ways of mimicking human language.

In artificial agents, substantive information drives automatic, frequency-based sensitization that has no need to be reorganized and modified by task-oriented feedback. That is, substantive information enables entrenching but not the construction of mechanisms. Neural networks set up bidirectional links with physical stimuli not through perceived sames but as statistically based memory functions in a normative way. Agents link physical and social distinctions to parameters that serve in coordination. Although necessarily automatic, they also consolidate memory, master chunks, and learn from each other. Given a pragmatic capacity, Stanford and Kenny's (2013) agents use social regularities (the observer's "phonetic knowledge") to exploit a spread of exemplars—collective memory that enacts and tracks linguistic variation. Lacking understanding, the agents use substantive information to connect internally stored values with differences in (simulated) pronunciation: Like Steels and Belpaeme's (2005) robots, they mimic human-style behavior. However, unlike embrained systems, the artificial agents cannot use entrenching to develop skills. In contrast to rats and pigeons, they neither detect affordances nor perceive the results of action. Humans, like rats and pigeons—and in contrast to artificial agents—both detect affordances and make more or less willful use of repetition with variation. This serves, for example, to make social distinctions or gauge and hone understanding. As people willfully create affordances (and signs) by linking entrenchment to understanding (whatever that is), people appropriate and construct routines. By hypothesis, the CNS combines probability with functional information. Although people use expressions as automatic chunks, they also develop skills. Accordingly, there is a parallel with decision making whereby 50 years of intense study show that people do not know how they find ways of "going on." Not only do they use biases and heuristics, but they also generate insights and rationalizations. For March (1999), decision making relies on not just choice but also interpretation. I now apply the same logic to language by arguing that observers link functional information to ways of acting (and perceiving).

18.7 Entrenchment: What Artificial Agents Can't Grasp

Artificial agents rely on entrenching substantive information. Although able to build "data" stores that map onto what observers see as linguistic patterns, that is all they do. Unsurprisingly, the same applies in simulating social agents who track speech practices. Without functional information, they can build neither predictive mechanisms nor novel modes of speech and action. Because they cannot perceive sames, the agents can grant no value to linguistic doings. It is likely that the same argument applies to brains. Indeed, evidence for identifying sames may be limited to organism–environment systems such as frogs, rats, and, of course, human observers who draw on language. In short, functional information supplements entrenching by enabling systems to link the accumulation and sorting of substantive information with agent-driven modes of action.

Although lacking space to pursue the view, Pattee (2012) argued that historically derived information coevolved with the measuring systems that use extracellular messages to prompt folding and protein synthesis that uses transcribed DNA. The lineage has an evolutionary history that renders substantive information functional for the living being. Further, because genes serve many functions, they can use functional information and, from an observer's perspective, drive memory consolidation and automatization. Indeed, this is why entrenching grants little flexibility—it works at a population level in which individual choices are limited. For a linguist, this

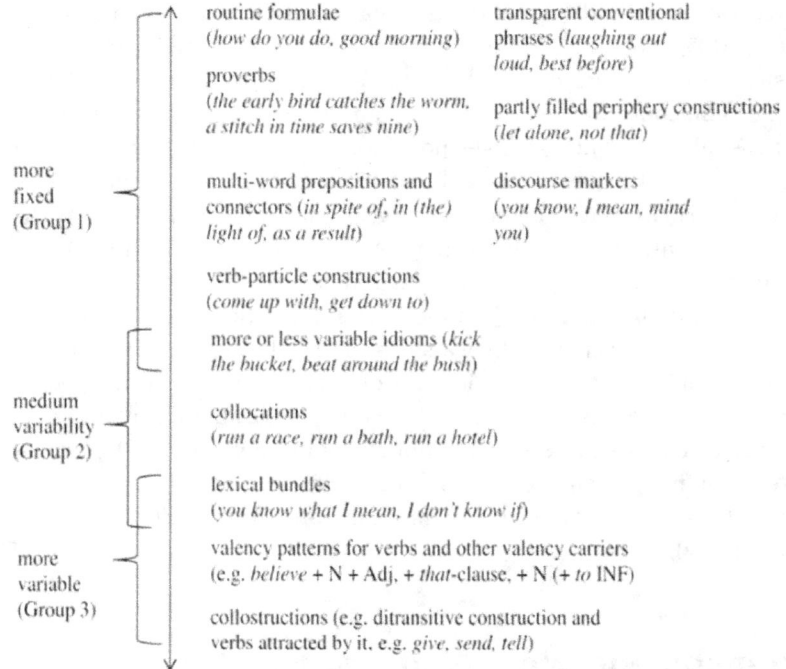

Fig. 18.2: Types of lexicogrammatical patterns arranged to show frozenness versus variability. Reprinted from *Constructions Collocations Patterns* (p. 256), by T. Herbst, H.-J. Schmid, and S. Faulhaber (Eds.), 2014, Berlin, Germany: De Gruyter Mouton. Copyright 2014 by De Gruyter Mouton.

resonates with the view that a language system constrains people who act as if following rules.[13]

Measures of entrenchment can be applied to lexis, grammar, and pragmatic aspects of language. However, strikingly different entrenchment measures characterize kinds of language activity. One finds, for example, a continuum between more or less frozen pragmatic facts (see the model by Schmid, 2014), as in Figure 18.2. Whereas the more frozen types (on top) readily disambiguate settings, those lower down apply to settings of use that are, typically at least, rather harder to imagine. Perhaps this is why, as Schmid (2014) noted, "literally all readers of earlier versions" (p. 256) of his chapter were moved to offer rich comments. Below, I pursue

---

[13] In a distributed view, disembodied aspects of language can function as constraints. By implication, they depend on acting as if following rules by drawing on synergies (see Anderson, Richardson, & Chemero, 2012) or task-specific devices (Bingham, 1988; Golonka, 2015).

the claim's importance by suggesting that re-entrenching—how functional information is used in a community—characterizes the systems that manage speaking and acting. Above all, they combine modes of use with varying degrees of subtlety or, as I prefer, how a person's rhetorical and *intellectual skills exploit delicacy* in the use of wordings.

Like proverbs, routine formulas tend to be rather frozen. However, although formulae are common, proverbs are relatively rare. If that is not surprising, why are both as frozen as "transparent phrases"? For, whereas "laugh out loud" or "best before" hint at new media and advertising, proverbs may sound old-fashioned. Nor are puzzles restricted to frozen items. Looking down Figure 18.2, one can ask, say, why "collocations" show flexibility. Accordingly, let us return to the points implied by the cognitivist model (Figure 18.1).

Recall the following five assumptions: (a) Brains use input to extract distributed information. (b) Brains identify linguistic patterns and use entrenching to construct stores of (what an observer sees as) linguistic data as a result of further processes (discussed below). (c) Entrenched information enables a person to conform to local practices by replicating conformist ways of speaking and hearing (and, perhaps, innate devices for intention recognition). It is striking that, if "input" is interpreted as substantive information (i.e., meaningless distinctions), robots perform as brains are hypothesized to do. Specifically, like search engines, they extract distributional information, identify and store "linguistic" patterns, and, using the data set, enact sound change that mirrors human practice. Robots show—and the point is exceedingly important—that "referential" and "formal" aspects of language can derive from sensitivity to physical distinctions maintained by not brains, but populations. Yet, before turning to implications for pragmatics, I turn to sticking points that beset autonomous agents that lack any kind of functional information. In terms presented above, they cannot meet the following criteria: (d) By linking stores based in entrenching to speech production, brains are able to repeat the cycle of production and entrenching. And (e) iterated cycles give rise to entrenched mechanisms that self-construct new (predictive) mechanisms and ways of producing linguistic output. Agents fail because they rely on digital tokens of what a designer treats as "linguistic data." Indeed, this is what ensures that, without seeing, robots can use color data "referentially" and an algorithm can shape the changing "speech" of software agents. Given an inability to separate entrenching from production, they cannot repeat the cycle while drawing on action or gaining sensitivity to a changing world.

Entrenching cannot build mechanisms because artificial agents cannot set up iterated cycles to perform in ways likely to bring off effects. Unlike frogs or infants, they rely on programmed sames. Like brains, agents lack a lineage that sensitizes them to a changing world and experience that is analogous to embodied action or, indeed, cuddles, teasing, or reprimands. Artificial models replace skills and ways of acting with output; they cannot show delicacy. However, even if using substantive information, a living robotlike CNS might perform differently. In rats, sensed bodily action could hone action and perception. In a world of conformist practices, entrenching might enable humans to discover both observing and thus acting with delicacy. Indeed, as people undertake activities such as using cutlery or making jewelry, they adjust how they act as they experience their moves (Baber, Parekh, & Cengiz, 2014). Further, as attested by self-repair and other conversational regularities, monitoring contributes much to language (or languaging). Let us ask how this affects freezing and, specifically, the fact that entrenchment measures show consistency in a population's use of kinds of expressions.

To approach freezing, one can compare robots, frogs, and humans. When robots do not break down, they are massively self-consistent: Although frogs show variation in identifying flies, their lineage guarantees much conformity. This is because whereas robots use substantive information, frogs draw on functions fixed by embodiment. Thus, the interest of pragmatics is precisely that it shows neither massive consistency nor too much freedom. Yet, predictable degrees of freezing apply to the use of expression: For example, agents can recognize a proverb as a proverb. Indeed, this is why one can generalize its freezing.

How is this recognition performed? Plainly, a system must link frequency information to nonfrequency pattern.[14] Generally, this has been posited as something that is performed by an inner language faculty. Indeed, theorists have offered ingenious solutions to the puzzle. For Fodor (1975), brains might use innate ("semantic/linguistic") information to ground concepts—they might possess innate knowledge of, say, proverbs. Alternatively, in appealing to Chomsky's (1986) I-language, just as brains might deduce information about the properties of nouns or pro-drop languages, they might identify proverb strings.

Objections are readily supplied. First, although a computational model would ascribe automatized knowledge to proverbs, collocations, collostructions, and so forth, the expressions have pragmatic flexibility. Second, if freezing is, in some sense, innate, computation explains nothing. Third, it can be objected that the argument confounds a person who uses a proverb (or pragmatic type) with a part of a person that is said to know (i.e., a brain or mind). The model falls afoul of the mereological fallacy. At very least, one should consider whether persons, not brains, use substantive information to master verbal patterns (making them functional information). If one allows this, it seems that the link between frequency information and its nonfrequency counterpart can depend on embodiment.

Phenomenal experience offers a challenge to the computational view. Each of us can learn a language, and as we do so, we pick out recurrent patterns. Although

---

14 It is circular to explain frequency by freezing (or vice versa); frozen expressions can be unusual (e.g., "a stitch in time saves nine"), and many frequent expressions are frozen (e.g., "good morning," "best before"). The metaphor of freezing is, nonetheless, evocative.

the CNS is necessary to the process, much depends on acts of observing. In learning to talk, children do not apply sames after they have picked them out. Rather, they gradually master the subtleties of behavior. For example, around their first birthday, English-speaking infants may wave "bye-bye" and Italian infants say or wave *"ciao."* They orient to greetings *before* they initiate, regulate, and otherwise enact the same. Even if we leave neural modulation aside, it is clear that pragmatic phenomena take on functional value before coming to ground behavioral routines. In learning to greet, moreover, performance is delicate—that is, far from reduction to types of act, greetings connect up subtle kinetic, pragmatic, and social nuances. Even for infants, they serve as openings and closings—not, say, talk initiators triggered after every 5-second silence. As is characteristic of pragmatic moves, they require delicacy in timing, tone, discourse context, multimodal accompaniment, and so on. When performance shows delicacy, functional neural mechanisms are usually tuned by sensory–motor skills. Such behavior contrasts with the automatized output of robots or artificial agents. The claim applies right across pragmatics. For example, although the phrase "best before" is familiar, most readers would hear its use as jocular in response to enquiries about health (e.g., "best before breakfast"). Thus, even if based in substantive information that has functional roles, it can be used and construed willfully. Far from resembling computational output, it is like Sally's turning left because she is going to the seaside.

Further freezing links many kinds of delicacy. Thus, although some items are vague (e.g., "good day"), their timing (or mistiming) can index fluency. In other cases, skilled use depends on remarkable precision—when, exactly, is it appropriate to say "a stitch in time"? In contrast to the view that this is possible because such information is encoded, I stress that delicacy depends on judgments. When one posits coding and a language faculty, these crucial aspects of language disappear. Competence models miss both delicacy and linguistic fluency because, by definition, pragmatic regularities link rules with meaning (whatever that is). The general problem is illustrated by collocations like "run a bath" and "run a race," which, it seems, have comparable frequency measures; however, even if a super-brain had miraculously calculated how frozen such expressions should be, it would still have to "know" their delicacy in comparison to, for example, "run a Facebook page" and "run a car." How could that be done?

To posit a robotlike autonomous system (whether a mental unit or an individual) that manages utterance types masks a dubious assumption that a brain can identify, classify, tag, and cross-reference "forms" to balance a degree of freezing with context flexibility. Thus, in relation to, say, utterance types such as "I don't know," the brain would have to gauge that "run a bath" fits fewer circumstances. This is bizarre. So, if entrenching shapes mental representation, it is staggeringly complex and needs principles that are unavailable to robots and, it seems, unknown in neuroscience. Although there are many views on the topic (see Jost & Christiansen, Chapter 10, this volume), one should not assume that what brains (or minds) "store" is indexed by measures of entrenchment. Observers may be picking out not neural mechanisms, but the frequency of ways of acting and perceiving or, simply, using routines.

18.8 Is Entrenchment "Real"?

It is clear that although real, reliable, and informative, measures of entrenchment lack explanatory value. Their value lies in describing facts of memory consolidation, chunking, and automatization. In this sense, entrenchment is real—and can be found in domains that reach far beyond language. In genes, frogs, and rats, I have suggested, mechanisms use functional information that is, at once, also substantive. Yet, as applied to language (and much other human behavior), much depends on an observer. Both the rat in a maze and Sally use entrenching in the sense that their behavior can be richly described by statistical measures. However, unlike the rat, Sally can justify her behavior and choose to modify it by using linguistic resources. Thus, just as the rat's behavior is irreducible to substantive information (as I argue), Sally's is also irreducible to its functional counterpart. Because entrenchment is real for an observer, it pertains not to a CNS but to a person-in-the-world. In other terms, people learn to *do* what entrenchment *measures*—Sally's turning left or right attests to her familiarity with her town. However, entrenchment does not index learning; it does not tell us why she turns left or right. Nor does comparing the freezing of linguistic items tell us about neural mechanisms or how putative types are used by different people at different times. These things should be obvious to any careful observer.

Given an observer's skills, there is more to entrenchment. People monitor—and improve—memory consolidation, chunking, and automatization. For humans, what entrenchment measures serves as a cognitive resource. Further, a contrast with artificial agents reveals the power of distributed control. Such agents exploit entrenching, in the one case, to code reference and, in the other, to track slow changes in formal aspects of a language. Both use statistical correlations that describe social outcomes. Although this does not scale up, the finding is indicative about human language, especially in its disembodied aspect. It makes it likely that humans link ways of using substantive information with body-based functionality as they learn to talk or, as Maturana (1978) would say, as they self-construct as observers. Their brains need not "represent" linguistic forms because people track how others orient to the verbal patterns (and other impersonal structures) in their life world. In short, *people* carry out re-entrenching.

When the brain's entrenching is reused as body-based functional information, the results are learning like that of rats and pigeons. However, by re-entrenching functional information, people use distributed control to master routines, automatize behavior, consolidate memory, and switch courses of action. In this view, to say, as Arnon (2015) does, that high-frequency items "tend to be acquired earlier" is to note that, all things being equal, people often adopt similar routines. Similarly, picking out "error patterns" confirms that overshoot is amenable to everyday observation. However, this occurs not in the brain, but as conscious performance is managed around order and disorder.

What Dennett (1993) called the "person level" is crucial to achieving delicate effects in a world where expectation influences language (and languaging). Chunks are social moves—that is, they render substantive information a functional part of interpersonal coordination. And so when they are automatized, they influence the systems that contribute to memory consolidation, aid prediction, and render anticipation possible. In short, what entrenchment measures grants a person access to ready-made resources for organizing activity—chunks of speech (or text) evoke events, situations, and ways of speaking.

18.9 Conclusion

Measures of entrenchment can be treated as showing the sensorimotor roots of human language. People use skilled action–perception to gain functional power from substantive information. By hypothesis, human flexibility arises as a CNS uses embodiment to grant functionality to bodily movements. Accordingly, I trace entrenchment measures to how people structure and regulate action–perception that, in the case of language, allows them to observe and use the results to build techniques for understanding and living. Linguistic routines draw on, not content, but social and pragmatic practice that grounds skill and judgment (Harvey, 2015). Humans master activity in which wordings play a part. Language thus connects individuals and collective resources with cultural practices (and languages) that spread across populations. As a consequence, measures of entrenchment index not just neural processes, but also a history of human observation. One rediscovers the primacy of pragmatics and finds, perhaps surprisingly, that this is in line with how artificial agents mimic entrenching. Indeed, it is likely that all living systems depend on entrenching that is based, ultimately, in substantive information.

Yet, metabolism and the bidirectional coupling of "intelligent" bacteria already depend on functional information. One should thus be skeptical of any model that treats culturally embedded primates that use language—living human beings—as robotlike users of substantive information. No measure of frequency or frequency differences can, I suggest, pick out a neural "mechanism." To think otherwise is to take the mentalist view that brains (or minds) are (like) von Neumann devices. In rejecting representations, I claim that the more and less frozen state of different pragmatic phenomena demonstrates the collective nature of language. The delicacy with which frozen phenomena can be used attests to the living human subject's flexibility; language is thus partly constitutive of human existence. As activity in which wordings play a part (Cowley, 2014), language and languaging enact social and cultural events. Such events, like the persons who enact them, are to be "explained" by neither processes within brains nor the slavish use of second order language systems.

Routines are partly automatic. Even in monologue, people act under distributed control as they connect their experience to that of others. As activity, persons share modes of attending while orienting to a community's expectations. In making this case, I sketched how artificial agents use entrenching to gain control over impersonal (digital) resources. Although inflexible, such devices mimic and track "linguistic" routines— and do so without granting functional value to distinctions. Accordingly, I argued that the sensorimotor basis of language enables brains to select distinctions that, over time, take on functions. For this reason explanations of sensorimotor activity capture how functional information can be engendered (i.e., through neural plasticity).

In pragmatics, cultural aspects of language (formal patterns) constrain how people speak and hear. Given entrenchment's sensorimotor roots, these allow people to create habits. They may come to use even proverbs with delicacy. Enculturation permits modes of acting that draw on projecting what *can* be said and done, as well as how it *might* be understood. Within cultural ecosystems, people learn about, say, engineering, cooking, or football, modes of activity that link language with a body's potential for action–perception. Given a sensorimotor history, physical distinctions come to function within routines and variations on routines. People perform as engineers, cooks, or footballers as entrenching connects an individual history, language experience, and subjective modes of action and perception. By tracing entrenchment to routines, individual use of verbal patterns re-evokes a history of sensorimotor activity. Coordinated activity and human action depend on substantive information, albeit indirectly. By using a history of entrenching, people gain skills that shape the routine and flexible modes of acting that are, I suggest, the hallmark of a living human soul.

References

Anderson, M. L. (2010). Neural reuse: A fundamental organizational principle of the brain. *Behavioral and Brain Sciences*, *33*, 245–266. http://dx.doi.org/10.1017/S0140525X10000853

Anderson, M. L., Richardson, M. J., & Chemero, A. (2012). Eroding the boundaries of cognition: Implications of embodiment. *Topics in Cognitive Science*, *4*, 717–730. http://dx.doi.org/10.1111/j.1756-8765.2012.01211.x

Arnon, I. (2015). What can frequency effects tell us about the building blocks and mechanisms of language learning? *Journal of Child Language*, *42*, 274–277. http://dx.doi.org/10.1017/S0305000914000610

Baber, C., Parekh, M., & Cengiz, T. G. (2014). Tool use as distributed cognition: How tools help, hinder and define manual skill. *Frontiers in Psychology*, *5*, 116. http://dx.doi.org/10.3389/fpsyg.2014.00116

Baronchelli, A., Gong, T., Puglisi, A., & Loreto, V. (2010). Modeling the emergence of universality in color naming patterns. *Proceedings of the National Academy of Sciences of the United States of America*, *107*, 2403–2407. http://dx.doi.org/10.1073/pnas.0908533107

Bateson, G. (1979). *Mind and nature: A necessary unity*. New York, NY: Dutton.

Belpaeme, T., & Bleys, J. (2005). Explaining universal color categories through a constrained acquisition process. *Adaptive Behavior*, *13*, 293–310. http://dx.doi.org/10.1177/105971230501300404

Belpaeme, T., Cowley, S. J., & MacDorman, K. F. (Eds.). (2009). *Symbol grounding*. http://dx.doi.org/10.1075/bct.21

Bennett, M. R., & Hacker, P. M. S. (2003). *Philosophical foundations of neuroscience*. Oxford, England: Blackwell.

Bernstein, N. A. (1967). *The co-ordination and regulation of movements*. Oxford, England: Pergamon Press.

Bickhard, M. H. (1992). How does the environment affect the person? In L. T. Winegar & J. Valsiner (Eds.), *Children's development within social contexts: Metatheory and theory* (pp. 63–92). Hillsdale, NJ: Erlbaum.

Bingham, G. P. (1988). Task-specific devices and the perceptual bottleneck. *Human Movement Science*, *7*, 225–264. http://dx.doi.org/10.1016/0167-9457(88)90013-9

Chemero, A. (2003). An outline of a theory of affordances. *Ecological Psychology*, *15*, 181–195. http://dx.doi.org/10.1207/S15326969ECO1502_5

Chemero, A. (2011). *Radical embodied cognitive science*. Cambridge, MA: MIT Press.

Chomsky, N. (1965). *Aspects of the theory of syntax*. Cambridge, MA: MIT Press.

Chomsky, N. (1986). *Knowledge of language: Its nature, origin, and use*. New York, NY: Praeger.

Collier, J. (2011). Kinds of information in scientific use. *TripleC*, *9*, 295–304.

Cowley, S. J. (2007). From bodily co-regulation to language and thinking. *Linguistics and the Human Sciences*, *3*, 137–164.

Cowley, S. J. (Ed.). (2011). *Distributed language*. http://dx.doi.org/10.1075/bct.34

Cowley, S. J. (2014). Linguistic embodiment and verbal constraints: Human cognition and the scales of time. *Frontiers in Cognitive Science*, *5*, 1085. http://dx.doi.org/10.3389/fpsyg.2014.01085

Cowley, S. J. (2016). Cognition beyond the body: Using ABM to explore cultural ecosystems. In D. Secchi & M. Neumann (Eds.), *Agent-based simulation of organizational behavior* (pp. 43–60). http://dx.doi.org/10.1007/978-3-319-18153-0_3

Cowley, S. J., & Gahrn-Andersen, R. (2015). Deflating autonomy: Human interactivity in the emerging social world. *Intellectica*, *63*, 49–63.

De Jaegher, H., & Di Paolo, E. (2007). Participatory sense-making. *Phenomenology and the Cognitive Sciences*, *6*, 485–507. http://dx.doi.org/10.1007/s11097-007-9076-9

Dennett, D. C. (1993). *Consciousness explained*. London, England: Penguin.

Fodor, J. A. (1975). *The language of thought*. Cambridge, MA: Harvard University Press.

Fowler, C. A. (2010). Embodied, embedded language use. *Ecological Psychology*, *22*, 286–303. http://dx.doi.org/10.1080/10407413.2010.517115

Gibson, J. J. (1979). *The ecological approach to visual perception: Classic edition*. New York, NY: Psychology Press.

Golonka, S. (2015). Laws and conventions in language-related behaviors. *Ecological Psychology*, *27*, 236–250. http://dx.doi.org/10.1080/10407413.2015.1068654

Harnad, S. (1990). The symbol grounding problem. *Physica D: Nonlinear Phenomena*, *42*, 335–346. http://dx.doi.org/10.1016/0167-2789(90)90087-6

Harris, Z. (1998). *Language and information.* New York, NY: Columbia University Press.

Harvey, M. I. (2015). Content in languaging: Why radical enactivism is incompatible with representational theories of language. *Language Sciences, 48,* 90–129. http://dx.doi.org/10.1016/j.langsci.2014.12.004

Herbst, T., Schmid, H.-J., & Faulhaber, S. (Eds.). (2014). *Constructions collocations patterns.* Berlin, Germany: de Gruyter.

Keijzer, F. (2015). Moving and sensing without input and output: Early nervous systems and the origins of the animal sensorimotor organization. *Biology and Philosophy, 30,* 311–331. http://dx.doi.org/10.1007/s10539-015-9483-1

Kravchenko, A. V. (2007). Essential properties of language, or, why language is not a code. *Language Sciences, 29,* 650–671. http://dx.doi.org/10.1016/j.langsci.2007.01.004

Labov, W. (2007). Transmission and diffusion. *Language, 83,* 344–387. http://dx.doi.org/10.1353/lan.2007.0082

Lettvin, J. Y., Maturana, H. R., McCulloch, W. S., & Pitts, W. H. (1959). What the frog's eye tells the frog's brain. *Proceedings of the IRE, 47,* 1940–1951. http://dx.doi.org/10.1109/JRPROC.1959.287207

Love, N. (2004). Cognition and the language myth. *Language Sciences, 26,* 525–544. http://dx.doi.org/10.1016/j.langsci.2004.09.003

March, J. (1999). *The pursuit of organizational intelligence.* Oxford, England: Blackwell.

Maturana, H. (1978). Biology of language: The epistemology of reality. In G. Miller & E. Lenneberg (Eds.), *Psychology and the biology of language and thought* (pp. 28–62). New York, NY: Academic Press.

Noë, A. (2004). *Action in perception.* Cambridge, MA: MIT Press.

Pattee, H. H. (2012). Evolving self-reference: Matter, symbols, and semantic closure. In H. H. Pattee & J. Rączaszek-Leonardi (Eds.), *Laws, language and life* (pp. 211–226). http://dx.doi.org/10.1007/978-94-007-5161-3_14

Pattee, H. H., & Rączaszek-Leonardi, J. (Eds.). (2012). *Laws, language and life.* http://dx.doi.org/10.1007/978-94-007-5161-3

Rączaszek-Leonardi, J., & Kelso, J. A. (2008). Reconciling symbolic and dynamic aspects of language: Toward a dynamic psycholinguistics. *New Ideas in Psychology, 26,* 193–207. http://dx.doi.org/10.1016/j.newideapsych.2007.07.003

Raimondi, V. (2014). Social interaction, languaging and the operational conditions for the emergence of observing. *Frontiers in Psychology, 5,* 899. http://dx.doi.org/10.3389/fpsyg.2014.00899

Saffran, J. R. (2009). What is statistical learning, and what statistical learning is not. In S. Johnson (Ed.), *Neuroconstructivism: The new science of cognitive development* (pp. 180–194). http://dx.doi.org/10.1093/acprof:oso/9780195331059.003.0009

Schmid, H.-J. (2014). Lexico-grammatical patterns, pragmatic associations and discourse frequency. In T. Herbst, H.-J. Schmid, & S. Faulhaber (Eds.), *Constructions collocations patterns* (pp. 239–293). Berlin, Germany: de Gruyter.

Shapiro, L. (2010). *Embodied cognition.* London, England: Routledge.

Sinclair, J. M., & Mauranen, A. (2006). *Linear unit grammar: Integrating speech and writing.* http://dx.doi.org/10.1075/scl.25

Skinner, B. F. (1957). *Verbal behavior.* East Norwalk, CT: Appleton-Century-Crofts. http://dx.doi.org/10.1037/11256-000

Stanford, J. N., & Kenny, L. A. (2013). Revisiting transmission and diffusion: An agent-based model of vowel chain shifts across large communities. *Language Variation and Change, 25,* 119–153. http://dx.doi.org/10.1017/S0954394513000069

Steels, L., & Belpaeme, T. (2005). Coordinating perceptually grounded categories through language: A case study for colour. *Behavioral and Brain Sciences, 28,* 469–489. http://dx.doi.org/10.1017/S0140525X05000087

Steels, L., & De Beule, J. (2006). Unify and merge in fluid construction grammar. In P. Vogt, Y. Sugita, E. Tuci, & C. Nehaniv (Eds.), *Symbol grounding and beyond* (pp. 197–223). http://dx.doi.org/10.1007/11880172_16

Tomasello, M. (2003). *Constructing a language: A usage-based theory of language acquisition.* Cambridge, MA: Harvard University Press.

Varela, F. (1979). *Principles of biological autonomy.* Dordrecht, the Netherlands: Elsevier Science.

Wilson, A. D., & Golonka, S. (2013). Embodied cognition is not what you think it is. *Frontiers in Psychology, 4,* 58. http://dx.doi.org/10.3389/fpsyg.2013.00058

Wittgenstein, L. W. (1980). *On certainty.* Oxford, England: Blackwell.

VI Synopsis

Hans-Jörg Schmid
19 Linguistic Entrenchment and Its Psychological Foundations

19.1 Introduction

The aim of this chapter is to distill the essence of linguistic and psychological aspects of entrenchment. In line with the suggestions made in the Introduction to this volume, this account will be structured in terms of four different types of association—symbolic, syntagmatic, paradigmatic, and pragmatic—which are considered to "represent" linguistic knowledge. For each of these types of association, linguistic evidence for entrenchment processes will be juxtaposed with their psychological substrates.

19.2 Different Conceptions of Entrenchment

The concept of linguistic entrenchment makes sense only within the scope of usage-based frameworks that view linguistic knowledge as emerging from language use. Within such frameworks, however, the process of entrenchment plays a key role in explaining how usage eventually translates into knowledge. A good understanding of entrenchment is therefore of utmost importance for filling the gap between linguistic and other communicative activities in social situations, on the one hand, and the cognitive representations that constitute linguistic knowledge, on the other.

Langacker's view of entrenchment also provides a good starting point for the discussion of different conceptions of this notion. For him, entrenchment relates to neural adjustment processes—mainly Hebbian learning—resulting from prior activity and leading to a strengthening of connectivity. Established patterns of neural activity are *units* (in the technical sense of cognitive grammar), which are defined as "complex neural event[s] with a significant potential for recurrence owing to entrenchment (adjustments in the substrate)" (Langacker, Chapter 2, this volume, Section 2.2). Well-established units are claimed to run largely uncontrolled. It is important to note that for Langacker, language consists of a structured inventory of units, which entails that all knowledge of words, fixed expressions, and variable syntactic schemas owes its existence in the mind of a speaker to the process of entrenchment.

Langacker's account highlights the main facets associated with entrenchment:

- the role of repetition and rehearsal,
- the resulting strengthening and "streamlining" of patterns of neuronal activity,
- the concomitant increase in ease and fluency of processing and composition,
- the resulting potential for the formation of units of different types, and
- the (controversial) relation to the emergence and strengthening of generalized schematic representations.

This set of features can serve as a benchmark to identify the scopes and foci of other conceptions of entrenchment.

Some researchers subscribe to fairly wide definitions of entrenchment: Hilpert and Diessel (Chapter 3, this volume), for example, characterized entrenchment as a domain-general process that strengthens any type of knowledge, including, of course, linguistic knowledge. Having to rely on historical corpus data, De Smet (Chapter 4, this volume) operationalizes entrenchment as frequency. Geeraerts (Chapter 7, this volume) equates entrenchment with onomasiological salience, which is in turn defined as the relative frequency of competing expressions. Other authors favor narrower conceptions: While agreeing with Langacker on the important role of Hebbian learning, MacWhinney (Chapter 15, this volume) recommends that we keep apart entrenchment—understood as "the emergent result of network computation" (Section 15.3)—from chunking. Theakston (Chapter 14, this volume) emphasizes the tension between entrenchment and abstraction, but considers entrenchment essentially as a process that strengthens the representations of fixed strings rather than variable schemas. Thus, for Theakston, entrenchment corresponds closely to the strengthening of chunks; for MacWhinney, chunking is different from entrenchment.

Stefanowitsch and Flach (Chapter 5, this volume) focus on the product of the entrenchment process and define the notion as "the degree to which a linguistic structure of any degree of complexity or schematicity forms an established unit of the mental grammar of a speaker" (Section 5.1). Like Langacker and Hilpert and Diessel, but unlike Theakston and MacWhinney, Stefanowitsch and Flach thus consider variable schemas as being subject to entrenchment processes. Hartsuiker and Moors (Chapter 9, this volume) highlight the ambiguity of the term *entrenchment*, which is used to refer to a predictor (equivalent to repetition and frequency), a process (unit formation), and a product (the unit or the automaticity of processing it). Part of this ambiguity could be resolved if, as suggested by Cowley (Chapter 18, this volume), the term *entrenching* is used to refer to the process, a practice also followed by Cordes (Chapter 12, this volume).

In Chapter 1 (Section 1.5) of this volume, I opted for a wide definition that characterizes entrenchment as a general process of reorganization and adaptation of individual communicative knowledge subject to the exigencies of the social environment. I regard this knowledge as being represented in the form of associations. This definition not only encompasses the elements attributed to entrenchment above—including the emergence and strengthening of schemas—but also makes reference to the social variables that affect neural and cognitive entrenchment processes. Further justification for this decision is given in Sections 19.5.2 and 19.5.3. I now turn to the principal psychological processes considered responsible for linguistic entrenchment.

19.3 Routinization, Automatization, Statistical Learning, and Memory Consolidation

Routinization is a domain-general process resulting from the repetition and rehearsal of activities. Linguistic routinization can affect the four major types of activities involved in the use of language (Schmid, 2015):

1. motor activity required for language production,
2. sensory activity required for the perception of features of contexts and language comprehension,
3. cognitive and neuronal activity required for language processing, and
4. social activity inescapably involved in communication.

The main effects of routinization are increased fluency (i.e., ease), speed, and efficiency in carrying out these activities. In the case of motor activity, routinization shows in the fluency and speed of articulation typically achieved by adult native speakers of a language. The routinization of sensory activity shows in effects like the categorical perception of the phonemes of one's native language and the extremely fast and efficient recognition of frequent words. Examples of routinized social activities include accommodation effects in conversation (Pickering & Garrod, 2004) and the unconscious group-membership allocation of interlocutors on the basis of social clichés and stereotypes. Finally, the routinization of cognitive and neuronal activity leads to the strengthening of patterns of associations in the associative network involved in language processing and the neuronal circuits subserving these patterns. This type of routinization—that is, the routinization of cognitive and neuronal activity—will be in the focus of the more detailed discussion in Section 19.4.

It is often claimed that the routinization of very frequent activities involved in language use contributes to their *automatization* (e.g., Langacker, 1987). As Hartsuiker and Moors (Chapter 9, this volume) showed, however, automaticity is neither a one-dimensional nor an all-or-none characteristic of mental activities. Processes like lexical retrieval, syntactic planning and parsing, and phonological encoding and decoding can be more or less fast and more or less conscious, controlled, and controllable, as well as more or less capacity consuming, depending on a large number of factors over and above rehearsal, repetition, and frequency. This insight is also emphasized in many other contributions to this volume (e.g., those by Cowley; Herdina; MacWhinney; Steinkrauss & Schmid).

In light of this complexity, it seems advisable to refrain from leaping to rash claims concerning the automaticity of the processing of more or less highly routinized linguistic elements or constructions. Instead, it seems mandatory to have a close look at the evidence from all possible sources—psycholinguistics, neurolinguistics, corpus linguistics, historical linguistics, and computational modeling, but also pragmatics and discourse analysis—and to make a differentiation according to levels of linguistic processing, modes of language use, and other variables such as linguistic complexity and, of course, all types of contexts.

Routinization and automatization are subserved by a number of basic psychological and neurological mechanisms. Because the effects of these mechanisms on different types of associations are described in greater detail in Section 19.4, they are explained only in a broad-brush manner here:

- *Hebbian learning and synaptic strengthening*: "The Hebbian principle states that simultaneous (or at least near-simultaneous) activation of multiple neuronal circuits promotes the formation of connections between them" (Takashima & Bakker, Chapter 8, this volume, Section 8.3.1). This strengthening of synaptic connections caused by repeated reactivation contributes to memory consolidation on the microlevel of brain connectivity (see also Langacker, Chapter 2, this volume, and MacWhinney, Chapter 15, this volume).
- *Systems memory consolidation*: On the macrolevel, consolidation takes the form of system consolidation from episodic memory (mainly processed in the hippocampus) to semantic and procedural memory in neocortical areas (Takashima & Bakker, Chapter 8, this volume). Possibly, entrenchment also involves the streamlining of procedural memory resulting in proceduralization, which is one key aspect of automaticity.
- *Statistical learning*: According to Jost and Christiansen (Chapter 10, this volume) statistical learning is a process by which learners implicitly form associations between stimuli by tracking and storing the underlying statistical relationships between such elements. These associations are strengthened by repetition over the course of a person's lifetime as a function of frequency and further variables including meaningfulness, predictability, salience, and resonance.
- *Weight changes and the emergence of attractors in the associative network*: A key effect of these learning processes is that the weights of links and associations in the associative network representing linguistic knowledge change, with repeated associations gaining stronger weights than rarer ones. Strong associations of any type (see Section 19.4 for details) acquire the role of attractors in the network (Langacker, Chapter 2, this volume; Herdina, Chapter 17, this volume), showing a higher "resting level" of activation. They represent the linguistic routines resorted to in default spontaneous language use.

- *Integration, abstraction, and generalization*: A concomitant effect of systems memory consolidation is the integration, abstraction, and generalization of information (Takashima & Bakker, Chapter 8, this volume). Abstraction arises from recognizing analogies between multiple episodes sharing similar characteristics (Cordes, Chapter 12, this volume).

Keeping these general processes in mind, I now turn to a description of the differential effects of entrenchment on the four different types of association.

19.4 Entrenchment as Strengthening of Different Types of Linguistic Associations

As argued in the Introduction to this volume, the multifarious linguistic effects that have been attributed to entrenchment processes can be explained and, where they conflict, reconciled if entrenchment is seen as operating over four different types of association: symbolic, syntagmatic, paradigmatic, and pragmatic. In what follows, I discuss the strengthening of each type of association in turn. In doing so, I relate the various types of linguistic evidence to psychological and neurological processes.

19.4.1 Symbolic Associations

Symbolic associations link forms and meanings of linguistic signs. These associations apply to fixed linguistic elements—that is, words (e.g., *engine*, *walk*) and fixed expressions (e.g., *happy birthday*)—and variable schemas, both low-level ones such as individual affixes (*un*-Adj or V-*ment*) and high-level ones such as argument-structure constructions.

Evidence for a more or less strong entrenchment of symbolic associations comes from a variety of sources, most of which are related to frequency (for details, see the Introduction to this volume). Frequent words and constructions are processed faster and with less effort than less frequent ones. In oral comprehension, simple and frequent words are prime candidates for automatic processing from perceived form to meaning in terms of not only speed but also controllability (we cannot help but understand; see Hartsuiker & Moors, Chapter 9, this volume) and efficiency (it requires no or very little capacity).

In production, especially in the written mode, processing is much less likely to be automatic, in particular when variable and complex schemas are involved. The routinization of symbolic associations has also been claimed to cause some diachronic processes, mainly bleaching (i.e., the expansion of the extension of a word or construction) and meaning diversification (i.e., the addition of new related meanings resulting in increasing polysemy; De Smet, Chapter 4, this volume). The fundamentally skewed frequency distributions of lexical items and grammatical patterns in corpora (e.g., Zipf's law) are also interpreted as indicating that symbolic associations show different strengths of representations (Stefanowitsch & Flach, Chapter 5, this volume). Note, however, that it is very likely that all of these frequency effects are modulated by further factors in addition to frequency (see Section 19.5.1 for more details).

The neurocognitive sources of these effects can be derived from the general account given in Section 19.3. Symbolic associations can become more or less entrenched by means of statistical learning (Jost & Christiansen, Chapter 10, this volume; Saffran, Aslin, & Newport, 1996). The more often a certain form is encountered and used in connection with a certain meaning, the stronger the symbolic association between them, again, of course, subject to many additional factors, including the knowledge of previous words (Takashima & Bakker, Chapter 8, this volume) and the salience (Günther, Müller, & Geyer, Chapter 13, this volume) and resonance (MacWhinney, Chapter 15, this volume) afforded by the cotext, context, and the current state of the associative network itself.

In terms of memory, the early phases of the entrenchment of a new word or expression involve the consolidation from episodic memory centered on the hippocampus to semantic memory in dedicated neocortical areas, with the left posterior middle temporal gyrus serving as a key "association area" involved in lexical learning and integration (Takashima & Bakker, Chapter 8, this volume, Section 8.4.4). Lexical processing, especially in casual conversation, is likely to be highly automatic. This can be explained in terms of an increasing proceduralization (i.e., a shift from semantic to procedural memory).

In production, frequent and contextually relevant words and fixed expressions acquire the role of strong attractors in the associative network. These frequency and recency effects explain why we tend to resort to habitual linguistic routines while encoding recurrent communicative intentions (Schmid, 2014). The subjective impression that words stand for familiar concepts (i.e., stored and hypostatized units of conceptual knowledge) seems to be accounted for very well by these processes.

Whereas the available evidence seems quite robust and convincing for the way lexical knowledge is "represented" in the network, we know much less about the entrenchment of variable schemas, which also unite linguistic forms and meanings by means of symbolic associations. Mainly on the basis of developmental data and experiments manipulating input conditions (Theakston, Chapter 14, this volume) and the observation of diachronic change (De Smet, Chapter 4, this volume), it is generally assumed that the distribution and dispersion of tokens and types affect the tendency for variable schemas to become abstracted by means of an integration of multiple episodes. Experiments reported by Jost and Christiansen (Chapter 10, this volume) suggest that statistical learning can operate over patterns reaching beyond immediately subsequent words and can tolerate a certain degree of variation. This is a fundamental prerequisite for the assumption that more schematic constructions such as argument-structure constructions can be learned and continuously refreshed.

Unlike fixed elements and units, the entrenchment of variable meaning-carrying schemas also requires cooperation of other types of associations, over and above symbolic ones: the strengthening of the syntagmatic associations between the component parts and slots and of the paradigmatic associations linking the elements competing for activation in the variable slots. These routinization processes in turn require the abilities to identify similarities and analogies and abstract over input (Cordes, Chapter 12, this volume). Although it may be possible that, once abstracted and generalized, such schematic symbolic associations can become entrenched in ways very similar to simple elements or repeated lexically filled sequences, to date not much research using adult participants has been done in this field. In large part, this is because of the methodological challenges involved in the systematic and controlled study of variable patterns.

19.4.2 Syntagmatic Associations

Evidence for linguistic effects of the strengthening of syntagmatic associations comes from the existence of phenomena such as collocations and other co-occurrence tendencies like collostructions in corpora (Hilpert & Diessel, Chapter 3, this volume; Stefanowitsch & Flach, Chapter 5, this volume); from diachronic processes such as constructional split, conservatisms, fusion, and phonological reduction (De Smet, Chapter 4, this volume); and from psycholinguistic and neurolinguistic experiments (Blumenthal-Dramé, Chapter 6, this volume). The catchword frequently used to describe these processes is of course *chunking*—the facet perhaps most strongly associated with entrenchment in the minds of many researchers in the field.

The discussion of chunking in many contributions to this volume has demonstrated that it is in fact quite a risky term. For one thing, it is used in a systematically ambiguous way to refer to three different phenomena: (a) the psychological process of grouping information (explained in Gobet, Chapter 11, this volume), (b) linguistic grouping tendencies taking place within the lifetime of an individual (e.g., in language learning; see Theakston, Chapter 14; and MacWhinney, Chapter 15, this volume), and (c) the long-term collective processes bringing about the types of language change mentioned above (e.g., constructional split; phonological, morphological, and orthographic fusion; loss of compositionality; De Smet, Chapter 4, this volume).

Second, as pointed out by MacWhinney, the understanding of chunking as the strengthening of syntagmatic associations must not be confused with the phenomenon of wholesale *chunk extraction*, the process responsible for the existence of a lot of fixed expressions such as idioms, proverbs, and winged words. In the case of chunking, what was a sequence of individual items gradually merges into a more or less holistic unit (e.g., *and so on, the thing is, you know what I mean*), whereas in chunk extraction, a sequence of items (e.g., *don't judge a book by its cover*) is grabbed wholesale and acquires new meanings and functions because of its use in new cotexts and contexts.

Third, the notions of *chunking* and *chunk* suggest the existence of one holistic unit that is accessed and retrieved as one piece of information, thus barring, or at least impeding, access to its components parts. Although such a scenario seems plausible for totally opaque compounds like *daisy* (*day's eye*) or linking words (e.g., *nevertheless, however, anyway*), it is much more controversial for less strongly chunked items such as *get carried away with* or *by means of*. Whether or not a more or less fixed sequence is indeed processed as one unit of information is thus much less clear than it may seem (see Blumenthal-Dramé, Chapter 6, this volume).

What, then, are the psychological and neurological processes involved in the strengthening of syntagmatic associations? As suggested by Gobet (Chapter 11, this volume) and Jost and Christiansen (Chapter 10, this volume), linguistic chunking effects are best traced back to automatic—as opposed to deliberate—grouping based on implicit statistical learning. From a psychological point of view, chunking is thus a perceptual and conceptual information grouping process facilitated by tracking transitional probabilities between frequently co-occurring elements in running speech or text. As pointed out above, these co-occurring elements do not have to be immediately adjacent in the speech stream, thus opening up the possibility of strengthened syntagmatic associations between elements occurring repeatedly within a certain span and, eventually, also variable schemas. As before, the general disclaimer that frequency tracking is flanked by other predictors of chunking effects applies here as well.

In terms of the association model proposed here, chunking is explained as the strengthening of syntagmatic associations between the components of recurrent sequences of items. In the course of this process, the whole sequence can begin to acquire a symbolic association of its own, while the symbolic associations of the components parts and their paradigmatic relations to competitors weaken to a point where they are lost. Lexicalized compounds exhibiting partly idiomatic meanings such as *fire engine* ('a large vehicle that carries material for putting out a fire') and *firework* ('a small object containing explosive material') are cases in point. This scenario seems compatible with the computational models of associative networks described by Gobet (Chapter 11, this volume) and MacWhinney (Chapter 15, this volume). Increasing weights of syntagmatic links go hand in hand with decreasing weights of symbolic and paradigmatic links.

One open question in this field is whether highly predictable sequences can be considered as holistic units or are simply marked by extremely strong syntagmatic associations (Blumenthal-Dramé, Chapter 6, and Gobet, Chapter 11, this volume). Although the holistic model is certainly convincing for the *daisy* case described above, which is no longer able to be decomposed and therefore does not invoke any internal syntagmatic associations, and also for the process of chunk extraction described by MacWhinney (Chapter 15, this volume), the evidence on more transparent and compositional groups reported by Blumenthal-Dramé (Chapter 6, this volume) is less conclusive. As pointed out by Hartsuiker and Moors (Chapter 9, this volume), the processing of highly frequent chunklike sequences seems to meet a number of the criteria associated with automaticity. The proceduralization effected by frequent repetition contributes to a largely uncontrolled and highly efficient processing of the later parts of a composite expression. The phonological symptoms of the strengthening of syntagmatic associations—phonological reduction and fusion—are caused not only by faster cognitive processing, but also by increasing routinization of the articulatory gestures required for pronunciation (Langacker, Chapter 2, this volume).

19.4.3 Paradigmatic Associations

Paradigmatic associations supply the substrate of paradigmatic choices on all linguistic levels, from phonemes, morphemes, and lexemes to discourse moves. What is more, in cooperation with syntagmatic and pragmatic associations, paradigmatic associations subserve the linguistic knowledge of all grammatical categories, including inflectional morphemes, word classes, and phrasal and syntactic structures, as well as schematic constructions involving variable slots. All these categories rely on the availability of paradigmatic associations between forms and meanings competing for occurrence in a given slot opened up by syntagmatic or pragmatic associations.

The key psychological mechanisms responsible for the processing and routinization of paradigmatic associations are analogy, abstraction and generalization, and categorization (Cordes, Chapter 12, this volume). All of these processes rely on the recognition of concrete or relational similarities between options in a given environment. Crucially, identity relations do not give rise to the emergence of paradigmatic associations, which is why token repetition does not contribute to the emergence of variable schemas in children and adults.

By definition, paradigmatic associations must rely on memory-based information resulting from prior processing experience. This is because competition can come into play only when there is a selection from at least two alternative ways of encoding a communicative intention (see Günther, 2016). If this is the case, then the available paradigmatic competitors can be activated from semantic memory by means of paradigmatic associations. The activation potential of these associations is determined both by their general strength in the network (i.e., their frequency-based onomasiological salience; see Geerearts, Chapter 7, this volume) and by the recency and priming effects exerted by the processing of prior linguistic cotext (i.e., syntagmatic associations) and situational context (i.e., pragmatic associations).

This insight has strong repercussions on our understanding of the entrenchment of symbolic associations: The context-free entrenchment of any given symbolic association—which could be approximated by counting raw frequencies of words and constructions (Stefanowitsch & Flach, Chapter 5, this volume)—is inevitably superseded in online processing by cotextual entrenchment and contextual entrenchment (Schmid & Küchenhoff, 2013; see Section 19.5.1 for more details).

Elements that stand out among the potential competitors in a given syntagmatically or pragmatically defined selection situation are salient (Günther, Müller, & Geyer, Chapter 13, this volume). It is especially from such a perspective that entrenchment can be conceptualized and operationalized as onomasiological salience (Geeraerts, Chapter 7, this volume), that is, as the relative frequency with which a given form is associated with a given meaning. According to this view, forms that are more frequently used to denote a given meaning acquire stronger weights in the network and therefore win out against weaker forms when it comes to the activation of symbolic associations.

19.4.4 Pragmatic Associations

Although context-dependent by definition, pragmatic associations have a central role to play in the emergence of linguistic knowledge in usage-based approaches (Schmid, 2014). The reason is that pragmatic associations mediate between the activation of linguistic forms and meanings based on the other types of associations in the service of current communicative intentions, on the one hand, and the perception of physical and social aspects of the current communication situation, on the other. In this way pragmatic associations have a very strong priming effect on the activation of symbolic, syntagmatic, and paradigmatic associations and the resulting selection of linguistic forms and meanings. In addition, in terms of entrenchment, traces of pragmatic associations can also become routinized and sedimented in the other types of associations. This way situational characteristics of past processing events can eventually become part of linguistic knowledge.

Evidence for this effect can be found in many linguistic phenomena: the social dynamics of language change, as well as semantic change triggered by invited inference and pragmatic strengthening (De Smet, Chapter 4, this volume); the dynamics of the connotations and ultimately denotations of words, expressions, and even schematic constructions depending on frequent user groups and usage situations (e.g., the replacement of the meaning of *gay* as 'happy, cheerful' by 'homosexual'); the sensitivity of speakers for situationally appropriate use of language, such as style and register awareness (Schmid, 2014); the ability of speakers to assess social characteristics of interlocutors, such as education and regional background, on the basis of their linguistic choices; and, of course, the effects of the immediate situational environment on the choice of referential language (i.e., deixis). All these aspects of linguistic knowledge and language use require that language users are able to not only take in information about usage situations (e.g., interlocutors, setting, objects) while processing language but also store traces of this information by routinizing these associations to some extent.

The way in which pragmatic associations work and ultimately affect entrenchment is subject to the psychological processes of perception and attention and to the salience effects they bring about (Günther, Müller, & Geyer, Chapter 13, this volume).

The complex link between different types of salience and entrenchment is best understood in terms of a feedback loop (Günther, 2016) accounting for the reciprocal effects of high salience of stimuli on intensity of processing and of strong entrenchment on likelihood of activation. In such a framework, *salience* can be defined as

> a multidimensional set of processes which effect that cognitively represented information (variably originating from sensory input or long-term memory) becomes selected for current processing by a particular individual at a particular point in time in a particular constellation of external (social and situational) and internal (cognitive) contexts. (Günther, Müller, & Geyer, Chapter 13, this volume, Section 13.3.2)

Context, as mediated by pragmatic associations, of course also strongly affects unit formation (Langacker, Chapter 2, this volume), memory consolidation, and the automaticity of processing. Because of its unpredictability, it is the prime confounding variable when it comes to predicting pathways of entrenchment (Cowley, Chapter 18; and Herdina, Chapter 17, this volume). As far as memory is concerned, the sedimentation of pragmatic associations described above could in principle be explained in two ways. First, it could be possible that semantic memory is able to reactivate traces of episodic information. Although this was in fact predicted by early versions of the multiple trace theory of lexical memory by Moscovitch et al. (2005), later versions of the theory are less supportive of this idea (Takashima & Bakker, Chapter 8, this volume).

This leaves the second option: the claim that semantic memory retains quite specific information about prior processing events. This is in fact what Takashima and Bakker (Chapter 8, this volume) concluded with regard to the role of memory in entrenchment: "From the point of view of memory research, entrenchment can therefore be seen as the transformation of the episodic features of linguistic experiences into semanticized lexical and grammatical knowledge" (Section 8.5). Importantly, this conclusion not only applies to the consolidation of lexical knowledge but also encompasses the integration and generalization processes required for variable schemas. It thus opens up the possibility that contextual information about previous processing episodes does not have to be stored in the form of myriads of individual exemplar representations (i.e., a massive "cloud") but can be retained in the distilled form of rich symbolic associations activated from semantic memory. The insight that automatization, categorization, and category learning are strongly determined by context—and thus pragmatic associations—was also emphasized by Hartsuiker and Moors (Chapter 9, this volume), Cordes (Chapter 12, this volume), and Ramscar and Port (2015).

19.4.5 Interim Summary

I have argued that entrenchment should be regarded as operating over different types of associations. This idea is supported, or at least found fruitful as a starting point, in some of the contributions to this volume (e.g., those by Cordes; De Smet; Hilpert &

Diessel; and Herdina). The main advantage of this approach is that it affords a differentiated perspective on the ways in which memory consolidation, learning, proceduralization, and automatization affect the emergence and consolidation of linguistic knowledge. The association-based view of entrenchment is also compatible with the discussions of first-language acquisition (see Theakston, Chapter 14, this volume), second-language learning (MacWhinney, Chapter 15, this volume), and language attrition (Steinkrauss & Schmid, Chapter 16, this volume).

19.5 Challenges and Controversies

The previous sections highlighted some of the major links between linguistic phenomena that have been connected to or explained by entrenchment processes and their psychological underpinnings. I now turn to the main challenges and controversies that have emerged from the present volume.

19.5.1 Role of Frequency and Lack of Predictability of Pathways of Entrenchment

Although there can be little doubt that repeated processing and frequency of exposure are the main predictors of entrenchment, many issues revolving around frequency are still unresolved (see also Divjak & Caldwell-Harris, 2015). I single out three of these issues for a brief discussion.

First, what is to count as *frequency*? In the contributions to this volume by Stefanowitsch and Flach (Chapter 5), Hilpert and Diessel (Chapter 3), Geeraerts (Chapter 7), and others, it is emphasized that raw frequency counts in corpora do not constitute a very useful approximation to the effects of repetition on entrenchment. The only exception mentioned by Stefanowitsch and Flach could be counts of fixed units and strings, but even here the effects of the frequencies of elements in direct onomasiological competition should not be underestimated (Geeraerts, Chapter 7, this volume; Schmid & Küchenhoff, 2013). As soon as what is to be counted is variable, simple frequency-based measures are prone to be misleading and should be replaced by probability-based measures (e.g., transitional probability, cue availability) or statistical measures derived from contingency tests (e.g., the G^2 of the log-likelihood test). In fact, to do justice to the competition between symbolic, syntagmatic, paradigmatic, and pragmatic associations, even more sophisticated measures currently under debate (see Gries, 2012, 2015; Küchenhoff & Schmid, 2015; Schmid & Küchenhoff, 2013) that keep track of the dispersion of potential competitors and their frequencies may be required.

A potentially mundane but methodologically very important side issue is the way in which the exact formal and semantic properties of variable schemas are to be determined. Such operationalization problems are one main reason why the entrenchment of variable schemas has been researched much less intensively than that of simple elements and fixed strings and is also much less well understood (see Blumenthal-Dramé, Chapter 6; Stefanowitsch & Flach, Chapter 5; and Theakston, Chapter 14, this volume).

Second, how does frequency come about in the first place? This question takes center stage in the contributions to this volume by Herdina (Chapter 17) and Cowley (Chapter 18), who emphasize the shortcomings of using discourse frequency (e.g., as measured by frequency of occurrence in corpora) as a proxy for entrenchment. Both authors stress the importance of the contexts behind frequency counts. In addition, Cowley declares that measuring *entrenchment* in terms of frequencies must not be confused with *entrenching* as an ongoing process performed by human agents. In a similar vein, Geeraerts (Chapter 7, this volume) points to the danger of circularity involved in conceptions of entrenchment that do not try to transcend the feedback loop linking increased frequency and increased entrenchment. For him, the main ways out this "infinite regress"—the more frequent, the more entrenched; the more entrenched, the more frequent; and so on—are understanding entrenchment as competition between alternatives and actively embracing the sociocommunicative side of entrenchment. In my own attempt to come to grips with this issue (Schmid, 2015), I propose to separate effects of frequency and repetition on the cognitive system of individuals (i.e., entrenchment) from those on the social systems of collectives (i.e., conventionalization).

Third, what are the limits of the predictive power of frequency for entrenchment? This question was a running theme in many contributions to this volume. In short, the upshot is that we should have little trust in the potential of frequency to serve as an exclusive predictor of entrenchment because likely covariables are numerous and potentially powerful. These copredictors vary in their forces and effects not only between speakers but also as a function of the properties of linguistic structures and situational and social parameters. Speaker-related variables include the status ante quo of the associative network of an individual processing a given linguistic structure (determined by, among other things, age and individual linguistic experience), as well as general cognitive abilities such as attention span, capacity of working memory, and ability for statistical learning. Language-related factors include the level and complexity of linguistic elements and structures to be entrenched and the typological properties of the language. Situational and social variables affecting entrenchment are particularly varied and therefore difficult to control. They include all parameters of linguistic cotexts and situational contexts of prior events of processing identical or similar linguistic structures, the structures and densities of social networks, degrees of the meaningfulness and communicative utility of linguistic structures and patterns, and degrees of cognitive and affective resonance for individuals.

Although there is little doubt that all these factors affect the time courses and depths of entrenchment processes, it remains unclear to what extent they have a direct impact on entrenchment or only modulate frequency effects, which in turn remain the main determinant. And although many researchers would presumably agree with proponents of complex adaptive theories (see Herdina, Chapter 17, this volume) that frequency has neither a linear effect on entrenchment nor a simple logarithmic one, but is instead subject to unpredictable influences and ad hoc effects, the challenge of how to do justice to this complexity methodologically has also remained unanswered so far.

19.5.2 Role of Schemas

As I have pointed out, researchers are divided over the question of whether abstraction, generalization, categorization, and schema formation are to be included within the scope of the notion of entrenchment or better pitched against it. In the field of language acquisition, for example, there is a strong tradition of separating entrenchment from schema formation (see Theakston, Chapter 14, this volume), mainly because explanations of overgeneralization phenomena require keeping apart the effects of fixed-string strengthening and the acquisition and productive application of variable schemas. In contrast, Langacker's (Chapter 2, this volume) current position, summarized above, allows for including the emergence of schemas as a part of entrenching. This is supported by other contributors to this volume (e.g., Blumenthal-Dramé; Cordes; Stefanowitsch & Flach; Hilpert & Diessel) and, perhaps most forcefully, by myself in the introductory chapter. The question is whether the psychological evidence collected in this volume can help arbitrate between the two positions. If the two processes were based on the same or highly similar cognitive mechanisms, and if they were intertwined to such an extent that it turns out to be impossible to keep them apart, this would speak in favor of allowing the notion of entrenchment to encompass schema formation.

In fact, there seems to be some evidence in favor of a wide view of entrenchment. Theakston herself (Chapter 14, this volume) states that it is very difficult to disentangle the interplay of entrenchment and abstraction in language acquisition because the way in which children proceed from chunks to schemas still is not well understood. Jost and Christiansen (Chapter 10, this volume) point out that the general mechanism of statistical learning seems to operate not only over fixed sequences of immediately neighboring elements but also over variable and discontinuous patterns. According to Takashima and Bakker (Chapter 8, this volume), memory consolidation is facilitated and sped up if newly incoming information can be related to a schema representing coherent pieces of available knowledge. What's more, the very process of systems memory consolidation (i.e., the transfer of episodic to semantic memory) requires the abstraction of information from individual episodes to a more schematic form of retention. This entails that the strengthening of traces of prior processing episodes is invariably accompanied by a generalization process resulting in the formation of a schema. In fact, as argued by Cordes (Chapter 12, this volume) and Takashima and Bakker (Chapter 8, this volume), it is very likely that the recognition that incoming stimuli are similar or identical to previously experienced ones rests on the availability of an existing category or schema generalized after exposure to a very small number of episodes.

These observations seem to indicate that the emergence and strengthening of schemas is an inevitable corollary of fundamental and undisputed entrenchment mechanisms such as statistical and Hebbian learning, as well as systems memory consolidation and proceduralization. They thus speak in favor of integrating schema formation within the purview of entrenchment. What remains unclear, however, is how the system reacts to linguistic processing events that have the potential to refresh more or less fixed and more or less variable representations that can license them—which presumably constitute the vast majority of processing events. For example, will the receptive processing of the expression "he's driving me crazy" (Stefanowitsch & Flach, Chapter 5, this volume) contribute to the entrenchment of the fixed sequence 'he's driving me crazy,' of the semifixed pattern 'X is driving Y crazy,' of the highly schematic resultative construction 'X verbs Y resultant state,' of a schema on an intermediate level, or of all of these "representations" to various degrees, depending on other factors? Although Blumenthal-Dramé (Chapter 6, this volume) suggested a number of ways of how these effects could be teased apart, these await implementation. The associative framework of entrenchment suggested in the Introduction and in Section 19.4 does go some way toward modeling the competition between different types of association, but it is certainly also far from being able to cope with this methodological challenge.

19.5.3 Differential Effects of Entrenchment on Different Linguistic Levels and Modes

A final largely unresolved issue concerns the question of whether entrenchment processes work in similar ways across different linguistic levels—from phonetics and phonology to morphology, lexis, syntax, and discourse—and across different modes (i.e., written, spoken, and signed production and comprehension). The differentiated discussion offered by Hartsuiker and Moors (Chapter 9, this volume) certainly indicates that the different features associated with automaticity do not apply the same way across linguistic levels and modes. This may have important implications for our understanding of the links between entrenchment, memory, and automaticity, as well as salience. Because systematic research into this issue does not seem to be available so far (see the Introduction to this volume for some references), it appears to be legitimate to offer some general deliberations.

To begin with, categorical perception of phonemes and access to frequent lexical items in auditory and visual comprehension are among the best candidates for fast, uncontrolled, uncontrollable, and efficient processing. This would mean that these types of processing are highly automatic, do not reach consciousness, and are therefore extremely unlikely to be salient (in the sense of being likely to catch attention). This, in turn, raises the question of whether such strongly entrenched associations are still refreshed by repetition, and whether they are in need of being refreshed in the first place or are, instead, so strongly entrenched that they will not disentrench even if they are not continuously re-entrenched. The evidence from language attrition (Steinkrauss & Schmid, Chapter 16, this volume) suggests that refreshment is needed at least in cases in which one language enters into competition with another one that is used more frequently by the same speaker.

An opposing scenario is constituted by the composition of complex syntactic structures in written production, which is very unlikely to be "automatic" in any of the senses of this term. Instead, it requires a lot of conscious processing effort and thus reaches a high level of salience. Does this mean that the structures involved in such situations are more likely to become entrenched? Intuition clearly goes against such a conclusion, because even a lot of practice does not turn elaborate written production into an effortless task, which would be expected if entrenchment is supposed to lead to ease of processing. The reason why higher salience and conscious attention do not translate into deeper entrenchment presumably lies in the much lower degree of repetitiveness of elaborate written production. Most writers do of course avail themselves of their favorite (i.e., entrenched) linguistic moves and patterns, but norms of written style demand a more variable and versatile use of language. Professional writers such as journalists may in fact stand out by two characteristics: (a) their ability to take fast and efficient recourse to a much wider range of entrenched routines than lay writers and (b) their more strongly entrenched associations representing linguistic structures typical of written news-media style. This highlights the social dimension of entrenchment.

Articulatory phonetics in spoken production seems to be yet another good candidate for automatic language processing based on entrenched routines. However, the status of the routines of our articulatory gestures seems to differ considerably from the routines subserving symbolic units such as words and schemas. Although there is little doubt that articulatory routines shape and change both the speech patterns of individuals and the phonological properties of items on the macrolevel of the speech community, it is unlikely that the psychological processes contributing to these effects are the same as those responsible for the entrenchment of lexical, morphological, and syntactic items and schemas.

Finally, coming back to the question of the effects of processing episodes on the strengthening of associations on different levels of abstraction, which was addressed at the end of the previous section, it seems that entrenchment could well be subject to considerable individual differences. Speakers may differ with regard to their propensity to entrench lexically fixed sequences or variable schemas. Because people differ in terms of their working memory capacities and statistical learning abilities, what suits one speaker may be less helpful for another. This would indicate that one and the same expression may be processed and entrenched in a more "lexical" format (i.e., as a chunklike unit) by one speaker and in a more "syntactic" format (i.e., as a variable schema) by another.

19.6 Conclusion

The aim of this volume was to bring together views of the nature of linguistic knowledge and linguistic learning from usage-based linguistics and cognitive psychology. The notion of linguistic entrenchment and the traditional conception of its cognitive underpinnings in terms of strengthening, chunking, and unit formation have provided the starting point for engaging in a more thorough dialogue between linguistics and psychology.

As this synopsis has demonstrated, both sides have a lot to gain from such a dialogue. Usage-based linguists have been offered an opportunity to learn more about psychological processes and mechanisms—neural strengthening, memory consolidation, automatization, proceduralization, chunking, attention, salience, abstraction, and generalization—that many of them routinely invoke in their descriptions and explanations of language structure and change. Cognitive psychologists have been given an opportunity to realize that the study of language has a lot to offer to them if they accept that language is subject to the same domain-general mechanisms as other cognitive abilities. In addition, they have had a chance to become familiar with the rather more differentiated and fine-grained view of linguistic elements and structures prevalent in linguistics and with some of the methodological tools linguists make use of. In view of the large number of open questions identified in the contributions to this volume and in the synopsis in this chapter, it is to be hoped that the two fields of inquiry will continue to join forces in interdisciplinary cooperation and step up efforts to increase opportunities for young researchers to feel at home on the boundary between linguistics and psychology.

References

Divjak, D., & Caldwell-Harris, C. L. (2015). Frequency and entrenchment. In E. Dąbrowska & D. Divjak (Eds.), *Handbook of cognitive linguistics* (pp. 53–75). http://dx.doi.org/10.1515/9783110292022-004

Gries, S. T. (2012). Frequencies, probabilities, and association measures in usage-/exemplar-based linguistics: Some necessary clarifications. *Studies in Language*, 36, 477–510. http://dx.doi.org/10.1075/sl.36.3.02gri

Gries, S. T. (2015). More (old and new) misunderstandings of collostructional analysis: On Schmid & Küchenhoff (2013). *Cognitive Linguistics*, 26, 505–536. http://dx.doi.org/10.1515/cog-2014-0092

Günther, F. (2016). *Constructions in cognitive context: Why individuals matter in linguistic relativity research*. Berlin, Germany: de Gruyter Mouton.

Küchenhoff, H., & Schmid, H.-J. (2015). Reply to "More (old and new) misunderstandings of collostructional analysis: On Schmid & Küchenhoff" by Stefan T. Gries. *Cognitive Linguistics, 26*, 537–547. http://dx.doi.org/10.1515/cog-2015-0053

Langacker, R. W. (1987). *Foundations of cognitive grammar: Vol. 1. Theoretical prerequisites*. Stanford, CA: Stanford University Press.

Moscovitch, M., Rosenbaum, R. S., Gilboa, A., Addis, D. R., Westmacott, R., Grady, C., . . . Nadel, L. (2005). Functional neuroanatomy of remote episodic, semantic and spatial memory: A unified account based on multiple trace theory. *Journal of Anatomy, 207*, 35–66. http://dx.doi.org/10.1111/j.1469-7580.2005.00421.x

Pickering, M. J., & Garrod, S. (2004). Toward a mechanistic psychology of dialogue. *Behavioral and Brain Sciences, 27*, 169–190. http://dx.doi.org/10.1017/S0140525X04000056

Ramscar, M., & Port, R. (2015). Categorization (without categories). In E. Dąbrowska & D. Divjak (Eds.), *Handbook of cognitive linguistics* (pp. 75–99). Berlin, Germany: de Gruyter Mouton.

Saffran, J. R., Aslin, R. N., & Newport, E. L. (1996). Statistical learning by 8-month-old infants. *Science, 274*, 1926–1928. http://dx.doi.org/10.1126/science.274.5294.1926

Schmid, H.-J. (2014). Lexico-grammatical patterns, pragmatic associations and discourse frequency. In T. Herbst, H.-J. Schmid, & S. Faulhaber (Eds.), *Constructions collocations patterns* (pp. 239–293). http://dx.doi.org/10.1515/9783110356854.239

Schmid, H.-J. (2015). A blueprint of the entrenchment-and-conventionalization model. *Yearbook of the German Cognitive Linguistics Association, 3*, 1–27. http://dx.doi.org/10.1515/gcla-2015-0002

Schmid, H.-J., & Küchenhoff, H. (2013). Collostructional analysis and other ways of measuring lexico-grammatical attraction: Theoretical premises, practical problems and cognitive underpinnings. *Cognitive Linguistics, 24*, 531–577. http://dx.doi.org/10.1515/cog-2013-0018

Index

Abbot-Smith, K., 278, 320–321
Absolute frequency, 394
Abstract expressions, 120
Abstraction
– and automatization/routinization, 439
– in entrenchment, 3, 436
– in language used by children, 317
– lexical frames in, 318–321
– and paradigmatic associations, 443
– with prototypes, 277
– and token frequency, 322–323
– and type frequency, 14
Abstract levels of representation, in experimental perspective, 142–145
Abstract morphosyntactic patterns, collocations and, 62
Accommodation, 19, 23
Action(s)
– chunks as conditions of, 258
– dialogue as joint, 217
– perception and, 291–292, 409–410
Activation
– co-, 47–48, 53
– interactive models of, 139
– of linguistic units, 45–49
– memory trace reactivation, 183–185
– of neural system, 192
– schema, 143–145
Activation threshold, 372
Actual category member, prototype as, 277
Adaptation, 19, 23, 42, 43
Adjacent dependencies, 231, 236–237
Adjective–noun combinations
– frequency-based measures of, 110–111
– probability-based measures of, 111–115
– statistical measures of, 115–116
Adults
– language learning for children vs., 349–351
– linguistic corpora for, 103, 104
– second-language learning by, 345, 347
– sleep and grammar learning for, 190
– statistical learning for, 234–236
Affixes
– complexity and schematicity of, 107
– in construction grammar model, 68–69
– usage intensity of words containing, 109–110

Affordances, 421
Age. See also Unified Competition Model (UCM)
– as determinant of entrenchment, 21, 345
– and language attrition, 370
– and language learning, 343–345
Agent models of entrenching
– limitations on, 421–426
– social context in, 419–421
Agreement, 211–212
Alignment, 19, 23
Allen, K. V., 211
Alliterative patterns, 398
Allophones, conditioned, 43
Alphabet recitation, 255
Alzheimer's dementia, 180
Ambiguity, structural, 201–202
Ambridge, B., 14, 66, 326, 332
Amnesia, 179, 181–182
Amso, D., 234
Analogical leveling, 76, 86
Analogy(-ies)
– in entrenchment, 3, 270, 283–284
– and exemplar model, 54
– formation of, 270–275
– in language learning, 279–281
– paradigmatic, 92–93
– and paradigmatic associations, 443
Analytic learners, 146
Analyzability, in cognitive grammar model, 43
Anchoring, 397–398
Anderson, J. R., 218–219
Anderson, R. W., 376–378
Animals
– action and perception by, 409–410
– entrenchment for, 426
– functional information for robots/artificial agents vs., 419, 421
– recognition by artificial agents and humans vs., 424
Anterograde amnesia, 179, 181–182
Apprehension, of targets, 45–47
Argument-structure errors, 326–327, 332–333
Aristotelian theory of categories, 276
Arnon, I., 135, 136, 219, 416–418, 426
Articles, 88–89, 398
Articulation, 105n1, 346, 352

Articulatory phonetics, 450
Artificial agents. *See also* Robots
– modeling entrenching with, 419–421
– use of functional information by, 423
– value of entrenching for, 426
Artificial-language learning, frequency effects in, 325–326
As good as, 87–88
Aslin, R. N., 227–228, 259
Assemblies, 39, 44, 53
Association areas, 191
Associative network, 438
Attention, 3, 206, 289
Attractors
– and automatization/routinization, 438
– in categorization, 278
– in dynamic complexity theory, 404–405
– and frequency effects, 16, 18
– linguistic units as, 41
– and symbolic associations, 440
Attributional metaphors, 273–274
Attrition, language. *See* Language attrition
Audition
– entrenchment effects in, 346–347, 351–352
– statistical learning in, 230, 232
Auditory feedback, 214–215
Autobiographical memory, 183
Automatic chunking, 251, 255–260
Automaticity of language processing, 201–222
– classic view of, 204–206
– and classic view of automaticity, 203
– contemporary view of, 208–217
– and contemporary view of automaticity, 206–207
– factors influencing automatization, 217–218
– future research directions, 221–222
– for language comprehension vs. production, 220–221
– and language processing framework, 202–203
– mechanisms underlying automatization, 218–220
– and psychological foundations of entrenchment, 22–23
Automatic processes, 203, 228
Automatization, 4
– elements of entrenchment in, 10
– factors influencing, 217–218
– in integrated entrenchment model, 23, 437–439

– and language change, 15
– and linguistic units, 41
– mechanisms underlying, 218–220
– repetition effects in, 19

Baayen, R. H., 61, 136
BAD lexeme, suppletion with, 93, 94
Bakema, P., 158
Bakker, I., 188
Baldinger, Kurt, 155
Balkenius, C., 214–215
Bannard, C., 135
Barkhuysen, P. N., 211
Basal ganglia, 357
Base rate problem, 394
Basic-level model, 162–164
Basser, L. S., 344
Bateson, G., 412
Behrens, H., 320–321
Belapeme, T., 418, 421
BE lexeme, suppletion with, 93
Belpaeme, T., 418
Bennett, M. R., 416
Berant, J., 139–140, 146
Berlin, B., 276
Bertalanffy, L., 405
Bilalic, M., 250
Bilingual advantage, 379
Bilingualism, language attrition and, 369
Bilingual mode, 373
Birch, H. G., 249
Birdsong, D., 345
Bistable precept, 246
Blank, Andreas, 166
Bleaching, 15, 80–83, 392, 439
Bleys, J., 418
Blocking, 49
Blood oxygen–level dependent (BOLD) signals, 135, 137, 140–141
Blumenthal-Dramé, A., 21, 23, 122, 137, 140–141
BNC. *See* British National Corpus
Bock, K., 210, 211
Bod, R., 135
BOLD signals. *See* Blood oxygen–level dependent signals
Booji, G., 67
Booth, J. R., 343
Bootzin, R. R., 189
Borges, Jorge Luis, 275

Borovsky, A., 188
Bottom-up salience, 290–292, 304
Bounded frequency, 394–395
Bounded rationality, 260
Bowerman, M., 65, 316, 317
Bowers, J. S., 187
Boyd, J. K., 66
Brain. *See also specific structures*
– in cognitivist view of entrenching, 416–419
– linguistic processing areas in, 351–352
– memory systems in, 178–180
– and perception of language, 415
– plasticity of, 343–345, 348–349
Braine, M. D. S., 316, 317
Braun, C., 291
Breidegard, B., 214–215
Bresnan, J., 61
British National Corpus (BNC), 104, 108–114, 117, 121
Brooks, P. J., 65
BROWN (A Standard Corpus of Present-Day Edited American English), 119, 120
Brown, P., 329
Bühler, Karl, 261
"Building-block" view of semantic construction, 41, 52, 53
Bybee, J. L., 67, 68, 80–81, 89, 132, 141

Caldwell-Harris, C., 139–140, 146
Cameron-Faulkner, T., 316, 331
Campbell, L., 86–87
Can, bleaching of, 80–81
Caplan, D., 205
Capture, of targets, 45, 46
Caramazza, A., 215
Cardinal numbers, 167–168
Carpenter, P. A., 204–205, 211
Casenhiser, D. M., 324
Case system, 86
Catastrophic interference, 348, 351
Categorical identification, 162–164
Categorization
– in cognitive grammar model, 45–49
– in entrenchment of associations, 270, 283–284
– in language learning, 279–281
– and paradigmatic associations, 443
– psychological background on, 275–279
– and type frequency, 14
Central nervous system (CNS), 409–411, 413

Cerebral equipotentiality, 343–344
CG model. *See* Cognitive grammar model
Chang, F., 14
Changes in language. *See* Language change
Chase, W. G., 254, 257, 261
Child Language Data Exchange System (CHILDES), 238
Children. *See also* First-language learning
– analogy, categorization, and generalization for, 281–283
– grammatical errors of, 326–328
– language development for, 343–344
– language learning for adults vs., 349–351
– linguistic corpora for, 103
– overgeneralization errors of, 14, 65–66
– second-language learning for, 343–345
– sleep and grammar learning for, 189–190
– statistical learning for, 234
Chomsky, N., 3, 416, 417n11, 420
Chow, K. L., 250
CHREST (Chunk Hierarchy and REtrieval STructures), 258–262
Christiansen, M. H., 208, 233, 236, 238
Chunk(s)
– defined, 252, 356, 427
– fixed multiword, 17
– and formation of productions, 258
– as holistic units, 442–443
– identifying, 261
Chunk extraction, 356, 441
Chunk Hierarchy and REtrieval STructures (CHREST), 258–262
Chunking, 251–261. *See also* Syntagmatic association
– automatic, 255–260
– and automatization, 219
– and conception of entrenchment, 436
– and context effects, 19–20
– defined, 84
– deliberate, 251–255
– and elements of entrenchment, 10
– in first-language learning, 319
– formalisms from computer science for, 260–261
– and frequency effects, 16–18
– in implicit vs. statistical learning, 229
– and language, 262
– and perception of language, 415
– and psychological foundations of entrenchment, 23

– for schemas, 142
– in second-language learning, 356–357
– and statistical learning, 238–239
Chunking theory, for problem solving, 257–258
Chunk status, 130, 138–141
Claes, J., 170
Clahsen, H., 352
Classic view of automaticity, 203–206
Clay, F., 187
Closed word classes, 119–120
Closure, law of, 246
Cloutier, R., 78
CLS model. *See* Complementary learning systems model
Clustering, lexical, 399
CNS (central nervous system), 409–411, 413
Coactivation, 47–48, 53
Co-adaptation, 19, 23
Coalescence, 16
Coates, J., 81
COCA (Corpus of Contemporary American English), 117
Code-switching, 355, 373, 379
Cognates, 397
Cognition
– in linguistic corpora, 102–104
– in radical embodied cognitive science, 411
– and salience, 297
Cognitive control, 350, 378–379
Cognitive crowding, 344
Cognitive development, experience and, 235
Cognitive-functional linguistics, 50
Cognitive grammar (CG) model, 39–54
– activation of units in, 45–49
– development of units in, 42–44
– linguistic units in, 39–42
– theoretical issues with, 50–54
Cognitive linguistics, 3
– entrenchment in, 129–132
– and language attrition, 367–371
Cognitive modularity theories, 230
Cognitive precedence, 138–139
Cognitive psychology, 245, 289
Cognitive salience, 20, 284, 298
Cognitive sciences, 3, 411, 412. *See also* Radical embodied cognitive science view
Cognitive semantics, 156
Cognitive styles, 146
Cognitivist views of entrenching, 416–419, 423

Collective memory, 420–421
Collective perspective on salience, 303
Collexeme analysis, 63
Collier, J., 412
Collocations
– and chunking, 17–18, 262
– in construction grammar model, 62
– delicacy of, 425
– in first-language learning, 315–318
Collostructional analysis, 62–64
Collostructions, 18, 62–64
Common ground, 216
Competition
– constructional, 170
– in entrenchment model, 154
– and suppletion, 94
– testing memory consolidation with, 187, 188
Competition-model framework, 325. *See also* Unified Competition Model (UCM)
Competitive Chunker, 259
Complementary learning systems (CLS) model
– and grammar learning, 190–191
– lexical learning in, 186–188, 191–192
– memory consolidation in, 177, 182–185
Complex-adaptive models of language, 3, 23
Complex categories, 44
Complex functions, 403–404
Complexity(-ies)
– and automatization, 217–218
– in dynamic complexity theory, 395–396
– of linguistic units, 105–107
Complexity theory, 395–396
Complex linguistic units
– comparing measurements for, 116–117
– frequency-based measurement of, 110–111
– measuring entrenchment of, 110–117
– probability-based measurement of, 111–115
– statistical measurement of, 115–116
Componential analysis, 208
Composition
– ease of, 142
– fluency of, 135–138
Compositionality, loss of, 90
Compression, of information in STM, 252–253
Computational model, 412, 424–425
Computer science formalisms for chunking, 260–261
Conceptual frequency, 158
Conceptual onomasiological profiles, 165

Conceptual onomasiological salience, 157, 161–165, 168–170
Conditional probability, 111, 112
Conditioned allophones, 43
Conjunctions, temporal, 20
Conklin, K., 136
Connectionist models, 70–71, 208, 278
Consciousness, 203, 206, 215, 220
Conservatism, language change and, 86–87
Consolidation, memory. See Memory consolidation
Constraint-based models of sentence comprehension, 218
Construals, 164–165, 299
Constructional competition, 170
Constructional idioms, 107
Constructionalization, frequency effects and, 16
Constructional splits, 85–86
Construction grammar model, 57–71
– collostructions in, 62–64
– described, 57
– and entrenchment in morphological constructions, 67–69
– entrenchment of constructions vs. links in, 70–71
– negative entrenchment in, 66–67
– networks of interlinked constructions in, 58–62
– no negative evidence problem with, 65–66
Constructions, 283
– Children's learning of, 324
– defined, 50
– entrenchment of links vs., 70–71
– in integrated framework for linguistic entrenchment, 25
– onomasiological salience in study of entrenchment of, 168–169
Constructs, 61
Contemporary view of automaticity, 206–217, 221
Context
– and first-language learning, 329–333
– and language attrition, 371–375
– and linguistic entrenchment, 18–20
– and salience, 303
Contextual entrenchment, 121, 169
Control
– in classic view of automaticity, 203
– cognitive, 350, 378–379
– of language comprehension, 209–210

Conventionality, of linguistic units, 46
Conventionalization, 15, 24, 122
Conversational patterns, repetition effects in, 20
Conway, C. M., 233, 236
Cook, A. E., 213
Cordes, A.-K., 280
Core language processes, 221–222
Corpora. See Linguistic corpora
Corpora from the Web, English Version, Release 2014, Slice AXO3 (ENCOW14), 118, 119
Corpus-as-input view, 103
Corpus-as-output view, 102–103
Corpus-based perspective on entrenchment, 101–123
– and cognition in linguistic corpora, 102–104
– complexity and schematicity dimensions in, 106–107
– criticisms of, 120–123
– linguistic corpora and entrenchment in, 104–105
– and measuring entrenchment, 105–120
– usage intensity in, 108–120
Corpus-based research
– collostructions in, 62–64
– frequency effects in, 14–15, 18
– types and tokens in, 390
Corpus frequency, 377
Corpus of Contemporary American English (COCA), 117
Cortical areas, 349
Costa, A., 214
Cotextual entrenchment, 169
Covarying collexeme analysis, 63
Critical period, 21, 343–345
Critical problems, 249
Croft, W., 91n5
Cross-linguistic similarity, 375–378
Cross-mapping tasks, 274
Cue availability, 112–113
Cueni, A., 61
Cue reliability, 111–113
Cue validity, 113
Cuyckens, H., 130

Dąbrowska, E., 146, 317
Dallenbach, K. M., 183
D'Arcy, A., 78
Davidow, J., 234

Davis, C. J., 187
Davis, M. H., 186, 189
DCT. *See* Dynamic complexity theory
Decision making, 421
Decision tasks, 134, 135
Declarative (explicit) memory, 178–179, 183
Decontextualization, 52–53
Decoupling, 354–355
Deep encoding strategies, 180
Degree of entrenchment, 10, 42, 48–49
De Groot, A. D., 257
De Houwer, J., 207
Deliberate chunking, 251–255
Delicacy, 415, 423–425, 427
Delimitation, of linguistic units, 41
Dell, G. S., 210
Dementia, 180
Denison, D., 91
Dennett, D. C., 427
Dense switchers, 379
Dependencies, 231, 235–237
Derivational affixes, 68–69
Derivational splits, 85–86
Derivations, frequency effects for, 13
Derwing, B., 135–136
De Smet, H., 82, 91, 92, 130
Determiners, 88
Deuker, L., 184
DevLex model, 345, 351, 352
Diachronic perspective on entrenchment, 15–16. *See also* Language change
Dialogue, 205, 216–217, 219–221
Di Biase, B., 354
Dice coefficient, 113
Diessel, H., 317
Differentiation, in cognitive grammar model, 44
Digit span task, 254
Dimension-weighting account (DWA), 292–293
Direct approach to categorization, 161–162
Direct memory retrieval mechanism, 218
Discourse, second-language learning, 351
Discourse-focused approaches to cognitive salience, 298
Discourse frequency, 15, 77. *See also* Frequency effects
Discrimination, 256
Discrimination network, 256
Disentrenchment, 370
Disfluencies, in second-language learning, 356–357

Distinctive collexeme analysis, 63
Distractor interference, 292
Distributed cognition models of language, 23
Distributional information, in statistical learning, 228
Distributions, in cognitive grammar model, 53
Ditransitive constructions
– collocations with, 62
– collostructional analysis of, 64
– instance links for, 61
– polysemy links with, 59
– prepositional dative construction vs., 63
– in studies of negative entrenchment, 66
– in studies of no negative evidence problem, 65–66
– subpart links with, 60–62
DIVA model, 351
DOD (double-object dative) construction, 143–144, 331
Dodson, K., 65
Domain-generality of statistical learning, 230–233
Double-object dative (DOD) construction, 143–144, 331
Drift, 376, 396–397
Dumay, N., 187
Duncker, K., 249
Dusseldorp, E., 373
DWA (dimension-weighting account), 292–293
Dynamic complexity theory (DCT), 387–405
– anchoring and priming in, 397–398
– attractors in, 404–405
– complexities in, 395–396
– described, 387
– embeddedness and isolation in, 398–399
– entanglement in, 399–400
– entrenchment and variation in, 396–397
– and frequency as complex function, 403–404
– frequency hypothesis in, 388–395
– language retention and interaction in, 402
– and stability of entrenchment, 400–402
Dynamic usage-based models, 53

Ease of activation, 143–144
Ease of composition, 142
Ease of processing, 133–137
– in definition of entrenchment, 130
– experimental paradigms for, 134–135

– and fluency of composition, 135–138
– interpreting, 133–134
Ebbinghaus, H., 353
Economy (cognitive principle), 15
Edelman, S., 139–140, 146
Efficiency
– in classic view of automaticity, 203
– of language comprehension, 208–209, 220
– of language production, 211–213, 220
Einstellung effect, 249–251, 261
Elaboration, 44, 278
Electrophysiological studies, of lexical learning, 188–189
Elementary Perceiver and Memorizer, Model IV (EPAM-IV), 254–256, 261
Ellis, N. C., 146–147
Elman, J. L., 188, 347
Embeddedness, 398–399
Emulation, 4, 23
Encoding strategies, 180
ENCOW14 (Corpora from the Web, English Version, Release 2014, Slice AX03), 118, 119
Entanglement, 399–400
Entrenched linguistic structures, 10
Entrenching
– agent models of, 421–426
– entrenchment vs., 436, 447
– mechanisms of, 416–419
– value of, 426–427
Entrenchment, 9–26. *See also specific topics*
– conceptions of, 435–437
– of constructions vs. links, 70–71
– contextual, 121, 169
– cotextual, 169
– defined, 3–4, 23, 24, 40, 57, 75, 101, 130–132, 219n3, 269
– degree of, 10, 42, 48–49
– differential effects of, 449–451
– dis-, 370
– elements of, 9–10
– empirical evidence for, 10–22
– of form frequency, 329–333
– frequency effects on, 13–18
– irreversible, 348–349
– long-term, 146–147
– measuring, 105–120
– negative, 66–67, 121
– other determinants of, 20–22
– pathways of, 447–448

– as proxy for language, 414–415
– psychological foundations of, 22–23
– repetition effects on, 18–20
– stability of, 400–402
– statistical learning as mechanism of, 229–230
EPAM-IV (Elementary Perceiver and Memorizer, Model IV), 254–256, 261
EPAM-VOC, 262
Episodic memory, 20, 179–180, 183
Ericsson, K. A., 254
ERPs (event-related brain potentials), 134–136
Estrogen levels, 347
Euphemisms, 392
Event-related brain potentials (ERPs), 134–136
Executive function, 350, 379
Exemplar-based models, 19, 54, 277–278
Expectation-driven salience, 304
Experience
– cognitive development and, 235
– intersubjective differences due to, 145–146
Experience-independent theories of language acquisition, 227–228
Experiential frequency, 158
Experimental perspective on entrenchment, 129–148
– abstract levels of representation in, 142–145
– chunk status in, 138–141
– corpus-based vs., 120–122
– and definition of entrenchment, 130–132
– ease of processing in, 133–137
– individual differences in, 145–146
– long-term entrenchment and online processing in, 146–147
Experimental psychology, salience in, 290–296
Expertise, 249–250, 257–258
Explicit memory, 178–179, 183
Expressions
– complexity of, 106
– fixed (formulaic), 50
– frequency effects for, 13
– fully abstract, 120
– referring, 332
– semifixed, 117–119
Expressive learners, 146
Extension, 43–46, 278
External information, bottom-up salience and, 291
Extinction problem, 249
Eye tracking, 134–136

Face cues, salience of, 294
Faloon, S., 254
Familiarization, 256
Fayol, M., 211
Feedback loops, 21, 154, 304
Feldman, J., 255
Felser, C., 352
Ferreira, V. S., 205, 213
Fictive radiation problem, 271–272
Field, S. L., 236
Figure-ground segregation, law of, 246, 251
Fillmore, C., 61–62
Finkbeiner, M., 215
Finke, K., 293
First articulation, 105n1
First-language learning, 315–334
– chunking in, 17, 18
– determinants of entrenchment in, 22
– entrenchment of form frequency in, 329–333
– frequency effects in, 13–14, 321–325, 368
– and grammatical errors of children, 326–328
– lexical frames in, 318–321
– lexical strings in, 315–317
– mechanism for, 328–329
– neural system activation in, 192
– and type/token frequencies, 321–326
First order complexity, 395
Fisher–Yates test, 63n1
Fixed expressions, 50
Fixed multiword chunks, 17
Flexibility
– in first-language learning, 319–320
– of lexicogrammatical patterns, 422–425
Flikeid, K., 95
Fluency
– of composition, 135–138
– and delicacy, 425
– and phonetic reduction, 89–90
Fluent switchers, 379
fMRI studies, 135, 137, 140–141, 188
Focal colors, 276
Fodor, J. A., 201, 424
Folia, V., 190
Folk genera, 162
Folk specifics, 162
Forkstam, C., 190
Formal onomasiological salience, 157–161, 165–166, 168
Form-focused linguistic research, 296
Form frequency, entrenchment of, 329–333

Form–meaning pairings
– in construction grammar model, 50, 58, 67
– frequency effects on, 14
– schemas as, 142
Formulaic expressions, 50
Frames, lexical, 317–321
Freezing, of lexicogrammatical patterns, 422–425
Frequency. *See also* Token frequency; Type frequency; Usage intensity
– absolute, 394
– bounded, 394–395
– as complex function, 403–404
– of complex linguistic units, 110–111
– conceptual, 158
– corpus, 377
– discourse, 15, 77. *See also* Frequency effects
– experiential, 158
– form, 329–333
– in integrated framework for linguistic entrenchment, 446–447
– lexical, 158, 375–378
– measuring entrenchment in terms of, 101
– relative, 15, 137, 155, 394
– and strengths of representation, 14–15
– usage, 130–132
Frequency effects
– and chunking/holistic units, 16–18
– in cognitive grammar model, 50
– in dynamic complexity theory, 404–405
– in experimental view of entrenchment, 135–137
– on first-language learning, 321–325, 368
– on language attrition, 371–375
– on linguistic entrenchment, 13–18
– repetition effects vs., 18–19
– on second-language learning, 368
– and strength of representation, 13–16
Frequency hypothesis, 388–395
– bounded frequency in, 394–395
– described, 388–389
– and frequency paradox, 392–394
– type and token frequency in, 389–391
Frequency-induced chunk status, 139–141
Frequency paradox, 392–394
Fricatives, voicing of, 404
Friederici, A., 357
From-corpus-to-cognition principle, 105
Fully abstract expressions, 120
Functional approaches to linguistics, 299–300

Functional fixedness, 249
Functional information, 412–415
– artificial agents' use of, 420, 421, 423
– and flexibility with entrenching, 421–422
– re-entrenching of, 423, 426–427
– robots' use of, 419
Fusion, 16, 17, 443

G^2 statistic, 115–116
Garnsey, S., 210
Garrett, Merrill, 201
Garrod, S., 18–19, 216–217, 219–221
Gaskell, M. G., 186–189
Gaze direction, 294–295
Gaze following, 210
Géant, 91–92
Geeraerts, D., 158, 160, 163, 165, 169, 298
Generalization. *See also* Bleaching
– in association entrenchment, 270, 283–284
– and automatization/routinization, 439
– in language learning, 281–283, 324
– in memory consolidation, 177, 184–185
– and paradigmatic associations, 443
– and symbolic association, 80
– and type frequency, 14
Genitive form, 78
Gentner, D., 273, 274, 281
Gerund complements, 92–93
Gerundive complement clauses, 63
Gestalt psychology, 245–251
– and language, 261–262
– mechanisms for phenomena in, 250–251
– perception in, 246
– problem solving in, 246–250
Gevers, W., 206
Geyer, T., 293
Ghesquière, 2014, 85
Gibson, E. J., 227
Gibson, J. J., 227
Gick, M. L., 271–272
Gilmartin, K., 258
Give, 64
Global cognitive precedence, 138–139
Go, grammaticalization of, 77
Goals, automaticity of processing and, 206, 213–214
Gobet, F., 250, 251, 260
Gökce, A., 293
Goldberg, A. E., 59, 64, 66, 324, 332
GO lexeme, suppletion with, 93

Gómez, R. L., 189
GOOD lexeme, suppletion with, 93, 94
Goodman, N., 401, 404
Gordon, M. B., 252
Gordon, P. C., 209
Gozli, D. G., 293
Graduated interval recall, 353
Grammar
– conceptualization of language change in, 75
– hypercorrection in, 95
– lexical frames in abstraction of, 318–321
– memory consolidation in learning of, 189–191
– in second-language learning, 347
Grammar patterns, 107
Grammatical categories, universality of, 52
Grammatical errors, of children, 326–328
Grammaticality, of linguistic units, 46
Grammaticalization, 77, 169, 390, 391, 393
Grammatical structures, 20, 299–300
Great time, 106
Greetings, 425
Gregg, L. W., 255
Gries, S. T., 62–64
Groisman, M., 205
Grondelaers, S., 158, 160, 169
Grosjean, F., 373
Grouping, 245, 260
Günther, F., 146

Hacker, P. M. S., 416
Hahne, A., 357
Håkansson, G., 354
Hall, L., 214–215
Halliday, M. A. K., 388
Hanley, D. A., 187
Harris, A. C., 86–87
Hartsuiker, R. J., 211, 214
Haspelmath, M., 81–82
Hay, J., 69
Hebbian principle, 40, 47, 181, 346, 438
Heine, Bernd, 167
Held, R., 250
Hendrick, R., 209
Herman, R. E., 211
Hernandez, A., 374
Heylen, K., 165
Hickock, G., 351
Hierarchical predictive coding paradigm, 139
High-concrete similarity, 273
Hilpert, M., 60, 63

Hippocampus
– in lexical learning, 186–187, 189, 191
– in systems consolidation, 181–183
Historical linguistics, 75–76, 102
Holcomb, P. J., 214
Holistic learners, 146
Holistic meta-concept of salience, 302–305
Holistic units, 9–10, 16–18, 23
Holistic views of usage and memory representation, 130–132
Holyoak, K. J., 271–272
Hommel, B., 292
Homonymy, 51
Hooper, J., 86
Hopper, P., 70, 391
Horizontal links, 60
Houston, D. M., 236
Humans
– action and perception by, 409–410
– recognition by artificial agents and animals vs., 424
– social practices of, 415
– value of entrenching for, 426–427
Hypercomplex systems, 396
Hypercorrection, 94–95

I, suppletion with, 93
Idealized member, prototype as, 277
Idioms, 17–18, 59, 106–107, 262
Imitation, 4, 23
Implicit learning, 227–230, 258–260
Implicit memory, 178–179
Indefinite articles, 88–89
Indirect approach to categorization, 162
Individual variation
– in corpus-based perspective, 122
– in experimental perspective, 145–146
– in language change, 77
– in salience, 297, 299, 303
– in statistical learning, 235–237
Infants, 234–236, 350
Infinite regress, 153
Infinitive markers, bleaching of, 81–82
Inheritance links, 59–62
Inhibition, 378–379
Innovation, 16, 76, 87–88
Insight, 247, 250, 251
In spite of, 85
Instance links, 59, 61
Instantiations, 44, 278

Integrated framework for linguistic entrenchment, 435–451
– conceptions of entrenchment in, 435–437
– and differential effects of entrenchment, 449–451
– features of, 24–26
– frequency's role in, 446–447
– predictability of entrenchment pathways in, 447–448
– routinization and automatization in, 437–439
– schemas in, 448–449
– strengthening of linguistic associations in, 439–446
Integration, 185, 187, 439
Intended actions, vision and, 291–292
Intensifiers, 82–83
Intensity, usage. *See* Usage intensity
Intentionality, 203, 213–215, 220
Interactive activation models, 139
Interleaved learning, 185
Interlinked constructions, 58–62
Intermediate mode, 373
Internal information, top-down salience and, 291
Internalization, 371
Internal theories, prototypes as, 277
Interpretation processes, automaticity of, 204
Intransitive verbs, gerund complements with, 93
Irregular verbs, frequency of, 86
Irreversible binomials, 17
Irreversible entrenchment, 348–349
Isolation, 358, 370, 398–399
Isomorphism hypothesis, 250
-ive suffix, 68–69
-ize suffix, 68–69

Janzen, G., 188
Jarvis, S., 376–377
Jenkins, J. G., 183
Jensen, O., 190
Jescheniak, J. D., 212
Jiang, N, 135
Johansson, P., 214–215
Johns, C. L., 209
Johnson, J. S., 345
Joint action model of dialogue, 217
Just, M. A., 204–205, 211

Kawaguchi, S., 354
Kay, P., 61–62, 276
Kemper, S., 211
Kennings, 391
Kenny, L. A., 419–421
Kirjavainen, M., 327
Klahr, D., 255
Knowledge, 412
Koch, Peter, 166
Köhler, W., 250
Kolmogorov, A. N., 252
König, E., 79
Köpke, B., 375
Kramer, A. F., 210
Kubose, T. T., 210
Kuhl, P., 346
Kutas, M., 188

L2 learning. *See* Second-language learning
Labov, W., 159–160, 276, 420
Lane, L. W., 205, 214, 216
Lane, P. C. R., 260
Langacker, R. W., 9–10, 76, 104–105, 120, 132, 142, 153–154, 270, 278, 372, 388
Language
– and chunking, 262
– defined, 270, 405
– entrenchment as proxy for, 414–415
– exposure to, 372
– and Gestalt psychology, 261–262
– interactions of, 402
– statistical learning and ability with, 236, 237
Language acquisition. *See also* Language learning
– experience-independent theories of, 227–228
– memory consolidation studies on, 192
– repetition effects in, 20
Language attrition, 367–380, 402
– and cognitive linguistics, 367–371
– defined, 367
– and frequency/context of use, 371–375
– and frequency of lexical items/cross-linguistic similarity, 375–378
– inhibition and cognitive control in, 378–379
Language Attrition Test Battery, 372–373
Language change, 75–96
– and analogy formation, 280n7
– in dynamic complexity theory, 396–397
– effects of entrenchment on, 76–77

– and entrenchment in historical linguistics, 75–76
– frequency effects in, 14–16
– paradigmatic association in, 91–95
– pragmatic association in, 78–80
– repetition effects in, 20
– symbolic association in, 80–84
– syntagmatic association in, 84–90
Language comprehension
– automaticity for language production vs., 220–221
– classic view of automaticity for, 204–205
– contemporary view of automaticity for, 208–210
– in language processing framework, 202–203
– symbolic associations in, 439–440
Language learning. *See also* First-language learning; Second-language learning
– analogy in, 279–281
– for artificial languages, 325–326
– categorization in, 279–281
– by children vs. adults, 349–351
– generalization in, 281–283
– and memory consolidation, 177, 186–192
– statistical learning in, 238–239
Language maintenance, 378–379
Language processing
– automaticity of. *See* Automaticity of language processing
– framework for, 202–203
– statistical learning in, 238–239
Language production
– automaticity for language comprehension vs., 220–221
– classic view of automaticity for, 205–206
– contemporary view of automaticity for, 210–216
– differential effects of entrenchment on, 450–451
– in language processing framework, 202–203
– onomasiological salience in, 170–171
– symbolic associations in, 439–440
Language-related factors, 447
Language retention, 402
Languaging, 409n2
Largy, P., 211
Lashley, K. S., 250
Law of closure, 246
Law of figure-ground segregation, 246, 251
Law of proximity, 246

Law of symmetry, 246
Learning. *See also* Complementary learning systems (CLS) model; Language learning; Statistical learning
– entrenching vs., 415
– implicit, 227–230, 258–260
– interleaved, 185
– lexical, 186–189, 352, 353
– perceptual learning theory, 227
– procedural, 347
– verbal, 256
Leibniz, Gottfried Wilhelm, 387
Lemaire, B., 252, 253
Lemaire, P., 211
Lemmas, 13, 107
Lenneberg, E., 343–345
Let alone, 61–62
Levelt, W. J. M., 201, 204, 213
Levine, W. H., 209
Lewis, L. B., 65
Lexemes, 43, 93, 94
Lexical categories, 52
Lexical clustering, 399
Lexical description, 50–52
Lexical diversity, 369
Lexical frames, 317–321
Lexical frequency, 158, 375–378
Lexical items
– differential effects of entrenchment on, 449–450
– language attrition and frequency of, 375–378
Lexicalization, 401
Lexical learning, 186–189, 352, 353
Lexical overlap, in first-language learning, 320–321
Lexical parasitism, 354
Lexical semantic analysis (LSA), 320
Lexical strings, 144, 315–317, 327
Lexicogenetic mechanism, salience of, 166–167
Lian, C. H. T., 211
Libben, G., 135–136
Lieven, E., 316, 327, 331
Lind, A., 214–215
Lindsay, S., 187, 188
Linguistic associations, 439–446. *See also specific types, e.g.:* Paradigmatic associations

Linguistic corpora
– cognition in, 102–104
– criticisms of measuring entrenchment with, 120–123
– defined, 101, 102
– and entrenchment, 104–105
Linguistic creativity, 331
Linguistic domain, 229–231
Linguistic entrenchment. *See* Entrenchment
Linguistic level (language processing framework), 202, 203
Linguistic relationships, tracking of, 237
Linguistic rules, 53–54
Linguistics
– in cognitive sciences, 3
– salience in, 289, 296–301
Linguistic structures, 39–41, 50
Linguistic units, 153, 401, 435
– activation of, 45–49
– assessing schematicity/complexity of, 105–107
– in cognitive grammar model, 39–42
– complex, 110–117
– in corpus-based perspective on entrenchment, 108
– development of, 42–44
– and language change, 75
– measuring entrenchment of, 108–120
– rules as, 53
– schematic, 117–120
– simple, 108–110
Links, constructions vs., 70–71
Literal similarity, 284
Loci, method of, 253, 254
Logan, G. D., 218
Logarithmically transformed relative frequency, 137
Long-term entrenchment, 146–147
Long-term memory (LTM), 251
LSA (lexical semantic analysis), 320
Luchins, A. S., 249

MacDonald, M. C., 208
MacWhinney, B., 349, 374
Maier, N. R. F., 248–249
Mainstream linguistics, 3
Makin, V.S., 277, 278
March, J., 421
Markedness, 393–394, 403
Martin, R. C., 211

Mǎ shàng, 78–79
Masked distractor studies, 215
Masked priming studies, 137, 140–141
Mathy, F., 255
Maturana, H., 409, 426
McCauley, S. M., 238
McClelland, J. L., 182, 191
McElree, B., 209
McLean, R. S., 255
McLeod, P., 250
McNaughton, B. L., 182
McQueen, J. M., 188
MDL (minimum description length), 252
MDLCHUNKER model, 252–253
Meaning diversification, 439–440
Mechanistic theory of dialogue, 221
Me-for-I errors, 327
Memory
– autobiographical, 183
– collective, 420–421
– co-occurrence patterns in, 64
– declarative (explicit), 178–179, 183
– in entrenchment, 3
– episodic, 20, 179–180, 183
– long-term, 251
– nondeclarative (implicit), 178–179
– and pragmatic associations, 445
– procedural, 178
– semantic, 20, 179–180, 445
– short-term, 251–253
– working, 201, 204–205, 211
Memory-based information, vision and, 292–293
Memory consolidation, 177–193
– and automatization/routinization, 438
– in complementary learning systems model, 177
– defined, 180
– and elements of entrenchment, 10
– generalization, integration, and prior knowledge in, 184–186
– and language learning, 186–192
– and language maintenance, 378–379
– and memory systems, 178–180
– and psychological foundations of entrenchment, 22–23
– repetition effects in, 19
– and schema, 448–449
– in second-language learning, 353

– sleep in, 183–184
– and symbolic associations, 440
– synaptic, 181
– systems, 181–183, 438
Memory palace, 253
Memory representation, 130–132
Memory retrieval, 17, 218
Memory systems, 178–180
Memory trace reactivation, 183–185
Mentalism, 416
Mental model construction, 352
-ment suffix, 68
Mereological error, 416, 424
Meringer, Rudolf, 158
Metaphors, 59, 273–274
Method of loci, 253, 254
Meyer, A. S., 212, 213
Milicka, J., 390
Miller, C. A., 211
Miller, G. A., 227, 253–255, 260
Milner, B., 179
Minimum description length (MDL), 252
Minimum sensitivity, 113
Misyak, J. B., 236
Mnemonics, 253–255
Modal auxiliary constructions, 63
Moder, C., 392
Modularity, 214, 222
Modularity of Mind (Fodor), 201
Modular models of sentence comprehension, 218
Monitoring systems, in dialogue, 216
Monomorphemic words, 106, 107
Monosemy, 51–52
Moors, A., 206–207, 221
Morphemes, 105n1
Morphological constructions, entrenchment in, 67–69
Morphological forms, 15, 16, 347
Morphosyntax, language attrition and, 371
MOSAIC, 262
MTT (multiple trace theory), 183, 187
Müller, G. E., 180
Müller, H. J., 210, 292–293
Multiple inheritance, subpart links and, 60
Multiple trace theory (MTT), 183, 187
Multiword expressions. *See* Expressions
Mutual exclusivity constraint, 261
Myelination, 344

N400 potential, 188–189
Nadel, L., 189
Naming processes, 214
Navon, D., 221
Navon figures, 138, 139
Negation, in first-language learning, 331
Negative entrenchment, 66–67, 121
Negative transfer, 370
Nekrasova, T. M., 135
Neocortical integration, in CLS, 191
Networks, of interlinked constructions, 58–62
Neural activity, linguistic units and, 40
Neural basis of lexical learning, 188–189
Neural network models, 343, 345–346, 351
Neural system, in first vs. second language learning, 192
Neurolinguistics. *See* Experimental perspective on entrenchment
Neuronal variation, 348
Newport, E. L., 227–228, 238–239, 259, 324–325, 345, 347
Nieuwenhuis, I. L. C., 190
Nikitina, T., 61
Node view of entrenchment, 70–71
Nonadjacent dependencies, 231, 235–237
Nonautomatic processes, 203
Nondeclarative (implicit) memory, 178–179
No negative evidence problem, 65–66
Non-Markov chains, 395
Nonswitchers, 379
Nontargets, visual search, 290
Noticing hypothesis, 394
NOUN-ful construction, 68
Noun–noun sequences, qualifying nouns in, 91–92
Nouns. *See* Adjective–noun combinations

Object clitics, 323
Object relative clauses, 331–332
Object similarity, 274–275, 282
Oblique construals, 164–165
Observer-relevant applications of information, 414, 415, 426
Occam's razor principle, 252
O'Connor, C., 61–62
Olson, M., 78
Om, 81–82
ONE lexeme, suppletion with, 93
One-to-one mappings, 272
Online processing, 146–147

Onomasiological profiles, 160, 165
Onomasiological salience, 153–171
– in conception of entrenchment, 436
– conceptions for studying, 156–159
– conceptual, 157, 161–165, 168–170
– defined, 155–156
– formal, 157–161, 165–166, 168
– future research directions, 168–171
– and paradigmatic associations, 444
– typological, 156, 159, 165–168
Onomasiology, 155, 158–159
Onomasiology-based lectometry, 161
Ontological salience, 284
Open word classes, 119–120
Operant conditioning, 409
Opitz, C., 374
O'Reilly, R. C., 182
Orthography, in second-language learning, 353
Osman, M., 206
Over, 59
Overanalysis, 355–356
Overgeneralization errors, 14, 65–67, 324, 332
Overlap, with target, 48–49
Overregularization, 323–324
Overspecification, 205

Pacton, S., 229
Paired-associate paradigm, 256
Pallier, C., 370
Paoletti, D., 291
Paradigmatic analogy, 92–93
Paradigmatic associations
– defined, 269, 284
– effects of entrenchment processes on, 12, 25–26
– in integrated framework for entrenchment, 25, 76n1
– in language change, 91–95
– in schematization, 14
– strengthening of, 443–444
Paradis, M., 357, 371, 375
Parallel connectivity, 272
Parasitism, 349
Parkinson disease, 179
PARSER, 259, 262
Parsing
– and automaticity of language processing, 201–202
– frequency effects for, 13
– and morphological constructions, 69

– in sentence comprehension models, 218
– and subpart links, 61–62
Partial sanction, 76–77, 89
Participation, 358, 370
Pashler, H., 213
Past-tense formation, 49, 86
Pattee, H. H., 412, 421
Pattern-finding, 270
Pattern recognition, 258
Patterns of activity, linguistic units as, 40–41
Paul, H., 271n1, 280n7
Payne, J. D., 185
PCA (principal component analysis), 373
PDH (proceduralization deficit hypothesis) (PDH), 357
Peirce, C., 390, 391
Peirsman, Y., 165
Perception. *See also specific types, e.g.:* Audition
– and action, 291–292, 409–410
– in entrenchment, 3
– in Gestalt psychology, 245, 246
– of language, 415
– salience in, 290–296
– of third formant, 347
Perception shaping, 259
Perceptual identification, 140
Perceptual learning theory, 227
Perceptual magnet hypothesis, 346
Perceptual salience, 20, 329–330
Perkins, S. J., 277
Perruchet, P., 229
Petersson, K. M., 190
Phi phenomenon, 246
Phoneme inventory, 375
Phonemes, differential effects on, 449–450
Phonetic attrition, 392
Phonetic drift, 376
Phonetic duration, 136
Phonetic forms, 15, 16
Phonetic gestures, 410
Phonetic reduction. *See* Reduction
Phonology, language attrition and, 371
Phrasal verbs, chunking with, 17
Phrase contraction, 75
Pickering, M. J., 18–19, 216–217, 219–221
Pienemass, M., 354
Pilzecker, A., 180
Pine, J. M., 14
Pinker, S., 66

Plag, I., 69
Planning scope, 212–213
Plasticity, of brain, 343–345, 348–349
Plural constructions, 68, 92, 95, 401
pMTG. *See* Posterior middle temporal gyrus
Poeppel, D., 351
Polysemy, 51, 59, 61, 83–84
Port, R., 276
Posterior middle temporal gyrus (pMTG), 188, 189, 191
Post-selective view of visual search, 293
Poststructuralist conception of onomasiological salience, 156, 159
Potrat, S., 253
Poverty of stimulus argument, 227
Pragmatic associations
– defined, 269, 284
– effects of entrenchment processes on, 12, 25–26
– in integrated framework for linguistic entrenchment, 25
– in language change, 78–80
– repetition effects for, 20
– strengthening of, 444–445
Pragmatic conception of onomasiological salience, 155–156
Pragmatic facts, 422–423
Pragmatic salience, 82–83
Pragmatic strengthening, 78–80
Prägnanz, principle of, 246
Pratt, J., 293
Predictability, of entrenchment pathways, 447–448
Predictive-coding models, 293–294, 296
Preemption, 49
Prefixes, 398. *See also* Affixes
Prepositional dative construction, 63, 66
Preselective view of visual search, 293
Prestige forms, 78, 94
Prestructuralist conception of onomasiology, 158–159
Primary categorization for lexemes, 52
Priming
– and chunking, 17
– and context, 19
– in dynamic complexity theory, 397–398
– in first-language learning, 328–329
– and grammatical errors by children, 327
– masked priming studies, 137, 140–141
– repetition, 104–105

– semantic, 187, 188
– syntactic (structural), 19, 21, 90, 145
– whole-to-part, 140
Principal component analysis (PCA), 373
Principle of Prägnanz, 246
Principle of Semantic Coherence, 64
Principle of simplicity, 252
Prior knowledge
– in Gestalt problem solving, 248–250
– memory consolidation with, 185–186
– and paradigmatic associations, 443
– remembering information using, 253
Priva, U. C., 136
Probability-based measurement, of linguistic units, 111–115
Problem solving, 246–250, 257–258
Proceduralization, 356–357, 440
Proceduralization deficit hypothesis (PDH), 357
Procedural learning, 347
Procedural memory, 178
Procedure strengthening, 219
Processing activities, as linguistic structures, 39
Processing mode, 21
Processing-related entrenchment factors, 20–21
Productions, chunks and formation of, 258
Productivity
– in first-language learning, 319–320
– of schema, 119, 145
– and type frequency, 16, 48
Professional use of language, attrition and, 373–374
Progressive-alignment hypothesis, 274
Progressive form, 63, 90
Pronouns, 322–323
Prototypes, 277
Prototype theory, 156, 276–277
Proverbs, 423
Proximity, law of, 246
Pseudohomophone effect, 138–139
Psycholinguistics. *See also* Experimental perspective on entrenchment
– corpora in, 102
– critical period research in, 345
– frequency effects in, 13
– salience research in, 289
Psychosocial processes, 23

Qualifying nouns, 91–92
Quantitative Lexicology and Variational Linguistics (QLVL), 159
Quantitative paradigm, 388
Quatre-vingts, 43

Rabinowitz, H. S., 249
Radical embodied cognitive science view, 409–428
– described, 410–411
– entrenchment as proxy for language in, 414–415
– on entrenchment mechanisms, 416–419
– entrenchment studies in, 411–414
– and limitations of agent models of entrenching, 421–426
– social influence on entrenchment from, 419–421
– on value of entrenching, 426–427
Raimondi, V., 409n2
Ramscar, M., 276
Rasch, B., 184
Rationality, 260
Reading time, 236–237
Ready, 53
Reber, A. S., 227, 230, 234, 235
Recitation, alphabet, 255
Recognition, 45, 46, 424
Recommend, 66
Reconfiguration, in streamlining, 42–43
Recurrent alternations, suppletion and, 93–94
-*red*, 86
Red, 53
Reduction, 16, 42, 88–90, 443
Redundant information, compression of, 252–253
Re-entrenching, 423, 426–427
Referential dimension, for onomasiological salience, 156–159
Referential enrichment, 164
Referential language use, 205, 300, 305–306
Referential learners, 146
Referring expressions, 332
Regression to infinity, 154
Regularization, 86–87, 401
Relational-shift hypothesis, 273
Relational similarity, 273–275, 284
Relative frequency, 15, 137, 155, 394
Repetition, 18–20, 316. *See also* Token repetition; Type repetition
Repetition priming, 104–105
Replication, context effects and, 19

Representation(s). *See also* Strength of representation
– abstract levels of, 142–145
– of categories, 277–278
– format for, 130
– and memory consolidation, 187
– quality of, 207
Representational model of entrenchment, 417
Representational redundancy, 130
Resonance, 352–353, 355, 370
Resource theories, 208
Restructuring, in Gestalt psychology, 250
Retrieval structures, 253, 254
Retroactive interference, 183
Retrograde amnesia, 179, 181–182
Reversal errors, 140
Richman, H. B., 254
Robinet, V., 252, 253
Robots, use of information by, 418–419
Rosch, E., 163, 276
Ross, B. H., 277, 278
Routine formulas, 423
Routinization
– in dialogue, 219–220
– in entrenchment, 4, 269, 283, 437–439
– and language change, 15
– and symbolic associations, 441
Rowland, C., 14, 317

Saffran, J. R., 227–228, 232, 259, 416n8
Salience, 289–306. *See also* Onomasiological salience
– bottom-up, 290–292, 304
– and bounded frequency, 395
– carriers of, 295, 301–303
– cognitive, 20, 284, 298
– and contextual entrenchment, 121
– defined, 289
– as determinant of entrenchment, 20–21
– dimensions of variation for modeling, 301–302
– domains of, 302, 303
– and entrenchment, 284
– expectation-driven, 304
– in experimental psychology, 290–296
– foci of, 303
– future research perspectives on, 305–306
– holistic meta-concept of, 302–305
– in linguistics, 296–301
– loci of, 302
– manifestations of, 295, 302, 306
– ontological, 284
– perceptual, 20, 329–330
– pragmatic, 82–83
– and pragmatic associations, 444–445
– semasiological, 158
– situational, 284
– sources of, 295, 301–303
– surprisal-induced, 294, 304
– top-down, 290–291, 293, 304
– transfer of, 304
Sampling, in corpus-based perspective, 122–123
Sanction, partial, 76–77, 89
Sandwich technique, 137
Saturation threshold, 374
Say, 66
Scatter, 393
Schemas
– activation of, 143–145
– in cognitive grammar model, 44, 54
– and conception of entrenchment, 436
– in experimental view, 142–145
– in first-language learning, 318
– in integrated framework, 448–449
– in language learning by children, 281–282
– in memory consolidation, 185–186
– prototype as, 277
– and symbolic associations, 440–441
– in template theory, 258
– and type frequency, 14
– variable, 446–447
Schematicity, of linguistic units, 105, 107
Schematic linguistic units, 117–120
Schematization, 14, 18, 23, 44, 323–324
Schmid, H.-J., 105, 122, 145–146, 169, 284, 422
Schmid, M. S., 373–379
Schreifers, H., 212
Schreiner, T., 184
Schubö, A., 292
Schuchardt, Hugo, 158
Scoville, W. B., 179
Search, visual, 290–293
Second articulation, 105n1
Second-language learning, 343–359
– chunking in, 18
– critical periods for, 343–345
– entrenchment and problems in, 345–349
– frequency effects in, 13–14, 368
– isolation and participation in, 358

– neural system activation in, 192
– overanalysis, proceduralization, and chunking in, 355–357
– resonance and entrenchment in, 351–353
– transfer and decoupling in, 354–355
– Unified Competition Model of, 349–358
Segregation, figure-ground, 246, 251
Selectivity, in vision, 292
Self-generated movement, 293–294
Self-organizing feature maps, 345
Self-paced reading experiments, 134–136
Selfridge, J. A., 227
Semantic accretion, 392
Semantic coherence, 63–64
Semantic dementia, 180
Semantic divergence, in historical linguistics, 75
Semantic drift, 397
Semantic memory, 20, 179–180, 445
Semantic priming effect, 187, 188
Semantics
– in construction grammar model, 63–64
– and overgeneralization errors, 66–67
– in second-language learning, 354
Semantic similarity, 330
Semasiological salience, 158
Semasiology, 155
Semifixed expressions, 117–119
Semiprefabricated phrases, 17
Semmes, J., 250
Sensitivity, minimum, 113
Sentence comprehension models, 218
Set effect, 249
Sethuraman, N., 324
S-genitive, 59, 61
Shafto, C. L., 236
Shallow encoding, 180
Shallow structure hypothesis, 352
Shapiro, L., 409
Sheepish, 86
Shift, in dynamic complexity theory, 396–397
Short-term memory (STM), 251–253
Siegel, D., 69
Similarity
– in analogy formation, 273–275
– cross-linguistic, 375–378
– and entrenchment, 284
– high-concrete, 273
– and language attrition, 375–378
– literal, 284
– object, 274–275, 282
– of patterns of activity, 40
– relational, 273–275, 284
– semantic, 330
Simon, H. A., 257, 258, 260–262
Simple linguistic units, measuring entrenchment of, 108–110
Simple present, 63
Simplicity, principle, 252
Sine-wave speech, 210
Single word production, automaticity studies of, 213
Situated referential language use, 300, 305–306
Situational context, for repetition effects, 19
Situational salience, 284
Situational variables, 447
Situation models, 217
Siyanova-Chanturia, A., 136
Skill development, 421
Skinner, B. F., 417n11
Sleep, 183–185, 189–190
Slot-and-frame patterns, 330
Snider, N., 135, 219
Social context
– in entrenchment, 22, 447
– in radical embodied cognitive science view, 419–421
– repetition effects in, 19–20
Social domain, statistical learning in, 233
Social dynamics for language change, 77, 78
Social-interactive behavior, 294–295
Social setting, in language processing framework, 202, 203
Social support, 350, 358
Sociocognitive models of linguistic knowledge, 23
Sociocommunicative view of entrenchment, 153
Sociolinguistics
– corpora in, 102
– pragmatic associations in, 78
– salience research in, 296–297
Sociolinguistic variables, 159–160
Speaker-centered entrenchment factors, 21–22
Speaker-related variables, 447
Speech rate, 89
Speed, in classic view of automaticity, 203
Speelman, D., 160, 165
Stability, 41, 401–402

A Standard Corpus of Present-Day Edited
American English (BROWN), 119, 120
Standard model of systems consolidation,
181–183
Stanford, J. N., 419–421
Staszewski, J. J., 254
Statistical learning, 227–239
– and automatization/routinization, 438
– defined, 228n1
– developmental changes in, 234–235
– domain-generality of, 230–233
– history of, 227–228
– and implicit learning, 228–229
– individual differences in, 235–237
– in language learning and processing models,
238–239
– as mechanism of entrenchment, 229–230
– and symbolic associations, 440
– and syntagmatic associations, 442
Statistical measurement, of complex linguistic
units, 115–116
Steels, L., 418, 421
Stefanowitsch, A., 62–66
Sternberg, R. J., 249
STM (short-term memory), 251–253
Streamlining, 42–43
Strength of representation
– and analogies, categorization, generalization,
281
– and context effects, 19–20
– and frequency effects, 13–16
– in linguistic entrenchment, 9
– and psychological foundations of
entrenchment, 22–23
– for schemas, 143
Strijkers, K., 214
Strings, lexical, 144, 315–317, 327
String token frequency, 16
Stroop effect, 209, 215
Structural ambiguity, 201–202
Structuralist conception of onomasiological
salience, 155–156
Structured inventory, in language, 39
Structure-mapping process, 272
Subpart links, 60, 61, 69
Substantive information, 412–414
– artificial agents' use of, 420, 421
– in cognitivist view, 417, 418
– robots' use of, 418
Suffixes, 68–69. *See also* Affixes

Suppletion, 93–94
Supporting constructions, 87–88
Surprisal-induced salience, 294, 304
Symbol grounding problem, 418
Symbolic associations
– defined, 269, 284
– effects of entrenchment processes on, 11,
25–26
– in integrated framework, 25
– in language change, 80–84
– in language learning by children, 281
– and paradigmatic associations, 443
– strengthening of, 439–441
Symmetry, law of, 246
Synaptic consolidation, 181
Synaptic strengthening, 438
Syntactic amalgams, 60
Syntactic (structural) priming, 19, 21, 90, 145
Syntactic processes, automaticity of, 204
Syntactic structures, 13, 450
Syntagmatic associations
– and chunking, 16–17, 262
– defined, 269, 284
– effects of entrenchment processes on, 11–12,
25–26
– in integrated framework for entrenchment,
76n1
– in integrated framework for linguistic
entrenchment, 25
– in language change, 84–90
– in masked priming study, 137
– strengthening of, 441–443
Syntagmatic sequences, constructional splits
for, 85–86
Syntagmatic views of usage and memory
representation, 131–132
Syntax
– and language attrition, 371, 377–378
– and second-language learning, 352, 354
Systematicity, in analogy formation, 272–273
Systems consolidation, 181–183, 438

Tagliamonte, S. A., 78
Takashima, A., 188, 189
Tanenhaus, M. K., 218, 324–325
Tao, L., 88–89
Targets, 45–47, 290
Taylor, J. R., 61
Tees, R. C., 346
Template theory, 258

Temporal conjunctions, 20
Temporally-graded retrograde amnesia, 181–182
Tenpenny, P. L., 277
Text-focused approaches to cognitive salience, 298
Tham, E. K., 187
Theakston, A., 317, 327, 330, 331
Third formant, perception of, 347
Third infinitives, 87
Third-person plural, 95
Thompson, S. P., 238–239
Throw a fit, 59
To-dative construction, 64
To-infinitive omission errors, 328
Token frequency
– in cognitive grammar model, 47
– defined, 14, 24, 321, 389
– in diachronic perspective on entrenchment, 15
– in first-language learning, 321–325
– in frequency hypothesis, 389–391
– as measure of entrenchment, 108–109, 116–119
– measuring of, 325–326
– string, 16
Tokenization, 390–391
Token repetition, 11, 12, 281, 283–284
Tokens, types and, 389–391
Töllner, T., 292, 293
Tomasello, M., 65, 278, 281, 316–318, 417
Tomblin, J. B., 236
Top-down effects, in cognitive precedence, 138–139
Top-down salience, 290–291, 293, 304
Torres Cacoullos, R., 90
Totally, 82–83
Touch, statistical learning with, 233
Trace-transfer theory, 183
Transfer, 183, 354, 370, 371
Transitional probability, 111–112
Transitive constructions, 66–67, 332–333
Transparency stacking, 281–282
Traugott, E., 79, 391
Tremblay, A., 135–136
Tsunami, 83–84
Tucker, B. V., 136
Tuggy, D., 51
Turn taking, in dialogue, 216
TWO lexeme, suppletion with, 93
Two-string problem, 248–249

Type frequency
– in cognitive grammar model, 47–48
– defined, 14, 24, 321, 389
– in diachronic perspective on entrenchment, 15–16
– in first-language learning, 321–325
– in frequency hypothesis, 389–391
– as measure of entrenchment, 118–119
– measuring of, 325–326
Type repetition, 11, 12, 281–282, 284
Types, tokens and, 389–391
Typological onomasiological salience, 156, 159, 165–168

UCM. *See* Unified Competition Model
Ullman, M. T., 347, 357
Unconscious processing of language, 201
Unconscious stimuli, 215
Unified Competition Model (UCM), 349–358
– described, 349–351
– entrenchment and resonance in, 351–353
– isolation and participation in, 358
– language attrition in, 369–371, 376
– overanalysis, proceduralization, and chunking in, 355–357
– transfer and decoupling in, 354–355
Unified theory of usage and linguistic knowledge, 75
Uniformity, 160–161
Unintentional parts
– of language comprehension, 220
– of language production, 213–215
Unique beginner, 162
Universality, of lexical categories, 52
Usage-based models of language, 3
– associative links in, 60–61
– chunking in, 238
– collocations in, 318
– context in, 19
– corpus-as-input view in, 103–104
– entrenchment in, 130, 132, 435
– and entrenchment of constructions vs. links, 70
– experiments related to, 141
– frequency effects in, 50
– and frequency hypothesis, 388
– integrated framework vs., 25
– morphological constructions in, 67
– no negative evidence problem in, 65, 67
– paradigmatic associations in, 91

– and pragmatic associations, 444
– salience in, 297–298
Usage events, 52–53
Usage frequency, 130–133
Usage intensity, 108–120
– of complex linguistic units, 110–117
– of schematic linguistic units, 117–120
– of simple linguistic units, 108–110

Vagueness, in lexical description, 51
Van Dyke, J. A., 209
Van Goethem, K., 91
Van Hell, J. G., 188
Van Heuven, W. J. B., 136
Van Opstal, F, 206
VanPatten, B., 347
Van Zoest, W., 291
Variable idioms, 107
Variable schemas, 446–447
Variant realizations, 89–90
Variation, of linguistic units, 43–44
Variation sets, 320
Varietal taxa, 162
Verbal learning, 256
Verb argument constructions, 65–66
Verbs
– in first-language learning, 321–322, 324–325, 329–330, 332–333
– lexicalization of, 401
Verguts, T., 206
Vertical links, 59, 60
Vigliocco, G., 214
Vision
– salience in, 290–296
– statistical learning in, 230, 232–233
Visual search, 290–293

Visual-world paradigm, 206, 300–301
Von Ehrenfels, C., 245
Von Restorff effect, 256

Wagner, V., 212
Waters, G. S., 205
Weaver, M. D., 291
Weerman, F., 78
Weird word order studies, 321–322
Well-formedness, of linguistic units, 46
Wells, J. B., 237
Werker, J. F., 346
Westbury, C., 135–136
While, pragmatic strengthening with, 79–80
Whole, 85
Whole-to-part priming, 140
Whorfian linguistic-relativity view, 276
Wh-questions, collocations with, 62
Wh-relatives, 78
Wh words, phonetics of, 392
Wiese, E., 210
Wittgenstein, L., 277
Wonnacott, E., 324–325
Word classes, 91, 119–120
Word order, 325–326
Word superiority effect, 138
Working memory, 201, 204–205, 211
Wörter und Sachen movement, 158–159
Wykowska, A., 210, 292, 294–295

Yí, 88–89

Zauner, Adolf, 158
Zehetleitner, M., 292
Zhang, W., 165
Zwickel, J., 210

About the Editor

Hans-Jörg Schmid, DrPhil, holds the Chair of Modern English Linguistics at Ludwig-Maximilians-Universität München (LMU Munich). He obtained his doctorate and *Habilitation* from the same university and taught for many years at the Universities of Dresden, Bochum, and Bayreuth, before returning to Munich in 2005. Dr. Schmid's research interests lie in the fields of cognitive linguistics, lexical semantics, word formation, pragmatics, construction grammar, and corpus linguistics. He developed a linguistic framework known as the entrenchment-and-conventionalization model.

www.ingramcontent.com/pod-product-compliance
Lightning Source LLC
Chambersburg PA
CBHW080117020526
44112CB00037B/2760